John Charles Frémont as he looked about 1849. From a print in
Walter Colton's *Three Years in California* (New York, 1850).

THE EXPEDITIONS OF
John Charles
Frémont

VOLUME 3
Travels from 1848
to 1854

EDITED BY

MARY LEE SPENCE

UNIVERSITY OF ILLINOIS PRESS

URBANA AND CHICAGO

Publication of this work was supported in part by
grants from the National Endowment for the Humanities and the
National Historical Publications and Records Commission.

Quotations from the papers of the Hon. George Washington
Wright (1816–85) are published with the kind permission of
Mr. M. A. Goodspeed, Jr., of Chevy Chase, Md., a descendant
and the owner of these documents, which may be quoted
without permission.

This book is printed on acid-free paper.

Library of Congress Cataloging in Publication Data

Frémont, John Charles, 1813–1890.
   The expeditions of John Charles Frémont.

Vol. 3   edited by Mary Lee Spence
Includes bibliographies.
CONTENTS:—v. 1. Travels from 1838 to 1844.—v. 2.
The Bear Flag Revolt and the court-martial.—v. 2. suppl.
Proceedings of the court-martial.—v. 3. Travels from
1848 to 1854.
   1. United States—Exploring expeditions.   2. United
States—Description and travel—To 1848.   3. United
States—Description and travel—1848– .860.   4. Frémont,
John Charles, 1813–1890.   I. Jackson, Donald Dean,
1919–   ed.   II. Spence, Mary Lee, ed.   III. Title.
F592.F852   917.3'046   73-100374
ISBN 0-252-00416-7 (Vol. 3)

ACKNOWLEDGMENTS

I find it impossible to thank by name the many, many scholars and librarians who have assisted me in preparing the present volume. I wish to acknowledge, however, at the institutional level the continuing support of the National Historical Publications and Records Commission and the staff of the University of Illinois Press. At the personal level, I am especially grateful for the help of four persons: M. A. Goodspeed, Jr., of Chevy Chase, Maryland, who generously permitted me to use the papers of George W. Wright; Bertha Schroeder of Mariposa, California, who patiently answered many questions about the history of this area; and Patricia Joy Richmond of Crestone, Colorado, and Todd I. Berens of Santa Ana, California, who helped me follow the trails of Frémont's fourth and fifth expeditions respectively.

During the preparation of this work, the granddaughter of John Charles and Jessie Benton Frémont, Miss Jessie Frémont, died in Washington, D.C. Her enthusiasm for the project and her permission to use family papers are gratefully acknowledged.

MARY LEE SPENCE

CONTENTS

POLITICS AND ECONOMICS

The Fifth and Final Expedition, 1853–54

ILLUSTRATIONS

MAPS

INTRODUCTION

"I start suddenly for California tomorrow leaving many things unfinished," John Charles Frémont wrote to a scientist friend in late August 1854 as he prepared for his sixth trip to the Pacific Coast—this one by sea. The previous half-dozen years, covered by the documents in this volume, had not been easy for the handsome forty-one-year-old explorer. They had added to the breadth of his experience while mingling success, frustration, and bitter disappointment; throughout them Frémont had failed to exhibit the flawless character that an aspiring politician ought to possess.

There had been the disastrous fourth expedition, 1848–49, with the horrors of exhaustion, starvation, possible cannibalism, and ten men dead on the icy reaches of the San Juan Mountains. The experience was behind him; it reflected upon his leadership and he would not resurrect it with a report. Unfinished, too, was the report of his fifth expedition, 1853–54, across the Rockies into southern Utah and on into California. He fully intended to write one, but politics and the problem of obtaining title for Las Mariposas and other land interests in California, properties he optimistically thought held the key to his future wealth, would cause an indefinite postponement. Consequently, the results of that expedition are known largely through his 14 June 1854 letter to the editors of the *National Intelligencer*, which was subsequently published as a government document, and Solomon Nunes Carvalho's journal.

Another unfinished piece of business was with his agent, David Hoffman, who had worked hard to promote his Mariposa mining holdings in London, only to be callously treated by the explorer. Finished too soon for Frémont's and his wife's satisfaction was his senatorship in Washington, but the appetite for politics had been whetted. Not to be forgotten by either were Alexander von Humboldt's praises for earlier geographical discoveries and the award of the Founder's Medal by the prestigious Royal Geographical Society in London. Despite the "ups and downs," one point was clear: Frémont was in a much better economic and political position in 1854 than in 1848, when his court-martial and resignation from the army had stripped him of a career and a regular income.

At that point he had immediately gone to work obtaining fair adjustments of the accounts of the California Battalion and of the debts he had incurred as civil governor, at the same time completing the *Geographical Memoir* to accompany Charles Preuss's map of Oregon and California. But neither he nor his father-in-law, Senator Thomas Hart Benton, could relinquish the idea of his continuing exploration—especially exploration at government expense. After all, this was what had made him a national hero.

When the 9 May 1848 issue of the *National Intelligencer* noted that a whaler had been lost because of an error in the coastal charts "now in general use," the two saw an opportunity to recapture the limelight. Benton wrote immediately to indicate that the error, which set the California shore too far east, had already been detected by Frémont, whose soon-to-be-published map would show the correction. While he mentioned no names, Old Bullion really impugned the work of Charles Wilkes, then enjoying a reputation in the nation's capital as the leading expert on Oregon and the Pacific Coast. With his regular naval salary and congressional funds to keep his scientific work moving along every year, Wilkes's status was enviable.[1] It was highly unlikely that Congress would appropriate money to support the work of a second specialist in the same area, but perhaps Wilkes could be replaced. Benton and the naval officer had clashed before and now took up the cudgel again.

"Young Bullion," as Wilkes called Frémont, responded, and for almost a month the public read about erroneous survey positions in the Sacramento Valley, priority in accurate charting of the coast, and suppression of corrections. Near the end of the controversy Wilkes promised his wife that if Frémont replied again, he would give him a "homeopathic dose and have Col. Benton on one of the horns of the dilemma, either he made the claim [for Frémont] through ignorance or if he had knowledge of it then a wilful intention to deceive the public."[2] Frémont flatly stated that Wilkes's "entire surveys in Oregon and California as far as they follow his [Wilkes's] own observations, are erroneously laid down in his published work." That Wilkes's

---

[1] WICKMAN, 11, 130.
[2] Wilkes to his wife, 17 June 1848 (DLC—Charles Wilkes Papers).

blunders on the Sacramento River were not the exception, and that the expedition had not always gone "on its own hook," were acknowledged by a former naval officer, James Alden. Frémont emerged from the dispute with enhanced scientific credit, but Wilkes was too entrenched to be supplanted.

During the acrimony with Wilkes, Frémont sent his geographical memoir to the Senate. He noted that "one more year of labor" in the geographical field would fill in the map of Oregon and California, permit the drawing of topographical and descriptive charts of their most valuable parts and a general map of the whole area west of the Mississippi River. His closing was almost a plea: "Having been many years engaged in this geographical labor, and having made so much progress in it, I should be much gratified with an opportunity to complete it in the public employ."

Benton lobbied in the Senate for appropriations to permit this, while botanist John Torrey wrote a letter about the third expedition's discovery of new and rare plants, partly to support the argument for continuing the surveys and partly to assist Benton in his drive to have Congress allocate money for classifying plants and engraving drawings. Contacting some of his old followers, Frémont pushed ahead with preparations for crossing the continent on a central line intersecting the head of the Rio Grande. As the summer of 1848 wore on, there was increasing talk of a railroad from St. Louis to the Pacific; one objective of exploration would be to ascertain the practicality of a central route, especially in winter.

On 5 August, in an amendment to the civil and diplomatic appropriation bill, the Senate by an 18-to-16 vote approved $30,000 for Frémont's projected surveys and exploration. Five days later the House rejected the measure by an overwhelming margin of 128 to 29, thus assuring that the fourth expedition would be privately financed.[3] Accepting offers of nonofficial funding, Frémont also put himself forward as replacement for Consul Thomas O. Larkin as naval agent in California, a solicitation to which Secretary of State Buchanan failed to respond and which prompted Benton in his inimitable style to remind him of the Pathfinder's ever-present willingness to serve his government.

---

[3] Senate Committee Report 226, 30th Cong., 1st Sess., Serial 512; *Congressional Globe*, 30th Cong., 1st Sess., 5 and 10 Aug. 1848.

Mr. Frémont sets out to California in a few days. He goes on his own resources, Mr. Campbell, of St. Louis, advancing him $5,000; and the same number of his old followers going with him, and just as good, as went with Ulysses into the belly of the Trojan horse. He goes for two purposes: *first*, to finish up the surveys for his great work on Oregon & California; *secondly*, to pacify the Californians (Americans as well as Mexicans) and hold them on to the United States in spite of the loss of all their bills and the non payment of the expenses of the war. He goes to save California, for he is not Coriolanus. He goes at all events, and immediately, but he thinks it due to the President of the United States to let him know his design, and to offer to carry out any letter or proclamation he may wish to send, and to become the agent of the government (if deemed necessary) in observing the progress of events, and the conduct of people (foreign as well as domestic) and counteracting all evil tendencies. If not employed by the government he will act on his own views, and add $5,000 to the $4,000 already spent in the good work, and give another year to the several already employed in making California American.[4]

Benton's "Mr. Campbell" was Robert Campbell, a wealthy merchant and banking friend in St. Louis with whom Frémont had had previous business dealings. In addition to Campbell, two other substantial St. Louis businessmen supplied assistance, namely Thornton Grimsley, a saddler, and Oliver D. Filley, a Dutch oven manufacturer who would provide most of the camp equipment. Filley later became mayor of St. Louis and during the Civil War would support the Blair faction in their struggle with Frémont.[5] In 1848 the explorer could not have had much money of his own, but he may have obtained some funds from Benton. Many of the men in the fourth expedition, notably Henry King, Andrew Cathcart, Thomas E. Breckenridge, Micajah McGehee, and the Kern brothers, seem to have supplied much of their own equipment and most certainly furnished their services free.

About his own preparations for the expedition, Cathcart, the adventurous British Army officer, wrote at the time: "My own establishment will consist of 3 mules and 1 horse, and one mountain man, 'half horse, half alligator' sort of character whom I hire to assist me packing and who takes his share of camp duties; one of the mules I ride and is packed with my kit (a very small one), blankets, Buffalo robe &c. and the other is mounted by my Squire while the horse runs

[4] Benton to James Buchanan, 20 Aug. 1848 (PHi—James Buchanan Papers).
[5] UPHAM, 273; Charles P. Johnson, "Biographical sketch of O. D. Filley" (MoSHi—Filley Family Papers).

loose with the pack mules, ready for Buffalo chasing and that sort of thing."[6]

To some, Frémont apparently held out the hope that Tom Benton would ultimately persuade Congress to appropriate funds.[7] In the end, after the disaster in the mountains, Edward Kern reckoned that Frémont's own loss (from whatever sources) must have been between $8,000 and $10,000.[8]

The California accounts and aspirations for the appointment as naval agent kept Frémont in Washington until late summer, with Benton calling the government's attention to the urgency of the situation. "Every day's delay is throwing him deep into the winter snows in crossing the mountainous region to California. His baggage & men are all gone a head, waiting for him. . . . He will go; and with a few men; and through dangers from Indians & snows, which will leave his undertaking without a parallel in history."[9]

Giving Richard Burgess a power of attorney to settle his accounts with the government, Frémont was on his way in early September, accompanied by his wife, their six-year-old daughter Lily, and baby son Benton, age six weeks. From New York City, where arrangements were made to ship supplies to California, the party moved on to Buffalo to take passage on the lake steamer *Saratoga*,[10] ultimately reaching St. Louis.

The few days in St. Louis bustled with activity, including a visit to the German scientist George Engelmann. By 3 October the Frémonts (without Lily) and the thirty-five men and their accouterments for the expedition were aboard the *Martha*, which backed away from the wharf and steamed up the Missouri, arriving at Kansas Landing on 8 October without the infant Benton, who died en route. In a camp some three miles from Westport, the group was busily occupied buying and purchasing mules, making mule shoes, and packing gear, although one member, John Scott, found time to shoot quail for Mrs.

---

[6] Cathcart to C. J. Colville, St. Louis, 29 Sept. 1848 (National Register of Archives, Scotland). All of the Cathcart letters cited in this volume are from this archive.

[7] BRECKENRIDGE [1].

[8] Edward Kern to Mary Kern Wolfe, Taos, 10 Feb. 1849 (CSmH).

[9] Benton to "Dear Sir," 30 Aug. 1848 (DNA-92, LR, Consolidated Corres. File—John C. Frémont).

[10] Letter of T. C. Peters, Buffalo *Republic*, reprinted in New York *Evening Post*, 31 July 1856.

Frémont.[11] Jessie occupied a Sibley tent until the group broke camp 20 October, when she went to stay with Indian agent Robert W. Cummins and his wife, who were to put her aboard the steamer for St. Louis, the first leg of her trip by water to California. The night that camp was raised, Jessie later recorded, Frémont rode back for a few hours with her. The next morning "with our early tea for the stirrup-cup, 'he gave his bridle rein a shake,' and we went our ways, one into the mid-winter snows of untracked mountains, the other to the long sea-voyage through the tropics, and into equally strange foreign places."[12]

Thus began one of Frémont's most painful adventures. The story of the fourth expedition is simple and tragic. Led by Frémont and guided by a lean, eccentric veteran, Old Bill Williams, its thirty-three members challenged the elements—and lost. Ignoring warnings that the cold that year was unprecedented and that the San Juans were impassable in winter, they pushed on into the rugged La Garita range until waist-deep snow, knife-sharp winds honed by subzero temperatures, and exhausted supplies forced them to retreat. With food exhausted, mules collapsing, men numb and weak and sick, the tattered remnants struggled back, but ten of them and 120 mules had perished before the survivors reached safety.

Frémont left no daily record of his fourth expedition, but his 1848 and 1849 letters to his wife and Senator Benton, in the words of Cathcart, the Scotsman in the party, give a "pretty good account."[13] The original letters seem no longer to exist, but fortunately Jessie and Benton excerpted them for the *National Intelligencer*; from its columns they were copied into many western journals and are now reprinted in this volume. Somewhat different and longer versions were transcribed in 1856 in John Bigelow's and Charles W. Upham's campaign biographies of Frémont. In many instances the additions were of personal thoughts and reminiscences. In 1849, "tact" may have caused the deletion of an implication that the men of the expedition were second-raters, at least in courage; in 1856 political expediency—the necessity to show a faultless leader—may have forced its restoration. No reference to his having ordered agricultural equipment appears in the 1856 printing, leading one to suspect that in 1849 it was a

[11] MC GEHEE [1], 1–11; E. M. Kern diary, 8–21 Oct. 1848 entries (CSmH).

[12] P. 96 of Jessie B. Frémont's unpublished memoirs (CU-B); J. B. FRÉMONT [3], 55:907.

[13] Cathcart to Colville, St. Louis, 29 April 1849.

Benton addition. Curiously, in his 1849 comments on Frémont's letters, the senator acknowledged that his son-in-law knew of the gold discoveries in California before he left the frontier, a fact which Benton had denied some two and a half months earlier in private correspondence.[14] Edward F. Beale had arrived in Washington 16 September 1848 with news of the discoveries; a bit later it was in all the Missouri newspapers, and was remarked upon by Cathcart, who had just joined Frémont in St. Louis.[15] Gold was not the motive for the fourth expedition, but it may have been the compelling impulse for proceeding as rapidly as possible to California after the rescue in the San Juans. Two days after the last of his men straggled into Taos, Frémont, with his outfit renewed, was on his way. True, delay would have gained nothing but additional expense, and Jessie was expected to arrive in San Francisco in April.

Some years later, perhaps in the 1850s, possibly as late as the 1880s, Frémont made notes on his fourth expedition and these begin the documentation of that fatal venture. They are used primarily because they list the names of the men who went into the mountains with him; they are followed by Cathcart's letters to his friend in England and the Frémont letters already noted.

Jessie wrote an account of the expedition, probably for inclusion in the second volume of her husband's *Memoirs*, which was never published, but it adds nothing new to his notes and letters and is not reprinted here. Like the explorer, she blamed the guide, Old Bill Williams, for the expedition's failure and added the charge of "evil character." "'In starving times no man who knew him ever walked in front of Bill Williams,'"[16] she quoted Kit Carson as having said.

At least seven of Frémont's fellow travelers left records of all or part of the expedition. The manuscripts of the sketchy diaries of the Kern brothers, Benjamin, Edward M., and Richard H., are in the Henry E. Huntington Library, San Marino, California. They were published in 1960[17] and are not reprinted in this volume, except for the abbreviated journal of Richard, which was printed immediately after the expedition in Quincy, Illinois.[18] Its chief interest lies in the adverse

[14] Benton to "Sir," Washington City, 28 Jan. 1849 (NHi).

[15] Cathcart to Colville, St. Louis, 29 Sept. 1848, takes note of the gold fever that held California in its grip.

[16] "Great Events during the life of Major General John C. Fremont," 84 (CU-B).

[17] HAFEN & HAFEN.

[18] Quincy *Whig*, 22 May 1849, Doc. No. 39.

comments on Frémont, none of which appear in the Kerns' manuscript diaries or in their first letters home after the rescue. In fact Edward had written to his sister, "The whole business may be laid down to error in judgment to whom attributable I am not now prepared to say." But in a few days he was unleashing his fury at Frémont. In the words of one of his biographers, the Kerns' admiration of their leader "had cracked like spring ice, leaving sharp, jagged disillusionment." In Taos and Santa Fe the two surviving brothers became the center of an anti-Frémont circle.[19]

Both Andrew Cathcart and Henry King seem to have kept diaries, but these have not been found. Richard Kern wrote to Cathcart requesting a short extract from his journal "from Dec. 12 until Jany. 28" and an estimate of how much it had cost him for provisions.[20] And from Philadelphia, John Kern related having received a letter from the sorrowing Mrs. Christina King in which she stated that "upon Frémont's arrival in California, he admitted to her two sons who are out there that he had their brother Henry's journal, and requested the privilege of looking over it, which they very inconsiderately granted. On his arrival at Washington (as senator), when called upon for it, he stated that he left it with his brother-in-law, Jones; when Jones arrived he said he gave it to Mrs. Frémont. Now Frémont says that it was stolen from out of his camp."[21]

Charles Preuss left a short record of his experiences with the Fourth between 15 December 1848 and 12 February 1849. Published by Erwin and Elisabeth Gudde, it adds little to Frémont's letters and Richard Kern's account. Preuss does record that King's comrades had eaten part of his body.[22]

The one member who left a running narrative of the expedition from St. Louis to California was Mississippian Micajah McGehee,[23] but unfortunately it is a reconstructed account and not a day-to-day journal. Entitled "Rough Notes of Rough Times in Rough Places," it may have been written from notations taken on the spot. A family member, James Stewart McGehee, reports that a few penciled scraps with such an appearance were found among Micajah's papers. For-

[19] HINE [2], 61.
[20] Richard H. Kern to Andrew Cathcart, Santa Fe, 30 Sept. 1849 (CSmH).
[21] John Kern to Richard H. and Edward M. Kern, Philadelphia, 30 May 1850 (CSmH).
[22] PREUSS, 149, entry of 17? Jan. 1849.
[23] See Doc. No. 30, n. 13, for a biographical sketch.

tunately, he had a typewritten transcription of the narrative prepared in 1913, for apparently a second volume of the manuscript journal has not survived. The James Stewart McGehee transcription is a full account of the trip from its beginning in St. Louis in October 1848 to its termination in Los Angeles in April 1849.[24] The 218-page handwritten narrative, which was given to the Library of Congress in 1975 by Ann Landis McLaughlin and Ellen Landis McKee, ends abruptly with the party resting at the Pima villages on 27 March 1849. Because of the existence of the transcription, there is every reason to assume that the handwritten account was continued into a second volume, which probably disappeared sometime between 1913 and 1935. Novelist and drama critic Stark Young, in an 1935 *Saturday Evening Post* article entitled "Cousin Micajah," refers to one journal only—218 pages—and notes that for many years it had lain in a bank vault in Micajah's home town, Woodville, Mississippi.[25]

An extract dealing with the disaster in La Garita Mountains was published in the March 1891 issue of *The Century*.[26] It had been sent to the journal by Charles G. McGehee, the brother who had bidden farewell to Micajah in St. Louis in 1848. In 1910 *Outdoor Life* brought out James Stewart McGehee's amplified account of the freezing and starving time. Utilizing the two McGehee versions, the Hafens published yet a fuller account in 1960 in their documentary volume of the fourth expedition and expressed the opinion that McGehee had written his account within ten years of the events reported.[27] Because the "mountain portion" of the journal has been published so many times, it is not reprinted here, although it is probably the most valuable part of the entire account. Nor are other portions of the journal reproduced. While Micajah seems to be quite accurate in his information about the expedition per se, he actually relates very little about its day-to-day activities. He does not name the individual who suggested that his little group feed on the body of their dead companion, or state how his party, which included Cathcart, learned that members of the first rescue party had eaten part of the remains of Henry King, if they did; nor does he enlighten us as to the men's attitude toward Frémont, or when the latter left for the Mariposa region.

---

[24] LU—James Stewart McGehee Papers.
[25] YOUNG.
[26] For a reprint of the article, see JOHNSON & DAVIS.
[27] HAFEN & HAFEN, 143–73. For an opinion on composition, see their notes 143 and 172.

For yet another reason Micajah's journal is used simply for documentation and summary information. His fascinating descriptions of the terrain, the buffalo and other forms of wildlife, the Indian tribes and their customs, and the settlements in New Mexico and Arizona rely too heavily on *Adventures in Mexico and the Rocky Mountains* (1847) and *Life in the Far West* (1849) by George Ruxton and on a work by Frémont's old foe, William H. Emory, entitled *Notes of a Military Reconnaissance from Fort Leavenworth, in Missouri, to San Diego, in California*. Indeed, some of the passages are borrowed almost verbatim, and perhaps it should not surprise that McGehee turned to these superb earlier writers when years later he began fleshing out his own rough notes. Ruxton's name was well known among the expedition members; Cathcart for one would have talked about him. He and the twenty-seven-year-old Ruxton had been planning a hunting trip into the West when the latter fell ill with dysentery in St. Louis and died within two weeks. Cathcart then decided to join Frémont's Fourth. Emory's route from Albuquerque to Warner's Ranch in California in 1846 was followed closely by Frémont and Micajah in 1849.

In addition to the seven members who appear to have kept some actual records, Alexander Godey, Thomas S. Martin, and Thomas E. Breckenridge gave later accounts. Godey's was in the form of a long letter written during the presidential campaign of 1856 and was specifically designed to answer Richard Kern's criticisms of 1849, which were being re-circulated.[28] Martin dictated his reminiscences in 1878 to Edward F. Murray for the H. H. Bancroft collection, and these were published in 1975.[29] Breckenridge's story is in the Western Historical Manuscripts Collection at the University of Missouri. With Frederick Remington illustrations and high polishing by J. S. Freeman and Charles W. Watson, it fascinated readers of *Cosmopolitan* in August 1896. The applicable portions of these three narratives have been relegated to notes, since the passage of time, old age, and—in the case of Godey—political motives eroded memory and, consequently, historical accuracy.

Historians have long been intrigued by several questions arising from the fourth expedition. First, who was responsible for the disaster? Was it Frémont? Or did old Bill Williams, the colorful and expe-

---

[28] For example, see the Washington *Daily Union*, 31 July 1856, which reprinted the diary of Richard Kern as first published by the Quincy (Ill.) *Whig*, 22 May 1849.
[29] MARTIN.

rienced mountain guide, mislead the party, as Frémont charged? Perhaps both were to blame. In his gripping book *The Men and the Mountain*, William Brandon argues that Williams did indeed lose his way, but that Frémont had given him an "insurmountable assignment." Another who has spent many years studying the expedition notes that the routes Williams chose were routes to where Frémont wished to travel, but that they were not the best routes, especially in the atypical winter of 1848–49, with its heavy snow and savage winds which took the chill factor to −75°.[30]

Intertwined with the first is a second question: what pass was Frémont using to cross the Continental Divide? At the time there were three possibilities. One, a southerly route, followed the old Spanish Trail through Abiquiu. Farther north were Carnero (presently Cochetopa) and Cochetopa (presently North Cochetopa). Brandon contended that there was a fourth—Pass of the Rio del Norte—which since the 1850s had faded from memory. Presumably it was the shortest of the northern passes, but also the highest, steepest, and roughest. This, he wrote, was Frémont's objective.

Brandon charts Frémont's route across the Sangre de Cristos by way of Mosca Pass and around the giant sand dunes in San Luis Valley. He tracks the men as they struggled westward across that valley's level, treeless floor, maintaining that killing temperature forced them to swing over to the more sheltered Rio Grande River, which they followed as far up as Alder Creek. After turning off the Rio Grande, the route seems to have "led up the narrow cañon of West Alder Creek, past the present Round Park, on across the area of a feeder stream now known revealingly as Difficult Creek, and swung to the right up Long's Gulch, which brought them up against the flat-topped summit of Pool Table Mountain. They went around this and followed the extreme headwaters of Trujillo Creek (the highest fork of East Bellows Creek) to the ridge above its rincons and crossed this ridge to the head of Wannamaker Creek."[31]

Brandon did careful field work for *The Men and the Mountain*, but Patricia Joy Richmond believes that his tracing of the expedition's route into the mountains is not entirely accurate, probably because he was given erroneous information by a ranger who had been in the San Juans a short time and did not know the history of the area. Rich-

---

[30] BRANDON, 308, and RICHMOND.
[31] BRANDON, 306.

mond, who lives in Crestone, Colorado, has spent fourteen years absorbing local history and studying the extant documents and the terrain. In all seasons she covered the same ground, viewed the same sights, and experienced the same stresses as the intrepid explorers of 1848–49. So thorough have been her on-site inspections of campsites that this editor has accepted her conclusions about the route.

Richmond agrees with Brandon that the expedition reached Wannamaker Creek, but she maintains that it did so by a more northern passage than the Rio Grande. Details of her Frémont route are supplied in the notes to the documents. She is also firmly convinced that historians have interpreted too narrowly early references to the Rio del Norte. They are not to just that part of the river that flows from Rio Grande Reservoir through Del Norte and Alamosa but to the entire river system of the San Luis Valley. This interpretation in effect makes all the streams of the San Luis Valley the headwaters of the Rio Grande. And finally, she maintains that Frémont intended to use presently named Cochetopa Pass to reach the waters of the Colorado. It was the lowest in altitude, the most easily accessible for wagons, and under normal conditions would be free of snow.[32]

Statements after the destruction of the expedition reinforce Richmond's insistence that Cochetopa Pass had been the explorer's destination all along. Benton believed it; Antoine Leroux said so;[33] so did Gwinn Harris Heap, who for a time had been guided by Leroux and who had been Frémont's agent on the Mariposa. From the San Luis Valley, on 3 July 1853, Heap wrote: "We encamped on the Rio Grande del Norte, as the sun was setting behind the pass in the Sierra de San Juan, at the head of the Del Norte. This pass was in sight of us, and is the one which Colonel Frémont met with so terrible a disaster in the winter of 1848–49, so near was he to the object of his search, the Coochatope."[34]

A third question has also perplexed historians. After the failure— the defeat by the elements—why did Frémont waste time and further dissipate the strength of his men by having the baggage, including pack and riding saddles, hauled from their Christmas camp on the west slope of Rincones Creek down to La Garita Creek, while he sent a "relief" party of four exhausted men more than a hundred

---

[32] RICHMOND.

[33] Leroux's statement in *Letter from Col. Benton to the People of Missouri* (Washington, D.C., 1853).

[34] HEAP, 173–74.

miles on foot to procure animals and supplies for the stranded expedition? The answer is that his pride—the need to achieve victory after the court-martial humiliation, plus the memory of the triumphal winter crossing of the Sierras five years before—made him unwilling to accept the idea of surrender. Probably he hoped to use the station to mount another assault on the high mountains when the relief animals appeared. But unless aid came promptly, not only would he be unable to continue but he would also have to abandon the expensive equipment in order to save the lives of his men. Thus, after sixteen days of waiting, he decided to go himself in search of the relief party, but so tenaciously did he cling to the tattered hope of blazing a new route that he instructed his camp to wait three days, then follow him down the Rio Grande River. If he met the relief party immediately, all could yet be saved. Unfortunately, he found one of the party dead and the other three floundering and half-starved. An additional eight would perish in the mountains before help reached them.[35]

As the emaciated survivors straggled into Taos, Frémont re-outfitted and on 13 February set out for California, going down the Rio Grande and then westward along the Gila route to Los Angeles. His "Notes" list some of the incidents of the trip and some of the places through which his party passed; as far as present-day Pembroke or Tacna his route is marked on the map in his *Memoirs*.

Touted as having been "drawn and engraved especially for Frémont's *Memoirs*," the map seems to have been prepared much earlier than the *Memoirs*, a book of the 1880s, or at least based on one that was prepared earlier. Since it shows the additions to cartography that Howard Stansbury, Lorenzo Sitgreaves, and others had made during the 1850s, it was probably drawn at the end of that decade.[36] At least three names applicable for the fourth expedition would indicate so. The present-day San Carlos River appears as the San Francisco on the map, a designation given to the old Rio de Carlos by William H. Emory in the late 1840s. By 1874 the Public Survey maps and by 1875 the military showed it again as Rio San Carlos.[37] As governor of Arizona Territory between 1878 and 1881, Frémont would have been familiar with the later name change, especially as he was riding over the country, prospecting for minerals. His 1848 map had labeled the

[35] Raphael Proue died before JCF left the party on 11 Jan. Altogether he lost ten men.

[36] WHEAT [1], 3:203, discusses the problems of dating the map.

[37] BARNES, 115–16.

present-day Salt River by that name, but the *Memoirs* map calls it Salinas, which, along with Salado, was a common designation for the stream in the 1850s. Fort Buchanan, another name on the *Memoirs* map, existed only between 1856 and 1861.[38]

Analysis of the map with respect to the 1853–54 expedition also argues strongly for its preparation in the late 1850s. Lacking is the cartographical detail for southern and southwestern Utah—the region traversed by Frémont in 1854, which George M. Wheeler had been able to include on his map of the region as a result of his explorations in 1869 and 1871.[39] Presumably a Frémont map "drawn and engraved" in the 1880s would have included such detail, but the whole trail from the Cedar Mountains to California is deficient in the names of peaks, passes, and streams. Additional support for argument that the map was begun in the 1850s is a letter of Jessie's to Francis Preston Blair noticing that her husband was "making out his calculations for his map" and would "take some on to Mr. Hubbard at the Observatory."[40]

To return to the fourth expedition: by 20 April 1849 Frémont's party had reached Isaac Williams's magnificent Rancho del Chino—more than 35,000 acres, stocked with 15,000–20,000 head of cattle, 1,000 horses, and numerous mules, sheep, and hogs. Frémont reputedly contracted to purchase the property for $200,000, a reasonable sum, thought McGehee, who expansively wrote that cattle were selling at $100 a head in the mines. The arrangement fell through, the New York *Herald*'s correspondent reported, because the first payment had not been made on time. McGehee believed that "certain conditions of possession" prevented the fulfillment of the contract; William R. Hutton reported to his uncle that the sale "cannot hold as the property belongs to Williams' children by his first wife. . . ."[41]

[38] *Ibid.*, 314.

[39] I am indebted to Todd Berens for calling my attention to Atlas Sheet 59, "Southern and Southwestern Utah," *U.S. Geographical Survey West of the 100th Meridian*, which was prepared by Wheeler about 1872 or 1873.

[40] Jessie B. Frémont to F. P. Blair, 18 Nov. 1855 (NjP—Blair-Lee Papers).

[41] MC GEHEE [2], 166–67; MARTIN, 28; William Rich Hutton to William Rich, Los Angeles, 14 July 1849 (CSmH); T. F. to editor, Rancho del Chino, 24 Aug. 1849, New York *Herald*, 12 Nov. 1849; BEATTIE, 127. Williams's first wife had been the daughter of Antonio María Lugo, who in 1841 deeded his son-in-law a half-interest in the ranch, which then comprised some five leagues or approximately 21,000 acres. In 1847, "as a gift of inheritance," Lugo ceded the other

It was probably at Williams's ranch, although Breckenridge says John Rowland's, that Frémont broke up his expedition. Breckenridge also recalled that the explorer gave each member a pony and a pack animal, "but nothing more as he had nothing more to give," although he made arrangements at Los Angeles for food and an outfit and invited each to try his luck on the Mariposa.[42] It may have been here, too, that Alexander Godey took twenty-eight of the many Sonorans who had joined Frémont on the trail and headed for Mariposa, where they would wash out gold on a contractual basis.

Frémont paid a hurried visit to Los Angeles before pushing on to the Mariposa.[43] He soon recognized that money was to be made in supplying cattle to the mushrooming mining camps and sent Godey back to Los Angeles to make purchases, while he went on to Monterey and then to San Francisco to meet Jessie and Lily, whose steamer had already arrived. He found them occupying a part of the residence of the late Vice-Consul Leidesdorff, now a club for wealthy merchants. Shortly they moved to the more genial climate of Monterey and occupied a wing of the home of former Governor José Castro.[44] Monterey was better for Jessie's lungs, it was closer to the Mariposa to which Frémont was making frequent trips, and it was to be the site of the constitutional convention called for 1 September. Already the rumors were widespread that Frémont was anxious to become governor.[45]

In late August Edward F. Beale arrived with a letter from the president appointing Frémont to the Mexican Boundary Commission. He found the explorer in San Jose on the portico of Grove C. Cook's

---

two and one half leagues to his granddaughters, Maria Mercedes and Francisca. Williams acquired adjacent property, and by 1849 the ranch embraced eight leagues or 35,000 acres.

[42] BRECKENRIDGE [1].

[43] W. R. Hutton wrote to William Rich, 19 Aug. 1849, that he had been shown the beautiful steel ruler and fine telescope, made in Munich, which JCF had left in Los Angeles before going on to the Mariposa (CSmH).

[44] Jessie gives a delightful description of her Isthmus crossing and the early months in California in "A Year of American Travel" (J. B. FRÉMONT [3]). She writes of their traveling carriage, which "Mr. Aspinwall had . . . built under his own directions in New Jersey" and of their many trips in it from Monterey to San Francisco, "stopping at different ranches and farms to see and be seen by the people who wished Mr. Fremont to bring me to them. We would turn out of our way to accept the invitation of some of the old Californians to visit them at their ranches." JCF was building political strength.

[45] William Rich to Mrs. J. R. Hutton, Monterey, 30 July 1849 (CSmH).

home, wearing a sombrero and a Californian jacket. He had just returned from the Mariposa River and showed no trace of the terrible hardships of the previous winter. With Beale was the correspondent of the New York *Tribune*, Bayard Taylor, who remarked of the explorer that he had "seen in no other man the qualities of lightness, activity, strength and physical endurance in so perfect an equilibrium. . . . A stranger would never suppose him to be the Columbus of our central wilderness, though when so informed, would believe it without surprise." He noted that Frémont had established a steam sawmill at Pueblo San Jose, close to the redwoods that made fine timber, which promised a business more secure than the digging of gold. Lumber was then bringing $500 per thousand feet and he had a year's work engaged. Taylor stayed at the Miner's Home, where also lodged two of Frémont's men, Preuss and Creutzfeldt. He made a brief trip to the "diggings" on the Mokelumne, but when he returned to San Francisco in early September, he encountered Frémont at the United States Hotel and heard from him the particulars of the magnificent discovery on the Mariposa. He saw specimens too. "The stone was a reddish quartz, filled with rich veins of gold, and far surpassing the specimens brought from North Carolina and Georgia. Some stones picked up on top of the quartz strata, without particular selection, yielded two ounces of gold to every twenty-five pounds. Col. Frémont informed me that the vein had been traced for more than a mile. The thickness on the surface is two feet, gradually widening as it descends and showing larger particles of gold. The dip downward is only about 20°, so that the mine can be worked at little expense."[46]

Frémont returned to Monterey, but as soon as the constitutional convention was over, he took his family to Happy Valley, about half a mile east of the old city of San Francisco, where he had a Chinese house erected and whence he commenced his campaign for a seat in the U.S. Senate. He assured the public "that by association, feeling, principle and education," he was "thoroughly a democrat," and that he would work hard for the immediate location and construction of a central, national railroad from the Mississippi to the Pacific. He also

---

[46] TAYLOR, 69–70, 110–11. Taylor is the only source the editor has located for JCF's activity in the sawmill industry. Since he liked later to pose as a conservationist, he probably wished not to remember his destruction of the redwoods, however brief it might have been. Some documentation for the Frémonts' residence in the area is a letter of Charles V. Gillespie to his brother: "I forgot to mention that Mrs. Fremont is for the present residing at Pueblo San José" (1 Sept. 1849, CLU—Gillespie Papers).

explained why he had accepted, then resigned, a place on the commission to determine the boundary with Mexico; he discussed his purchase of the Mariposa claim; and he defended his financial transactions during his brief governorship and embroglio with Gen. Stephen Watts Kearny in 1847.

Eastern newspapers noted that Frémont's political character was not clearly understood and that "he has warmer friends and more unrelenting enemies than any man in California." Among the "enemies" was Charles V. Gillespie, brother of that Archibald Gillespie who in 1846 had pursued Frémont into the Oregon wilderness to urge him and his exploring expedition to return to California. As a supporter of T. Butler King, Gillespie complained that the Frémonts were too "haughty," and asked, "Who that has any interest in California would like to see it represented in the Senate by Col. Benton & Mrs. Frémont?" After the legislature, meeting in San Jose, elected the explorer on the first ballot, he grumbled that the action was "the influence of rowdies & gamblers."[47]

The new senator promptly displayed both political finesse and an appreciation of the honor by presenting 100 volumes of valuable books to the state, a collection that became the nucleus of the California State Library.[48] A physician and politician from Mississippi, William M. Gwin, was elected on an early ballot as the state's second senator.

When the *Oregon* cleared the Golden Gate for Panama on New Year's Day, 1850, she was carrying over $1,000,000 in gold and 280 passengers, among them the Frémont family, Gwin, and the two other members of the California congressional delegation, Edward Gilbert and George W. Wright. A close friendship developed between Frémont and Wright that was to endure until the latter's death some thirty-five years later. The significance of this relationship can be appreciated when it is remembered that Wright was one of the four founders of the San Francisco banking firm of Palmer, Cook & Company, which was to play so important a role in shaping Frémont's financial and political future. Wright himself was a true entrepreneur, ever promoting someone or some enterprise and rarely seeking the limelight for himself. He and Frémont were kindred spirits: both had

---

[47] Charles V. Gillespie to Archibald Gillespie, 1, 15, 28 Sept., 31 Oct., 31 Dec. 1849 (CLU—Gillespie Papers).

[48] *California Senate Journal*, 19 Jan. 1850. The presentation was made by John Bidwell.

visions of grand fortunes and both were willing to take inordinate speculative risks in the hopes of making their dreams come true.

Detained in Panama by serious illness, the Frémonts did not arrive in Washington until the second week of March.[49] In the interim between his arrival and the admission of California to the Union on 10 September 1850, the explorer kept his name before the public and was as active as "Chagres fever" would permit. He sent a long letter to the Mississippi and Pacific Railroad Convention in Philadelphia, urging the route between the 38th and 39th parallels; he promoted the establishment of a mint in San Francisco; he defended his "state" against Henry Clay's charges that some Californians lacked loyalty to the Union; and he made arrangements for the development of Las Mariposas, which in the end, as Allan Nevins has so accurately written, was to prove " a thorny and profitless maze," a "perfect Pandora's box of complications."[50]

When California's star was added to the flag, three weeks of the first session of the 31st Congress remained—time enough for Frémont to introduce at least eighteen bills, mostly routine and designed to establish the normal federal functions within the new state. None passed immediately, and since Frémont had drawn the short term and would fail at re-election, it would fall upon Senator Gwin to shepherd the legislation through Congress. The measures pertaining to the settlement of private land claims and to mining were of special interest to Californians.

On the land question, the Treaty of Guadalupe Hidalgo ending the Mexican War had guaranteed resident Californians protection and security in the "free enjoyment" of their property as well as of their liberty and religion. Many American settlers, however, were convinced that the grants were not only excessively large but also spurious, being made in the waning hours of Mexican hegemony and to personal friends of the Mexican governor, perhaps even backdated. Capt. Henry Wagner Halleck, who had been on Governor Richard B. Mason's staff, reported in 1849 that a large number of the titles were imperfect, but Frémont's brother-in-law, William Carey Jones, who had been sent to California specifically to procure information on the subject, found a majority of the land titles in conformity with Mexican law.

---

[49] *National Intelligencer*, 13 March 1850.
[50] NEVINS, 394.

Frémont's land bill provided for a board of commissioners to examine all claims. Its decision against the United States was to be final, but the claimant was given the right to appeal to the federal courts. Benton was critical of the bill, feeling that it was much too stringent and would subject the country to confusion and grantees to protracted and excessive litigation. He would simply provide for the registration of land claims in California and the patenting of all claims in which there was no clear evidence of fraud. Neither Benton nor Frémont's measures passed and the Land Act of 1851 was largely the handiwork of Senator Gwin, whose sympathies lay with American land seekers. It permitted both the claimant and the United States to appeal a decision of the Land Commission. Frémont spent scarcely five minutes in Congress on "his" land bill. When he returned to California, he assured his constituency that his purpose had been "to quiet titles, not to disturb them; to prevent, not promote litigation; to make every owner of property, or who contemplated owning property, secure in the tenure by which he should hold." Many suspected he was not completely pure in his motives. He was known to be a political favorite of the native Californians and the claimant to Las Mariposas.

He was more attuned to the prejudices of his constituents when he voted in favor of confining mining privileges to American citizens. On the floor of the Senate he pointedly criticized the flood of Mexicans pouring into the Mother Lode mines: they were "a class of population of very doubtful character," he said, composed largely of "uncivilized Indians and inferior castes." With time, he would come to regret these nativistic remarks. In 1856, hoping to make his presidential candidacy more appealing to the foreign-born, he had his biographer Charles Upham revise the senatorial chapter to eliminate this offensive statement before the manuscript went to the printers.[51]

Once the Congress had adjourned, Frémont and his family sailed from New York on the *Cherokee*, arriving in San Francisco via Panama in late November aboard the *California*. Already he had written

---

[51] *Congressional Globe*, 31st Cong., 1st sess., 19, Appendix, pt. 2, pp. 1362–72. As amended, the Senate bill reserved mining to U.S. citizens or "such foreigners from Europe or the British North American possessions as have filed their declaration of intention to become citizens," which caused the editor of the Stockton *Times* to wonder why the "sallow emigrants" of Old Spain or Italy were more desirable than the Mexicans (16 Nov. 1850). For Isaac Sherman's concern about JCF's early Americanism, see Sherman to Upham, 2 and 11 June 1856, and Frémont to Upham, 24 June 1856 (Hugh Upham Clark Collection, Arlington, Va.).

friends of his desire to be returned to the Senate and enlisted the support of young James Blair, who was then living in California and whose wife and young daughter the Frémonts were escorting to the Pacific Coast. James was the son of the politically powerful Francis Preston Blair, a staunch supporter of Benton and the editor of the Washington *Globe* until 1845. The friendship between the Bentons and the Blairs was so close that Jessie considered Silver Spring a second home and was a frequent correspondent of "Father" Blair and of his daughter Elizabeth. Because his father wished it, James worked assiduously for Frémont, even borrowing money to further his political cause.[52]

In January 1851 Frémont made his headquarters in San Jose, the capital, and quietly established the *Argus* to promote his campaign. That journal avowed its interest in "principles not men" and pledged itself to be "democratic to the core" in politics.[53] Among Frémont's opponents were Democrats Solomon Heydenfeldt and John B. Weller; in addition, T. Butler King, John Geary, and James A. Collier also coveted the Senate prize.

When the legislature met, suspicion, liquor, and lobbyists were rife. Countless little secret caucuses and postponements hampered the business at hand. According to the *Alta California*, the selection of a senator and the proposal to move the seat of government to Vallejo were the "two huge grizzly questions" hanging like a spell over the lawmakers. Finally, after much maneuvering, the two legislative houses met in joint convention on 18 February. After the ninth ballot, it was noted that the native Californian members were solidly behind Frémont, who usually ran second or third. Four more days of voting continued, including Washington's Birthday, and a compromise caucus, which Frémont supporters refused to attend, failed to settle upon a single Democratic candidate. Finally on February 27, after the 142nd ballot, the legislature was dissolved and the election of a senator was carried over to the next term. "The city looks like a deserted town," a reporter wrote the following day. "The lobby has been evacuated; half

---

[52] Montgomery Blair to Minna Blair, 27 May 1854 (DLC—Blair Papers).

[53] See J. Winchester (editor of the *Argus*) in New York *Tribune*, 19 June 1856. Rare copies of the San Jose *Daily Argus* (it was published briefly as a weekly before it folded shortly after the adjournment of the legislature) may be found in the American Antiquarian Society and the New-York Historical Society. C. M. Blake and Co. are listed as the "Editors and Proprietors."

the members are gone, and the other half look like Lucretia Borgia's victims after her feast of poison."[54]

A hostile San Francisco banker reported that Jessie blamed James Blair for her husband's defeat, but Montgomery Blair, who had gone out to San Francisco to settle the estate of his brother after his premature death in December 1852, believed Frémont held William Carey Jones responsible. By 1856 the explorer was attributing it to the nullifiers, but slavery seems not to have been an issue in the election.[55] In any case, Frémont decided that for the moment politics was "too costly an amusement" and was not a candidate in 1852.[56]

He now became completely absorbed in business ventures, many of them speculative. One such was his contracts with the federal Indian commissioners to supply beef to the Indians, whose hostility and depredations had increased with the influx of miners into their old homes and hunting grounds. By early 1851 the situation had become especially acute in the Mariposa region and a general war seemed imminent. Volunteers were being called out when the commissioners finally arrived in California and adopted a policy of peace through food. At first the three commissioners acted jointly in negotiating treaties of peace and friendship whereby the natives ceded their old lands in exchange for specially reserved land and stated amounts of beef, flour, breeding stock, farm equipment, and clothing.[57] After 1 May the agents divided California among them, but in their separate capacities continued to negotiate at least eighteen treaties that set aside a total of approximately 7,488,000 acres and promised substantial supplies of food and clothing—perhaps worth as much as $800,000 or $1,000,000.[58] To make these agreements effective, ratification in Washington was necessary, but the commissioners believed that delay might bring actual hostilities and thus contracted directly with individuals to supply provisions immediately. With only $50,000 available to the commissioners at the time, contractors were compelled to accept payment in the form of drafts upon the Secretary of the Interior.

Frémont's proposals to supply some of the beef are dated 12 and 19

---

[54] For the attempts to elect a senator, see *Alta California*, 10 Jan.–3 March 1851.

[55] Montgomery Blair to Minna Blair, 27 May 1854 (DLC—Blair Papers); JCF to Charles Robinson, 17 March 1856, printed in BIGELOW, 447–48; BARTLETT.

[56] JBF to F. P. Blair, 14 Aug. 1851 (NjP—Blair-Lee Papers).

[57] See MITCHELL, 102–7, for the text of the treaty signed 29 April 1851 at Camp Barbour on the San Joaquin.

[58] ELLISON.

May 1852; the acceptance of George W. Barbour, the commissioner responsible for the southern district, is dated 28 May. And yet on 11 May Frémont had been able to write his London agent that he had "made some large cattle contracts."[59] The probability of an Indian market for beef had undoubtedly been a consideration in his offer to purchase Los Alamitos from Abel Stearns in late April and in his decision to establish a substantial cattle ranch on the Mariposa, where he went in mid-May. From there he proceeded south to acquire cattle, part of which seem to have come from Eulogio de Célis, who probably took them out of the herd which Frémont had left in trust with Stearns in the spring of 1847.[60] Antonio José Côt, William Workman, and Francisco Ocampo furnished some and probably also Henry Mellus and John Rowland; all of them were paid, at least in part, by checks drawn on Palmer, Cook & Company.

Frémont or his agents delivered some cattle directly to the different Indian tribes and a large herd of 1,900 to Barbour on the San Joaquin River. Barbour turned them over to the subagent, Adam Johnston, who in turn passed them along to James D. Savage, the Indian trader, for transfer to the Indians. Altogether from Barbour Frémont received a total of $183,825 in drafts drawn on the Secretary of the Interior. A large part of this—$153,575—he used to obtain an immediate advance from a San Francisco banker with the peculiar name of James King of William, who was affiliated with Corcoran & Riggs in Washington.[61] He also agreed to give Beale $29,376 when the drafts were paid—presumably because Beale was carrying his Indian contracts east and, with Benton, would lobby for their acceptance, although there may have been other reasons as well.

California bankers presented Frémont's "Indian drafts" for collection along with those of other contractors who had been paid in similar fashion. All were protested by the federal government, an action which came as no surprise to Frémont. In fact, such hostility developed toward all of the Indian treaties under which the contracts had been negotiated that the agreements themselves were never ratified. Californians were opposed because they removed such large areas of

---

[59] For the May 1851 contracts, see Doc. Nos. 139 and 140.

[60] As governor of California JCF had entered into contracts (involving money and cattle) with Eulogio de Célis and Abel Stearns. See Vol. 2, pp. 407–21.

[61] See Doc. No. 161 and "Contract between J. King and Corcoran & Riggs," 29 July 1854, which mentions the 9 Sept. 1851 advance to JCF (DLC—W. W. Corcoran Papers, Lbk, pp. 275–76). W. W. Corcoran came to have a three-fourths interest in the sum advanced by King.

public land from private use and because there was evidence of fraud in many of the contracts. One of the few claims allowed was Frémont's $183,825, which with 10 percent interest from 14 June 1851 made a total of $242,036.25. This was paid after special appeals and a special authorization by Congress in 1854.[62]

Since many of the debts Frémont had incurred as military commander and governor of California were still unsettled by the government, one might wonder why he would embark on similar tenuous transactions. He and his friends simply hoped to make a great deal of money out of the overpriced beef, and they felt they had the necessary political influence to guarantee payment from a generous and charitable Uncle Sam, whose treatment of the Indian was beginning to disturb the national conscience. At first Frémont was pained that his contractual arrangement with one of the commissioners, Oliver M. Wozencraft,[63] went awry, but later was careful to note that his transaction with Barbour was in no way connected with the other two commissioners. He could not ignore charges like those of Joel H. Brooks, who testified that he was instructed by Savage to take receipts for double or even triple the number of cattle actually delivered to the tribes and that over 500 head had been delivered to Alexander Godey, who sold them to miners or settlers or herded them "elsewhere"; and that an additional 800 went to Savage, who used some to feed the Indians working for him and others to stock his ranch on the San Joaquin.[64] Indeed, Frémont believed that a portion had become the "spoil of unfaithful agents trusted by Mr. Barbour," but of this he

---

[62] Following the advice of Montgomery Blair, the Frémont memorial claimed not only the actual delivery of the beef but also the absolute necessity of the supply to the Indians, the great moral obligation of the United States to furnish it, its good effects in pacifying the Indians in the San Joaquin area and saving the peace by preventing their incursions to rob or find food, and the low terms upon which the beef had been furnished (JBF's printed memorial in Senate Misc. Doc. 69, 33rd Cong., 1st sess., Serial 705). In the handwriting of JBF, the memorial of four California congressmen further maintained: "Throughout all this section, extending southward from the Stanislaus river about two hundred and fifty miles, and occupied by many tribes of Indians, peace has been uninterrupted since the period in question, when they were furnished with food" (J. B. Weller, W. M. Gwin, J. McDougall, and M. S. Latham to the chairman of the Committee on Indian Affairs, House of Representatives, Washington City, 30 June [1854], DNA). For the authorization of payment and the payment, see *United States Statutes*, 33rd Cong., 1 sess. (Private Acts); DNA-217, Misc. Treasury Accounts, Account No. 115–310.

[63] See Doc. Nos. 184 and 185.

[64] Brooks's testimony, 21 Sept. 1852, Senate Ex. Doc. 4, 33rd Cong., Special sess., pp. 369–70, Serial 688.

knew nothing himself, "having immediately left the country." Savage had been dead a month when Brooks gave his testimony and could not speak in his own defense. Barbour admitted that he had received more beef than the Indians were specifically authorized for the year 1851, but justified the larger amount on the ground that the Indians must be placated during the rainy season, from October or November until May, lest they commit depredations on the whites during that time.[65]

Almost all of those who had or came to have an interest in Frémont's beef contracts were men close to him: L. D. Vinsonhaler; Alexander Godey and his nephew, Theodore McNabb; Edward F. Beale and his brother-in-law, Henry B. Edwards; and George W. Wright. Frémont had posted surety for Savage and Vinsonhaler in May, and for a fee of $1,200 they were licensed on 20 June 1851 to trade with the Indians over the entire San Joaquin reservation, which had been recently created by treaty.[66] Godey and his nephew were in charge of the drovers who brought the cattle from Los Angeles to Allsbury's Ferry at Four Creeks, there to be met by Edwards and Vinsonhaler.[67] Frémont sought further to both protect and enhance his economic interests by having Beale, his old and intimate friend, appointed Superintendent of California Indians. His business associate Wright had direct ties into the banking house of Palmer, Cook & Company. Just returned from a mine promotion visit to England, Wright in November signed a contract with subagent Adam Johnston by which he and Frémont would deliver an additional 1,200 head of beef cattle "now on the little Mariposa" and 1,000 half-sacks of flour to the tribes of the San Joaquin Valley. Just eleven days later Johnston acknowledged delivery and paid with the usual Interior drafts, part of which Wright then used to purchase additional cattle required to meet the terms of the original agreement. These drafts, too, were protested and became the center of controversy, with petitions to Congress urging they be honored and others condemning their speculative nature, and a round of lawsuits were filed against Frémont, Wright, and the federal government.[68]

[65] G. W. Barbour to Luke Lea, n.d., *ibid.*, p. 259.

[66] Letter of Adam Johnston, San Joaquin Indian Reservation, Fresno River, 20 June 1851, printed in *ibid.*, pp. 101–2.

[67] Godey's testimony, 24 June 1858, pp. 133–34 in Argenti v. United States (CHi—Wright Papers).

[68] For notice of petitions and cases, see the notes to Doc. Nos. 167 and 235. Better than the legal cases, the Wright Papers show rampant speculation.

The involvement of Palmer, Cook & Company in the beef drafts and in various Mariposa mining schemes much disturbed Senator Gwin, who urged Palmer to turn his back when Satan presented himself in the form of such speculation. "You all know that from the first," he wrote, "I have warned you to beware of these Indian drafts and quartz speculations and the Mariposa grant which I solemnly believe will never be confirmed." He wished they had concentrated all their "energies to the business in hand on the 1st August last," when he believed they "had not seen one of those cursed Indian Agent drafts."[69]

Having succeeded in being appointed Superintendent of Indian Affairs in California, Edward F. Beale was charged, ironically and much against his own wishes, with investigating possible fraud in the cattle contracts. He did find some irregularities, most of which he blamed on Savage.[70] When Montgomery Blair talked with Beale in San Francisco in the spring of 1854, hoping to gather evidence to bolster Frémont's claims for payment on the beef contracts, he was surprised at Beale's ambivalence. "Beale said he would do anything . . . I would suggest to serve Frémont, consistent with his honor, for the sake of Old Bullion [Benton] for whom he was ready to lay down his life. As respects Frémont, he was glad he had not met him here &c. &c. I was rather discouraged you may suppose by this talk of Ned's & altho he said emphatically that Frémont ought to be paid his money &c. &c. there was something kept back as if he thought at the same time he ought not to receive it."[71]

Many years later a friend of Savage who had also been a member of the Mariposa Batallion, which discovered Yosemite Valley, implied the existence of a California Indian "ring." He had, he maintained, warned Savage that he was surrounded by greedy men "endeavoring to use him as a tool to work their gold mine."[72]

Litigation surrounding the drafts would swirl around the U.S. government for more than two decades, especially after Congress, by a series of enactments (of which the private bill compensating Frémont was one), gave legislative recognition to the obligation of government

---

[69] Gwin to Joseph C. Palmer, "private and confidential," n.d., but probably late spring 1852 (M. A. Goodspeed, Jr., Collection).

[70] *Congressional Globe*, 6 Aug. 1852, pp. 2103–10; Senate Ex. Doc. 57, 32nd Cong., 2nd sess., Serial 665.

[71] Montgomery Blair to Minna Blair, 10 May 1854 (DLC—Blair Papers).

[72] BUNNELL, 270–83.

to provide for the wants of the Indians and an implied ratification of the unauthorized acts of their agents. Frémont would ultimately make a partial collection on his and Wright's November 1851 contract with Johnston but it was a thorny business.

Even more demanding and more complex were the issues connected with Las Mariposas. Juan B. Alvarado's own title to the ten-league grant had been doubtful when he sold it to Frémont in 1847. The transfer had lacked departmental approval; nor had Alvarado occupied, improved, or even located the boundaries of the property as required by Mexican law. In addition, one of the conditions of his grant forbade its sale or alienation. For several years, then, there was a real question whether Frémont had a valid title to this large, somewhat vaguely defined "floating" grant that was susceptible of being extended into the Mother Lode country.

At best, the intricacies of mining law are perplexing, the more so when, as in California, segments of several existing systems were being brought together. Compound the situation with a superimposition of many elements: claims and claim jumpers, leases and subleases, original companies and reorganized companies, sales and resales of both mineral claims and surface lands, authorized agents and unauthorized. Add three decades of time, and the maze of California land and mineral claims, often hazy and overlapping, becomes even more confusing.

The first placer strikes had brought a flood of miners into the Mariposa area. During part of 1849 Frémont's twenty-eight Sonorans washed out about a hundred pounds of gold per month—the equivalent of $25,000—half of which went to the explorer. In the autumn came the sensational discovery of the rich Mariposa Lode, graphically described by Bayard Taylor in *Eldorado* and by a geologist in October as more than five miles long.[73] Early in 1850, when Frémont left California to take up his Senate seat, prospects seemed bright indeed: specimens returned such rich assays that Frémont estimated that the lowest-yielding ore would return more than $16 million a year, based on the same quantity of ore crushed in 1849 by the Morro Velho Mine in Brazil. All that was needed were men, money, and machinery. Toward this end, Frémont resorted to seven-year leases with almost any-

[73] New York *Daily Tribune*, Supplement, 12 Nov. 1849.

one who would promise to begin work on a vein within six months or a year, the lessor to receive the traditional one-sixth of all gold and other minerals extracted.

By the end of July 1850 he had leases with seventeen parties. In general, these were "unlocated" or "scramble" leases, which gave the recipient the privilege of locating his own mine on ground not already occupied by others. Ordinarily grants were for a square of mineral land measuring either 200 or 600 feet on each of the four sides. Very few of the early leases made directly by Frémont are extant.[74] The amount of mineral land covered by all of these early leases was "about 3600 yards in length by 200 yards in breadth," Frémont wrote, this in a domain of more than 43,000 acres.

A lease, however, was not a prerequisite for mining gold on the Mariposa; hundreds simply invaded the estate and filed claims by right of discovery. Palmer, Cook & Company, for example, first entered as squatters, then received a lease, and by September 1851 owned an undivided one-half of the estate.

At the same time that Frémont was leasing at home, Richard Robert was convincing him that European capital and mining experts, especially the British, could develop the California property. Robert had been engaged in commercial and mining pursuits in various parts of the world and was familiar with the organization of joint-stock companies. When he approached Frémont, he was associated with David Hoffman, likewise an American, who was in London promoting land and immigration companies. A former professor of law at the University of Maryland, Hoffman had been casually acquainted with Frémont since 1839 when the young explorer visited in Baltimore with his mentor, Joseph N. Nicollet. That city's distinguished citizens, Brantz and Charles F. Mayer, were friends of both Hoffman and Frémont and were responsible for introducing Robert to Frémont in 1850 and for the business union that resulted between the California senator and the aging law professor.

Frémont sent Robert back to London with a power of attorney and a letter authorizing him and David Hoffman to grant leases and organize mining companies; Charles F. Mayer would act as intermediary and as Frémont's American solicitor. Initially a large joint-stock enter-

---

[74] One is printed as Doc. No. 67 and an incomplete list is given in the appendix, p. 609.

prise seems to have been contemplated, but when Hoffman reported that the London market was slow and that it might take as long as a year to organize it, the impatient owner of the Mariposa backed off and even considered abandoning the entire European effort. Much to Hoffman's delight, he decided to continue, but opted for smaller companies.

Hoffman not only financed his entire agency out of his own pocket but also underwrote Robert and his work on the Continent. His personal monetary outlay and his unflagging effort to publicize Frémont and his property led Hoffman to develop a proprietary attitude toward the agency and even toward the Mariposa. As a result, he bitterly resented others who sought to hawk their Mariposa leases or to compete for capital in Europe. Often their leases called for a lower royalty than he asked for Frémont, and he looked upon himself as Frémont's "sole representative" abroad. Any lessee wishing to extend his seven-year rights as an inducement to investors should work through Hoffman, who exacted "a consideration" for his role, a fee that would be credited to Frémont, although undoubtedly the London agent hoped to realize an ultimate percentage.

Among those with whom Hoffman would have difficulties were William King Smith, Thomas Denny Sargent, and the two who were attempting to float the Agua Fria: George W. Wright and Gen. Hiram Walbridge. He reached a quick accommodation with Smith, who sold his two "direct leases" from Frémont to the Nouveau Monde Mining Company, originally one of Hoffman's blue-ribbon concerns. Without knowing the exact relationship between Frémont and Wright, Hoffman tried to exercise diplomatic restraint where the Agua Fria was concerned, but eventually he attacked the veracity of some of Walbridge's advertisements and reported with mingled jealousy and suspicion that Wright and Walbridge and their co-workers were undercutting Frémont by organizing a firm devoted wholly to the interests of Palmer, Cook & Company.

Palmer, Cook & Company had located the Agua Fria under a lease from Frémont in September 1850 and now sought to enlist British capital in the formation of a company to purchase the property. Prominent in assisting Wright and Walbridge in this effort were the Englishman Stephen Charles Lakeman and William A. Jackson, who was also preparing an elaborate map of the mining district of California. Jackson, Wright, Palmer, and the two Cook brothers had been old associates in the Mariposa Mining Company, which they and seven others had created shortly after the banking firm had obtained the Frémont lease.[75]

Wright had already returned to California when the British concern, the Agua Fria Gold Mining Company, was chartered to develop the mine of the same name. Nominally capitalized at £200,000 (subsequently reduced to £100,000 in shares of £1 each), the company was typical of the era. Its trustees and directors were well-known Englishmen of wealth and station—the "Guinea Pigs" of corporate organization, so called because they were willing to lend their names to promotion and to attend board meetings for a nominal fee of a guinea a meeting. But behind the scenes their holdings were minimal. Palmer, Cook & Company held a full one-third of the allocated shares, while Lakeman, Walbridge, and Jackson owned lesser amounts. If periodicals like *Britannia* acclaimed the luster of those heading the company, they also gave careful attention to more germane matters. The consulting engineer was a professor of geology at King's College; the managing director in California, James Hepburn, was "a Kentish landowner, well known for his scientific attainments." Three assays of Agua Fria ore had been made: one by the U.S. Mint, one by the Bank of England, and one by a private London bullion firm. "The result of the three trials is—it is no fairy tale, but simple truth—that the quartz ore produces gold of the value of £370 sterling per cwt., and therefore £7,000 per ton. Thirty tons have already been raised, and await crushing— or upwards of £220,000 worth of ore."[76]

---

[75] The articles of association of the Mariposa Mining Company, 27 Sept. 1850, list the founders: Joseph C. Palmer, Gregory Yale, Charles W. Cook, Robert F. R. Allen, Jonathan Walker, Ebenezer Eliason, Barker Burnell, A. D. Merrifield, G. W. Wright, John Cook, Jr., William A. Jackson, and Edward Jones. It was organized in San Francisco with a capital stock of $1 million in 2,000 shares worth $500 each. Its primary purpose was to open and work gold-bearing quartz veins, but other rocks and ores were not excluded nor did it necessarily confine its operations to the Mariposa area (Mariposa County Records, Book 1, pp. 1–3).

Jackson's 1851 map of the mining district of California, published by John Arrowsmith, was based on his smaller map issued the previous year in New York by Lambert & Lane's Lith. Under the title *Carte du district aurifere du San Joaquin*, an undated French edition showed the southern portion of Jackson's 1850 work (WHEAT [2], 162).

There was a public report that the Chilean mill put up by Messrs. Cook & Jackson on the big Mariposa vein commenced work in July 1851, crushing about 500 pounds in twelve hours, really too small an amount to be profitable (*Hunt's Merchants Magazine and Commercial Review*, 27 [July–Dec. 1852]:445–46).

[76] *The Britannia*, Supplement, 7 Feb. 1852. For official records of the com-

Meanwhile, Palmer, Cook & Company negotiated an extension of time for fulfilling the terms of its 1850 lease, an extension which for an additional consideration was passed on to the Agua Fria Company. The banking house had also acquired an undivided one-half of the Mariposa for one dollar and "other good and valuable considerations" not stated in the contract. In time, after Frémont came to London, the Agua Fria Company was granted exclusive right to work all of the Agua Fria Vein within the bounds of the Mariposa grant, in return for which it promised immediate payment to Frémont and Wright of £4,656, an additional £1,344 later, and royalties of one-sixth of all minerals found.[77]

Although Hoffman was convinced that Wright was an important and mischievous meddler and responsible for much of the disrepute into which Frémont and his estate later fell, it was another rival promoter, Thomas Denny Sargent, who became the principal target of his salvos. A mustachioed Massachusettsan of some thirty-five years, and like Wright a fancier of bold schemes, Sargent had received two leases from Frémont in the spring of 1850. Assigning a two-thirds interest in one of these to Alexander H. Harper and James Eldridge, he traveled with them to Mariposa to locate the San Carlos and the Santa Maria mines. Subsequently he sailed to London to solicit British capital, boasting, as Wright and Walbridge did of the Agua Fria, that his was a located mine whereas Hoffman's were not. Hoffman countered that an unlocated lease was preferable, since selection could be made by an experienced mining engineer after a careful examination of the veins. In June 1851 Sargent left suddenly for the United States to complete negotiations for the reacquisition of the interests of Eldridge and the now-deceased Harper, so his solicitor, John Duncan, later informed Frémont.

---

pany, see British Registrar of Companies Archive, Hayes, Middlesex (Papers of the Agua Fria Gold Mining Company), Film Z-61, Reel 58 (CU-B). See also two signed documents in the Frémont Papers (CU-B). One, dated 16 April 1852, is his grant (with George W. Wright) to the Agua Fria Gold Mining Company of the exclusive right to work the Agua Fria Vein in the Mariposa estate. The second, dated 17 April 1852, is the deed of contract with the Agua Fria Gold Mining Company relative to the amount of royalty payable under lease and mining license.

[77] The extension of Palmer, Cook & Company's Agua Fria's lease is dated 11 Sept. 1851 and is mentioned in the 16 April 1852 document cited above. Palmer, Cook & Company's second lease to the British company is dated 29 Jan. 1852.

Before long, Hoffman received a letter from Thomas Hart Benton, informing him that J. Eugene Flandin, a former agent of Frémont on the Mariposa, had been authorized to sell one-half of Las Mariposas and that he—Benton—had recommended that Frémont sell the whole, "for he is not adapted to such business and it interferes with his attention to other business to which he is adapted." The "other business" was probably politics. Next came a letter from Flandin informing Hoffman that a conditional sale of the Mariposa had been made and advising a stay of leasing. On 12 July Benton notified the London agent that the purchaser was a "Mr. Sergeant," who would soon be back in England to raise the advance payment of $100,000, if Frémont ratified the transaction.

Hoffman found the news incredible. Was not Frémont breaking faith with him and with the British lessees? How could Flandin sell the entire estate when he was authorized to sell only half? He considered Benton and Flandin's suggestions to stop leasing as merely advisory, since only Frémont could curtail or broaden his powers. These thoughts, reflected in his letters of fear and inquiry, brought an ambivalent response from Frémont, who intimated that a sale was contemplated, but requested that a notice be published in the London *Times* warning against sales, leases, or any other transactions pertaining to the Mariposa except with Benton or Hoffman. Hoffman placed the notice but by signing himself Frémont's "sole representative in Europe" managed to shake the confidence of investors in the Agua Fria and in Sargent's West Mariposa Gold Quartz Mining Company. Persistent rumors of impending sale, uncertainty about leasing authority, and news of the failure of the Stockton and Aspinwall mine on the Mariposa combined to make lessees nervous, and they insisted that money and shares due Frémont be deposited in a bank with Hoffman as "trustee" until the actual selection of locations had been made and Frémont's formal approval obtained.

Hoffman insisted that he could sell the estate for five or even ten times Sargent's price. When the London *Globe* carried an extract from a Benton letter terming the Hoffman leases since 7 July "not only void, but fraudulent," Hoffman screamed "libel" and threatened to sue. Late in December 1851 he had published a notice of suspension of his own leasing powers, but insisted that all his leasing contracts to that time were valid. On the same day he issued a sixty-three-page pamphlet which analyzed various documents to indicate that no sale to Sargent had taken place, that Benton had no legal power to conclude such a transaction, and that his own authority from Frémont had been complete.

Nonetheless, across the Atlantic Benton was preparing to complete arrangements with Sargent, although Frémont had reportedly urged him not to do so "if he can get off honorably," advice Old Bullion shrugged off. On 15 January 1852 Frémont wrote Hoffman that he was coming to London and that he had made every effort to halt the sale of Las Mariposas. Two weeks later Benton concluded the million-dollar transaction, with the proviso that Frémont might annul the contract within fifteen days after Sargent's agent asked for possession of the property. Twenty-five thousand dollars were to be paid in cash, another $75,000 in London once Frémont's confirmation was obtained. Then a deed to the inchoate title to the estate was to pass to Sargent, whose mortgage on the property Frémont would receive, with annual payments to follow and the final settlement due one year after the delivery of a perfect title.

Before leaving for England, Sargent started his agent, Gwinn Harris Heap, to California to take possession. Heap was thoroughly acquainted with Las Mariposas: he had been Frémont's agent there in the summer of 1850 and had opened the mineral vein that came to bear his name. At the Isthmus Heap met the Frémonts, who were en route to Britain. At that time Frémont may have denounced the sale; in any case, Heap turned back, traveling to New York with them.

In New York Frémont conferred with Wright at the Irving House. He telegraphed Charles F. Mayer that he did not confirm the sale and sent a friend immediately to reassure Hoffman that the Mariposa remained unsold. Without seeing Benton, who was in Missouri, Frémont, his family, Wright, and Heap all embarked for England in the *Africa*, arriving 22 March. Hoffman wrote an enthusiastic letter of welcome, in which he urged Frémont to set aside several days for business discussion with him. But the explorer ignored the old man who had labored so industriously on his behalf for more than two years and who had looked forward with eagerness to this visit. Through Wright, Frémont made it clear that the Agua Fria was to have priority on the British market. Hoffman was both surprised and hurt and was convinced that rumors and innuendo had poisoned Frémont's mind against him. On their part, the Frémonts had been alienated by his prolific writings and felt that the Mariposa and those involved in its affairs had been thrust too much in the public eye, sometimes in an unsavory light. Jessie especially disliked the attacks on her father.

In London she had anticipated acceptance into court society, and her hopes were not disappointed. Dressed in pink satin, lace, and pearls, she was thrilled and delighted when she was presented to Queen Victoria. With her husband, she was swept up in a pleasant round of teas and dinners at important London houses and with figures like Joshua Bates, an American connected with the Barings, and Sir Roderick Murchison, president of the Royal Geographical Society.[78]

But the splendor was tainted by humiliation. Thomas Sargent filed a bill of complaint against Frémont in the British Chancery on 27 March for repudiation of the Mariposa sale. A few days later, as the explorer stepped into a carriage to attend a dinner with Jessie, he was arrested for nonpayment of drafts he had drawn upon the Secretary of State when governor of California, drafts that had subsequently passed into the hands of Anthony Gibbs and Sons, who now instituted the charges. While Jessie frantically sought bail money—ironically, from Hoffman—Frémont spent the night in Sloman's Lock-up on Cursitor Street, Chancery Lane. In the end the American investment banker George Peabody and his junior partner came to the financial rescue. Soon Frémont wrote Benton, asking help in obtaining an appointment as chargé to some neighboring power "to protect me from further arrests & to help pay expenses." By the end of April he had taken up residence in Paris, occasionally slipping back across the Channel to conduct business or to attend social affairs, including the elaborate dinner for a hundred guests that George Peabody held to celebrate the anniversary of Bunker Hill at the Brunswick Hotel in Blackwell, overlooking the Thames.[79]

Frémont publicly advertised that he was ready to carry into effect all contracts made by Hoffman prior to 20 December 1851, but little activity resulted. Of the twenty-one companies Hoffman claimed to have organized, only three—Le Nouveau Monde, the Quartz Rock Mariposa Gold Mining Company, and Les Mineurs Belges—actually sent men and equipment to the Mariposa. Andrew Smith, lessee and engineer of the Golden Mountain, also went. Hoffman's sense of betrayal deepened when Frémont became a party to the 16 April 1852

[78] J. B. FRÉMONT [2] contains chapters on their life in London and Paris.
[79] PARKER, 1:281–82, 277–78.

indenture, noted earlier, by which Palmer, Cook & Company sold their original lease to the Agua Fria Mining Company.

Thus relations between the Mariposa owner and his agent steadily disintegrated. When Frémont and his London attorney requested the papers and accounts of the agency, Hoffman refused to relinquish them, in part because he had been paid nothing for his outlays and services, and in part because he believed that Frémont wanted the records in order to find petty flaws by which to break the contracts already concluded. Losing patience, Frémont soon filed suit to obtain the materials as well as money that he insisted Hoffman had received on his behalf. Although Hoffman, too, hired solicitors, he hoped for an out-of-court settlement to avoid the heavy expense and long delays of litigation. Repeatedly negotiations broke down. Hoffman barely escaped arrest and in June 1853 the Vice Chancellor's Court ordered him to surrender the agency papers to Frémont, who seems never to have compensated him or his widow for his services or expenditures.[80]

While his case against Hoffman and the Gibbs draft suit were grinding through the judicial machinery, Frémont had the help of the distinguished French astronomer François Arago in selecting the finest surveying instruments money could buy. Another exploring expedition was on the horizon.

In March a letter from Benton indicated that Congress had authorized surveys of the principal routes to the Pacific to determine the most practical and economical route for a railroad. Benton urged Frémont to return and to ask for a place on the survey of the central region between the 38th and 39th parallels. Indeed, the Missouri senator went so far as to suggest to Secretary of War Jefferson Davis that Frémont and Edward F. Beale be given joint command of that particular survey. Having elected to return overland to his California Indian superintendency, Beale would be able to enter upon his duties immediately. Since Frémont had already surveyed both ends of the projected route, only the area from the mouth of the Huerfano River on the upper Arkansas to the Mormon settlements near Little Salt Lake and the Vegas de Santa Clara, including Cochetopa Pass, needed special investigation.

---

[80] See Vice-Chancellor's Courts, Fremont v. Hoffman, London *Times*, 6 June 1853. See SPENCE for an account of Mrs. Hoffman's suit in the New York Supreme Court in 1856 to recover $40,000 from Frémont.

But Secretary Davis was deaf to Benton's special pleading and appointed Captain John W. Gunnison to command the official expedition. Before that group could leave the Missouri frontier, Beale and his cousin, Gwinn Harris Heap, now returned from England, headed west from Westport Landing with a small party on 10 May 1853. Their letters and journals, sent back to Benton, were published in the newspapers and further publicized the middle route, as did Heap's more formal account of the expedition printed the following year in Philadelphia under the title *Central Route to the Pacific, from the Valley of the Mississippi to California*.

That same spring saw Frémont clean up his affairs in London. The Gibbs case was decided on 6 May in the plaintiff's favor and the explorer was finally released from bail.[81] Crossing the Channel to consult once more with his attorneys, he borrowed £13,000 from Stephen C. Lakeman, securing it by a mortgage on all of his one-half interest in Las Mariposas.[82] Then he sailed for the United States from Liverpool, leaving Jessie and the three children to follow from Le Havre on the *Arago* with his niece, Nina, and two French servants.[83] The family took a house near Benton's, but heat and the illness of the baby caused Jessie to seek relief at the Francis Blair estate at Silver Spring, just outside Washington. On 12 July sorrow visited again when the infant died suddenly in her arms, as had little Benton five years before.

Frémont spent the summer giving additional explanations to the board examining the California claims, wrestling with Mariposa business affairs, and preparing for what would be his fifth expedition. The latter, according to the press, was to be made without the financial aid of the government to test the practicality of the central route during the snowy season. Benton may have contributed funds, but observers noted a coolness between him and the explorer. The senator no doubt remembered the cancellation of the sale to Sargent, but other reasons may have contributed to his aloofness—possibly a growing

<hr />

[81] Senate Ex. Doc. 109, 34th Cong., 1st sess., Serial 825. On 3 March 1853 Congress had approved an act for the relief of Frémont. See *Laws of the United States*, 10:759.

[82] Indenture between Stephen C. Lakeman, 3 June 1853, Mariposa County Records, Book A of Deeds, pp. 254–59.

[83] P. 76 of Jessie B. Frémont's unpublished memoirs (CU-B).

mistrust of Frémont's judgment, a feeling Jessie thought her brother-in-law, Jones, had encouraged.[84]

Late in August in New York, Frémont met Wright and Palmer, who clearly saw that new laurels for the explorer might benefit them all economically and politically, though they were not unconcerned about the physical hazards of the proposed venture. Perhaps this was one consideration in sending Palmer's brother, William H., on the expedition, while the two bankers returned to California by sea.

Also in New York Frémont made arrangements with Solomon Nunes Carvalho to accompany him as artist and daguerreotypist. Whether he or Carvalho paid for the camera and supplies is not clear, but all the daguerreotypes were to belong to Frémont, who probably forbade the artist to keep a journal of the expedition. Like Isaac Cooper in 1845, James F. Milligan, a young Saint Louisan who traveled with the expedition as far as Bent's Fort, wrote about the prohibition on journals and public communications:

Col. Frémont at supper informed us that during his illness in St. Louis that he had seen communications from some gentleman in the camp to the newspapers. I informed him that I was that individual. He requested me not to again do it as it was never customary in any of his former expeditions for any person but him, and also that to give up all journals that he would not allow one being kept by any person of the expedition. Mr. Fuller complyed [*sic*] with this exceedingly modest request but I did not. The sequel of this selfish demand of the Col. remains to be seen.[85]

When Carvalho returned from California, the editor of the *Photographic Art Journal*, H. H. Snelling, requested information about his experiences on the fifth expedition, but Carvalho replied: "I am very sorry I am unable to respond to your request for the particulars of my tour with Colonel Frémont, in his late Exploring expedition across the mountains, not having taken any private notes. But this much I am at liberty to say that I succeeded beyond my utmost expectations in producing good results and effects by the Daguerreotype."[86]

Carvalho was then reportedly quite critical of his former leader,

[84] Montgomery Blair to Minna Blair, San Francisco, 10 May 1854 (DLC—Blair Papers); JBF to Elizabeth Blair Lee, 8 March and 18 April [1856?] (NjP—Blair-Lee Papers).

[85] Unpublished diary of James F. Milligan, courtesy of David H. Miller.

[86] Printed in STURHAHN, 124–25.

but Frémont's nomination for the presidency brought a rapid change of attitude and ardent support for the Republican ticket. Carvalho's nephew noted his uncle's economic aspirations: "He says if Frémont is elected he will have the office of Collector of the Port of Baltimore, or anything else he wants."[87] When John Bigelow collected the materials for his campaign biography of Frémont, it was Carvalho who provided—undoubtedly with the explorer's permission—information about the journey, reconstructing the details from "letters," he maintained, but perhaps in actuality from a journal he may have kept secretly. A few months later his own book, *Incidents of Travel and Adventure in the Far West; with Col. Frémont's Last Expedition . . .*, was released, first in England, then in the United States.[88] In it the Bigelow account was incorporated without significant change, except for the addition of laudatory comments about Frémont. Added also, as "an exact copy" from the Carvalho diary, was a description of the artist's own travel from Salt Lake City to San Bernardino, together with views on Mormonism.

Why Frémont did not give Bigelow access to his own journal is a mystery; perhaps his contract with publisher George W. Childs prohibited it.[89] It appears to be permanently lost save for the two entries printed in the *Memoirs* and included here as Doc. No. 262. Ironically, Carvalho's illustrations embellish Frémont's *Memoirs* but do not appear in his own book, which remains the principal account of the fifth expedition.

Unlike earlier occasions, Jessie did not accompany her husband to the frontier in 1853 when the group was assembling, but when the telegraph brought word of his illness—"neuralgic sciatica," Benton told the public—she rushed to his side at St. Louis, where Dr. Ebers was soothing the pain, eradicating the inflammation, and literally getting Frémont "on his legs." No doubt she was relieved when Ebers agreed to accompany the expedition, but her husband made it known he did "not quite like its being said that he carries a Homeopathetic physician with him."[90]

Frémont rejoined the main party camped on the Saline Fork of the

---

[87] Jacob S. Ritterband to a cousin, 11 Sept. 1856, printed in KORN, 37–38.
[88] See Doc. No. 261 for the commentary on its publication.
[89] See Vol. 1, pp. xxxiii–xxxiv.
[90] JBF to Elizabeth Blair Lee, St. Louis, 14 Oct. [1853] (NjP—Blair-Lee Papers).

Kansas on 31 October. Included were twenty-two members, of whom ten were Delaware Indians and two were Mexican. Moving out through buffalo country, the expedition would spend a week resting and reprovisioning at William Bent's new fort near Big Timbers before moving up the Arkansas to the mouth of the Huerfano at the end of November, leaving the physician and another member behind. The Huerfano would be followed into the mountains, but at one point Carvalho and Frémont temporarily left the main party to examine Robidoux Pass, although the expedition would use a more northern defile—present-day Medano Pass—to cross the Sangre de Cristo Range into the San Luis Valley.

Neither Carvalho's journal nor Frémont's communications to newspapers after the completion of the expedition are very specific about the route; nor is the tracing on the *Memoirs* map complete or entirely in accordance with the extant documents. Fortunately for posterity and for Frémont, too, he connected up in the San Luis Valley with the trail made by Captain Gunnison and his large party a few months earlier. Since trees felled to clear a path for Gunnison's wagons plainly marked the way, the explorer was able to follow the route easily, even with snow on the ground.

Like Gunnison, Frémont crossed the valley, led his men up the gradually ascending Saguache Creek to North Cochetopa Pass, then worked westward to reach the little Mormon town of Parowan, sixty miles from the Nevada line. Carvalho chronicles vividly their sufferings as they doggedly pushed through a wintery wilderness, sometimes in raging snowstorms, sometimes in temperatures thirty degrees below zero, sometimes reduced to a diet of porcupine, coyote, and cactus leaves from which the spines had been burned. While the party was attempting to avoid the deep chasm of the Gunnison River, the lead mule slipped on an icy mountain slope and tumbled heels over head, carrying fifty others with him several hundred feet to the bottom; fortunately only one was killed. As they entered the Parowan Valley, one man died. Little wonder that the *Daily San Joaquin Republican* noted wryly that in his fourth and fifth expeditions, Frémont had "enjoyed more suffering and privation in surmounting nature's protest against" the central railroad route than all other expeditions combined over the previous seven years.[91]

---

[91] *Daily San Joaquin Republican*, 7 July 1854.

When Almon W. Babbitt brought to Washington the letters Frémont had given him in Parowan, Benton saw "Failure" looming behind the written assurances of "general good health" and "reasonable success." The harshness with which he told his anxious and overwrought daughter of her husband's safety reflected Benton's own disappointment and bitterness. To the *National Intelligencer*, however, he sent the most optimistic of reports. Grateful for word from the expedition, Jessie arranged a dinner party. In her invitation to Frank Preston Blair, Sr., and his son-in-law she requested that they forget that Babbitt "has lots of wives [which he did not] and look upon him only as I do in his last character as friend & banker to Mr. Frémont."[92]

Parowan was a break in the expedition's work. By 21 February, without the services of Carvalho and several others, the party was on the move again, although rumors of desertion reached San Francisco and caused Palmer no little anxiety. When they also found their way into the *National Intelligencer*, Benton issued a heated denial: "No man ever deserted him. His men die with him, as for him, but never desert."[93]

The route from Parowan was "a little south of West," or roughly across central Nevada, with his trail and the tracks of the Death Valley Forty-niners alternately merging and diverging several times before Frémont reached California. An early report had him crossing the Sierra Nevada near the head of the Merced River, a parallel of Joseph R. Walker's northern penetration of 1833;[94] in reality, he traversed the mountains below the 36th parallel, probably at Bird Spring Pass or Walker's southern pass.[95]

An aura of mystery surrounds the fifth expedition. Frémont was never explicit; he promised details but gave none. According to the Los Angeles *Star*, he "remained two days between the Kern and the Tule Rivers; and when visited by some settlers on Tule River and asked why he did not come into the settlements, he evasively answered that he was out of funds, and though he was in need of provisions, he knew he could get none without money." Frémont was never

---

[92] Undated invitation (NjP—Blair-Lee Papers).
[93] Letter of Benton, printed in *Daily Missouri Democrat*, 31 May 1854.
[94] *Daily Alta California*, 17 April 1854; FARQUAHAR, 6–7.
[95] See Doc. Nos. 269 and 274 for the contradiction in his reports and historians' interpretations.

known to be averse to credit. The *Star* maintained it had "some items of interest concerning the expedition," but never gave them.[96] Jessie wrote that Judge George Belt and another Californian named Stone offered hospitality and money and that Belt invited him to his ranch where he and his party might recuperate.[97] For some reason, perhaps because of the beef contracts to feed the Indians, Edward Beale was glad to have arrived in San Francisco after Frémont had left for home.[98]

Frémont's stay in California was brief. He left his Delawares camped on a ranch near Stockton while he went to San Francisco, arriving there on a Sunday evening, 16 April. Montgomery Blair remarked that he was staying with Palmer and that he was "as fat as a buck. So much so, that his clothes seem too tight for him," and that he made "no account of his hardships." Blair would see much of him during his short visit and helped put his affairs "in some sort of shape." On 23 April the explorer returned to Stockton for his Delaware Indians and a week later, having borrowed money "to get away" and having declined a public dinner tendered by the Society of California Pioneers, he took passage for Panama on the Nicaraguan steamer *Cortés*.[99]

He arrived in New York on 25 May 1854, about a week after Jessie had given birth to another son, Frank Preston, and soon his accomplishments were being lauded by his father-in-law. "The return of Mr. Frémont, (perfectly successful in his winter expeditions) emboldens all the friends of the central route, and shows that nature has prepared that route in every particular for the great national highway between the Mississippi River and the Bay of San Francisco," wrote Benton in an open letter to his constituents.[100] In June Frémont made a report of his expedition to the *National Intelligencer*, an adventure which the *Daily Missouri Democrat* hailed as settling "the question of the excellence, the superiority, the pre-eminent advantage of the Central route, over all the routes to the Pacific."[101]

[96] Los Angeles *Star* as printed in *Alta California*, 15 July 1854.

[97] Printed prospectus for JCF's *Memoirs of My Life*, xi (CSmH).

[98] Montgomery Blair to Minna Blair, 10 May 1854 (DLC—Blair Papers).

[99] Montgomery Blair to Minna Blair, 17 and 18 April, 25 May, 13 June 1854 (DLC—Blair Papers); *Daily San Joaquin Republican*, 24 April and 1 May 1854; *Daily Alta California*, 1 and 2 May 1854.

[100] *National Intelligencer*, 27 May 1854; letter of Benton, 30 May 1854, printed in *Daily Missouri Democrat*, 9 June 1854.

[101] *Daily Missouri Democrat*, 26 June 1854.

Late in August, when Frémont again left Washington for California, the *National Intelligencer* reported that he went to fix astronomically the position of the crossing he had discovered the previous spring, reputedly "north of the Walker and Tejon passes."[102] In reality, it was not scientific exploration but Las Mariposas and other business affairs that called him back to the Pacific Coast.

Las Mariposas had been the first case taken up by the California land commissioners under the Land Act of 1851.[103] They were sitting in San Francisco in January 1852 when they received Frémont's petition for a confirmation of his title from Alvarado. With his petition, he submitted a rough sketch of the area bounded by the Sierra Nevada and the rivers Chowchilla, Merced, and San Joaquin within which Alvarado had been given the privilege of locating his grant of ten Spanish leagues (approximately 44,000 acres). The approximate boundaries had allegedly been given to him by Alvarado in 1849 and were known as the Pico-Gulnack *diseño*, although it had probably been prepared by Frémont's cartographer, Charles Preuss. Marked in red lines on the map was the land Frémont wished to have patented as Las Mariposas. Shortly before he sailed for Europe, the commissioners accepted a motion of his attorneys and ordered the Surveyor General of California to make a preliminary survey of the grant, at the claimant's expense, as was customary. Allexey W. Von Schmidt ran the survey and followed very closely the petitioner's wishes, that is, the red lines sketched on the Pico-Gulnack *diseño*. The result was a pan-handle-shaped claim and map embracing the whole watershed of the Mariposa River, the gold mines near Mariposa and Agua Frio, and a good slice of the grazing and farming lands in the San Joaquin Valley. By 1856, when Frémont's economic interest had changed, the boundaries of the grant described in his patent would be considerably different from those depicted by the Von Schmidt map.[104]

[102] *National Intelligencer*, 26 Aug. 1854.

[103] Many of the documents and testimony relating to Las Mariposas are printed in Supreme Court Case No. 3338, U.S. v. John C. Frémont, DNA-267; a fuller record of the proceedings, but largely handwritten, is in DNA-49, California Private Land Claims Dockets, Docket No. 1. The latter includes not only the judicial records but also the protests of the Mariposans, some of the correspondence of the claimants' attorneys, the Secretary of the Interior and the Attorney General, and JCF's printed memorial to President Franklin Pierce.

[104] In 1983 the original Von Schmidt 1852 survey map was owned by Louis Milburn of Mariposa, Calif.

When the commission began examining the documents relating to the title and sale of Las Mariposas, Frémont was in Europe, his movements circumscribed by his legal difficulties, but he had the counsel of the brilliant attorney Rufus A. Lockwood and the support of many sympathizers, including William Carey Jones and George W. Wright, who undoubtedly returned from England for the specific purpose of giving testimony.[105] Wright admitted that he had been a lessee under Frémont in 1850 but had assigned his interest in 1851. He probably committed perjury when he swore that he had "no interest, present or contingent, in the result of the case."[106]

The commission confirmed title to Frémont on 27 December and in a lengthy opinion addressed objections to the claim of Juan B. Alvarado, who had sold the property to Frémont. If there was no evidence that the Departmental Assembly had approved Governor Manuel Micheltorena's original grant to Alvarado, the commission found no evidence that it had not; in any event, equity, usages, and customs and the Treaty of Guadalupe Hidalgo protected his title. The prohibition on Alvarado's disposal of the property was ruled invalid, inasmuch as the whole tenor of Mexican legislation was historically opposed to any restriction against alienation. Objection to the sale to Frémont on the ground that he was not a Mexican citizen was irrelevant because the transfer was made after the full sovereignty of the United States had been established. Alvarado's failure to build a house upon the tract within a year did not bring forefeiture, but merely made it subject to denouncement, which had never been done. His failure, too, to measure out ten leagues did not bar title, since the larger tract had been temporarily separated from the public domain until actual selection of the smaller grant could be made. The right of selection was thus incident to the grant. The commissioners gave scant attention to the argument that mineral rights on the property be reserved to the U.S. government. The Mexican government had not reserved the mines on the estate, hence had transferred only a general power of sovereignty to the United States, not a proprietary interest. Moreover, the Land Act of 1851 had not empowered the commission to protect any interest the government may have had in mineral lands.[107]

---

[105] Lockwood's written agreement for confirmation is MS 1289/2 in CHi.

[106] See Doc. No. 160 for JCF's 5 Sept. 1851 deed of an undivided half-interest in Las Mariposas to Palmer, Cook & Company. Wright's testimony is pp. 55–56 in Supreme Court Case No. 3338, DNA-267.

[107] For the opinion of the Board of Land Commissioners, see *ibid.*, 9–34.

Confirmation of title failed to bring the foreign investment Frémont had anticipated. No doubt the London scenario involving Hoffman, Sargent, and the supporters of the Agua Frio had evoked distrust and wariness about risking capital in the stock of companies intending to operate on the Mariposa. Further doubts were raised in mid-August 1853, while Frémont prepared for his fifth expedition, when the Attorney General of the United States, Caleb Cushing, served notice that the commissioners' decision would be appealed to the District Court for the Northern District of California. Additional testimony was taken and in January 1854, while Frémont was slogging through the winter storms of Colorado, Judge Ogden Hoffman reversed the Land Commission's opinion, holding that because Alvarado had not met the conditions of his grant, the claim had no legal basis.[108] Palmer thought that attorney Volney E. Howard, then managing the case, was an inept lawyer, but Montgomery Blair was convinced that the explorer would have lost anyway before Hoffman, whom he saw as "a violent partizan and unfriendly to Frémont, Benton & that whole political connection."[109]

Frémont immediately appealed the case to the U.S. Supreme Court, where it came up for a hearing during the December 1854 term. Montgomery Blair had been able to add to the legal services of William Carey Jones, those of the venerable George M. Bibb and John J. Crittenden, former senator and Attorney General.[110] Together they were able to convince a majority of the Court of the validity of the floating grant to Alvarado—and thus to Frémont—and a precedent was established that for a time prevailed in confirming other questionable titles in California. Chief Justice Roger Taney, an old friend

---

[108] *Ibid.*, 60–109.

[109] Montgomery Blair to Minna Blair, 9 April 1854 (DLC—Blair Papers).

[110] See DLC—John Jordan Crittenden Papers, especially letters of Montgomery Blair to J. J. Crittenden, 8 and 18 May 1855, referring to the fee due Crittenden "as counsel for Fremont." Present in the collection are a five-page statement of Frémont's case and a seventy-eight page brief. Crittenden was still trying to collect fees in 1861. Frémont insisted they had been paid; the sons were unconvinced and, after the death of their father, pressed the claim. Thomas wrote that the matter could be adjusted by arbitration or suit; Robert proposed squaring the account by arbitration or a duel (E. L. Fancher to T. L. Crittenden, 24 Dec. 1861; T. L. Crittenden to Frémont, 28 Dec. 1864; and R. H. Crittenden to E. L. Fancher, 29 Dec. 1864). Montgomery Blair also had difficulty collecting. In a letter to Col. Leonidas Haskell, 11 Aug. 1863, he details ten years of service and influence ón JCF's behalf and expressed a willingness to settle for the small sum of $3,000 (DLC—Blair Papers).

of Benton's, read the decision on 10 March 1855 and ordered the land "surveyed in the form and divisions prescribed by law for Surveys in California, and in one entire tract." When the case was returned to the California District Court, Frémont's lawyers moved for an exception on the survey, arguing that that confirmation of the claim should be in general terms, with location of the land to be left to the Surveyor General without any instructions.

The survey now became the all-important question. Conceivably it might be entirely different from the earlier tract marked out by Frémont and surveyed by Von Schmidt in 1852. It might even disregard his mining interests and locate on vacant lands, as the U.S. Attorney and many Mariposans wished. In denying the plea for an uninstructed survey, Judges Hall McAllister and Ogden Hoffman tacitly agreed that the district court had no power to restrict the survey to vacant lands, even if it interfered with the rights of third parties. This decision on 27 June 1855 prompted the U.S. Attorney to move for appeal, which was granted a month later, but by then the Mariposa survey had taken place.

Even before the final decree of the district court, Frémont and his associates had begun making plans for the survey. George Wright wrote about the project to Joshua E. Clayton, the engineer whom he had sent to the Mariposa to map out a water canal and who would shortly become manager of the property. "The Col.," he noted, "will put our friend on to the Survey and will probably look to you for all his help, he paying for all except yourself and Jonathan [Wright]." [111] "The Col." was probably the Surveyor General of California, John C. "Jack" Hays, of Texas Ranger fame, although possibly it was his chief clerk, Col. Leander Ransom, who would accompany Horace Higley and counsel with him on the mode and manner of conducting the actual survey. Frémont was not on the Mariposa or even in the state at the time, but Wright had been on the grant in June either before or after he wrote Clayton.

The survey—a clandestine one, opponents charged—took place

---

[111] George W. Wright to Joshua E. Clayton, 16 June 1855 (M. A. Goodspeed, Jr., Collection). One of the items in Clayton's 28 May 1856 bill to Palmer, Cook & Company was "$1,500 for 5 months active service making selection for location of Mariposa grant and prelim ditch surveys" (CtY—Clayton Papers). The survey party consisted of Horace Higley, Leander Ransom, Clayton (not really an official member), Twichel, two chainmen, and a Mexican by the name of Pasquel.

between 1 and 15 July. The plat of the survey was certified on 31 July, but since the government's appeal was pending, it could not be a final certification nor could a patent be issued. Frémont was impatient and appealed to President Pierce to stop the interminable delay. The chief executive was sympathetic and asked for all the documents relating to the case. While they were on his desk, the U.S. Supreme Court considered the Mariposa case once more and decided to dismiss the appeal because the government's attorney had failed to file the record and docket the cause within the first six days of the term. It issued a writ of procedendo to the district court and two days later—19 February 1856—Frémont visited the White House and was handed the letters patent to Las Mariposas by President Pierce, who had also personally signed them.[112] The special treatment was undoubtedly a recognition of the fact that Frémont might well be a presidential nominee, but Palmer, Cook & Company's enormous stake in the patent was recognized by John W. Dwinelle, who wrote to Wright: "I congratulate you that you have succeeded in getting the Frémont patent into your *possession*. . . ." However, in March 1856, before the firm went bankrupt, it released to Frémont all of its interest in Las Mariposas.[113]

The boundaries of the patented Mariposas were quite different from those marked out by Frémont in 1849 and by Von Schmidt in 1852. The main portion of that survey was retained, but the surveyors, conscious of the necessity for a compact form, cut off the long handle that had extended thirty miles down and along both sides of the Mariposa River to a width of about one and one-quarter miles. Owners of land on either side of the elongated claim would have been denied access to the stream. To compensate, the upper part of Bear Creek Valley was included. The whole tract measured 44,386.83 acres and in addition to the town of Mariposa included Frenchtown and Mormon Bar in the valley of the Mariposas; Simpsonville, Oso, and Mount Ophir in the Great Bear Valley; Princeton, Upper Agua Fria, Lower Auga Fria, and Carsonville in the valley of Agua Fria Creek; and Bridgeport, Guadalupe, and the Chinese settlement of Canton in the Guadalupe Valley. Running through the new area of the Bear

[112] New York *Herald*, 24 Feb. 1856.
[113] John W. Dwinelle to G. W. Wright, Rochester, N.Y., 23 Feb. 1856 (M. A. Goodspeed, Jr., Collection); Palmer, Cook & Company to Frémont, Indenture, 28 March 1856, Vol. C of Deeds, pp. 94–96, Mariposa County Court House.

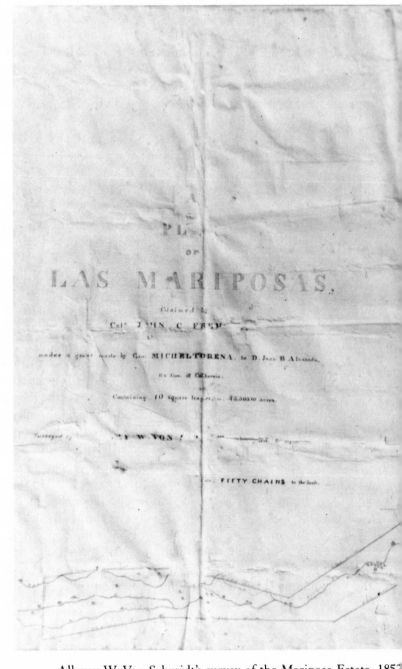

Allexey W. Von Schmidt's survey of the Mariposa Estate, 1852

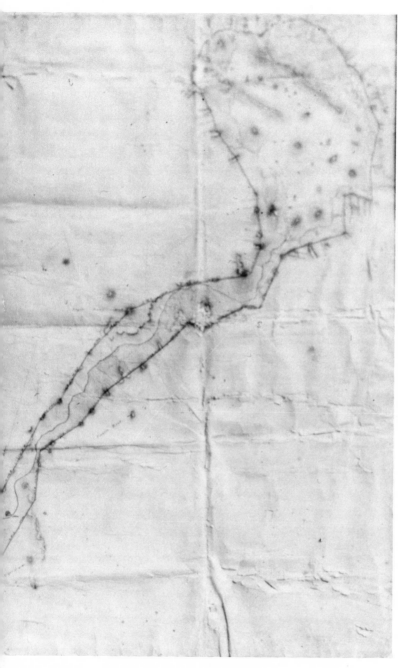

Courtesy of Louis T. Milburn, Mariposa, California.

LAS MARIPOSAS ESTATE MARIPOSAS COUNTY CALIFORNIA.

CONTAINING 44.386 86 ACRES

OR 70 SQUARE MILES.

Lith. of Sarony Major & Knapp, 449 Broadway N.Y.

The patent boundaries of the Mariposa Estate. Courtesy of the Bancroft Library.

in noticing the suggestion of the difficulty arising out of the former survey, says:

"The right which the Mexican Government reserved to control this survey passed with all other public rights to the United States, and the survey must now be made under the authority of the United States in the form and divisions prescribed by law for surveys in California, embracing the entire grant in one tract."

When the mandate of the Supreme Court confirming

tion of said decree directing the mode of survey, the said John C. Fremont, by his counsel at the proper time duly excepted and prayed that his exception be signed and sealed by the Court, and made a part of the record of this cause, which is accordingly done.

[SEAL]   HALL McALLISTER,
       Circuit Judge U. S. for the Dists. of California.

[SEAL]   OGDEN HOFFMAN, JR.,
       U. S. Dist. Judge, Northern Dist. of California.

MAP REFERRED TO IN COL. RANSOM'S LETTER.

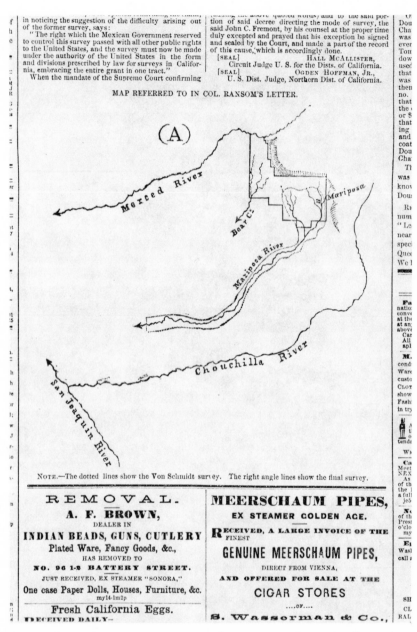

NOTE.—The dotted lines show the Von Schmidt survey. The right angle lines show the final survey.

Map of Frémont's Mariposa Estate showing the relationship between the original claim as surveyed by Allexey W. Von Schmidt in 1852 and the final location of its boundaries. From the San Francisco *Bulletin*, 8 June 1858.

Valley was the central vein of the Mother Lode, including the works and mines of the Merced Mining Company at Mount Ophir, and the rich Josephine and Pine Tree mines farther north, as well as many other valuable gold-bearing properties. Ironically, it was the Nouveau Monde Mining Company, originally planned by David Hoffman to work on Frémont's property, that had done so much to put the Merced Company's mines in a favorable working condition before it surrendered its lease.

Frémont had never before claimed some of this property, and many considered the final location of Las Mariposas "an outrageous barefaced piece of downright stealing." [114] Suits were filed, passions ran high, and at one time rifles, shotguns, and revolvers bristled on both sides, a story beyond the scope of the present volume. [115]

While Frémont was seeking to patent Las Mariposas, he was also trying to keep it out of the hands of his creditors. The District of Columbia's banking house of Corcoran and Riggs and its San Francisco affiliate, James King of William, posed the most serious threat. Frémont had borrowed $40,000 from them in September 1851, giving as security bills of exchange in the amount of $153,575 that he had received as payment for the beef furnished by him to the Indians in California. Since the drafts had been repudiated by the Secretary of the Interior, Frémont had been unable to meet his debt. There also seem to have been other loans from James King of William, who on 16 February 1854 obtained a judgment in the Fourth Judicial District against Frémont in the amount of $84,320. This occurred while the explorer was on his fifth expedition and after the Federal District Court had denied the Mariposa patent. On reaching San Francisco, Frémont met with Palmer and Montgomery Blair, their conversations revolving around the court judgment, Mariposa affairs, and the beef contracts. Since he had no money, he did not call upon King, who took this as a contemptuous slight. Shortly after Frémont left, the Mariposa "claim," except for block four in the town and section sixty-three of the whole rancho, was advertised for public sale to satisfy the judgment. James King of William bought it for $952. Montgomery Blair was convinced that King, whose brother Henry had been lost on the fourth expedition, was motivated by malicious feelings, although

---

[114] San Francisco *Bulletin*, 27 March 1858.
[115] For a partisan view of the struggle, see J. B. FRÉMONT [1]; CRAMPTON, 240–53, gives a balanced summary of the feud.

King assured Blair that he was acting under orders from his principles, Corcoran and Riggs. In view of the adverse decision of the court on Frémont's title, Palmer was not especially eager to advance money to redeem the property from Corcoran and Riggs.

For the next few weeks, Montgomery Blair worked hard and long on Frémont's affairs, collecting evidence and drawing up legal documents. Before August he was able to send east a large package and letter which he expected the explorer to read "with more delight than he ever did a love letter from Jessie," for it revealed to him "a mode of wrestling the Mariposa from Corcoran & Riggs." Before its arrival, however, Frémont had reached a settlement. He agreed to pay the Washington bank $56,500 out of the monies appropriated by Congress in the summer of 1854 for his special relief in the matter of the Indian beef contracts, but he was to pay any legal and court costs over $2,500. This ultimately amounted to more than $2,209 and seems to have been covered by Palmer in his settlement with King.

Perhaps Palmer's banking firm was following the original "plan" of Montgomery Blair, or perhaps it was erecting an additional safeguard against the tentacles of James King of William and Corcoran and Riggs when it obtained a judgment against Frémont in the Twelfth Judicial District of California. The court ordered the sheriff to seize and sell Frémont's interest in the Mariposa, save again for block four in the town and section sixty-three. The public auction was on 28 October 1854 and Palmer bought the property for $579. In June 1855 he paid $2,200.15 for all of James King of William's interest in the Mariposa, which included the 10 June 1854 certificate of purchase and interest by reason of unpaid court costs. The property had been saved from Corcoran and Riggs, but Palmer, Cook & Company's grip on the Mariposa had tightened.[116]

Although Las Mariposas was Frémont's most important land inter-

<hr />

[116] For a summary of JCF's debt and the settlement worked out by the three parties, see W. W. Corcoran Papers, Letterpress books for 1854 and 1855, especially 29 July 1854, pp. 275–76, but also Corcoran and Riggs to Frémont, 31 March, 13 and 17 April, 12 July, 12[?] Aug. 1855, pp. 547, 614, 639, 316, and Corcoran and Riggs to James King of William, 17 April and two Aug. 1855 letters, pp. 638, 348, 376 (DLC). The 6 June 1855 indenture between James King of William and Joseph C. Palmer not only indicates the final settlement between King and Palmer but also gives information on the judgment and 10 June 1854 sale. For Palmer's 28 Oct. 1854 purchase of JCF's interest to satisfy the judgment, see indenture between John Boling and Joseph C. Palmer, 5 June 1855. Both indentures are in Book B of Deeds, pp. 421–25, Mariposa County Court House.

est in California during this period, it was by no means the only one. Alcatraz, commanding the entrance to the Bay of San Francisco, was a will-of-the-wisp tantalizing him with the prospect of ownership for more than forty years and glowing especially bright when other economic assets fell off. As with the Mariposa, Joseph C. Palmer acquired a heavy stake; indeed, for a time Frémont seemed to relinquish to him all claim, but he succeeded in procuring a reconveyance, and 1882 found him writing to former Governor John G. Downey: "I am about to bring before Congress my claim to the Island of Alcatrases and if possible obtain a fair payment for it. I have been informed that you understand and appreciate the justice of my claim and that you are willing to aid me. . . ." He subsequently sold his shadowy claim to W. W. Jenkins and A. K. Moropolous, who were no more successful than he had been with the federal government.[117]

In San Francisco proper Frémont owned at least three valuable lots. The largest of 100 *varas*, or about 275 feet on a side, was located on Mission Street and had been marked no. 7 on the original town plan. A second was lot no. 90 of fifty *varas* at the corner of Broadway and Stockton, and the third, also of fifty *varas*, was near the corner of Sansome and California streets. It had already been subdivided and marked on the town plat as nos. 197, 198, and 201. William Leidesdorff had acted as the explorer's agent in the acquisition of all these properties in 1847 and, after his death, Frémont had to sue his estate to gain a clear title to the third, which was a valuable water lot.[118]

The explorer also claimed an undivided interest, with Abel Stearns, in the orchard lands of Mission Dolores. The original grant had supposedly been to José Andrade in 1846; the tenuous claims were proba-

---

For Montgomery Blair's comments on the situation, see his letters to Minna, 25 May and 9 Aug. 1854 (DLC—Blair Papers).

[117] For a history of the purchase, see Vol. 2, Doc. No. 153. Palmer's interest is noted in JCF to Caleb Cushing, 10 May 1855 (DNA-77), and in Doc. 261 n. 7, this volume. The Jenkins Family Papers (CU-B) contain many letters on Alcatraz, including JCF to John G. Downey, 4 March 1882.

[118] WHEELER, Schedule B, p. 28; BOSQUI, 82; and the Frémonts' indenture to John Pointer, 18 April 1851 (CHi), refer to the 100-*vara* lot. WHEELER, Schedule B, p. 40, notes the grant of lot no. 90; *Daily Alta California*, 3 March 1851, observed that auctioneers were scheduled to sell the property for failure to pay street assessments. The Transcript of Records, Court of 1st Instance, in Fremont v. Howard, California Supreme Court #47, State Archives #561, Sacramento, identifies the third property. Helpful in locating the properties is William M. Eddy's Official Map of San Francisco (1849).

bly acquired for him by Leidesdorff, who also seems to have had an interest and may have taken some action to improve the property before his death in May 1848. The Andrade claim was rejected by the land commissioners in 1855, by which time Frémont seems to have sold his share, although it is not clear that he and Stearns ever reached an agreement on the division and location of their respective portions.[119] In conflict with their claims were those of José Prudencio Santillan, to whom Governor Pío Pico allegedly granted all the property of Mission Dolores on the condition that he pay the debts of the mission. Frémont also tried to hedge his bets by acquiring "Santillan stock" in the San Francisco Land Association, which his business cohorts, Wright and Palmer, had done so much to float and which was trying to patent the Santillan/Bolton claim as well as that of the Noe Ranch.[120]

Away from the Golden Gate, Frémont claimed as early as August 1850 to be part owner of a league of land on the San Joaquin. If this were an interest in the José Castro claim of eleven leagues on that river, as it may have been, it vanished with the Supreme Court's rejection of the entire Castro case in 1860,[121] although possibly Frémont had already disposed of his share.

In November 1851 he purchased from the widow of José Dominguez for $2,000 a half-interest in the more than 17,000-acre San Emigdio rancho in what is now Kern County. Two months later for $5,000 he acquired an undivided half-interest in El Pescadero, a ranch twice as large in San Joaquin County, belonging to Antonio María Pico. Patents were eventually obtained for both properties and the Frémont family held its interest in them for many years.[122]

The three San Francisco lots; the claims to Mission Dolores, to Alcatraz Island, and to land on the San Joaquin River; and the extensive lands of the Mariposa, San Emigdio, and El Pescadero constitute the

---

[119] See Doc. Nos. 177, 268, 273, 276, and 281; GATES [1]. Apparently JCF borrowed money on 7 Nov. 1854, using the Mission Dolores property as collateral. See excerpt printed in Dawson's Book Shop Catalog 462, "Copy of Summons, Rowland G. Hazard *v.* John C. Fremont, J. S. Howard and Francisco Ocampo in the District Court of the 12th Judicial District, San Francisco, March 12, 1859."

[120] William Lippincott to George W. Wright, 4 March 1857, and an undated document, both in the M. A. Goodspeed, Jr., Collection, indicate JCF's ownership of Santillan stock. See Doc. No. 178, n.1, for a history of the Santillan/Bolton claim and its relationship to the Andrade claim.

[121] See Doc. No. 103, n.2.

[122] See Doc. Nos. 173 and 198.

known real estate assets of Frémont in California during the 1848–55 period. Another holding, the one that was so dear to Jessie's heart, was a thirteen-acre tract on Point San Jose (Black Point) overlooking Alcatraz, which Frémont purchased for her in 1860 for $41,000 in gold from the San Francisco banker Mark Brumagin, the presumed owner.[123] The property included a Gothic cottage, built by a neighbor and probably once occupied by Charles W. Cook; Joseph C. Palmer, also of Cook, Palmer & Company, lived on the point, too. Once the family was settled in the house, Jessie spent $20,000 on improvements, enlarging the parlor, adding a glass veranda on three sides, and building a stable and summer house on the grounds.[124] It was her pride and joy. To Elizabeth Blair Lee, she ecstatically described the home as "more beautiful than any Sea Dream that Tennyson or any poet ever fancied"; it was much preferred to Las Mariposas, with its isolation, grizzly bears, rattlesnakes, and miners.[125]

But the federal government had never conceded that Black Point was private property and, during the Civil War, took it over for defense purposes, removed the improvements, and erected fortifications. At the time Jessie was in the East, having rented the house to old friend Edward F. Beale, then Surveyor General of California and Nevada. In 1867 Frémont petitioned the Secretary of War to restore the property to Jessie; when this failed, she prosecuted her case all the way to the Supreme Court. Denied redress there, through her attorney, lobbyists, and friends she kept the claim before Congress: by 1892 House or Senate committees had investigated and reported at least twelve times on proposals for her relief. As late as 1895 she was writing to the daughter of the original developer: "You see I hold to living until we get Black Point, after that my pension will not be needed."[126]

The years from 1848 to 1855 were times of contrast. As in Fré-

---

[123] See DNA-77, Land Papers, Point San Jose, for documents relating to the claim, including JCF's 1867 petition and congressional committees' reports and bills. The Frémonts seemed to have occupied and improved the property before the formal purchase from Mark Brumagin on 28 Sept. 1860. The previous day, JBF had mortgaged the property to Leonidas Haskell and his wife for $16,000 and to William Dana and Haskell for $5,000 (Senate Report 898, 52nd Cong., 1st sess., Serial 2915).

[124] RATHER, 28, 32; JCF to Albert Tracy, 23 Sept. 1863 (NN).

[125] JBF to Elizabeth Blair Lee, Black Point, 2 June 1860 and 14 June [1860] (NjP—Blair-Lee Papers).

[126] JBF to "Dear Nell," Los Angeles, 18 March 1895 (CU-B).

mont's life in general, they brought both success and failure, high points and low points. On the one hand, there was the glamor of a seat in the U.S. Senate, fleeting though it was, but fueling his ambition for the presidency. There was the social whirl in London and Paris, in which Jessie so delighted. If Frémont was the holder of the vast Las Mariposas, he found its use difficult. Confirmation of title was ultimately achieved, but only after years of struggle. To raise capital by leases or by sale was not easy, either at home or in England. To be sure, Indian beef contracts were lucrative but payment was another matter. Even with substantial holdings, Frémont was never wealthy; he often borrowed money and was often sued for debt.

And if the earlier years had established his reputation as explorer, the horrors of the fourth expedition tarnished the luster, adding little to geographical and scientific knowledge of the West but providing melodrama and a wealth of material for future studies in psychohistory, motivation, and leadership. Not even the fifth and final one would bring full redemption, although Carvalho tried mightily to make it "original" and his leader a "Caesar." Out of a total route of 1,550 miles in 1853–54, Frémont had traveled the first 700 miles over old ground and at least another 300 in the wagon tracks of John Gunnison. By his own admission the results had been meager— principally daguerreotypes, meteorological observations, barometrical readings, and geological fragments. He would hardly call the latter a collection: snow, fatigue, and anxiety had left room for only the most scanty gleaning.

Warranting the scrutiny of perspective are the first three expeditions, which established forever Frémont's place in history. The first in 1842—which eventually reached South Pass and the rugged Wind River Mountains in Wyoming—had not been especially pathbreaking, but by his spectacular unfurling of the national flag on one of the highest peaks in the chain and by his remarkable report, he stirred the imaginations of Americans and did more than Benton's rhetoric or any previous explorer or mountain man to point the way west. The Senate ordered printed and distributed a thousand copies of his report, which included a kind of road map as far as South Pass.

He became even more famous when, two years later, Americans read the report of his fantastic 1843–44 circuit of the West, which his wife had again helped him prepare. They also pored over the accompanying map of the West, drawn like the first with the help of Charles Preuss, his topographer on both expeditions. Three times the length of the first, the report was to become a classic of exploring literature and with the map changed easterners' conception of the West. Both the House and the Senate ordered printings of 10,000 (in combination with the first report), and very shortly it was taken up by commercial publishers in America and abroad with editions appearing in French and German. When in 1850 Londoners viewed a grand moving painted panorama of the western expeditions and read a twenty-one page "Thrilling Sketch" of his life, prepared by his father-in-law, Frémont was well on the way to becoming not merely a national but a world hero.

Part of Frémont's appeal lay in his reports—in their charm and readability. Together he and Jessie had been able to capture his love of adventure, his enthusiasm for the natural environment, and to involve readers vicariously in the shooting of the canyons of the Sweetwater, the navigation of the Great Salt Lake in an eighteen-foot India rubber boat, the month-long battle with snow in crossing the Sierra Nevadas in mid-January, and other exciting adventures. The reports were lively, filled with human touches, even frontier gossip, and provided curious Americans with a wealth of miscellaneous information about the West: the superiority of Indian buffalo-skin lodges to American tents, Sutter's Fort on the Sacramento River, the size of the redwoods, and the importance of acorns in the diet of the California Indians.

More important, the reports gave utilitarian information about terrain, campsites, water, vegetation, wildlife, and weather. Many set out for the West "guided," as Sarah Royce remembered, "only by the light of Frémont's *Travels*." [127] In coming home from California at the rear of Stephen Watts Kearny's column in 1847, the explorer's spirits had soared when in the great emigration he had met many strong and warm friends. "They were using my maps on the road, traveling by them," he wrote Pierson B. Reading, "and you may judge how gratified I was to find that they found them perfectly correct & could do so."

Frémont's participation in the Bear Flag Revolt and his subsequent court-martial for refusing to acknowledge Gen. Kearny's authority gave a million dollars worth of publicity to him and to California. His *Geographical Memoir* upon the former Mexican province to accompany the map of Oregon and California, which Preuss was drawing, added another measure. While the *Memoir* was never as popular or

---

[127] ROYCE, 3.

lxxv

influential as the two reports, it enhanced Frémont's reputation as a scientist and, in Dale L. Morgan's words, "the map was a cartographical monument." [128]

In addition, Frémont's image as a dashing young explorer was undoubtedly enhanced by the fact that he was known largely through his own writings and those of Jessie and Benton. It is rather extraordinary that five expeditions, involving at least 175 men, left so few letters and journals by the participants. None at all relating to the first three were published during his lifetime. William H. Emory took a few swipes at him in the press in 1847, but these stemmed from the controversy with Kearny and did not impugn Frémont's work as an explorer. Nor was the personnel of the expeditions of a kind likely to write. He seldom took scientists with him, indeed, few educated men at all. As far back as December 1844 the German scientist in Saint Louis, George Engelmann, noticed that Frémont had objected to adding a botanist or geologist on the second expedition and suspected that he was reluctant to let anybody share in his discoveries, being "anxious to reap all the honour, as well as undertake all the labour himself." Both Isaac Cooper and James F. Milligan noted Frémont's prohibition on the keeping of journals or other memoranda.

With such a minimum of expert help, it is amazing that he was able to accomplish as much as he did. His scientific contributions were more than respectable and were recognized at home and abroad. He discovered and named the Great Basin as a geological and geographic entry. Because he explored the area's perimeters, he knew that no rivers ran from it to the sea, although large streams flowed in; his perceptive analysis of this phenomenon was the first recognition of the great power of evaporation in the region. He aptly compared the Great Basin with the interior of Asia. He also established the correct elevation of Great Salt Lake at 4,200 feet, and his description of the valleys along Bear River were undoubtedly influential in the Mormons' decision to settle in Salt Lake Valley. As Vols. 1 and 2 noted, he collected specimens of rocks, minerals, fossils, soils, and plants for eastern scientists to analyze and classify. One such botanical collection was made in the Uinta Basin, an area not again botanized until the twentieth century.

He was also the first to describe and explain so succinctly the great climatic difference between the east and west sides of the Cascade

---

[128] NEVINS & MORGAN, XXX.

Mountains. He recognized that the Oregon country was geologically different from the other regions of the United States, partly because of the great lava flows and partly because of the Columbia River, the mighty watercourse that tied the Rocky Mountains to the Pacific. When he saw submerged trees at one place in the Columbia, he recognized that this was the result not of rising waters but of complicated landsliding, and he was able to find the actual shear surfaces on which the shifts had occurred.

He was among the first to emphasize the agricultural possibilities of California, noticing the importance of wheat in the north and the potential for cotton further south. Among the arid brush-covered hills south of San Diego, he had found "little vallies converted by a single spring into crowded gardens, where pears, peaches, quinces, pomegranates, grapes, olives, and other fruits grew luxuriantly together. . . ."

Some of the names Frémont bestowed upon the land did not possess much staying power, but others were permanently transmitted; among the most famous are the Golden Gate, the Humboldt River and Mountains, Carson River and Lake, Walker River and Lake, Owens River and Lake, and the Kern River. Eventually twelve towns—east and west of the Mississippi—and countless city streets would bear the name Frémont.

More than in the earlier volumes, the documents here show Frémont to be complex, distant, and on occasion unscrupulous, but in 1856 most Americans would still agree with Thomas Oliver Larkin: "I considered Mr. Frémont a just, correct and moral man, abstemious, bold and persevering."[129] Without a doubt he was intelligent and ambitious, a true product of the mid-nineteenth century, manifesting that same faith in his own destiny as Americans did collectively in theirs and in their nation.

EDITORIAL PROCEDURES

THE DOCUMENTS

I have continued the editorial procedures established by Donald Jackson and myself in Vols. 1 and 2 of *The Expeditions of John Charles Frémont*. The original text is followed as closely as the demands of typography will permit, with several departures based on common

---

[129] LARKIN, 10:290–91.

sense and the current practice of scholars. In the matter of capitalization the original is followed, unless the writer's intention is not clear, in which case I resort to modern usage. Occasionally, in the interests of clarity, a long, involved sentence is broken into two sentences. Missing periods at the ends of sentences are supplied, dashes terminating sentences are supplanted by periods, and superfluous dashes after periods are omitted. In abbreviations, raised letters are brought down and a period supplied if modern usage calls for one. Words underscored in manuscript are italicized. The complimentary closing is run in with the preceding paragraph, and a comma is used if no other end punctuation is present. The acute accent mark on the *e* in Frémont is supplied when it appears in the document and omitted where it does not appear, but it is used in all headings and references to Frémont. Procedures for dealing with missing or illegible words, conjectural readings, etc. are shown in the list of symbols, pp. lxxx–lxxxii. When in doubt about how to proceed in a trivial matter, I have silently followed modern practice; if the question is more important, the situation is explained in a note.

Because Jessie B. Frémont wrote and signed so many of her husband's letters, I have continued to indicate this to the reader, as set forth in the list of symbols.

When a related document or letter is used—that is, not one directly to or from Frémont—extraneous portions are deleted and the deletion is indicated by a symbol. The present volume contains fewer related documents than did Vol. 2. Space and printing costs have forced the calendaring of some documents. Frémont's many powers of attorney are not printed in full but are summarized. So also are the long and often repetitious letters of David Hoffman, Frémont's agent in London, but Frémont's letters to him are printed in full.

The Notes

The first manuscript indicated is the one from which the transcription has been made; other copies, if known, are listed next. If endorsements or addresses are routine, their presence is merely noted, but if they contribute useful information, they are quoted in full. For example, see the endorsement on the copy of the letter of Jessie B. Frémont to David Hoffman, 8 April 1852, Doc. No. 230, concerning Mrs. Frémont's appeal for bail money for her husband following his arrest in London.

Material taken from printed texts is so indicated (printed in BIGE-

LOW), but no attempt is made to record other printed versions.

Unless previously done in Vols. 1 and 2, senders, receivers, and persons referred to in the documents are briefly identified at first mention. For senders and receivers, this identification is made in the first paragraph of the notes and no reference number is used. The reader can easily find the identification of an individual by locating in the index the page on which he or she is first mentioned.

With the exception of H. H. Bancroft's *Register of Pioneer Inhabitants of California, 1542 to 1848*, no source is cited for the kind of biographical information to be found in standard directories, genealogies, and similar aids.

Names of authors in SMALL CAPITALS are citations to sources listed in the bibliography on pp. 611–17. This device enables me to keep many long titles and other impedimenta out of the notes. In the case of two or more works by the same author, a number is assigned, as in GATES [1]. When a published work is being discussed, not merely cited, I often list it fully by author and title in the notes.

To avoid the constant repetition of the Frémont names, I have freely used the initials JCF and JBF for John Charles and Jessie.

Most of the papers of George W. Wright used in this volume are from the M. A. Goodspeed, Jr., Collection.

SYMBOLS

C	California State Library, Sacramento
CHi	California Historical Society, San Francisco
CLU	University of California at Los Angeles
CSf	San Francisco Public Library, San Francisco
CSmH	Henry E. Huntington Library, San Marino, Calif.
CtY	Yale University, New Haven
CU-B	Bancroft Library, University of California at Berkeley
DLC	Library of Congress
ICHi	Chicago Historical Society, Chicago
IU	University of Illinois, Urbana-Champaign
LU	Louisiana State University
MB	Boston Public Library
MHi	Massachusetts Historical Society, Boston
MoSB	Missouri Botanical Garden Library, St. Louis
MoSHi	Missouri Historical Society, St. Louis
MoU	University of Missouri, Columbia
NHi	New-York Historical Society, New York
NjP	Princeton University, Princeton, N.J.
NN	New York Public Library
NNNBG	New York Botanical Garden, Bronx Park, New York
NNPM	Pierpont Morgan Library, New York
OrHi	Oregon Historical Society, Portland
PHi	Historical Society of Pennsylvania, Philadelphia
PPAN	Academy of Natural Sciences, Philadelphia
Vi	Virginia State Library, Richmond

DNA-15	Records of the Veterans Administration
DNA-49	Records of the Bureau of Land Management—General Land Office
DNA-59	General Records of the Department of State
DNA-75	Records of the Bureau of Indian Affairs
DNA-76	Records of Boundary and Claims Commissions and Arbitrations
DNA-77	Records of the Office of the Chief of Engineers
DNA-92	Records of the Office of the Quartermaster General, California Claims Board, 1847–55
DNA-94	Records of the Adjutant General's Office, 1780s–1917
DNA-104	Records of the Bureau of the Mint
DNA-107	Records of the Office of the Secretary of War
DNA-217	Records of the U.S. General Accounting Office (T-135 denotes a collection of microfilm documents in this record group.)
DNA-267	Records of the Supreme Court of the United States—Appellate Case Files
DNA-393	Records of U.S. Army Continental Commands, 1821–1920

OTHER SYMBOLS AND EDITORIAL AIDS

AD	Autograph document
ADS	Autograph document, signed
ADS-JBF	Autograph document, Frémont's name signed by Jessie
AL	Autograph letter
ALS	Autograph letter, signed
ALS-JBF	Autograph letter, Frémont's name signed by Jessie
D	Document
DS	Document, signed
DS-JBF	Document, Frémont's name signed by Jessie
JBF	Jessie Benton Frémont
JCF	John Charles Frémont
Lbk	Letterbook copy
LR	Letter received
LS	Letter sent
RC	Receiver's copy
RG	Record Group

SC	Sender's copy
[ ]	Word or phrase supplied or corrected. Editorial remarks within text are italicized and enclosed in square brackets.
[?]	Conjectural reading or conjectural identification of an addressee.
[. . .]	A word or two missing or illegible. Longer omissions are specified in footnotes.
⟨ ⟩	Word or phrase deleted from manuscript, usually by sender. The words are set in italics.
. . . .	Unrelated matter deleted by the editor. The symbol stands alone, centered on a separate line.

The 1848–49 Expedition:
Disaster in the Garitas

1. Frémont to John Torrey

WASHINGTON CITY, March 22d. 1848
MY DEAR SIR

After taking the trouble to gather plants I do not think we ought to lose them, even the scattered fragments which I find here & there in my note books. I shall therefore send you such as I find, and will beg you to return them to me with a name if you have leisure. It may happen that I can make the knowledge useful. Very truly yours,

J. C. FRÉMONT

ALS-JBF (NNNBG).

2. Frémont to John Torrey

WASHINGTON CITY, May 3d. 1848
MY DEAR SIR,

I have just received with much pleasure your interesting note of the 1st.[1] to which I will reply more at length. In the mean time I beg you to give me the name of the flower enclosed. Very truly yours,

J. C. FRÉMONT

Dr. Torrey

ALS-JBF (NNNBG).
1. Not found.

3

3. Frémont to John Torrey

Washington May 5. 1848

My dear Sir,

I mentioned to you that I am drawing up to be presented to Congress a *brief* memoir upon California. It is intended to give some *data* for forming an estimate of the real value of the country, particularly required at this time, and will contain what facts I am able to give in (the absence of journals and collections) climate, general appearance, elevation and vegetation in different seasons. I therefore am obliged to make use of what little botanical knowledge is in my possession. If you have no objection I will mention the oak under the name *Quercus longiglanda*. The fruit in the drawing sent is of the natural size, and the tree a very large one frequently 6 feet in diam[eter].

In mentioning trees I am anxious to be as exact and definite as possible, and will thank you for the name of the large cedar of the Sierra Nevada, *California*, (juniperus) brought home on our previous voyage, and also of a large tree belonging to the division of cypresses probably brought in at that time. It is called *Palo colorado* by the Californians, or Red wood. During our last journey I measured some 15 & 17 feet diameter and 285 feet high. Our present collection has many specimens in almost every stage of growth. The fruit grows on the upper parts and is a sort of small cone. [*JCF draws a small cone.*]

This memoir I expect to send in next week, and would be glad to hear from you immediately. I have not yet received Mr. Brackenridge's[1] note. Probably the plant is already in our collection, but as I shall not know any thing on this point I will do what I can to find it. In looking over the few notes I have here I find that our collection is very rich, containing in addition to the plants, many seeds. Col. Benton will see that it reaches you safely. It is on board a ship of war [the *Erie*] now on her way home, and which is expected to reach Norfork in the next month. When the immediate press of business is over, we will arrange our plans for the coming enterprise. Very truly yours,

J. C. Frémont

Dr. John Torrey

ALS (NNNBG).
1. William Dunlop Brackenridge (1810–93) had served as assistant naturalist on Charles Wilkes's exploring expedition in the Pacific. He was on board the *Peacock* when it was wrecked at the Columbia River in 1841 and had to travel

overland to join the rest of the Wilkes squadron anchored in San Francisco Bay (MALONEY). He thus had an opportunity to collect and record in the Shasta region and Sacramento Valley, and presumably Brackenridge's note would deal with *Libocedrus decurrens* Torr., incense cedar, later described by Torrey and illustrated by Isaac Sprague (see pp. 578 and 601).

4. Thomas H. Benton to the Editors of the *National Intelligencer*

C Street, May 14, 1848

GENTLEMEN:

We read in the *National Intelligencer* for May 9 as follows:

"The United States sloop of war Portsmouth, Commander [John B.] Montgomery, arrived in Boston, on Friday from the Pacific Ocean.

"Commander Montgomery states that the British frigate Herald and the brig Pandora are engaged in making a new survey of the Gulf and coast of California.

"The whaleship Hope, of Providence, [Rhode Island], was recently lost on the coast in consequence of an error in the charts now in general use, which locate the coast and islands from Monterey to Cape San Lucas from fifteen to forty miles too far to the eastward."

On reading this notice in your paper, I have to say that the error in question has already been detected by Mr. Frémont and corrected in his map of Oregon and Upper California, now in course of preparation, and nearly ready to be laid before the Senate, by whom its construction was ordered. In his last expedition, Mr. Frémont made a series of astronomical observations across the continent, terminating at Santa Cruz, near Anno Nuevo, the northwestern point of the Bay of Monterey. It was found, on laying down these positions on his map, that the west end of the line went beyond the coast, as given in Vancouver's charts (the basis of all in use), and that it projected ten miles into the sea. His own map was immediately corrected accordingly, placing the coast and islands of Upper California ten miles further west.

Mr. Frémont's observations were made in the winter and spring of 1845 and 1846. They were calculated by Professor Hubbard,[1] of the Washington City Observatory, during the past winter; and were laid down on the map by Mr. Chas. Preuss, in February last.

This map, with a memoir to illustrate it, and the calculations of Prof. Hubbard, will be laid before the Senate in a few days.

Respectfully, gentlemen, your obedient servant,

THOMAS H. BENTON

Printed in *National Intelligencer*, 15 May 1848.
1. Professor of mathematics in the U.S. Navy and stationed at the Naval Observatory, Joseph Hubbard (1823–63) had been doing calculations for JCF since 1844.

5. William L. Marcy to Frémont

War Department
WASHINGTON May 18, 1848

SIR,

The Chairman of the Committee on Military Affairs of the House of Representatives[1] has called on the Department for all papers on file relative to the accounts or claims arising in California. On looking at them, I find some of such character as induced me to think that you might wish to see them, and probably may desire to accompany them with some remarks.

Should you think proper to call at the Department, I will submit them to your examination. I am, with great respect, Your Obt. Servt.,

W. L. MARCY
Secretary of War

Lbk (DNA-107, LS, 28:294).
1. The chairman was Congressman John M. Botts (1802–69) of Virginia.

6. Frémont to William L. Marcy

WASHINGTON CITY, May 19, 1848

SIR,

The contract with Celis for money & cattle, & two per cent. a month interest, communicated to you by Col. Mason, was one of those alluded to in my letter to you of October last,[1] & brought before the Senate Committee of Military Affairs in February, & the evidence in relation to it printed in the document of evidence.

In my letter to you, I said, in reference to this class of claims remaining to be provided for:

"2. Payment to citizens of that territory of money loaned to me by them, required and expended in the administration of the government and partial payment of the troops. . . .

Amounts of money required for civil and military purposes were at different times loaned to me by different individuals, principally Mexican citizens, as the governor of the territory, acknowledged as such by them. The sums of money are not large, but having been obtained under the high rate of interest usual in that country, public interest is suffering by a delayed payment."

See the whole letter, pages 3 & 4 of document, a copy in full of which is herewith furnished.

This contract with Celis was made by the commissary, Capt. [Samuel J.] Hensley, with my approbation, & was fully brought before the Military Committee of the Senate. The testimony of Capt. Hensley, at pages 35 & 36, says:[2]

"After the formation of the civil government of California by Commodore Stockton, in January, 1847, I was appointed by Governor Frémont, commissary of subsistence to the California battalion, in which capacity I made such purchases as were necessary for the subsistence of the troops, paying for the articles purchased by giving my official certificate of the amount due. In discharge of this duty, I purchased of Eulogio de Celez [Célis] six hundred head of beef cattle, at $10 cash, Celez also furnishing as part of the same transaction, twenty-five hundred dollars in cash to Governor Frémont, for the use of the United States government, the whole amount of the loan and the price of the cattle, was agreed on our part, to be paid to him within six months thereafter, if not, to bear interest from that date till paid. Soon after this purchase the California battalion was disbanded, and Governor Frémont ordered me to retain possession of these cattle until he could know whether those succeeding him in command would become responsible for the contracts made under his authority. When it was ascertained that his successor would not become thus responsible, Governor Frémont directed me to place the cattle in safe keeping, where they might remain as some security to Celez for the amount due him. I accordingly placed the cattle in charge of Abel Sternes [Stearns], a responsible man, who agreed to keep and be responsible for them, for one half of their increase. There was also left in that country about sixteen hundred pounds of sugar, in the possession of John

7

Rowland, near the city of Angels, and also a quantity stored in Santa Barbara."

The statement of Celis, forwarded by Col. Jonathan D. Stevenson to the War Department confirms the testimony of Capt. Hensley. After Genl. Kearny informed me that he would not assume my liabilities as Governor, the cattle, for the security of Celis, not knowing what would be done, were placed in deposit with a responsible man (Mr. Abel Stearns) & without expense to the United States. I went up to Monterey to see Genl. Kearny about these liabilities, in the latter part of March, 1847, when the interview was of such a character as to induce me to offer my resignation to him (page 107 of the printed record of the trial.)

To a question if he had not then been asked whether he would assume these liabilities? he answered that he did not recollect the question, but if it had been put he would have answered in the negative. It was put, & was answered in the negative, & hence the arrangement to put the cattle in deposit. The following from the printed trial shows this: (page 107)

"Question. Did not Lieutenant Colonel Frémont in that interview make known to you that he wished to know whether you, as governor, would assume the government responsibilities, accruing during the time that he was governor, under Governor Stockton's appointment?

Answer. I have no recollection of his having asked me. If he had, I should have answered in the negative.

Question. Did you not *tell* him that you would not assume one cent of those liabilities? and do you not know that his drafts on account of those expenses are now protested to the amount of some twenty thousand dollars, and subject to be doubled, and he to be sued for the whole?

Answer. I do not remember of telling him as stated in the question. I do not know, at this time, that his drafts have been protested.

Question. Did he not immediately offer his resignation of his commission in the army? and did you not refuse it? and, if so, please relate all that passed?

Answer. In the conversation with him at Monterey, I think he did offer to resign his commission, which I refused to accept."

It was notorious in the country that Genl. Kearny refused to recognize these liabilities, & even depreciated their value by disparaging remarks, & Messrs. [Henry] *King* & [Edward M.] *Kern*, left behind in California, when he brought me away, & now just arrived here, can prove it.

The interest to be paid after the note became due (2 per cent. per month) appeared high to the Committee of the Senate, & many witnesses were examined on that point, of whom, Mr. [Frank] Ward, a merchant of San Francisco, testified (page 60, of the document of evidence) as follows:

"Question. Do you know of the rates at which bills were selling while you were at California, and what per cent. was paid for money?

Answer. Government has paid from 12 to 20 per cent. on bills of the United States; and it is my impression that there has been paid as high as 25 per cent.

The legal interest for money in California is two per cent. a month, and three per cent. a month is very often paid."

And Mr. [Daingerfield] Fauntleroy, a purser in the Navy, & a witness before the Committee (same page) testified as follows:

"Answer. I was a purser in the navy of the United States on the California station on board the frigate Savannah, from the 2d of February, 1846, to the 26th March, 1847. The rate of exchange, I believe, was twenty per cent; that pursers of the squadron had drawn at that rate; and, I believe, a higher rate of interest had been given in other instances. I had occasion to draw, myself, several times, first in favor of Mr. Frank Ward, a gentleman from New York, and merchant of Yerba Buena, who very liberally reduced the exchange to twelve per cent., much to the annoyance of capitalists of that country; but on the ship leaving for the United States, I was compelled to give fifteen per cent. in favor of another person.

The rate of interest for money loaned, I think, was two per cent. a month."

In this case, the contract was at eight months, & interest only payable after that time, if not paid when due. If so paid, there was no interest: if not, the *legal* interest, & the *common* interest was two per cent. a month. I was then acting as Governor, under commission from Comm. Stockton, who had sent to Callas to raise money, & the contract was expected to be met when due.

The price of the cattle is said by Col. Mason to be 40 per cent. too high. The testimony of Capt. Hensley (page 36 of the document of evidence) shows the error of that statement—that beef cattle were $8 to $10.

"Statement of the average prices of military supplies of all descriptions in California before and during the war.
Horses and mules, from . . . . $25 to $35.

9

```
Saddles, complete, from . . . . . . . . . . . . . . . . . . . . . . . . . . . 30 to 40
Bridles . . . . . . . . . . . . . . . . . . . . . . . . . . . . . . . . . . . . . . . . . 6 to 10
Spurs. . . . . . . . . . . . . . . . . . . . . . . . . . . . . . . . . . . . . . . . . . . 6 to 10
Botas. . . . . . . . . . . . . . . . . . . . . . . . . . . . . . . . . . . . . . . . . . .  4 to 8
```
   All of which are necessary in that country
```
Rifles, from . . . . . . . . . . . . . . . . . . . . . . $50 to $100; very scarce
Powder . . . . . . . . . . . . . . . . . . . . . . . . . 2 per pound
Lead . . . . . . . . . . . . . . . . . . . . . . . . . . . 37½ cents per pound
Percussion caps . . . . . . . . . . . . . . . . . . . $10 per thousand
Beef cattle. . . . . . . . . . . . . . . . . . . . . . . 8 to $10 per head
Flour . . . . . . . . . . . . . . . . . . . . . . . . . . . 10 per hundred pounds
Sugar. . . . . . . . . . . . . . . . . . . . . . . . . . . 37 to $50 per hundred pounds.
Coffee . . . . . . . . . . . . . . . . . . . . . . . . . . 50 per hundred pounds"
```

The contract with Celis was a good one for the United States, & entered into by him as an act of friendship to the United States. He was a wealthy Mexican gentleman of California, remained neutral during the war, & lent the money & furnished the cattle to me as Governor, & ought to be faithfully repaid, with thanks for his friendly aid. The cattle are kept by Mr. Stearns without expense to the United States, to secure the parties concerned from loss. The following statement of Col. Russell (page 50 of the document of evidence) relates to contracts like that with Mr. Celis:

"Your deponent states that, in consequence of the wise and humane treatment of Colonel Fremont towards the conquered population, his popularity became very great in the country, and enabled him to do what no other man, I confidently believe, could have done, to obtain supplies on credit, and simply by pledging his word that his acts would be ratified by his government."

Col. Mason says there was a quartermaster at Monterey, who had been more than a month in the country, with a supply of money, applicable to the proper expenses of the army in California. Such might have been the fact at Monterey, but I was at Los Angeles 400 miles distant, & on account of the conflicting claims of Commodore Stockton & Genl. Kearny, derived no benefit from that quartermaster. What little I received, came from Comm. Stockton, who did what he could to support the civil government he had created.

The contract with Celis was made on the 3d. of March, 1847, which was *two days before* Genl. Kearny, at Monterey, 400 miles distant, had issued his proclamation dated 1st of March, to assume the government of California, as shown in his own testimony before the Court Martial. At page 100 of the printed record, these facts appear:

"Question. You state in your letter of the 15th of March, that you issued a proclamation on the 4th, dated on the 1st of March; now, when and where was that proclamation promulgated?

Answer. It was promulgated throughout California; it was given in manuscript to the printer on the 4th of March; many copies of it were printed and distributed immediately after; the copies were sent by the printer to me; and Mr. Larkin, at whose house I was staying, took them from me to distribute; the printers, as I understood him, distributed some; I believe they were printed, on the 5th. If the object of the accused is to inquire of me whether Captain Turner, when he went below, took a copy of that paper, I will say that he did not."

This shows that the Proclamation assuming the government of California was not printed at Monterey until the 5th. of March, & that even then it was not sent to me. In the meantime, I had fulfilled the duties of Governor under the commission of Commodore Stockton; & the question now is, whether my contract as such shall be complied with? The papers given to Celis by me, in April, 1847, was to verify the contract of March 3d. after I knew that Genl. Kearny would not assume it, & to enable a just settlement to be made. I was about to be brought out of the country, & wished to make the transaction. The money was delivered on the 3d. of March, most of the cattle soon after; the rest secured to be delivered to Mr. Stearns, & a certificate given to Mr. Celis that his contract was complied with, on his giving security to deliver the few remaining cattle. The transaction was thus authenticated both in California, for the security, & before the Military Committee of the Senate, for the information of the Government at home.

Col. Mason also gives information of the loan from Antonio Cot, at what he calls an "enormous rate of interest." The interest was *three* percent. for *two* months, & *two* per cent. for *four* months more, if not repaid at that time, & the sum was $3000. The date of the loan was the 4th of February, 1847, soon after I became Governor under Commodore Stockton's appointment, & when his purser, Mr. [William] Speiden, was endeavoring to raise money on bills to defray the expenses of the civil government which he had established. This case is one of those referred to in my letter to the Secretary at War in Oct. last, as money borrowed for the service of the government at the high rates of interest common in the country. It is proved that *two* per cent.

a month was the *legal* interest of the country, that three was sometimes given & that the naval pursers raised money on bills on the
United States at from 12 to 25 per cent. discount. Reducing this discount to interest, & supposing the bill to be six months (a usual time)
in getting round the Cape Horn & the rate of interest would be from
two to four per cent a month. A letter from Mr. Larkin, U.S. consul at
Monterey, to Genl. Kearny, written to obtain payment of claims, and
dated May 30th, 1847, and printed at page 17 of the document of evidence, says that, in consequence of the non payment of the claimants,
merchants were then paying two per cent. a month on borrowed
money.

Col. Mason says, Genl. Kearny, my superior, was then in the country, (to wit, February 4, 1847). Genl. Kearny's testimony before the
Court Martial says that his controversy with Commodore Stockton
took place at Los Angeles about the middle of January—that he left
Comm. Stockton & myself there on the 18th.—that he went off, without notice to me, or orders, or message, or taking leave, or saying
where he was going—& that afterwards at Monterey, 400 miles distant, he assumed the civil government of California, by a proclamation written the 4th of March, dated the 1st, printed the 5th, distributed afterwards, & no copy sent to me. From the time he left Los
Angeles, (18th January) till the 11th of March, (when he sent me an
order by Capt. Turner) I was without information from him. Where
he was, was to me unknown, nor did it make any difference in my
administration of the government, as Genl. Kearny had not then assumed it.

The third, & last thing, communicated by Col. Mason, is the order
to the Collector of the Customs, at San Pedro "to receive depreciated
paper ($1700) signed by individuals in no way responsible to the gov-
ernment." This information from Col. Mason, was information of
what has also been the subject of examination here, & received its judicial answer. (The precise sum was $1731.41 1/2). The order to the
collector was to receive the certificates *given in payment for supplies for
the use of the United States*, in payment for duties. It was a mode of
paying for the supplies. The certificates were then at a discount of
about thirty per cent. I presume they are much more depreciated now,
& will sink to a mere trifle if not paid under a law of this session. The
depreciation was no loss to the government, which had received the
value in supplies: it was a loss to the original holder, who took it in

place of money, which the government had not there to give, & who sold it at a discount. The *payment* was no loss to the government but an act of justice in taking its own paper in payment of its own debts. The amount received was $1731.41 1/2, & diminishes to that extent the claims to be provided for under this bill. The order to the collector was in my character of governor—was at first verbal—afterwards given in writing, to authenticate the transaction, which written order it is probable Col. Mason had not seen, otherwise he would have known that it was a mere receiving of government paper in payment of government dues. The order to receive it was *official*, through the Secretary of California, Col. Wm. H. Russell. It was in these words:

"CIUDAD DE LOS ANGELES,
March 21, 1847.

Sir: You are hereby ordered and permitted, in the case of F. Hultman [Hüttmann], to receive government payment in payment of his custom-house dues. Very respectfully,

J. C. FRÉMONT,
Governor of California
By Wm. H. Russell,
Secretary of State

To David W. Alexander,
Collector of the port of San Pedro.

N. B. Mr. Hultman will be entitled to the usual discount by prompt payment.

WM. H. RUSSELL, for
J. C. FRÉMONT, Governor"

The only loser in the transaction was the original holder—but even thirty per cent. loss then might have been better for him than to have held it to the present time.

My situation in California was difficult & arduous—3000 miles distant—without money—carrying on military operations—administering a civil government—getting supplies & small loans on the best terms possible—& actually getting supplies & loans from the conquered inhabitants, as an act of friendship to the United States. Myself & my staff officers know every transaction—authenticated many before I was *brought away* from the country, & would have authenticated all just demands if I had remained, & they would have been paid, by orders of Commodore Stockton, if he had remained, out of naval funds as he paid other expenses of the conquest.

The U.S. consul, Mr. Larkin, at Monterey, addressed a letter to Gen. Kearny, to be shown to the President—another to Mr. Buchanan, both printed in the document of evidence, page 17 &c., & of which the following are extracts:

"The claimants made their advances, and performed their services, with good will and readiness, which our government will always find among our citizens; they had every reason to expect that their demands would be approved of and paid by the United States government. For some reason this has not been done, and the distress caused to the merchants is too plainly visible, in their having to pay 2 per cent. per month on their borrowed money.

Emigrants who, in October and November, 1846, arrived here, singly and with families, with scarcely more than arms and ammunitions, wagons, oxen, mules, and harness, came forward and lent or sold this little, all to fight for their country, and secure California to the United States and make a home for themselves under our flag, as well as those who may come after them. The crush of their hopes, their own poverty—some of them even returning to their families on the Sacramento without decent clothing—are the sorrowful results. As regards the claimants of the campaign, you are fully informed of."

"Commodore Stockton and Colonel Frémont have now superior officers in California, and from this reason, or some other, the greatest confusion relative to money affairs prevails in this territory. I have seen the prime of the last emigration travelling from the south to the Sacramento; some of them almost in rags, having spent their services, and sold their guns and wagons to government, for which they now suffer. I have given General Kearny a statement of facts, and have requested him to have an interview with the President on this subject."

Policy, as well as Justice, requires these claims to be now paid with the least possible delay. Very respectfully, Sir, Your obt. servant,

J. C. FRÉMONT

To the Hon. Mr. Marcy
Secretary at War

ALS (DNA-92, LR, 1852–54). This letter may be found as an enclosure in the letter of Charles M. Conrad, Secretary of War, to C. F. Smith and other members of the board for the examination of claims contracted in California under Frémont, 27 Sept. 1852. JCF's letter was endorsed, "Rec. May 27 '48."

1. See Vol. 2, pp. 428–29.

2. JCF's quotations for the remainder of this letter are from "Report on Memorial of J. C. Frémont," Senate Report 75, 30th Cong., 1st sess., Serial 512, and from "Message of the President of the United States communicating the proceedings of the court-martial in the trial of Lieut. Col. Frémont," Senate Ex. Doc. 33, 30th Cong., 1st sess., Serial 507. His quotations are in the form of pasted clippings from the documents.

7. Jessie B. Frémont to John Torrey

WASHINGTON CITY
May 29th. 1848.

MY DEAR SIR,

Mr. Frémont is so pressed to finish his little memoir for the Senate, that he has asked me to send you the enclosed remnants of plants. They are the earliest flowering plants of the Joaquin valley (Cal.) and he would be much obliged if you could send him very soon, their names.

Mr. Fréculo [sic][1], the French botanist, made Mr. Frémont a visit in which he talked over his intended explorations, so he has seen him.

As he will have to go to the North Mr. Frémont hopes to see you before leaving for California, which he trusts will be in the coming month.

Your wishes for my successful journey are a little premature. I shall go by the isthmus after the steamers commence running, a much less interesting, but shorter & safer way for women & children. I should have written to your daughter some time since in answer to her kind message but for some months I have been unwell & since the last of April I have not left my room, but have had a battle with a violent bilious fever, which like Bunyan's fight with Apollyon was the dreadfullest fight I ever had. Like him, however I have gained the victory & I am more than willing not even to remember it. Very truly yours,

JESSIE BENTON FRÉMONT

ALS (NNNBG—Torrey Correspondence).
1. The French botanist Auguste A. L. Trécul (1818–96) was on his way to Kansas to collect specimens for the Muséum National d'Histoire Naturelle in Paris. By September he was working on the Arkansas and Little Arkansas (MC KELVEY, 1048–52).

8. Frémont to John Torrey

My Dear Sir,

I send you this sketch,[1] *from memory* of the tree about which I wrote you, & which you thought was probably *Abies Douglassii*. It is called the Redwood in California, and I have measured them 275 feet high and 10 to 15 feet in diameter.

I shall be glad to send you the proof sheets of the short memoir I am finishing, that you may pass judgment on the few botanical remarks which are introduced. I suppose they will reach you at Princeton? Very truly yours,

J. C. Frémont

ALS (NNNBG—Torrey Correspondence).
1. Not found.

9. Charles Wilkes to the Editors of the *National Intelligencer*

[Washington, 6 June 1848]

Messrs. Gales & Seaton:

On my return to the city, after a few weeks' absence, your paper of the 15th of May, containing some remarks on the errors existing in the charts of the northwest coast of California, by Col. Benton was brought to my notice.[1] Although I have no desire to detract from any one, yet I think it due others, as well as to the United States Exploring Expedition, to place the following facts before the public respecting the errors which *did exist* in the longitude of this coast, the "discovery" of which is now claimed to have been first made, and the errors corrected by Col. Frémont, "through a series of astronomical observations across the continent."

Shortly after the publication of Vancouver's charts in 1798, errors were suspected to exist in them (his points were determined by lunar observations, and several chronometers, which latter performed but indifferently, and from these his results were obtained) from a difference which was found between him and the Spanish surveying vessels, employed at the same time on the coast of California. The amount of error was not, however, truly ascertained until some years after this, when Captain [Frederick William] Beechey, of H. B. M. S. the Blossom, visited this coast in 1826. His observations were confirmed by Captain De Petit Thouars, in the French frigate La Venus, in 1836 and 1837, and again by Captain Sir Edward Belcher, in H. B. M. surveying ship the Sulphur, in 1835; and it was again confirmed by the United States Exploring Expedition in 1841.

These corrections were all made on the general charts published by order of Congress in 1844, from the surveys and examinations of the Exploring Expedition, and have been in possession of our ships navigating the Pacific Ocean since that time.

By comparing dates, it will be perceived that these *"discoveries"* were known long since, and that the actual amount of error was ascertained some twenty years ago by both the English and French expeditions, and were published by our own Government in the results of the Exploring Expedition, a year prior to the earliest date claimed by Col. Benton as the time when the observations of Lieut. Col. Frémont were made. With great respect, I am, yours, &c.,

CHARLES WILKES

Printed in *National Intelligencer*, 8 June 1848.
1. See Doc. No. 4.

10. Frémont to the Editors of the *National Intelligencer*

WASHINGTON, June 8th, 1848

MESSRS. GALES AND SEATON:

In the absence of Col. Benton, and as the matter relates specially to myself, I desire to take some notice of the publication made in your paper of to-day by Captain Wilkes of the Navy, concerning the rectification of an error on our western coast.

Capt. Wilkes could not have examined with much care the note of Col. Benton, which he undertakes to criticise, or he would have perceived that it is not against anything stated by Col. Benton, or claimed for the observations made by myself, that his strictures apply: but that his sole dispute, if he had any, is with the reports brought in by the sloop of war Portsmouth, Commander Montgomery, and only quoted in the note of Col. B. He must also have perceived, with a little more attention, that the word "*discovery*," which he has introduced as a quotation italicized, does not exist in Col. Benton's note: and hence that his use of the word, as if copied from Col. Benton's notes, is, in both instances unwarranted.

The plain facts in the matter in question are these: In my map published in 1845, accompanying the report of the first and second expeditions under my command, the line of the Pacific coast was laid down (and so stated) according to the survey of Vancouver. It was introduced merely with a view to give a necessary completeness to the map of my reconnoissance, and without any attempt at a rectification of errors, which I supposed to come properly within the province of the naval exploring expedition which had recently surveyed the coast.

In a recent expedition, having reference particularly to the geography on the Pacific coast, I was enabled to make "a series of observations" in that country, depending on two main positions in the Sacramento valley established by lunar culminations. These observations were made in 1845 and 1846; they were calculated during the last winter by Professor Hubbard of the Washington Observatory. On laying down the positions thus ascertained on the map, they were found not to correspond with the coast line as before projected. I was aware that there had been various surveys of the coast, and discrepancies between the observations of the different navigators there. My observations agreed nearly with those of Capt. Beechey; and I immediately wrote to the city of New York to procure, if any such had been published, a chart of the coast founded on the surveys of either Beechey or Belcher; but was informed that there was nothing of the kind known there. This being the case, I caused the line to be erased, and projected further west, in conformity with my own observations. The fact of this alteration was confined to myself and to Mr. Preuss, who was engaged in draughting a map, and was not intended to be brought to the public notice in any more prominent way than by the publication of the map and observations, to go for what they are worth, whether by themselves or in comparison. In the beginning of May, however, the arrival of the sloop of war *Portsmouth,* Commander Montgomery, from the Pacific Ocean, was announced with the information, brought by her, that the whale ship *Hope* had lately been lost on that coast in consequence of this same error *still existing "on the charts in common use."* In connection with this, it was also stated that two British naval vessels were engaged in a new survey of the coast. The correction made in my map (then nearly completed, and since laid before the Senate) was then mentioned, and it was thought proper, for public information, to make a statement of the fact of the correction, which was accordingly done in the note of Colonel Benton, certainly without the intent to detract from the labors of Capt. Wilkes, or any one else, or to offer a remark that could have that effect. I had had the good fortune to find my observations in the Sacramento valley agree with those made in the same valley by Captain Belcher, but they differed with Capt. Wilkes by about a third of a degree of longitude. These recurring discrepancies presented an additional reason, as I judged, at a moment when a new survey, by foreign authority, was going on, for a public notice being made of my observations, which I conceived I had a right to give, with the rest, to be taken at their value.

The purpose of Capt. Wilkes' note, as I understand it, is to show that the error in the geography of the coast was known many years ago, and is corrected on the charts published in 1844 by the Exploration Expedition under his command, and "in the possession of our ships navigating the Pacific Ocean since that time." This being admitted, it only brings Captain Wilkes in conflict with the information given to the press by the officer of the sloop *Portsmouth,* as this was the sole authority on which it was supposed that the "charts in common use" were erroneously projected, and that a note of correction of the error might be of interest and importance.

It does not appear, however, why Captain Wilkes should have felt called upon to open a controversy on this matter in any shape. Certainly, whatever merit the Exploring Expedition which he commanded may have entitled itself to in the *publication* of corrections, it cannot claim any share of the making of them upon the coast in question, (that of Upper California). In his card of to-day, Captain Wilkes refers to and professes to have agreed with the observations of Sir Edward Belcher. But, in point of fact, the discrepancy between positions of Captain Belcher and of Captain Wilkes is so great, as to have left the true geography of the coast more unsettled than before. Captain Belcher's observations, like those of Captain Wilkes, were extended into the Sacramento valley. Point Victoria, at the junction of Feather River with the Sacramento, is placed by Captain Belcher in longitude 121° 35′ 35″ (Belcher, vol. 1, p. 122). As laid down by Captain Wilkes in his map, the same spot is about 30′ or half a degree further west; so that Captain Wilkes must say either that he is himself wrong by a half a degree, or that Captain Belcher is. This is a large error to make in the position of a navigable river, within two degrees of the coast, parallel to it, affecting the position of the whole valley, five hundred miles in length, at the foot of the Sierra Nevada, and necessarily impairs confidence in the position of the coast itself, with which it is connected.

Previous to the publication of map of 1845, Captain Wilkes was good enough to furnish me with the position established by himself at New Helvetia, as is acknowledged in my report of that date, and as it is laid down upon the map then published. The results of my own observations made during a recent journey to California, compelled me materially to change this position, removing it about twenty miles to the eastward. The observations connected with these at this point extended through the Sacramento and San Joaquin valleys, which, with the dependent country, are accordingly placed upon the present map twenty miles further east. As already said, these positions agreed with Captain Belcher, and, being thus supported by his authority, and aware that my observations did not agree with those of Captain Wilkes, I did not further consult his maps or charts. I find to-day, however, by his map of Upper California, accompanying the fifth volume of his Narrative, that he has laid down the whole extent of the Sacramento River more westerly than the longitude in which he had placed New Helvetia, and differing consequently by half a degree from Captain Belcher, whom he professes to concur with and corroborate.

It is true that the line *of the coast* appears to have been laid down by Captain Wilkes in the position which the observations of Captain Beechey and Captain Belcher would assign to it. But it is very strange that, if he agreed with those officers so exactly on the coast, he should in the extention of his surveys through the short space of a degree differ with them by half a degree of longitude. Had Captain Wilkes referred the coast, by the true difference in longitude, to his observations in the Sacramento valley, it would have been thrown as much too far west as Vancouver had placed it too far east. It would seem, then, that Captain Wilkes' observations do not form a connected "series" which depend on each other, and that they do not corroborate or confirm previous surveys, except insomuch as they copy them.

I infer from Captain Wilkes' card, that neither Captain Beechey nor Captain Belcher's survey caused the proper corrections to be made in the charts of the coasts, and that *his* publications of 1844 were the first to give the benefit of those older surveys to the seamen of the Pacific. In that case, the cause must have been that the true position of the coast was considered still uncertain at the Hydrographic Office in London; and this is the more probable from the fact that a new survey was being made last November. That Captain Wilkes added anything he does not pretend, and that our seamen need something more accurate than they have is shown by the recent fate of the ship Hope, and the report of her loss brought in by a naval vessel, whose officers may be supposed to know what are the charts most in use and most authentic.

In conclusion, I would state that the observations which I have made, and on which the positions I have adopted depend, will be *published*, in connection with a geographical memoir of California, laid before the Senate a few days ago; and since Captain Wilkes has thought proper to raise a controversy with me, I hope he will see the propriety of also publishing the observations, which, with his large equipment of instruments, he was so well prepared to make with accuracy. I have not learned that any such have been published, and have not the leisure to read through his work.

J. C. Frémont

Printed in *National Intelligencer*, 10 June 1848.

11. Charles Wilkes to the Editors of the *National Intelligencer*

[Washington, 12 June 1848]

Gentlemen:

With much pleasure I avail myself of the call of Lt. Col. Fremont to give the public the required information in relation to the observations made by the Exploration Expedition on the coast of California. It has been my constant desire to publish the astronomical and hydrographical results ever since the return of the Exploration Expedition, but from circumstances beyond my control the publication has been and will be delayed for some time.

As Lt. Col. Fremont wishes the public to know why I controverted the first detection of the error in the longitude of the coast of California, I will state that it arose from my desire to do justice to others and ourselves on an interesting point of geographical history, deemed of such high importance by Col. Benton as to cause him to claim, through the columns of your journal, that the merit of its detection was due to the labors of Col. Fremont, and also from a sense of duty to the public, to state what I knew had been previously done by others and ourselves. I am well satisfied the public will deem me justified in doing so, without impugning my motives.

With reference to the longitudes on the Northwest Coast determined by the Exploring Expedition, the limits of your whole paper would not more than suffice to give the details. I shall therefore content myself with giving a general outline of the manner in which the duty was performed, so as to be intelligible to every one, and refer to the actual results when they are published.

Two observations were established, one at Nisqually, in Puget Sound, Oregon Territory, in latitude 47°, and the other at Sausalito, on the north side of the entrance in the bay of San Francisco, California, in 37° 51′ 00″. At these positions, series of moon culminating stars, with both limbs of the moon, were taken, and the longitude deduced from intervals observed by W[illia]m Cranch Bond, Esq., at the Observatory, Cambridge, Massachusetts; by Lt. [James M.] Gillis, of the Navy, at Washington; and from those also at Greenwich, both calculated in the Nautical Almanac and observed. The first position, Nisqually, was by 46 moon culminating stars, and the second, Sausalito, by 68. These two points, thus astronomically determined, were also connected by meridian distances through our chronometers, and found to correspond satisfactorily. All the intermediate points between these two latitudes have been referred to one or the other, and most to both, through the agency of our chronometers. The longitude resulting from the mean of the 68 moon culminating stars at Sausalito places it in 122° 26′ 06″ 221′″.

The survey of the river Sacramento was intrusted to able officers, and seven boats, including the launch, with provisions, were employed on this duty. To the untiring exertions and zeal of the party we are indebted for the accurate survey of the river, from its mouth at San Pablo, to head of navigation for boats. The survey was made by triangulation until the river became too narrow to work by that method; above that it was accomplished by azimuths and distances by sound. Four stations were occupied for longitude and latitude, the former being determined by chronometers through equal altitudes of the sun, and the latter by circum-meridian observations and by polaris. These positions have been compared with the surveys and proved satisfactory. The chronometer used was No. 972, Arnold and Dent, an excellent instrument. It was compared with the standard time at the Observatory before leaving, and after their return, a period of eighteen days; and its rate (which was small) determined during that interval by the Observatory time. The four positions I refer to above were Karguines [Carquinez] Straits, Capt. Sutter's Landing, Feather river, and the Fish weir at the head of navigation for canoes, and the resulting longitudes, from applying the meridian distances to that of Sausalito Observatory, were as follows: Karguines camp, 122° 10′ 58″ 95′″; Capt. Sutter's Landing, 121° 22′ 23″ 55′″; Feather river, 121° 29′ 02″ 60′″; Fish weir 121° 48′ 38″ 25′″.

The original chart of the river was plotted during the progress of the survey on a large scale, and is 27 feet in length. This I had the pleasure of showing to Col. Benton, Capt. Frémont (just after his return from his second trip), and two or three other gentlemen, who called at my house to see it. This chart has been reduced, and is now engraved on a sufficiently large scale to show all the windings of the river. In February, 1845, Capt. Frémont wrote me a letter requesting I would give him the positions I had assigned Fort Vancouver and Capt. Sutter's Fort. The letter was forwarded to me at Philadelphia, where I was then engaged reading the proofs of my Narrative. The longitude given to Col. Frémont of Fort Vancouver was 122° 39′ 34″ .6W., and Capt. Sutter's Fort 121° 40′ 05″—the same as given in the Narrative, and which was then believed to be correct. Subsequent calculations proved it to be erroneous. When this was discovered, one of the officers (Lt. [Henry] Eld), who was on very intimate terms with Capt. Frémont, asked me if he was at liberty to communicate it to Col. Frémont, and explain to him how it had occurred. To this I of course assented, and having since presumed it had been done, though I have no further knowledge of the fact.

The above longitude of Feather River differs from that given by Belcher some five or six minutes, and not as stated by Col. Frémont some thirty minutes. In respect to the observations made on the Sacramento, by the able officers intrusted with that duty, I am satisfied that every confidence is to be placed in them both for longitude and latitude.

I must here take exception to Col. Frémont comparing and measuring our longitudes from a small map eleven inches by eight, covering seventeen degrees of longitude.

Exception is also to be taken to his treating the minor points of our surveys as though they were principal ones, and governed our coast line; this cannot be permitted; he must well know that all points of longitude in a survey are derived from and referred to that occupied as an observatory, and that there is no other true course, and none other can with fairness be adopted in comparing the longitudes of different surveys.

Capt. Beechey gives his longitude of Yerba Buena Cove from the results of twenty-two moon culminating stars, as 122° 27′ 23″. (See his Appendix, page 667, quarto, London). It will be seen that this differs from ours, and with all due deference to so able an observer, I have not the slightest doubt but that Capt. Beechey himself would, in weighing the testimony of the two, decide that the preference was to be given to our longitude, the result of sixty-eight culminations. Although we do not agree with Capt. Beechey, yet I consider we confirm his longitudes.

An inference may be drawn from a part of the remarks of Col. Frémont that the Exploration Expedition had depended for its results upon others. I have to inform him as well as others (to make use of a common expression), that the Expedition, wherever it did go, went on its *own hook*.

Having thus considered the operations of the Exploring Expedition, let us return to the point at *issue* before the public. Capt. Beechey established his observatory in November, 1827, near the fort at Monterey, from which can be seen "*Santa Cruz*, near *Anno Nuevo*, the northwestern point of the bay of Monterey," where Col. Benton claims that Lieut. Col. Fremont made the observations which detected the error in the coast-line of California. Capt. Beechey has given the longitude as 122° 51′ 46″, obtained from seven moon culminating stars. (See Appendix, page 668). Lieut. Col. Fremont admits that he agrees with Capt. Beechey in his longitudes, and it is, therefore, to be presumed that it is with the longitude of Monterey or that of Yerba Buena Cove, which have been connected by Beechey and found to correspond. If he had a knowledge of these observations the public must be satisfied that Col. Benton was not authorized to claim the detection of an *error* for Lieut. Col. Fremont in the longitude of the coast of California that had been previously known to him. The surveys reported to be in prosecution by Commander Montgomery, of the Portsmouth, relate no doubt to the *Gulf* of California and its coast, and not to the Pacific coast of California, between Monterey and Cape San Lucas. This part of the coast is well known, and there are ample materials for its delineation in the possession of the British Admiralty. It is usual to account for the loss of a ship by imputing errors to the charts. No vessel ought to encounter wreck on a coast, except through stress of weather; it might happen on an insulated reef, rock, or islet; but on a coast, in fair weather, it must result either from ignorance or culpable neglect.

As you, Messrs. Editors, truly observe, "this discussion is a matter purely scientific; difference of opinion cannot be any cause of quarrel, not even of unkind feeling." I therefore trust that, having felt none myself, I have been successful in avoiding giving cause for any to others. I am, very respectfully, your obedient servant,

CHARLES WILKES

Printed in *National Intelligencer*, 14 June 1848.

12. Frémont to the Editors of the *National Intelligencer*

[WASHINGTON, 14 June 1848]

MESSRS. GALES AND SEATON:

I should not deem it necessary to trouble you or your readers with any further remarks on the subject which Capt. Wilkes has thought proper to invite a controversy with me, were it not for the very extraordinary position taken in his letter this morning, and which goes to the extent, in effect, of imputing unfairness in my references to his observations, because I tested them by the map and books which he has published, and not by the results of certain "subsequent calculations," which are now for the first time made public.

Not long after Captain Wilkes had been polite enough to furnish me, as stated in my former letter, with the position he had established for New Helvetia, I left the country on my third expedition; and neither before my departure nor at any time until now, in the Intelligencer of this morning, did I ever learn that Capt. Wilkes had discovered the erroneousness of that position, nor do I now find that there are any errata or other memoranda in his book by which the correction is indicated; and I had not the power of clairvoyance to discover those "subsequent calculations" that seem to have been meantime secure in his bureau.[1] Capt. Wilkes knew the use I was to make of the position with which he furnished me, and if, in fact, he made the discovery which he now announces at the time he states, while I was still here and my report and map open to correction, the indifference which, according to his own showing, he manifested, was neither more nor less than wilfully to permit (or rather cause) the further propagation of error on his authority. I had applied to Captain Wilkes, in a written communication, for positions which would enable me to connect my reconnoissance across the country with his surveys. His reply and the positions he furnished me came in the same shape. I received them and gave them to the public in full confidence; and I must confess my surprise—not to use a stronger term—now to learn that, on discovering that he had led me into so important an error, he had not at once given me the proper correction in the most authentic form.

Undoubtedly the positions *now set* down by Capt. Wilkes for the Sacramento valley agree closely with the fact; but he gives them now for the first time, and it is most unwarrantable, his assertion that it was with reference to these *new positions* that I had said he differed half a degree of longitude from Capt. Belcher. I had never heard of these new positions and could not have spoken of them. It was with reference to Capt. Wilkes's *published works*, which have now been before the public uncorrected for the space of *three years*, that I said and repeat that his positions differ half a degree from those of Capt. Belcher, whom he assumes, in his letter of Thursday last, to agree with and corroborate.

I wish it to be borne in mind that it was not in an invidious spirit, or for any purpose of attack, that I pointed out this remarkable discrepancy. Capt. Wilkes claimed in his note to have published a correct delineation of the western coast prior to any observations which I had made there; and my only object was to show why, if such were the fact, I was not aware of it. The reason was this, that on comparing the position he has given me in the Sacramento valley with my own observations, I perceived that there was the wide difference of twenty miles of longitude between us, and I supposed that his observations would agree with each other, and of course the same disagreement between his positions and mine would exist on the coast. I did not know that he had published maps or charts on other surveys than his own, and hence did not further consult his labors. When, however, he raised this controversy, and referred in his note to Capt. Belcher's observations as being in agreement with his, I found it proper to consult his published works, and to show, in self-defence, that in the discrepancy between us he was not thus supported by Capt. Belcher, but differed widely from him.

If Captain Wilkes intends, by taking exception to my reference to his map, published with the fifth volume of his narrative, to say that his map is incorrect and of no authority, then I admit it would be improper to use it against him hereafter. But this disavowal comes too late to affect anything that has gone before; and, moreover, if the map is to be thus discarded, and also the positions given in the text, now, after a lapse of three years, to be erased and different ones substituted, in what part of the eight magnificent volumes can we be certain that "subsequent calculations" have not detected inaccuracies hereafter to be exhibited? It is idle to intimate that in a map, on the scale of that given in the narrative of Captain Wilkes (volume 5, beginning of chapter 5), and executed with so much precision and neatness, with the meridians and parallels of latitude drawn at distances of single degrees, discrepancies in position of such an extent as twenty to thirty minutes, cannot properly be examined. For what purpose are the lines of longitude and latitude drawn upon the map at all, if the position of places and objects given are not to be measured and ascertained by them? If the differences in question were slight, no notice would have been taken of it; but this broad discrepancy of half a degree is as palpable and as open to criticism as if the map which shows it were twenty times its actual scale; and this more especially when it relates to a section which was the object of a particular, extended, and careful survey, as Captain Wilkes informs us was the case with the river Sacramento, and embraces not an isolated point, but the whole of that section.

But Captain Wilkes further takes exception, and "cannot permit" that I shall "treat the minor points of his survey as principal ones." Nor have I done so; but surely there ought to be some degree of accordance between the minor points and the principal ones, and if a large error be found in the minor, a corresponding error will be inferred in the principal. Besides this is not the error of a single "minor point," but a series of errors running through the observations made in some hundreds of miles. And, furthermore, Capt. Wilkes informs us in his narrative, that a prominent point in the Sacramento valley—the *Prairie Buttes* (isolated mountains)—formed "one of the *connecting links*" between two surveying parties of his expedition, one coming from the north, the other from the south, and "*served to verify their respective observations.*" Surely it was fair to conclude that the observations thus "connected" and "verified," whether made at minor points or principal ones, were intended to be taken for correct, and the positions laid down accordingly. Again, these *Buttes*, "particularly described" in the narrative, and thus forming a "connecting link" and point of "verification" for the surveys of the expedition, are conspicuously laid down by Captain Wilkes on his map, with the meridian of 122° passing through them. Now, does Captain Wilkes wish us to believe that all this stands for nothing? Does he mean to intimate that positions thus noted by him, and conspicuously brought forward in the book and on the map, are not to be criticised because they are minor, not principal parts in his surveys?

Considered with relation to the position assigned to the Sacramento River, the Buttes are rightly placed on the map; but, "connecting link" and point of "verification" as they are, they require, along with the whole extent of the river, to be removed many miles (in no part less than twenty) further east, in order to correspond with their true longitude. The errors, therefore, cannot be laid to the execution of the map, which is thus shown to be drawn with care, and to agree with itself. It will also be noted that, as two surveys were here "connected" and "verified"—if, in fact, the errors, which run through the line, were the result, as we are now informed, of wrong "*calculations*," instead of wrong "observations," they involve a most remarkable series of blunders, embracing the surveys of the parties both from the north and the south.

I will copy here the longitude given by Capt. Wilkes in *his book*, contrasted with those he now, for the first time, offers as from "subsequent calculations." In his book (4th edition), he places New Helvetia in longitude 121° 40′ 05″; in his letter of today he gives 121° 22′ 23″ 55‴′; as the longitude of a point, (Sutter's landing) near two miles west of New Helvetia. The "Fish weir, at the head of navigation" he gives in his book at 122° 12′ 17″—his present correction brings it 121° 48′ 38″ 25‴′. The mouth of Feather River I do not find noted in his book; in his new correction he assigns it 121° 29′ 02″ 60‴′—on his map it is placed *some minutes west of* 122°. A relative position given to the coast, I repeat, would have thrown it as much too far west as Vancouver has placed it too far east.

I will not, however, here question Capt. Wilkes' observations on the coast, or further inquire whether they ought to be said to copy or corroborate those of Capt. Beechey; neither will I question that the longitudes *now* given by Capt. Wilkes for his positions in the Sacramento valley are the true results of his observations there, corrected by "subsequent calculations;" but I will say that, after suppressing the discovery of the errors he now announces for a space of three years, he has lost any right to plead then for any purpose; least of all, for the purpose of finding fault with those who have innocently taken his book and map for authentic records. I must, moreover, be allowed to inquire what degree of credit can further attach to a work which, got ready with four years' preparation, its author, three years subsequent to its publication, thus comes forward to discredit?

J. C. Frémont

Printed in *National Intelligencer*, 16 June 1848.
1. By these statements JCF appears to deny that Lieut. Eld had informed him of the corrections, as Wilkes had implied in his 12 June letter.

13. Charles Wilkes to the Editors of the *National Intelligencer*

[16 June 1848]

Gentlemen:

It is not my intention to trespass upon your columns, or to weary the patience of your readers; but I feel constrained to offer a few words in reply to Lieut. Col. Frémont's article in your paper of this morning.

As the object which was *at issue* before the public is not touched upon in Lieut. Col. Frémont's last article, I consider it therefore as ended, and that the testimony that I have adduced of Capt. Beechey's observations at Monterey and Yerba Buena are entirely satisfactory to show that Col. Benton was not authorized to claim for Lieut. Col. Frémont the detection of the error in longitude of the coast of California.

Lieut. Col. Frémont's absence from the country on arduous duty may perhaps be a sufficient apology for his being uninformed of what has been done or published during the time, but I do not think he can be held justified for making against me so sweeping a charge as he had done, of withholding and suppressing corrections from the public, when a slight examination or some little inquiry would have satisfied him he was in error, especially as it is a fact that the desire to meet his inquiries and oblige him was in part the cause of the errors of the longitude he makes mention of on a small map, the corrections of which errors were made a short time afterwards, and I fully believed had been furnished to Lieut. Col. Frémont by Lieut. Eld, as stated in my last communication. Respectfully, yours, &c.,

CHARLES WILKES

Printed in *National Intelligencer*, 19 June 1848.

14. Frémont to the Editors of the *National Intelligencer*

[WASHINGTON, 20 June 1848]

MESSRS. GALES & SEATON:

I must confess my inability to understand what Capt. Wilkes intends to signify, in his letter of yesterday, by stating that his desire to oblige me was one cause of the errors in his map of California. I do not perceive what connection I had with those mistakes, other than to have been grossly misled by placing confidence in the positions which he furnished me. Apart from those I never saw any observations or calculations of Capt. Wilkes, and I never saw his publications till since the beginning of the present correspondence. If he means that in his haste to furnish me with positions I had requested, the erroneous calculations were made, to which he now attributes his mistaken longitudes, I answer that his expedition had been nearly four years returned, his publications were nearly through the press, and it is extraordinary if his calculations had not been made, and even the identical map (which he would thus seem disposed to hold me responsible for the blunders of) both drawn and engraved. Moreover, I had understood from Capt. Wilkes' first letter that his charts had been published the year previous to my application to him, and it would seem that his positions ought to have been calculated previous to the making of his charts. The truth is Capt. Wilkes led me into error. According to his present showing, he discovered very soon after that he had done so. I must be permitted to believe that had his desire to oblige me been so strong as is now intimated, he would have taken the trouble to apprise me of his mistake, which he never did. I discovered the error of the position he had given me in the Sacramento valley from observations made during my late tour. I did not suspect, and had no reason to suspect, that he had made any subsequent rectification, and hence I was led into the second error (if it be an error) of supposing that the coast was still erroneously laid down. I ascertained, as far as I was able to make inquiry, that no chart of the coast had been issued by Beechey or Belcher; I knew that Capt. Wilkes was the last surveyor there; I knew that my observations differed from what he had furnished me as his by about twenty miles, in the Sacramento valley, and took it for granted that forty miles further west the same disagreement would exist; and so corrected the outline of my map according to my own observations. The report shortly after brought in by one of our public vessels of the wreck of a ship on the coast in consequence of error in "the charts in common use," was considered good reason for making known that a different projection of the coast would appear on the forthcoming map. If, then, there was any error in this, or in the manner of its announcement, it is attributable entirely to the wrong information given me by Capt. Wilkes, and his failure to inform me of the fact, if he afterwards discovered the error he had led me into, and which I had published on his authority; for I could not be expected to look to his publications for a correct delineation of the coast, when I knew that forty miles off he had made so large an error.

But it is clear that, if, as Captain Wilkes informs us, he has made a publication of charts which give the necessary correction of the coast, he must have *abandoned his own survey* for the purpose, and *proceeded entirely by the observations of others.* He published his charts, according to his note of the 6th instant, inviting this controversy, "in 1844." Now, it was in the winter of 1844–45, that he furnished me the positions which, according to his own showing, are so erroneous; and, still later, his own books contain the same and many corresponding errors. His positions, Capt. Wilkes informs us, were determined by the establishment of two observations—one at Nisqually, in Puget's Sound (the longitude of which, nevertheless, he does not furnish us with), and the other Sausalito, at the north side of the entrance to the Bay of San Francisco—and the reference of all the intermediate points to *one or the other*, and most of them to *both* of these main positions. Now, I will venture to say that all these "intermediate points," thus "referred," and, as appears by the narrative, "connected" and "verified," *could not* contain a common error, as they do, both in the map and text of Capt. Wilkes' book, without a like error in the main positions. Hence, if Capt. Wilkes published a correction of the coast, in charts of 1844, he must have done it on the labors of others; for he does not pretend to have discovered the erroneousness of his own calculations till after the issuing of his book in 1845.

I apprehend, Messrs. Editors, that, notwithstanding the charts published by Capt. Wilkes, and the labors of the British officers, whom he quotes and seems to have copied, when the whole truth comes to be investigated, it will be found that the proper position of the coast is not much better ascertained now than it was near sixty years ago. My occupation has been that of reconnaissance and survey *inland*, and my attention had not been directed to the state of the surveys on the *coast* beyond the very narrow inquiry—when I found my observations to be at variance with those of Vancouver, and still more so with those of Capt. Wilkes—whether Beechey or Belcher had published a corrected chart. Since the commencement of this correspondence, however, I have given the subject some more examination. The Spanish navigator, [Alessandro] Malaspina, to the merits of whom Humboldt bears such honorable testimony, and whose subsequent misfortunes and political persecution gave a peculiar interest to such portion of his labors as they did not destroy, made a survey of this coast in 1791. His longitudes, as far as I have been able to examine them, were nearly correct. Vancouver followed immediately after, and his surveys, disagreeing with Malaspina's, threw the coast from a third to a half degree too far east; subsequent surveys, as far as they have made any change, are but little more than restoring the positions of Malaspina.

As for Capt. Wilkes' renewed objection to having his "small map" taken for a test, I have to remark, that corresponding errors with those in his "small map," appear *in his larger map of Oregon, and in the text of his Narrative*, and I am not acquainted with any other publications he had made. If he objects to having it said that he has suppressed or withheld his corrections, surely he ought to point where and when he has made them public.

I wish again to make the remark that this controversy is not of my seeking. When I discovered the great erroneousness of the positions Capt. Wilkes had given me, I contented myself by quietly making the corrections on my map.[1] I had received them in good faith as the result of his observations, and supposed them to be given the same way, and should have studiously avoided, therefore, any mention of the discrepancy. Had I known, however, what he now informs us of, that he had shortly afterwards found those positions to be incorrect, and yet left me in ignorance of the rectification, to make an erroneous publication, I should not have been so silent.

I stated in my first letter that I did not see why Captain Wilkes had thought himself called on to provoke this controversy, since whatever his merit in *the publication* of corrections on the coast of California, he could not claim any share in the making of them. I am now still more at a loss to know why he felt concerned in the matter, for it has become still more plain that he could not have supposed himself in any way wronged. His surveys not only do not make any corrections on the coast of California, but I feel warranted in saying that his entire surveys in Oregon and California, as far as they follow his own observations, are erroneously laid down in his published works.

J. C. FRÉMONT

Printed in *National Intelligencer*, 22 June 1848.
1. WICKMAN, 146, notes that Frémont had engaged in the same kind of activity of which he accused Wilkes—not notifying him of corrections. If Frémont had discovered that some of Wilkes's positions were incorrect, why did he not inform Wilkes?

15. Charles Wilkes to the Editors of the *National Intelligencer*

[WASHINGTON, 22 June 1848]

MESSRS. EDITORS:

Lieut. Col. Fremont deems that I have provoked this controversy relative to the correction of an error in the longitude of the coast of

California. If any provocation has excited it, it was the publication of Col. Benton's card in your papers of the 15th of May, which I well knew to be a mistake, and which Lieut. Col. Frémont fully admits in his article of to-day, having discovered, on examination (since this controversy began,) that Malaspina's observations on the coast of California, made in 1791, were correct. If this search had been made, the claim of Col. Benton on behalf of Lieut. Col. Frémont would not have been put forth, for it would have resulted, as it had done, in finding the authorities spoken of in my first article, and settled all priority in his mind as to the claim of subsequent explorers, and avoided the appearance of his being on either horn of a dilemma.

The public mind, I think, will be satisfied now that there was no ground for the claim set up, and my end has been obtained, notwithstanding some sharp firing has been directed against the Exploring Expedition.

In concluding this subject, I cannot subscribe to the idea entertained by Lieut. Col. Frémont that when the Exploring Expedition agree with him it must be *correct*: but, when it differs, in *error*. I am, very respectfully,

CHARLES WILKES

Printed in *National Intelligencer*, 23 June 1848. This final letter in the controversy was not reprinted in BIGELOW.

16. Frémont to John Torrey

Washington City 22d June 1848

MY DEAR SIR,

I have referred in the pamphlet on California, now being printed, to the Red wood tree as "Cypress (Thuya)." I sent you the drawing in order that you might be satisfied that it was not an *abies*. The Cedar to which we have referred in the report, as being from 120 to 130 feet high belongs to a different tribe; it, must certainly be a *juniperus*—, its foliage is much the same as that of the redwood, but it bears berries like those of the common cedar.

You will see by the pamphlet that it is not owing to particularly favorable locality that the redwood I mentioned attained such great size.

I have frequently measured them nine, ten and eleven feet diameter, and they are the tallest forest trees on the western coast. I have been looking over Douglass' notes on California, and think that he refers to the same tree, when he speaks of a species of *taxodium*.

I daily expect our plants. The vessel which has them on board having put into Rio Janiero on her way home on the 28th of March. Please let me know if you think it safe to let the words "a cypress (Thuya)" remain. I think it is about the truth.

I shall soon obtain leisure now to arrange for the journey west and will try to see you before going. Yours truly,

J. C. FRÉMONT

Dr. Torrey

ALS (NNNBG—Torrey Correspondence).

17. Excerpt from a Letter of John Torrey to Frémont

[ca. 1 July 1848]

After incessant working on the California plants, from the time they were received till this moment I have secured all that were not decomposed, and have the entire collection in clean dry paper.[1] The loss of one or two boxes, and the partial injury of some others, we can well bear, when the rest are so valuable. Of those that were spoiled I trust there were duplicates of the greater part in the rest of the herbarium. No doubt there are many new species among your discoveries. The pines are well represented and most of them can be drawn so as to show all the essential parts. As soon as I get Captain Wilkes' plants off my hands, I shall attack these with vigor. How much I regret not having a botanical artist at my elbow, as my friend Dr. [Asa] Gray has. Now that the doctor has undertaken the great bulk of the exploring expedition botany, he will, I fear, need the whole of Mr. [Isaac] Sprague's (his artist's) time.

The only way to have our work properly executed is, either to import an artist (and one could be got at a very moderate salary) or to send the specimens from time to time, to Europe, where they might be drawn and put at once upon the stone. . . .

Please let me know what I am to do about drawings of your new and rare plants. They ought to be put in hand soon, as it will take a long time to get them properly done. At any rate, I will send a few to Europe immediately, and have then drawn under the eye of Professors Jussieu and Decaisne.[2] We can then find exactly what they will cost. Do you not think that the forest trees ought to be done in a style and size with Michaux's Sylva? A supplementary volume, or distinct work rather, on the trees of California and Oregon, would be a most acceptable gift, not only to botanists, but to men of trade and lovers of nature generally.[3]

Was I right in supposing the *Taxodium sempervirens* to be your great cedar? The *Thuya* does not grow to the enormous size that you mention; but the *Taxodium*[4] does. What a pity there was not time to get a figure of it ready for your report.

Printed in Senate Committee Report 226, 30th Cong., 1st sess., pp. 7–8, Serial 512; also *National Intelligencer*, 5 Aug. 1848. As chairman of the committee, Senator Sidney Breese attached the letter to his report in order to indicate to the Senate the scientific richness of JCF's work, and hence the expediency of having it continued by the government.
1. On 1 July Torrey had written a fellow scientist, Jacob Whitman Bailey, an interesting account of the arrival of the plants, how they had been packed, and the value of the collection:

"Two days ago the long-expected plants of Frémont's last expedition arrived. One of his people was sent on to the Navy Yard in Brooklyn to take them out of the Erie, lately arrived–& bring them here. There were two huge cases—filled with the tin cases, which were just in the state they were in when taken from the backs of the mules in California. The cases were soldered up after being filled with dried plants—then guarded by a strong frame of wood, & finally sowed up in a green cowhide. Some of the specimens were damaged owing to the cases having been broken, but most of the contents were in good order. A great many of the plants are quite new. You would have been amused to see the unpacking under the shade of trees in our lawn. Frémont's man, & my two small boys had business for several hours. It was quite difficult to cut away the hard & tough skins, & then to open & examine the boxes. There must be a thousand species of plants in the collection. Also several cases of pine cones, fruit &c. Fremont is going out again, & will doubtless be as active & zealous as ever in observing the Botany of his favorite regions. His plants will all fall into my hands, & I shall give account of them in a work on California which he intends writing" (Museum of Science Library, Science Park, Boston, Mass.—J. W. Bailey Papers).

2. French botanist Adrien de Jussieu (1797–1853) had succeeded his father as professor of rural botany in the Museum of Natural History in 1826 and in 1845 had become professor of vegetable organography to the Faculté des Sciences. For a time Joseph Decaisne (1808–82) served under Jussieu as aide-naturalist at the museum, but in 1850 was made director of the famous Jardin des Plantes of Paris.

3. Benton attempted unsuccessfully to get Congress to appropriate $4,000 to

compensate Torrey for his services in classifying the plants and to defray the costs of engraving (*Congressional Globe*, 5 Aug. 1848)

4. The *Taxodium* was JCF's cypress. See *Sequoia sempervirens* in Index.

18. James Alden to Frémont

Navy Yard, Boston
July 2d. 1848

My dear Sir

Although I have not the pleasure of a personal acquaintance with you, I cannot refrain from expressing my satisfaction at the manner in which you have exposed in your recent letters to the Editors of the National Intelligencer, misstatements published by Commander Wilkes in his account of the U.S. Ex. Expedition. I take the liberty of enclosing in the form of a letter a few statements of the truth of which I am positive, proving that Comr. Wilkes' error with regard to the position of the Sacramento R. was by no means a solitary instance of the kind, but that in his case, blundering and misrepresentation of the grossest kind, were the rule, and not the exception.

The interest I feel in the subject will, I hope, induce you to excuse the liberty I take in thus addressing you.

The enclosed is entirely at your service for any use which you may feel inclined to make of it. With great respect I am your Servt.

James Alden
Lt. U.S. Navy

To
Col. J. C. Frémont
Washington, D.C.

[*Enclosure*]

James Alden to Frémont

Navy Yard, Boston
July 1st. 1848

Sir,

At the close of one of your letters to the Editors of the National Intelligencer upon the subject of your controversy with Comr. Wilkes, I find the following remark "I must moreover be allowed to enquire what degree of credit can further attach to a work which got ready with four years preparation, its author, three years subsequent to its publication thus comes forward to discredit."

No doubt you and all persons who have read the correspondence above referred to have made up your minds very conclusively as to the precise degree of credit to be given to statements resting on the sole authority of Comr. Wilkes, but as I was an officer of the Exploring Expedition during the whole period of its absence from the U.S. and a careful observer of all its proceedings, I take the liberty of stating a few facts that came under my own observation, which may show that the blunders of Comd. Wilkes in relation to the position of the Sacramento River was by no means the only one of the kind that he committed during the cruise, and which may also show how far the U.S. Ex. Expedition is entitled to the credit so confidently claimed for it by Capt. Wilkes of having always gone "on its own hook."

During the entire absence of the Expedition it was the constant practice whenever an opportunity at sea or in port to compare the Chronometers of the different vessels with those of the Flag Ship, and from these comparisons Comr. Wilkes always furnished the Comrs. of each vessel with the rate and error of their Chrors. These comparisons were frequently made at Orange Harbour near Cape Horn, where an observatory was established and where Comr. Wilkes asserted that he had discovered an error of some thirty or forty miles in the position assigned to that place by that celebrated Hydrographer Capt. Ring [King] R. N. Shortly after leaving Orange Harbour and by the first land that was made (The Island of Mocha and the Coast of Chili) it was discovered that the chronometers of the Vincennes— the standard by which all the other vessels of the Squadron were navigating, the unfortunate Sea Gull among the number, was greatly out of the way, and would have soon run her high & dry on that coast. The Vincennes, however, escaped destruction by giving the land about Cape Horn a wide berth, but I would ask, if this great error, for which Comr. Wilkes is solely responsible, may not have occasioned the loss of the ill fated Sea Gull with all on board.

The sailing directions for the entrance of the Columbia River which were furnished by Comr. Wilkes to Commodore [Alexander James] Dallas, the late commander of the Pacific Squadron, when applied to the chart of that entrance published by Comr. Wilkes, and made by Messrs. [Samuel R.] Knox, [William] Reynolds & [James L.] Blair, three officers of the Expedition in whom skill & accuracy of the utmost reliance can be placed, will inevitably carry a vessel upon the middle ground, the most dangerous part of that entrance, and the very place which Comr. Wilkes says should be most carefully avoided. This I have proved by a comparison of the sailing directions with the chart, and several officers, whose attention I have called to the subject, have arrived at the same conclusions as myself.

The Fiji Islands were surveyed by the Expedition in the usual manner & plotted on a plain scale: afterwards Mercators projection was applied to it, and Comr. Wilkes insisted upon allowing *sixty miles* to a degree of longitude instead of making the necessary correction for the diminution for the degrees of longitude corresponding to the latitude of the place, the obvious effect of this error is to assign incorrect dimensions to the whole group.

Commander Wilkes has asserted in one of his letters that the Ex. Ex. "went entirely on its own hook" probably meaning that he was indebted to no one for any of the charts or surveys published in the account of that Expedition. But he has published a chart of the Soolo [Sulu] Sea & Archipelago together with a quantity of miscellaneous information connected with it, as if the chart, and nearly all of the information were the fruits of his own great labor and a long and careful examination, while it is notorious that the Vincennes & the Flying Fish merely sailed through that extensive Sea, the first named alone making only a few hasty observations & was employed about *one fortnight* making a chart now wholly claimed as the title shows *"By the U.S. Ex. Expedition."*

He has also published under the same authority charts of the entire group of the Sandwich, and other Islands, and a great portion of the map of Oregon as if he had thoroughly surveyed and examined all these places, which he never did, but has borrowed or stolen, whichever may be the proper expression the greater part of these charts and of that information from the abler and more honest navigators who have preceded him.

A map of Upper California is also published by Comr. Wilkes under the title, *"By the U.S. Exploring Expedition and best authorities."* Now the only part of Upper California actually surveyed by the Expedition is the Sacramento River, & Comr. Wilkes has committed an error of some twenty or thirty miles in the position he has assigned to this River in his published map. The whole remaining part of Upper California, comprising an extent of seventeen degrees of longitude & ten degrees of latitude with its *entire coast*, is borrowed from the "best

39

authorities," and it is perhaps fortunate that no blunders of C. Wilkes can unsettle the geography of any other part of this country.

I have taken the liberty of addressing these remarks to you from a feeling that it is my duty as an officer of the Ex. Expedition to do all in my power to expose a few of the gross blunders & misrepresentations that abound in every part of the account published by Commander Wilkes.

Most of the officers of the Ex. Expedition, many of whom are now in Washington, can vouch for the correctness of the statements that I have made. I am very respectfully Your Obt. Servt.

James Alden
Lt. U.S. Navy

To
Col. J. C. Frémont
Washington D.C.

ALS (CSmH). James Alden (1810–77) had served as a lieutenant in the South Sea Exploring Expedition, and Wilkes's *Narrative* in effect had blamed Alden's inattention to duty for the Fijians' murder of two of the officers at Malolo. Alden, however, was not the only officer who felt he had been unjustly and cruelly libeled by Wilkes (see Memorial of the Officers of the Exploring Expedition, 11 Jan. 1847, 29th Cong., 2nd sess., Senate Doc. 47, [Serial 494]). Wilkes had already been court-martialed for illegally punishing some of his men (STANTON, 281–89).

19. Frémont to J. J. Abert

Washington City, July 13th 1848

Sir,

During my connection with the various geographical expeditions west of the Mississippi, a considerable amount of property was purchased on account of the Government.

As you are aware, the greater part of this property was of a perishable nature, being intended solely for the support and carrying on of the expeditions, and from the nature of the duty subject to constant waste and loss. A greater part of this property has been expended in the public service and what has not been so expended has been accounted for by bills of sale, and by receipts from Quartermasters, Ordnance and other officers.

Being now on the eve of an absence from the country, and desirous as far as possible to close my accounts with the Departments, I have to request that you will produce for me the necessary credit for such expenditures, or in any other proper way release me from my present responsibility. I have the honor to be very respectfully Your Obt. Servt.

J. C. Frémont.

Copy (DNA-217, T-135).

20. Frémont to James Alden

Washington City August 11th. 1848

My dear Sir,

I have had the gratification to receive your letter [Doc. No. 18] and in the press of business on the eve of a departure from the country, together with a desire to acquaint you with the use I had made of it, have delayed a reply longer than I had intended. Had it arrived in time it would have most fully sustained me before the public, but, as my correspondence with Capt. Wilkes had already finished when it reached me, I availed myself of your permission to give your letter to Col. Benton, who used it in the Senate a few days since in connection with one of a similar character from Capt. Montgomery.[1]

I have been much gratified to find that the officers of the Expedition have correctly understood the nature of the controversy with Capt. Wilkes, which was wholly personal to himself, and directed on my part only to the operations which he claimed exclusively as his own.

I will avail myself of a future occasion to publish the letter, as together with the facts already made public, it wholly justifies the charges which I felt warranted to make. In the meantime I beg you to accept my acknowledgments for your kindness which I shall be very happy to reciprocate whenever the opportunity offers. I am with regard Very respectfully yours,

J. C. Frémont

Lt. James Alden
U.S. Navy

ALS-JBF (CSmH).
1. The editor was unable to find in the *Congressional Globe* the use Benton had made of the letter.

21. Frémont to George Engelmann

WASHINGTON CITY, August 13th. 1848

MY DEAR SIR,

Yours of the 27th I received only yesterday. A few days after you receive this I expect to see you in St. Louis and therefore only write briefly to say that your letter arrived too late to do anything for [Charles] Schreiber this session. It found Congress in the last days of the session battling its most important bills, & when no other business could possibly be introduced. I will leave it with Mrs. Fremont and if any thing can be done for him the coming winter it will give her pleasure to have it done.

Until seeing you, with regards to Dr. Wistlizenus [Wislizenus], I am Very truly yours,

J. C. FRÉMONT

Dr. Engelmann

ALS-JBF (MoSB). Endorsed: "Rec'd. Aug. 21."

22. Committee of the Citizens of Charleston to Frémont

[18 August 1848]

DEAR SIR:

It was a privilege, as a committee of a public meeting of the citizens of Charleston, brought together for the purpose of expressing their sense of the distinguished services rendered by you to our common country and the cause of science, to communicate, in anticipation of your arrival from California, through Mrs. Fremont, the complimentary resolutions to which we have referred.[1]

One of these resolutions contemplated the gift and presentation to you in person of a sword ornamented with such devices as would indicate to you, and your children after you, that as citizens of South Carolina, we take pride in greeting you as a son who has done *her* honor, and honor to our common country, by sustaining, under difficult, delicate, and trying circumstances, calling for the most self-possessed courage, prompt sagacity, and fertility of resource, the glory of the national colors; and in another field, not less exalted by labors attended with scarcely less peril, exposure, and hardship, wrought out for your country and the world, as an explorer and discoverer in wild and inhospitable regions, a most valuable contribution to the cause of science.

We[2] regret that circumstances deny to us the pleasure of welcoming you to our city, and rendering to you in person this humble token of our sense of your distinguished merit, and shall be compelled to beg your acceptance of it at the hands of another; but we trust that, though we shall not [be] permitted the gratification of delivering it directly into your keeping, yet that it will come to you none the less acceptably, but with added value, from our patriotic representative, the honorable Robert Barnwell Rhett.

We cannot, dear sir, feel that we have fully discharged our pleasant duty, without expressing the fervent wish that you may be long spared to the country you have so well and so faithfully served; and that in whatever field it may be your lot in future to labor, that success in keeping with past achievement and desert may crown your efforts and cheer you in an ever onward and upward career.

We have the honor to be, most truly, your friends and fellow-citizens.

[Signed by the committee]

Printed in Washington *Daily Union*, 25 Aug. 1848. Although this letter was obviously written before 18 Aug. 1848, it has been given this date in order that it may appear immediately before JCF's reply (Doc. No. 23).

1. In a letter dated 1 March 1847, the committee had conveyed the resolutions to JBF. In addition to authorizing a sword, the citizens of Charleston had expressed appreciation to JCF for his explorations, and applauded his conduct in California.

2. The committee was composed of John E. Carew, Henry Gourdin, W. C. Gatewood, E. H. Trescott, G. H. Bryan, S. Y. Tupper, and the chairman, Henry W. Conner.

23. Frémont to a Committee of the Citizens of Charleston

WASHINGTON, August 18, 1848.

GENTLEMEN:

I have had the pleasure to receive the sword and belt, with which you have conveyed to me, on the part of my fellow-citizens of Charleston, the expression of their approbation of my conduct during some recent years of my life, and the further gratification to receive them from the hands of a Representative, the Hon. Mr. Rhett.

I cannot imagine any honor which I would consider greater than that you have conferred upon me, or any circumstances in which that honor would have been more valuable. Arriving on our frontier after a long absence, and in circumstances most humiliating and mortifying, I first learned that you had honored, with a public expression of your approval, my geographical labours in our remote Western Territories, and my subsequent conduct in aid of American citizens during the revolutionary movements in California. From the country which had been the scene of the one, and across the region which had been the subject of the other, I had been brought a degraded prisoner. My situation had been studiously aggravated by every humiliation to which I could be exposed, and my whole journey homeward was one continued indignity.

In these circumstances, and at the first frontier village, I received your letter accompanying the resolutions of the meeting in Charleston. In the sudden revulsion of feeling, I felt indebted to you for the moment of highest gratification I have ever experienced, in which the distress and pain of unmerited disgrace were entirely forgotten in the awakened feelings of gratitude and devotion to my country.

With all the strength of feeling so created, I offer to you my thanks, and through you to the citizens of Charleston whom you represent. I have been educated among them, and grown up together with many of them. Some were the associates and friends of my early youth. It will probably be long before I can have the pleasure to take them by the hand, and personally make them my acknowledgments. I beg, therefore, through you to express to them my grateful sense of their kind remembrance, and my great pleasure in having been able to do any thing which has given them gratification, and which they can think worthy a public expression of their approbation.

To my friends, the ladies of Charleston, I beg you to make acceptable my warmest and most respectful thanks; to assure them that I feel highly honored by their gift, and deeply grateful to them for the sympathy which prompted them to make it. With great pleasure I found exercised in my behalf the generous spirit which has so often distinguished them, and which has given them a place so honorable in the history of the State. The consciousness of having once been distinguished by their notice will always be an incentive to honorable exertion.

Having now offered to my fellow-citizens the earnest expression of my gratitude for the honor with which they have distinguished me, and of which I am as deeply sensible as if that honor had been really earned by myself, I could not remain satisfied were I to pass over in silence those to whom the distinction properly belong, and so appropriate to myself the fruits of their good conduct.

The exploring parties under my command, and the volunteer force of California, were composed of men whose courage and energy had made them pioneers in the wilderness country beyond our western frontier, or whose spirit of enterprise had carried them to find new homes on the shore of the Pacific. They were tried men, experienced in difficulty and danger, accustomed to self-reliance, and full of resources. What their matured experience aided me to plan, their courage always enabled me to accomplish. With inferior men, the services which had received your approbation would never have been performed; and to them, therefore, the praise you have awarded justly belongs. They have certainly deserved well of their country, and earned for themselves an honorable mention. I trust that you will allow me to make it here, and respectfully ask that you will further permit me to receive, in their name, and as their representative, the public testimonial with which you have honored me.

In taking leave of you, on the eve of a long absence from the country, I beg you to receive the assurance of my warm regard and most earnest wishes for your continued happiness.

With much respect, gentlemen, your friend and fellow-citizen.

J. C. FRÉMONT

To Messrs. Conner, Bryan, Gourdin, Carew, Trescott, Gatewood, and Tupper, a committee, &c.

Printed in Washington *Daily Union*, 25 Aug. 1848.

24. Frémont to George Engelmann

MY DEAR SIR,

Major [Thomas Beasley] Linnard has been ordered to St. Louis to pay the accounts of my party out of the appropriations just made.[1] I therefore return you Schriebers [Schreiber's] receipt, and will immediately forward you another, which with my certificate subscribed, will be presented to Major Linnard. Yours truly,

J. C. FRÉMONT

P.S. Enclosed I send the bills. Major Linnard will retain out of the whole amount the sum advanced by me to Schreiber, and place it to my credit at the Bank of Missouri.

Dr. Engelmann
St. Louis, Mri.

ALS-JBF (MoSB).
1. Benton had tried to procure the appointment of his and JCF's good friend, Robert Campbell, to adjust the claims, but Col. Abert refused on the grounds that Campbell was "the principal creditor in the case" and, furthermore, not a public officer (Abert to Benton, 18 Aug. 1848, Lbk [DNA-77, LS, 10:458–59]).

25. Frémont to Walter R. Johnson

WASHINGTON CITY, August 19th. 1848

SIR,

I have had the honor to receive your letter informing me that I had been elected a correspondent of the Academy of Natural Sciences in Philadelphia. I beg you to accept my apologies already offered through Mr. Kern for my unintentional delay in replying to your letter. With assurances of respect & regard I am Sir Your obedient Servant,

J. C. FRÉMONT

Dr. Walter R. Johnson
Corresponding Secty.
Academy of Natl. Sciences, Philadelphia

LS (PPAN).

26. James Buchanan to Frémont

WASHINGTON, 29 August 1848

MY DEAR SIR:

I regret to inform you that the President does not think that any sufficient reason exists for the removal of Mr. Larkin as Navy Agent at Monterey. The allegations against him have not yet assumed any authentic form. I am very sorry that I have been innocently instrumental in delaying you until this day, & I hope that my motive will be my apology.

Wishing you success & prosperity, I remain Sincerely & respectfully Your friend,

JAMES BUCHANAN

Colonel John C. Fremont

ALS, SC (PHi—Buchanan Papers). Buchanan made heavy corrections that are difficult to decipher. His original version read approximately: "I regret to inform you that whilst the President is anxious ⟨well-disposed⟩ to confer upon you the appointment and would be pleased to appoint you the Navy Agent at Monterey, yet he is unwilling to remove Mr. Larkin without more ⟨accurate⟩ authentic information than he possesses respecting that officer's conduct." The allegations against Larkin were not found.

27. Frémont to Richard Burgess

WASHINGTON, 31 Aug. 1848

[Richard Burgess of the City of Washington is given the power to settle and prosecute whatever claims JCF may have against any of the departments of government. He may receive and receipt for all monies due JCF. The original power of attorney was placed on file in the Third Auditor's Office, but a copy may be found in DNA-217, Roll 10, Manning File: Receipts.]

28. Frémont to John Torrey

My dear Sir,

The settlement of my affairs in order to [provide for] my long absence has so totally engrossed me that I have been forced to neglect my friends, and with them, other more agreeable business. Nothing which had in it the name of California could pass the House this session, and with other things, our appropriation for the survey was lost there. I set out from this place on Wednesday or Thursday morning, remain one day in N.Y. and go on to Missouri from which I shall set out for California about the end of this month. Being in the Winter our journey will be a severe one, but I hope to reach California early in December. I shall send you plants such as the season may afford by the first or second steamer (February or March) and you may rely on my exploring the country about Mt Shasté (Shastl) early in the next spring. All our plans will be carried out. Col. Benton desires me to say to you that at the next session (this winter) he will procure the means sufficient to cover all the expense attendant upon the examination of the plants, and upon the Engraving and publishing our work in the style you suggest. He will want a letter from you upon the value of the plants and the value of the work, and will communicate with you for that purpose. So that you may be confident of our ultimate success, and in the mean time I will make a good harvest in California. Prof. Henry told me some weeks since that he would publish any thing you could furnish him with from the plants.[1] In all this please act as you judge best. I would be glad to have a line from you, and letters sent to Col. Benton here will be forwarded to me. Mrs. Frémont will send you (from my journal) the localities &c. of the plants of California. Some brief memoranda of plants gathered between Bent's fort and the Salt Lake are sent by this mail. They refer to such plants only as I had not had time to label when they were gathered on the march or in my absence. I will afterwards send you the list of the plants gathered between the Missouri frontier and California.

I do not think that I have told you that I have a son[2] about five weeks old—Mrs. Frémont is doing well. I will write again and I am my dear Sir most truly yours,

J. C. Frémont

Prof. John Torrey,
Princeton

ALS (NNNBG—Torrey Correspondence).
1. Joseph Henry (1797–1878), secretary of the Smithsonian Institution, had been a professor of natural philosophy at Princeton from 1832 to 1846. Torrey's description of the plants collected by JCF in California, known as *Plantae Frémontianae*, was published in the *Smithsonian Contributions to Knowledge* (April 1853).
2. Benton Frémont, born 24 July 1848, died on 6 Oct. in the Missouri River steamer that was carrying his parents to Kansas landing, whence JCF would leave on his fourth expedition (PHILLIPS, 353, and Doc. No. 30).

29. Frémont's Notice to California Claimants

[WASHINGTON, 7 Sept. 1848]

The undersigned gives this notice to persons holding claims against the United States, for military or civil operations under his authority, and which claims were ascertained and authenticated while he was in the country in 1846–'47, that, on receiving an abstract of such claim, in duplicate, he will make the remarks upon it which justice and truth require to be made, and return one copy to the claimant, and retain the other for the benefit of the United States. No person need be at the trouble to come personally to see the undersigned on this business; his remarks will be made upon his own knowledge, and that of ex-officers of the California battalion. The undersigned gives this notice for three reasons:

1. For the benefit of the honest claimant, that he may eventually get what is due.

2. For the benefit of the United States, that it may have a check upon false claims.

3. For the protection of his own reputation that unjust claims shall not be presented under his name.

A compliance with the request will cost no expense, and but little trouble; non-compliance will be a serious detriment to any claimant, as I shall advise the proper authorities that all such non-presented claims must be held, *prima facie*, to be fraudulent. I shall be in different parts of California during the spring and summer of 1849, so that a compliance with this notice will be easy to every claimant.

I send this notice to California by Mr. [Frank] Ward to be published in the newspapers. I will publish a similar notice upon arrival.

J. C. Fremont

Washington City, Sept. 7, 1848.

Printed in *Alta California*, 15 March 1849.

30. Frémont's Notes on the 1848–49 Expedition

A winter expedition—about snow obstacles & home for family. Preparations at St. Louis—Campbell and Filley. Journey up the river—death of the child. Mrs. Frémont at Maj. Cummins Camp on the frontier—Mrs. Frémont's visits to the camp. Scott & the quails. Capt. Cathcart. Personnel (*33 men*) of the party. Godey—the Kerns —King—Breckenridge. Creutzfeldt (when was he with me?). The two Indian boys—Gregorio &——Proue. The 3 Canadians.[1]

Route up the Southern Kansas—the Arkansas bare of timber fuel and exposed to snow storms. For 400 miles abundant timber, game and excellent grass. Valley of the Kansas best approach to the Mountains. The valley soil of superior quality, well timbered, abundant grasses, the route direct. Would afford good settlements for 400 miles. The Big Timber, 30 m below Bents Fort. Fitzpatrick & the Indians. 600 lodges. Talks and feasts. Indians report snow deeper than for many years.[2]

Nov. 17. Mountains show themselves for the first time, covered with snow, the country around also. Not discouraged. Plan of the forward journey—Extract from letter of 17th Nov. Journey continued. Halt at Pueblo (San Carlos?) on the Fontaine qui Bouit.[3] Purchase here mules and provisions—load animals with corn.[4] Leave Pueblo, party & animals all in fine order. The Sierra Mojada (plate here) The Robidoux Pass (plate here)—The San Louis Valley—the Del Norte (Plate). The San Juan Mtns. The disaster—wreck of party (Xmas Camp)[5]—the look over the fields of snow in the west. The relief party under King—the long waiting for news tidings that did not come.[6] Give them up for lost and go for relief. Down to the Del Norte—travelling easy on the frozen river—strike lodge trail. Godey and the bit of bacon. Kill a hawk. Surprise a Utah Indian. Go with him to Utah lodges—feast on venison and barley *pot-au-feu*. Hire horses and Indians to go to Red River Settlement with us. Start again next day. Indians tell us of a starving [party] in the snow. Guided to them by the smoke of their camp fire. Prove to be King's party. Find King dead and the others starving. Put these on the Indian horses and continue journey. Snow disappears fast as we go down the valley—sheep ranchos—reach Taos—after nightfall—go into Beaubien's shop—find Owens, Maxwell, and Carson. Owens fails to recognize me. Maxwell does instantly—Why don't you know the Captain? Hospitable reception. Carson takes me to his house. Send back Godey to meet the party with horses & supplies. Horses furnished by Maj. Beale [Beall]. How Godey met the men. Re-organize the party. Capt. Cathcart goes back—health not warranting further venture, with him return [*blank line*].[7]

With 25 men all told[8] and outfit renewed I resume journey, following down the Del Norte and intending to reach the Rio Grande [Colorado] by a route south of Gila river. The snows this season too heavy to insist on a direct route through the mountains. Engage a New Mexican for guide. Spring weather in the valley—fruit trees in bloom—hospitality. Leave the river.[9] Open country—snowed on again. No wood and weather cold. Retreat into the Mimbres Mountains. Pleasant country, well wooded, resembling the oak region of the Sierra Nevada—color of soil—grass and water abundant. Travel along foot of mountains. Apaches around the camp—watch and watch. McGee [McGehee] fired on. Halt and have parley with chief —make friends. The Indians go to Mimbres River with us. Breakfast and presents. Indians direct us to watering place in the open country—appoint to meet us there—their war parties out in Sonora and Chihuahua. I push forward and avoid them. The Apache visitor—Santa Cruz. The Mexican and the bundle of grass. Follow down the Santa Cruz river—Tucson.[10] Spring on the Santa Cruz—peach orchards—the ruined missions. Reach the Gila river. The Pimah Village. (*See Johnson's report*) Indian faces painted with black lead. Follow the river around the Bend. Meet large party of Sonorians going to California for gold.[11] Their pleasure in meeting us. Their fear of Indians. They urge me to travel with them. I consent. Many presents of fruits and provisions in various forms. Reach the Gila river. Determine position of the Junction with the Rio Grande. Make Bullboat[12]—ferry women & children of the Sonorians across, with my party, and leave the Bullboat for men to complete their crossing. Some of the Sonorians decide to go to the Mariposa with me to look for gold which I told them would be found there.

Names of the party of 1848[13]

Cathcart	Taplin
Godey	+Sorel
Vincent Haler	+Morel
The Three Kerns	Godey's nephew
Preuss	+Carver
+Proue	Saunders
Creutzfeldt	+Manuel (Cosumne Indian)
+Wise	+Andrews
Ferguson	McKie
+Rohrer	Stepperfeldt
Martin	Bacon
Scott	+King
+Beadle	Gregorio
+Hubbard	Juan [Joaquin] } Tularé Indians

AD (CU-B).

1. For more details on preparations for the expedition, see the Introduction, pp. xxii–iv. Short biographical sketches of the personnel of the party are given in n. 13 below. Thirty-five men left Westport with JCF; three dropped out along the way. At the Pueblo de San Carlos on the Fontaine qui Bouit (present Pueblo, Colo.), JCF recruited William S. Williams as guide, and thus entered the rugged San Juans with thirty-three men.

2. For details of the journey to Bent's Fort, see Andrew Cathcart's letters to C. J. Colville (Doc. Nos. 31 and 32) and JCF to Benton, 17 Nov. 1848 (Doc. No. 34).

3. The halt was made at Mormontown at the mouth of the Fountain River. Located across the river was El Pueblo de San Carlos, whence came Bill Williams to offer his services as guide.

4. It was at a little settlement on the Hardscrabble affluent of the Arkansas, twenty-five miles distant, that sacks of shelled corn were loaded on the backs of mules. The party left Hardscrabble on 25 Nov. and went up the north branch of Hardscrabble Creek. After passing parallel walls of red rock, located just west of Wetmore, the men entered the canyon of North Hardscrabble Creek with its huge outcroppings of red and green rocks. Water was made from snow. RICHMOND notes when they crossed from the drainage of North Hardscrabble Creek onto the Williams Fork of the Huerfano River they found themselves near the Gardner Butte, "standing like a 'bastion' at the gap of the Huerfano. Across the river were the 'little Spanish Peaks,' Sheep and Little Sheep Mountains, resembling their better known neighbors to the south." They moved along the Huerfano. Battling wind and deep snow, they crossed the Sangre de Cristos by way of Robidoux (Mosca Pass) on 3 Dec., and using the narrow, rocky, timber-choked canyon of Mosca Creek, descended into the San Luis Valley, "the valley of the

Rio del Norte." Camp was made in a grove of trees by a small stream, probably Medano Creek. On 6 Dec. King, Preuss, and Creutzfeldt went with JCF to examine Medano or Sand Hills Pass. The next day, the entire party rounded the giant sand dunes and in killing temperatures struggled westward across the level, treeless valley floor. The exhausted men and mules rested in the cottonwoods on the Rio de Tres Tetones, presently named Crestone Creek, before moving west to the Saguache, which Richard Kern in his manuscript diary (CSmH) mistakenly called the Rio Grande. His 1849 published diary (Doc. No. 39) and JCF's 27 Jan. 1849 letter to JBF (Doc. No. 36) recount their subsequent trials; the tall hacked-off stumps, bones, and other artifacts showed later hunters and foresters the charred sites of their camps on Wannamaker, Rincones, and Groundhog creeks, and the maps here (pp. 106–8) indicate their wanderings. No railroad has ever gone through the San Juans where JCF attempted to lead his men.

5. Of all the plates mentioned here, the Sierra Mojada illustration is the only one that appears in the *Memoirs*. In fact, two views of it are included in that volume. Two other plates relating to the Sierra Mojada are also in the prospectus for the *Memoirs* (CSmH), as well as engravings entitled "San Luis Valley, near Sand Hill Pass" and "Christmas Camp." BIGELOW published a different view of the Christmas Camp, one painted by Jacob A. Dallas and engraved by Nathaniel Orr's company. The prospectus has no plate for Robidoux Pass (presumably Mosca Pass across the Sangre de Cristo Mountains), but does contain an engraving for Cochetopa Pass and one for the San Juans. Virtually all of the expensive artwork for the *Memoirs* was done in the 1850s, with the daguerreotypes of Solomon Nunes Carvalho forming the basis for much of it.

6. For details of JCF's story, see his long letter beginning on 27 Jan. 1849 (Doc. No. 36).

7. Those remaining behind, besides Cathcart, were the three Kern brothers, Old Bill Williams, Taplin, and Stepperfeldt.

8. Pencilled between the lines of McGehee's manuscript chronicle, as though an afterthought of his—or perhaps added by a reader of his diary—are the names of Lindsay Carson and "Thos. Boggs, son of Ex-Gov. of Mexico." The men were additions to the old party of seventeen, including JCF. After the party reached Santa Fe, the names of Carson and Boggs are again interlined in the McGehee chronicle, except Boggs is now correctly identified as the son of the "Ex.-Gov. of Mo., now of Cal." The names of Edward Perry, a relative of Godey's, and "Joaquin LeRue, guide" are also added (MC GEHEE [1], 150, 167).

"Joaquin LeRue" is undoubtedly Antoine Leroux (1801–61), as Joaquin, sometimes spelled Joachin, was one of his given names. He may have guided the JCF party as far as Albuquerque, but he certainly did not go on to California. PARKHILL, 116–20, notes that Leroux was the guide for J. H. Whittlesey's expedition against the Utes, which left Taos on 11 March and returned on 14 March 1849.

Omitting Leroux and including JCF, we know the names of twenty members. The other five were probably Mexican muleteers.

9. Four days' travel below San Antonio, they left the Rio Grande and used Leroux's trail, "which cuts off more than 100 miles from the route taken by Colonel Cook in 1846" (MC GEHEE [1], 185).

10. They entered Tucson on 23 March and four days later were at the Pimah Indian village on the Gila (MC GEHEE [1], 208, 214).

11. MC GEHEE [1], 203, writes that it was after they left the Spanish town of Santa Cruz that they "fell in" with the Sonorians.

12. It was about 8 April that the mules were driven across. The men constructed the bullboat of six oxhides, which they had packed along for that purpose, and attached five oars. Two trips were sufficient to carry their possessions across (MC GEHEE [2], 151).

13. JCF's roster of the fourth expedition is incomplete, but of the thirty men he lists, fourteen had been associated with him in one way or another on previous expeditions, and only passing notice need now be taken of those who have been identified in Vols. 1 and 2. Such a one is Alexander Godey, the gay and practical French Canadian from St. Louis who had been on two previous expeditions. JCF wrote that under Napoleon, Godey, Kit Carson, and Richard Owens might have become marshals (MEMOIRS, 427), and indeed, Godey seems to have been genuinely admired and respected by all the men even in their severest days of trial. He did not replace Bill Williams as a guide as some writers have indicated.

The forty-one-year-old Vincent Haler's real name was Lorenzo D. Vinsonhaler, although it was often written as Vincenthaler. A native of Ohio, he had emigrated to California in 1846, served as sergeant in Company C of the battalion, and joined JCF's homeward-bound expedition late in the spring of 1847 (*National Intelligencer*, 3 Nov. 1847; DNA-92, microfilm roll 7). The Kerns did not like him and events of the expedition convinced them that he was a coward and an unscrupulous opportunist. When the party broke up in Taos, Vinsonhaler continued on to California, working for a time for JCF, who thought him a "sterling man" and went his surety on a bond when he applied, along with James D. Savage, for a license to trade with the Indians ("Correspondence between the Department of Interior and the Indian Agents and Commissioners in California," Senate Ex. Doc. 4, 33rd Cong., 1st sess., p. 106, Serial 688). In 1851 Vinsonhaler served as a guide to the Mariposa Battalion (ECCLESTON).

Of the three Kerns of Philadelphia, Edward M. was the veteran explorer. He had been the artist-topographer for the third expedition and had commanded Sutter's Fort after the American flag was raised there. He was instrumental in signing up his two brothers: Richard H., also an artist, and Benjamin, a physician, who was to act as surgeon and assistant naturalist to the expedition. All three had hoped the expedition would improve their professional opportunities. While nursing his body back to health in Taos, Edward wrote bitterly about JCF and their disappointments: "He has left us without even his good wishes or a thought of our future and owing *me money*. . . . I have lost a start that I never expect to recover again" (E. M. Kern to Mary, Feb. 1849, CSmH). Worse was yet to come. Within a few days Benjamin, and Bill Williams also, were murdered by the Utes when the two returned to the mountains with a few Mexican helpers to try to recover the abandoned property. Four years later Richard met a similar fate when, as a member of Captain John W. Gunnison's topographical party, he was massacred by Utes in Sevier Valley. The HINE [2] and HEFFERNAN biographies of Edward give many details on the lives of Richard and Benjamin.

When the Utes attacked Gunnison, they also killed the botanist Frederick Creutzfeldt, who had served JCF in a similar capacity on the fourth expedition. Being a tall, strong, active man, weighing 180 or 190 pounds, he had broken a lot of trail in the deep snow of the mountains (BRECKENRIDGE [1])

Yet a third member of JCF's Fourth joined up with Gunnison—Charles Van Linneus Taplin—and served as a wagonmaster until, fortunately for him, poor health forced him to drop out when the expedition was still in San Luis Valley. Thus he was not present at the Ute attack and managed to live another two years. Taplin's ties to JCF went back a long time, as he had served in both the second and third expeditions but not the war in California. Leaving JCF on the Sacramento River on 3 April 1846, he had gone east to seek JBF's aid in securing a second lieutenancy in the regular army (J. B. Frémont to the President, 16 Feb. 1847, Copley Collection). He resigned this commission just a week after JCF submitted his own resignation following the court-martial verdict (HEITMAN).

The German cartographer Charles Preuss endured the perils of this expedition as stoically as he had those of the first and second, and yet there was a difference. He neglected to comment in his journal on the blunders of Americans in general and the stupidity of JCF in particular.

An old man and a native of France, Raphael Proue was making his fourth expedition with JCF (Charles Taplin's report, St. Louis *Weekly Reveille*, 30 April 1849, reprinted in HAFEN & HAFEN, 195). Sorrel, whose proper name seems to have been Vincent Tabeau, may have been a kinsman of Jean Baptiste Tabeau, who had been killed by the Indians near Littlefield, Ariz., while serving on JCF's second expedition. The man whose name JCF gives as Morel was Antoine Morin from Illinois and a veteran of the third expedition. Another old mountaineer, Longe, not listed by name by JCF but registered by Micajah McGehee, went along as far as Hardscrabble when the "prospect of deep snow upon the mountains replenished by continual storms" caused him to break off from the party and to predict "evil to those who continued" (MC GEHEE [1], 11, 92–93). Longe, Tabeau, and Morin were undoubtedly JCF's "3 Canadians."

Godey's nephew was fourteen-year-old Theodore McNabb, and Jackson Saunders was a free Negro servant in the Benton household who went as JCF's personal chef and orderly.

Henry J. Wise, Henry Rohrer, Benjamin Beadle (sometimes the newspapers have it "Beddell"), George Hubbard (McGehee writes "Hibbard"), Elijah T. Andrews, and Carver were all new recruits, and they all died on the expedition. Formerly a tax collector for St. Louis County, Henry J. Wise has often been confused with the Marion Wise of the third expedition (Saint Louis *Daily Reveille*, 30 March 1849). Marion was from St. Louis and was still living there in 1888 when he signed an affidavit before the clerk of the circuit court stating that he had known Thomas E. Breckenridge for over fifty years, having been "raised with him from childhood" (DNA-15, Mexican War Pension Files, Margaret E. Breckenridge, 10901).

Rohrer was a family man and a millwright who had suffered pecuniary losses on a contract in Georgetown and hoped to repair his fortunes in California where skilled mechanics were in great demand (Baltimore *Sun*, 16 April 1849). Beadle was from St. Louis County, Hubbard from Milwaukee, and Carver from Chicago (Charles Taplin's report, St. Louis *Weekly Reveille*, 30 April 1849, printed in HAFEN & HAFEN, 195–96). Tubercular midshipman Elijah T. Andrews was from the city of St. Louis; so was William Bacon, a new recruit but one who survived to mine gold with Breckenridge (*ibid*.; BRECKENRIDGE [1]).

Missourian Josiah Ferguson and Thomas Salathiel Martin, a Tennessean who had lived in St. Louis since 1840, were veterans of both the third expedition and the California Battalion. After his travels with JCF were over, Martin settled near Santa Barbara, Calif., and married a Mexican woman who bore him children. For a time he worked as a city marshal and a deputy sheriff and later became a rancher and a breeder of fine horses (MARTIN, iii). John Scott had joined the Third at Bent's Fort in 1845 as a *voyageur* and two years later returned with JCF to St. Louis as a hunter. That city's Missouri Hotel listed him as being from Elk Mills, Mo. (*Daily Missouri Republican*, 28 Sept. 1848).

Henry King of the Georgetown district of Washington had also been a faithful and responsible member of the third expedition and had served the California Battalion as commissary officer with the rank of captain. When going became rough for the Fourth, it was King whom JCF selected to lead a small party in search of assistance. After the interview with Taplin, the reporter for the St. Louis *Weekly Reveille* wrote: "The fate of Mr. King was most heart-rendering. He was, says Mr. Taplin, a man in the spring time of life, of cultivated mind, and of the most engaging manners. He had been married but two weeks previous to his departure on the expedition, and was only a short time with the company where he had gained the friendship and esteem of every member" (30 April 1849, reprinted in HAFEN & HAFEN, 195–96).

"McKie" was Micajah McGehee (1824–80), a twenty-two-year-old graduate of Transylvania University and the son of Judge Edward McGehee, the owner of Bowling Green Plantation near Woodville, Miss. His brother Charles was with him in St. Louis when he joined JCF, and family tradition has it that it was his girl's love for the brother that sent Micajah in search of western adventure. After the disaster in the mountains, Micajah went on to Las Mariposas with JCF to wash gold and had his first nugget made into a pin for the girl back home (Lieut. Col. John H. Napier III to Mary Lee Spence, 20 Aug. 1975). He soon settled at Big Oak Flat in Tuolumne County, where he continued to mine and also began a merchandise business. When he was not immediately moved by family pleas to come home, an older brother wrote, "Some said you did not come home because you were making money so fast you disliked to leave and others equally stoutly avered that it was because you had had reverses and were too proud to come home under their pressure." But he thought Micajah occupied the middle ground. "You had not got so high as some said not so low (in finance) as others feared but that you were pleased with the fresh life that California offered you and meant to stay and enjoy it" (Edward McGehee to Micajah McGehee, Cold Spring, 14 June 1854, copy courtesy of Mrs. H. B. McGehee). In time, Micajah became a justice of the peace, a circuit judge, and in 1856 a member of the California legislature. He finally returned permanently to Woodville in 1872. Copies of some of the family correspondence may be found in the James Stewart McGehee Papers (LU).

One of the new recruits was thirty-six-year-old John S. Stepperfeldt, a blacksmith from Quincy, Ill. He, his wife, and two children had migrated there from New York sometime after 1839 (U.S. Census, 1850, for Adams County, North Ward of Quincy, Ill., pp. 214 A & B give the name as Stepperfield).

The three California Indian boys, Manuel, Gregorio, and Juan (Joaquin), seem to have had previous service with JCF. Identified by JCF as being "a Christian Indian of the Cosumne tribe in the valley of the San Joaquin" (Doc. No. 36), Manuel had been connected with the third expedition and was known to JBF. Gregorio was probably the young Indian whom JCF had brought home in 1844 and who subsequently, as a member of the 1845–47 expedition, endured all the hardships and glory of the marching and fighting in California. The identity of the third boy is a problem. Two of the 1848–49 Kern diaries repeatedly indicate that his name was Joaquin and not Juan as JCF much later lists here. But "Juan" is the name given in the MEMOIRS, 411, to the second Indian boy brought home by JCF in 1844, and Jessie implies that Juan was on the Fourth (J. B. FRÉMONT [3], 56:95). Breckenridge does claim to have brought home in 1847 a fourteen-year-old Indian boy who had been given to him by his mother (BRECKENRIDGE [1]).

Capt. Andrew Cathcart (1817–82), who heads JCF's list, was an Ayrshire Scot who had served in the 10th and 11th Hussars before leaving the army in 1846. He had come to St. Louis in Aug. 1848 with a fellow Britisher, George

Frederick Ruxton, the author of *Adventures in Mexico and the Rocky Mountains* (London, 1847) and *Life in the Far West* (London, 1849). While Ruxton waited in St. Louis for an opportunity to travel to Santa Fe, Cathcart joined Gen. George Brooke, who had been ordered from his command in New Orleans to Minnesota to establish two new military posts in the heart of Sioux country. Brooke had been president of the board for the court-martial of JCF and it is entirely possible that he made a few comments about him to the British officer. While he was at Fort Snelling preparing for a buffalo hunt, Cathcart received news that Ruxton had died of dysentery. He hastened back to St. Louis to arrange his poor friend's affairs, and then, hearing of JCF's plans for expedition, asked to go along and was accepted into the party (Cathcart to C. J. Colville, 20 Aug., 20 and 29 Sept. 1848, National Register of Archives, Scotland).

After the San Juan fiasco, Cathcart seems not to have been as bitter as the Kerns. According to JBF, he had sent some letters and a Damascus sword, and there had been a meeting with the Frémonts in France in 1852 (Jessie Benton Frémont's draft manuscripts of her "Memoirs," p. 96, and of "Great Events during the life of Major General John C. Frémont," p. 178, both at CU-B).

In 1967 Charles Hill of Hermosa Beach, Calif., located the sword in a restaurant in Chula Vista, Calif. It had been made by the Wilkinson Company in London and etched on the blade, along with an eagle, stars, and "E. Pluribus Unum," is the presentation inscription: "The Honorable Col. Fremont from A. Cathcart 1850" (Charles Hill to Donald Jackson, 12 Oct. 1967, personal files).

After meeting the Frémonts in Paris, Cathcart went off to Australia, where he spent some time in the "gold diggings" and cruised about the South Seas in Turkey; in 1858 he was chief of police at Mauritius and in 1859 consul in Albania. Cathcart died of cancer. For some of the details of his life, see the obituary notice clipped from a newspaper in the Cathcart Papers, National Register of Archives, Scotland.

Omitted from the roster of the men who actually entered the San Juans with JCF are Julius E. Ducatel, Thomas E. Breckenridge, and his guide, William Sherley Williams. Ducatel was the son of Baltimorean Julius T. Ducatel, who had been state geologist of Maryland and a friend of JCF's mentor, Joseph N. Nicollet. The young man must have heard of his father's death soon after his arrival in California. He returned to the Atlantic states in 1852, but in 1854 Micajah McGehee reported Ducatel's death at the California rancho of Vinsonhaler (W. C. Jones's testimony before the California Land Commission, DNA-49, Docket 1, p. 101; Micajah McGehee to Charles G. McGehee, Big Oak Flat, 7 April 1854, copy, LU—James Stewart McGehee Papers).

Breckenridge (1825–97) was young too, but, like his comrades Ferguson and Martin, a veteran of the third expedition and of the war in California. He had not returned with JCF in 1847, but had come east earlier in the year with Carson and Beale. When the fourth expedition broke up in Taos, Breckenridge went on to California and with Billy Bacon mined gold somewhat successfully for a time. By 1851 he was back in St. Louis, married to Margaret E. Ritner, and making claims for bounty land (BRECKENRIDGE [1]). When *Cosmopolitan* obtained his story, he was living in the mining town of Telluride, Colo. (BRECKENRIDGE [2]).

With Williams (1787–1849), JCF acquired a guide who had spent his entire life on the cutting edge of the frontier or in the mountains and who had close associations with the Indians, particularly the Osage and Utes. Popularly known as "Old Bill Williams," sometimes as "Parson Bill," or even as "Lone Elk" in later life, he had been born in a cabin on Horse Creek, old Rutherford County, N.C., and had been brought to a farm near St. Louis when he was about eight and when Louisiana still belonged to Spain. At sixteen he began living with the Big Hill band of the Great Osages and in time married one of their girls and acted as interpreter and translator for various U.S. Indian agents, generals, and missionaries, and even produced an Osage-English dictionary. In 1825 he became a member of the government expedition which had the responsibility for marking the road from Fort Osage to Santa Fe. At Taos he left the expedition and for the next twenty years ranged far and wide over the West, trapping beaver, hunting buffalo, "collecting" horses, and trading. His activities took him over the Southwest into California, up to the Columbia River, into the Wind River Mountains, and to Salt Lake, but he was seen most often in the southern Rockies of Colorado.

As we have noted in Vol. 2, he was no stranger to JCF, having accompanied his 1845 expedition from the Pueblo to Great Salt Lake. When JCF came again to the Pueblo in 1848, Bill Williams was recuperating from a wound the Apaches had given him when they encountered Major W. W. Reynold's forces, for which he was acting as scout and guide. See VOELKER and FAVOUR for biographical treatments of this eccentric and complex mountain man who, McGehee wrote, "was a dead shot with a rifle, though he always shot with a 'double wabble'" (MC GEHEE [1], 87).

In addition to Longe, two other men quit the expedition before it entered the mountains. One was James McDowell, a St. Louis physician and nephew of Mrs. Thomas Hart Benton. He sold his mule to McGehee and left the party on 27 Oct. when it was three days beyond the Kansas Methodist Mission near Union Town and two days away from crossing the Smoky Hill near present Saline. The second was Amos Andrews, father of Elijah, who withdrew at Bent's Fort (MC GEHEE [1], 12, 20, 73). According to Thomas Fitzpatrick, two men, whom he does not identify, tried to join JCF after he left the Pueblo, but the explorer had no need of their services and they returned. Contrary to Breckenridge, who had a faulty memory, "Dick" Wootton was never a part of the expedition.

31. Andrew Cathcart to C. J. Colville

FREMONT'S CAMP.
Oct. 16th, 1848

DEAR COLVILLE.

We had a very good voyage up the Missouri, very slow though in consequence of the hundreds of snags (which we were lucky enough to escape). The whole party came up in the same boat, an advantage to me as I made their acquaintance all in a bunch. They really are very good fellows and very well disposed, some are superior in education; one, a German, acts as topographer, a little, squat man with an eternal pipe and three heathen Americans who act respectively as Doctor, artist and one as Head man[1] of the party under Frémont.

Richard Hovendon Kern. From a daguerreotype.
Courtesy of the Henry E. Huntington Library.

Edward Meyer Kern. From a daguerreotype.
Courtesy of the Henry E. Huntington Library.

Benjamin Jordan Kern. From a daguerreotype.
Courtesy of the Henry E. Huntington Library.

Alexander Godey. From a print in *Century Magazine*,
March 1891.

Charles Preuss. From a print in *Century Magazine*,
March 1891.

We have been out here camped for a week on the Prairie, preparing to start. I like the life very much and it agrees with me; the roughing it would astonish you, I assure you. I have abandoned all vestige of polished life now. You would laugh to see me *roasting* meat on a pointed stick draped in a leather hunting shirt, or as I had to do the other day leading a d——d obstinate mule for ten miles. Heavens, that was a job. I have been chiefly employed during the week in sewing up stuff for the tents, little things, just for shelter in the snow, and after the first attempt I took famously to tailoring. We expect to start in two days so I shall now close this letter. I want you to do me a particular favor, as early as possible, which is to procure a package of seeds either from the Botanical Garden of Saharanpore or Calcutta including all the Hymalayan Pines—creepers—Flowers & Fruit—and in fact anything rare that Indian Botany offers, also some Grane and Dhol. All these must be properly ticketted and the package Hermetically sealed and when received by you, sent on as quick as possible by the Cunard Steamer to the address I give below.

Colonel J. C. Fremont.

care of Messrs. Howland and Aspinall.

New York.

They are for Fremont to whom I wish to give them as some return for his kindness and to whom they will be most acceptable as he is a great botanist and I have no doubt that most of them would do well in the fine climate of California. If you see Sir G. Clarke[2] he could assist in getting them as he understands these matters. Give him my kindest remembrances. If not Bacon[3] could put you in the way; the great thing is to get the seeds as quickly home as possible—I will repay you any expenses when we meet. Pray set about it as early as possible. I must now stop; my writing is worse than usual, but I am sitting on the ground writing on my knee which partly accounts for it. God bless you, old boy—Ever your sincere,

A. CATHCART

P.S. Best regards to Bacon and Arthur.[4] I will write by the first opportunity. I wish you were here. I had the satisfaction of hearing from poor Ruxton's brother. He had seen the account of his brother's death in the paper and came to St. Louis not being aware that I had made all the arrangements. I only missed him by one day.

A. C.

ALS (National Register of Archives, Scotland—Cathcart Papers). Charles John Colville (1818–1903) was a close friend and fellow officer of Cathcart's in the 11th (Prince Albert's own) Regiment of Hussars. In 1849 he succeeded his uncle as the eleventh Baron of Scotland and in 1885 was created a peer of the United Kingdom (HART'S ANNUAL ARMY LIST, 7 [1846]:137; WHO WAS WHO).

1. Benjamin, Richard, and Edward Kern.
2. At the time of Cathcart's letter, Sir George Clerk (1787–1867) was representing Dover in Parliament. In 1862 he became president of the Zoological Society.
3. Not identified.
4. Not identified.

32. Andrew Cathcart to C. J. Colville

"FREMONT'S CAMP".
Oct. 30th, 1848

DEAR COLVILLE.

I am very glad to have an opportunity of letting you know that I am getting on famously. Some of our Indians return tomorrow to the settlements and I send a few letters by them. We have now been eleven days out and have hitherto made a good journey. The first week the d—d mules and new hands ("greenhorns") were troublesome but now all men and beasts have settled to their work. We travelled South of the Santa Fe trail up the Kanzas and are now on the Smoky Hill Fork some where about the 38th parallel of Latitude (West of Washington, 101 Greenwich), and the 24th of Longitude and 250 miles from Settlements. We came through the Pottawatomie Indians and are now on the Great Indian War Ground, daily and rightly looking out for an attack from the Pawnees. We yesterday reached Buffallo.

I had such a chapter of accidents and killed nothing. I was with three of the hunters and we all got bogged in the river; I lost my six shooter pistol, spurs, broke my wiping stick and had to cut my reins to prevent my mule being drowned. I did not discern the loss of the pistol for some time, when I returned on the trail and waded above my middle twice through the river in the vain hope of finding my pistol. I had taken my boots off to wade and not being able to get them on again had to ride my mule in stockings and with a halter ten miles to camp. Today I had better luck and killed two bulls. It was great fun. I brought a mule load of meat into camp. There are few cows about as yet and the grass is so wretched that we cannot afford to "run them," at least have to be careful, but approach them, easy work; after all I shot one fellow today off my mule, having cut him off. I brought him down at the first go at about 30 yards and soon had some society about in the shape of wolves, licking their chops and squatting about.

The life is damned hard; we start at sunrise, having breakfasted by star-light and travel till near sun down, always camping in a strong position and keeping guard. Our danger now (except Indians) is snow; it looks like it and if we catch it here on the Prairies it will kill our animals. It is infernally cold, I wish you could feel the Mercury. I can hardly write, my hands are in such a state, all due to bruises by working. I assure you I do harder work than any private in the Cherrybums; you ought to see my plight, *such dirt*. I quite like it and consider my red flannel shirt which I have only worn 14 days as being *quite* clean. I assure you one learns to turn his hand to anything out here, and tonight I have to make myself leather pockets to my trousers, a pr. of moccasins and clean my gun, run bullets, cut up some meat and I catch, saddle, water and tie up my mules. Give my love to Peel, Noel[1] and Arthur. I will write when I can. Ever yours,

A. CATHCART

We expect to reach Bent's Fort, a trading post on the Arkansa, in 12 days. There we stop 2 days and thence we start to cross the mountains. If we are snowed up we shall have to eat our mules. Frémont, who has twice had to do it before, says it is not bad feeding; he is a very nice fellow, very gentlemanlike and quiet. If all goes right we shall reach the Pacific by the end of the year. Write me to Canton—I shall certainly try to get there. I wish I could hear from you, or that you were here; you would enjoy the life, rough but very pleasant and full of excitement. Adieu.

A. C.

ALS (National Register of Archives, Scotland—Cathcart Papers).
1. Edmund Peel and Gerard James Noel had been lieutenants in the 11th Regiment of Hussars (HART'S ANNUAL ARMY LIST, 7 [1846]:317).

33. Andrew Cathcart to C. J. Colville.

"CAMP" ON THE SOUTHERN BANK
OF THE ARKANSA. LAT. 38.
(WASHINGTON), LONG. 104.
Nov. 17th, 1848

MY DEAR COLVILLE,

If you take the trouble to look out in a map the above address you will see pretty nearly whereabouts I now am, 640 miles west of the Frontier. We have accomplished that distance in 25 days and all the time across the Prairies. I wrote you a few lines some weeks ago when some of our Indians returned and trust that you received them, as I knew that it would afford you pleasure to hear of my progress, and I was also desirous of showing you that I had not forgotten my promise of keeping you "au fait" of my movements. I only wish I could get some of your letters, but not a shadow of a chance exists of my being able to hear in any shape from Europe for many months, and I assure you that I find the absence of all intelligence of friends a very great blank. This letter goes with Frémont's to an Indian agent at a little miserable trading post near this, who will forward them by the first opportunity.

I told you in my last that we had just reached the Buffallo range and of my mishaps. That accursed river played the devil with me. I lost my Pistol, powder horn, spurs and broke my ramrod; however I made shift as I best could and made determined war on the "Savage Buffallo," of whom I laid a good many low. My riding mule turned out first rate for the sport, as I could fire off her back. All were fish that came to my net and I peppered anything, whether cow, calf or bull that I could get near. I gruelled my animal terribly, as I never followed the camp march but went away on the flanks. Once I lost myself and was rather panicked, not having a compass. I got back to the trail.

How you would have enjoyed the sport and the eating (the cows at least) are excellent; the Prairie air gives a tremendous appetite. I was regularly "chivied" one day by an old bull whose shoulder I broke; I thought he could not move but on my going pretty close made such a charge that in three yards more I should have been tossed. You ought to have seen me kicking my mule along with all the vigour of desperation. His head for some lengths was close at her tail, but as she was regularly "scared" she saved me from a gore or two. I can assure you that they look very ugly, particularly when you approach on foot. I did not at all relish such crawling work, going a mile on ones belly and cutting your hands and knees to ribbons.

The weather has been and is very cold. Our great danger was in meeting snowstorms and the Pawnees, and we did both.

Our route lay up the Smoky Hill Fork, which the Pawnee trail crosses leading down to the Arkansa. The temperature was tolerably mild up to the 2nd Nov. when it changed and after two days threatening we were caught one morning in a tremendous snow storm and forced to take refuge in a little creek in the bush; here we spent a wretched day, a hurricane blowing all the time. Buffallo came close into the camp and I went after them. I got one of my hands rather frostbitten in holding my rifle without a mitten on but by snow rubbing got it right again.

The storm cleared in afternoon and we found some Indians near us who expressively made signs to us that they meant to "take our hair." We immediately set to work and "forted," that is, felled trees and formed an enclosure where we placed the animals and made every preparation for defending ourselves, but no attack took place, our precautions being too good for them to risk it. We always chose good camps, and Fremont picked out very stony places. The requisites of a good camp are water, grass and wood, the latter both for fires, shelter for the animals in storms and to enable you to make enclosures for defence.

For the first 300 miles the Prairie was diversified in character, long slopes, little ravines and knolls. We were surrounded with fires and once or twice had difficulty in getting round them. One evening our camp was on fire and we had to burn against other fires that the wind was bringing rapidly on us. These lines of *miles* of flames are a magnificent sight, but (especially at night) keeps you in perpetual anxiety.

The morning after the snow storm (Nov. 4th) was intensely cold; the Therm. before sunrise marked 12 and after sunrise 16. How should you fancy eating your breakfast by star light with the air 22 degrees below freezing point? There was a keen mist too and our march over the freezing plain was a painful one. We lost several animals, the storm and wretched grass having exhausted them.

You will readily believe the life is not one of great ease. We always rise before the sun, breakfast by star light, travel all day and eat again in evening. Heavens, how I enjoy the *tea*; we have a little with us. As long as we met Buffallo we lived on them, afterwards on bacon, and one day I had the luck to kill four *racoons* which we devoured with relish; they were immensely fat and I had a deuce of a job to bring them into camp as they weighed altogether upwards of 80 lbs. Some badgers which the men killed were also pronounced excellent. If you wish to try one boil him over-night and eat him cold; he does not otherwise do.

You have no idea how this rough life finds out the weak parts of your garments. I am all shreds and patches and every day employed sewing and repairing damages. It is really a life of labour but I get on very well. We passed close to some very large Pawnee villages, luckily for us abandoned, and that in a hurry, as tomahawks &c. were scattered about. They had probably been surprised by a war party. We made some very long marches of 40, and one of 50, miles, when we struck this river. These long days used up many animals. We travelled down the Santa Fe trail for the last ten days close on heels of some Indians. Every night nearly we forded the river to the Islands for shelter, as they have a little wood on them. The river banks are perfectly bare.

One evening we had a bad crossing and both Fremont and I got sousings, our animals falling backwards with us. Our clothes were instantly frozen stiff and he got his feet slightly frostbitten. I stuck mine into the fire in time and saved them. We rested on the 12th with the Indians in front, having popped most unexpectedly right into a large village of some hundred lodges. They received us as friends, strange enough too as they were Comanches, a dread tribe as Windham[1] can tell you. We travelled some days in company without molestation, but they pestered us greatly. They were fine looking men, very handsome Roman profiles all painted and ornaments. The village had quite a chivalric appearance, each lodge having in front on a tripod the lance, shield, bows and arrows of the inmates. They had a good many Spanish captives. Poor devils! they use them as slaves. I wanted to trade for one little child but they did not fancy the few goods we had. We got some dried meat from them, on which we are now living. It is very like shoe leather boiled but better than salt.

On getting near this place we found three tribes of Indians assembled for trade, the Arapahoes, Apaches and Kiawos. Great feasts &c were going on and a new Indian agent[2] was making them a talk. I have had quite enough of these red men; they bother one to death and are dirty enough. Our camp looked like Catlin's gallery let loose, or rather animated. We wanted to trade, but did very little. Not an animal could we get and we want them, otherwise we shall have to walk over the mountains. I have lost one of mine.

We traded an Indian lodge, a great comfort, I assure you. I now write in it, squatted at the little fire in the centre. They are heavy to carry as the poles, 20 in number, are dragged by mules trailing on the ground. We made a halt here yesterday to refit a little.

How Gerard[3] would laugh to see me washing my flannel shirt and other things but out here you must work for yourself. I am pretty certain I lead a harder life than can be led in Europe but it is wonderful how easy one comes into it. I am very fortunate in being with Fremont. I like him very much; he is very gentlemanlike and quiet and genial; we get on very well. However, I should enjoy it more if I had a friend with me, as former associations add so much to one's enjoyment.

I sincerely trust that some day you and I may pass some pleasant days together. I wonder if you are hunting this winter or what you are about. I wish you were settled down. Remember when you write to give me all your history. I shall certainly, if I can accomplish it, go to Canton so write me there; you will have plenty of time; I do not suppose that I can, if all goes well, get there before May, probably much later. We march from here today up the river and shall probably follow it to its head water. Where we cross the mountains depends on the snow; it fell heavily yesterday.

There are some very "ugly" Indians in our way about 200 miles from this; they defeated a 150 Americans a short time back, but perhaps our hitherto wonderful luck may still stick to us. I must now stop—I can hardly write for the cold, and though close to the fire, the ink keeps freezing. Give my love to Peel and Noel, Arthur &c. and Windham. Goody Bye, old boy, God bless. Ever yours,

A. Cathcart

P.S. I forgot to say that we have seen great numbers of elk; one band consisted of several hundred, a splendid sight. We have also killed antelope and as for wolves I am sick of firing at them. I hope Cox[4] will pay my subscription to Pratts[5] and the Kay; when you happen to go down there mention it to the clerk, I suppose I shall have some money sent there. The Rocky Mountains are now in sight, 200 miles distant, so I can now say that I have seen both the Himalayas and this great range in the *same year*.

I wish you a merry Xmas; tell Arthur to take care of his hair— mine is coming out like the deuce. I have not had a squaw yet; some were offered by the Comanches but such brutes, lousy, all of them and the "Children of the Forest" suffer from severe Poxes, I discovered that Snooks (Cardigan)[6] is very Indian like in features: shave his moustache, dye him brown and daub his face with red and he would make a capital "White Buffallo," as one of the Chiefs was called. Another rejoiced in the name of the "Kettle-The Fat Meat Is Boiled In." Some of them were most hideously attired in coats and caps. We had some singular scenes but I must postpone them till we meet. Remember me to Windham, he can give you an idea of the Prairies. I shall write a line to Jocelyn.

A. C.

ALS (National Register of Archives, Scotland—Cathcart Papers).

1. Charles Ashe Windham (1810–70) and six fellow British officers stationed in Canada had come to St. Louis in 1840 and had gone farther west to hunt game and to study the habits of the Indians. Windham later became commander of the forces in Canada (SUNDER).

2. Thomas Fitzpatrick (see Doc. No. 34).

3. Lieut. Noel, referred to in Doc. No. 32.

4. Messrs. Cox & Co. were the agents for the 11th Regiment of Hussars, i.e., held the soldiers' pay for them.

5. Probably founded about 1841, Pratt's was a little club in London, just off St. James' Street (NEVILL, 36).

6. James Thomas Brudenell (1797–1868), the seventh Earl of Cardigan, was the lieutenant colonel of Cathcart's old regiment (HART'S ANNUAL ARMY LIST, 7 [1846]:137). He later took part in the charge of the Light Brigade at Balaclava. The cardigan jacket style was named after him. WOODHAM-SMITH has an account of this ruthless aristocrat and his brother-in-law, George Charles Bingham, the third Earl of Lucan.

34. Frémont to Thomas H. Benton

CAMP AT BENT'S FORT, UPPER ARKANSAS,
November 17, 1848

We have met with very reasonable success and some good results in this first long step in our expedition. To avoid the danger of snowstorms upon the more exposed Arkansas route, I followed the line of the southern Kanzas,[1] (the true Kanzas river), and so far added something to geography.[2] For a distance of four hundred miles, our route led through a country affording abundant wood, game, and excellent grass. We find that the valley of the Kanzas affords by far the most eligible approach to the mountains. The whole valley soil is of very superior quality, and the route very direct (between thirty-eight and thirty-nine degrees). This line would afford continuous and good settlements certainly for four hundred miles, and is therefore worthy of consideration in any plan of approach to the mountains. We found our friend Major [Thomas] Fitzpatrick (United States Indian agent) in the full exercise of his functions, about thirty miles below this point, in what is called the "Big Timbers," and surrounded by about six hundred lodges of different nations—Apaches, Cumanches, Kiowas, and Arapahoes. He is a most admirable agent, and has succeeded in drawing out from among the Cumanches the whole Kiowa nation, with the exception of six lodges, and brought over among them a considerable number of lodges of the Apaches and Cumanches; and in a few years he could have them all farming on the Arkansas. We found him holding a talk with them, making a feast, and giving small presents. They were all on their good behavior, and treated us in a friendly manner, and gave us no annoyance; nor did we lose anything. We were three or four days among them. (The number of their lodges would indicate about six thousand.)[3]

Both Indians and whites here report the snow to be deeper in the mountains than has for a long time been known so early in the season, and they predict a severe winter. This morning, for the first time, the mountains showed themselves covered with snow, as well as the country around us; for it has snowed steadily the greater part of yesterday and the night before. They look imposing and somewhat stern; still I am in nowise discouraged, and believe that we shall succeed in forcing our way across. We will, after crossing the chain before us, ascend the *Rio del Norte* to its head,[4] descend to the Colorado, and across the Wah-satch mountain and the Great Basin country, somewhere near the 37th parallel, and seek a (believed) pass between 37° and 38°, in the Sierra Nevada, which I wish to examine. The party is in good spirits and good health; we have a small store of provisions for hard times, and our instruments, barometer included, all in good order. We are always up an hour or two before light, and the breakfasts are all over, the horses and mules (about one hundred in number) saddled and packed, and the camp preparing to move before sun-rise. This breakfasting before day in the open air, in a cold of from twelve to twenty degrees of freezing, contrasts strongly with home, but is necessary for the day's labor.[5]

Very few of our animals have given out, and the whole band is now in good condition. A new storm—a *pouderie*—overtook us on the 4th, but we were looking out for it, and took care to be in wood, so that did us no harm.* Some men who arrived here from the *Pueblos*, near the *Fontaine qui Bouit*, (Boiling Springs river,) say they have never known the snow so deep in the mountains so early, and that there is every prospect of a severe winter. But this does not deter us. I have my party well prepared, and the men all made as comfortable as possible, and expect to overcome all obstacles.

I was able to procure a good lodge (a conical skin tent, admitting of a fire in the centure, and with a hole at top to let out the smoke) from the Indians, which we put up yesterday for the first time, greatly to the delight of our *compagnon de voyage*, Captain Cathcart,** who is eloquent in its praise for the comfort it secures. It was indeed wanted, for I found it almost impossible to work in a tent. After the fatigue of a day's ride, with the anxieties which winter exploration in an un-known country bring upon me, and with the demand upon one's strength which the mere resistance to cold always makes, it requires an exertion of courage to take astronomical observations, and then calculate them at night, in a linen tent, tired and cold, and make up the notes of the day. These observations and calculations are necessary to our safety, indispensable to our safe advance in a wild unknown country, and the lodge enables us to work with comparative pleasure. Besides my labors, the Kerns have their drawings and paintings to make—Preuss his field sketches to finish. We are all busy now round the fire, writing letters home—Cathcart also. He stands it well, and sends his letters to your care. The men can sleep under linen tents, but the lodge is indispensable to all who have to work.

From this place we continue up the river to the *Pueblos*—seventy and one hundred miles above—where we shall get some supplies, and then bear south to cross the mountain range—a branch of the

---

*Large trains of oxen, returning from the Mexican war, were caught in this storm, and sixteen hundred perished in it.
**An English gentleman—an officer and traveller in India—and now a traveller with Fremont, whom he joined in St. Louis.

Rocky Mountains—which divides the upper Arkansas from the upper Rio del Norte; and, after crossing that, we shall have to cross the mountain chain—the mother chain—Sierra Madre—at the head of the Rio de Norte. A vigorous effort we trust, will carry us over.

Printed in *National Intelligencer*, 26 Feb. 1849. The letter is probably a combination of letters to both Benton and JBF, since the journal labeled its column "Mr. Fremont's Letters—Extracts." The major part of the letter is also published in BIGELOW, 359–60, and in UPHAM, 274–76.

1. This is today's Smoky Hill Fork of the Kansas.

2. By pre-arrangement, a party of Delaware Indians, some of whom had been on JCF's third expedition, had joined them near the Wakarusa on 22 Oct. and guided them to the Smoky Hills. They turned homeward on 31 Oct. (CSmH-Edward M. Kern Diary).

3. In the campaign biographies the paragraph continues: "I hope you will be able to give him some support. He [Fitzpatrick] will be able to save lives and money for the government, and knowing how difficult this Indian question may become, I am particular in bringing Fitzpatrick's operations to your notice. In a few years he might have them all farming here on the Arkansas."

4. Historians have taken this statement to indicate that JCF wished to cross the Continental Divide by way of a pass which they have called Rio del Norte or Williams Pass, not by the better-known passes of Carnero (presently Cochetopa) and Cochetopa (presently North Cochetopa) in the Cochetopa complex.

5. As published by JCF's biographers, the letter does not contain the three paragraphs which follow, but concludes with a personal observation that did not appear in the *Intelligencer*; "I think that I shall never cross the continent again, except at Panama. I do not feel the pleasure that I used to have in those labors, as they remain inseparably connected with painful circumstances, due mostly to them. It needs strong incitements to undergo the hardships and self denial of this kind of life, and as I find I have these no longer, I will drop into a quiet life. Should we have reasonable success, we shall be in California early in January, say about the 8th, where I shall expect to hear from all by the steamer. Referring you for other details to Jessie, to whom I have written at length, I remain, most affectionately yours, J. C. Fremont."

35. Jessie B. Frémont to John Torrey

WASHINGTON CITY—December 8th. 1848

My Dear Sir,

Mr. Frémont left me a list of plants to copy out for you, but until now I have had neither the quiet nor the strength to do it. A few days will bring it to a close, and you may derive fresh interest for examining those from Feather river by reading the accounts of the great wealth of that region. Are there any flowers or plants peculiar to a gold region? One flower, 209, which Mr. Frémont supposes may be the "Cumas" may be belonging to that kind of earth. I have as you know very vague botanical ideas. Your daughter [Margaret] would laugh at me, but Mr. Frémont encourages my questionings and I am a sort of privileged person in the family which must excuse my questioning you also.

By some Indians who are to be sent back from Bent's Fort I shall get letters from Mr. Frémont before the New Year. Then, or at any time you wish to know anything I can inform you of, I hope you will let me have the pleasure of doing so. Father reserves for his part the sending of documents—none of any interest are out yet, but Mr. Frémonts memoir is just coming in from the last session, and shall be sent to you. Very respectfully yours,

JESSIE BENTON FRÉMONT

Dr. John Torrey

ALS (NHi).

36. Frémont to Jessie B. Frémont

[27 Jan.–17 Feb. 1849]
TAOS, NEW MEXICO, January 27, 1849

I write to you from the house of our good friend [Kit] Carson. This morning a cup of chocolate was brought to me, while yet in bed. To an overworn, overworked, fatigued, and starving traveller, these little luxuries of the world offer an interest which, in your comfortable home, it is not possible for you to conceive.[1]

I have now the unpleasant task of telling you how I came here.[2] I had much rather speak of the future (which plans for which I am already occupied), for the mind turns from the scenes I have witnessed and the sufferings we have endured; but as clear information is due you, and to your father still more, I will give you the story now, instead of waiting to tell it to you in California; but I write in the great hope that you will not receive this letter. When it reaches Washington you may be on your way to California.

Former letters will have made you acquainted with our progress as far as Bent's Fort, and, from report, you will have heard the circumstances of our departure from the *Upper Pueblo* [the Hardscrabble settlement], near the head of the Arkansas. We left that place on the 25th of November with upwards of one hundred good mules and one hundred and thirty bushels of [shelled] corn, intended to support our animals in the deep snows of the high mountains and down to the lower parts of the Grand river * tributaries, where usually the snow forms no obstacle to winter travelling At *Pueblo* I had engaged as a guide an old trapper, well known as "*Bill Williams*," and who had spent some twenty-five years of his life in trapping in various parts of the Rocky Mountains.

The error of our expedition was committed in engaging this man. He proved never to have known, or entirely to have forgotten, the whole country through which we were to pass. We occupied (after passing the mountain) more than half a month in making the progress of a few days, blundering along a tortuous course, through deep snow, which already began to choke up the passes, and wasting our time in searching the way. The 11th of December we found ourselves at the mouth of the *Rio del Norte* cañon,[3] where that river issues from the *Sierra San Juan*—one of the highest, most rugged, and impracticable of all the Rocky Mountain ranges, inaccessible to trappers and hunters, even in summer. Across the point of this elevated range our guide conducted us; and, having still great confidence in this man's knowledge, we pressed onwards with fatal resolution. Even among the river bottoms the snow was already breast deep for the mules, and falling frequently in the valley and almost constantly in the mountains. The cold was extraordinary. At the warmest hours of the day (between one and two) the thermometer (Fahrenheit) stood, in the shade of a tree trunk, at *zero*; and that was a favorable day, the sun shining and a moderate breeze. Judge of the nights and the storms!

We pressed up towards the summit, the snow deepening as we rose, and in four or five days of this struggling and climbing, all on foot, we reached the naked ridges which lie above the line of the timbered region, and which form the dividing heights between the waters of the Atlantic and Pacific oceans. Along these naked heights it storms all winter and the raging winds sweep across them with remorseless fury. On our first attempt to cross we encountered a *pouderie*—(dry snow driven thick through the air by violent wind, and in which objects are visible only at a short distance)—and were driven

---

* A fork of the Colorado of the Gulf of California.

back, having some ten or twelve men variously frozen—face, hands, or feet. The guide came near being frozen to death here, and dead mules were already lying about the camp fires. Meantime it snowed steadily. The next day (December—)[4] we renewed the attempt to scale the summit, and were more fortunate, as it then seemed. Making mauls, and beating down a road, or trench, through the deep snow, we forced the ascent in defiance of the driving *pouderie*, crossed the crest, descended a little, and encamped immediately below in the edge of the timbered region. The trail showed as if a defeated party had passed by—packs, pack saddles, scattered articles of clothing, and dead mules strewed along. We were encamped about twelve thousand feet above the level of the sea. Westward the country was buried in snow. The storm continued. All movement was paralyzed. To advance with the expedition was impossible: to get back, impossible. Our fate stood revealed. We were overtaken by sudden and inevitable ruin. The poor animals were to go first. The only places where grass could be had were the extreme summits of the *sierra*, where the sweeping winds kept the rocky ground bare, and where the men could not live. Below, in the timbered region, the poor animals could not get about, the snow being deep enough to bury them alive. It was instantly apparent that we should lose every one. I took my resolution immediately, and determined to recross the mountain back to the valley of the *Rio del Norte*, dragging or packing the baggage by men. With great labor the baggage was transported across the crest to the head springs of a little stream leading to the main river.[5] A few days were sufficient to destroy the fine band of mules which you saw me purchase last fall on the frontier of Missouri. They generally kept huddled together; and, as they froze, one would be seen to tumble down and disappear under the driving snow. Sometimes they would break off, and rush down towards the timber till stopped by the deep snow, where they were soon hidden by the *pouderie*.[6] The courage of some of the men began to fail.

In this situation I determined to send in a party to the Spanish settlements of New Mexico for provisions, and for mules to transport our baggage. With economy, and after we should leave the mules, we had not two weeks' provisions in the camp; and these consisted of a reserve of maccaroni, bacon, sugar, &c., intended for the last extremity. It was indispensable to send for relief. I asked for volunteers for the service. From the many that offered I chose King, Brackenridge, Creutzfeldt, and the guide, Williams; and placed the party under the command of King, with directions to send me an express in case of the least delay at the settlements. It was the day after Christmas that this little party set out for relief.[7] That day, like many Christmas days for years past, was spent by me on the side of the wintry mountain, my heart filled with anxious thoughts and gloomy forebodings. You may be sure we contrasted it with the Christmas of home, and made warm wishes for your happiness. Could you have looked into Agrippa's glass for a few moments only! You remember the volumes of Blackstone's Commentaries which I took from your father's library when we were overlooking it at our friend Brant's?[8] They made my Christmas *"amusements."* I read them to pass the time, and to kill the consciousness of my situation. Certainly you may suppose that my first law lessons will be well remembered.

The party for relief being gone, we of the camp occupied ourselves in removing the baggage and equipage down the side of the mountain to the river in the valley. Now came on the *tedium* of waiting for the return of the relief party. Day after day passed, and no news from them. Snow fell almost incessantly in the mountains. The spirits of the camp grew lower. Life was losing its charm to those who had not reasons beyond themselves to live. Proue laid down in the trail and froze to death. In a sunshiny day, and having with him the means to make a fire, he threw his blanket down on the trail, laid down upon it, and laid there till he froze to death! We were not then with him.

Sixteen days passed away, and no tidings from the party sent for relief. I became oppressed with anxiety, weary of delay, and determined to go myself, both in search of the absent party, and in search of relief in the Mexican settlements. I was aware that our troops in New Mexico had been engaged in hostilities with the Spanish Utahs, and with the Apaches, who range in the valley of the *Rio del Norte* and the mountains where we were, and became fearful that they (King and his party) had been cut off by these Indians. I could imagine no other accident to them. Leaving the camp employed with the baggage, under the command of Vincenthaler, with injunctions to follow me in three days, I set off down the river with a small party, consisting of Godey, his young nephew, Preuss, and Saunders (colored servant).[9] We carried our arms and provisions for two or three days. In the camp (left under the command of Vincenthaler) the messes only had provisions for a few meals, and a supply of five pounds of sugar to each man. If I failed to meet King my intention was to make the Mexican settlement on the *Colorado*, a little affluent of the *Rio del Norte*, about half a degree above Taos (you will see it on my map), and then send back the speediest relief possible to the party under Vincenthaler.[10]

On the second day after leaving camp we came upon a fresh trail of Indians—two lodges, with a considerable number of animals. This did not lessen our uneasiness for our long-absent people. The Indian trail, where we fell upon it, turned and went down the river, and we followed it. On the fifth day (after leaving camp) we surprised an Indian on the ice of the river. He proved to be a Utah, son of a Grand River chief whom we had formerly known, and he behaved towards us in a friendly manner. We encamped near them at night. By a present of a rifle, my two blankets, and other promised rewards when we should get in, I prevailed on this Indian to go with us as a guide to the Little Rio Colorado settlement, and to take with him four of his horses to carry our little baggage. The horses were miserably poor, and could only get along at a slow walk. On the next day (the sixth of our progress) we left the Indians lodges late and travelled only some six or seven miles. About sunset we discovered a little smoke, in a grove of timber, off from the river, and, thinking perhaps it might be our express party (King and his men) on their return, we went to see. This was the twenty-second day since that party had left us, and the sixth since we have left the camp under Vincenthaler. We found them—three of them: Creutzfelt, Brackenridge, and Williams—the most miserable objects I had ever beheld. I did not recognize Creutzfelt's features, when Brackenridge brought him up and told me his name. They had been starving! King had starved to death a few days before. His remains were some six or eight miles above, near the river.[11] By aid of the Indian horses we carried these three with us, down to the valley, to the *Pueblo* on the Little Colorado, which we reached the fourth day afterwards (the tenth after leaving the camp on the mountains), having travelled through snow, and on foot, one hundred and sixty miles.[12]

I looked upon the feeling which induced me to set out from the camp as an inspiration. Had I remained there, waiting the return of poor King's party, every man of us must have perished.

The morning after reaching the Little Colorado *Pueblo* (horses and supplies not being there), Godey and I rode on to the *Rio Hondo*, and thence to Taos, about twenty-five miles, where we found what we needed; and the next morning Godey, with four Mexicans, thirty horses or mules, and provisions, set out on his return to the relief of

Vincenthaler's party. I heard from him at the Little Colorado Pueblo, which he reached the same day he left me, and pressed on the next morning. On the way he received an accession of eight or ten horses, turned over to him by the orders of Major [Benjamin L.] Beall, of the army, commanding officer of this northern district of New Mexico. From him I received the offer of every aid in his power, and such actual assistance as he was able to render. Some horses, which he had just recovered from the Utahs, were loaned to me, and he supplied me from the commissary's department with provisions, which I could have had nowhere else.[13] I find myself in the midst of friends. With Carson is living [Richard] Owens. [Lucien B.] Maxwell is at his father-in-law's, doing a prosperous business as a merchant and contractor for the troops. I remain here with these old comrades, while Godey goes back; because it was not necessary for me to go with him, and it was necessary for me to remain, and prepare the means of resuming the expedition to California as soon as he returns with the men left behind. I expect him on Wednesday evening, the 31st instant, this being the 17th [27th].

Say to your father that these are my plans for the future:

At the beginning of February (Godey having got back at that time) I shall set out for California, taking the southern route—the old route—by the *Rio Abajo*, the *Paso del Norte*, the south side of the *Gila*, entering California by the *Agua Caliente*, thence to *Los Angeles* and immediately to San Francisco, expecting to get there in March, and hoping for your arrival in April. It is the first time I have *explored* an old road,[14] but cannot help it now. I shall move rapidly taking with me but a part of my party.[15] *The survey* * * *has been uninterrupted up to this point, and I shall carry it on consecutively.* As soon as possible after reaching California I shall go on with it [i.e., the survey of the coast country]. I shall then be able to draw up a map and report of the whole country, agreeably to our original plan. Your father knows that this is an object of great desire with me.[16] *All my other plans remain entirely unaltered.* A home in California is the first point, and that will be ready for you in April.

Evening—Mr. [Ceran] St. Vrain and Aubrey, who have just arrived from Sante Fe, called to see me.[17] I had the gratification to learn that St. Vrain sets out from Santa Fe on the 15th of February for St.

* * With a view, among other great objects, to the Mississippi and Pacific highway.

Louis; so that by him I shall have an early and sure opportunity of sending you my letters—the one I now write, and others after the return of Godey, and up to our departure for California. Lieut. Beale left Santa Fe on his way to California on the 9th of this month. He probably carried on with him any letters that might have been in his care, or at Santa Fe, for me.[18]

Monday, January 29.—My letter assumes a journal form. No news from Godey. A great deal of falling weather—rain and sleet here—snow in the mountains. This is to be considered a poor country, mountainous, with but little arable land, and infested with hostile Indians.[19]

I am anxiously waiting to hear from my party, and in much uneasiness as to their fate. My presence kept them together and quiet: my absence may have had a bad affect. When we overtook King's famishing party, Brackenridge said to me '*He felt himself safe.*'

Taos, New Mexico, February 6, 1849

After a long delay, which had wearied me to a point of resolving to set out again myself, tidings have at last reached me from my ill-fated party.

Mr. Vincent Haler came in last night, having the night before reached the Little Colorado settlement, with three or four others. Including Mr. King and Mr. Proulx [Proue], we have lost eleven of our party.[20]

Occurrences, since I left them, are briefly these, so far as they came within the knowledge of Mr. Haler: I say briefly, because I am now unwilling to force my mind to dwell upon the details of what has been suffered. I need reprieve from terrible contemplations. I am absolutely astonished at this persistence of misfortune—this succession of calamities which no care or vigilance of mine could foresee or prevent.

You will remember that I had left the camp (twenty-three men) [twenty-four] when I set off with Godey, [Godey's nephew], Preuss, and my servant in search of King and succor, with directions about the baggage, and with occupation sufficient about it to employ them for three or four days; after which they were to follow me down the river. Within that time I expected relief from King's party, if it came at all. They remained seven days, and then started, their scant provisions about exhausted, and the dead mules on the western side of the great *Sierra* buried under snow.

Manuel—(you will remember Manuel—a Christian Indian of the Cosumne tribe, in the valley of the San Joaquin)—gave way to a feeling of despair after they had moved about two miles and begged Vincent Haler, whom I had left in command, to shoot him. Failing to find death in that form, he turned and made his way back to the camp, intending to die there; which he doubtless soon did.

The party moved on, and at ten miles Wise gave out—threw away his gun and blanket—and, a few hundred yards further, fell over into the snow, and died. Two Indian boys—countrymen of Manuel— were behind. They came upon him—rolled him up in his blanket, and buried him in the snow, on the bank of the river.

No other died that day. None the next.

Carver raved during the night—his imagination wholly occupied with images of many things which he fancied himself to be eating. In the morning he wandered off, and probably soon died. He was not seen again.

Sorel on this day (the fourth from the camp) laid down to die. They built him a fire, and Morin, who was in a dying condition, and snow-blind, remained with him.[21] These two did not probably last till the next morning. That evening (I think it was) Hubbard killed a deer.

They travelled on, getting here and there a grouse, but nothing else, the deep snow in the valley having driven off the game.

The state of the party became desperate, and brought Haler to the determination of breaking it up, in order to prevent them from living upon each other. He told them that he had done all he could for them—that they had no other hope remaining than the expected relief—and that the best plan was to scatter, and make the best of their way, each as he could, down the river; that, for himself, if he was to be eaten, he would, at all events be found travelling when he did die. This address had its effect. They accordingly separated.

With Haler continued five others—Scott, Hubbard, Martin, Bacon, one [two] other[s] [Ducatel and Rohrer], and the two Cosumne Indian boys.[22]

Rohrer now became despondent, and stopped. Haler reminded him of his family, and urged him to try and hold out for their sake. Roused by this appeal to his tenderest affections, the unfortunate man moved forward, but feebly, and soon began to fall behind. On a further appeal he promised to follow, and to overtake them at evening.

Haler, Scott, Hubbard, and Martin now agreed that if any one of them should give out the others were not to wait for him to die, but to push on, and try and save themselves. Soon this mournful covenant had to be kept. But let me not anticipate events. Sufficient for each day is the sorrow thereof.

At night Kerne's party encamped a few hundred yards from Haler's, with the intention, according to Taplin, to remain where they were until the relief should come, and in the mean time to live upon those who had died, and upon the weaker ones as they should die. With this party were the three brothers Kerne, Captain Cathcart, McKie [McGehee], Andrews, Stepperfelt, and Taplin. I do not know that I have got all the names of this party.[23]

Ferguson and Beadle had remained together behind. In the evening Rohrer came up and remained in Kerne's party. Haler, learnt afterwards from some of the party that Rohrer and Andrews wandered off the next morning and died. They say they saw their bodies.

Haler's party continued on. After a few hours Hubbard gave out. According to the agreement he was left to die, but with such comfort as could be given him. They built him a fire and gathered him some wood, and then left him—without turning their heads, as Haler says, to look at him as they went off.

About two miles further Scott—you remember him; he used to shoot birds for you on the frontier—he gave out. He was another of the four who had covenanted against waiting for each other. The survivors did to him as they had done for Hubbard, and passed on.

In the afternoon the two Indian boys went ahead—blessed be these boys!—and before nightfall met Godey with the relief. He had gone on with all speed. The boys gave him the news. He fired signal guns to notify his approach. Haler heard the guns, and knew the crack of our rifles, and felt that relief had come. This night was the first of hope and joy. Early in the morning, with the first gray light, Godey was in the trail, and soon met Haler and the wreck of his party slowly advancing. I hear that they all cried together like children—these men of iron nerves and lion hearts, when dangers were to be faced or hardships to be conquered. They were all children in this moment of melted hearts. Succor was soon dealt out to these few first met; and Godey with his relief, and accompanied by Haler, who turned back hurriedly followed the back trail in search of the living and the dead, scattered in the rear. They came to Scott first. He was yet alive, and is saved! They came to Hubbard next: he was dead, but still warm. These were the only ones of Haler's party that had been left.

From Kerne's party, next met, they learnt the deaths of Andrews and Rohrer; and, a little further on, met Ferguson, who told them that Beadle had died the night before. All the living were found—and saved—Manuel among them—which looked like a resurrection—and reduced the number of the dead to ten—one-third of the whole party which a few days before were scaling the mountain with me, and battling with the elements twelve thousand feet in the air.

Godey had accomplished his mission for the people: a further service had been prescribed him, that of going to the camp on the river, at the base of the great mountain, to recover the most valuable of the baggage, secreted there. With some Mexicans and pack mules he went on; and this is the last yet heard of him.[24]

Vincent Haler, with Martin and Bacon, all on foot, and bringing Scott on horseback, have just arrived at the outside *Pueblo* on the Little Colorado. Provisions for their support, and horses for their transport, were left for the others, who preferred to remain where they were, regaining some strength, till Godey should get back. At the latest, they would have reached the little *Pueblo* last night. Haler came on to relieve my anxieties, and did well in so doing; for I was wound up to the point of setting out again. When Godey returns I shall know from him all the circumstances sufficiently in detail to understand clearly every thing. But it will not be necessary to tell you any thing further. You have the results, and sorrow enough in reading them.

Evening[25]—How rapid are the changes of life! A few days ago, and I was struggling through snow in the savage wilds of the upper Del Norte—following the course of the frozen river in more than Russian cold—no food—no blanket to cover me in the long freezing nights—(I had sold my two to the *Utah* for help to my men)—uncertain at what moment of the night we might be roused by the Indian rifle—doubtful, very doubtful, whether I should ever see you or friends again. Now I am seated by a comfortable fire, alone—pursuing my own thoughts—writing to you in the certainty of reaching you—a French volume of Balzac on the table—a colored print of the landing of Columbus before me—listening in safety to the raging storm without!

You will wish to know what effect the scenes I have passed through have had upon me. In person, none. The destruction of my party, and the loss of friends, are causes of grief; but I have not been injured in body or mind. Both have been strained, and severely taxed, but neither hurt. I have seen one or the other, and sometimes both, give way in strong frames, strong minds, and stout hearts; but, as heretofore, I have come out unhurt. I believe that the rememberance of friends sometimes gives us a power of resistance which the desire to save our own lives could never call up.

I have made my preparations to proceed. I shall have to follow the old Gila road, and shall move rapidly, and expect to be in California in March, and to find letters from home, and a supply of newspapers and documents, more welcome perhaps, because these things have a home look about them. The future occupies me. Our home in California—your arrival in April—your good health in that delightful climate—the finishing up my geographical and astronomical labors—my farming labors and enjoyments. I have written to Messrs. Mayhew & Co., agricultural warehouse, New York, requesting them to ship me immediately a threshing machine; and to Messrs. Hoe & Co., same city, requesting them to forward to me at San Francisco two runs, or sets of mill stones. The mill irons and the agricultural instruments shipped for me last autumn from New York will be at San Francisco by the time I arrive there. Your arrival in April will complete all the plans.

[These extracts in relation to Colonel Fremont's intended pursuits are given to contradict the unfounded supposition of gold projects attributed to him by some newspapers. The word gold is not mentioned in his letters from one end to the other, nor did he take gold mining the least into his calculation when he left Missouri on the 21st of October last, although the authentic reports brought in by Lieut. Beale, of the navy, were then in all the newspapers, and fully known to him.][26]

February 11.—Godey has got back. He did not succeed in recovering any of the baggage or camp furniture. Everything was lost except some few things which I had brought down to the river. The depth of the snow made it impossible for him to reach the camp at the mountain where the men had left the baggage. Amidst the wreck I had the good fortune to save my large *alforgas*, or travelling trunk—the double one which you packed—and that was about all.

Sante Fe, February 17, 1849.—In the midst of hurried movements, and in the difficult endeavor to get a *party* all started together, I can only write a line to say that I am well, and moving on to California. I *will* leave Santa Fe this evening.

I have received here from the officers every civility and attention in their power, and have been assisted in my outfit as far as it was possible for them to do. I dine this evening with the Governor, (Col. Washington) before I follow my party.[27] A Spanish gentleman has been engaged to go to *Albuquerque* and purchase mules for me. From that place we go on my own animals, and expect no detention, as we follow the old Gila route, so long known, and presenting nothing new to stop for.

Printed in *National Intelligencer*, 14 and 16 April 1849. The letter presented here is made up of a series of excerpts from a number of letters written from Taos and Santa Fe by JCF and addressed to JBF in Washington, and in her absence to Senator Benton, and in his absence to William Carey Jones. JBF was on her way to California, but Benton showed the originals to the editors of the *National Intelligencer*, who published excerpts in order of their dates. The letters had been carried to St. Louis by Ceran St. Vrain and forwarded on to Washington.

BIGELOW, 365–76, and UPHAM, 279–96, print a slightly different version of the letter or letters. Significant differences are noted in the footnotes below.

1. In BIGELOW, 366, and UPHAM, 279, the paragraph continues: "While in the enjoyment of this luxury, then, I pleased myself in imagining how gratified you will be in picturing me here in Kit's care, whom you will fancy constantly occupied and constantly uneasy in endeavoring to make me comfortable. How little could you have dreamed of this while he was enjoying the pleasant hospitality of your father's house. The furthest thing then from your mind was that he would ever repay it to me here."

2. BIGELOW, 366, and UPHAM, 279–80, continue: "I had much rather write you some rambling letters in unison with the repose in which I feel inclined to indulge, and talk to you about the future with which I am already busily occupied; about my arrangements for getting speedily down into the more pleasant climate of the lower Del Norte and rapidly through into California; and my plans when I get there. I have an almost invincible repugnance to going back among scenes where I have endured much suffering, and for all the incidents and circumstances of which I feel a strong aversion. But as clear information is absolutely necessary to you, and to your father more particularly still, I will give you the story now instead of waiting to tell it to you in California. But I write in the great hope that you will not receive the letter. When it reaches Washington you may be on your way to California."

3. In BIGELOW, 367, and UPHAM, 281, the clause reads: "About the 11th December we found ourselves at the North of the Del Norte Cañon." This is undoubtedly the correct rendering and places JCF on Carnero Creek. Specifics of the movements of the expedition in the mountains are given in the notes to Doc. No. 39.

4. December 17 according to Benjamin Kern (Diary, CSmH). JCF thought he had crossed the Continental Divide and that his party had been on the Colorado River drainage. This had not been true. The men had merely crossed to the headwaters of Wannamaker Creek, a tributary of the Saquache, and had re-

mained in the Rio Grande watershed. Wannamaker Creek would have eventually led into Carnero Pass. When Patrica Joy Richmond visited the Wannamaker site in 1981 she walked the ridge toward the west "and suddenly was struck by the practicality of that as a summer route to the Coochatope" (Richmond to Mary Lee Spence, 17 Jan. 1983).

5. The expedition had established a camp in the protection of trees on the west slope of Rincones Creek, about three and a half miles from the Wannamaker Creek camp. The new base was sometimes called Christmas Camp or Camp Hope.

6. As printed in BIGELOW and UPHAM the letter continues: "The courage of the men failed fast; in fact, I have never seen men so soon discouraged by misfortune as we were on this occasion; but, as you know, the party was not constituted like the former ones. But among those who deserve to be honorably mentioned and who behaved like what they were—men of the old exploring party,—were Godey, King, and Taplin; and first of all Godey."

7. According to Preuss, their destination was Abiquiu, about one hundred miles away at Rio Chama. King was supplied with money and "everything was thoroughly discussed until late in the night" (PREUSS, 146, 27 Dec. entry). Godey went a short way with them to ascertain how the main party could get down from the mountains with the baggage.

It took the relief party three days to reach the Rio Grande, which they followed out into the plains of the San Luis Valley. Then, at the point where the river makes a great bend to the south, they struck off across the country, possibly to save mileage or possibly to avoid a camp of Ute Indians, whose enmity Williams had recently incurred (see BRECKENRIDGE [1] and [2]). Later, Thomas S. Martin remembered hearing that Williams had left the river to attempt to reach a small settlement on the Conejos River called Socorro (MARTIN), although it is doubtful that this little Mexican town still existed in 1849. If so, help would have been nearer than Abiquiu. Whatever the motive for the shortcut, the party suffered "all the agonies of Hell," and King never made it to the Rio Grande.

8. Joshua B. Brant, the husband of Jessie's cousin, Sarah Benton of St. Louis.

9. The entire party might have been saved had JCF abandoned the baggage at this time, 11 Jan., and taken all the men with him.

10. In place of this sentence ending the paragraph, BIGELOW and UPHAM print: "Failing to meet King, my intention was to make the Red River settlement about twenty-five miles north of Taos, and send back the speediest relief possible. My instructions to the camp were, that if they did not hear from me within a stated time, they were to follow down the Del Norte."

11. JCF does not write that Creutzfeldt, Breckenridge, and Williams had eaten part of King's body. Nor does he indicate that he and members of his party actually saw the body, but Preuss recorded: "King had died of exhaustion four days before, and the others had eaten part of his body" (PREUSS, 149, [17? Jan.] entry). And at the little Red River settlement of Questa, awaiting the results of Godey's rescue efforts, Preuss noted, "Yesterday there was a rumor that a Utah Indian had seen a man wandering through the prairie with two human legs on his back. After what I have experienced, I am inclined to believe this." When Vinsonhaler's party got in with news of the others, Preuss recorded: "Human flesh, to be sure, was not eaten again as far as I could learn" (PREUSS, 151–52, 3 and 6 Feb. entries). Very early, 2 Feb. 1849, before the arrival of Vinsonhaler's advance party at Questa, the Santa Fe *Republican* reported cannibalism among the party. Presumably their correspondent at Taos had received the information

from JCF (reprinted in HAFEN & HAFEN, 237–38). Benjamin Kern wrote that a member of the first rescue party "was all eaten by the others," and Taplin reported in St. Louis that King's companions had eaten his body. "A dire necessity had left them no choice, and it was done in self protection" (Benjamin Kern to Joe, 20 Feb. 1849, CSmH; Charles Taplin's report in Saint Louis *Weekly Reveille*, 30 April 1849, reprinted in HAFEN & HAFEN, 195–97). Kern's and Taplin's information could only have come second hand. Breckenridge ignores the charge in both his versions of the story (BRECKENRIDGE [1] and [2]). Thomas Martin stated from hearsay not only that King's companions had eaten part of his body but also that there had been cannibalism among the Kern-McGehee party (MARTIN). For a discussion of his charge, see n. 22 below.

12. In old age, Breckenridge maintained that JCF had left him, Williams, and Creutzfeldt to make the fifty-mile trip to Questa as best they could. This was not true. Preuss and Edward Kern confirm JCF's statement that he picked them up on the way down (PREUSS, 150, 23 Jan. entry; E. M. Kern to Mary Wolfe Kern, 10 Feb. 1849, CSmH).

13. As early as 19 March 1849, Richard Kern charged that the provisions had not been turned over to the men (Doc. No. 39). The charge was resurrected during the presidential campaign of 1856 and answered in a letter over Godey's signature. With reference to the regrouping for California, he stated: "Our party was at once formed, and started down towards Albuquerque, at which place, some 200 miles south of Taos, we for the first time were enabled to procure military stores, showing the looseness of the assertion made by Kern that Frémont obtained rations for his party (from the Carnero Pass), which he appropriated to his own use. He neither procured, nor was he provided with any rations at Taos, nor, after he left that place, and until he had made some two hundred miles on the route to California, did he have an opportunity of obtaining any, and these were furnished by myself, with funds furnished by him for the use and purposes of the trip to California. Thus much for the ration business.

"The supplies which were sent back to the Carnero Pass were purchased by me, with moneys furnished by Col. Fremont, and the Messrs. Kern freely participated in them, and alike with the others were amply cared for upon their arrival in Taos" (Godey to John O. Wheeler, 12 Sept. 1856, as printed in the New York *Evening Post*, 30 Oct. 1856, and republished in HAFEN & HAFEN, 263–75).

In view of JCF's letter and of two documents found among the Fort Sutter Papers (CSmH), not all of Godey's statement is convincing. In February Henry Casey of the commissary at Taos furnished the starving men "580 lbs. of bacon, 850 lbs. of flour, 75 lbs. of rice, 50 lbs. of coffee, 100 lbs. of sugar, 35 lbs. of soap, 8 lbs. of candles, and 15 qrts. of salt." On 28 March 1849 Major Beall certified, probably truthfully but undoubtedly at the request of the Kerns, who were collecting anti-Frémont ammunition, that they had been supplied on his order and with no charge to JCF. He added, "These provisions were not furnished for individual *benefit*, but for the whole party." In a "return," dated 11 Feb. 1849, Casey lists a smaller quantity of supplies that JCF purchased from the commissary "for the purpose of rationing his men to California." Undoubtedly, the men who went on to California took their rations with them, leaving the six "drop-outs" meager pickings and certainly not enough to last thirty days.

14. JCF's reference to exploring an "old road" does not appear in BIGELOW and UPHAM.

15. In BIGELOW and UPHAM the sentence reads: "I shall break up my party here and take with me only a few men."

16. In BIGELOW and UPHAM the sentence continues, "and I trust it is not too much to hope that he may obtain the countenance and aid of the President (whoever he may be) in carrying it on effectually and rapidly to completion. For this I hope earnestly."

17. In BIGELOW and UPHAM the reference to the visit of St. Vrain and Aubry appears before JCF outlines his California plans. François Xavier Aubry (1824–54) was a prominent southwestern trader and explorer. In 1852 he began driving New Mexican sheep to the California market, but this activity was cut short by Richard H. Weightman, who during an argument stabbed him fatally with a bowie knife (BIEBER, 38–62).

18. See Doc. No. 61, n. 3.

19. Between here and the final paragraph of the 29 Jan. entry, BIGELOW and UPHAM print: "To hold this country will occasion the government great expense, and, certainly, one can see no source of profit or advantage in it. An additional regiment will be required for special service here.

"Mr. St. Vrain dined with us today. Owens goes to Missouri in April to get married, and thence by water to California. Carson is very anxious to go there with me now, and afterwards move his family thither, but he cannot decide to break off from Maxwell and family connections."

20. Ten died on the expedition. Vinsonhaler, who brought JCF the first news, did not know of Manuel's rescue by Godey.

21. According to Taplin, Morin had wandered around in search of game, and then finally "followed in the footsteps of Col. Fremont, with a desperate hope of overtaking him" (Taplin's report in Saint Louis *Weekly Reveille*, 30 April 1849, reprinted in HAFEN & HAFEN, 195–97).

22. In a sentence he has marked through, as though he wished to delete it, McGehee records that Joaquin and Gregorio "had left the mess that they were in [the Kern-McGehee mess], for fear, as they said, that certain men in it would kill them to eat when it came to the worst" (MC GEHEE [1], 119).

It could be that Vinsonhaler's remarks about breaking up the party so as to prevent them from living upon each other, if indeed he did make them, had instilled a general suspicion and fear in the Indian boys—aimed at no one in particular—but causing them to conclude that their greater safety lay with the man who had made them. After his rescue Benjamin Kern charged that "the stronger party [Vinsonhaler's] containing the hunters enticed away our two Indian boys and deserted us" (B. Kern to Joe, 20 Feb. 1849, CSmH). And Edward Kern wrote to his sister: "The strongest and most experienced men went ahead, leaving the weaker ones to get along as they could" (E. M. Kern to Mary Kern Wolfe, 10 Feb. 1849, CSmH). Richard Kern had condemned Vinsonhaler's breaking up of the party as "a piece of rascality almost without parallel" (Diary, 21 Jan. 1849, CSmH).

BRANDON, 262–63, concludes that Vinsonhaler alleged "cannibalistic intent" against the Kern-McGehee party in order to justify to JCF his own callous and cowardly conduct in abandoning the weaker members of the party. Undoubtedly Edward Kern had Vinsonhaler and his accusation in mind when he wrote to his sister about JCF's weaknesses, one of them being his propensity to believe "lies carried to him by others prejudicial to us. Another amiable weakness he has, that of believing the reports of the meanest in his camp" (E. M. Kern to Mary Kern Wolfe, Feb. 1849, CSmH).

23. Micajah McGehee wrote that a member of his group had suggested to him, Taplin, and Stepperfeldt that they sustain life by eating the dead Andrews, but the proposition was rejected. Rohrer had joined them, but as he was dying,

the suggestion must have been made by Cathcart or one of the Kern brothers (MC GEHEE [1], 123–24).

24. This paragraph is obviously Benton's summary of a portion of the letter.

25. The balance of the letter or letters, as printed in BIGELOW and UPHAM, is quite different, although many of the same ideas are embodied in it and a few of the sentences are the same. The 1856 version reads:

"As I told you, I shall break up my party here. I have engaged a Spaniard to furnish mules to take my little party with our baggage, as far down the Del Norte as Albuquerque. To-morrow a friend sets out to purchase me a few mules, with which he is to meet me at Albuquerque, and thence I continue the journey on my own animals. My road will take me down the Del Norte, about 160 miles below Albuquerque and then passes between this river and the heads of the Gila, to a little Mexican town called, I think, Tusson [Tucson]. Then to the mouth of the Gila and across the Colorado, direct to Agua Caliente, into California. I intend to make the journey rapidly, and about the middle of March; hope for the great pleasure of hearing from home. I look for a large supply of newspapers and documents, more perhaps because these things have a home look about them than on their own account. When I think of you all, I feel a warm glow at my heart which renovates it like a good medicine, and I forget painful feelings in strong hope for the future. We shall yet, dearest wife, enjoy quiet and happiness together—these are nearly one and the same to me now. I make frequently pleasant pictures of the happy home we are to have, and oftenest and among the pleasantest of all I see, our library with its bright fire in the rainy stormy days, and the large windows looking out upon the sea in the bright weather. I have it all planned in my own mind. It is getting late now, La Harpe says that there are two gods which are very dear to us, Hope and Sleep. My homage shall be equally divided between them: both make the time pass lightly until I see you. So I go now to pay a willing tribute to one with my heart full of the other."

The Frémonts' correspondence with Charles Upham reveal that the original letter did contain Jean Françoise De La Harpe's dictum about the two gods of "Hope and Sleep," but that they were expressed in French. It is impossible to determine whether Benton's 1849 renderings of the letters or the 1856 printings are the most authentic. If the latter, then JCF's reference to the orders for agricultural implements was a Benton creation. On the other hand, when JCF returned galley proof to his biographer, he wrote: "But this portion, comprising my own original letter [the 1849 letter from New Mexico] and the Senatorial Chapter I had sound reasons for reading and correcting, & I hope nothing will prevent the corrections being made" (JCF to Charles Upham, New York, 24 June 1856, Hugh Upham Clark Collection, Arlington, Va.).

26. This seems to be a Benton editorial.

27. Lieut. Col. John M. Washington (1797–1853) was also the military commander of New Mexico, and it was during his administration that a campaign against the Navajos was undertaken (CULLUM, 1:178; TWITCHELL, 2:263, 266, 268).

37. Andrew Cathcart to C. J. Colville

Taos, New Mexico
Feby. 10th 1849

Dear Colville,

After enduring frightful misery since the 16th Decr. I reached this today, one of the survivors of Fremont's ill-starred expedition. We lost all our animals (101 mules) in the deep snow and lofty mountains, 200 miles N.W. of this—and after living for sometime on their carcases and no relief which we had sent for arriving, the last party, 22 in number,[1] left the camp on the "Rio del Norte" (which we had reached down to) on the 16th Jany., then starving, and moved down the river; ten of us perished by the 24th of the most horrible of all deaths— starvation. What agonies I endured and witnessed, but God's mercy carried me through, while stronger men died. I was determined not to give in till the last and thank God my mental energy never failed. I am a perfect skeleton, snowblind, frostbitten and hardly able to stand, but rest will recruit me, when I shall as soon as able return across the Prairies to the States and thence home. How happy I shall be to see you, my dear boy, again. You were often present to my mind, I assure you, during my miseries. I *saved* the Shakespeare you *gave me* and to the last carried my rifle and one blanket—conceive such a covering with the Therm. below Zero in many feet of snow, which we lived in for two months. God bless you, my dear fellow. Ever your attached friend,

A. Cathcart

P.S. I will write details soon, this goes by any opportunity which offers tomorrow. My love to [erased]. What would they say to living on *hide* ropes and leather for weeks, and then no *food* for days. We all scattered when going down the river and some of the survivors fed on dead bodies of comrades. I saw some awful scenes. This is a disgraceful scrawl, I wanted to tell you I was still alive.

ALS (National Register of Archives, Scotland). Addressed "to Captain C. J. Colville, St. James Street, London (By British Steamer)." The letter with minor changes was printed in the London *Times*, 3 May 1849.
1. He apparently considers Manuel (as well as Proue) to be dead.

38. Frémont to Thomas H. Benton

SOCORRO, RIO DEL NORTE, February 24, 1849

MY DEAR SIR:

I write a line from this place in the hope that by way of Chihuahua and Vera Cruz, it will reach you sooner than letters by the direct mail from Santa Fé, and so be in advance of exaggerated reports of the events which have delayed my journey, and turned me in this direction. Letters which I have forwarded by Mr. St. Vrain, will inform you that we were overtaken and surrounded by deep and impracticable snows in the Rocky Mountains at the head of the Del Norte. We lost all our animals and ten men, the mules frozen, and the men starved to death, Proue only excepted. He was frozen. The miscarriage of an express party, sent in under Mr. King, was a secondary cause of our greatest calamity in the loss of our men. In six days after leaving my camp in the mountains, I overtook his party, they having been out twenty-two days, and King having been starved to death. In four days afterwards I reached the settlements, in time to save many, but too late to rescue all the men. Relief was immediately sent back, but did not meet them in time to save all. An attempt, made with fresh animals, to get our baggage out of the snow, failed entirely, resulting only in the loss of ten or twelve animals more.[1] On the main river bottoms at the foot of the mountains, the snow was five feet deep, and in the mountains impassable. Camp furniture of all descriptions, saddles, pack-saddles, &c., clothes, money, &c. all lost. I had the good fortune to recover one of my baggage trunks, which Jessie will remember to have packed for me, and so saved some clothes, &c. My instruments, which I always carry with me, were in greater part saved.

The officers of the army stationed in the country have been uniformly prompt and liberal in their attentions to me, offering me all the assistance in their power. In this country, where supplies are scarce and extravagantly high, this assistance was of great value to me in prosecuting my journey. Among those whom I ought particularly to mention is Major Beale [Beall], who is in command of the Northern District, Capt. [Henry B.] Judd, Lieut. [Francis John] Thomas, Dr. Webb,[2] and Capt. [John] Buford. I mention their names particularly, knowing that you will take pleasure in reciprocating it to them.

Colonel Washington desired me to call on him without reserve for anything at his command. He invited me to dine with him one out of the two days I spent at Santa Fé, and dined with me at the officers' quarters on the other. Major Weightman (of Washington, son-in-law of Mr. Cox) was very friendly in his attentions to me,[3] and Capt. [Thomas Lee] Brent, of the quartermaster's deputy [department] gave me some most effective aid in my equipment. Among the citizens who have treated me with some attention, I make it a duty to recommend to your attention, when you may meet him, our fellow-citizen of St. Louis, Mr. F. X. Aubry. You will remember him as having lately made an extraordinary ride from Santa Fé to Independence.[4] We have been travelling together from Santa Fé to this place. Among other acts of kindness, I received from him a loan of $1000, to purchase animals for my journey to Calfornia.

I reached this town at half-past eight o'clock this morning, by appointment to breakfast. Capt. Buford, who commands here, received me with much kindness, and I am staying with him. This is a military post, and with the exception of a little village or two, a few miles below, the last settlement we see until reaching Tusson, even should we pass by that route. We go on this afternoon, and perhaps reach California in twenty-five days. The weather here is warm, and the people engaged in opening the ground for sowing. I will write a brief note to Jessie, and conclude this, as I shall be much pressed to get through the business set apart for this day. Very affectionately,

J. C. FREMONT

Hon. Thomas H. Benton,
Washington City

Printed in BIGELOW, 376–78, and UPHAM, 296–99.

1. This was the effort of Godey, mentioned in JCF's letter to JBF, 27 Jan.–17 Feb. 1849 under 6 and 11 Feb. dates.

2. Probably the New Englander James Josiah Webb (1818–89), who had started his career as a trader but was now a prominent Santa Fe merchant with a permanent establishment there. See WEBB.

3. After serving in the Mexican War, Richard H. Weightman (1816–61) became New Mexico Territory's first delegate to Congress and editor of the *Amigo del Pais* newspaper of Albuquerque. (BIOG. DIR. CONG).

4. In referring to Aubry's Sept. 1848 ride in five days and sixteen hours, JCF no doubt had in mind his own accomplishment of the previous year, namely a ride of 400 miles from Los Angeles to Monterey in three days and ten hours.

39. Diary of Richard H. Kern
John S. Stepperfield—Frémont's Disaster in the Mountains

Mr. Stepperfield, who was one of Frémont's men, and who suffered with others of the company, in the attempt to cross the mountains of New Mexico, last winter, returned to his home in this city on Tuesday last. From a conversation with Mr. S. we are led to believe, that the sufferings of the party were not fully detailed (even if known) by Colonel Frémont; and as the public will probably never have any authentic account of the disaster from his pen, it rests with the men who composed the party, and who shared the suffering, to give the details as events transpired from day to day. A daily Journal of the transactions was kept by some of the men, which may be of some interest to the public. Mr. S. has left a transcript of the Journal with us to make such disposal of it as we deem best. We find it very interesting, and believing our readers will also find it so, we give it a place in our paper, with the remark that further accounts of the expedition may be furnished by Mr. S. for publication.

It will be seen that Col. Frémont is much censured in these pages, and with considerable justice, if the testimony of the men of his party is to be relied on. The journal appears to have been kept by Richard H. Kern:

Struck the river Dec. 8. Course West and South-west. Snowed all day. Camped on the river; plenty of timber and snow.

Dec. 9. Moved in the valley of the river, on its eastern bank. Entered a small canon of the river, but on account of the deep snow,[1] were forced to turn back and pass over the top of the hill;[2] crossed the river and camped. *The deep snow of today should have warned Col. Frémont of his approaching destruction, but with the wilfully blind eyes of rashness and self-conceit and confidence he pushed on.* Course N. and W. Elk sign abundant.

Dec. 10. Lay in camp until 12 o'clock, then moved three miles further up the river and camped in fine grove of Cotton-wood. Course W. by N.

Dec. 11. Trail today very hilly and difficult, the hills being steep and rugged. Day clear and windy. Made 12 miles and camped in deep snow on the river. Course same as yesterday.

Dec. 12. Passed through a little valley that lay to the right of the camp, and had some very difficult canons to contend with—the sides in many places almost perpendicular. Camped on the sloping side of the canon. Made from 5 to 7 miles, course nearly North.

Dec. 13. Had very difficult hill to climb at start; road better after. Passed through large Pine forests and camped in beautiful valley, with another running from it to the right. Made about 7 miles; course N.

Dec. 14. Road over pine hills and through deep snow valleys. Passed over a high bald mountain, from the summit of which, one of the finest mountain views in the world can be seen.[3] Camped in a deep pine forest near the head of a fine little valley;[4] some little grass; course north. Made about 5 miles.

Dec. 15. Very bad hill at start; afterwards the trail passed over the summit of hills. Snowed all day; camped on a hill side. Made about 3 miles; course east.[5]

Dec. 16. Made start to pass what was supposed to be dividing ridge between the waters of Rio del Norte and those of Grand river.[6] Passed dead mules, and riding and pack saddles lying beside the trail. After hard work, reached hill summit, but the wind and *poudre* were so dreadful we had to return. Eleven more men were frostbitten in various places, the cold being so intense. Returned to our old campfires amid a furious storm of wind and snow, which continued all day and night.

Dec. 17. A party of men went ahead to beat a trail, whilst those remaining in camp were to bring the animals up. After hard labor reached the top of the hill, and saw the trail winding up the opposite hills, on whose summit some grass could be seen; the trail passed through snow from 3 to 15 feet deep. We unpacked the mules on a little point, after which some were driven to the hill top and those that were too weak, left to perish.[7] *This was the last time we packed them. Every animal should have been butchered, and we would have plenty in camp.*[8] Camped in small pine grove in which we remained until the 24th, when we moved southwest[9] about 3 miles, to a fine large pine forest. The snow 6 feet deep. Meanwhile, camp was employed portaging the baggage from the last to Christmas camp.

On the 26th, Henry King, W. S. Williams, F. [T.] Breckenridge and ———Creutzfeldt, were sent to the settlements to bring us relief.

Remained in Christmas camp until the 28th, when we moved three miles further towards the [Rio Grande] river, and the two Messes [of] Toplin's [Taplin's] and Kern's camped in small valley whilst the rest remained on the hillside.

Dec. 31. Moved on about three miles nearer the river.[10]

Jan 1. Reached, with the Colonel's packs, what was called the Quaking-asp camp, about 3 miles beyond the last.[11]

Jan 2. Moved the Col. to the Rio del Norte, about 7 miles, and *East of where we* LEFT *the river Dec. 12th.*[12] Continued portaging the packs to the Colonel's camp of Jan. 1st—and to some Cotton-woods a mile beyond,[13] until Jan 11, when we were ordered to come and camp on the river—the Colonel, with Mr. Preuss, Godey, and nephew, and Jackson, having left early same day, to meet and hasten Mr. King's party.

Raphael Proulx died on the 9th; *death caused by Frémont's harsh treatment.*[14]

[The following letter was left by Col. Frémont as directions for the party—Vincenthaler in command:]

"L. D. Vinsonhaler. I am now going to start for Abaca [Abiquiu]. I want all the men to bring their baggage down, and put it in the lodge. If no relief comes then, let them take their guns and blankets, and follow the river down to Rabbit Creek [Conejos River], and if no relief at Rabbit creek, then come to Abaca, and come quick, or you will not find me there, as I shall have left for California."[15]

Jan. 16. All camp moved down river about two miles. Manuel turned back.

Jan. 17. Moved about 8 miles. *Wise died today.*

Jan 18. Moved about a mile and half and remained in camp, whilst the hunters went to look for game.

Jan. 19. Made camp near where we first camped on the river; a deer was killed by Hibbard, and ten men received as their share the two fore shoulder blades, and eleven men all the rest, including blood, hide and entrails. Vinsonhaler intended to have kept the deer from the rest of us, pack it among his party and press on to the settlements. *Scott refused to agree, and so we got our small portion.*

Jan. 20. Moved 3 miles further down the river.

Jan. 21. Made about 15 miles. All the strong men together and ahead.

This camp was made with the hope that some of us would be left on the trail. Lord [Sorrel] and Moran did not come up and when Vinsonhaler (commonly called Hayler), was informed of it he observed, that if two of us had not fallen into the river (alluding to Scott and himself) there would have been more of you left.[16] This day he gave up all command and declared the party dissolved, and that we should divide in parties of two and three to hunt small game.

Jan. 22. Vinsonhaler, Hibbard, Ducatel, Martin, Scott, Beadle [Bacon] and the two Indians Gregorio and Joachim all strong men, started ahead accompanied by Ferguson and Beadle, determined to leave us—Taplin, Rohrer, Stepperfield, Andrews, McGehee, Capt. Cathcart, Dr. Kern, Edward M. Kern, and R. H. Kern, to get along as we could, or perish. We weak ones made four miles. (Rohrer and Andrews did not come up).

Lay in this camp until the 28th, when Godey came with relief.

Feb. 9. Reached Rio Colorado. Reached Taos on the 10th. Colonel left on the 13th.

Raphael Proulx died Jan. 9th, 1849; Henry Wise, Jan 17; Henry King, Jan.—: Vincent Sorrel, probably Jan. 22; Joseph Moran, between Jan 22nd and 28th;———Carver, probably Jan. 22; E. T. Andrews, U.S.N., probably Jan. 22; Henry Rohrer, probably Jan 22; Benjamin Beadle Jan. 26, George Hibbard, Jan. 27.

The above dates are copied from my Journal, and are believed to be correct. Under the circumstances, of course, in some instances, definite information could not be obtained.

Upon Col. Frémont's arrival at Taos, Major Beall, commanding that post, ordered the Commissary to issue to the Colonel thirty days full rations, for the twenty-five men then in the mountains, and expected in. These rations were never turned over to the men, and were probably taken on to California by Frémont. The men were obliged to buy their own provisions from the people of the country, who came to their relief.[17]

RICHARD H. KERN

Rio Honda, March 19, 1849.

Printed in Quincy (Ill.) *Whig*, 22 May 1849. Note that the newspaper editor refers to the bearer of Richard Kern's journal as John S. Stepperfield, the anglicized version of Stepperfeldt. He was probably a kinsman of the Joseph Stepperfeldt (often known as Joseph Stepp) who had served JCF's third expedition as a hunter and gunsmith and who had returned to St. Louis in 1847 with the Beale-Carson-Talbot party.

As published in the *Whig*, the journal is a shortened version of the diary that Richard H. Kern began on 20 Oct. 1848 on Boone Creek near Westport. The diary is owned by the Henry E. Huntington Library and is published in HAFEN & HAFEN, 109–34. Important statements, largely strictures on JCF, not appearing in the original are italicized here.

Richard Kern wrote Cathcart that Stepperfeldt had had a terrible time getting home. He "had started off alone [from New Mexico] and was picked up on the prairie perfectly crazy; he however got in safe and published Fremont" (Santa Fe, 30 Sept. 1849, CSmH). From Taos Edward Kern had already written his sister that JCF, for all his dislike of them, would have had them continue on to California with him, "for he did not wish a man of his party with any influence to remain here. The greatest dread he has at present is that a true and correct account of the proceedings *above* and *here* may be made public" (E. M. Kern to Mary Wolfe Kern, Feb. 1849, CSmH).

1. The expedition struck the canyon of Rio de Carnero, approximately twelve miles north of the main branch of the Rio Grande del Norte. The steep cliffs of Hell's Gate as well as the deep snow made it impossible for them to continue along the Carnero.

2. RICHMOND maintains that after crossing the pine-forested hills, the men should have returned to the South Fork of Carnero Creek and followed it, which would have led them ultimately into Cochetopa Park. Instead they became mired in a series of canyons, whose walls in places were almost perpendicular. RICHMOND notes that a sketch of rock outcropping in Richard Kern's diary (CSmH) resembles the one that juts from the stone walls of Cave Creek.

3. RICHMOND identifies the "high bald mountain" as twin-peaked Boot Mountain with an elevation of 12,400 feet. It was not the dividing ridge as they had hoped, but looking back from the summit the men had a spectacular view of the Sangre de Cristo Range and the sand hills, framed by Medano and Mosca passes.

4. Camp was near the head of La Garita Creek (RICHMOND).

5. They had moved up the steep sides of the valley into the tableland at the head of Perry's Creek. Camp was made at the head of West Benino Creek, a quarter of a mile below the summit of Mesa Mountain, which they would attempt to cross the next day (RICHMOND). At the head of East Benino Creek where the trail left the ridge, Richmond found a small stone shelter built against a volcanic outcropping. The year 1848 was inscribed upon the smooth surface of the great rock.

6. Mesa Mountain did not separate the waters of the Rio Grande and the Colorado, but did divide the tributaries of the Saguache from those of La Garita Creek.

7. In moving over the bowl-shaped summit of the ridge, El Bole de Hilda, the expedition had crossed to the headwaters of Wannamaker Creek, a tributary of the Saguache within the Rio Grande watershed.

8. Some of the mules were butchered. On 18 Dec. the men began eating mule meat on a regular basis; JCF's animal was eaten on Christmas Day and Benjamin Kern's on 29 Dec. Later Godey defended JCF against Kern's charge, maintaining that at the time (17 Dec.) there were sufficient provisions for eighteen or twenty days and that the loss of King's relief party was the cause of extreme destitution (Godey to John O. Wheeler, 12 Sept. 1856, printed in New York *Evening Post*, 30 Oct. 1856, and republished in HAFEN & HAFEN, 263–75. By 11 Jan. the men were boiling parfleches and rawhide tug ropes for breakfast.

9. The original diary does not give the direction, but they moved southeast— not southwest—across the mountains to the protection of the trees on the west slope of Rincones Creek. It took the men several days to drag the baggage three and a half miles into the new camp, which became known as Christmas Camp or Camp Hope.

10. The men had started out 28 Dec. along the same route used by the rescue party, that is, to follow Rincones Creek down to its juncture with Embargo Creek. But the canyon was too steep; they fell down often, sliding with the bag-

gage twenty or fifty feet at a time. Since it was impossible to continue with their bundles, they retraced their steps up the hard road and during the next few days made a new trail across the ridge, going into camp on East Embargo Creek (Diary of Benjamin Kern, CSmH). One writer estimates that the twenty-nine men and a boy had to carry three hundred man loads—the equivalent of the loads left by eighty mules (BRANDON, 234).

11. The expedition began to splinter into camps, with JCF's being the most forward. From the east ridge and terraces of Mesa Mountain in mid-December, he had spotted the gently sloping open expanses of Groundhog Park. He established a temporary mess in an isolated aspen grove at the head of Groundhog Creek (RICHMOND).

12. On 2 Jan. JCF moved his camp to the valley floor following the drainage of the Rio de La Garita, which had less snow (RICHMOND). The men toiled in relays to move the baggage. Their camps and fireholes came to be strung out for a distance of ten miles. On 3 Jan. the Kerns burned some of their books and the least valuable of their property. They moved to JCF's vacated Groundhog Creek camp and erected a shanty; a storm soon tore it down, but they gathered saplings and started another.

13. A cache was being prepared, although it seems to have been beyond these particular cottonwoods. RICHMOND puts it at a large rock outcropping on the La Garita. Its visibility from the floor of the San Luis Valley would assist in retrieving the baggage.

14. In the original, under the 9 Jan. entry, Richard Kern notes that Vinsonhaler, on his way to JCF's camp on the river, had met Proue, "his legs frozen," and had helped him as much as possible, wrapping his blankets around him.

15. In 1856, denying that JCF ever intimated that he would start for California, Godey wrote, "On the contrary, it was understood that no attempt would be made either to renew our present, or enter upon any new expedition before the next season, as Fremont supposed that he would have to revisit the States for the purpose of procuring scientific instruments; and not until the entire party had got back to Taos, was a word said by Colonel Fremont, or any one else, of an expedition to California" (Godey to John O. Wheeler, 12 Sept. 1856, printed in New York *Evening Post*, 30 Oct. 1856, and republished in HAFEN & HAFEN, 263–75). Any idea of returning to the States that JCF might have had while in the mountains was relinquished immediately on reaching Taos. The second paragraph of his 27 Jan. letter to JBF makes clear that his destination is California. In extracting the letters for the newspapers, Benton was also anxious to emphasize that the survey was uninterrupted.

16. The meaning of the latter part of this sentence is not clear to the editor.

17. For a discussion of this charge, see Doc. No. 36, n. 13.

San Juan Mountains, 1848. From the "Prospectus"
for Frémont's *Memoirs*. Courtesy of the
Henry E. Huntington Library.

Hardscrabble Canyon, 1848. Watercolor by Richard H. Kern,
who erroneously identifies it as "Robidoux's Pass."
Courtesy Amon Carter Museum, Fort Worth.

Cave Creek, 1848. Watercolor by Richard H. Kern, who labels it Courtesy Amon Carter Museum, Fort Worth.

Jacob A. Dallas' sketch of Frémont's Christmas Camp in the San Juans,
1848. From a print in John Bigelow's *Memoir of the Life and
Public Services of John Charles Fremont* (New York, 1856).

Headwaters of Embargo Creek, 31 December 1848. Watercolor by
Richard H. Kern. Courtesy Amon Carter Museum, Fort Worth.

The Relief Camp, 29 January 1849. Watercolor by Richard H. Kern.
Courtesy Amon Carter Museum, Fort Worth.

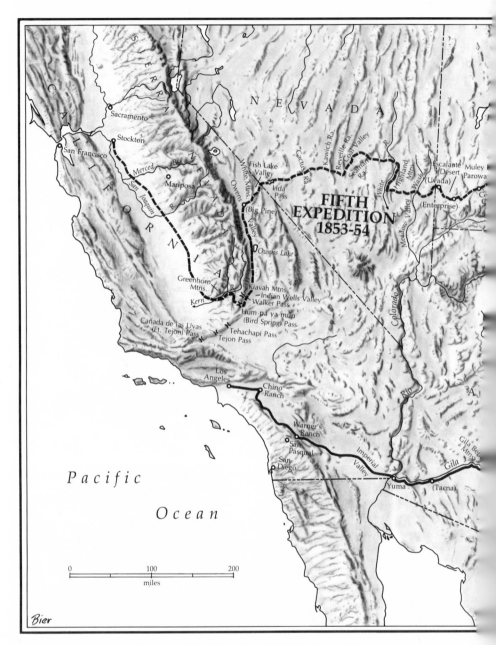

Routes of the Fourth and Fifth Expeditions.

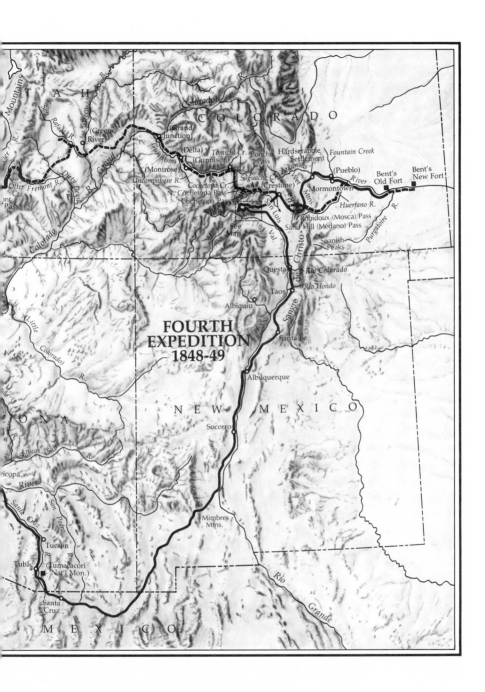

FOURTH
EXPEDITION
1848-49

Frémont's route in the San Juan Mountains, 1848–49.

Politics and Economics

40. Frémont to Benjamin D. Wilson

My dear Sir,

This note will be handed to you by Mr. Alexander Godey, whom I have sent to your neighborhood to purchase cattle, the kind which I require being to be had on much better terms then about Monterey. He may probably make use of all the funds he carries in the purchase of cattle, in which I have directed him to apply to you for supplies or any other assistance he may need. I will therefore be much obliged to you to furnish him on my account with all he may require.

I refer you to him for particulars of our journey[1] and future intentions as the mosquitoes torment me here so much that I absolutely cannot write. You have passed here yourself and know them by experience.

Should there be any thing of interest I will write to you from Monterey to which place I am now on my way. Very truly yours,

J. C. Frémont

Capt. B. Wilson
Los Angeles

ALS (CSmH—Benjamin David Wilson Papers). JCF had not yet made contact with his wife, who had crossed the Isthmus of Panama and at this very time was off the California coast in the *Panama*, which would steam through the Golden Gate on 4 June. According to PHILLIPS, 140–42, JCF was ten days late in meeting her.

1. Presumably the journey from Los Angeles to Las Mariposas—not that of the expedition from Westport to California.

41. John M. Clayton to Frémont

Department of State
Washington, 26th. June 1849

Sir:

The President having thought proper to appoint you the Commissioner on the part of the United States for running and marking the Boundary line under the Fifth Article of the Treaty of Guadalupe Hidalgo, I transmit your Commission in that character. You will also receive herewith a copy of the several instructions which this Department had addressed to your predecessor.[1] It is not considered that you will need any further instructions at this time. I would, however, invite your special attention to the necessity of the regular transmission of your accounts and vouchers for settlement at the Treasury Department as those instructions require. Any drafts also, which you may have occasion to draw on account of the expenses of the Commission, must be addressed to the Secretary of State and not to the Secretary of the Treasury. You will also forward to this Department a full list of the persons (other than military or naval) in the Service of the Commission, on our part, with the rates of compensation allowed to each, and will apprize the Department of any changes therein which may from time to time take place.

Your compensation as well as that of your predecessor will be settled by Congress at this next session. I am Sir &c.,

John M. Clayton

Lbk (DNA-59, Domestic Letters, 37:239–40). Addressed to Frémont at San Francisco.

1. Not printed is the copy of Clayton's letter to Ohioan John B. Weller (1812–75), JCF's predecessor. The Secretary of State expressed his displeasure that Weller had not furnished a list of persons he had employed or an account of his first quarter's expenses. He noted that the president had thought "proper to appoint" JCF to mark the boundary, and instructed that all papers and public property be transferred to his custody. Clayton to JCF, 28 June 1849, indicates that it would really be JCF's decision as to when Weller should leave office. This unusual method of attempted dismissal plus the removal of other Polk appointees caused considerable debate in and out of the Senate (see the Bradbury Resolutions, *Congressional Globe*, 31st Cong., 1st sess., 15 Jan., 21–23 March, 23 April, 8 May, 12 and 18 Dec. 1850, and 31st Cong., 2nd sess., *Appendix*, 7 Jan. 1851; Snyder to Frémont, 11 Dec. 1849). As successive documents show, JCF never took up his duties, and it was not until 19 Dec. 1849 that a letter was written removing Weller. Weller subsequently started a legal practice in San

Francisco, was elected to the U.S. Senate in 1852, and won the California gubernatorial election in 1857 (DAB).

42. Excerpt from a letter of Frémont to Thomas H. Benton

MONTEREY, June 27, 1849

I shall be anxious to receive the least information relative to your plan for the railroad—what the prospects are for its adoption, and towards what point of this country it will probably be directed. In conversation with Mr. Butler King and Gen. Persifor Smith, a few days since, this road was a subject of great interest.[1] I mentioned that the line explored in my last journey was admirably calculated for the road, passing the mountains between the Arkansas and the Del Norte, with scarcely an inequality of profile, and which knowledge obtained since our disaster showed would have been the character of its extension further west to the Great Basin. A reference to the map will show you that this line crosses the valley of the Del Norte at the northern edge of the New Mexican settlements (a handsome and fertile country), whence a branch road might be thrown down the valley of the river and through the settlements to Santa Fe, &c. This road would enter the basin at the southern end of the Mormon settlements, and cross by way of Humboldt river. About midway of that river's course a large valley opens into it, and up this an excellent way to a low pass near the head of the lower Sacramento valley. Before reaching this pass, a way, diverging to the north, affords a very practicable valley road into Oregon, and, in my opinion, far the best by which you can reach that country. Immediately after this conversation, Gen. Smith determined upon sending a party to explore that part of the route which I have last described, with a view to report upon it at the ensuing session of Congress. He afterward called upon me to request that I would send him a written communication to the same effect, in order that hereafter credit of the suggestion might remain with me. It is not pleasant to see the work pass into other hands, but private means are inadequate to such undertakings here.

Printed in St. Louis *Daily Reveille*, 17 Oct. 1849, as a part of the speech delivered on 16 Oct. 1849 by Senator Benton to the St. Louis Pacific Railway Convention.

1. Thomas Butler King (1800–1864) was a Whig congressman from Georgia when President Taylor sent him to California, ostensibly to acquire information about the country but in reality to work for the admission of California as a free, and Whig, state. He arrived in California on 4 June and within a short time made arrangements to go with the commander of the Pacific Division, Persifor F. Smith (1798–1858), "to the interior of the country, for the purpose of examining the gold region, and other interesting and important portions of it." A few months later King made an unsuccessful bid to be one of California's first U.S. senators; in Oct. 1850 President Fillmore appointed him collector of the Port of San Francisco. For a biography of King, see STEEL.

43. John M. Clayton to Frémont

Department of State
WASHINGTON, 28th June 1849

SIR:

In a letter from this Department under the 26th Instant, you were informed of your appointment as Commissioner of the United States under the 5th Article of the Treaty of Guadalupe Hidalgo. With that letter one addressed to your predecessor was also transmitted which, however, it is deemed advisable you should not deliver or forward to him until you are about to enter upon the duties of the office. The letter for him which is herewith transmitted, you will consider as addressed to yourself when you shall have communicated to him that above referred to.[1] I am Sir &c.,

JOHN M. CLAYTON

[Enclosure]

John M. Clayton to John B. Weller

Department of State
WASHINGTON, 28th June 1849

SIR:

Your letter from Panama of the 15th. Ultimo with the accompanying lists of persons in the service of the Commission was received at this Department of yesterday the 27th Instant.

The difficulties which you anticipate in regard to running and marking the boundary line from the Pacific toward the Rio Grande may be realized, but without actual experience of them it would be premature even to take into consideration your suggestion as to reversing that course and beginning the demarcation at the eastern end of the line. Inasmuch, however, as the starting point for tracing the boundary as well as the proceedings of the joint commission with reference thereto are prescribed by the Treaty it would seem that the Executive of neither government has any discretion in regard to them, or any more right to change them than they would have to change the direction of the line itself. If it should be found to be impracticable to execute the duties of the Commission as the Treaty contemplates and enjoins, a supplementary article will be necessary to impart validity to any deviations therefrom.

It may, as you suggest, be advisable, occasionally to make presents to the Indians who may be met with along the route of the Commission. Careful discrimination however will be necessary in selecting articles for this purpose. They should be acceptable to the Indians but not such as would enable them to injure the Commission in case their permanent good will should not be secured. The cost of the presents also should be moderate and our share thereof should have just proportion to the fund appropriated by Congress for the expenses of the commission. Upon this subject, however, you had better consult and make some arrangements with the Mexican Commissioners. If presents should be indispensable they would be for the common benefit of both parties and both should equally share the expense. I am Sir, &c.,

JOHN M. CLAYTON

Lbk (DNA-59, Domestic Letters, 37:241–43).
1. See Doc. No. 41, n. 1, for a summary of Clayton to Weller, 26 June 1849.

44. Frémont to John M. Clayton

PUEBLO OF SAN JOSÉ, August 1849

To THE HON. J. M. CLAYTON,
SECY. OF STATE
SIR:

I have had the honor to receive, by the hands of Mr. Beale,[1] U.S. Navy, your letter conferring upon me the post of Commissioner of the

United States for the determination of our boundary line with Mexico.

I feel much gratification in accepting the appointment and beg to offer through you to the President my acknowledgments for the mark of confidence bestowed upon me and which he may be assured is fully appreciated.

Col. Weller is now at San Francisco, having just arrived from the South. His reports of the actual state of the Survey will probably suggest instructions for me. I will see him within a few days, and having made myself acquainted with the condition of the work shall be able to communicate understandingly with the Department. I have the honor to be with much respect your obedient servant,

J. C. Frémont

LS (DNA-76, Records Re International Boundaries. Records Re U.S.—Mexican Border, Entry 405—Applications, Recommendations, Acceptances, Resignation). Body of letter in hand of JCF. Endorsed: "Recd. & filed Oct. 16. 1849."
    1. A good friend of JCF's and identified in Vol. 2, Beale had just married Mary Edwards of Chester, Pa., when he received orders to carry government dispatches to the West Coast. He took his wife with him as far as Havana and on 22 Aug. arrived with Bayard Taylor in California in the *Panama* (*Alta California*, Supplemental, 23 Aug. 1849; TAYLOR, 1:54).

45. John B. Weller to Frémont

MONTEREY, CALIFORNIA, September 27, 1849

DEAR SIR:

Having failed in obtaining funds from General Riley,[1] I have been compelled to send an express to San Francisco, with a view to negotiate the drafts herewith inclosed. Justice to the employees of the commission, as well as the interests of the Government, demand that funds to the amount of $10,000 should be raised, if possible, before you go to San Diego. Very little has been paid to them since the 1st of April, and as some of them will doubtless desire to leave, it is necessary they should be paid. Besides, there are some debts contracted for supplies, house-rent, &c., which should for the honor of the Government, be paid *at once*. As the public understand that I am superseded, your explanation will be necessary in obtaining funds.

I send four bank drafts, supposing they might be more conveniently negotiated at different houses. If any are used as duplicates, please see that they are so marked. As a deposit of a portion of the money in that place will, perhaps, answer the purpose. Whatever sum is obtained in money should be placed on the "Oregon," unless you will take personal charge of it.

If any draft is sold below par, be good enough to take receipts in my name. I send my instructions of the 24th January last, from which I derive authority to draw the appropriation specified.

Mr. Plume,[2] of the firm of Burgoyne & Co., is charged with the execution of some orders for me, and will, I have no doubt, aid in raising funds.

As I regard this business of the utmost importance to the Government, as well as myself, I must beg your attendance to it as soon as practicable. Very respectfully, your obedient servant,

JOHN B. WELLER
UNITED STATES COMMISSIONER

Printed in *Congressional Globe*, 32nd Cong., 1st sess., *Appendix*, 6 July 1852, p. 798.

1. Bennet Riley (1787–1853) had relieved Richard B. Mason as military governor of California on 12 April 1849 and had convened the constitutional convention that was meeting at Monterey when Weller penned this letter (DAB and GRIVAS).

2. John V. Plume and his partner, W. M. Burgoyne, had established themselves as bankers and commission merchants in San Francisco on 5 June 1849 (CROSS, 1:51).

46. Frémont to John B. Weller

SAN FRANCISCO, October 31, 1849

DEAR SIR:

After a long delay in endeavoring to sell your drafts on favorable terms, I have this day found myself obliged to sell them at 10 per cent. discount. No better terms could be obtained, and the necessity which exists for your payments to be made did not appear to admit further delay. I have sent to you (through Messrs. Burgoyne & Co.) by the steamer California, which sails tomorrow, $5,000 in specie, and have deposited to your order at the same house, the other $4,000 in specie. Of this about $50 will be required for the freight, and $300 more will be required to pay your carpenter, whom you directed to call upon me. The remainder will be subject to your order.

Hoping that this will arrive in time to meet the necessities of your people, I am, very truly yours,

J. C. FRÉMONT

Printed in *Congressional Globe,* 32nd Cong., 1st sess., *Appendix,* 6 July 1852, p. 799. Weller indicated that the letter was received on 3 or 4 Nov. and that it and his 27 Sept. letter to JCF constituted the entire correspondence between them. He stated that as early as 20 Aug., he had heard rumors that JCF was holding letters superseding him as commissioner, that he had actually seen JCF in Monterey on several occasions, and that the explorer had introduced the subject but declined to deliver the letters. Weller reported that in the last days of November he went to San Francisco to seek his discharge from JCF. "There I learned that he had accepted the commission, subsequently resigned, and declined relieving me, by returning the letter to the Department." Frémont thus never delivered Clayton's order of 26 June 1849. See Weller's speech in the Senate, *ibid.,* 797–802.

47. Frémont to Benjamin D. Wilson

MONTEREY, Novr. 15th. 1849

MY DEAR SIR,

This note will be handed to you by my brother-in-law Mr. Jones[1] about whom we have already had some conversation. Business of the government brings him to Los Angeles and I will be obliged to you for any facilities or kindness you can afford him. He has also charged himself with some business of mine[2] in which he may need your counsel and for which I will be much indebted to you. I have put into the hands of Mr. Packhard[3] of your city one hundred and sixty-six dollars in payment of a bill which Godey made with you. I understand that your town lots are to be sold in December. Please purchase one for me exercising your judgment as to the locality. I will write to you again soon and in the meantime remain Yours truly,

J. C. FRÉMONT

Capt. B. Wilson

ALS-JBF (CSmH).

1. On 12 July 1849 President Taylor had appointed William Carey Jones to procure information on Mexican land titles in California. He arrived on 19 Sept., visited Monterey, San Jose, San Francisco, Los Angeles, and San Diego, spent eighteen days in Mexico City, and was back in Washington on 1 Feb. where he soon afterward submitted his report.

2. The specific nature of JCF's business is not known, but a reasonable assumption is that it related to the acquisition of land—a subject of extreme interest to both of Benton's sons-in-law. In fact, while Jones was conducting his investigation of land titles, he purchased the twelve-league San Luis Rey and Pala Mission rancho in San Diego. Although confirmed by both the Board of Land Commissioners and the district judge, it was rejected by the Supreme Court in 1863, some seven years after the final confirmation of JCF's Las Mariposas title. For a revealing letter and article on the Frémont-Jones scramble for California land, see Jones to Wilson, San Diego, 7 Dec. 1849 (CSmH), and GATES [1].

3. Albert Packard and Wilson were partners in a store in Los Angeles (GUINN).

48. Frémont to John M. Clayton

MONTEREY, November 15th, 1849

TO THE HON. J. M. CLAYTON
SECRETARY OF STATE
SIR:

Having become a candidate for the Senate of the United States, it has become necessary that I should tender to the President, as I hereby do, a resignation of the office of Commissioner of the Boundary Survey, which I recently had the honor to receive.

Col. Weller is now at San Diego, to which place he returned after a conversation with me, for the purpose of discharging his liabilities to his party. So far as I have been able to understand, the outstanding liabilities necessary to be now discharged will exhaust the appropriation and leave nothing for carrying on the work. If this be the case it may be difficult to avoid an interruption of the work and will render the duties of the Commissioners embarrassing.

I had judged it proper to relieve Mr. Weller at San Diego and for that reason delayed delivering him your letter. It accordingly remained undelivered leaving him still in the exercise of the duties of Commissioner.

It suggests itself to me that until the Department have the time to make its arrangements, it will best subserve the public interest to leave affairs in their present situation and withhold the letter, which I shall accordingly do. With much respect, I am Sir, your obedient servant,

J. C. Frémont

LS (DNA-76, Entry 405).

49. Jacob R. Snyder to Frémont

San Francisco, Dec. 11th, 1849

Dear Sir:

Your name has been long before the people of California as a candidate for the U.S. Senate. As an old resident of California, and a personal friend of long standing, I feel the deepest interest in your election, and take the liberty of asking of you information on certain points which I discover to be much agitated by some who are not your friends. Are you a believer in the distinctive tenets of the democratic party? What are your views in relation to an overland communication by railroad or otherwise, from the Pacific to the Atlantic and through the territory of the United States? What is the true history and real nature of your title to a certain tract of land which you are said to claim on the Mariposa River? What have you done, and what do you propose to do, to establish that claim?

What has been your course in reference to a commission which you are said to have received to run the boundary line called for by the late treaty with Mexico? Was that appointment solicited by yourself or your friends, and have you accepted it? and if not, how long did you hold it under consideration?

What was the real nature of the transaction with D. Eulogio de Célis, concerning which, certain publications were sometime since made in the newspapers of this place and of some of the Eastern States? On all of these matters I would respectfully submit that as full an answer as this short notice will allow, is due to your friends and supporters, and that in regard to your political principles, a declaration would come from you with peculiar fitness, seeing that your occupations, honorable as they have been, and serviceable to your country, have not been of a character to call for an expression of your opinions on matters of government, and that your friends, though well persuaded themselves of your soundness, are yet daily met with the question, "how do you know that Mr. Frémont is a democrat, and how long has he been one?" Yours, &c.,

Jacob R. Snyder

John C. Frémont, Esq.

Printed in *Alta California*, 15 Dec. 1849.

50. Frémont to Jacob R. Snyder

San Francisco, Dec. 11th, 1849

My Dear Sir:

I have the pleasure to acknowledge the receipt of your letter to-day, and to make you my kind thanks for the gratification I find in being called to make some reply to the vague accusations in circulation against me.

I presume that it will be a sufficient answer to your first question, simply to state, that by association, feeling, principle and education, I am thoroughly a democrat; and with out entering into any discussion of the question at issue between the two great parties, I have only further to say, that I adhere to the great principles of the democratic party as they are understood on this and the other side of the continent.

I am strongly in favor of a central, national railroad from the Mississippi River to the Pacific Ocean. Recent events have converted the vague desire for that work into an organized movement throughout the great body of our fellow citizens in the United States, and in common with them, I am warmly in favor of its immediate location and speediest possible construction. Its stupendous magnitude—the immense benefit which it will confer upon our whole country—the changes which it will operate throughout the Pacific Ocean and eastern Asia—commingling together the European, American, and Asiatic races—spreading indefinitely religious, social and political improvement—characterize it as the greatest enterprise of the age, and a great question proposed for the solution of the American people. There never has been presented an enterprise so calculated to draw together in its support all classes of society; and the perpetual and always increasing benefits which it will confer upon the human race in addition to the weighty national considerations, military, political, and commerical, which more immediately concerns us, call upon us for immediate and efficient action. Ardently in favor of the work, it follows of course that I am entirely satisfied of its practicability, and believe fully in its ultimate and speedy construction. Many years of labor and exploration of the interior of our continent, and along a great part of the way the road will necessarily pass, have conclusively satisfied me not only of its entire practicability, but of extraordinary advantages offered for its construction. A late journey across the continent from the frontier of Missouri was solely directed to an examination of the country in reference to the railroad communication, and was undertaken in the season of winter in order that all the obstacles which could exist to the construction of the road might be known and fully determined. The result was entirely satisfactory. It convinced me that neither the snow of winter nor the mountian ranges were obstacles in the way of the road, and furnished me with a far better line than any I had previously known. From the frontier of Missouri along the line of the Kansas River, 400 miles of rich wooded country, well adapted to settlement—by the upper waters of the Arkansas into and through the rugged mountains in which they rise, to the valley which lies around the head waters of the great Del Norte—the profile of the route presents a regularly ascending plain, without a perceptible inequality to break the uniformity of its surface. Lying between the 38th and 39th parallels of latitude, commencing on the frontier of Missouri at the 39th and ending in the Del Norte valley at the 38th—the route presents a comparatively straight line, running for a greater part of the way through a country capable of settlement, and cultivation, and passing through the Arkansas chain (one of the most rugged in all the Rocky Mountain ranges), by a pass of imperceptible grade, and in every respect one of the best with which we are acquainted in those difficult mountains. Beyond the Del Norte that region yet remains to be explored, well known from reliable information to afford through the mountains which separate the valley of the Del Norte and Colorado, an excellent pass, traveled by the Mexicans at all seasons of the year, which gives every reason for believing that the character of the country is equally favorable. Its further progress would carry it by the southern extremity of the country now occupied by the people of Deseret, and thence by the line of the Humboldt River around into the head of the lower Sacramento valley, by a pass in the

Sierra Nevada, but little above the general level of the great basin. Such a location would be entirely central, passing by the northern edge of the Mexican settlements, going through the southern part of Mormon—and branching into Oregon from the confines of California.

Some months since, in conversation with Gen. Smith, I had the honor to propose this plan for the location of the road, I further indicated to him the existence of this favorable way and pass from the Humboldt River into the head of the lower Sacramento Valley. Gen. Smith decided immediately to send an exploring party to examine the route, and requested me to send him a letter recapitulating the information, in order, as he had the kindness to say, that any credit which might hereafter belong to the origin of the line, should inure to me. The expedition was immediately sent, and although it terminated in the death of the gallant officer who commanded it, I am informed that his journal and sketches fully establish, so far as he went, the practicability of the road.[1] You are aware that among the indefinite objections which have been raised against me, are some of a sectional character. Such objections I think may be fairly met with the statement above.

The "Mariposa claim" is a tract of land ten leagues in extent lying upon a creek of the same name in the San Joaquin valley. It was purchased for me by Mr. Larkin in the beginning of 1847, and during my absence with the battalion in the south, from D. Juan B. Alvarado, to whom it had been granted in consideration of his public services. Mr. Larkin paid for it $3,000. I had never seen the place, and know nothing of its character or value. The purchase was made before California was ceded to the United States, and long before any gold had been discovered. I had always intended to make my home in the country if possible, and for this purpose desired a foothold in it. On my return to the country in the present year I visited the place in company with Dr. Corrie, Mr. Reid,[2] and several other gentlemen, and for the first time saw the land. Two-thirds are adapted only to farming; on the other third gold was discovered, and we went to work to dig it out. So soon as it was known that we were there, hundreds—soon becoming thousands—crowded to the same place, and to this day from two to three thousand persons have been regularly employed. They have worked them freely; no one has ever offered them the slightest impediment, nor have I myself, ever expressed to any one or entertained an intention of interfering with the free working of the mines at that place. I regard the claim to the Mariposa in the same light as any other vested right. It was a purchase fairly made, and I have always supposed that at some future time the validity of the claim would be settled by the proper courts. I am satisfied to wait that decision, whether it be favorable or otherwise, and in the meantime to leave the gold, as it is now, free to all who have the industry to collect it.

I was at San José, when I had the honor to receive from President Taylor, by the hands of Mr. Beale, the commission to run the boundary line with Mexico. I regarded that commission as a disavowal on the part of the President of the proceedings recently held against me. Respect to the President, together with a full appreciation of the consideration which had induced him to make the appointment, did not, in my judgment, permit me to decline, and I accordingly accepted the commission, with the intention *which I then expressed* to Mr. Beale and others shortly afterwards to resign. I immediately went to San Francisco, where I had been informed Col. Weller had arrived. He had left that place and I shortly afterwards joined him at Monterey. The Secretary of State had made me the bearer of the letter which superseded Col. Weller. To present it was a disagreeable office, and from motives of delicacy I did not immediately present him the letter, but waited until I was about to leave the town. I then called upon Col. Weller, in order to ascertain from him, at what time and place it would be most agreeable to him, that I should relieve him. I learnt that the object of his journey to San Francisco had been to procure funds with which to discharge the liabilities of the government to his party; and that it would best suit his purposes to obtain the necessary sum, return to San Diego, and be relieved by me at that place. I then informed him that my instructions left me at liberty to relieve when I should be ready to do so, and that accordingly he might proceed to San Francisco, and it was agreed, that if Col. Weller did not succeed in obtaining money from Gen. Riley, to whom he intended to apply, an express should be forwarded to me, and the money obtained at San Francisco and brought down by me in the steamer.

On the eve of leaving San Francisco and too late to negotiate drafts, I received an express informing me that General Riley had declined furnishing the money. When the steamer reached Monterey, I found Colonel Weller on the landing, ready to embark for San Diego, and fully expecting to receive the money; understanding the embarrassment of his situation, I offered, if he determined to go on to San

Diego, that I would return to San Francisco, to procure the money and bring or send it to him.

I had, in the mean time, resigned my appointment, informing the secretary that I should withhold the letter relieving Mr. Weller, and leave the department at liberty to make its own arrangements.

It had become unnecessary for me to go to San Diego in the public service, and the management of my private affairs did not otherwise leave me the necessary time. I suppose that Colonel Weller was not detained at San Diego, as he returned to this place as soon as could be expected after the receipt of the money. This is a brief statement of the course I have pursued. It was dictated altogether by a disposition to promote the interests of Colonel Weller, and to make my concern in his removal as little unpleasant as possible. The office was never sought after by me, and never sought or expected by any of my friends for me.

In reply to your inquiry for information regarding the "real nature of the transaction with D. Eulogio de Célis," I have to state, that, at a time when the troops under my command were destitute of provisions, and we were able to procure them only in small and desultory supplies, on a precarious credit, Major Samuel Hensley, then commissary for the battalion, called upon me with an offer from Mr. Célis, which I was glad to accept immediately.[3] The offer was to furnish me with 600 head of cattle, at ten dollars per head and a loan of $2,500, payable all in six months, with the usual interest, if not paid at that time, we were to return him the hides as the cattle were killed, and the difference in price of the cattle ($8 being the cash price then), being a *bonus* for the loan and for the relief afforded by the provisions. D. Andres Pico was charged to bring the cattle from San Louis Obispo to Los Angeles. In the interval of his absence, General [Stephen Watts] Kearney issued his proclamation, taking out of my hands the partial direction of affairs which I had retained, and destroying the confidence which the people of the South had been disposed to place in me. Desirous to know for the satisfaction of those to whom I was indebted, how far Gen. Kearney designed to fulfill my contracts previously made, I *immediately* visited him for that purpose at Monterey. As I have already asserted, on my trial before the court martial at Washington, he refused to assume any responsibility or to fulfill any contract. I immediately returned to Los Angeles, and make known his reply to Mr. Célis, Mr. Cot., D. Andres Pico, and other gentlemen then at that place. D. Andres Pico had, in the meantime, brought a portion of the cattle (between 400 and 500 I believe), to the mission of San Fernando, near Los Angeles, where they were waiting to be delivered—what disposition should be made of the cattle was for some days a subject of discussion between Mr. Célis, D. Andres Pico, Major Hensley, and myself. It was at first proposed to leave the cattle with D. Andres; but agreeably to the suggestion of Major Hensley, it was decided to place them with Mr. Stearns, as a security both to Célis and to the government, until we should be able to know what course would be pursued by the government. They were to be kept by Mr. Stearns on the terms usually allowed for keeping cattle, viz: one half the increase, and they were not placed in his hand for any fixed time, but only to await the action of the government.

It had been made a matter of charge against me, that I gave to Mr. Célis a full receipt for the delivery of *all* cattle, when I had received only a part. I had the right to do so. I had the right to complete my own contracts, when others, whose duty it was to resume them, endeavored rather to invalidate them. As Mr. Célis had had sufficient confidence in me to advance me money, and I was under order to leave the country immediately, I chose to have sufficient confidence in him to give him a receipt for all the cattle, and to bind the government to him, so far as I possibly could. These cattle were all delivered as soon as they could be brought to Los Angeles.

Since my return to this country I have received a number of affidavits to all the occurrences of the foregoing transaction, from Mr. Wilson, Mr. Temple, and other gentlemen, citizens of Los Angeles. These, with some other papers, were designed for another occasion, and are now at Monterey, but they shall be published as soon as I can conveniently do so. Mr. Célis is now in this city. I have thus, my dear sir, briefly and hurriedly answered your several inquiries; I should have been better satisfied if there had been time sufficient to give each particular point a well-digested reply, but I trust that they may answer the present purpose of removing some erroneous impressions; and in any event, I beg you to receive my thanks for the kindness of the motive which dictated your letter, and which, in every way is consistent with the same friendly spirit which has always influenced your conduct to me. With respect and regard, I am yours truly,

J. C. Frémont

J. R. Snyder, Esq.

Printed in *Alta California*, 15 Dec. 1849.

1. The officer, William Horace Warner, was killed by hostile Indians on 26 Sept. 1849.

2. "Dr. Corrie" was Benjamin Cory, an Ohio physician who had immigrated to Oregon before coming south to California. In Dec. 1849 he was representing San Jose in the Assembly. "Mr. Reid" is undoubtedly Hugo Reid (1810?–52), who was then living in Monterey and was keenly interested in mining as well as in the life and customs of the Indians. DAKIN, however, gives no evidence to associate him directly with JCF's trip to the Mariposa.

3. For documents and editorial notes relating to the contract between Célis and JCF, see Vol. 2, pp. 407–22.

51. Thomas H. Benton to Frémont

WASHINGTON, 4 Jan. 1850.

[Introduces Professor [George C.] Pratt, "late of the University of the State of Missouri," who was going to California with views of permanent settlement. ALS (NHi). Pratt in fact returned to Missouri and became active in the location and construction of railroads and ultimately railroad commissioner (STEPHENS and VILES).]

52. Frémont to James Blair

PANAMA, N[EW] G[RANADA], Feby. 6, 1850

MY DEAR SIR,

The object of this note is to ask the advantages of your acquaintance and friendly regard of the bearer, C. Garvey, Esq. of St. Louis, Mri.

Mr. Garvey is an old resident of that city and a democrat, and therefore will have claims on your attention. Any kindness you may be able to show to him will [be] very gratifying to me. He will be able to give you some recent intelligence of your brother Judge [Montgomery] Blair. With regard yours truly,

J. C. FRÉMONT

Lt. James Blair

ALS (DLC—Frank Preston Blair Family Papers). The son of Frank Preston Blair, James L. Blair (1819–53) had been on the Wilkes expedition. He took a year's leave from the Navy in 1849 and went to San Francisco, where with $10,000 from his father he started a small shipping business in partnership with the Aspinwall brothers. The Frémonts would escort his wife and little daughter to California when the first session of Congress ended, and still later the settlement of young Blair's estate would bring west his brother, Montgomery, who did so much to help JCF with his business and legal affairs following the fifth expedition (SMITH, 184–88).

On the same day JCF also wrote on Garvey's behalf to Jacob R. Snyder (calendared at p. 43 in the Northern California Historical Records Survey Project, Works Project Administration, *A Calendar of the Major Jacob Rink Snyder Collection in the Manuscript Collection of The Society of California Pioneers* [San Francisco, 1940]).

53. Frémont to John Torrey

WASHINGTON CITY, March 28th. 1850

MY DEAR SIR,

I received yours of the 20th yesterday with the same pleasure that I always hear from you. I have not yet left my room after a relapse into the Chagres fever and therefore write only briefly. I shall be able to send you a few plants by your daughter,[1] which I have no doubt are of much interest, as being, some at least, entirely new. I had collected many fine plants along the Gila and in Sonora but the man to whom I entrusted their collection although professing to be a botanist, permitted them to get wet repeatedly and many are ruined & the rest he did not even label.[2] I will however try to locate some, and such as I am certain of will try to send you.

We shall still be able to do a great deal in that country (Sonora & California) as I am satisfied there are a great many new plants and my interest has rather increased than diminished in the pursuit.

I notice you have given to Emory one of the plants (with flower) which we brought with us in our first return from California.[3] I will send you another specimen which I bring home this time.

I was much pleased with the plates you sent and glad to see we were able to rescue so many new plants. I am not able to send you the drawings; they have been left in California. I shall send for them by Adams express & hope to receive them.

As soon as able, I will send you the notes necessary to the plants I will send by your daughter.

Mrs. Fremont will see Miss Torrey today it will give her pleasure to extend her acquaintance in your family. Yours very truly,

J. C. FRÉMONT

LS (NHi).

1. Torrey's youngest daughter, Margaret, "was at Washington where she will remain till Spring" (Torrey to Asa Gray, 11 Jan. 1850, extract printed in ROB-BINS, 598).

2. Undoubtedly Frederick Creutzfeldt.

3. Probably *Hymenoclea monogyra*, which had been found by Emory on the Gila River.

54. Frémont to Messrs. B. Gerhard and Others, Committee

[ca. 1 April 1850]

GENTLEMEN:

It would have given me great pleasure to have been able to accept your kind invitation, and to have met the interesting Mississippi and Pacific Railroad Convention on Monday, but the remains of a Chagres fever confine me to my room, and leave me no other mode of showing my sense of your attention, and manifesting the interest I take in the great object which assembles this convention, than to contribute, so far as I can, to the mass of the information which will be laid before it. In doing this, I regret that the state of my health does not permit even the labor necessary to give the distances and barometrical elevations along the route which I shall offer for your consideration; but I have caused a skeleton map, rudely sketched, to be prepared to accompany this communication, and which in exhibiting the prominent features of the country, and general direction of the line, will be found sufficiently full and accurate to illustrate what I have to say.[1]

Many lines of explorations through the wilderness country, from our inhabited frontier to the Pacific Ocean, have conclusively satisfied me that the region or belt of country, lying between the 38th and 39th parallels of latitude, offer singular facilities and extraordinary comparative advantages for the construction of the proposed road.

I propose, therefore, to occupy your attention solely with this line; for the clearer understanding of which, it will aid to keep under the eye of the accompanying map, upon which the unbroken red lines are intended to show that the regions which they traverse have been already explored, while the broken red lines what is known only from reliable information.

The country to be traversed by the proposed road exhibits but two great features—the prairies reaching to about the 105th degree of longitude; and the mountains, with which it is bristling from that point to the shores of the Pacific ocean. Some years of travel among these mountains, during which I was occupied principally in searching for convenient passes and good lines of communication, gradually led me to comprehend their structure, and to understand that among this extended mass of mountains there is nowhere to be found a great continuous range having an unbroken crest, where passes are only to be found in the comparatively small depressions of the summit line. Throughout this great extent of country stretching in each way about 17 degrees, all these apparently continuous ranges are composed of lengthened blocks of mountains, separate and detached of greater or less length, according to the magnitude of the chain which they compose—each one possessing its separate, noted, and prominent peaks, and lying parallel to each other, though not usually so to the general direction of the range, but in many cases lying diagonally across it. Springing suddenly up from the general level of the country, sometimes rising into bare and rocky summits, of great height, they leave openings through the range but little above the general level, and by which they can be passed without climbing a mountain. Generally these openings are wooded valleys, where the mountain springs from either side collect together, forming often the main branches of some mighty stream. Aggregated together in this way, they go to form the great chain of the Rocky Mountains and Sierra Nevadas as well as the smaller and secondary ranges which occupy the intervening space. With the gradual discovery of this system, I became satisfied, not only of the entire practicability, but of the easy construction of a railroad across this rugged region. As this peculiarity forms the basis of my information, I desire to state it clearly at the outset, in order that I may be more readily understood in proceeding to show that this continent can be crossed from the Mississippi to the Pacific, without climbing a mountain, and on the very line which every national consideration would require to connect the great valley of the West with the Pacific Ocean.

In describing the belt of country through which the road should pass, it will be found convenient to divide the entire line into three parts—the Eastern, reaching from the mouth of the Kansas to the head of the Del Norte; the Middle, from the head of the Del Norte to the river of the Great Basin; and the Western, from the rim of the Great Basin to the ocean. Beginning near the 39th parallel of latitude, at the mouth of the Kansas, the road would extend along the valley of that river some three or four hundred miles, traversing a beautiful and wooded country of great fertility, well adapted to settlement and cultivation. From the upper waters of the Kansas, falling easily over into the valley of Arkansas, the road strikes that river about a hundred miles below the foot of the mountains, continuing up it only to the mouth of the Huerfano River. From this point the prairie plains sweep directly up to the mountains, which dominate them as highlands to the ocean.

The Huerfano is one of the upper branches of the Arkansas and following the lines of this stream the road would here enter into a country magnificently beautiful—timbered, having many bays or valleys of great fertility; having a mild and beautiful climate; having throughout the valley country short winters, which spend their force in the elevated regions of the mountains. The range of mountains in which this stream finds its head springs is distinguished by having its summits almost constantly enveloped in clouds of rain or snow, from which it obtains its name of Sierra Mojada, or Wet Mountain. This chain is remarkable among the Rocky Mountain ranges for the singular grandeur of its winter scenery, which has been characterized by travellers who have seen both as unsurpassed either in the Alps or the Himalayas. Their naked rocky summits are grouped into numerous peaks, which rise from the midst of black piny forests, whence issue many small streams to the valley below.

Following by an open wagon way the valley of the Huerfano, the road reaches the immediate foot of the mountain at the entrance of a remarkable pass, almost everywhere surrounded by bold rocky mountain masses. From one foot of the mountain to the other, the pass is about five miles long; a level valley from two to four hundred yards wide, the Mountains rising abruptly on either side. With scarcely a distinguishable rise from the river plains, the road here passes directly through or between the mountains, emerging in the open valley of Del Norte, here some forty or fifty miles broad or more properly a continuation northward of the valley in which the Del Norte runs. Crossing the flat country, or opening between the mountains, and encountering no water course in its way, the road would reach the entrance of a pass in the Colorado Mountains, familiarly known to the New Mexicans and Indian traders, who are accustomed to traverse it at all seasons of the year, and who represent it as conducting to the waters of the Colorado River through a handsome rolling grass-covered country, affording practical wagon routes.

Of this section of the route, so far as the entrance of this pass, covering twelve degrees of longitude, I am able to speak from actual exploration, and to say that the line described is not only practicable, but affords many singular facilities for the construction of a railway, and offers many advantages in the fertile and wooded country through which it lies in the greater part of its course.

In the whole distance there is not an elevation worthy of the name, to be surmounted; and a level of about 8,000 feet is gained almost without perceptible ascent. Upon the Kansas and Huerfano River valleys, the country is wooded and watered: the valley of the Del Norte is open, but wood is abundant in the neighboring mountains, and land fit for cultivation is found almost continuously along the water courses, from the mouth of the Kansas to the head of the valley of the Del Norte.

A journey undertaken in the winter of 1848–49 (and interrupted here by entering more to the southward the rugged mountains of St. John's, one of the most impracticable on the continent), was intended to make a correct examination of this pass and the country beyond to the rim of the Great Basin. The failure of this expedition leaves only for this middle position of our line such knowledge as we have been able to obtain from trappers and Indian traders. The information thus obtained had led me to attempt its exploration, as all accounts concurred in representing it practicable for a road, and these accounts were considered sufficiently reliable.

According to this information, the same structure of the country to which I have called your attention above, as forming a system among the mountains, holds good here; and I accordingly found no difficulty in believing that the road would readily avoid any obstacles which might be presented in the shape of mountain ranges, and easily reach the basin. In pronouncing upon the practicability of a road through this section, I proceed therefore upon my general knowledge of the face of the country, upon information received from hunters and residents in New Mexico, and upon the established fact that it has not only been travelled, but at all seasons of the year, and is one of the travelling routes from New Mexico to California.

The third section of the map is from the Wahsatch Mountain to the Sierra Nevada, and thence to the Bay of San Francisco. This route traverses the Great Basin, presenting three different lines, which you will find indicated on the map. Repeated journeys have given me more or less knowledge of the country along these lines, and I consider all of them practicable, although the question of preference remains to be settled. The northern line is that of the Humboldt River, which although deflecting from the direct course of the bay, commands in its approach to the mountains several practicable passes, the lowest of which is 4,500 feet above the sea. The southern line, which in crossing the Basin has not the same freedom from obstruction enjoyed by the open river line of the North, is still entirely practicable, and possesses the advantage of crossing the Sierra Nevada at a remarkably low depression, called Walker's pass, more commonly known as the *Point of the Mountains*, and being in fact, a termination of one of the mountains which go to form that chain.

This pass is near the 35th degree of latitude, and near the head of the beautiful and fertile valley San Joaquin, which the road thence would follow down to its junction with the Sacramento, or to some point on the bay. This route deflects to the south about as much as the other does to the north, but secures a good way, and finds no obstacle from the Sierra, turning that mountain where it has sunk down nearly to the level of the country. Among the recent proceedings of the California legislature, resolutions were introduced in favor of beginning in [*sic*] the railway at that pass.

The third line, which is the middle and direct line, and that to which I give a decided preference, is less known to me than either of the others: but I believe fully in its practicability, and only see the principal obstacle to be overcome is the Great Sierra itself, which it would strike near its centre. That obstacle is not considered insurmountable, nor in the present state of railway science, sufficient to turn us from the direct route. A pass is known as indicated by the line upon the map, which labor would render practicable. Other passes are also known to the north and south, and if tunneling became necessary, the structure of the mountains is such as to allow tunnels to be used with the greatest advantage. Narrow places are presented where opposite gorges approach each other, and a wall of some two or three thousand feet often separates points which may not be more than a quarter of a mile apart at its base. It will also be remembered that the Great Basin east of the Sierra Nevada, has a general elevation of over 4,000 feet, so that the mountains would be approached on the east at that elevation; on the west the slope is wide, though descending too near the level of the tide water.

The foregoing remarks embody all the general information I am now able to give upon this line. The first section of it, from the Missouri frontier to the head of the Del Norte is explored, and needs no further reconnaissances. It is ready for the location of the road by a practical engineer. The second and third sections require further explorations, to determine, not upon practicability, but upon the preference due to one over the others.

A party of 300 men, skillfully directed, with the assistance of three or four practical road engineers, would be sufficient to lay out the whole routes, and clear and open a common road in the course of next spring and summer, so as to be passable for wagons and carriages, and as rapidly traversed as any of the common roads in the United States.

The obstacles I have not mentioned are the winter impediments of snows, and the temporary one from the hostility of the Indians. The latter can be surmounted by military stations sending out military patrols to clear and scout the line. The snows are less formidable than would be supposed, from the great elevation of the central part of the route. They are dry, and therefore more readily passed through; are thin in the valleys, and remain only during a very brief winter. The winter of my last expedition was one of unprecedentedly deep and early snows, yet in the valley of the Kansas and Arkansas it was thin; in the valley of Huerfano, none; and in the valley of Del Norte the snow was only three feet deep; the thermometer at zero near midday.

The weather in these high mountains and deep valleys is of a character adapted to such localities—extremely cold on the mountains, while temperate in the valleys. I have seen it storming for days together on the mountains in a way to be destructive to all animal life exposed to it, while in the valley, there would be a pleasant sunshine, and the animals feeding on nutritious grass. Beyond the Rocky Mountains, the cold is less and the snows become a less and more transient obstacle. These are my views of a route for the road or roads (a common one is first wanted), from the Mississippi to the Pacific. It fulfills, in my opinion, all the conditions for a route for a national thoroughfare.

1st. It is direct. The course is almost a straight line. St. Louis is between 38,39; San Francisco is about the same; the route is between these parallels, or nearly between them, the whole way.

2nd. It is central to territory. It is through the territorial centre west of the Mississippi, and its prolongation to the Atlantic ocean would be central to the States east of that river. It is also central to business and population, and unites the greatest commercial point in the valley of the Mississippi with the greatest commercial point on the coast of the Pacific.

3rd. It combines the advantages for making and preserving the road, wood, water, and soil, for inhabitation and cultivation.

4th. It is a healthy route. No diseases of any kind upon it; and the valetudinarian might travel it in his own vehicle, on horse, or even on foot, for the mere restoration of health and recovery of spirits.

It not only fulfills all the conditions of a national route, but it is preferable to any other. It is preferable to the South Pass from being nearly four degrees further south, more free from open plains, and from the crossing of great rivers. Its course is parallel with the rivers, there being but one (the Upper Colorado), directly crossing its line. There are passes at the head of Arkansas, in the Three Parks, and north of them, but none equal to this by the Rio del Norte. There is no route north of it that is comparable to it; I believe there is no practicable route south of it in the United States. The disaster which turned me south from the head of the Del Norte and sent me down that river, and to the mountains around to the Upper Gila, enabled me to satisfy myself on that point.

I went a middle route—a new way—between the Gila River and the wagon-road through the Mexican province of Sonora, and am satisfied that no route for a road can be had on that line, except going through Mexico, then crossing the Great Colorado of the West, near the mouth of the Gila, to cross the desert to arrive at San Diego, and still be six hundred miles by land, and three or four hundred by water, from the Bay of San Francisco, which now is and forever must be, the great center of commerce, wealth and power on the American coast of the Pacific Ocean.

In conclusion, I have to say that I believe in the practicability of this work, and that every national consideration requires it to be done, and to be done at once, and as a national work by the United States. Your obliged fellow-citizen,

J. C. FREMONT.

Printed in *National Intelligencer*, 8 April 1850, *Daily Alta California*, 23 May 1850, and BIGELOW, 399–407.
1. The *Missouri Daily Democrat*, 14 Sept. 1853, maintained that the map never reached the president of the convention, but "strangely" fell into the hands of John Loughborough of the Saint Louis bar, who, it thought, had pirated the information for his essays promoting a Pacific railway. JCF is supposed to have gotten the map back in the fall of 1852 (*Missouri Daily Democrat*, 23 Nov. 1853), but the reader should remember that JCF was then in Europe. WHEAT [2], 56, notes that the California portion of Loughborough's map was based largely on JCF's map.

55. Robert M. Patterson to Frémont

MINT U.S.
PHIL. April 2, 1850

DEAR SIR,

I send herewith a copy of the communication which I mentioned to you as being sent to the Secretary of the Treasury in Jan. last *.[1] It has been obtained in the hope that I could accompany it with a draft of a bill for the establishment of an assay office at San Francisco. This subject, however, has been found to produce some difficulties that I had not anticipated; yet I hope to be able to send my views to you in a few days.

R. M. P.

Hon. J. C. Frémont
Washington

(*Letter dated Jan. 16, 1850)

SC, initialed (DNA-104, Records of the U.S. Mint at Philadelphia, General Correspondence).
1. As this is Patterson's copy, no enclosure was found. JCF had seen Patterson on 19 March 1850 when he had presented his letter of introduction from Dr. Joseph W. Farnum, a former assayer at the U.S. Mint at Dahlonega, Ga. Farnum had undoubtedly seen JCF when the *Oregon* called at Mazatlan, where the letter was written on 9 Jan. 1850. In all likelihood they were already acquaintances, since Farnum had resided in San Francisco in 1849, advertising

himself as "Assayer and Metallurgical Chemist, Refiner of Gold, Silver and Platina." He was an old friend of Benton's and he is undoubtedly the "Dr. Farnham" whom the Frémonts saw later in Paris. "Through him," JBF wrote, "the scientific world was open to Mr. Frémont, who, in this way acquired the best results of knowledge in mining and in treating gold" (Whitfield J. Bell, Jr., Librarian, American Philosophical Society, to Mary Lee Spence, 5 July 1978; *Alta California*, 25 Oct. 1849; "Great Events,"174).

56. Frémont to Robert M. Patterson

WASHINGTON CITY, April 3d. 1850

DEAR SIR,

Your note of yesterday enclosing a copy of the letter to the Secy. of the Treasury, I have just received. It has reached me in good time as I am just recovering from a relapse of Chagres fever. As it will [be] some ten days or so before we are admitted,[1] your letter on the subject of an assay office at San Francisco will reach me in good time to use it in Congress. I beg you to accept my thanks for your kindness to myself and for the information which will be of material benefit to California. I am with regard Yours truly,

J. C. FRÉMONT

Dr. R. M. Patterson,
Director U.S. Mint
Phila., Penn.

ALS (DNA-104, Records of the U.S. Mint at Philadelphia, General Correspondence). Endorsed: "Recd. 5th."
1. JCF was overly optimistic; California was not admitted into the Union until 10 Sept. 1850.

57. Robert M. Patterson to Frémont

MINT U.S., PHILADA.
April 5, 1850

DEAR SIR,

I have to acknowledge the receipt of your letter of the 3d inst. We have had under consideration the subject of the proposed assay office at San Francisco, but we gladly take advantage of the further delay which you think may be admitted, in the hope that we may have in time the important advantage of an interview with Dr. Farnum.

R. M. P.

Hon. J. C. Frémont
Washington

SC, initialed (DNA-104, Records of the U.S. Mint at Philadelphia, General Correspondence).

58. Frémont to Thomas Ewing

WASHINGTON CITY, April 6th, 1850

SIR:

I this day received from Mr. A. B. Gray, Surveyor of the Boundary Commission at San Diego, the enclosed letter, with a request that I would deliver it to you.[1]

As I am not able to call upon you, I comply with his wish in sending it to you. Very respectfully, Your obedient Servant.

J. C. FRÉMONT

ALS (DNA-76, No. 170, Entry 429). After the attempted recall of Weller through the appointment of JCF the previous June, the supervision of the Mexican boundary survey had been transferred from the Department of State to the Department of the Interior. Its Secretary, Thomas Ewing, would have no compunction about "butchering" Weller, his old political rival in Ohio, according to a charge made by Senator Gwin of California (*Congressional Globe*, 31st Cong, 2nd sess., 18 Dec. 1850, pp. 70–82).

1. On 10 Jan. 1849 President Polk had appointed civilian engineer and Texas emigré Andrew B. Gray (1820–62) as principal surveyor of the Mexican Boundary Commission. Gray's letter, dated San Diego, 20 Feb. 1850, is not printed here, but related to his authority to fix points for drawing the boundary. He was later dismissed from the commission largely because of differences with his new chief, John R. Bartlett, who, he charged, had sacrificed the interests of the South and Texas by placing the initial point on the Rio Grande farther north by thirty-five miles than called for by the Treaty of Guadalupe Hidalgo and the Disturnell map. For the issues and the controversy, see GOETZMANN, 173–75, and HINE [1], 31–32, 38–45.

59. Frémont to the Editors of the *National Intelligencer*

[Tuesday, 9 April, 1850]

MESSRS. EDITORS:

Everything coming from Mr. Clay carries with it so much weight, and goes so quickly to form the public opinion, that I feel called upon to make without delay the following correction.

An injurious imputation is intimated by Mr. Clay against the State of California, in the following passage of his remarks of yesterday, in the Senate:

I am not disposed to charge on a community the misconduct or peculiar opinions of any individual of that community, but I must say, what I have been constrained to feel, that I am pained to see with what contumacy, with what disregard of the allegiance due from the States, old and new, they sometimes treat the parental and paramount authority. And I was lately—I will not say provoked, for the annoyance was too slight—somewhat grieved at seeing some letter-writers from California talking already of breaking off from this Union and setting up for themselves. They will venture on no such hazardous experiment as that. If they do, I venture to say the common authority of the Union will recall them to obedience and a sense of their duty very quickly.[1]

This intimation, and the conditional menace of the power of the Government, I feel bound to say, are both gratuitous, because there is nothing in the present occasion, nor in the conduct of the people of that State, to warrant them. So far from exhibiting any feelings of contumacy or disrespect to the Union, the people of California, in all their public assemblages and public acts, have steadily manifested an enthusiastic affection and perfect respect for the country and Government of the United States. The great body of people in California are American citizens, who have recently left this portion of the country—many of them temporarily, and all of whom are connected with it by ties of family and business. It was a thing of course to regard California as a part of their common country, and no doubt or question regarding her future condition as a component part of it has ever been raised there. In the formation of her constitution the Convention labored scrupulously to assimilate it with those of the other States of the Union, and to insert nothing, and to omit nothing, which might in any way retard her admission, or make a cause of opposition to it. Mr. Clay is not warranted in seizing upon the remark of an unknown letter-writer, which is contradicted by every public and authorized act of the People and the State, to hang upon it an implied charge of disloyalty, and a conditional threat of punishment.

The Government of the United States has been three years indebted to the people of California for property taken and services rendered, and during this time they have been paying taxes, without representation, and without protection.

In fact, the only connexion, with a single exception, that now exists between this Government and the people of California is their loyalty and affection for the Union. The exception I allude to is the *taxation* which this government sends its ministers there to collect: the tax-law being the only law of the United States which the Government has been pleased to extend to them. The people there pay tribute to this government, and this is the only tie between them and it, except what their spontaneous sentiment creates, and manifests in their present patient application to be received into closer and assured connexion. Respectfully yours,

J. C. FRÉMONT

Printed in *National Intelligencer*, 10 April 1850.
1. See Senator Henry Clay's remarks in *Congressional Globe*, 31st Cong., 1st sess., 8 April 1850, p. 661. Clay was referring to a movement in Los Angeles to have the country from San Luis Obispo to San Diego established as a territory. The opposition to statehood came largely from the holders of old Spanish and Mexican land grants who feared, first, that the expenses of a state government would bring ruinous taxes on them since the public domain could not be taxed, and second, that the state legislature would favor the more populous north (BANCROFT, 23:349n).

60. Frémont to John Bidwell

WASHINGTON CITY
April 10th 1850

MY DEAR SIR,

I have received your letter including Marshall's petition.[1] This shall be presented and we will do what we can to get it admitted so soon as the State is received. The public papers will give you a fair idea of the state of things here, but almost every day presents a different phase, and it is difficult to say when we shall be admitted though probably within a month.

I send you a paper containing the debate of Monday which will let you see how the question stands in the Senate. In both houses we have a considerable majority. I go with the party which claims to have California admitted alone. You will find in one of the papers I send, a card from me in relation to some of Mr. Clay's remarks.[2]

I go off in the morning to New York in order to arrange some business for the steamer of the 13th and therefore write you briefly— but I shall write you frequently. We are prepared immediately on ad- mission, to urge the bills in reference to lands and other measures which the condition of California so much demands. We would have them brought forward now but nothing can possibly be done until the California question is settled.

We are able to see by the California papers that the question of land titles is becoming daily more involved and is a matter of deep regret to us here that we are made the battle ground for some dema- gogues to get capital from while the country is suffering. In regard to investing the county courts with jurisdiction to settle the land titles, it would be useless to send any such petition here, as the constitution expressly gives to the United States courts sole jurisdiction in all con- troversies to which the United States shall be a party, and therefore Congress can grant nothing of the kind.

I congratulate you on the amount of business your legislature is doing, and on the manner in which it is done. I shall be very glad to have from you any reports and other proceedings of your body. Very truly yours,

J. C. FRÉMONT

ALS (Sutter's Fort State Historical Monument).

1. There is no indication in the records that JCF ever presented the petition to Congress. It has not been found, but James Marshall undoubtedly asked for a large grant of land around the sawmill on the South Fork of the American River where he had discovered gold. GAY, 284–98, notes subsequent unsuccessful peti- tions, one of which was presented on Marshall's behalf by Commodore Robert F. Stockton in 1852.

2. See Doc. No. 59 and notes.

61. Frémont to Edward F. Beale

WASHINGTON, April 17th, 10 p.m. [1850]

MY DEAR MR. BEALE,

Yours of today is just received. My note of this morning will be agreeable to you as it informs you that there will be some delay in the Secretary's reply to your application for furlough. We will do what we can to delay it beyond the 27th.

You will see by the morning's papers that there was an occurrence today in the Senate which will necessarily keep me in Washington just now. Foote drew a pistol on Col. Benton, and although there will be no consequences to the affair, it would not be proper for me to leave.[1] In the meantime don't you leave your wife, as I will keep you well informed of what goes on here, and we will try to come and see you after a little. My wife sends her regards to Mrs. Beale,[2] and asks you to say to her that from long experience she knows well how to sympathise with her. Do not leave home, but let me hear from you. Are you writing up your Gila journey?[3] Yours truly,

J. C. FRÉMONT

Mr. Edward F. Beale
Chester, Penn.

ALS (DLC—Decatur House Papers, Box 4).
1. For some time the Senate had been debating Henry Clay's proposals with reference to slavery, the admission of California, the organization of territorial governments in New Mexico and Utah, and the Texas–New Mexico boundary—all of which later came to be called the Compromise of 1850. Mississippian Henry S. Foote wished the proposals referred to a select committee of thirteen; Benton wanted the power of the committee so limited that it could not discuss abolition, in this way permitting Congress to reassure southerners that it had no desire to oppress them or their institutions. When Benton referred briefly to Calhoun's Southern Address (1849) as "agitation," Foote, who had goadingly vilified the Missourian on a number of previous occasions, began a reply that was personally vindictive. At this point Benton left his desk and advanced toward Foote; the latter backed down the aisle toward the vice-president's dais, drawing and cocking a five-chambered loaded pistol as he moved. Pandemonium reigned in the Senate. A special committee was appointed to investigate the incident and when it questioned JCF as to Benton's motive in approaching Foote, the explorer replied, "As nearly as I can remember, Mr. Benton said he went to or towards Mr. Foote's desk, to hear what Mr. Foote should say" (Senate Report 170, 31st Cong., 1st sess., p. 31, Serial 565). Its report intimated that Benton had intended to intimidate or assault Foote and absolved Foote of "any design or desire to assassinate" Benton, but did condemn him for engaging in "offensive and insult-

ing" personalities. For details of this particular incident and of earlier Benton-Foote confrontations, see not only the report cited above but also the *Congressional Globe*, 31st Cong., 1st sess., 17 April, 27 March, 30 July 1850, pp. 751–64, 602–4, 1480–81; CHAMBERS, 356–62; and GONZALES, 69–71.

2. The Beales' first child, Mary, nicknamed "Mame," had been born in March.

3. The "Gila journey" was Beale's 1848–49 trip to California when he met the same winter conditions that almost destroyed JCF in the San Juans. Fifty miles below Socorro, he took the route which Stephen Watts Kearny had used in 1846 and which for a time follows the Gila River through deep gorges. Several times Beale's mules slipped off the narrow ledges and plunged to their deaths. In central Arizona his party was attacked by Apaches, and in the Mojave it suffered from a severe shortage of water. He seems never to have written an official account of his journey; in fact, he reported to Bayard Taylor on 28 March 1850 that he was finding it impossible to do so.

62. Frémont to C. Edwards Lester

WASHINGTON CITY, April 25, 1850

MY DEAR SIR,

I had the pleasure to receive your letter yesterday morning. My recent illness accumulated engagements so much upon me, that I find myself just now oppressed with business. I was therefore glad to thank Colonel Benton for offering to draw up the account you suggest,[1] and the more especially as he will use only more prominent circumstances, from want of acquaintance with details. Of course, you will model as you please the sketch he may send you, *striking* out and amending according as your particular view of the subject will require.

Making you many acknowledgements for the distinction of being placed so early in your work, I am, with regard, yours truly,

J. C. FRÉMONT

Charles Edward[s] Lester, Esqre.
New York

ALS (James S. Copley Collection, La Jolla, Calif.). Trained in both law and theology, Charles Edwards Lester (1815–90) was now engaged in writing popular biography and history and serving as a correspondent of the London *Times*.

1. For information about Benton's *Thrilling Sketch of the Life of Col. J. C. Fremont* . . ., see Doc. No. 72.

63. Frémont to Benjamin D. Wilson

My DEAR SIR,

Your letter of January 1st was received by the last mail from California, and probably too late to prevent payment of the draft, provided certain sales were made out of which payment was to have been made. You will probably see Mr. Jones shortly after the receipt of this letter, as he will sail for California in the steamer of May 4th, and his business will necessarily call him to your part of the country soon after his arrival.[1] It is not probable that the state will be admitted before the last days of the session, and we shall therefore have very little time to work for California in Congress, but we will [do] all that is possible. At all events if we can get no good laws passed, we will take care that no bad ones are. You will see from Butler King's report,[2] that he is against the old land titles in California; but he cannot do any harm, and has laid himself open to us by his great ignorance of the whole subject. His object is to gain popularity among the newcomers in California. The administration too have brought forward a bill hostile to the titles, but we shall have no difficulty in defeating it, whether we are in or out of Congress.

Since Mr. Calhoun's death[3] Clay has been endeavoring to get at the head of the Southern party, and so has acted with them against the interests & admission of California, but the voice of the whole country is rising against them, and newspapers of all parties are everywhere coming out against them.

I send you some of Col. Benton's speeches on the subject and some newspapers & other documents. Yours truly,

J. C. FRÉMONT

Capt. B. D. Wilson
Los Angeles, Cal.

ALS (CSmH).
1. With William Carey Jones went Gwinn Harris Heap, JCF's newly appointed resident agent for Las Mariposas (Testimony, DNA-49, California Private Land Claims Dockets, Docket 1, pp. 100–101). He was a cousin of Edward F. Beale and a discoverer of one of the early veins—the Heap Vein—on the estate. Also traveling to California in May with Jones and Heap was Beale's brother-in-law, Henry B. Edwards. From the time of his arrival until his temporary return in Oct. 1851, he was primarily on the Mariposa "doing business on his own account," and later assisting JCF in the delivery of cattle to the Indians

under the contract with George W. Barbour (Certificate of Henry B. Edwards, 24 Jan. 1852, DNA-75, LR, California B-10 1852 f/w Special File No. 266).

2. House Ex. Doc. 59, 31st Cong., 1st sess., Serial 577.

3. John C. Calhoun died 31 March 1850.

64. Frémont to Robert M. Patterson

WASHINGTON CITY, April 27, 1850

MY DEAR SIR,

Your note of yesterday is just received. I intended the specimens to be destroyed in making the examination. So far as my judgment could be formed from what excavations we had had time to make, I considered the different specimens which I sent on by Mr. Hunt[1] as representing about what would be the average product. He sent me yesterday some results which appear enormous. I desired him to ask you if you should find it convenient to ascertain more particularly in what proportion the gold was contained in such fragments of the rock as do not show *any*. May I hope soon to hear the result? Very truly yours,

JOHN C. FRÉMONT

Dr. R. M. Patterson,
Philadelphia.

ALS (DNA-104, Records of the U.S. Mint at Philadelphia, General Correspondence). Endorsed: "Recd. 29."

1. Possibly Alfred Hunt, who later testified that he was acquainted with JCF's handwriting (Testimony before J. B. Burns, 22 Feb. 1858, in connection with business of the Philadelphia and California Mining Company, Mariposa County Deeds, Book D, pp. 360–64).

65. Frémont to Jacob R. Snyder

WASHINGTON CITY, April 29, 1850

MY DEAR MAJOR,

Yours of the 26th I received yesterday. We regret to hear of the continued ill health of your mother, but hope it may improve in the present fine weather, and that we may soon have the pleasure of seeing you here. Mr. Larkin writes me that he will be here with others of our friends about the 5th.[1] I sent your message to Mr. Beale by his brother-in-law, Edwards.[2] He will be here himself tomorrow. Very truly yours,

J. C. FRÉMONT

Major Jacob R. Snyder
Philadelphia

ALS (The Society of California Pioneers—Jacob Rink Snyder Papers).
1. Ex-Consul Thomas O. Larkin had several reasons for bringing his influence to Washington. His war loans to JCF in California were still unpaid by Congress; he wished to have Benicia, where he had heavy investments, made a port of entry; and he recognized that his own land claims would be greatly benefited by the loose-claim legislation favored by JCF and Benton (GATES [2]).
2. See Doc. No. 63, n.1.

66. Frémont to Thomas O. Larkin *et al.*

WASHINGTON, 30 April 1850.

[Regrets that his "numerous and pressing engagements" will prevent his attending the reunion of so many old friends and fellow citizens. Printed in New York *Herald*, 2 May 1850. The *Herald* noted that the grand dinner and magnificent ball, costing $8,000–$10,000, took place at the Irving House on Broadway. "It was given by 24 Californians to their friends from California, and those at home who had taken a prominent part in the California movements. . . . It was the most choice, recherché, elegant, refined, tasty affair that had ever been got up in New York. . . . One hundred and fifty people of both sexes went there to be happy."]

67. Frémont to Thomas Denny Sargent

[30 April 1850]

An Indenture, made this thirtieth day of April in the year One thousand eight hundred and fifty between John Charles Fremont of the first part, and Thomas D. Sargent of the other;

Witnesseth that in consideration of the rents, provisos and agreements hereinafter Contained and Which on the part of the said Thomas D. Sargent are to be done and performed, he the said John Charles Fremont has demised and leased, and does hereby demise and Lease to the said Thomas D. Sargent his executors, Administrators and assigns a lot or square of land measuring six hundred feet on each of the four sides with all the Mineral property and issues therein Contained, quicksilver along [sic] excepted,—the Said lot or square of land, being upon a tract belonging to said John Charles Fremont, by Virtue of purchase from Don Juan B. Alvarado, ex-Governor of California the same situate near or on the Mariposas river, and its branches, The square of land to be selected by the party of the second part from any of the lands above described, not previously Occupied by Consent of said John Charles Fremont at the time of the Selection Which is to be made upon the ground,

To have and to hold the same to the party of the second part, to his heirs and assigns without let, hindrance or molestation from the party of the first part, or from any person or persons Claiming by, through or under him the said John Charles Fremont for and during the term of Seven years from the date hereof.

The party of the first part does further grant to the party of the second part a Section of land not exceeding One hundred Acres, the Selection of Which to be approved by said John C. Fremont provided said selection be not made on Mineral land And that no mining Operation of any description be Carried on upon it, but to be Occupied and improved for farming purposes, building houses, or any other purposes Connected with Mining Operations upon the aforesaid square of land, with permission to Cut such timber and Wood as may be necessary for his wants, and also to make use of such Water and Water privileges not previously Occupied as may be required for his Mining Operations,

It is further granted and agreed by the party of the first part that the party of the second part at any time exchange the lot of Which he shall at first Select for another of the same dimensions upon the aforesaid premises not leased to other parties nor improved by the party of the first part, for his own use.

And in Consideration of the above Lease, the party of the second part does hereby Covenant and agree to pay to the said John Charles Fremont, his heirs and assigns One sixth part of all the Gold and other Minerals Obtained from Mining, or any other Operations upon said square of land, the same to be paid or delivered, quarterly at the Mines,

The party of the second part agrees, that if the aforesaid square of land Occupied by him shall remain unimproved for Mining purposes, at any One time, for a period of Six months, the same shall revert with all the privileges appertaining to said lot to the party of the first part,

And it is understood that nothing herein Contained shall be Construed to imply a permission to work any Mine or Mines of quicksilver, Which are expressly reserved to the party of the first part, and the said Thomas D. Sargent, his heirs, executors and administrators does Covenant to and with the said John Charles Fremont, his heirs and assigns, that he will peaceably Yield up said lands, and all the privilege thereto belonging at the expiration of Seven Years from the Date hereof, together with all and singular the improvements which shall have been made, upon said lands, the same becoming the property of the said John Charles Fremont.

In Witness Whereof the parties to these presents have hereto set their hands and affixed their seals the day and year above written
Witness to the
Signatures of
J. C. Fremont &   J. C. Fremont [*Seal*]
T. D. Sargent.   T. D. Sargent [*Seal*]
G. H. Heap.

DS (Office of the Recorder of Deeds, Washington, D.C.). Lease recorded 16 May 1850.

Copies of JCF's early leases are rare, and biographical information on Thomas Denny Sargent must be pieced together from many sources. At this time he was thirty-four years old and had lived in Massachusetts (DNA-59, Passport Applications, vol. 72, no. 5457). Four days after obtaining this lease from JCF he assigned "two undivided thirds" of all his interest in it to two fellow residents of the District of Columbia, Alexander H. Harper and James Eldridge (Sargent to Harper and Eldridge, 3 May 1850, Office of the Recorder of Deeds, Washington, D.C.). He then obtained a second lease from JCF on 21 May 1850 and with Harper and Eldridge went out to the Mariposa to prospect and locate their leases. The one in which all three had an interest was located on the banks of the Mariposa River and was called the Santa Maria Mine; the second lease was located on a quartz vein, situated on the banks of the Ave Maria River, and came to be known as the San Carlos Mine.

Sargent then went to England in an attempt to interest Britishers in forming companies and raising capital for working the two mines. His operations were vigorously resisted by David Hoffman, who had been authorized by JCF to form companies and grant leases. In the meantime Harper died, and in a quick trip to the United States to arrange for the retransfer of the Eldridge-Harper interests to himself, Sargent negotiated with J. Eugene Flandin and Thomas H. Benton to purchase the entire Mariposa estate for a million dollars (DUNCAN). JCF repudiated the sale; Sargent lodged a bill of complaint against him in the British Court of Chancery and JCF settled "privately" (Sargent v. Frémont, British Court of Chancery, 27 March 1852, and Frémont v. Hoffman, Brief, Bill and Answer, 24 Dec. 1852, p. 13; copies of both of these long documents are in NHi—David Hoffman Papers).

In 1861 Sargent wrote the Secretary of War that he had a strategem for "bagging" Jefferson Davis and other prominent secessionists "without much cost comparatively" (Sargent to Simon Cameron, 8 July 1861, DNA-107, LR S-183 [98]).

68. Robert M. Patterson to Frémont

MINT U.S. PHIL. May 2, 1850

DEAR SIR,

Your specimens of California gold ore has been carefully examined, and has led to the following results.

The whole weight of gold in the piece was 34 grains.

It was divided into two parts. One the quartz with visible gold, and the other quartz without visible gold.

The gold in the first was in the proportion of 459.38 grs. in one lb. avoirdupois.

The gold in the second was in the proportion of 3.15 grs. per lb. avoir.

The fineness of the gold was 888.5 thousandths.

Hence it follows that the value of 100 lbs. avoir, (compounding to about a bushel in volume), of the first portion, is $1755.

And the value of 100 lbs. of the second part is $12.11.

R. M. P.

SC, initialed (DNA-104, Records of the U.S. Mint at Philadelphia, General Correspondence).

69. Frémont to William M. Gwin

C STREET, WASHINGTON, May 8th [1850]

MY DEAR SIR,

Thinking you may perhaps need Dr. Chamberlin's letter at the Senate,[1] I send it up immediately.

I had been for some time aware that such a movement was intended, & am glad to know that it found such small support. Yours truly,

J. C. Frémont

Hon. Mr. Gwin
Senate Chamber

ALS (CU-B). William McKendree Gwin (1805–85) was the other senator-elect from California. After its admission he drew the long term, to JCF's great disappointment. Gwin was likewise very ambitious and his primary motive in going to California was to obtain the senatorial office and return to Congress, where he had already represented Mississippi in the House (THOMAS, 23–29).

1. Elected from the San Diego district and like Gwin a physician, E. Kirby Chamberlin was president pro tem of the California senate. An extract of his letter is contained in Senator Foote's remarks as printed in the *Congressional Globe*, 31st Cong., 1st. sess., 9 May 1850, p. 967. Dealing with the opposition of the southern Californians to state government noted in Doc. No. 59, n. 1, Chamberlin termed the disaffection slight, coming largely from the old American Spaniards with "not a single new resident or emigrant" participating. The Hungarian Agoston Harazthy, however, was behind the opposition in San Diego, which Edward Gilbert termed "little short of treason" (*ibid.*; Gilbert to *Daily Alta California*, Washington, D.C., 10 May 1850).

70. Robert M. Patterson to Frémont

U.S. Mint, Philada.
May 10, 1850

Hon. John C. Frémont
Dear Sir

You are aware that I have been delaying compliance with your request for the draft of a bill organizing an Assay Office in California in the hope of conferring personally with Dr. Farnum, whose judgment and experience would render essential aid. He has not arrived; and I must therefore beg you to give me your views, as a preliminary step, upon the alternative which I have to propose.

Do you, on the one hand, think it best that the proposed Assay Office should be solely for the accommodation of custom-house transactions, so that the Collector should first receive the grain-gold, subject to the determination of its value by the Assayer; or, on the other hand, should the Office be constituted upon a large plan, and for general accommodation, so that the grain-gold should first be carried *there*, assayed, cast into bars, and stamped, and *then* be receivable at the Custom House, and for public lands, and perhaps for debts between individuals?

The two bases here suggested would require very different schemes of legislation, and I do not feel prepared to proceed upon either, without your advice and direction. Very respectfully,

[*Unsigned*]

SC (DNA-104, Records of the U.S. Mint at Philadelphia, General Correspondence).

71. Frémont to Robert M. Patterson

WASHINGTON CITY, May 15, 1850

MY DEAR SIR,

I was gratified with the receipt of yours of the 10th inst. as it is probable that we shall in a few weeks be able to do something for our state, and I would be glad to have things in the best possible condition for taking most advantage of what little time will remain for our share of business. I am clearly of opinion that we should adopt the larger of the two plans you propose. It provides for the general accommodation and will be most serviceable to the country.

Please let me hear as soon as your many other avocations conveniently permit, and oblige. Yours very truly,

J. C. FRÉMONT

Dr. R. M. Patterson,
Director U.S. Mint
Philadelphia

ALS (DNA-104, Records of the U.S. Mint at Philadelphia, General Correspondence). Endorsed: "Recd. 17."

72. Frémont to C. Edwards Lester

My dear Sir,

Your note of the 15th was received last night. I have been for several days tied down to business connected with California and therefore did not read, until after the receipt of your note, what Col. Benton had drawn up.[1] I am not satisfied with it because it is altogether too eulogistic giving too much *point* to small things, and if I were to make any correction of it, I would do so by rewriting the whole. But as your letter is urgent—leaving no time for me to write—I send you Col. Benton's sketch, earnestly requesting you to use it, as you say in your note as *material*, and clothing the facts you may select in your own language, I regret that you have this labor, which I certainly intended should have been spared you.

I remarked to Col. Benton that his article is altogether beyond the length contemplated by your sketches. He therefore expects that you will only use prominent points, and asks that the manuscript may afterward be returned to him as he designs extending it for other purposes.

I send you, accompanying the manuscript, a July number of the Southern [Quarterly] Review which contains a notice of myself by Govr. Hammond of South Carolina.[2] It is a well written article, and may furnish you with some material. Knowing that your own excellent taste will make the proper use of Col. Benton's sketch, I leave it in your hands & am very truly yours,

J. C. Frémont

C. Edwards Lester
New York

ALS (ICHi).
1. Benton's short biography of JCF was published in London in several editions with varying titles. J. Field printed it as a twenty-one-page pamphlet entitled *Thrilling Sketch of the Life of Col. J. C. Fremont*, . . . and also combined it with a more lengthy description of his overland route to Oregon and California. R. S. Francis and J. K. Chapman put out similar enlarged editions. All four were designed to attract the public to John Skirving's moving panorama which opened in Egyptian Hall, Piccadilly, on 27 April 1850. It attracted 35,000 patrons and ran until 6 Dec. 1851 before being dismantled for showing in the provincial cities and towns of Great Britain. The panorama was painted by American art-

ists—Skirving, Joseph Kyle, Jacob A. Dallas, and J. Lee—who based a large portion of their work on sketches from Frémont's expeditions (ARRINGTON).

A similar JCF tableau opened at the Théâtre des Variétes in Paris on 8 Aug. 1850 (HULBERT).

2. JCF errs in attributing authorship of the unsigned article to the former governor of South Carolina, James Henry Hammond. Written by his brother, Marcus Claudius Marcellus Hammond, the article was entitled "The Conquest of California and the Case of Lieut. Col. Fremont," and was published in the *Southern Quarterly Review*, 15 (July 1849):410–44 (SIMMS, 2:484–85, 530–31).

73. Frémont to C. Edwards Lester

WASHINGTON CITY, May 17, 1850

MY DEAR SIR,

Since writing the note of this morning I have sent you by Adams Express the volume containing Govr. Hammond's sketch[1] of myself in the article headed "Conquest of California."

I write to call your attention particularly to the latter part of it— thinking you might not have time to read the whole. I think this concluding part written with force and beauty & I will be gratified if you find yourself able to draw upon it for some of your material.[2]

The volume I send is borrowed from the Congressional Library— please return it as sent, as soon as you have done using it. Yours very truly,

J. C. FRÉMONT

ALS-JBF (CSmH).

1. For correct authorship, see Doc. No. 72, n. 2.

2. The article was extremely laudatory of JCF, who Hammond noted was no mere "mushroom hero." He conceded that Benton's support had not always been favorable to his cause, but wrote: "He [Frémont] will probably shake off the dust from his garments, and, by new and more noble achievements in science and discovery, clear his escutcheon from every stigma. . . . His endowments are large and solid, highly cultivated and constantly expanding. . . . If Generals Scott and Taylor are historically immortal for capturing the city of the Montezumas and subduing the northern provinces, Frémont must be equally distinguished for *his* conquest, which, intrinsically, is incomparably superior to them all" (*Southern Quarterly Review*, 15 [July 1849]:410–44).

74. Frémont to Richard Robert

WASHINGTON CITY, May 19, 1850

DEAR SIR:

A reference to the large map published in 1848,[1] and which is amongst the Papers I have given, will shew you the position of the Mariposas upon a small affluent to the Upper San Joaquin. The smaller sketch, altho' not a topographical plan, is a survey of the place, and is sufficient to shew its general features.[2] It is divided into sections, according to the nature of the ground, the upper or mountain section containing about 25 square miles being the gold bearing part; and the lower section that which is more especially suited to agriculture. In the middle section, there are small and fertile vallies, very suitable for cultivation. The middle and upper sections are wooded with oak and pine, and the lower or valley section is wooded with oaks, only along the immediate valley or bottom lands of the stream.

This stream runs directly across the valley of the San Joaquin, but reaches the main river only in the rainy season. At other times and throughout the course in the valley section, the stream bed has water only in holes, or springs, which remain all the year. The soil of the immediate valley of the stream in this the plain or valley section is a rich vegetable mould covered with luxuriant grass and wild oats, which latter remain green until the end of June, later than is generally the case in other parts of the Country. This is an evidence of a large share of moisture in the soil and favorable to its cultivation. In the mountain section the water runs all the year in the eastern branches of the stream and is sufficient for all mining purposes, and if collected by a small aqueduct, could be carried below to irrigate the valley section, which the large body of fertile land there would well justify.

You will remark noticed upon the Plan of the place particular points where gold has been found most abundant. We suppose it to be distributed in greater or less quantity throughout the soil of the mountain section (25 square miles) and very probably further still. This part of the tract is intersected by many lines of quartz rock, but there have been and a few of them only, very slightly examined.

The particular vein which we have opened is in a ledge of quartz rock in the hill[?] on the east side of the Eastern Fork of the Mariposa Creek. You will find it marked upon the plan by the words "Quartz

Rock." This rock has a very great inclination and extends some three or four miles in length to where it terminates in a hill of quartz. When I left California in January last, this rock had been opened but in one point and only to a depth of about two feet. The gold showed in the side in a thickness of about two feet.

Examinations made upon what we judged to be ordinary specimens from this rock gave the results which are stated in the letters from Mr. Hunt and the Director of the Mint at Philadelphia.[3] How far this character of the rock may continue we cannot say, as no examination has been made. The stream which runs parallel with it is throughout rich in gold, and this circumstance warrants the opinion that the rock is in the same condition.

By the steamer of the 4th instant I sent agents[4] there for the purpose of further examination.

The above comprise the most material facts in relation to the place.

During the quarter part of the year and probably all the year, small steamers may run within 45 miles of the Mine, and experience so far shows that it is a remarkably healthy region.

Other information may be furnished you as points arise from time to time. Yours truly,

J. C. FREMONT

Richard Robert, Esq.
Washington City

Copy (NHi—David Hoffman Papers). Endorsed: "Mr. Andrew Smith. Copy letter by Col. F. of information and instruction to his Agents." Richard Robert, an American residing in London, was in Baltimore on a business mission for David Hoffman when Charles F. Mayer introduced him to JCF. Robert was able to convince the latter of the value of having British capitalists develop Las Mariposas. Within a short time he and Hoffman had a power of attorney to act together as JCF's agents in forming associations, raising money, and giving leases for the development of the California estate (Doc. No. 75).

1. The map of Oregon and California was published as part of Senate Misc. Doc. 148, 30th Cong., 1st sess., Serial 511, and as Map 5 in the Map Portfolio accompanying Vol. 1.

2. Charles Preuss had surveyed the grant in the summer of 1849 and made a map (see Vol. 2, p. 299n, and TYSON, 29).

3. See Doc. Nos. 64 and 68.

4. Gwinn Harris Heap and Henry B. Edwards left from New York (see Doc. No. 63, n. 1).

75. Frémont's Power of Attorney to Richard Robert and David Hoffman

[21 May 1850]

Whereas, I, John Charles Frémont, of California, am proprietor of Lands in that Territory containing Gold ore, and also, as it is believed, Quicksilver ore, and desire that said Gold and Quicksilver ores should be mined and be made available, and am, therefore, willing to convey and assure to any Associations, or Joint-Stock companies, for that object, to be formed in England and on the Continent of Europe, full mining privileges for said metals in said lands, or in such portions thereof as may be set apart for such associations or companies, but to such extent as shall afford occupations for all the workmen and machinery that any such Associations, or Companies, shall employ and be prepared to use and apply at any time:

Now these Presents witness that to carry into effect my above declared objects, I have appointed and hereby constitute and appoint Richard Robert, Esquire, of London and about to go thither from these United States of America, my Attorney for me to proceed to England and to the Continent of Europe and in my name to propose for subscriptions to stock for an Association or Associations as aforesaid—the Capital for any one association's stock not being less than

Hundred Thousand Pounds Sterling—such subscriptions to be taken and stipulated for on such terms with reference to any share of the monies yielded by the subscription, and in regard to any share of the nett profits of the mining aforesaid, in my behalf and for my benefit, as my said Attorney, in conjunction with David Hoffman,[1] Esquire, of 41 Conduit Street, London, shall fix and ordain, and said Richard Robert and David Hoffman, Esquires, also stipulating in my name that the Mining privileges aforesaid shall be only and effectually granted and assured to such associations for terms of years extending to the period of Seven years, and to be exercised within such limits in my said Lands as shall be fixed by said Robert and Hoffman under any Letter or Letters of Instruction from me or from Charles Frederick Mayer,[2] Esquire, of Baltimore, counter-signed by me; it being, however, understood that such limits shall afford adequate scope for the employment as aforesaid of all workmen and machinery that may be had and prepared by said Associations for mining as aforesaid: in the term "mining" I embrace all washings from streams. And I do hereby empower my said Attorney Richard Robert, with the advice and under the direction of said Hoffman, to take all proceedings and do all things and enter into all contracts for and toward, organizing Associations as aforesaid and, so far as may be practicable, in such manner that the members thereof shall be held to no personal responsibility for any operations, or contracts, of such associations; and it being hereby provided that said David Hoffman, Esquire, shall be a Trustee and Director of, and in respect of any such Associations that may be formed in England.

And I do hereby provide and declare that, until the Associations to be formed as aforesaid shall respectively be perfected in organization so as to be entitled to act in their respective associate or corporate names and capacities and in that character to take charge of monies subscribed, the monies to be subscribed for stock as aforesaid shall be deposited with, and by the Stock subscribers paid to, such Bankers as may be designated by said Hoffman and Robert, to be held for the Associations forming as aforesaid, and ultimately to be applied as the proposed terms of subscription, or Association, may require or allow.

And I do hereby require that in respect of the share, or interest, that shall be fixed and specified for me in the profits and operations of any such associations, provisions be made for a representation of my concern as aforesaid, or that of my Executors, Administrators, or Assigns, in the Directory or Board of Management or of Trustees, or other Administrative authority of such Associations, according to the form of the organization aforesaid.

And to the effect and toward the fulfillment of what I have herein before declared, I do hereby, for myself and my Heirs, covenant with all Members of Associations to be created and organized as aforesaid; and also that all that I shall direct, and assent to by any Letter, or Letters, of Instructions from me or countersigned by me, in any wise concerning the objects or interests of such Associations, or of any of the members as such of said Associations shall to all purposes be deemed as part of these presents and as if here embodied.

In witness whereof I do hereto, at the City of Washington, in the District of Columbia, set my Hand and Seal, this Eighteenth Day of May in the year of Our Lord Eighteen Hundred and Fifty.

[*Signature cut out and the following paragraph added:*]

And I do hereby further declare that no privileges or rights granted to any Association or Associations formed in pursuance of powers and instructions given in the above instrument to my said attorney

Richard Robert in conjunction with David Hoffman, Esquire, shall be considered binding upon me until their acts shall have been duly ratified and approved by me. In whereof I do hereto at the City of Washington in the District of Columbia set my Hand and Seal this twenty-first day of May in the year of our Lord Eighteen Hundred and Fifty.

JOHN CHARLES FRÉMONT

Signed, Sealed, and delivered
in presence of
John M. Clayton
W. S. Derrick [?]

DS (NHi—David Hoffman Papers). Attached to the power of attorney is a certificate to the effect that JCF's signature is genuine and entitled to full faith and credit. It is signed by John M. Clayton, Secretary of State.

1. David Hoffman (1784–1854) had been professor of law at the University of Maryland, but had been living in London since 1847, where he sometimes promoted land and emigration companies. He and JCF were casual acquaintances of long standing, having been introduced by Joseph N. Nicollet.

2. Charles F. Mayer, a brother of the more famous Brantz, was an attorney in Baltimore and had served a term in Maryland's senate (SCHARF). Hoffman and the Mayer brothers were lifelong friends.

76. Frémont to David Hoffman

WASHINGTON CITY, May 22. 1850

DEAR SIR,

After some consultation with our mutual friend Charles F. Mayer, Esquire, I have decided to request you to become a Trustee in England of all my interests in an association which I desire to form there for the purpose of carrying on mining operations upon a certain property held by me in the gold region of California. I have deputed Richard Robert, Esquire, of London, who will hand you this note, to confer with you upon this subject, and have also commissioned him to act in conjunction with you, should you conclude to accept the trust. In that event you will please draw upon me for the necessary and reasonable expenditures which Mr. Robert may contract in the formation of the association. Mr. Mayer, who has consented to act as my solicitor will send on from time to time such farther information and instructions as may present themselves here, or may grow out of your own suggestions.

As our mining interests require immediate action, I would be glad to have your views as early as suits with your convenience. Hoping therefore to hear from you about the end of June, I am very respectfully yours,

J. C. Frémont

David Hoffman, Esquire
Conduit Street, London

ALS (NHi—David Hoffman Papers). Endorsed: "Recd. June 5th. London. 1st Letter."

77. Frémont to Charles F. Mayer

Washington City, May 28, 1850

My Dear Sir,

Your note was received on Sunday. Enclosed I send you a draft for the fifty dollars.

Intelligence by the last mail from California is very favourable. I send you the Intelligencer of today with a marked page, altho' you will have noticed that item in other papers. The Intelligencer contains a fair summary of what I see in the Californian.[1]

I have heard by letter at second hand by Mr. McG from his Son at the Mariposas,[2] that a piece of rock was broken from my vein *containing several pounds of Gold in one mass.*

This, in fact is only what we, from analogy have good reason to expect, as the condition of the rock. Very truly yours,

J. C. Frémont

Copy in Hoffman v. Fremont, Statement, pt. I (NHi—David Hoffman Papers).
1. The *National Intelligencer*, 28 May 1850, noted that the newly created city in the gold diggings—Mariposa City—had been surveyed by C. Armstrong, fifteen to twenty stores were established, a hotel was operating, 1,500 people were in the gulch and 3,000 settled nearby. While operations on the Frémont vein had not yet commenced, it predicted a "rich harvest," since several fragments broken from the veins appeared "high grade."

2. "Mr. McG" is probably Edward McGehee, father of Micajah. A brother had written Micajah that their father had seen JCF in Washington "and heard from him a vague account of your suffering" (C. G. McGehee to Micajah McGehee, 26 June 1850, LU—James Stewart McGehee Papers, 2:237–41).

78. Frémont to Charles F. Mayer

WASHINGTON CITY, May 30, 1850

DEAR SIR,

I have just received your note of yesterday, and send you immediately the enclosed note to Mr. Hoffman.[1]

We have been successful with our Bill for a mint at San Francisco, together with an Assayer's office *ad interim*, in the Senate, and we have not any doubt of its success in the House.[2]

I will forward you all I hear of interest in relation to California & remain Yours very truly,

J. C. FRÉMONT

Mr. Mayer
Baltimore

ALS (NNPM). Endorsed.
1. See Doc. No. 76.
2. It was to be two more years before a bill to establish a branch mint at San Francisco would pass both houses of Congress (*Congressional Globe*, 32nd Cong., 1st sess., 23 June 1852, p. 1602). The mint began operations on 3 April 1854 (CROSS, 1:142).

79. Abbott Lawrence to Frémont

LONDON, May 31st, 1850

DEAR SIR,

On the 27th Inst., I had the honor to receive from the President of the Royal Geographical Society[1] the Founder's Medal, which was awarded to you by the Council of that Society, for your pre-eminent services in promoting the cause of Geographical Science. The Meeting was public, and the reasons for according the Medal to you were set forth with ability by the President. It became my duty to reply on your behalf which I did very briefly.[2] The proceedings of the Meeting will be published at an early day, when I shall transmit a copy to you. I assure you that I feel a proud satisfaction in having the opportunity of being present at the Annual Meeting of the Society, and receiving this complimentary testimonial of merit to a citizen of the United States,[3] who has done so much not only in the cause of science, but in every department of duty to which he has been called to promote the honor of his country.

It is my fervent hope that your life may be long spared to enjoy your well earned fame in Science, and that your success in your new and high position may be commensurate with the name and fame acquired by arduous labor in your brief, but brilliant career. I am dear sir, Most faithfully, Your Serv,

ABBOTT LAWRENCE

P.S. I have sent the Medal to the Secretary of State.

ALS (James S. Copley Collection, La Jolla, Calif.).
1. A founder of the Royal Geographical Society, geologist Roderick Impley Murchison (1792–1871) was its president at the time of the award to JCF.
2. The Copley Collection contains the manuscript of Abbott Lawrence's reply.
3. The first American to receive the society's gold medal was Charles Wilkes in 1849.

80. Frémont to Christian and David Keener

WASHINGTON CITY, June 1, 1850.

GENTLEMEN,

I have just received your letter of yesterday, asking some information relative to a mine formerly owned by the Santa Clara mining Asscn.[1] In reply I have to inform you that Quicksilver ore of a very rich quality has been found and is known to exist at several places in the range which contains Forbes' mine.[2] A new mine has been recently opened on the road from San José to Monterey, and about 7 miles from the former place.[3] The ore in this mine, which was being worked when I was last there in Decr. last, is said to be of the same quality as Forbes'. The Santa Clara mine [i.e., the Guadalupe Mine] so far as I know its locality lies between the two [i.e., the New Almaden and San Juan Bautista], and although I have not its exact locality, I have no doubt that it is of the same quality as the others.[4] They are all within a few miles of each other, in the same mountain,[5] and I suppose are all pretty much alike. I have never had any occasion to examine the title, but that is one of the oldest settled sections of the country, the titles are in my opinion good, and will doubtlessly be maintained.

Any further information that I may have is at your service & I remain yours respectfully,

J. C. Frémont.

To Messrs Christian & David Keener,
Baltimore, Md.

ALS (Honnold Library, Claremont, Calif.) Endorsed. The Keeners have not been identified.
1. The mine referred to is probably the Guadalupe, which was owned by the Santa Clara Mining Association of Baltimore (HALL, 414).
2. "Forbes' mine" is a reference to the New Almaden Mine. By 1850 Alexander Forbes, British vice-consul at Tepic, Mexico, had acquired controlling interest in this extraordinarily rich mine, which was situated about four miles southeast of the Guadalupe (K. M. JOHNSON, 24–25).
3. The "new mine" to which JCF refers is the San Juan Bautista, located on the floor of the valley and isolated from all other mountainous formations. It was really about four or five miles, rather than seven, from San Jose (information from Clyde Arbuckle of San Jose, Calif.).
4. No quicksilver mine in the area was as rich as the New Almaden.
5. The mines were not in the same mountain.

81. Frémont to John M. Clayton

WASHINGTON CITY, June 10th 1850

To THE SECRETARY OF STATE,
SIR,

I respectfully ask leave to bring to the notice of the Department the name of Mr. Edward F. Beale as a suitable person to be appointed the United States Marshal for California. Mr. Beale's well known courage and energy, together with the great popularity among the people, would make his appointment a peculiarly fit one. His laborious services and heroic conduct in California and the Indian country entitle him to the consideration of the government, while his appointment would be serviceable to the State and gratifying to his numerous friends, and most especially to myself.

Requesting that you will at the proper time lay this application before the President, I am very respectfully Sir, your obedt. servt.,

J. C. FREMONT

Mr. Benton, from a personal knowledge of Mr. Beale and of his great merits and fitness, joins in this recommendation.

ALS (DNA: Letters of Application and Recommendation during the Administration of James Polk, Zachary Taylor and Millard Fillmore, 1845–53, Microcopy No. M-873, Roll 30). Endorsed: "Cont'd." On the same day JCF wrote President Taylor about Beale and on 3 Sept. wrote the new Secretary of State, Daniel Webster, on Beale's suitability for the marshalship of California (*ibid.*).

82. Frémont to Jacob R. Snyder

WASHINGTON CITY, June 11, 1850

MY DEAR MAJOR,

I drop you a line this morning to say that nothing in the shape of a vote has yet been had. Col. Benton made a strong speech yesterday, and I think that the Compromise Bill cannot possibly pass. I send you several copies of his speech.[1]

I will write every day till I know you have left and telegraph if any thing of interest occurs. Yours very truly,

J. C. FRÉMONT

Major Snyder,
New York

Copy (Society of California Pioneers—Jacob Rink Snyder Papers).
1. Benton's anticompromise speech of 10 June 1850 was delivered in connection with his motion to postpone Henry Clay's omnibus bill until the sitting of the next Congress and was printed in a fifteen-page pamphlet for public circulation. JCF was a poor prophet; by mid-September all the bills known as the Compromise of 1850 had passed, and he and Gwin were able to take their seats as California's senators on 11 Sept. 1850.

83. David Hoffman to Frémont

41 CONDUIT ST., HANOVER SQUARE, LONDON, 12 June 1850.

[Hoffman has read the papers submitted to him by Richard Robert and ascertained from him "your probable views and wishes in regard to the important and very responsible trust you have reposed in us, which I shall endeavor to execute with all faithfulness, zeal, and industry."

The papers are in a more crude state than Englishmen were accustomed to seeing, but Hoffman would prepare other papers, and perhaps a more formal power of attorney for JCF's approval or modification.

He will also prepare a short statement for a few gentlemen-capitalists whom he hopes to interest in organizing a joint-stock company. Presently the market is very slow, but he is confident "that so fresh and really brilliant an enterprise" in time will be received kindly by them. Signed copy.]

84. Frémont to Pierson B. Reading

WASHINGTON, 15 June 1850.

[Requests his friendly offices "for a gentleman now in California," Cantine Hoes, a nephew of President Van Buren. ALS (C). Addressed to Reading in Sacramento. According to the 1850 U.S. Census for California, the twenty-nine-year-old Hoes was mining in Calaveras County.]

85. John M. Clayton to Frémont

Department of State
WASHINGTON, June 15, 1850

My DEAR SIR:

I have the honor, to enclose, herewith, an extract[1] from a despatch received at this Department, yesterday, from the Hon: Abbott Lawrence, our Minister in London, from which you will perceive that the Royal Geographical Society has awarded you the "founder's medal" for the distinguished services, which you have rendered to Geographical Science.

The messenger, who bears you this letter, will also deliver you the medal.

It affords me pleasure to be the immediate instrument in conveying to you this high tribute of respect, so well earned by the valuable and distinguished services, which you have rendered, not only to your own country, but to the whole scientific world. I am, sir, very sincerely & truly, yours,

J. M. CLAYTON

Hon: J. C. Frémont

ALS (James S. Copley Collection, La Jolla, Calif.). JCF's reply, 25 June 1850, with signature torn away, is in the DLC—John M. Clayton Papers, 9:1744.
    1. Not printed.

86. Frémont to Cyrus Powers

WASHINGTON CITY, June 16, 1850

DEAR SIR,

Yours of the 13th is just received. I have been engaged, as the article you send me says, in making leases to companies of certain trusts of land for a term of years, they paying to me one sixth of the gold obtained from their mining operations. Until we have further advice we are not able to say whether the leases already made will, or will not, cover the veins. But if you desire it, such an arrangement might be made as would give you the right to mine on my land, if there remain sufficient extent of vein open. With acknowledgements for your good wishes I am respectfully yours,

J. C. FRÉMONT

Dr. Cyrus Powers
Moravia, [N.Y.]

ALS (MHi—C. E. French Collection). Cyrus Powers has not been identified.

87. Frémont to A. M. Auguste Moxhet

WASHINGTON CITY, 17 June 1850

DEAR SIR,

I have the honor to acknowledge receipt of your letter of the 14th of this month concerning the project proposed to me by Mr. Colson[1] which has as its aim the sending of a group of Belgian miners to California.

I, myself, at the present moment am preoccupied with a similar idea and I am going to make the initial preparations to begin our operations in the Spring of 1851.

I am willing to enter into an arrangement with Mr. Colson, and since, he proposes to come to California, I shall be delighted to meet with him. Agréez, etc.

J. C. FRÉMONT

Translated from the French as printed in *Journal des Mineurs Belges Compagnie* (Paris), 20 June 1851. Copy of the newspaper may be found in the Hoffman Papers. A. M. Moxhet was consul-general of Belgium in New York.

1. Presumably the Mr. Colson referred to by Robert in his 29 July 1851 letter to JCF (Doc. No. 147). Jean-Nicolas Perlot, who had been associated with the bankrupt French company La Fortune, noted that a Belgian by the name of Colson had arrived on the Mariposa two days earlier than he. He had a fine new greatcoat, nicely polished boots, neatly combed hair, and was freshly shaven (Howard Lamar's manuscript "Jean Nicolas Perlot, Gold Seeker: Adventures of a Belgian Argonaut in California and Oregon . . .," 247–49).

88. Frémont to Orlando Brown

WASHINGTON CITY, June 17. 1850

SIR,

I have to acknowledge the receipt of your letter of the 14th. instant, and take pleasure in replying to your enquiries, according to my information.

Within the State of California, to which exclusively I understand your letter to refer, there are probably forty thousand indians. These consist of very numerous, and small tribes, speaking many different languages and dialects of the same language; are much broken up and probably intermixed; so that, in making a distribution, the agencies cannot now be assigned to particular tribes. Leaving the tribes entirely out of consideration, the country should be divided into sections, to be placed under the control of respective agencies. Of these there should be three, having at their disposal eight subagents; all under the direction of a superintendent, and to be distributed as follows, viz:

The superintendent to reside at Sacramento City, or some other central point, from which the agencies could be conveniently furnished with supplies.

A principle [*sic*] agent to be stationed at or near "*Reading's rancho*," in the head of the lower Sacramento valley, having under his supervision the entire Sacramento valley, comprehending all the country drained by its numerous branches; and having at his disposal three subagents. These could be pushed into the Upper Sacramento valley, among the mountains below the Sierra Nevada, and across that range into communication with the Indians of the Basin.

The Indians of the coast country lying north of San Francisco Bay might be placed under the care of a subagent, resident at Sonoma, and reporting directly to the superintendent at Sacramento City.

A second agent should be established at or near King's river of the Tulárè lake, having under his supervision the entire valley of the San Joaquin river & the lakes, and including the mountains, within the State, on both sides of the Sierra Nevada. Within this section the Indian population is large, and would require that three subagents be placed at the disposal of the agent.

The remaining country, extending to the southern line, should be under the supervision of a third agent, resident at Los Angeles, and having at his disposal two subagents, with whom he would be able to control the strong mountain tribes of that section, and extend his supervision to the Colorado river & mouth of the Gila.

For his services the superintendent should receive a salary of three thousand dollars, each agent two thousand and upwards, and each subagent fifteen hundred dollars.

These indians are generally docile, in greater part already disposed by missionary teaching and their mode of subsisting, to agricultural labor. Simple farming materials; grain and other seeds; stock, horses & cattle; provisions, blankets and light readymade clothing, would be among the presents most suitable to them at the present time.

These suggestions appear briefly to meet the points of your enqui-

ries. They grow out of my knowledge of the country, and may indicate to you a plan best suited to the condition of the indians and the
character of the country. With this note I send you a map[1] on which
you will find marked the boundaries of the state and the sectional
divisions recommended for the location of agencies. Very respectfully,
Your obedt. servt.

J. C. FRÉMONT

Orlando Brown, Esqre.,
Commissioner Indn. Affairs, Washington City.

ALS (DNA-75, California F-159, LR 1850). Endorsed.
1. Map was not found.

89. Frémont to J. J. Abert

WASHINGTON CITY, June 18. 1850

DEAR SIR,

I would be much indebted to you if you can have Chapman paid.
He left me at the Dalles of Columbia, no account has ever been presented for him, and he did good service while with me. His name is
recorded in the list of the party near beginning of the published Report of that expedition. Very respectfully yours,

J. C. FRÉMONT

Col. Abert

ALS (DNA-77, LR). Endorsed.
1. A member of JCF's second expedition, Manuel Chapman settled in Oregon.

90. Frémont to Daniel A. Baldwin

WASHINGTON CITY, June 22, 1850

DEAR SIR,

Yours of yesterday is received. I send today the Report of Mr. Jones[1]
as you request. I am glad to learn that you design pushing into the

field at once, & think that in doing so you protect your own interests. Some very active men, with large capital, have lately taken leases & are sending out machinery immediately by the Isthmus, & go themselves by first steamer. Of those Werth & Co. of Richmond go on the 28th.[2] I have received an account of cost transportation of Stocktons machinery. It weighed 13000 lbs, & Mr. Beale wrote me from Cruces[3] that he was getting on well, & would have the machinery at the Mariposas in six weeks. Freight from San Francisco to Mariposas is varying, & gradually lessening. Our agents at San Francisco & Mariposas will give you the best suggestions. I believe you have letters to them but forget. Yours truly,

J. C. FRÉMONT

D. A. Baldwin, Esqre.
New York

ALS (James S. Copley Collection, La Jolla, Calif.). Daniel A. Baldwin had obtained a lease from JCF on 30 May 1850, and his mine, known as "Baldwin's Mine," was located and surveyed on 20 Nov. 1850 by Robert S. King. The mine was in Missouri Gulch about three-fourths of a mile west of the city of Mariposa. Baldwin subsequently sold the property to the Nouveau Mining Company (Prospectus, Nouveau Mining Company, London, Nov. 1851).

1. See Doc. No. 47, n. 1. William Carey Jones's 136-page report on California land titles was dated 10 April 1850 and published as Senate Ex. Doc. 18, 31st Cong., 2nd sess., Serial 589.

2. With some money supplied by J. R. Anderson of the Tredegar Company, John J. Werth took an engine (another was supplied to him later) and men, including a Negro, Manuel O'Moery [?], and sailed for California. He met his son, William H. Werth, and together they located a mine on the Frémont or Mariposa Vein. When results proved disappointing, Werth moved to Agua Fria and eventually gave up altogether. He then wrote a series of articles for the *Alta California*, which JCF, Beale, and others persuaded him to put in a more permanent form. The result was *A Dissertation on the Resources and Policy of California* (Benicia, Calif.: St. Clair and Pinkham, 1851). Anderson lamented that he had engaged in the costly enterprise of shipping men and machinery to California before first sending Werth to survey the situation (J. R. Anderson to Werth, 18 and 29 June, 23 Aug., 23 Nov. 1850, 24 March, 21 April 1851, Tredegar Company Letter Books, Vi; Mariposa County Census [1850], p. 57).

"Worth's Mine" is shown on an 1852 map issued by the Nouveau Mining Company and on Thomas Denny Sargent's sketch map of the Mariposa in the Hoffman Papers; mining claims filed in Mariposa County give "Worth's Mine," "Worth's Vein," and "Worth's & Co." as reference points. This editor thinks that all are references to John J. Werth's operations on the Agua Fria, but it should be noted that Henry C. Worth, born in Nantucket in 1815, sailed to California with George W. Wright. The latter, on returning from his mission to sell mines in London, paid Worth $3,691.80 for specimens, indicating that somehow and somewhere Henry C. Worth had acquired gold-bearing quartz rock (Settlement between G. W. Wright and Hiram Walbridge [1851], and 27 June 1841 receipt of H. C. Worth, M. A. Goodspeed, Jr., Collection). The California Census for 1850 (roll 28, p. 800) lists Worth as a merchant in Coloma, which is the settlement that developed around Sutter's Fort after the discovery of gold by John Marshall. It was 200 miles from the Mariposa.

3. At the mouth of the Chagres River in New Granada, vessels from the East Coast often unloaded their California-bound passengers, who would paddle by small boat to Cruces, where they hoped to find mules and guides to lead them the rest of the way to the City of Panama, where they would again embark on a ship (NIEMEIER, 1).

91. Frémont to Sir Roderick Murchison

WASHINGTON CITY, June 22, 1850

SIR:

I have had the gratification to receive, through the hands of the American Minister and the Secretary of State, the honourable medal with which the Royal Geographical Society has distinguished me.

In making my acknowledgments for this high testimonial of approbation, I feel it a particular pleasure that they are rendered to a society which I am happy to recognize as my *alma mater*, to the notice of whose eminent members I am already indebted for much gratification, and in whose occasional approval I have found a reason and a stimulus for continued exertion. I deem myself highly honored in having been considered a subject for the exercise of a national courtesy, and in being made one of the thousand links among the associations and cordial sympathies which unite our kindred nations.

With feelings of high respect and regard for yourself, I am, sir, very respectfully, your obedient servant,

J. C. FRÉMONT

To Sir Roderick Murchison,
President of the Royal Geographical Society, London

ALS (James S. Copley Collection, La Jolla, Calif.). Also printed in BIGELOW, 332–33.

92. Frémont to Buckingham Smith

WASHINGTON CITY June 26, 1850

DEAR SIR,

In the press of occupation I have accidently delayed to acknowledge yours of the 24th inst. At such time as best suits your convenience I will esteem it a favor to hear the reading of the manuscript[1] you describe, and am very respectfully Yours,

J. C. FRÉMONT

Buckingham Smith Esqr.
National [Hotel]
Washington city.

ALS (DLC—Peter Force Papers).
1. Possibly the manuscript was Smith's translation, published the next year in Washington, of Alvar Nuñez Cabeça de Vaca's odyssey through the interior of Florida, Texas, New Mexico, Arizona, and northern Mexico between 1527 and 1535. De Vaca's account is unparalleled in the history of exploration and would have appealed to JCF.

93. Frémont to Charles F. Mayer

WASHINGTON CITY
June 29th. 1850

MY DEAR SIR:

I received last night your note accompanying the letters from Mr. Hoffman & Mr. Robert.

I was disappointed in their contents. I know very little about formation of Stock companies generally, & less still of their formation in England, but Mr. Robert expected when he left that this business of ours would be a simple affair, & concluded in time for him to return by the end of August.

We spoke of arranging for him to meet me at that time at Chagres.

In this Country Companies are formed, & men & machinery on their way to California & all in two months time under crews. Besides the increase of expenditure occasioned, I may suffer losses in various ways by the delay & certainly am in some. On the whole it seems to me best to abandon the enterprise.

You are all aware that the additional safeguards they require are impossible. As to procuring any action of Congress upon the subject, it is entirely out of the question.

I cannot think of leaving the property derelict while the subject is undergoing long discussion in England and it is certainly advisable that I should immediately make arrangements in this country for sending out machinery & commencing operations myself.

I shall not leave this City during the coming week, & should you come here, I will be very glad to see you. Very truly yours,

J. C. FRÉMONT

Copy (NHi—David Hoffman Papers). This letter importing stay of proceedings was revoked by letters of 25 and 28 July. JCF's 29 June letter was a reply through Mayer to Hoffman's 12 June letter, which had noticed the inactivity in the market.

94. Robert M. Patterson to Frémont

Mint of the United States.
PHILADELPHIA, July 3d. 1850

DEAR SIR,

I thank you for recalling my attention to the proposed establishment of an Assay Office in California. When you first requested our views with regard to it, the subject was referred to our Assayers here. They have given it attention, and have consulted with Dr. Farnum, who is now here. They promise to give me their views in a short time, and their conclusions shall be communicated to you. Very respectfully and truly yours,

R. M. PATTERSON
Director

Hon. H. C. Frémont,
Washington

SC (DNA-104, Records of the U.S. Mint at Philadelphia, General Correspondence).

95. Frémont to Mr. Gray

WASHINGTON CITY, July 3, 1850

MY DEAR SIR,

I very much regretted that I did not see you before you left, as I had much to say to you. I enclose a letter to my brother-in-law, Mr. Jones which is of particular importance, and will be greatly obliged to you to deliver it to him.[1]

I have promised Mr. Jones to send him some members of my portrait contained in a recent number of the National Gallery.[2] Can you find room in your trunk for a dozen of them? If you can, please call at Brady's Daguerreotype Rooms, No. 205 Broadway, and ask either Mr. Brady, or Mr. Lester for them. This note will be a sufficient order to enable you to procure them. I will send you before you leave N. York several other letters & newspapers for our friends in Calforina.

Sometime in September I shall have the pleasure to see you there, & in the meantime I remain very truly yours,

J. C. FRÉMONT

Mr. Gray,
at New York

Please drop me a line to let me know if you receive this letter in order that I may not have any anxiety about it.

ALS (NN—Miscellaneous Papers). Addressed and endorsed. "Mr. Gray" not identified.

1. JCF's letter to his brother-in-law, William Carey Jones, not found.

2. C. Edwards Lester's literary interest in JCF, expressed in Doc. Nos. 62, 72, and 73, had borne fruit. The explorer was one of "twenty-four of the most eminent citizens of the American republic, since the death of Washington" which the triumvirate—Lester, Mathew B. Brady, and F. D'Avignon—photographed and wrote about under the title *The Gallery of Illustrious Americans* (New York, 1850). Since there was no museum in America at the time with the name "National Gallery," JCF may have had in mind a lavish compilation of portrait prints known as *The National Portrait Gallery of Distinguished Americans*, which James Longacre and James Herring had begun issuing in 1834.

96. David Hoffman to Frémont

41 CONDUIT STREET, LONDON, 5 July 1850.

[Writes of his plans to present the Mariposa estate to the British capitalists, notes how unacquainted the public is with California and how many—even Sir Charles Lyell and Sir Roderick Murchison— are striving to convince that the gold in California is confined to the surface and will soon be exhausted. His first interview with capitalists is on 19 July. He is forwarding three papers under the title of *The Messenger* and especially recommends that JCF look for an item in the "Varieties" column in the third paper. Signed copy.]

97. Robert M. Patterson to Frémont

Mint of the United States
PHILADELPHIA, July 6, 1850

DEAR SIR,

In my note to you of the 3d inst., I stated that the subject of an Assay Office in California had been referred by me to our Assayers for their judgment. They have now sent to me a communication of which a copy is enclosed.

I have to add to it only my conviction that Dr. Farnum is peculiarly suited as the Agent of Government for carrying this Assay object into execution. He is thoroughly practiced in assaying, and, by his residence in California, is well acquainted with the means of acting there. He is now in Philadelphia, but is about going to Europe, where he intends to stay only for a short time. If he can be charged with the arrangements required for the Assay Office, he could gain many advantages by his presence in England particularly.

R. M. P.

[*Enclosure*]

[6 July 1850]

In reply to Col. Fremont of July 1. Memorandum from the Assayers of the Mint

John C. Frémont as he looked in 1850. Daguerreotype by Brady,
engraved by D'Avignon. Courtesy of the National
Portrait Gallery, Smithsonian Institution.

George Washington Wright. From a print in Walter
Colton's *The Land of Gold; or, Three Years in
California* (New York, 1860).

We were engaged in preparing a bill, with Dr. Farnum's aid, for the establishment of an assay office in Cala. when the rapid and decisive action of the Senate, upon Col. Benton's amendments to the N.Y. bill, seemed to supersede our plan. This is the reason why no communication has been made.

On the whole, the provisions proposed by Col. B. appear to be appropriate & practicable, and there was much wisdom in providing for an Assay Office as precedent to a branch mint. Two suggestions only appear to be necessary, and they refer to the Assay Office.

1. To give it public confidence, and to make it duly responsible, it ought to be subject to the regulation and control of the Director of the Mint, as well as the Secretary of the Treasury, thus putting it in the attitude of an office subsidiary to the Mint.

2. It should be provided "that the bars melted and assayed at the Assay Office, shall have their weight, fineness and value stamped upon them, the value to be at the same rate as is provided by law in the gold coin of the United States, but without respect to the silver contained; and the said bars shall be receivable for public dues in any part of the United States, and for debts or contracts in California and Oregon; provided, that it shall be lawful to refuse to melt and assay any less quantity of gold than fifty ounces."

This limit is of course referred to Col. F.'s judgment. If it be much less, the labour & expense of the office will probably be too great a burden, and will only cause miners and others to get into the practice of carrying their little parcels to the office as soon as they reach the limit; which thing is, as we are informed, much practised at Dahlonega.[1]

SC, initialed (DNA-104, Records of the U.S. Mint at Philadelphia, General Correspondence).

1. Dahlonega is a small gold mining and sawmilling city in the northern part of Georgia. It was settled in 1829 with the opening of the mines and from 1836 to 1861 had a U.S. Mint.

98. Frémont to Robert M. Patterson

WASHINGTON CITY, July 9, 1850

MY DEAR SIR,

I have to thank you for the notes relative to a law for assayers of the mint, which with your letter were duly received.

The amendment offered by Col. Benton to the New York Mint Bill was offered in the shape least objectionable, in order not to provoke debate, as any new thing would.[1] We have it in our power, afterwards, to modify and amend. I fully concur in your views in regard to Dr. Farnum, to whom I have always looked as a most suitable person for the management of our mint. I will act in the matter as early as I can do so efficiently, & remain Yours truly,

J. C. FRÉMONT

Dr. Patterson
Director of U.S. Mint,
Phila.

ALS (DNA-104, Records of the U.S. Mint at Philadelphia, General Correspondence).
1. The original bill had simply provided for a branch mint in New York City. The amendment offered by Benton would also establish a branch in San Francisco *Congressional Globe*, 31st Cong., 1st sess., 4 and 22 Jan., 24 May 1850, pp. 103, 210, 1063).

99. William M. Gwin, Edward Gilbert, and Frémont to John Bidwell and Henry A. Schoolcraft

WASHINGTON, D.C.
July 24, 1850

GENTLEMEN:

The undersigned take great pleasure in acknowledging the receipt of the block of gold-bearing quartz and accompanying specimens, destined as the tribute of our young and cherished State to mark her interest in the fame and glory of the "Father of his Country," and her desire to perpetuate his great name and virtues so far as earthly monuments can accomplish that object.[1]

The undersigned also acknowledge the receipt of a communication from Peter H. Burnett, Esq., the Governor of the State of California, enclosing a copy of the Joint Resolutions passed by the Legislature in relation to this subject. And they beg that you will be pleased to forward to His Excellency the accompanying letter of acknowledgment.

The undersigned have the honor to inform you that they will at once take the necessary steps, under the direction of the National Monument Association, to have the wishes of the citizens of our State fulfilled, according to the instructions contained in the Joint Resolutions of our Legislature.

It is proper the undersigned should state that the Hon. George W. Wright[2] is absent from the city at the present moment; and that we have no doubt that it will be a source of regret to him, as it is to us, that he is not enabled to join us in this pleasing duty. We have the honor to be With Sentiments of high esteem, Your Obdt. Servants,

WM. M. GWIN
EDW. GILBERT
J. C. FRÉMONT

To Messrs. John Bidwell and Henry A. Schoolcraft, Committee
Washington, D.C.

LS (C). Endorsed with the notation that it was "recd. July 1st, 1851"—almost a year later than the date of the letter. One of California's two congressional representatives, Edward Gilbert was the editor of the *Alta California*. He was killed in a duel with James Denver in 1852. A senator in the first state legislature and one of the best-known pioneers of northern California, John Bidwell (1819–1900) had been closely associated with John A. Sutter until he left his employment to mine on Feather River. Henry A. Schoolcraft, too, had been an employee of Sutter's. His death occurred at sea in 1853 when he was returning to California with an appointment as collector of Sacramento (PIONEER REGISTER).

1. In his 25 July 1850 letter to Hoffman, JCF says the block of quartz came from "his place" (Doc. No. 100). Although perhaps not formally rejected by the Washington Monument Society, California's representatives and other citizens in Washington decided that this particular block of quartz was "unworthy" of the state, and the legislature was asked to furnish a suitable specimen. Acting under its authority, Governor John Bigler procured three pieces of different shades, representative of the three different periods in California history. Fire in Sacramento destroyed two, but the third, in Bigler's words, was "beautiful" (*Journals of the California Legislature*, 1st sess. [1850], 28 Jan.–2 Feb., 7–11 Feb.; 4th sess. [1853], Governor's message to the Assembly, 3 Jan.).

2. George W. Wright (1816–85) was California's other elected representative. A native of Concord, Mass., he had spent the summer of 1849 traversing the foothills of the Sierra Nevada from the Feather River to the Mariposa collecting specimens of gold-bearing quartz. He was one of the four founders of the San Francisco banking firm of Palmer, Cook & Company and for many years was to be closely associated with JCF in business matters and to have great influence on him (BIOG. DIR. CONG. and documents in this volume).

100. Frémont to David Hoffman

WASHINGTON CITY, July 25, 1850

My dear Sir,

Since the receipt of your first letter I have been waiting for other advices from you in order to see if there was any probability of prompt action upon the enterprise in which I desired to engage. When Mr. Robert went out to England it was understood & believed by us, certainly by me, that an association for working mineral lands could be formed *immediately*. It was understood that Mr. Robert should endeavor so to arrange the business as to meet me about the 20th August at Chagres where I should be on my way to California. I designed by the aid of the capital of the association forthwith to put a large working force upon the place, to be occupied in blasting & excavating work, and to erect immediately such machinery as might be at hand, until better could be procured from England. It did not occur to me to imagine that any difficulty was to be met in the incredulity of British capitalists as to the notorious fact of the existence of valuable mines on the Mariposas. My object was to procure the means of prompt, & strong action upon the premises, and for this end I was willing to associate others with myself & divide the results. If this object could not be accomplished, then there existed no reason for a connexion with British capitalists. Your letters, written shortly subsequent to Mr. Robert's arrival, at once almost entirely destroyed all such expectations. I therefore immediately proceeded to take or rather prosecute other measures which I had held in abeyance.

As Mr. Robert is aware, previously to his leaving this place I had executed leases to Commodore Stockton & some other parties, for certain small portions of the mining land. These leases I now continued to grant until the present day, when such are held by about *seventeen* different parties, with heavy capital, who go out with machinery, men, wagons, provisions, and every thing necessary to commence immediate operations. Stockton & Aspinwall's[1] machinery must be today upon the ground, probably that of others, and by the recent steamers the machinery &c. of other parties left New York, to be transported across the Isthmus of Panama, on the way to the mine.[2]

Now, it is to be remarked that the ground covered by these leases, occupies but a *small* portion of my domain; perhaps what they hold may be about 3600 yards in length by 200 yds. in breadth, in all. I have for the present stopt [*sic*] here and will do nothing more until I return to California.

In the meantime new discoveries are constantly being made upon the place, and from the exploring [party] which I sent there I expect interesting reports in *August*.[3] A block of gold bearing quartz, sent by the state of California to form a stone in the national monument now being erected to Washington accompanied by some rich specimens of ore, came from *my place*.[4] That you may see the development now being made of the gold veins throughout the state, I enclose you a piece cut from the Nat. Intelligencer of today, and send you also several California newspapers.[5] You will at once see how extensive are these gold mines, and how immense the results are to be. And you will likewise understand how utterly impossible it is for me to wait. I should be involved in collisions & interminable law suits were I longer to leave the land derelict in a densely peopled country. My interest absolutely requires me to cover the land with working parties this *coming winter*. We can be employed in fencing, putting up buildings, excavating ore &c. Our farming lands should be put under fence, and crops begun to be put in the ground in October. What I have here said will be sufficient to let you understand the actual position of things. Mr. Robert's recent letter speaks of the formation of the association as a thing to be favorably influenced by Mr. Andrew Smith's company going out to the Mariposas.[6] That is looking far ahead. If any association is to be formed at all, it must of necessity be *immediately*. I understand clearly the difficulties with which you have had to contend, and understand the necessary caution with which the British capitalists advance. But we can only regret their want of knowledge, and take other measures. Later in the day such an association would be useless to me—there must always be a *quid pro quo* in matters of business. To conclude this part of my letter, I have to say that I will do nothing farther until I hear from you, except to authorize Mr. Robert to conclude the offered contract with Mr. Smith.

We are constantly receiving intelligence which goes to confirm the extent and value of our mines. To people in England their extraordinary richness would seem incredible. I have to thank you, among other things, for the Report of the St. John del Rey Mining Company.[7] I found it very interesting.

The quantity of ore stamped by that company in '49 would yield upon my place, and at the lowest result obtained from our ore by Dr. Patterson, nearly seventeen millions of dollars, and if we take the mean result per one year would be $1,215,000,000! And really, my dear Sir, if we judge of the work by what we have seen only, these results are not at all incredible, but this I would say to yourself only. My own opinion formed by what I saw and knew of the rock as far as we had opened it was, that it would yield about fifty cents to the pound of rock. This for the quantity of ore above cited would be 69,000,000$ yearly. You ask in one of your letters something about a ball of gold weighing about two ounces, and which is among the specimens I sent you. Its history is this. When the vein on the Mariposa was first opened about twenty five pounds of rock were given to an Indian to pound up, which he did as a day's work. The fragments of the rock were *picked* out, those which showed gold being taken, and those which did not, being rejected. After he had pounded the rock, the gold was collected from it by quicksilver. It was a day's work for the Indian, but of course rudely done. Still it may give a very good idea of the rock, as according to recent experiments the gold is disseminated entirely through the rock in minute, as well as grosser particles.

How would it do to organize a smaller company—something like what is proposed for himself by Mr. Smith? Say, several gentlemen of those you have mentioned who have abundant means, to be associated with me, and giving me a strong voice in the directing or managing the business, and making you also a director. I hold now, *specially reserved*, the point where I first opened the vein in sufficient extent and ground round about it, for carrying on very handsome and large operations. I would add to this say 500 acres of fertile land for cultivation. If such an association of gentlemen can be formed, who will immediately send out some miners with some capable men at their head together with means to commence operations this fall, I think it might be the best thing to be done. We could then regard this company as the nucleus of a more extended operation. I shall await your reply with some anxiety, and in the meantime beg you to receive my thanks for the friendly promptness with which you took charge of my interests in this matter, and for the zeal and ability you have brought to the task. With much regard I am very truly yours,

J. C. FRÉMONT

ALS (NHi—David Hoffman Papers). Endorsed: "Received 12th Augt."
1. The Mariposa County Records contain no record of a lease to Stockton & Aspinwall, but the company undoubtedly had one, or perhaps JCF's lease to Beale (mentioned in Doc. No. 138) formed the basis of operations. For notices of

the operations and of their failure, see Doc. Nos. 156 and 166. Stockton's patent machinery was too light to work effectively the quartz of the Mariposa.

2. In addition to Stockton & Aspinwall or Beale, JCF's seventeen parties undoubtedly included Thomas Denny Sargent (Doc. No. 67); Daniel A. Baldwin (Doc. No. 90); John C. Clark and George W. Guthrie of Washington, D.C. (28 May 1850 lease referred to in their 5 Sept. 1851 lease, Mariposa County Records, Book 1, pp. 267–71); and Capt. William K. Smith, 3 July 1850 (referred to in the memorandum of agreement between David Hoffman and the Nouveau Monde Gold Mining Company, 8 Nov. 1851, M. A. Goodspeed, Jr., Collection). Hoffman's letter of 7 Feb. 1851 indicates that William K. Smith had two leases from JCF. This 7 Feb. 1851 letter also mentions a Thomas La Chausne as having a lease.

3. He is referring to Heap and Edwards, who sailed from New York with William Carey Jones on 4 May.

4. See Doc. No. 99.

5. *National Intelligencer*, 25 July 1850 (quoting San Francisco *Herald*, 17 June 1850), notes that gold quartz had been found near Los Angeles but, like that of the Mariposa, science and machinery were needed to get it out.

6. The proprietor of twenty-six patents, Andrew Smith of London, whose occupation was listed as "Engineer," obtained a lease for auriferous and agricultural land on the Mariposa (lease of Hoffman [for JCF] to Smith, 31 Dec. 1851, CSmH). Smith and his sons, William and Andrew, Jr., went out to California, and one of their claims is recorded in Mariposa County Records, Book 2, p. 179. Andrew Smith was also the promoter of the Golden Mountain of Mariposa Mining Company of California, which was organized in Nov. 1851 with a capital stock of £50,000 and 50,000 shares (Hoffman to George Sutton, 29 Sept. 1852, NHi; Papers of Golden Mountain of Mariposa Mining Company, CU-B, Film Z-G1, Reel 58).

7. The San Juan del Rey Mining Company worked the rich Morro Velho Mine in Brazil.

101. Frémont to Richard Robert

WASHINGTON CITY, July 28th. 1850

MY DEAR SIR,

Your letter of the 5th Inst.[1] was received on the 26th. For my opinion as to what has been done, and what the actual position of things, makes it expedient to do, I refer you to my letter of this date to Mr. Hoffman and reply at once to that portion of your letter which refers to Mr. Andrew Smith.

The account which you have previously given me of this gentleman and occasional notice you sent me of his works, had satisfied me of his value and excited a strong desire to have him on my place.

He no doubt would set up admirable works on the ground leased to himself, and to me his genius and knowledge would render the most valuable assistance. I therefore desire to make with him some such contract as that proposed, whether it would be agreeable to the contemplated Association or not. What we want is to develop the place with power and its value is now ascertained to be so great that once upon the ground Mr. Smith would be the very man to do it. And now as to the terms and before we go to that let me call your attention to what experiment gives us as our very lowest figure.

Take Dr. Patterson's result obtained from the rock which exhibited no visible gold and which of necessity we consider our lowest figure. Take the quantity of ore, stamped in the year 1849 at the Morro Velho Mine, 69,004.4 tons as the least quantity, which would be stamped yearly at such a mine as Mr. Smith would work and what is the result 16,700,000 Dollars.

Now in no case would I like the trouble of having anything to do with the net profits, and certainly not when the outlay bears so small a proportion to the product. My portion therefore must be of the gold produced, and this is a *sine qua non*. The leases I have already made are on these terms. The lease should provide that the day books be at all times subject to the inspection of myself or Agent, that if after being opened the mine should be left unworked in good faith for six consecutive months, the lease is forfeited thereby *ipso facto*. And that the lease shall also be forfeited if mining operations be not commenced upon the ground in good faith within one year from its date.

The mining lots which I have hitherto leased are 200 yards square, to be located upon the veins whatever the Lessee may choose. To Mr. Smith I am willing to give a parallelogram of 600 yds. by 200 yds. to be located as he may judge best upon the vein or lode and one hundred Acres of land, for cultivation, building houses, &c. which shall not be selected upon the mineral land, and the selection of which be subject to my approval.

He shall of course be entitled to water privileges and to the use of timber for building purposes & fuel.

These are the general terms. If he does not think a sufficient quantity of land is granted, we might afterwards go farther into the business, but this is all I can do now. Therefore if he desire to have such a lease and will take it and commence operations immediately, let him have it. But it must be *immediately*, as I shall go to California about the middle and last of September at farthest, and if this arrangement is made it ought to be before I go. He ought to take efficient steps at once, and either himself go out or send someone out about the time that I do in order to examine the ground, and select and take possession of his ground this winter. These is abundance of preliminary work which he might do this winter, such as enclosing his mining lot, putting up buildings, excavating ore, and he might fence in (perhaps a wire fence is best) his farming ground and put in a crop which there ought to be done in October.

And now for another subject. I foresee that I cannot wait the time required for the formation of the large Association, but will go into the business myself. If convenient for you, please immediately on the receipt of this see Mr. Smith, and ask him if he can get up for me a light steam engine, burning the smallest possible amount of fuel, together with a stamping machine, amalgamator, &c. and to give me an estimate of the cost, and how much time it will require from receipt of the order until it be ready for shipment. Let it be on terms as economical as possible because my expenditures are heavy. I do not wish to sacrifice any property as I might be obliged to do before I can get this business started.

And now to speak freely I have to say to you that I care little about the large Association, or whether it is formed or not. According to what I can see it would not be possible for me to have that voice in the Directory without which I would not be willing to make it. But Mr. A. Smith's company pleases me, and I hope you will at once make an arrangement with him. In regard to what both yourself and Mr. Hoffman have done, and the devoted and energetic manner in which you have applied your abilities to this business, I have to express my great satisfaction, and take pleasure in making you acknowledgements.

In conclusion I have to inform you that intelligence from California confirms our previous examinations and extends our knowledge. New discoveries are constantly being made, showing greater extent and proving its most extraordinary riches. My great anxiety is that we cover all my tract with working parties before the great value of the place become generally known and this I must make the first object & cannot wait. Please show to Mr. Hoffman. Yours truly,

J. C. FRÉMONT

Copy (NHi—David Hoffman Papers).
1. Not found.

102. Frémont to Robert M. Patterson

MY DEAR SIR,

I have here some tolerably large fragments of the gold bearing quartz, in which no gold is perceptible, and which would consequently give about the lowest product of the rock. There is no part of the rock belonging to the vein which is poorer in appearance than this. I have also a small specimen of slate, in which, I suspect the existence of gold, and which I desired to ascertain. The object of this note is to ask whether or not the analyses of these specimens could be conveniently made at the mint. I would be glad in forming an opinion of the productiveness of the quartz to have the authority of the mint to base myself upon, and I suppose that you yourself feel the same interest in these examinations. If it should be entirely convenient for you to have these analyses made, I would be glad to hear from you & remain with regard Yours truly,

J. C. FRÉMONT

Dr. Patterson,
Director of the Mint,
Phila.

ALS (DNA-104, Records of the U.S. Mint at Philadelphia, General Correspondence). Endorsed: "Recd. 31st & ansd. Aug. 3. Stating that the assayers undertake the task, with such time as their public duties will permit."

103. Frémont to David Hoffman

MY DEAR SIR,

I have just received from Mr. Mayer a pacquet containing letters from yourself and Mr. Robert, of the dates July 20 and 19th respectively, & accompanied by certain documents.[1]

In order to get an answer off by this afternoon mail to go by the Boston steamer of Wednesday, I answer immediately & necessarily briefly.

Mr. Mayer gives me a *resumé* of enquiries by yourself to points which he says you have much at heart, & to these I answer first.

1. The plat, I forwarded by Mr. Robert, of the Mariposas Region, exhibits the whole of my domain in the San Joaquin Valley, containing,

I. The "gold region"—25 square miles

II. The other three sections, named "valley," "middle," & "Hill."

As you will see by the boundary line on the plat, the tract does not extend to the San Joaquin, but I am part owner of a league of land in that vicinity upon the San Joaquin.[2] A division of this could be made & my share be made available if thought proper. Or, a place much more eligible, & to which I have had my attention turned, as a good port for the Mariposa, could be secured by pre-emption, if we do not wait too long.[3] You see that delay works against us in every way. But my own tract of sixty-seven squares miles certainly, in such a country, is abundantly large for a most noble enterprise.

I now answer Mr. Robert's questions *seriatim*.

1. "*The geographical situation of the property &c.*" Answered by the map of the Mariposas.

2. "*Where and how situated with respect to water communication.*" Answered by the general map I gave to Mr. Robert, as being about 40 miles from the San Joaquin, and about the same distance from a newly established town on the *Merced* or Auxumné river, at the head of good steamboat navigation. These distances understood to be from the place where the mine has been opened.

3. "*As to the kinds of ore discovered.*" Gold only has been discovered by me; silver has been reported to me by Mr. Lamartinie,[4] an engineer whom I sent to examine the place. Quicksilver has been reported to me by my agent, and a specimen from the place exhibited to me by Mr. G. W. Wright, a representative elect from California to the U.S. Congress.

4. "*As to quarries of freestone, limestone, &c.*" I cannot answer with certainty as to the kinds of stone. Sandstone I think there certainly is, probably limestone. There is very fine granite in the Sierra near, but I am not certain if there is any immediately on the place. There is clay & marl for making bricks &c.

5. "*If well timbered &c.*" It is well timbered & is in one of the finest timbered regions in America; oak, pine, *juniperus &c.* of course applicable to the usual purposes.

6. "*With respect to soil &c.*" All good. The greater part of the very best kind, and lying well for cultivation.

7. "*What distance is the property from a sea port.*" The valley part of the property, say the western boundary of the estate, is 106 miles (by reckoning) from the seaport of Monterey, all land carriage.

It is about 90 miles from Stockton, to which come three masted vessels—and about 170 miles from San Francisco, in both cases all of water with exception of the 10 or 15 miles.

8. "*The extent of the vein, if easy of access, near to the surface, &c.*" All very difficult to answer, requiring much exploration to answer with certainty. *But*, the vein was reported by Mr. Lamartinie as extending three miles. When I left California I had opened it in but one point. I *believe* that there are two other lines of veins parallel to this one, and my belief is formed from my own examination, & with myself amounts to a certainty. In the meantime daily accounts bring information of the great abundance of the ore. My own agents, sent specially to make farther examination, and about whom or whose examinations Mr. Robert enquires, did not reach San Francisco until the 20th of June. They had then to go to the Mariposas & make their examination before reporting & then it requires 35 days for their letters from San Francisco to this. And in the mean time, and while we are enquiring about the existence of the ore, powerful companies are putting up their machinery on the place!

9. "*With respect to stream washing &c.*" I did have a company of Sonoranians (they are good working men) at work last year, 28 in number. I gave them protection & provisions, and they gave me half the gold they obtained from the washings. The gross amount which they obtained from the washings was about one hundred pounds (in gold) per month. The stream washings belong to me, of course, & to *nobody else*.

10. "*As to the samples of ore &c.*" I have none here, neither had I given direction to have any sent to me. I did not found my English operation on any thing so far ahead. If I should meet with any I will send them.

11. "*As to an advantageous position for laying off a town.*" There is one, highly advantageous, which we are hazarding by OUR DELAY.

These were Mr. Robert's enquiries. I have answered them frankly. He seems to think that I had found fault with what had been done. By no means; it would have been very unjust. It was the prospect ahead which discouraged me, the apparent improbability of that instant action, that instant employment of men & capital (even a comparatively small one) which would enable us to secure present advantages, to sweep on with the current, and to save myself from a long train of annoyance. You know well how slow is the action of the U.S. Congress, and you have present to your mind its tantalizing delays, ruinous to landholders, in its investigations of the Louisiana & Florida land. You will remember its unconstitutional & illegal acts. Against these delays I wish to protect myself by a full possession, co-extensive with the land.

In the full possession & enjoyment of the property we should not care for their delays, knowing that when the Congress did take final action it could only be to confirm. Our title is as legal a one as the Mexican Govt. could give, and was issued by Micheltorena in obedience and conformity to an express decree of the Mexican Congress & which you will find in the Report of Wm. Carey Jones, Esq. and of which Mr. Robert has a copy. I will send you a copy of the title with the deraignment. You will now see, as in my recent letter I told you, that in the British negociation the advantage which I am to derive is mainly in the PRESENT APPLICATION of men & money to the Mariposas. You will understand that my presence in the Congress as a member is important to the landholders of California. There (on the Mariposas, even with small means at the beginning) my presence would be invaluable, and I would need an association. *Away* from it, the country new, the property new, the absolute necessity of making imposing expenditures—all render it necessary for me to call capitalists to my aid, and for this they are offered a generous equivalent. I remain, now, as I said in my last, waiting to hear definitely from you. I think £300,000 more capital than we need. £200,000 and a restricted number of gentlemen would be better. I prefer a smaller company to go upon a mining ground of restricted dimensions (but still abundantly sufficient for very large operations) to a very large company. For the rest I coincide with your views entirely, and expressing to you my earnest thanks for the able manner in which you are conducting this business, I conclude this letter expecting to write after the arrival of the Califa. steamer. Very respectfully yours,

J. C. FRÉMONT

ALS (NHi—David Hoffman Papers). Endorsed: "Get admitted" (presumably as a part of Hoffman's answer in Chancery).

1. These letters were not found. In a 20 July 1850 letter to Mayer, marked "wholly private," and with a request that it be "locked up," Hoffman expresses his eagerness for the agency. But he is also concerned why JCF, reputed to be extremely rich, is so reluctant to spend money on machinery and developmental

work. He wonders a bit about his stability, since the least intimation of delay or an obstacle had caused him to consider abandoning the entire project. He fears, too, that the explorer possesses "a little of the leven of humbug" and might "prove deficient in that common sense which is, after all, the brightest jewel in the character of any man." With all these reservations, Hoffman was yet too proud to use JCF's authority "to draw for a shilling" until he had worked in his cause "some months."

2. Many parties besides JCF were interested in the eleven-league grant on the San Joaquin River which José Castro obtained from Pío Pico on 4 April 1846. The petition of Castro and others for confirmation was filed on 2 March 1853, confirmed by the commission two years later, but ultimately rejected by the U.S. Supreme Court (DNA-49, Record of Petitions, 11:81–82 [Case 693]; 65 *U.S. Reports*, 346–52; GATES [1], 33). JCF never names the shareholder or shareholders of "his" league of land. According to Dr. William F. Edgar, others besides JCF having interest in the Castro grant were: Beale, Samuel J. Hensley, R. P. Hammond, and a Mr. Crosby of San Francisco (Edgar to Henry W. Halleck, Fort Miller, Calif., 21 Feb. 1853, CU-B—Halleck, Peachy and Billings Correspondence). In 1849 Hammond had laid out the town of New York of the Pacific, at the mouth of the San Joaquin, for Col. Jonathan D. Stevenson (BANCROFT, 6:673–74).

3. The place would have been either on the San Joaquin River several miles below a fort that was established the next year—Fort Miller—or possibly on the lower Merced River near present-day Cressey (information form Bertha Schroeder, Mariposa, Calif.).

4. Probably Mr. La Martini, but he has not been identified. A number of low-grade silver mines, including the Silver Bar Mine, a few miles south of the town of Mariposa, were opened and operated for some years, but they are no longer active.

104. Frémont to Horace P. Hitchcock

WASHINGTON CITY, Augt. 30, 1850

DEAR SIR,

Yours of the 21st is received.

I find a difficulty in answering such enquiries as yours. If I answer them favorably, all the responsibility in case of failure would rest on me. I send you the only thing I have which I know to be reliable.[1] When I left California such a man as you describe yourself to be, could do what you ask. How it may be now I cannot say. There are a greatly larger number at work in the diggings, and machinery before long will take the place of the work of digging. But the gold cannot, in many years, be exhausted, & the early product will be comparatively immense.

A farmer's business there [is better] than in any part of the world that I know any thing of. If you should make California your home you would be certain of independence. By choosing your location you can have a fertile soil, healthy & pleasant climate & the best market in the world. Respectfully yours,

J. C. Frémont

Mr. Horace P. Hitchcock
Hillsdale, Mich.

ALS (Mason County Historical Society, Ludington, Mich.). Horace Philock-less Hitchcock did not go to California, but remained in Hillsdale to become a prosperous farmer.
1. Not found.

105. Frémont to John Torrey

Washington City, Sepr. 1, 1850

My dear Sir,

Yours of the 24th. was some five or six days in reaching me. I was just thinking to write & inform you that I am in a few weeks to set out again for California. I shall remain there so very short a time that I cannot do any thing for myself for plants, but will direct a person in my employ there to collect the Spring plants of our neighborhood. If there is any particular thing you would like done, please mention it to me. Is the *Taxodium*[1] yet decisively known? or would you want something from that tree?

The Engravings you sent reached me safely, & quite revived a recollection of old times. I regret that I have not yet received any of the drawings from Cal[iforni]a. As you remember, they were all left there, & I am afraid now will not reach you in time to be of any service. I will bring them all back with me when I return in December.

The family join me in remembrances to you. Perhaps you may be in New York when I pass through & I will try to find you. Yours truly,

J. C. Frémont

Dr. John Torrey,
Princeton

ALS (PPAN).
1. *Sequoia sempervirens* (JCF's cypress).

191

106. Frémont to William Crutchfield

WASHINGTON CITY, Sepr. 5, 1850

DEAR SIR,

Yours of the 26th ult. is received.

I have now been absent from California since the first of this year, and things there change so fast in the crowding population that I could not undertake to tell you what it would be best for you to engage in. Without a trade or profession immediately available, I would recommend you not at present to undertake to establish yourself in California. But I do recommend to you, that you endeavor to obtain through Mr. Clay, or other of your Whig friends, some Custom House or other appointment, however small, as a foothold. Take your family with you, and start from that; and you cannot reasonably fail to obtain the independence which your exertions here have failed to procure. It will give me pleasure to give you letters to friends there, & if you find yourself able to go, I would be glad to know. Respectfully Yours,

J. C. FRÉMONT

Wm. Crutchfield, Esqre.
Sharpsburg, [Ky.]

ALS (MB).

107. David Hoffman to Frémont

43 Upper Brooke Street, Grosvenor Square, LONDON,
5 Sept. 1850.

[Notes that the preliminaries of company no. 2 (the Anglo-California Gold Mining and Dredging Company) will be settled "tomorrow" and transmitted by Saturday's steamer of the 8th. "Mr. Smith's Company No. 1 is delayed a few days by the absence of a material person. Company No. 3 (which, for the present promises to be the largest) met me twice, and a final meeting for preliminaries to be forwarded to you will probably take place about Tuesday the

11th. Company No. 5 is only in embryo—at the head of which is Mr. Powles [president of the San Juan del Rey Mining Company], but he seems to be playing a game for a larger slice by far, and yet on far less advantageous terms. He speaks of miles instead of yards, but he also speaks of a capital of £350,000 and a gross royalty to you of not exceeding 8 to 12 percent!" Hoffman encloses a "Scale of Royalty."

All the companies were surprised at the smallness of the extent of land, but Hoffman had convinced them that the Brazilian and Mexican notion of miles or many acres was erroneous for California. Still, they looked for about 300 or 400 yards by 200 yards breadth for every £20,000 of capital furnished.

They were also "greatly astonished" that Charles F. Mayer had failed to name the minimum royalty or to send a complete form of JCF's lease; a plat of his land showing known and conjectured veins; the exact form, locality, and extent of each of his leases; and his general ideas as to the staff and capital required of each company. They hoped for particulars by 10 or 15 Sept.

The companies were pleased with the idea of having their own commisariat for the first six months, independent of California provisions, and thereafter of relying on the products of their own little farms, which they supposed would be from 100 to 125 acres, supervised and worked by five Englishmen and five Indians.

A Molineus Seele had £3,000 to establish his two sons (twenty-one and twenty-three years old) in an agricultural enterprise on the Mariposa in the vicinity of JCF's lessees and desired through Mayer all sorts of information, including the minimum price per acre if JCF would sell or the terms of a lease if he would not.

Chafes because the recent steamer had not brought a line from Mayer, whose duty is "to think for us all (on his side of the water) as Mr. Robert and myself have endeavored to do on our side." "Had I possessed the forms of your leases, with all of their stipulations, terms and conditions, I should have been enabled to settle preliminaries before this time." Notes that he and Robert have handled all correspondence "with slight aid" since 10 July, but that soon he must have an "experienced" secretary.

Suggests that a general smelting establishment be erected in the midst of JCF's leases. It was to be "the property of all the American and British lessees," financed by a contribution from each, in the ratio of their respective capitals. Suggests also that a London office, to be partly financed by JCF, be established for dealing with the concerns of lessees on both sides of the Atlantic. Sender's copy.]

Scale of Royalty [1]

	£	s	d
1/2	50		
1/3	33	6	8
1/4	25		
1/6	16	13	4
1/8	12	10	
1/10	10		
1/12	8	6	8
1/16	6	5	
1/20	5		

---

[1] If the yield of gold per ton of quarts was 18 to 24 ounces, the royalty was to be 1/4 of the gold or in money, £25 per £100 Sterling; if the gold yield per ton was 2 ounces and not exceeding 4 ounces, the royalty was 1/10 of the gold, or in money £10 per £100 Sterling.

108. Frémont to Mrs. M. A. Edwards

SENATE CHAMBER, Sepr. 12. 1850

MY DEAR MADAM,

I have had the pleasure to receive your note of the 11th & will of course carry Mr. Beale his revolver.

It is my present intention to go out by the first steamer after the end of this month, but I am not sure that I shall be able to do so, & may be disappointed in going at all.

I will not fail to give you early information of my movements. We regret to know that Mrs. Beale suffers from her eyes. The salt air of the California climate I think would do them good. We intend to bring forward Mr. Beale's name in a few days for an honorable and lucrative office in California.[1] Will you please ask Mrs. Beale what she thinks of it? Mrs. F. joins in regards to her & your family. With regard I am very respectfully yours,

J. C. FREMONT

ALS (DLC—Decatur House Papers, unnumbered blue box). Addressed to Mrs. M. A. Edwards at Chester, Pa. The widow of Samuel Edwards, a former representative of Pennsylvania in Congress, Mrs. M. A. Edwards was Beale's mother-in-law.

1. Benton is probably included in JCF's "we." Frémont had requested that Beale be appointed marshal of California. See Doc. No. 81.

109. Frémont to P. Dexter Tiffany

SENATE CHAMBER, Septr. 12, 1850

MY DEAR SIR,

You will see by the journals of the day that I have drawn the term ending on the 3d March next & Dr. Gwin the term ending in 1855.

I desire to be a candidate for re-election at the meeting of the legislature and ask you at once for your friendly offices again. Will you do me the favor to have it made known that I am a candidate & use your influence among our friends? I have written a line to [William Carey] Jones on the same subject. Yours truly,

J. C. FRÉMONT

P. Dexter Tiffany, Esqre.
San Francisco, Cala.

ALS (CSmH). P. Dexter Tiffany had been a member of the St. Louis bar and owned a great deal of property in San Francisco (San Francisco *Daily Pacific Press*, 17 July 1850; WHEELER).

110. Frémont to Palmer, Cook & Company

[WASHINGTON, D.C., 17 Sept. 1850]

This Indenture made this Seventeenth day of September in the Year One Thousand eight hundred and fifty at the City of Washington, District of Columbia between John Charles Frémont of the State of California of the first part and Joseph C. Palmer, Charles W. Cook, George W. Wright and Edward Jones all of the City of San Francisco and State of California Partners under the Firm of Palmer, Cooke & Co. of the second part—Witnesseth that in consideration of the Rents provisions and agreements hereinafter contained and which on the part of the said Joseph C. Palmer, Charles W. Cook, George W. Wright and Edward Jones are to be paid done and performed He the said John Charles Frémont has demised and leased and doth by these presents demise and lease until the said Joseph C. Palmer, Charles W. Cook, George W. Wright, and Edward Jones their heirs executors administrators and assigns a lot or square of land measuring Six Hundred Feet on each of the four sides, with all and singular the Mines, ores, and minerals, on in or under the same, together with the appurtenances to the said Lot belonging, the said lot or square being a part of a certain Tract of Land called the Mariposas, and claimed by the said John Charles Frémont by virtue of a purchase from Don Juan B. Alvarado, Ex-Governor of California situated on, in and near the Mariposas River and its branches, in the said State of California agreeably to the Plat hereunto annexed the precise location of said Lot or Square of Land to be selected and determined by the above party of the second part or their Agent, within and upon any portion of the tract of Land above described which shall not be occupied at the time of selection by other lessees, acting by and with the consent of the said John Charles Frémont, and also saving and reserving to the said John Charles Frémont, that part of the Mariposas Tract which lies on the East side of the East Fork of the Mariposa Creek, and on which the words "reserved" are written on the annexed plot.[1] To Have and to Hold the said Lot or Square of Land above described, to them, the said parties of the second part, their heirs and assigns for and during the Term of Seven Years from the date hereof.

And in consideration of the Premises the said party of the second part doth hereby covenant and agree to pay to the said John Charles Frémont his heirs and assigns One Sixth part of all Gold or other metals or minerals obtained from the aforesaid Square of Land the same to be paid or delivered quarterly at the Mines upon the demand of the said John Charles Frémont or his Agent the amount or quantity of which said rents shall be ascertained by a book to be regularly kept at the Mines and subject at all times to the inspection of said Fremont or his Agent.

And the said Joseph C. Palmer, Charles W. Cook, George W. Wright and Edward Jones their Heirs, Executors, and Administrators do covenant to and with the said John Charles Fremont his Heirs and Assigns, that they will peaceably yield up said Lands and all the privileges thereto belonging, at the expiration of Seven Years from the date thereof together with all and singular the improvements which shall have been made upon said Lands the same becoming the property of the said John Charles Fremont except machinery. And it is further stipulated and agreed that the said party of the second part shall put up the necessary machinery for the purposes aforesaid on such square of land as they may select, and have the same in full operation within one year from this date or this lease shall be held to be forefeited.

It is further agreed that the party of the first part, shall have the ordinary legal lien of the Land Lord for his payments; and any breach of the stipulations of this Lease by the party of the second part shall be a forfeiture of the same.

In Witness whereof the parties to these presents have hereunto set their hands and affixed their seals the day and year above written.

JOHN CHARLES FREMONT [*Seal*]
Palmer Cook & Co. [*Seal*]

Signed sealed and deliverd in
the presence of ————
(part of the 22d. and all of the
23d. and 24th lines on the first
page erased before signing & also
part of the 5 & 6th Lines)
Charles de Selding

UNITED STATES OF AMERICA
DISTRICT OF COLUMBIA
CITY AND COUNTY OF WASHINGTON

Be it Known, That on the nineteenth day of September in the year of our Lord, One thousand eight hundred and fifty, before me, Charles de Selding, a Public Notary, in and for the County of Washington, in the District of Columbia aforesaid by lawful authority duly appointed, commissioned, and sworn, residing in the City of Washington came the Honble. John Charles Fremont and George W. Wright for himself and as Attorney in fact of the firm of Palmer Cook & Co. before named and acknowledged the foregoing lease to be their Act and Deed.

In Testimony whereof I have hereunto set my Hand and affixed my seal of office, at Washington aforesaid, the day and year aforesaid.

CHARLES DE SELDING
Notary Public

Copy (NHi—David Hoffman Papers). The copy does not indicate the seal of the notary public. Since this is a copy and the lines are not numbered, the omissions referred to do not appear.

This is JCF's first known formal lease to Palmer, Cook & Company and was the basis of that firm's lease to the Agua Fria Mining Company, which would be organized by George W. Wright and Hiram Walbridge in Great Britain. Originally, the San Francisco banking firm seemed to have entered upon the Mariposa as squatters. It may have had a lease earlier than the present one, as JCF referred to a ten-year lease to 200 feet square with a variable royalty (Doc. No. 121, 29 Nov. 1850).

1. This is a reference to the Mariposa Mine.

111. David Hoffman to Frémont

LONDON, 19 Sept. 1850

[The lack of information from JCF and Mayer has caused a disagreeable state and delayed the proposed leases. All he can do now is to send to JCF (which he does) unsigned preliminaries embracing the general notions of both lessee and JCF. "I therefore earnestly hope they will receive your earliest attention, and that on them I shall receive such instructions as may enable me to have signed preliminaries speedily sent to you." Sender's copy.]

112. William M. Gwin, Frémont, George W. Wright and Edward Gilbert to Millard Fillmore

WASHINGTON, 20 Sept. 1850

[Recommend the appointment of Rodman Price Lewis as a midshipman in the navy. ALS (CLU—Fillmore Papers).]

113. David Hoffman to Frémont

43 Upper Brooke Street, LONDON, 24 Sept. 1850

["Mr. Robert and I are apprehensive that our many and voluminous letters, &c. &c. have either not duly come to your hands, or that
your pressing occupations prevent the possibility of your making early
replies or that Mr. Mayer has consented to receive an office more
onerous than he anticipated or than he can perform." Laments that
lack of information and the ability to state precisely the terms of leases
are delaying the formation of companies. "If one Company be finally
agreed on, I shall know my course, and have plain sailing." Sender's
copy.]

114. Frémont to William L. Marcy

SENATE CHAMBER, 25 Sept. 1850

[Supports Dr. Charles M. Hitchcock, of the army, for a proposed
brevet because of his "meritorious service during the late War." JCF
expresses a high opinion of Hitchcock's worth. He is also "an old &
highly esteemed friend." ALS (DNA-107, LR, S-219 [72]). In the
same file were supporting letters for Hitchcock's promotion from
Maj. Gen. John E. Wool and from Congressmen Alexander H. Stephens and W. A. Gorman. It was unusual for an officer of the medical department (i.e., not of the line) to be brevetted. On 13 Feb. 1851
Hitchcock was promoted to major surgeon; he resigned from the
army two years later and died in 1885.]

115. Frémont to Edward Simmes

[28 Sept. 1850?]

DEAR SIR,

We have the pleasure to thank you for the bouquet you sent
Mrs. Frémont this morning.

Col. Benton could hardly believe that such beautiful flowers grew on the north side of the street.

With many thanks for the gratifying expressions of your note I am with regard, Yours truly,

J. C. Frémont
Sepr. 28

ALS (James S. Copley Collection, La Jolla, Calif.).

116. Frémont to the Editor of the Baltimore *Sun*

Monday, Sept. 30th. 1850

Sir:

Your paper of this morning contains a paragraph in a letter from this place, which it is obligatory on me to notice and in such a clear language as I believe the circumstances justify me in using. It appears under the well-known signature X, and I believe it to have been written by Mr. Grund;[1] but the paragraph which concerns me, I consider as the work of Mr. Foote himself, and shall accordingly treat him as the author.

The following is the paragraph:

The difficulty between Senators Foote and Fremont has been amicably arranged, as you will have seen by the card of those gentlemen's friends in to-day's *Union*.[2] This is as it should be. Mr. Fremont was wrong to attack Mr. Foote for words spoken in debate, which, as he (Foote) distinctly avowed at the time in the Senate, were not spoken with a view to wound the personal feelings of any senator present, but merely to protect the country against *ex parte* decisions of the California Board of Commissioners for the adjustment of land titles. All that Gen. Foote had observed was, that without Ewing's amendment, granting an appeal to the Supreme Court of the United States from the decision of the Board, he considered that the bill would disgrace the Republic, and that however inclined he was to support the bill *with* the amendment, he should assuredly vote against it without the amendment. Mr. Foote retracted nothing; but distinctly avowed that he did not intend any personal disrespect for those who were against the amendment. Col. Fremont could not be satisfied with this explanation. As a sensible man, and a man of honor, he must have seen his mistake in attempting to gag senators in regard to all legislative acts relating to California, and in constituting himself the heir apparent of a family feud which, for the benefit of the whole country, had better be buried than renewed.

This paragraph is false in many particulars, as I will endeavor briefly to show, but will first make a few remarks as to the authorship. When the friend[3] whom I had sent to Mr. Foote on Saturday morning brought back his letter, and joined with other friends in saying it was sufficient, and that I ought to be satisfied with it, and with the statement which had been agreed to be published, myself and others replied that this arrangement was not satisfactory, because the affair would not rest there, but that Mr. Foote was in communication with a letter writer, who wrote for him in the *Baltimore Sun* and *Philadelphia Ledger*, and that these two papers would soon contain untrue accounts of the affair to my prejudice, and which would compel me to take further notice of it. This was repeatedly and emphatically told to the gentleman; but it was finally concluded to receive Mr. Foote's letter as satisfactory, and to watch the letters in the *Sun* and *Ledger*. Accordingly, Monday morning's *Sun* brought the expected letter, which, as I have said above, I fully believe to be the work of Mr. Foote through Mr. Grund.

The letter opens with saying, that the difficulties between Mr. Foote and Mr. Fremont have been very "*amicably*" arranged. This word "amicably" is false, as was well known to the writer. I merely received Mr. Foote's letter as satisfaction, and no tokens of amity were interchanged between us, not even speaking to each other. He comes then to the cause of the difficulty, all of which is falsely stated, and is so proved to be by the record. The letter says, "Mr. Fremont was wrong to attack Mr. Foote for words spoken in debate, which as he (Foote) distinctly avowed at the time, were not spoken with a view to wound the feelings of any senator present, but merely to protect the country against *ex parte* decisions of the California Board of Commissioners." This is untrue. This bill for the California land titles was not under consideration at the time, and had been previously laid upon the table, with my approbation, till the next session, with a view to give it the full consideration, for which there was now no time.[4] Other measures had been taken up, and the naval appropriation bill was then under discussion; and it was on this bill—on the pretext of a motion from Mr. Gwin, having no relation to the land titles—that the words were spoken. It was not, therefore, to "protect" the country against any action under that bill that the injurious words were spoken, for the bill was not before the Senate, and had been laid over until the next session.

The letter says Mr. Foote retracted nothing. This is untrue, as will be seen by the copy of Mr. Foote's remarks, as furnished to me by the reporter for the *Intelligencer*, contrasted with his own letter to me; both of which are herewith given in their order. And to avow no retraction, is to re-affirm the original insult, by an insidious implication. I make no account of difference between *retraction* and *denial* in this case.

The letter says, "Mr. Fremont must have seen his error in attempting to gag senators in regard to all legislative measures in relation to California."[5] This is absurdly false—absurd in the idea that I should attempt to gag senators, and false in the fact. Much as the circumstances of the country required the bill to be passed to prevent violence and bloodshed in California, yet, when it was kept off until the afternoon of Friday, I gave it up for the session—said so, before the evening recess, to Messrs. Ewing and Benton, the two principal speakers on it—agreed to have it laid upon the table—and, satisfied that this would be done, did not return to the Senate until after the evening session had commenced, and until after the bill had been laid upon the table; and when I did come in, I was surprised to find Mr. Foote referring to the California land title bill, the naval appropriation bill being the one under consideration. It is, therefore, false, as well as ridiculous, to say that I attempted to gag senators; I laid it over the next session expressly to admit the fullest discussion, which is exactly the reverse of gagging.

The Baltimore letter says, "Mr. Foote did not intend to wound the feelings of any senator—but distinctly avowed at the time in the Senate, that he did not intend any personal disrespect for whose who were against the amendment." This is false again, and is proved to be so by all the circumstances of the case, and by the words themselves. This is the report of them, as furnished me by one of the *National Intelligencer* reporters:

We had some little admonition this morning as to the danger of hasty legislation in regard to California matters. Nevertheless, I say deliberately, I say it with due consideration of the matter and of the consequences of the declaration, that if the views which have been expressed in certain quarters this morning in regard to a portion of the legislation which is urged upon us for California, should be adopted in the same hasty manner in which it is now proposed to us to give our sanction to the present proposition, the admission of California into the Union would be productive of more detriment to the republic, and, in my opinion, be fraught with more real dishonor to the nation, than any event that has ever occurred in the historic annals of the country. Sir, we must be cautious about this California business. Not only is California a State of this Union, but she is a great State. Her resources are large. Her interests are vast. They are of vast importance to herself and to the country at large. In dealing with them we must act cautiously, circumspectly, vigilantly, and permit no man, or set of men, to urge us hastily and indiscreetly into the adoption of any legislation for which, hereafter, we may have reason to repent in sackcloth and in ashes.

Now, take this language, and see if there was not a design to be personal and insulting in it, and that upon a plan previously resolved upon. He avows deliberation—due consideration—disregard of consequences. What does this mean, but a pre-determined design to give both insult and defiance? And in that light it would doubtless have been represented, if I had not called him to account. Then the terrible consequences of passing the bill, the dishonor to the nation, the corruption, the repentance in sackcloth and ashes: what did all this refer to, but the bill which I had brought in? And why refer to it at all, when it was not before the Senate, nor under consideration—actually laid upon the table, to lie there until the next session? Why not wait till the next session, if he only wanted to speak against the bill? Why refer to it at all, under such circumstances, unless for a purpose unconnected with the bill? and in such language, except for insult? It is useless to pretend the contrary; and, therefore, the Baltimore letter is false in saying that Mr. Foote had no design to wound feelings—no intent to be disrespectful. The contrary was understood by every senator at the time, and is proved by the words themselves, and the circumstances under which they were spoken, and there is no disavowal, distinct or indistinct, of personal disrespect to anybody.

The Baltimore letter admonishes me not to make myself "*heir*" to a family feud. The admonition would be unnecessary, even if it came from a source entitled to respect; but, found where it is, it is both false and impertinent. I make myself "*heir*" to no one's feuds. I begin none of my own. I prefer to live in peace with the world. But everybody will see from the remarks of Mr. Foote in the Senate, in relation to the bill I brought in, and his letter to the *Baltimore Sun*, that it is intended to make me "*heir*" to his feelings towards Col. Benton.

I conclude this notice with giving Mr. Foote's letter to me, in answer to the note which I sent him by a friend:

Senate Chamber, Sept. 28, 1850

Sir: I do not feel that I should be doing justice to myself, did I not, in writing, (as I thought I did very explicitly last night, *orally*), deny that I said anything denunciatory of the bill to which you refer, or of those who introduced it. I was in favor of Mr. Ewing's amendment, and in favor of the bill itself, provided his amendment could be incorporated with it. This your colleague, well knows. I said that certain views had been expressed in the course of debate upon that bill, and in support of it, what if sanctioned by Congress would disgrace the republic. What I meant was, that the establishment of a Board of Commissioners in California for the adjustment of land titles, *without the privilege* of appeal to the Supreme Court of the United States, would, in my opinion, result in scenes of corruption, and acts of injustice, which would be seriously derogatory to the national character. So I think yet, and so I shall always think and say.

If after this statement, you persevere in the demand contained in your note, I shall certainly gratify you, though I shall, from certain prudential considerations, defer a formal *acceptance* of your proposition until I can leave the District of Columbia. Your obedient servant,

H. S. FOOTE.

Hon. J. C. Fremont.

This was the letter received. It contradicts the speech, denies the denunciation and insult which the speech contains, and is itself contradicted both by the actual words spoken in the Senate, and by the letter to the *Baltimore Sun*; and, although both of these are themselves untrue, yet it is not for Mr. Foote to say so, or to impeach their competency to invalidate the other. All three of these documents are given, and those who please may compare them, and see how entirely they convict each other. The letter to me, and the statement published by friends, would have been a *quietus* to the affair with me, if it had not been for the Baltimore letter. The letter to me, to be sure was untrue; but that was not my affair, provided nothing more was written. But I expected more—expected letters injurious to me in the *Baltimore Sun* and the *Philadelphia Ledger*, and so said at the time, as so the event was verified—and that has forced me to make this brief exposition of the threefold falsehoods of the premeditated attack upon me in the Senate, its denial in a letter to me, and its insidious implied repetition in the *Baltimore Sun*, by asserting that he retracted nothing.

To put the whole case into three words, it is this: Mr. Foote went out of his way when the subject was not before the Senate, to deliver a deliberately considered insult and defiance to me—then denied the insult and defiance, and disclaimed all disrespect, in a letter to me—then re-affirmed, by inevitable implication, the same insult and defiance in a letter to the *Baltimore Sun*, denying all retraction.

With this summing up of the case and the precedent proofs, I leave the affair to the judgment of the public.[6]

(SIGNED) J. C. FRÉMONT

Printed in Baltimore *Sun*, 5 Oct. 1850, and in BIGELOW, 422–26.

1. A correspondent of the Baltimore *Sun* and a frequent contributor to the Philadelphia *Public Ledger*, Francis Joseph Grund (1798–1863) was credited "with being the father of the journalistic sensational style, full of hints of best sources and information behind the scenes" (DAB). He had been a witness for Foote in the investigation following the pistol incident in the Senate (see Doc. No. 61, n. 1).

2. A. C. Dodge, William M. Gwin, Henry H. Sibley, and Rodman M. Price had indicated that they were authorized "to state that the difficulty between the Hon. H. S. Foote and the Hon. J. C. Frémont—growing out of certain expressions used by the former in relation to the California land bill in the Senate last evening—had been adjusted satisfactorily and honorably to both these gentlemen" (Washington *Daily Union*, 29 Sept. 1850).

3. JCF's note was carried by Rodman M. Price. It was virtually a challenge to a duel; the two senators had exchanged strong words the previous evening, and Foote struck JCF when the latter charged that the former was not a gentleman (GONZALES, 82).

4. JCF is accurate in noting that the California land bill was not under consideration when Foote made his remarks.

5. JCF proposed allowing a board of land commissioners to adjudicate claims. A decision favorable to a claimant was to be final against the United States; if unfavorable, the claimant was to have a right of appeal to the District Court and, if still unsuccessful, to the Supreme Court (*Congressional Globe*, 31st Cong., 1st sess., 27 Sept. 1850, p. 2045).

6. The 7 Oct. 1850 issue of the Baltimore *Sun* carried "X" or Grund's satirical reply, and on 11 Oct. it ran a pro-Foote editorial, speculating about why JCF would object to giving the U.S. government the right of appeal from decisions of the California Board of Land Commissioners.

117. Alexander von Humboldt to Frémont

[SANS SOUCI, 7 Oct. 1850]

TO COL. FREMONT, SENATOR

It is very agreeable to me, sir, to address you these lines by my excellent friend, our minister to the United States, M. de Gerolt. After having given you, in the new edition of my "Aspects of Nature," the public testimony of the admiration which is due to your gigantic labors between St. Louis, of Missouri, and the coasts of the South Sea, I feel happy to offer you, in this living token, (*dans ce petit signe de vie*) the homage of my warm acknowledgment. You have displayed a noble courage in distant expeditions, braved all the dangers of cold and famine, enriched all the branches of the natural sciences, illustrated a vast country which was almost entirely unknown to us.

A merit so rare has been acknowledged by a sovereign warmly interested in the progress of physical geography; the king orders me to offer you the grand golden medal destined to those who have labored at scientific progress.[1] I hope that this mark of the royal good will, will be agreeable to you at a time when, upon the proposition of the illustrious geographer, Cha[rle]s Ritter, the Geographical Society at Berlin has named you an honorary member. For myself, I must thank you particularly also for the honor which you have done in attaching my name, and that of my fellow-laborer and intimate friend, Mr. [Aimé] Bonpland, to countries neighboring to those which have been the object of our labors. *California*, which has so nobly resisted the introduction of slavery, will be worthily represented by a friend of liberty and of the progress of intelligence.

Accept, I pray you, sir, the expression of my high and affectionate consideration. Your most humble and most obedient servant,

A. v. HUMBOLDT.

Sans Souci, October 7, 1850

English translation as printed in BIGELOW, 327–29, who also publishes the letter in French. On the envelope: "A Monsieur le Colonel Frémont, Senateur, Avec la grande médaille d'or, Pour les progres dans les sciences. Baron Humboldt."

1. BIGELOW describes the medal as being "of fine gold, massive, more than double the size of the American double eagle, and of exquisite workmanship. On the face is the medallion head of the king, Frederic William the Fourth, surrounded by figures emblematical of Religion, Jurisprudence, Medicine and the Arts. On the reverse, Apollo, in the chariot of the sun, drawn by four high mettled plunging horses, traversing the zodiac, and darting rays of light from its head."

118. Frémont to Charles F. Mayer

Irving House [New York]
Oct. 12, 1850

My dear Sir,

I have been terribly pressed by business and have deferred writing to you until it is too late, but will do so from Chagres. Yours truly,

J. C. Frémont

Copy (NHi—David Hoffman Papers). This copy letter is a part of Charles F. Mayer's letter to Hoffman and Robert, dated 14 Oct. 1850. Mayer's own letter contained some severe strictures on JCF. He noted that it was the only answer he had as a result of "four earnest letters written within the last eight days"; in two he had offered to go to JCF. Mayer maintained that he had asked for leases and all details needed by Hoffman, for provisional instructions to meet the preliminary lease Hoffman was forwarding, and for authority to act definitely under the instructions. He had also asked for permission to supply money to Robert and Hoffman. In vexation with JCF, he added: "You see this beautiful illustration of this spoiled child of fortune and of too sudden and too superlative fame. He is the most provokingly dilatory and fussy man. . . . He has gone, I presume, to California. . . . But even in passing through Baltimore, he did not give me the chance of an hour's conference with him. I am left to have a line as he is on the wing." On 24 Oct. Mayer continued in similar vein and assured Hoffman that he had tried industriously to procure information: "I kept up a seige to him most fruitlessly and only to meet an indifference the most impenetrable and most impossible and laziness the most disreputable." On 22 Nov., in reference to the fact that JCF had not supplied money to Hoffman, Mayer wrote, "He *will do right ultimately*: but his *immediate remissness* is unpardonable and stamps him in my eyes as a spoiled child of public eulogy."

119. Frémont to John Torrey

Taboga, near Panama, Oct. 30, 1850

My dear Sir,

Your letter in relation to Dr. Ellet's proposal[1] to me was received just in time to prevent a conference to him. A proposal has been made to me through a friend in New York, and as the subject is one of great interest with me just now, I had intended to examine into the subject with the view of making some application of it to our mines: We are about to engage in extensive gold mining operations, & I would be glad to know from you if you think your discovery can be advantageously employed by us in our operations.[2]

I shall not leave California until the steamer of January 15th so that an immediate reply from you, leaving New York by the Decr. steamer, would reach San Francisco just in time. I should be glad to hear from you while there. This note will probably reach you about the 23d November. Yours truly,

J. C. Frémont

Profr. John Torrey,
Princeton

ALS (NHi).
1. The nature of Ellet's proposal is not known. One of the great civil engineers of his time, Charles Ellet (1810–62) had designed and built the suspension bridges over the Schuylkill at Fairmount and over the Ohio at Wheeling. In 1857 JCF would offer him the position of chief engineer for the survey, location, and construction of a mining canal which he expected would run fifty to seventy miles long. A number of routes were being surveyed with the idea of bringing water to the mining operations on the Mariposa from either the headwaters of the Merced or the San Joaquin. The decision ultimately was to take the ore to the water, and a railroad was built from the Pine Tree Mine down to the Merced River where a quartz mill was also constructed. For a biography of Ellet, see LEWIS.
2. The editor has been unable to find information on the "discovery." The botanist was also interested in chemistry, and RODGERS, 230, notes that early in 1850 Torrey had earned $250 doing "some valuable researches for a California Gold Company."

120. Frémont to David Hoffman

ISLAND OF TABOGA, NEAR PANAMA
October 30th. 1850

MY DEAR SIR,

A slight illness obliges me to use Mrs. Frémonts pen. We are here on our way to California & sail on the 1st expecting to reach there by the 20th. Accompanying this letter I return to you through Mr. Mayer the "preliminaries"[1] which you submitted to the Anglo-American Company, and your scale of royalties.[2] With some slight modifications which you will find noticed upon the first, I approve both these papers, and have endorsed my approval upon them. This puts it in your power to make arrangements so far definitive as will enable the Companies to go on with their arrangements without any delay whatever. I am now going to California with a view of informing myself of the condition of affairs, and the quantity of mining ground upon which we can safely calculate. Until I am in possession of this definitive information I am not willing to give the Anglo-American Company the privilege of any greater quantity of land than what is secured to them in the first instance. I shall write to you immediately upon my arrival in San Francisco, and afterwards, as I shall have information to communicate. The difficulties which we have had with the squatters are disappearing and will soon be done away with.

I understand that Capt. Sir Henry Huntley[3] of the Royal Navy, has been taking liberties with my property, employing men to work there & carrying off gold quartz from the place.[4] I trust this information (which I received here) is not correct, as it would render it necessary for me to have recourse to the proper authority against him. I just missed seeing him on the Isthmus, he being now on his way home to England having with him a large quantity of valuable specimens. I have to ask you to pay some attention to his conduct in England & I will write to you on the subject as soon as I obtain more information. Very truly yours,

J. C. FRÉMONT

David Hoffman, Esqre.
London

ALS-JBF (NHi—David Hoffman Papers). Endorsed.
1. In approving the preliminaries, which he did on 29 Oct. 1850, JCF noted: "I have disagreed to the 10th article for the following reason, *viz*: that I desire before granting any such additional privileges to lease holders, to ascertain clearly the amount of mining land. For such purposes I am now on my way to California. If the quantity shall be found equal to what we have anticipated, I shall have no objection to grant the additional quantity on the same terms, as the mining lot granted in these preliminaries." By the tenth article, the company, within eighteen months of the date of the first lease, would have had the right to double the quantity of mineral land first leased, upon the same terms as the original lease, but with only a capital increase of £20,000. The expansion could be either on adjoining lands (if not already leased) or elsewhere (NHi—Hoffman Papers).
2. See "Scale of Royalty," Doc. No. 107.
3. A captain in the English navy, Sir Henry Vere Huntly had been sent to California by the Anglo-California Gold Mining and Dredging Company with which Hoffman was negotiating in the late summer of 1850. The company had been formed early in 1850 and allegedly had title to rich property somewhere on the Stanislaus or Calaveras rivers. Huntly could not locate the property de-

scribed in the beautiful prospectus and went to the Mariposa region, where he examined the works of the Stockton & Aspinwall company "on the other side of the mountain" in which the Mariposa Mine was situated. He also visited the Agua Fria Mine, which had just been opened by a party of five young Englishmen and one American. It was seven miles from the Mariposa Mine. But it was the latter, then being worked by the newly formed Mariposa Company, which won his enthusiasm. He noticed "that the privileges of sharing in this mine would involve an outlay at once from £25,000 to £100,000, according to the quantity of interest purchased," but that all the factors argued for a rich return. He himself had been negotiating with JCF's agent, William Buckler, and hoped to obtain a lease on a vein about half a mile from the Stockton & Aspinwall mine (HUNTLY).

4. Huntly insisted that the proprietors of the mine had made a present of specimens to him (HUNTLY).

121. Frémont to Charles F. Mayer

SAN FRANCISCO, CALA. Nov. 29th/50

My DEAR SIR,

I wrote to yourself & to Mr. Hoffman from Tobago and hoped that the letters reached you safely. In those letters I authorized Mr. Hoffman to make definitive arrangements with certain companies in England upon the terms he proposed to me. It seems to me that, in such leases as to give to me a fixed proportion, one third of the gross product would hereafter produce dissatisfaction among the English companies for the reason that in the Leases executed in the U. States only one sixth of the gross product is given to me. The House of Palmer Cooke & Co., who entered upon my land as squatters, have received a lease by which they pay only four per cent of the gross product the first year and ten (10) per cent the remaining six years. They however have only about 200 feet square, have no privileges of wood &c. and were already in operation when the lease was executed.[1] All this however might produce dissatisfaction, & I therefore make you the following suggestions.—The quantity of mining land, privileges & duration of lease are all much greater then I have granted to parties in the United States. I therefore propose that the leases shall be executed to them (the English companies) on the terms laid down by Mr. Hoffman in his *project*, and that they shall pay to me in quarterly payments, one *sixth* part of the gross product of gold; together with a *present* consideration of ten thousand pounds, or, one *fifth* part of the gross product & present consideration of five thousand pounds—or, one *fourth* of the gross product and no consideration. To this scale I shall endeavor to bring the leases I may hereafter grant in the U. States.

Mr. Hoffman can either adopt these terms, or the sliding scale according to the product of the [ro]ck, which he proposed to me.[2] The above arrangements would suit me well, as additional capital would now be of great aid to me in carrying out my plans on the Mariposas.

I had the good fortune to meet here (recently returned from the Mariposas) the Agent whom I had sent out with machinery. He had succeeded in getting it safely up to the place, & in having it mounted.[3] On my way here, I had been attacked by Neuralgia in the leg, and could not immediately go up. I have therefore sent him back &, expect to see him here again in a week. I shall be able to write to you about the product of our machinery.

The information I have received from the Mariposas is very encouraging. It goes to prove that the whole place is more or less covered with gold veins, which you will remember was always my opinion. I am having a mineralogical survey made by competent miners (Hungarians).[4] They have already laid down up[on] their map, thirty three distinct veins, yielding upon the surface from four to thirty cents to the pound of ore, and this in the vicinity of the first vein, beyond which they have not yet progressed. In the meantime other veins have been discovered in other parts of the tract. What these veins shall disclose when we come to open them up we shall soon see. I hope to be able to give some satisfactory intelligence by the next mail. I shall not have time to write Mr. Hoffman by this mail, or rather it is not necessary, as you can send him this letter. You will understand that I give him hereby power to make definitive arrangements with companies (to the extent at present of ten leases, for which we know that we have room) according to the terms proposed by him in the projects which you transmitted to me at New York in October (which I have returned to him through you with my endorsements) & the modifications of this letter. Very truly yours,

(SIGNED) J. C. FRÉMONT

To Charles F. Mayer, Esq.
Baltimore, Maryland

The squatter difficulties are disappearing.

Copy (NHi—David Hoffman Papers). Endorsed.
1. This seems to be a reference to Palmer, Cook & Company's very early lease

on the Mariposa Vein (see Frémont to Hoffman, 1 May 1851). The lease has never been located. JCF's lease of 17 Sept. 1850 was the basis for the company's claim to the Agua Fria and granted a square of 600 feet with a stipulation that JCF was to receive one-sixth of all gold or other metals (Doc. No. 110).

2. Hoffman's sliding scale was based on the richness of the quartz. For example, if the yield of gold per ton of rock was from two to four ounces, the royalty should be one-tenth in gold, or if in money, £10 per £100 sterling; if the yield was eighteen to twenty-four ounces, the royalty should be one-fourth in gold, or in money £25 per £100 sterling.

3. At the end of Aug. 1850 J. Eugene Flandin had sailed on the *Philadelphia* with machinery for extracting gold (New York *Herald*, 28 Aug. 1850).

4. The principal Hungarian making the survey was Samuel Count Wäss (1814–79). He was possibly assisted by two army friends who came to California with him, Maj. Edward Theodore Danburghy and Capt. Charles Uzani. The *Daily Alta California*, 13 Jan. and 14 Feb. 1851, prints two letters from him dated from the Mariposa in which he extolls some of the veins of the estate. The next year Wäss, Molitor & Co. of San Francisco were issuing small coins bearing their initials which they guaranteed to be worth the value stamped thereon. Wäss returned to Hungary permanently in 1859.

122. Frémont to Abel Stearns

SAN FRANCISCO, Dec. 1, 1850

MY DEAR SIR,

I write to say to you that I hope you will be at San José in time for the election of U.S. Senator, which will take place shortly after the meeting of the legislature. The measures relating to the landed interests of this country, which I introduced recently at Washington, and more especially that relating to the adjudication of the land claims, I as a landholder, consider of vital importance to the security of our property. For these reasons, if for no other, I desire to re-election,— and having confidence in my own devotion to the true interests of the [state] I wish to see these measures carried out. My views on these subjects are well known to you, & trusting to the continuance of your friendly feelings, without further enlargement, I have written to express my hope that you will come up in time to give me your support, as there will be many candidates. Yours truly,

J. C. FRÉMONT

Hon. Able Stearns
Los Angeles

ALS (CSmH).

123. Frémont to the People of California

[ca. 24 Dec. 1850]

Particular circumstances which have been created by the unexpected termination of my senatorial term on the 4th of March next, and the magnitude of the interests entrusted to the California delegation, make it expedient and proper that I should render to my constituents some account of the manner in which I have proposed to discharge my portion of the trust: especially as the approaching election, in awakening the concern of patriotic citizens for the welfare of the state, exposes my conduct to a severer scrutiny and a stricter accountability than would otherwise have fallen to my individual share; and likewise renders it incumbent on me not to seem by my silence to acquiesce in the multiplied misrepresentations of myself and my measures, which have been devised and pressed with so much energy for electioneering purposes.

When the State of California was finally admitted to a representation in Congress the day for adjournment had already been fixed, and barely three weeks of the session remained. Although into this brief space was to be crowded the accumulated business of the session, and of the country, it was generally understood that a *day* or *two* would be set apart in the senate for the consideration of California affairs. With this restricted allowance—narrowed down, as it proved to be by the pressure of other interests to a few hours only—it was evident that little in the way of deliberate legislation was to be had for California. What I have to say, therefore, must be confined rather to a declaration of my views and a vindication of what I had proposed to do, than of what I have done.

Satisfied that in this condition of things you would require little at the hands of your delegation, but would be proportionably gratified with whatever they might succeed in accomplishing, I prepared myself to urge upon Congress the laws customary and necessary to our full political organization, and such other important and exigent measures as in our singular condition had become necessary. In carrying out these views I resolved to bring before Congress only such practical measures as I might reasonably expect to obtain the favorable consideration of, and while asking for California all that had ever been granted to any other state, to introduce no propositions for the selfish purpose of creating false expectations or unfounded hopes at home, or hazarding the good that I thought might be obtained by demands which in the present spirit of Congress I know would not be listened to. Immediately, then, upon my taking my seat in the senate, I introduced a series of measures, which, though in some instances designed for local benefit, in greater part comprehended general interests of the state. With the view of our urging these measures as far forward as possible, I had in presenting them—as measures vitally affecting our future interest—the special object of bringing directly before the people of the state, for their consideration, in order that at the ensuing session of Congress I might act with a decreased responsibility, and under the authority and enlightenment of their fully expressed opinions. Continued ill health since my arrival has defeated one of my objects in returning to the state at this season, by preventing me from making a personal inquiry into the views of my constituents, that I might more effectively represent them.

Among the questions involved in the bills proposed, were several which a familiar knowledge of the country and friendly relations with a large body of its inhabitants led me to regard with a particular interest. First in importance was the course to be adopted for adjusting titles to land, and for acquiring rights of property in the gold mines. Upon the early settlement of these questions, and upon the direction given to the legislation of the general Government upon them, depended, in my opinion, a large measure of the future quiet and prosperity of the country.

To the bills comprehending these two subjects—land titles and gold mines—public attention has consequently been chiefly directed, and electioneering ingenuity has been chiefly extended to procure erroneous and prejudicial opinions. On them, therefore, I propose to make some remarks, referring for details to the bills themselves. That which has been most frequently made the subject of remark and objection, is the bill for preserving order in the gold mines, which has been condemned in general terms for excluding foreigners, and misrepresented as a scheme for imposing taxes on the miners, and in other equally unfounded respects.

As the title avers, the measure is a temporary one. It introduces a subject entirely new in American legislation, which from its novelty, importance and intrinsic difficulty excited much interest and attracted a close and jealous examination. Its leading principles are to exclude all idea of making national revenue out of the mines—to prevent the possibility of their monopoly by moneyed capitalists—and to give to natural capital, to LABOR and INDUSTRY, a fair chance in fields of its own choosing; that is, to accomplish the double purpose of inviting the investment of moneyed capital and at the same time preventing it from driving out or overpowering the population who have no capital but their courage and industry, in the domain which they alone have developed and made available. It is the foundation of a system granting to individuals rights of property in the mines. Its passage would have been equivalent to a surrender on the part of the general government of all usufructuary interest in the mines, and must gradually have led to a relinquishment of their municipal control to the State; a result, in my opinion, imperatively necessary to be obtained, but not practicable at this time as a distinct proposition.

The original bill, as drawn up by myself, conformed to the character of our institutions and the general spirit of our laws. Its privileges were not reserved exclusively to the citizens of the United States, and no invidious distinctions were established against any particular people. But before the subject came up for debate in the Senate, the delegation of this State, on consultation, unanimously decided, that in deference to the expressions of public sentiment as declared by the legislature of the State, and endorsed in public meetings, and by the public press, a clause should be introduced, confining the mining privileges to American citizens. The action of your delegation was founded on what they had thus every reason to believe was the public sentiment here, and which it was their duty to represent. It appears, however, that the feeling here which made its impression at the capital, and influenced your delegation there, had already changed when the next steamer brought an account of their conduct, and your returning representative finds himself unexpectedly censured for a proposition which he did not originate, and for which he is only accidentally placed in a situation to be held responsible.

Exception is made to the machinery, as we may call it, of executing the system; to the agents, to the permits, and of course to the sum, small as it is, which is proposed to be paid for the permit. Laws must have officers to execute them, and it was the purpose of the bill to provide the cheapest, most convenient and suitable system. In the first place there are agents to reside each in a gold mine district, grant the permits to applicants, visit the mines, and with a jury of six disinterested men—miners themselves, and neighbors and friends of the disputants—settle disputes equitably, and without the delay and expenses of a resort to a court of justice for every little question. To see that the agents are faithful a superintendent of gold mines is proposed, to superintend all the agents, examine their books and accounts, hear complaints against them, take appeals from their decisions and suspend them and appoint others in case of misconduct. The superintendent would be thus armed with strong power, not over the miners but over the agents, and for the benefit of the miners. It was considered necessary to have this strong, controlling power present, that all possible attention should be paid to the faithful conduct of the agents, and the immediate redress of wrongs. The gorges of the Sierra Nevada are too remote from the metropolitan government—the President is too far off to observe the conduct of agents, to hear complaints, redress wrongs or dismiss the unfaithful. It would be equivalent to no redress for injuries, if a miner who is wronged were obliged to send his complaint to Washington, and prove it at that distance from the scene of his complaint.

I have heard that it is objected to this feature of the bill, that it does not provide a further appeal of disputes. It will be observed that the primary tribunal proposed, is a jury of six—two of whom chosen by each of the disputants, and two by the resident agent; from this tribunal it proposes that the party dissatisfied with the decision, may appeal to the Superintendent, who in his option may or may not refer it to a new jury of twelve. Probably it would have been better to have made it incumbent on him so to refer it, at the demand of either disputant; and perhaps also, it would have been expedient to provide for a final appeal to a Court of law.

In reference to all this, it is only necessary to say, that the bill does not pretend to be perfect; it was not in the nature of things that it should be. It was expected that in its progress through Congress, it would be improved by the ideas which the discussion of the subject would develop. Still more, that in its operation, important amendments would be suggested. And I think I may congratulate myself that on a subject of so much difficulty, affecting such great interests, and in which the past legislation of our country offered nothing to guide my labors, I was able to devise a measure in which those who find it to their interest to misrepresent me and it, are compelled to resort to such details of it as do not affect its principles, and only require an improvement to be suggested, in order to be adopted.

The quantity allowed to each person I supposed would be ample, considering the privilege of changing his location, and of selling his lot as often as he pleases. Thirty feet square is proposed as the size of a lot to be worked by manual labor in a placer; two hundred and ten feet, or about one acre, to be the size of a lot in a mine worked by machinery in the rock.

A placer lot, accordingly, contains nine hundred superficial feet. A cube of these dimensions would be twenty-seven thousand solid feet, and if a place of tolerable richness be found, an industrious man may say his fortune is made.

If he sells, he may take another permit, and work on until he makes another good discovery, and either sells this or exhausts it; and so on until he is satisfied, or the mining exhausted. Wherever he may plant his stake, exclusive possession is guarantied to the miner so long as he works his mining lot, or to his assignee if sold, or to his legal representatives in the event of his death. All that he finds is to be his own—there is no tax to be paid, no per centum, no fifth, or tenth, or twentieth to the government, no officer to stand over him and require him to give an account of all he made, and surrender up a part to the government.

For the more extended operations by machinery, the dimensions, of the parcel of mining ground fixed by this bill, are two hundred and ten feet square or about one acre. In a mineral country, reputed to be of such extraordinary richness, these dimensions were considered large enough for the mine itself, and for temporary buildings in the beginning of operations. Hereafter, when the mineral districts shall be better known, and the locality of the lodes or veins precisely marked out, it is probable that larger contiguous spaces should be granted for the construction of the buildings necessary for extensive works. In the meantime, it should be remembered that these veins will occur in tracts of ground rich in loose gold, and that all the advantages attending a permit to work a *placer*, apply to the permit to work a mine, of which the superficial content is about forty-four thousand feet, and thirty feet depth of which would be one million three hundred and twenty thousand solid feet.

The bill contains beneficial provisions in favor of *first discoverers*; they are to have double quantity without the payment of any fee, and with the privilege of a *preemptive right*. This would furnish inducements to prosecute researchers which would result in great benefit to the country, and the discoverer of a new placer, or of a new mine, will have a full reward for his enterprise.

Upon the principle of sales of the public lands, five per centum of the proceeds from the sale of the permits is to go to the state of California, to be expended in opening communications through the country.

The mode of taking effect of the system is equitable and proper, going into effect when the agent arrives in a district and promulgates the law; without any interruption to work going on, without any shock to existing operations, or any retroactive operation.

As already stated, the leading purpose of the bill is to leave LABOR and INDUSTRY a fair choice in all the benefits of the mines; to exclude the idea of a government revenue from them, and especially to avoid any system that would cause an espionage by government agents, into the amount of any man's earnings. Without intending to cast censure on any one, it is proper for me to say, that every other plan, as far as I know, for the regulation or working of the mines, which has been recommended either to or in Congress, must have operated to the reverse of the objects which I proposed. Most or all the different plans suggested have contemplated, first, the advantage of the government, either in a per centage on the gold extracted, or in sales of the mining region, in lots, after ascertaining their comparative values by scientific examinations, or finally by establishing government broker shops, to which every man should be compelled to bring the gold he should extract, to sell at a fixed price; and nearly the only objections urged to the bill which I introduced, and the reasons that its friends did not succeed in getting it taken up in the House of Representatives, was that it proposed too much for the miners, and too little for the government. From these facts, my fellow citizens who are engaged in mining operations, will better understand the real condition of their interests at Washington, and the alternatives likely to be left to their representatives there.

I believe it is very important to the interests of this State, that the determination of the General Government in regard to the mines, should be speedily known, and the manner and conditions on which they may be permanently held and worked, relieved of the uncertainty and doubt that now unhappily check expensive enterprises. It was my endeavor to anticipate less favorable legislation, (which I believe, is to be apprehended) by initiating and compromising the government to the support of a system having for its object the interests of the miner; but if any better plan were proposed for the accomplishment of the same end, and likely to be favorably received by Congress, I should with increased satisfaction substitute it for what I have proposed.

The leading principle of the Bill concerning LAND TITLES is to *quiet the country*, and to this great object its details are carefully directed.

The bill proposes a Board of Commissioners, whose business it would be to collect evidence, and to decide briefly and without the technicalities of legal proceedings on the great mass of cases which have come before them. They are required to travel through the country and carry justice and quietude to every man's door. Cases involving really any doubt or any question of law would go to the District Court of the United States with an appeal in the event of a decision against the claimant, to the Supreme Court at Washington. The great mass of cases, therefore, would be decided here and speedily.

The principle of this bill, I shall state frankly, was to procure the speediest, cheapest and least troublesome mode that was likely to receive the approbation of Congress, for the settlement of questions of title, and the separation of private lands from the public domain. The purpose of the bill was to quiet titles, not to disturb them; to ascertain and guaranty the rights of property, or who contemplated owning property, secure in the tenure by which he should hold. The only objections urged in Congress against this bill were to those very features that I think ought to recommend the bill itself to the people of the state, and to every one who has regard for its honor and welfare. The sole objections urged were to those provisions which contemplate a *speedy* ascertainment and assurance of titles, by tribunals on the ground; and nearly the sole amendments offered were for the prolongations of the questions which now so much interefere with the harmony and prosperity of the country, and for their removal to Washington. The object of these propositions is so obvious—so plainly for the purpose of levying mail on the property of this state for individual benefits in the eastern states—to secure, in short, fat fees to the lawyers who congregate at Washington—to compel the people here to part their heritage with the promoters of litigation abroad—the object of all propositions of this kind is so obvious, and the monstrous injustice and hardship of sending the great mass of land titles to a country to be litigated six thousand miles off by a people not acquainted even with the language in which they are written, and the disastrous effect such delays must have on the improvement of this country, are so striking, that I cannot suppose any one can advocate them, whose interests and affections are not elsewhere than with the honor, dignity and welfare of this state.

The bill is framed in its general character in conformity with the

219

customary legislation of our government; but with important modifications, looking to the main object, already developed, of a speedy and cheap rendering of justice and establishment of quiet. The principal of these modifications consists in making awards of the Board of Commissioners and of the local Federal Court final, when in favor of the claimant, and in making the law of prescription a foundation for title to be respected. The law of prescription, more just and equitable than our statute of limitations, ought in justice to be recognized in adjudicating upon titles which were acquired under it.

So, the United States ought to be CONCLUDED by the decisions of its own law officers. They are their own judges, their own arbitrators, and ought to be concluded by the first decisions against them, and not have *three* chances at the same man's property. Neither ought the people to be made to spend their substance and their lives contending at law with the government for their homes.

I am in favor of and shall gladly adopt any modifications of the bill I introduced, or any other plan that can be devised, likely to meet a favorable reception in Congress, which shall better answer the ends I have mentioned, of a speedy ascertainment and assurance of titles and establishment of quiet. But I shall never consent to any measure that may betray our government or people into the ignominy of confiscating the rights of a conquered people, or violating the stipulations of a treaty.

J. C. FRÉMONT

Printed in *Alta California*, 24 Dec. 1850.

124. David Hoffman to Frémont

43 Upper Brooke Street, LONDON, 10 Jan. 1851

[Fears that Mr. Robert, in his zeal, may have overwhelmed JCF with details. Notes that two of JCF's American leases have been brought on the British market and that the fifteen others were expected to follow. Since they offered a lower royalty to JCF than Hoffman had been trying to negotiate, they had hindered his conclusion of European leases, although he had tried to counter the underbidding by noting that the American leases were "experimental" and designed for instant execution. He still has hopes for the organization of a French company and that JCF would answer all his questions immediately and effectually. Sender's copy.]

125. Frémont to Persifor Smith

SAN JOSÉ, Jany. 12th. 1851

MY DEAR SIR,

The accompanying petition has been forwarded to me with the request that I should send it to you, enclosed in a note from myself urging upon you the necessity for relief.

I am very sure you will act as you feel authorized and with the hope that it may be favorably to the petitioners I am with respect Yours very truly,

J. C. FRÉMONT

To Genl. P. F. Smith, U.S.A.

LS (DNA-393, LR, Division of the Pacific, F-1-1851). Endorsed: "Recd. Jany. 15, 1851." The petition was not found with JCF's letter, but the white Mariposans asked for protection from hostile Indians.

The influx of prospectors and miners into the foothills and valleys brought the usual abuse of the natives and their retaliation by murder and plunder. There seemed danger of a general Indian war, especially in the upper valley of the San Joaquin where the Indians were notably independent and bold.

Before the petition could reach Gen. Smith and even before Governor John McDougal's authorization to do so, Sheriff James Burney of Mariposa County had raised volunteers. With the governor's approval, the battalion's force was increased to 200, but before it could start on an extended expedition, McDougal instructed it to suspend operations. The U.S. Indian Commissioners—George W. Barbour, O. M. Wozencraft, and Redick McKee—had finally arrived in San Francisco and there was hope that peace could be re-established in the mining country (CRAMPTON, 115–22).

126. Frémont to Charles M. Conrad

SAN JOSE, CALIF., 29 Jan. 1851

[Recommends the appointment of Francis Wright, "son of an old and highly respectable citizen of this state," as a cadet at the Military

Academy. ALS (DNA-94, Military Academy, Applications, 280–1851). George W. Wright had a brother named Francis who had come out to California in 1849, but since he would have been twenty-seven years old in 1851, it is unlikely that he was interested in "cadet" status at West Point. In 1852 Francis Wright, along with Charles Moss and Mark Herring, purchased the interests of some of the heirs of Felipe Hernandez in Rancho Laguna de las Calabazas in Santa Cruz County (see two deeds dated 1 Aug. 1852 and one deed dated 9 Sept. 1852, Santa Cruz County Deeds, Book 1, pp. 433 and 434).]

127. David Hoffman to Frémont

43 Upper Brooke Street, LONDON, 1 Feb. 1851

[Writes that the French company, "The Nouveau Monde," has sent their proposal, but he does not approve of it, since it does not come up to "our Terms." The royalty was only one-sixth, as in JCF's leases to Capt. Smith.[1] Furthermore, the French company also wanted a longer lease term and a larger extent of land without an adequate increase of capital, but Hoffman had "no doubt that with firmness this Company will be brought to materially improve their amount of offer." He cautions JCF about interfering and negotiating directly with individuals and requests "a correct list of every one of the Leases you have granted with particulars of the terms." Notes that the Anglo-California Company has failed to raise capital and that Sir Henry Vere Huntly's "Report," a copy of which Hoffman had earlier forwarded to JCF, introduced doubts about the Mariposa title. "You could by that see also (I shall write stupid) inclination of preference for giving to the Mariposa Company[2] a large premium. They have been knocking about the Country some time to get funds from the Public and we have every reason to believe they have succeeded but badly, and I will tell you frankly I am under the firm impression that they will not be able to support any real or cohesive mining operation." Sender's copy.]

1. Capt. William K. Smith, a man of about sixty and a former commander of merchant ships. A Cornish mining engineer, Thomas Phillips, had opened the Vaucluse Mine for him in Orange County, Va., in 1842 and Hoffman noted

that Smith still owned gold and copper mining property in that state. The captain later visited California and then went to Washington, where he obtained from JCF two small seven-year leases—200 feet by 200 feet—dated 3 July 1850. From there he had come to London and subsequently he would go to Paris, where he sold the leases to the Nouveau Monde Mining Company (the Liberty Mining Company, Report on the Vaucluse Mine [London, 1852], Appendix, p. 19; Dagger Brief, 79–81, in Hoffman Papers; articles of agreement between David Hoffman and the Nouveau Monde Gold Mining Company, 8 Nov. 1851, in M. A. Goodspeed, Jr., Collection).

2. It is not clear what Hoffman means by "giving to the Mariposa Company a large premium." The Mariposa Mining Company had been organized in San Francisco on 27 Sept. 1850 with capital stock touted at one million dollars. Its operations were not to be confined to Mariposa County or to gold either, although the gold of JCF's estate seems to have been its primary objective. Twelve men formed the company, but it was undoubtedly dominated by Palmer, Cook & Company, since all four partners were members as well as John Cook, Jr., the brother of Charles W. Cook (Mariposa Mining Company, Articles of Association, 27 Sept. 1850, Mariposa County Records, Book 1, pp. 1–3).

128. David Hoffman to Frémont

43 Upper Brooke Street, LONDON, 7 Feb. 1851

[Notes that he had come to a final agreement with the British Mutual Gold Mining Company (later the Quartz Rock Mariposa Gold Mining Company) of 30 George Street. Ultimately their capital was proposed to be £100,000, but he feels that one-half will be quite sufficient and that £25,000 will be enough to justify full operations. While they did not expect to have their forces in readiness before July, they were to send out geologists at once to make a selection. Lord Erskine was the active person in the Mutual and, although there were four others "of far better business habits," he would be extremely useful in swelling the capital. As he had met some initial resistance, Hoffman had not pursued the idea of a bonus or advance to JCF.

The Anglo-California Company, with which Sir Henry Vere Huntly was connected, is so odious that he does not think it would be safe for JCF "to deal in any way with that Company." It had advertised in the *Times* that it held a lease from him, but Hoffman could not believe it and had inserted a rebuttal in the same journal.

Mr. Robert would write the details of the two French companies. Final agreements had been delayed by the appearance in London and

Paris of three of JCF's leases—two to Capt. [William K.] Smith and one to Thomas La Chausne (not identified). The Nouveau Monde had purchased from Capt. Smith, but now needed a larger quantity of land. Sender's copy.]

129. David Hoffman to Frémont

43 Upper Brooke Street, LONDON, 21 Feb. 1851

[Sends the duplicate original of the contract "executed this day" to the British Mutual Gold Mining Company and notes that the Welsh company has been "vexatiously delayed" by the accident of Mr. Beckerleg, an agent employed by Andrew Smith. The large British company, "similar to the French one of which Mr. Robert has made you quite familiar under the name of Nouveau Monde," was at a standstill as Hoffman, by reason of his inability to obtain information from JCF, could not supply answers to questions.

Four other contracts for France, somewhat similar to the British Mutual, had been executed by Hoffman, "and the monies are all confidently expected to be in hand in 60 days hence." The Nouveau Monde had been delayed by the indisposition of Mons. Paganelli and by three of JCF's leases (referred to in Doc. No. 128, 7 Feb. 1851).

In contrast to Hoffman's more protective leases, JCF's contained no prohibitions on subleasing or assignment, no clause binding the lessee to be at work by a defined day, and provided for a royalty of one-sixth instead of one-fourth or the royalty of the scale (see Hoffman to JCF, 5 Sept. 1850).

Again the London agent reiterates that the Anglo-California Company "is a regular humbug or bubble" and was trying to obtain "in an oblique way" a lease from Mr. [William] Buckler (JCF's agent on the Mariposa in the fall of 1850) approved of by Mr. Jones (probably William Carey Jones, JCF's brother-in-law). Hoffman had not proceeded with a contract to the company, although JCF had approved the carefully drawn preliminaries.

Finds Mr. Robert invaluable. "He seems to know every body in London and in Paris and is much respected." Sender's copy.]

130. Frémont to J. W. McCorkle, H. S. Richardson, and C. Robinson

San Jose, Feb. 26th, 1851

Gentlemen:

I have the honor to acknowledge the receipt of your letter of this date, and hasten to reply.

In your first question, whether "If elected to the U.S. Senate, I would oppose the passage of any bill which may be presented to the Senate, providing for the sale or leasing of the mineral lands in this State," I have to reply, that I would oppose the passage of any such bill—that I am opposed to any system with regard to the mineral lands that looks to either leasing or selling them, and that both in my place in the Senate and in a recent address to the people of this State, have distinctly declared my opposition to that, or any other mode of making the mines objects of revenue.

A principal object of my return to this State, after the close of the last session of Congress, was to ascertain more clearly, after the changes that in the course of a year would necessarily occur in our rapidly advancing State, the views and wishes of the people, and particularly those engaged in mining, in reference to the proper (if any) legislation required with reference to the mines, and I was only prevented from going immediately into the mining districts, for that object, by a severe illness that kept me confined in San Francisco.

Should I be elected, it would be my intention during the coming summer to carry out that design, and to visit the mining districts for the purpose of being informed and guided by the practical views of the persons most interested in the subject, and whose interests only, I could possibly have in view.

To your second question, whether I prefer the bill in regard to land titles in this State, presented in the Senate by Mr. Gwin or that of Col. Benton, I am obliged to reply, that since their receipt here last evening, my time has been so much occupied, and not anticipating the reception of any inquiries in relation to them, I have not given them an examination, or had an opportunity to consider what would be their respective operation. From what I have learned of them, however, neither the one nor the other entirely meets my views. The main features of Mr. Gwin's bill I was before acquainted with, and I think it is objectionable in the indefinite, and, probably, universal litigation, it appears to me it would produce. Of the bill of Mr. Benton, I have only read a single section, to which my attention was particularly drawn, and which was as follows:

Sec. 8. And be it further enacted, That on the trial of any *scire facias* to try the validity of a claim, the decision of the court shall be conclusive in favor of the claimant in every case, except in cases in which John Charles Fremont may be a claimant; and in all cases in which he may be a claimant, an appeal may be taken in favor of the United States to the Supreme Court of the United States; and in all decisions against the claimant an appeal may in like manner be taken to the Supreme Court.

This section, as far as it relates to myself or any claim or title I have, I fully endorse, and shall endeavor to procure its incorporation into any bill that may be passed on the subject.

I am not prepared to say that there may not be other titles, on which, if the decision be adverse, the government ought to take appeals to the Supreme Court at Washington, though, as a rule, I think the State and people ought to be spared the expense and delay of that distant litigation.

From what I have learned of other portions of Col. Benton's bill, it would require many and important modifications for me to agree to it; and as I do not accord fully with either that or the bill of Mr. Gwin, perhaps it will be more satisfactory to state briefly, the views I myself entertain.

I am in favor of the ascertainment, recognition, and confirmation of all lawful and equitable titles in this State, in the speediest and cheapest manner consistent with the detection and exclusion of any that may have been simulated or fraudulently made. To effect this, I proposed, in the Senate, a bill, in which, as conformable to the general course of our government, I proposed a commission of three persons, to be appointed by the President and Senate. It has been objected to this bill, that it restricted the government from the right of appeal, and in making the decisions of the commission final in so many cases, opened the way to corruption and the admission of frauds. My object was not to prevent inquiry, but to hasten justice; and I am free to admit, that the objection I have stated has force. I think it would be proper for the government to reserve the right of appeal to the Federal Courts, with a requirement that such appeal *should* be taken, in all cases where fraud or simulation was suspected.

I am not attached, however, to any particular form of proceeding; but shall gladly accept the best that can be desired for the cheap and speedy settlement of genuine titles, and the effectual exclusion of all others.

I think the interests of the State every way require this, because uncertainty in land tenures, beside being a prolific source of contention and often violence, must retard to a great degree, permanent settlement and improvement. I may be permitted, in conclusion, to say, I should hope and expect enlightenment and instruction from the Legislature and the people of the State.

I hope you will pardon me, gentlemen, that in connection with the present inquiries, I must respectfully ask that I may not be held responsible, on those or any other subjects, for the views or opinions of any other person, or my own be supposed to be presented or colored by those offered in Congress whilst I am here, six thousand miles distant. Very respectfully, your ob't. servant,[1]

J. C. FRÉMONT

From the *Daily Standard*, 4 March 1851, as printed in Stockton *Times*, 12 March 1851. Joseph Walker McCorkle (1819–84), H. S. Richardson, and Charles Robinson (1818–94) were all members of the California State Assembly, which was then meeting in San Jose and which was attempting to elect a U.S. senator (*Journals of the Legislature of the State of California*, 1851). McCorkle had already been elected to represent California in the 32nd Congress (BIOG. DIR. CONG.). Richardson was from Mariposa. Robinson, who had been a leader in the squatter riot at Sacramento the previous summer, would soon return to Massachusetts and eventually become the resident agent of the antislavery New England Emigrant Aid Society in Kansas and the first Republican governor of that state (DAB).

1. The day after this letter was written, the legislative convention balloted for the 142nd time. There was no winner, and it decided to postpone the election of a U.S. senator to 1852.

131. David Hoffman to Frémont

12 Half Moon Street, PICCADILLY, LONDON, 1 April 1851

[His last letter from JCF was dated 29 Nov. His anxiety had been relieved by a note from William Carey Jones "at Washington" indicating that JCF is well and in California. He hopes to have dispatches directly from him soon. Gives the terms with the British Mutual Gold Mining Company and with the Nouveau Monde: "1/6 royalty with £11,000. Premium—£1,000 in Bills at 4, 8, 12 and 16 months and £10,000 in the shares of the Company for 2400 feet by 600 feet minimum ground for 21 years with 300 acres of agricultural land." Had he known JCF's terms, he could also have made contracts for large tracts of agricultural lands for emigrants. Sender's copy.]

132. Joseph G. Totten to Frémont

Engineer Department
WASHINGTON, April 11. 1851

SIR,

Your letter of the 29th January last to the Secretary of War, recommending Francis Wright for a Cadet appointment has this day been referred to this Department.

In reply I have the honor to inform you that there is no vacancy in the M[ilitary] A[cademy] from California. Cadet Greene[1] will not graduate before 1854 and Cadet Vallejo[2] before 1855.

Enclosed is a copy of the regulations for the admissions &c. of Cadets into the M.A.

Mr. Wright's name will, however, be entered on the register as an applicant for a Calif. appointment. I am &c.

JOS. G. TOTTEN
B. GL. & COL./ENGS.

Lbk (DNA-94, Military Academy, LS, 14:529).

1. Jackson W. Green, son of Thomas J. Green of Sacramento City, Calif. had been recommended by George W. Wright in Aug. 1850. He accepted cadet status, was later found deficient, and resigned in May 1853 (DNA-94, Adjutant General's Office, U.S.M.A., Cadet Applications #112–1850 and *Register of Cadets*).

2. Appointed to the Military Academy on 23 Dec. 1850, sixteen-year-old Adronico Vallejo was the son of Mariano G. Vallejo. As he was not yet proficient in English, he asked to delay his entry, and resigned when the request was refused (DNA-94, Adjutant General's Office, U.S.M.A., Cadet Applications #316–1850).

133. Frémont to Abel Stearns

[SAN FRANCISCO, 24 April 1851]

I make to Mr. Stearns the following propositions, viz:

I offer to purchase his rancho in the sum of three hundred thousand dollars ($300,000), to be paid in the following manner—[1]

Fifty thousand dollars ($50,000) to be paid within six months after date of purchase.

Permission to be granted me to drive off for sale during the present year three thousand beef cattle (steers or novillas) and the proceeds of such sale to be paid to Mr. Stearns on account of the purchase.

The remainder to be paid in three years by equal payments, with interest at 6 per cent. per annum.

The privilege to be granted me of using an amount of stock equal to the yearly increase of all the stock upon the place, until the purchase money is paid.

The purchase money to be secured to Mr. Stearns by him upon the rancho and stock.

It is further understood in making this offer that Mr. Stearns will turn over all the stock, improvements, implements &c belonging to the place, & that no sale will be made or stock drive off, provided these terms be accepted.

Ten thousand dollars ($10,000) to be forfeited by me in the event that I fail to comply with the terms of the contract. Mr. RueVel [?][2] is associated with me, and be constantly upon the place, or occupied in driving up cattle, & general management of the business.

J. C. FRÉMONT

ALS (CSmH).

1. The rancho JCF wished to purchase was Los Alamitos, one side of which bordered the Pacific Ocean south of present-day Long Beach. As finally patented, it contained 28,027 acres, which in 1850 was assessed at 37.5 cents an acre or $12,192, including the two houses, appraised at $1,500, and other improvements. In addition, the cattle, horses, and sheep on the rancho were assessed at $66,400. Stearns did not sell (GATES [1]).

Shortly before JCF made the offer to Stearns, JBF had written Frank P. Blair, Sr., that they were "just about going on a ranchero and described it as containing 6,000 head of cattle and horses and "soft enough in climate" for olives, figs, grapes, peaches, and apricots. The implication was that JCF was "going largely into farming"; she desired Blair to send seed via Adam's Express (JBF to F. P. Blair, San Francisco, 11 April 1851, NjP—Blair-Lee Papers). She added that the Mariposa was no place for her. "Indians, bears & miners have made it lose its good qualities as a country place & it is very out of the way." When he did not succeed in purchasing Los Alamitos, JCF turned to the development of a ranch on the lower part of the Mariposa tract, but he never set out fruit trees and vines.

2. The name is difficult to read. Since the editor has been unable to identify "RueVel," JCF may have been referring to Paul Leroy, whom he identifies as "a merchant of San Francisco" briefly associated with him in the contract to supply beef to the Indians (see JCF to Beale, 8 March 1852).

134. Frémont to David Hoffman

SAN FRANCISCO, CALIFORNIA, May 1, 1851

MY DEAR SIR,

I have to acknowledge the receipt of your several letters of February accompanying a lease, to the British Mutual Gold Mining Company, of lands on my Mariposas property. Reserving for another letter my reply to your various suggestions, I have in this the *special* object of signifying my entire approval of the lease, in all its particulars. In regard to agricultural land, you are authorized to grant whatever quantity may be judged necessary to the maintenance of their establishment. The sooner their *selection* is made the better it will be for the interests of the company. Yours truly,

JOHN C. FRÉMONT

David Hoffman, Esquire
London, Eng.

ALS (NHi—David Hoffman Papers). Endorsed.

135. Frémont to David Hoffman

SAN FRANCISCO, CALIFORNIA, May 1, 1851

MY DEAR SIR,

I received by the mail of the 22nd. ult. your three letters of February, dated from the 1st to the 21st inclusively. I am glad that we have it at last in our power to congratulate ourselves on the success of your exertions, and I trust that we shall soon see some of your companies on the ground. I recognize that the delay is principally attributable to me, but much of it also belongs to the difficulty or impossibility of procuring information required by you, and to the distance which makes communication uncertain and long. In view of this latter element, I think that as you are thoroughly possessed of my plans for the development of the Mariposas and as I have perfect confidence in yourself, it is altogether advisable to leave the farther management of the business to you in Europe and for that purpose to give you carte blanche to make the leases on such terms as you judge advisable. I will approve them when transmitted to me. I do this mainly because I am satisfied that European capital & European stability alone are competent to the development of our mines. Every American enterprise of the kind that I am acquainted with, has originated and been conducted in a spirit of speculation. Some of a more stable and better character are now being commenced, but with these I shall have nothing to do. Agreeably to my letter to you of many months since, I have refrained from granting any leases on the Mariposas, holding it right to leave the ground unoccupied for the really sound companies you might be able to form.[1] The only leases granted after those advices to you was the final confirmation of the lease to Palmer, Cooke & Co. who work what is called the Mariposas vein (which is the first vein I discovered) & constitute what is called the Mariposas Mining Company,[2] & a lease recently granted to my friend Lieut. Beale, of the navy. This latter lease was recently granted & is of the usual small dimension of one hundred yards. In all the leases which I had previously given the error to which you refer, of making no provisions against a transfer or sale of the lease, was committed, but they contained also a provision to the effect that if within one year from date their machinery should not be in full operation, the lease should be forfeited. As I find that most of these leases were obtained for purposes of speculation in Europe & elsewhere, I shall (as I have already done in several cases) enforce the forfeit which they have nearly all incurred. The only exception I make is in Mr. Lacharme's case,[3] who in company with Mr. Antoine,[4] & Mr. Swift,[5] have arrived & went up yesterday to the Mariposas. I have granted them an extension of time. I suppose Mr. Smith's leases will have the same provision in them. In regard to Sir Henry Huntly and the Anglo-California Company I can only say that the only correspondence I have had with the company has been through yourself, & none at all with Sir Henry H. If he has any lease it must be from some arrangement with the Mariposas

Company to which he refers in his report, & which company holds under me. That lease however, covers an insufficient quantity of ground, & is otherwise meager, as they have not even the privilege of getting iron on the place, or of agricultural ground. I have not recd. the letter you refer to, & which you say contains inquiries in regard to the Mariposas. So far as regards the agricultural lands these you can state that they are abundant, & of the most fertile character in California, which is saying a great deal. There are excellent grazing lands, admirably adapted to sheep. So far then as regards the vein, I am satisfied that analyses give no reliable indication, for the simple reason that they do not embrace a sufficient quantity of the work. Analyses give results of any degree of richess, but what we want is labor by machinery continued for months, & going to a sufficient depth & with machinery of sufficient power to give us a solid guaranty for heavy operations. I was occupied at the session of Congress last year & trusted to Mr. Wright in the purchase of the machine which he got up & recommended[?]. I found on my arrival here that we could not get steam enough on it to grind the rock at all, and I assure you in sober truth that it would not grind the coffee for the St. John de Rey Mining Company! Stockton & Aspinwall (who hold a lease under me) sent out a force of men which costs them three hundred dollars per diem, with a heavy outfit, and yet have a machine which ground only two tons per diem! What we require here is *heavy* machinery— 50 or a hundred horse power. With that we can make fortunes.

But of all this I will write you at more leisure by the next mail. I have but a moment left for this. The mining in quartz has just taken a start here, and results will be crowding in upon us. The only result of great importance that I have obtained in the examination of the Mariposas is that we have an abundance of veins, so that we can afford a good extent of ground to each company. About the richness of the veins no doubt appears to be entertained any where. Yours truly,

J. C. FRÉMONT

David Hoffman Esqre.

Still not a line from Mr. Robert

ALS (NHi—David Hoffman Papers).
1. See Frémont to Mayer, 29 Nov. 1850, which was transmitted to Hoffman.
2. JCF seems to be referring to Palmer, Cook & Company's lease on the Mariposa Vein, although it could be a vague reference to the 17 Sept. 1850 lease which the company located on the Agua Fria. It is obvious to JCF that the Mariposa Mining Company is dominated by the banking firm.

3. A French engineer, Louis Lacharme had mined gold in South America and had received a U.S. patent for his invention of a machine that would save gold in the washing process (San Francisco *Herald*, 17 and 28 Aug. 1852; Patent 6771 in *Report of the Commissioner of Patents for the Year 1849*, Pt. I, pp. 95 and 329, Senate Ex. Doc. 15, 31st Cong., 1st sess.). He became director and sole manager of Lacharme & Co. of the French Society which was formed at Paris on 15 Aug. 1850 to work on the Mariposa. Lacharme seems never to have taken advantage of JCF's extension of his lease; rather, on 20 May 1851, with several San Franciscans (T. Butler King, John L. Moffat, John T. Temple, Charles G. Scott) and John F. Johnson of Mariposa County, he formed the Adeline Mining Company to work the Adeline Vein. Lacharme was to have absolute control and management for three years. A few months later Patrice Dillon, Andrew Anthoine, and Henry Mathey were added to the company. On 27 March 1852 Lacharme leased the Mary Harrison Mine but sold the lease a year later to the Quartz Rock Gold Mining Company of London (Mariposa County Records Book 1, pp. 286–96 [Memorandum of Agreement and Articles of Association of the Adeline Mining Company, 20 May 1851]; Book A of Deeds, 27 March 1852 and 24 March 1853, pp. 161, 210–12).

4. Probably Andrew Anthoine, mentioned in the note above.

5. In the course of a few years Pratt Swift acquired interests in the Dahlia Vein near the Mary Harrison group southeast of Coulterville, in Lacharmeville, and in the Mariquita (Mariposa County Records, Book B of Deeds, pp. 550, 552, and Book A of Deeds, p. 162).

136. David Hoffman to Frémont

LONDON, 2 May 1851

[A vague letter referring to two gentlemen (George W. Wright and Hiram Walbridge)[1] who had arrived in England bringing rich specimens from California. He thinks the confidence that he and Robert have established will be shaken by the imprudence of these gentlemen, who seem "well intentioned but extremely unsuited to promote your or their own objects." "The only Lessee of yours who has been firm to your interest and who has fully apprehended the views of Mr. Robert and myself is Capt. [William K.] Smith. He understands the matter on your side of the Atlantic and on this side. And if full powers were originally given to Mr. R. and myself, we would have covered your land by this time with the cleverest talent and means known in Europe." Frémont's silence pains him. Sender's copy.]

1. Hiram Walbridge (1821–70) was a New York merchant who came to London with Wright to promote the Agua Fria for the partners in Palmer, Cook &

Company. His New York district subsequently elected him as a Democrat to the 33rd Congress, and in the fall of 1853 he toured the interior cities of California and attended the convention (of which Wright was one of the secretaries) being held in San Francisco for promoting the Pacific and Atlantic Railroad. His title of general had been acquired in 1843 during his residency in Ohio when he became brigadier general of militia. (BIOG. DIR. CONG.; San Francisco *Daily Herald*, 4 Oct. 1853).

137. David Hoffman to Frémont

LONDON, 13 Half Moon Street, Piccadilly, 10 May 1851, "Private."

[Hoffman's apprehensions about George W. Wright, who is in London, have disappeared. Notes that the Nouveau Monde is making great exertions to send out first-rate machinery and that the Mineurs Belges, whose contract is signed, will sail in about ten days. He has negotiated several others of 600 feet square, and three English companies are preparing their papers.

There is no possibility of his drawing on JCF in California. He must have credit in the United States, for example at Corcoran and Riggs (Washington, D.C., bankers).

The £1,250 note and the stock handed over by the Nouveau Monde are at his bankers and will be collected when due and deposited to JCF's account.

Grieved that he has not had a line since JCF's 29 Nov. letter. Sender's copy.]

138. Frémont to David Hoffman

SAN FRANCISCO, CALIFORNIA, May 11. 1851

MY DEAR SIR,

I have had the great satisfaction to receive your letter of the [*blank space*], and in return am able to advise you that every thing here is going on extremely well. I am not able to give you yet any thing in detail. Tomorrow I set out for the Mariposas, & I have more business on hand than I shall be able to get through with before leaving. I am just about establishing on the lower part of the Mariposas tract a large cattle rancho, & in connection with this shall be obliged to extend my journey as far south as Los Angeles. I have made some large cattle contracts, and shall consequently be obliged to remove to the north, cattle which I have in the south. This will interest you as you will perceive that I am concentrating my interests on the Mariposas. Messrs. Lacharme, Antoine & Swift have reached the Mariposas, and I will be able soon to give you an account of their proposed operations.[1] As I informed you in my last, theirs is the only lease except Mr. Beale's & that of the so styled "Mariposas Mining Company" of Palmer, Cooke & Co. which now holds good. When I speak of Beale I intend to include the whole concern for which he is agent, viz, Stockton & Aspinwall. Now in regard to Sir Henry Huntly I recognize fully the justice and soundness of your views in regard to him, but several points for reflection present themselves to my mind. Is it not, if for no other reason yet for the sake of public opinion in *this* country, very advisable to concentrate European capital upon the Mariposas? And will not the effect of this be good in Europe also? So far, the uncertainty of future tenure, and the absolute want of any at this time in the gold region except at the Mariposas, points out this place as the only secure point for the investment of foreign capital. Is it not greatly expedient to keep this capital there as far as it is possible? And not leash it to overcome the difficulties to investment elsewhere. If he does not work under a lease from us, he may enter into an arrangement with Palmer, Cooke of (the "Mariposas Company") which they are proposing to him, and which I should regret to see done. Huntly is now here.[2] I will think the matter over and act for the best. It will be well to advise you that the French company, Lacharme &c. is also called the "Mariposas Mining Company." In my next I will advise you, where agents for the companies you may contract with should address themselves on their arrival in this city. I shall be found at the Mariposas, where I shall reside with my family.

This fall I shall set out varieties of fruit trees, and commence agricultural operations on a scale sufficiently large to make the Mariposas known as a place where supplies can be had advantageously. I shall endeavor to send you in a few weeks a statement of what kind of vegetables or grains have been grown at the Mariposas—their size, &c., and any information of value in regard to veins. I have not hitherto been able to do this, because from bad health, & occupation in political business I could not myself examine on the spot, and I would not send it to you at second hand. My health is now fully established, and I am able to undergo all the fatigue necessary in managing the press of business which I now have upon me. Renewing to you the expression of my satisfaction, with many and earnest acknowledgements for your successful management of the Mariposas, I am very truly yours,

J. C. FRÉMONT

I hear that Wright of the firm Palmer, Cooke & Co. has gone to England. It is doubtless with the view of interesting capital there in the operation of the "Mariposas Mining Co." J.C.F.

May 12. I have decided that it will be the best to sustain you fully & have nothing to do with Sir Henry Huntly. Frémont.

ALS (NHi—David Hoffman Papers). Endorsed.
1. See Doc. No. 135, n. 3.
2. Henry Vere Huntly returned to California, worked for an English company at "Dicksburgh," above Marysville in Yuba County and in 1856 published anonymously in London a two-volume work entitled *California: Its Gold and Its Inhabitants, by the Author of "Seven Years on the Slave Coast of Africa. . . ."*

139. Frémont to Oliver M. Wozencraft

SAN FRANCISCO, CALA., May 12, 1851

SIR,

Being about establishing a cattle rancho on the Mariposas river, neighboring the Indian tribes of the Sierra Nevada, with whom you are engaged in treating, I submit to your consideration the following *proposals*.

I propose to furnish for the two fiscal years commencing the 30th of June *proximo* and ending June 30th eighteen hundred and fifty three, all the animals, beef cattle, brood mares, and brood cows, which you shall need for the execution of your treaties with the Indian tribes in the district under your direction, and which extends from the head waters of the San Joaquin river to the head of the Sacramento. I engage and bind myself to make the deliveries, in the course of the present and following years, at such times and places within the district as you shall indicate, and to commence the deliveries one month after the date of notification to me of treaties as they shall be successively made.

I propose to furnish beef cattle upon the hoof at fifteen cents per pound nett: brood mares, between the ages of four and six years, at seventy five dollars each: and brood cows, between the ages of three and five years, at seventy five dollars each. Very respectfully,

JOHN C. FRÉMONT.

ALS (DNA-75, LR, California B-17 1852 f/w Special File No. 266). Attached to the document is Wozencraft's acceptance: "I hereby accede to the foregoing proposal so far as the furnishing of *present* supplies of beef to those Indians with whom I may treat, and will urge on the Dept. the adoption of the entire proposal, so soon as the treaties are approved by the President and the Senate. Very Respectfully, O. M. Wozencraft." JCF's proposal, with Wozencraft's acceptance, was forwarded by Benton to Col. Luke Lea, Commissioner of Indian Affairs, on 30 Jan. 1852 with the request that "as soon as the treaties are ratified, Col. Frémont may be advised of the decision of the Department."

A physician, Oliver M. Wozencraft (b. ca. 1814) had been a member of the convention in 1849 to frame the constitution for California (COLTON, 412). He had gone east and then returned on the *Constitution* at the end of Dec. 1850 as agent, later commissioner, with ill-defined instructions to conciliate the natives and bind them by treaty (*Alta California*, 30 Dec. 1850). For a time he and his two fellow commissioners, Barbour and McKee, acted collectively in the negotiations whereby the Indians would be supplied with food and other comforts and given certain lands in return for the cession of others. For the text of the 29 April 1851 treaty signed at Camp Barbour, on the San Joaquin River, see MITCHELL, 102–7.

On 1 May 1851 the three commissioners exercised their right to divide California among them. Wozencraft received the middle district, which included all the territory east of the coast range from the San Joaquin on the south to the headwaters of the Sacramento on the north. JCF had every reason to expect—perhaps even assurance—that future treaties would also call for the delivery of both beef and breeding stock, and he was determined to be a primary supplier.

Wozencraft made his first treaty on 28 May with six tribes of Indians who met at Dent and Vantine's ferry on the Stanislaus River; the next was concluded with ten tribes at Camp Union on the Yuba River; another was made 1 Aug. with nine tribes near Bidwell's ranch on Chico Creek; five tribes entered into a treaty at Camp Colus on 2 Sept.; and four tribes on the Cosumnes River entered into a treaty on 18 Sept. All the treaties promised large amounts of beef (ELLISON, 54).

140. Frémont to George W. Barbour

MARIPOSAS, SAN JOAQUIN VALLEY
May 19th. 1851

SIR,

Having established a cattle Rancho on the Mariposas river, neighboring to the Indian Tribes, of the Sierra Nevada, with whom you are engaged in treating, I submit to your consideration, the following proposals.

I propose to furnish for the present and ensuing years (eighteen hundred and fifty one, and eighteen hundred and fifty two) all the animals (Beef cattle, Brood cows, and Brood mares) which you shall need for the execution of your treaties with the Indian Tribes, in the district under your direction, and which I understand to comprehend all that portion of the State lying between the parallel of the upper waters of the San Joaquin river, and the southern boundary line. I engage, and bind myself to make the deliveries in the course of the present, and following years, at such time, and place, within the district, as you shall indicate, and to commence the deliveries one month after the date of notification to me of treaties, as they shall successively be made.

I propose to furnish Beef cattle upon the hoof, at the price of fifteen cents per pound net: Brood cows, between the ages of three and five years, at the price of Seventy-five dollars each: and Brood mares, between the ages of four and six years, at the price of seventy-five dollars each.[1] Very Respectfully,

JOHN C. FRÉMONT

Copy (DNA-75, LR, California B-10 1852 f/w Special File No. 266). It was Benton, again, who left Frémont's proposals to Barbour with Commissioner Luke Lea.

In the division of Indian California, George W. Barbour from Princeton, Ky. had assumed responsibility for pacifying the Indians in the southern district, extending from the San Joaquin south, west, and east to the state boundary. Like Wozencraft, he rapidly entered into treaties with Indians that promised quantities of supplies and set aside large tracts of lands as reservations. On 13 May a treaty was made on King's River with twelve bands; on 30 May one was arranged with seven tribes on the Kaweah River; on June 3 another was made with four tribes on Paint Creek; and on 10 June eleven bands at Tejon Pass signed a treaty (ELLISON, 51–52).

1. JCF's terms are the same as those to Wozencraft (Doc. No. 139).

141. George W. Barbour to Frémont

Camp Keyes, Cahivia [Kaweah] river, CALA.
May 28th 1851

SIR:

I have received your letter of the 19th instant.[1] in which you propose furnishing Beef cattle, Brood mares, and Cows, to the Indians in this (the Southern) district of the State, according to the stipulations of such Treaties as have been, or may be, made with the different Tribes.

Having received no advices from the Indian Department at Washington, since my colleagues and myself adopted the policy of supplying those Indians with whom we might treat, with Beef and stock &c. I could not, except to a very limited extent, enter into any unconditional contract for supplying those Indians treated with in this (the southern) district of the State, but in view of the necessity for such supplies, and not doubting but that the proper authorities will readily acquiesce in the policy that we have adopted, I should not hesitate to make such Contracts as may be necessary to carry out, *in good faith*, the stipulations of such Treaties as may be made with the Indians, such contracts of course, being left subject to the approval or rejection of the Indian Department at Washington.

I have had many proposals offered me to furnish such supplies, but regarding your offer, as the best, and lowest, of any yet made by a responsible man, and believing as I do, that your offer is a fair one, I have concluded to close with your proposition, subject however to the approval or rejection of the same, by the Indian Department at Washington.

Should this arrangement be satisfactory you can confer with Col. A. Johnson[2] subagent for the San Joaquin Valley who is near you, and who will advise you of the time, and place, and number of Beef Cattle, wanted for the Indians in this vicinity with whom Treaties have been made. I will advise you as to what will be necessary after leaving this valley. Respectfully,

G. W. Barbour Comer &c.

ALS (DNA-75, LR, California B-10 f/w Special File No. 266).
1. See Doc. No. 140.
2. A former subagent stationed at St. Louis, in 1849 Adam Johnston had been the sole federal Indian agent in California. While he did not consider the making of treaties an effective method of dealing with the Indians, it became necessary for him to assume responsibility for certain reservations after the treaties had been made. He actually took upon himself the responsibility for furnishing greater supplies of beef than were stipulated in the treaties and was ultimately relieved from office after friction developed between him and Wozencraft and he began to neglect his duties (CRAMPTON, 110–11; ELLISON, 53).

142. David Hoffman to Frémont

LONDON, 17 June 1851

[A former partner of Senator Gwin of California, Absalam A. Halsey, was leaving for the Mariposa to report on his business conversations with Hoffman and to make two selections of land—600 by 600 feet each—for two leases. He was associated with Messrs. Stevens & Co. of No. 7 New Broad [?] Street, London, and with "American gentlemen of long standing and commercial repute here, who have associated with C. G. Anthony, Esq. of New York, recently established in No. 5 Wharf [?] Court, London." Sender's copy.]

143. Frémont to Abel Stearns

ANGELES, 20 June 1851

HON. ABEL STEARNS
SIR,

The three years have expired, for the term of which were placed in your care in trust, the cattle purchased by me, as military governor of California, from D. Eulogio de Célis, and the government having been fully informed by me of the existence and nature of the contract concerning them, and not having taken any measures for completing the same, or to provide for the payment of the purchase money, or to reimburse Mr. Célis in the money which he at the same time advanced for the use of the government, I consider that [it] would be unjust longer to deprive Mr. Célis of the use and enjoyment of his property. I have therefore determined that my obligations in the premises will be best fulfilled by requesting that the cattle be redelivered to Mr. Célis, together with one half of their increase, according to the agreement under which you received them, when the refusal of my successors in office here to conform to the contracts made by me for the benefit of the government, caused me to have them placed in your care for the security of the vendor. I request, therefore, that you will, on the demand of Mr. Célis, redeliver to him, or to his order, all the cattle which you originally received, and one half of all their increase, and thereupon you will be discharged of all responsibility concerning the same. Yours respectfully,

JOHN C. FRÉMONT

Copy (CSmH).

144. George W. Barbour to Frémont

TEXON [TEJON] PASS, July 7th. 1851

COL. FRÉMONT
SIR,

I reached this place yesterday in good health again and found the Indians quiet and contented. Today I called the Chiefs together and had a talk with them, told them you were coming through with a large drove of cattle, and that I would write you a note and request you to let them have some. I will therefore be obliged to you if you will turn them out some ten or fifteen head.

The Four Creek Chief[1] happened to be here, he seems favourably disposed and I think you need have no fear of passing through with your stock.

Hoping soon to see you on the San Joaquin or Frezno [Fresno] in good health &c. I am your Obt. Svt. and friend,

G. W. BARBOUR

ALS (M. A. Goodspeed, Jr., Collection). At the end of June news reached Barbour, who was in Los Angeles, of Indian disturbances in the Tulare Valley. He decided to travel there although it had been less than a month since he had arranged a treaty with seven tribes on the Kaweah River. Tejon Pass was one of his stops on the way to the valley.
1. A reference to Francisco, chief of a Yokuts tribe called Kawia (also Gawia and Kaweah). He had been reluctant to sign the treaty negotiated with twelve tribes on 13 May at Camp Belt, Kings River.

145. George W. Barbour to Frémont

Col. Frémont
D[ea]r, Sir,

Please to deliver to Francisco, Chief of the Cahwia Indians, five bullocks, he and his people appear well satisfied altho I have but little confidence in him; we reached here today all well. I shall leave in the morning for Kings River where we will probably spend a day and then move on to the Joaquin where I hope soon to see you in good health and spirits. Respectfully,

G. W. Barbour

ALS (M. A. Goodspeed, Jr., Collection). The Cahwia River, known today as the Kaweah, derives its name from the Yokuts tribe Kawia or Gawia. In the 1850s the river system and delta were so structured that it was commonly known as the Four Creeks (gudde [2]; Doc. No. 144).

146. David Hoffman to Frémont

12 Half Moon Street, Piccadilly, London, 18 July 1851

[Acknowledges receipt of JCF's letters of 1 and 11 May, but expresses anxiety that many of his and Robert's letters may have gone astray, since some of their questions are still unanswered and since the 1 May letter contained the postscript, "Still not a line from Mr. Robert." He is also concerned that he has not had a letter from JCF announcing "the arrival of the agent of the French Company, Le Nouveau Monde who should surely have reached you within 60 days of his departure hence on the 17th March last." Since the transmission to JCF of the contract of the Mineurs Belges, he and Robert have "other matters advancing," but the struggle to maintain the public's high esteem for the Mariposa property is difficult in view of JCF's infrequent communications. Others reported on his property and disposition of various parts of it; how much better it would have been had he and Mr. Robert been able to give their own versions "authorized by yourself direct." Sender's copy.]

147. Richard Robert to Frémont

[Robert reassures JCF that he had not neglected his correspondence as the postscript to one of JCF's 1 May 1851 letters to Hoffman had implied. While in Paris he had kept up a daily correspondence with Hoffman and had sent letters either directly to JCF or through Charles F. Mayer.

Robert writes that the Mineurs Belges will probably delay their departure because of the impracticability of sending thirty or forty tons of material across the Isthmus. "The best and most prudent plan of operation which has been suggested will be to ship all their heavy material by the way of Havre direct to San Francisco," and to send by the Chagres-Panama route ten or twelve miners and supervisors who would carry with them their mining tools only.

Expects that the first and second expeditions of the Nouveau Monde have arrived in California and located on JCF's estate. Notes that the company is progressing with "great prudence and caution" and is forming an English branch.

Paco [?][1] and Colson[2] Vander-Maesen's[3] Company of Mineurs Belges will raise £8,000 in Belgium and their London agent an additional £8,000 or £10,000. "When ready their first expedition of Miners, machinery, engineers, tools, etc. will all proceed direct via Cape Horn."

Roget's health was bad and he had suspended his operations in order to take the waters of Vichy, but he expected to finance his association with five or six capitalists in Paris.

La Garde, the Polish company, "will be proceeded with, as soon as the summer visitors to the Sea Side and to the sundry island watering places return to Paris."

The preliminary arrangements with these different associations and companies had been agreed upon, as well as for another united operation from Belgium and Paris.

"I have only to say that Mr. Hoffman and myself have fought hard for the promotion of your interest with the aid and help of a mutual friend [Mayer] in all business matters wherein yourself and property was in any way concerned." Initialed copy.]

1. Not identified.
2. Probably the Colson referred to in the letter of Frémont to A. M. Auguste Moxhet, 17 June 1850.

3. René Vander-Maesen had directed the mining operations of the Society of the New Mountain in the region of Liégé and had excellent relations with the workers (*Journal des Mineurs Belges Compagnie*, 20 June 1851, copy in Hoffman Papers).

148. David Hoffman to Frémont

LONDON, July 29, 1851.

MY DEAR SIR,

The shortness of the time before the mail closes, and the suddenness of the astounding revelation which the enclosed copy of correspondence with Mr. Flandin, and with Col. Benton, will disclose to you, will, perhaps, render it advisable for you to read *that correspondence* before you read the present letter through.[1] There are a variety of matters altogether proper for me to state to *you*, which I could not with the same propriety have written to either of those gentlemen, and those matters are quite too numerous for me to unfold in the short time allowed me, and yet quite too important to you not to be at least briefly alluded to, and they are the following:—

1. You are quite aware of the fact, that our surprise has to this hour been very great, that very many letters of Mr. Robert and myself, perhaps quite twenty letters, remained wholly unanswered, and that your valuable letters of the 1st and 12th May still make no allusion to them, and yours of the 1st of May concludes with saying, "still not a line from Mr. Robert," although he must have written quite 100 pages! This want of ability in me to make any reply to Mr. Powles, who desired to know *to whom*, to what *extent*, the minimum *terms*, and whether the promised exploration of your party *had been made*, cast that valuable Company wholly off for me. Mr. Powles is the president of the *San Juan del Rey Company*, and was disposed to go in very largely, and with an immense capital, or not at all; but he needed definite information upon those points, to *none* of which had I any satisfactory reply to make, your illness and subsequent political occupations being so numerous.

2. Then came, in continued succession, a thousand statements as to California in general, and quite satisfactory, but not a word of your property! owing to the causes just stated.

3. Then, again, came exaggerated accounts of leases made by you, for next to nothing, as to which I could (until yours of the 1st May) say nothing satisfactory in contradiction as to those tenants, their localities, &c. &c., and nothing very specific even now as to those *pioneer* leases.

4. Then, also, came some half-dozen lessees, wholly *faithless* to you, who came here with all sorts of tales, poisoning the public mind, and striving to extract money from the public for a seven-years' lease, one year gone, and possibly forfeited! Could anything be more destructive to your really good leases?

5. Next followed a succession of doubts raised by *unprincipled* or ignorant persons here, all which I had to beat down by force of arguments, which I was enabled to make from my growing familiarity with facts obtained from a hundred other sources, and also from my familiarity with land, and with Spanish grants, &c., &c.

6. Then came Mr. Wright and General Wallbridge, looming very large, with 30,000 dollars worth of brilliant specimens, full of indiscretions, and exciting in me all manner of doubts, as I knew they did not know the sober sensible habits of John Bull. This conduct greatly alarmed me for your interests, and I frankly wrote to you on the subject; that letter I subsequently qualified, in consequence of their own promises to me, and assurances of their friendship towards *you* and *your interests*, and as to their own prudence.[2]

7. A few more days revealed the fact that, although their specimens were making an impression favourable to California in general! yet that they were somehow or other making some impressions favourable to themselves *alone*, for they said to me things which I feared they would say to *others*; as,

First, that Wright's title was better than yours! Altogether ridiculous.

Second. That you had sold half of the whole to Wright! Not a word true.

Third. That your title was laid out upon lands fancifully, and merely at your own will!! If they said these things, how scandalous!

Fourth. That their only object was to strengthen California in general, and thus benefit *you*, and, of course, themselves.

Fifth. That Mr. Wright would promptly return to California, and that a Dr. Jackson[3] would be left by them here to prepare maps of California also to make analyses of specimens, also to see capitalists for general purposes in your favour, and not at all in collision with my duties to you; and, finally, that he would deliver to me copies of all papers I needed, and of all the reports made here of analyses made, and that *these* should be handed to me without delay, in a few days after Mr. Wright sailed for the United States, and also some *specimens* needed by me.

8. Mr. Wright did sail, and also General Wallbridge; and in a few days thereafter, I learned as follows, to my great astonishment and annoyance:—

First. That Dr. Jackson would not deliver to me any maps or papers!

Second. That he would not hand over to me the *promised* reports of the Philadelphia Mint, and of the Bank of England, through the *British* Mint as I understood, as to certain analyses, but which since are known.

Third. That he would not grant me the use of a single specimen, which I happened greatly to need for France at that time.

Fourth. That he, (Dr. Jackson) for Mr. Wright, was now acting solely for P. C. & C., in getting up a Company here, based on adverse grounds to you, and asking enormous sums, but keeping me in darkness as much as possible of all their plans.

Fifth. I then found that they had taken up with a certain very notorious speculator,[4] altogether in *bad odour here*: this at once assured me of three things, viz., that their association with *that* person must ultimately ruin their plans; that their boasting and exactions must either injure you equally, *or drive* all persons inclined to deal in your mines *to me*, as the only legitimate source; and hence of the *imperious* necessity of solid and specific information when they did come to me.

9. At length came again rumors of even their failure of success, and also of the return from the United States of General Wallbridge, who, though very civil indeed towards me before his departure with Wright, has not visited me, although he has been here more than three weeks, and before his departure promised much on his return.

10. After this came your letters, 1st and 11th May; these were of immense general service, especially in France; but emissaries from———— came once more to me, respecting your land, and spoke of a large operation as to them, but their specific inquiries could not be answered as to your lands in particular, that is, expressly from *yourself*, and for this they seem now to be waiting.

11. Some time before that period came also *Mr. T. D. Sargent*, a lessee of yours, with a located grant. He appeared to me entirely a

gentleman. I examined his papers, he told me he had suddenly made up an English Company of great respectability, and that he *knew* you would readily grant him an extension of his lease from seven to twenty-one years, and that he would hand over to me for you 2,000£. of stock in said Company, which would at once go into operation, to the very great advantage of yourself, &c., &c., &c. I examined all his papers, was much urged so to do by Captain William K. Smith, (most certainly the truest man to your interests in all respects, and who to this hour has *proved* himself faithful, honest, clever, and of weight in this community.) Now, as I had confidence *then* in Sargent, (through Mr. Smith), and as I had the power to lease absolutely for 21 years, I thought the equity of the case enabled me to extend the lease, provided the Company would take the chance of its not being forfeited by you, and of its being confirmed by you; and also provided I found that the Company *would proceed*. In this state of matters, Sargent suddenly disappeared, and went to the United States upon an object carefully concealed from Captain W. K. Smith and myself, and he indebted to Captain Smith for cash loaned to him, Sargent.

12th. Then followed a letter from Mr. Mayer, stating that *Mr. Flandin*, your agent, had arrived in Baltimore from California, and would probably visit England, to tender his services to Mr. Robert and myself. The object and nature of those services were not in the least intimated to Mr. Mayer, and that circumstance excited some apprehension in me, and caused my letter of the 13th June to Mr. Mayer, to be promptly shown to Mr. Flandin, as a preliminary to his coming to England at all; *because* those numerous *interferences* with all my operations could not but distract the public mind, which, *I am sure*, reposes with confidence on me, and is cast into doubts by such persons as Messrs.————, and certain other lessees, who only speculated in leases for the mere purpose of making something certain for themselves in England!

13th. Next followed Col. Benton's letter of the 4th, July, stating, that you had authorized Mr. Flandin to sell, *in fee*, half of your Mariposa property, but that *he* (Col. Benton), recommended Flandin to sell all, part cash.

14th. Then came Flandin's letter, 9th July, stating that he had sold all for more than double what he asked for the half, but the sum was not stated, nor the purchaser.

15th. A few days more brought me Col. Benton's letter, 12th July, stating that SARGENT was the purchaser!! who was *confident* he could raise 100,000 dollars as the first payment—but *where* to be raised (whether in New York, or in London), he does not state.

I have now given you a brief detail to the present hour, and beg leave to make some comments thereon, and with my candid opinion of the whole matter.

1. It is altogether certain (and I declare it to you without the least flattery), that it is the high prestige of *your name* alone, that induces any one (even greedy of wealth) to think of California as a place of investment. It is not possible for me, in this, the brief compass of a letter, to disclose to you how certain it is *here*, and everywhere on the Continent, and especially in France, that the United States, and the whole world, owe you a deep debt of gratitude for your geographical and other labours, and how effectually France *ridiculed* the first whisperings against your title, by a shrug of the shoulder, saying, "The United States is just—and this gold region and much more, would be heartily given to him, if he had no other title." Such remarks are often made,—and even in England the constant reply (as to title) is, "we care nothing about that, Col. Frémont's title, at all events, is good; and even if not, his tenants will never be disturbed." Now, my dear Sir, is it not altogether manifest that if *you sell*, three things must follow:

First. The whole *prestige* of your name (virtually pledged to them) must be taken away, and the Companies be panic-struck.

Second. The world will say, there is neither gold, title, nor truth, in all that has been said, nor any *gratitude* in the country towards you; and they will naturally ask,

Third. What became of the determination not to *sell* in fee an acre; but only to make short leases, at first, for seven years, then, from conviction, for twenty-one years.

Such, surely, would be the remarks; but *fancy* would, in such a case, go infinitely beyond truth, and those inclined to invest, or who have invested, would say, "The Colonel has *forsaken* us at the highest moment of our confidence—the news of the 11th of May was, that he was settled with *his family* at Mariposa. We regarded *that* as a protection, and now, by the letter of 12th July, all is sold to Americans, and we are left to the mercy of a *Wall Street Stock Jobbing Company*". Such would inevitably be their remarks, and such a state of things would, *of itself*, destroy such a Wall Street Company, not only here, but even in New York.

(2). Such a rumour of sale (if it *ever reaches* here) would prostrate every hope of *present* success. But, if you firmly adhere to your original plan, and resolve to contend through every real and imaginary difficulty, and take the cause of *all settlers* upon your land into your own hands and protection, success here and in the United States, and with the United States Government, and that of California, must be the inevitable result; but the least idea of parting with the property (or *any part* of it, except for *cash, which would be understood* every where as a very proper yielding to necessity, in order to *protect the residue*) must inevitably destroy the whole; for if *all* or *part* be sold mainly on credit, I feel convinced that the purchasers would pay you (if at all) only out of your own gold, but that they would not be able to do even this, because it *cannot be had* without much further expenditures and *cleverness* also, than you will find in New York.

(3). As to Mr. Sargent, the idea is truly ridiculous. It is impossible he can have either money or credit; he may summon around him some speculators *looming* large in New York and in London, but *here* with no effect, and in New York with only a temporary one.

(4). Now, upon the whole, it is altogether *certain* that if the information come to me (as asked for by my many letters,) if the *capabilities* of your property be stated in maps, and if some demonstrations be given of what *can be done*, I can make many good leases in addition to those made; all these will then proceed, for the English and French both would understand the matter, and be willing to take their chances, provided you remained owner of far the larger part, and provided, also, you continued at Mariposa, or, even if not, provided the gold results (even as a beginning) looked well. But, my dear Sir, *so far at least*, I have no authentic *specific* accounts from you, though I have volumes of my collections respecting California, from 1526 to July 1851. Such a property needed daily protection from 1848 to the present hour; but, as far as I can learn, it is not possible that any but the best, and most experienced, and industrious agents in America, can place your property before the public in such a point of view as its essential auriferous and agricultural worth *entitle* it to; and I have yet seen no American here to be compared in all respects to Capt. W. K. Smith. To me he was a total stranger, he has *worn well;* and, as a *Juror* in the present Exhibition, no name among the hundred stands higher for industry, cleverness, and good manners.

(5.) Your letters, 1st May and 12th May, will, as I hope, be followed by equally gratifying news to me. I shall carefully watch over your interests in every respect; and I do not at all believe that such letters are to be *cancelled* by the weak and inefficient exertions of Mr. Flandin and Mr. Sargent. I need not at all call in question Mr. Flandin's *motives*; but I must think that the most ordinary share of prudence *ought* to have suggested to him *two* things; *first*, to commune fully with me before he contracted with any body even conditionally; and *secondly*, not to jeopard every thing by trusting such a secret as your willingness *to sell even any part* to such a floating gentleman as Mr. Sargent, who, however civil and pleasing in his manners, never can exhibit that *solidity* requisite for *such a contract*; especially for the *whole*, and confessedly without the *shadow of power* so to do.

(6.) The whole recent affair has greatly wondered Mr. Robert, who, I must say, is a mild and honourable and indefatigable gentleman, worth a *distillation* of the said Mr. Sargent. May I again ask your patient recurrence to his and my letters, and *a brief* reply to all essentials. Such a man as Mr. Robert would make a *resumé* of our voluminous correspondence in the course of a few days. I duly appreciate and entirely feel the almost impossibility of *your* doing so now: I *know* your many occupations—it must be, that you are *extremely* occupied; but any one of your agents (*if entirely trustworthy* and clever with the pen) *could* read the whole, and suggest, in a short way, replies to all—leaving to your good self the more *important* matters. Your next letters (not in reply to this) I shall value on, as giving me some important results as to explorations—veins—depths—riches, &c.

(7.) And now, my dear Sir, as to a new subject. Do not smile at the idea; but I have set my heart upon your visiting England, (as suggested in several of my previous letters). Were you to visit London, I can assure you of three things—*first*, your reception would be a glorious one, from the throne down—*second*, in a day or two we could understand one another better than could be done in a year of correspondence—and *third*, we could in a few days together do more effective business than can be hoped for in a year, *unless* your coming letters, maps, &c., &c., be altogether to the purpose. Mrs. Fremont could not but be *delighted*; and all the distinguished *clever* women of Old England would be proud to welcome her. I am a thorough *American*, and only mention such things because they are your and her due. Yours truly,

D. HOFFMAN

P.S., on the 12th August, to my triplicate copy of Letter to Col. Fremont of the 29th July.

P.S.—12th August, 1851. During the past fourteen days I have only to say, that all my conjectures on the 29th July are thus far confirmed; and the subsequent correspondence establishes my conviction, but a few days more must reveal to me Sargent's actual condition. At present he continues *incog.*, he cannot appear; and though it is possible he may for a time *mystify* a few persons, it must end in a sheer bubble.

D. H.

Printed in HOFFMAN, 33–38. Not included in the list of papers received by Benjamin Rush from Messrs. Venning, Naylor, and Robins, solicitors.

1. The "astounding revelation" was Benton and J. Eugene Flandin's announcement to Hoffman that they had been authorized to sell the Mariposa and had sold it to Thomas Denny Sargent, one of JCF's early lessees. Hoffman outlines the sequence of events in articles 11–15 of this letter. Originals and/or copies of the Flandin-Benton-Hoffman correspondence may be found in the Hoffman Papers. Excerpts from those letters and some of Sargent's letters are printed in HOFFMAN.

2. See Doc. Nos. 136 and 137.

3. William A. Jackson had drawn a very early map of the mining district of California which had been published in New York the previous year. He was one of Wright's eleven partners in the Mariposa Mining Company.

4. Stephen Charles Lakeman, a Britisher, was distrusted intensely by Hoffman. Wright, acting for Palmer, Cook & Company, had subleased part of the firm's interest to him on 23 May 1851 and JCF gave another lease on 20 April 1852 (M. A. Goodspeed, Jr., Collection). On 3 June 1853, before leaving England to prepare for his fifth expedition, the explorer borrowed £13,000 from Lakeman and secured the loan with a mortgage on his remaining one-half interest in the Mariposa (Mariposa County Records, Book A of Deeds, pp. 254–59).

149. Jessie B. Frémont to Charles F. Mayer

SAN FRANCISCO, Augt. 1, 1851

MY DEAR SIR:

Will you please write to Mr. Hoffman who will I fear think Mr. Fremont a myth and let him know that letters to him have been mailed by Mr. Fremont as late as the 15th May. In the fire of the 21 June, I, among others, had my home destroyed, but as I had some half hour's time all Mr. Fremont's papers as well as the most valuable things in the house were saved. In the flutter of such a sudden removal I did not think to do what I hope is not now too late & write telling Mr. Hoffman of the safe arrival of several contracts and many letters. All that has been done Mr. Frémont approves of entirely. He

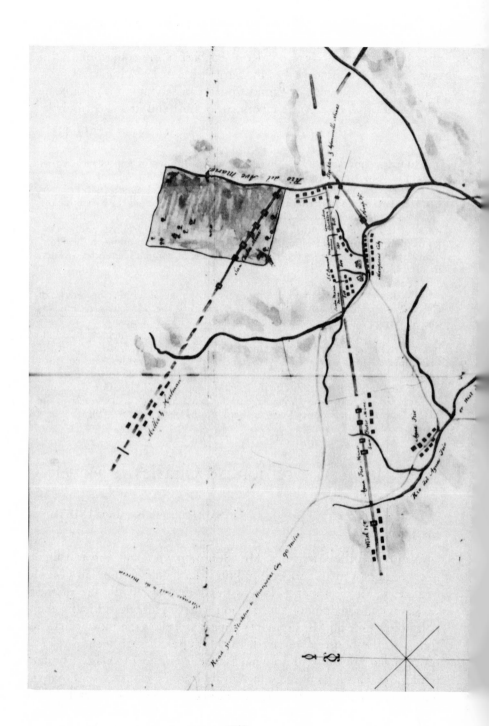

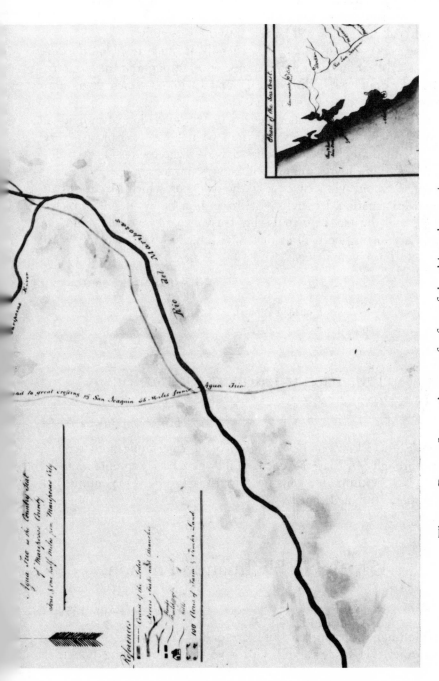

Thomas Denny Sargent's map of a few of the thirty-three veins on the Mariposa. From the David Hoffman Papers, New-York Historical Society.

will be here, I think, certainly before the Steamer of the 15th & having been now some time (since 14th May) in the Mariposa in the Mining Country to the South will be able to write very fully.

The papers of this place give generally as much reliable information as exists about the mining in operation throughout the Country. The only drawback is the want of Capital without which at the start the other expenditures are useless.

But that too will be alleviated by the consolidation of individual efforts & several companies and from what I was told by two very disappointed and reliable persons a few days ago the results even this summer from Quartz mining will be very immense.

Mr. Frémont will answer to all the points on which Mr. Hoffman asked information. I merely write to let him know the safety of his letters and the fact of their having been in part answered although from my having been ill at that time I heard no particulars. With respects, I am, yours truly,

Jessie Benton Frémont

Copy (NHi—David Hoffman Papers).

150. Richard Robert to Frémont

London, 1 Aug. 1851

[Wishes to know if he has received the communications sent to him through Mr. Mayer. Wonders if they have been kept intentionally from JCF. Within a few days he will proceed to Paris to continue his operations. Initialed copy.]

151. David Hoffman to Frémont

London, 2 Aug. 1851

[Hoffman dispatches a duplicate of his 29 July letter (with its enclosures) via Chagres and adds a postscript informing JCF that

Sargent had arrived in London. He notes that he is enclosing copies of Sargent's 1 Aug. letter to him and his own reply of the same date and adds: "His [Sargent's] anxiety to secure the confirmed extension of his lease for a few hundred feet is in flat contradiction of his having bought the whole of your property, or his hope that he can raise here or in N. York the proposed post payment! All seems to me a mere charlatan effort for sinister purposes. If Mr. Flandin be your partner, and also Mr. Wright (as I before wrote to you he says), I do not see how it is possible for me to defend your rights, or to prevent all kinds of strange doings on their part. . . . So far, Mr. Flandin does not present himself to me in any manner whatever as your agent. And my legal duty, therefore, is to conserve your rights in every possible way until your hand shall reveal to me your wishes and their respective powers. I confess, I doubt the whole matter, and rely fully on the letters you have addressed to me, in which you make not the least allusion to Mr. Wright, Mr. Flandin, or any one else as competent to instruct me but yourself." Signed copy.]

152. Frémont to John C. Parrott

[SAN FRANCISCO, 5 Aug. 1851]

[Gives Parrott a mortgage on the Mariposa in order to secure the payment of a bill of exchange in the amount of $8,000 which he has drawn upon Edward F. Beale in favor of Parrott. The loan is for sixty days with interest at the rate of 5 percent per month, payable monthly in advance. Default entitles Parrott or his assigns to have the property sold at public auction in the city of San Francisco after giving three days' notice in the public papers. The recorder of Mariposa County, Edward C. Bell, noted that the mortgage was filed in his office by J. G. Delamare on Monday, 8 Sept. 1851, at 2 P.M. (Book 1 of Records, p. 211, Mariposa County Court House). John Parrott acknowledged receipt from Edward F. Beale of the $8,000 on 6 Sept. 1851 in San Francisco before notary public P. Warren Van Winkle. The receipt was filed for record on Wednesday, 11 Feb. 1852, at 10 A.M. and recorded at the request of H. L. Parks (*ibid.*, p. 471).]

153. David Hoffman to Frémont

LONDON, 11 Aug. 1851

[Encloses duplicates (in some cases triplicates) of correspondence pertinent to the Sargent affair. Sargent "seems now upon his last legs." The idea of the sale of a single acre by him, or his purchase of one, is preposterous.

The New York *Herald*'s publication (12 July 1851) of the sale of the Mariposa had "astounded" Hoffman's companies, but he hopes his firmness has restored confidence. JCF needs to publicly deny the sale and firmly support him.

Sargent does not make known his residence in London from fear of arrest for debt. His name in any connection with JCF's must be prevented. "Messrs. Green and Edmunds[1] (as I should think), are only waiting for further developments, before they venture to cast him wholly off. But, even if Mr. Sargent should be still retained by them, I cannot ascertain that *they* have the least power to aid him in such a matter.

"Your affairs are all in a healthy state here and on the Continent, and they await nothing more than *two* things—*first*, your own replies to some of the most important questions heretofore propounded; and *second*, the denial of any sale of your property contemplated, beyond a small part for cash, in order to make more effectual your developments of your property by yourself. The *title* does not at all disturb them; but the more important questions to be answered are the following:

"1. Can heavy machinery be taken to the mines, and how?

"2. Of what weight can be taken by water, say to Stockton?

"3. Of what weight, and how, are things carried from Stockton to the Mariposa mines?

"4. Specimens authenticated by yourself or agents, as from your veins.

"5. Maps of your veins.

"6. What leases by you (not forefeited), to what extent, where located, and the terms of each?

"7. What number of veins, extent, direction, &c. &c.

"8. Is there protection present, or expected, for sound and industrious persons against intruders?

"9. Is there any water power in connexion with you, what, and where?

"10. Are there coals, foreign and domestic, and what average prices?

"11. What are the elevations of your locations of mines, and of those not located, also grades to be passed over?

"12. What facilities for transporting timber, stone, &c., from the agricultural to the mining lands, and what distances?

"13. Is there any iron on your lands; and if not, can it be easily obtained from other places, for various machinery purposes?

"14. Are there any machine shops for adjusting machinery at the Mariposas?

"15. Can honest workmen be had, so as to be united with the forces that each Company shall bring, and on what terms?

"16. Can Chinese, Mexican, and native Indian labourers be had, and on what terms?

"17. Can machinery, &c., be transported across the Isthmus, and of what weight, and on what terms, and the best route? And finally, any other information as to the Isthmus, the Cape, the veins, &c. &c.

"18. The prices of agricultural lands per acre.

"19. Will you sell any AGRICULTURAL lands in fee simple, and if so, at what price per acre?"
Printed in HOFFMAN, 44–45. This letter was not included in the list of papers received by Benjamin Rush from Messrs. Venning, Naylor, and Robins, solicitors.]

1. Edmunds not further identified. Green was probably Thomas Green of No. 4, Trafalgar Square, who accompanied Sargent to New York in Dec. 1851 (Sargent v. Frémont [in Chancery], Hoffman Papers).

154. Richard Robert to Frémont

LONDON, 12 Aug. 1851

[Expresses the fear that if JCF has not received his communications, they have been "interrupted by some interested, designing and victimizing person or persons," and hopes that JCF will make a careful investigation.

Expects to have the pleasure of writing to him again by Mr. Vander-Maesen and Mr. March [?][1] who will travel by the West India Royal

Mail via Southhampton and Chagres on 18 Aug. "These two gentlemen will take with them 12 or 18 miners, and, on the 2nd of September, Mr. Coulombier [2] will follow with the remainder of the expedition by the same route."

The reported sale of his estate may injure JCF and his property
momentarily. Signed copy.]

1. Mr. March [?] not identified.
2. Thomas Coulombier was co-gérant of the Mineurs Belges (*Journal des
Mineurs Belges Compagnie*, 20 June 1851, copy in Hoffman Papers).

155. Frémont to Pablo de la Guerra

SAN FRANCISCO
August 15, 1851

HON. PABLO DE LA GUERRA,
MY DEAR SIR,

I take pleasure in making you acquainted with my particular
friend, Joseph C. Palmer Esqre,[1] of this City, who will hand you this
note. I owe it to your former kindness to say that I am not a candidate
for the office of Senator, but have entirely withdrawn my name from
the political field, and so far as my good wishes and active exertions
go, both are entirely in favor of Mr. [T. Butler] King for that office.[2]

I have been talking with our friends on the subject and they all
agree with me that putting aside party questions, Mr. King is altogether the best man to represent us at this time.

I do not know what your own feelings may be, but we are all solic-
itous to engage them in favor of Mr. King, knowing the extent of
your influence among our Southern friends. Mr. Palmer visits Santa
Barbara as his friend, and I have given him this letter with the object
of obtaining for him your friendly attentions.[3]

Being desirous to act in concert with you, I should be glad to have a
line from you in order to know your sentiments on this subject which
so nearly concerns us all. Yours truly,

J. C. FRÉMONT

ALS (Santa Barbara Mission Archives—De La Guerra Collection). Except
for his father, Don Pablo was the most prominent member of the Guerra family

of Santa Barbara and served as a member of the constitutional convention, state senate, and judicial system.

1. Married to Martha Field, Joseph C. Palmer (1819–82) had been a tailor in Nantucket before coming to California in 1849. He and his New England friends Charles W. Cook and George W. Wright quickly became successful. They purchased a schooner, laden with lumber, which they sold at a fabulous profit; entered into the express business; and finally, with Edward Jones, went into banking and real estate. At first the firm enjoyed an excellent reputation and handled the early state bond issues, but speculation and politics brought failure to Palmer, Cook & Company in 1856. JCF was always a heavy borrower and Palmer maintained a close connection with him to the end of his life, even visiting him in Arizona to investigate the opportunities for investment in mining (Nantucket Vital Records; CROSS, 1:72–73, 173–75; BOSQUI, 68; Providence *Post* as printed in New-Bedford *Daily Mercury*, 2 May 1850; *Weekly Arizona Miner*, 31 Jan. and Feb. 1879; San Francisco *Call*, 2 May 1882).

2. The day before JCF penned his letter to Guerra, JBF had written Blair: . . . "He [JCF] says I must tell you to prepare yourself for a Whig Senator in his place, politics being too costly an amusement in this country just now, but that he will come to it with renewed vigor by the next election" (JBF to F. P. Blair, San Francisco, 14 Aug. 1851, NjP—Blair-Lee Papers). The Frémonts erred, however, in declaring that the state "is decidedly Whig." For the second time in twelve months King failed in his quest for a U.S. Senate seat; John B. Weller, a Democrat, was elected when the legislature met in Jan. 1852.

3. Dated the same day and likewise written in Spanish and in the same vein, JCF gave Palmer another letter of introduction to a person whom he refers to as "Muy amigo mio" (CU-B).

156. David Hoffman to Frémont

LONDON, 15 Aug. 1851

["This will be handed to you by Mons. Bourginon of Paris,[1] who proceeds to the Mariposas as Director of the Company called 'Le Mineur,' being a sublessee of Le Nouveau Monde Company, and with excellent machinery as I am informed." Requests that he extend Bourginon every possible aid.

"I deeply regret to learn today that Stockton and Aspinwall has been very unsuccessful. I shall study out the matter before you can write to me about it, and duly inform the public (of necessity) of the reason of its failure."

He is still waiting with anxiety for something official from JCF. "As to the Sargent affair it seems nearly forgotten, he being still in 'durance vile,' and if he can pay his paltry debts, I suppose he will return to N. York. He cannot do anything here. . . . I hope by next steamer to hear from Col. Benton repudiating his connection with Sargent.

"The Prospectus of the Nouveau Monde will be published in a few days. All seems to be admirable, but your expected intelligence will greatly stimulate them." Signed copy.]

1. Bourginon not identified.

157. David Hoffman to Frémont

LONDON, 16 Aug. 1851

[Writes that his many previous letters will have informed him of the state of things in London. "The Mineurs Belges Company sail today—also the Mineurs Français. The Nouveau Monde will send a third vessel shortly. No less than 9 other companies are on the tapis and are actively employed." The "shocks" and "fresh difficulties" to his and Robert's proceedings were caused by the report of the sale of the Mariposa and the failure of Stockton & Aspinwall's mine. He reassures JCF that he has "in Europe a vast field of good operations provided three things are right. First, that you have not sold your lands; second, that the failure of the Stockton & Aspinwal mine is owing to causes clearly distinguishable from the rest of your property; third, some reply to my questions propounded in my letter of the 11 August. As to the Sargent purchase of your whole estate, I pronounce it the most shameful humbug that was ever practiced by any one, he being wholly without means, and absolutely without credit here and elsewhere." Sender's copy.]

158. Frémont's Indian Beef Contract— Receipt 1

Receipt for Drafts drawn on the Secretary of the Interior (1)

[28 Aug. 1851]

The United States to John C. Fremont
    To two hundred and seventy head of beef cattle,

averaging each five hundred lbs net weight, left by Alexander Godey at different points in the Valley of the San Joaquin for the use of the Indians agreeably to the treaties, as follows, viz

at the Texon	82
Tulare Lake	50
Cahivia River	36
Kings River	34
San Joaquin	34
River Fresno	34 amounting to

135000 lbs. $20,250.00

Received at the Military post of Fort Miller, on the San Joaquin River, from Col G. W. Barbour, Indian Agent for the United States in California, the twenty eighth day of August 1851, the sum of twenty thousand, two hundred and fifty dollars in drafts on the Hon. Secretary of the Interior in full of above amount

JOHN CHARLES FRÉMONT

Copy, enclosure in G. W. Barbour to Luke Lea, 5 Jan. 1852 (DNA-75, LR, California B-6 1852 f/w Special File No. 266).

159. Frémont's Indian Beef Contract— Receipt 2

Receipt for Drafts drawn on the Secretary of the Interior (2)

[28 Aug. 1851]

The United States to John C. Fremont

To					
22000	lbs beef furnished		Indians at Texon	3,300.00
2500	”	”	”	Juans Rancheria	375.00
30000	”	”	”	Indians at Cahivia	4,500.00
21000	”	”	”	Kings River Indians	3,150.00
13000	”	”	”	San Joaquin Indians	1,950.00
16000	”	”	”	at the Fresno by Alexr. Godey	2,400.00
7500	”	”	”	At the Fresno by V. D. Haler [Lorenzo D. Vinsonhaler]	1,125.00

28500	"	"	"	at Fresno from Mariposa Rancho			4,275.00
950000	"	"	delivered Augt. 27th at San Joaquin[1]				142,500.00

$$163,575.00$$

By draft on Hon. Alexander H. H. Stuart[2]   10,000.00

$$\$153,575.00$$

Received at the Military post on the San Joaquin River, from Col. G. W. Barbour, Indian Agent for the United States in California, this twenty-eighth day of August 1851, the sum of one hundred and fifty three thousand, five hundred and seventy five dollars, in drafts on the Hon. Secretary of the Interior, in full of the above amount.

JOHN CHARLES FRÉMONT

Copy, enclosure in G. W. Barbour to Luke Lea, 5 Jan. 1852 (DNA-75, LR, California B-6 1852 f/w Special File No. 266).

1. The Indian subagent for the San Joaquin Valley acknowledged receipt as follows: "G. W. Barbour Indian Agent for California has this day delivered to me nineteen hundred head of beef Cattle to be distributed among the Indians south of the Chowchilla River with whom treaties have been formed in accordance with the stipulations of said treaties. Adam Johnston, Sub Indn. Agt. for San Joaquin Valley. Fort Miller San Joaquin River 28th August 1851" (*ibid.*).

2. Before deliveries were complete, JCF had asked Barbour for an advance payment in the form of $10,000 worth of drafts drawn on the Secretary of the Interior (*ibid.*). This document and Doc. No. 158 indicate that JCF received from Barbour drafts on the Secretary for a total of $183,825.

160. Frémont to Palmer, Cook & Company

[5 Sept. 1851]

This indenture made and concluded this fifth day of September A.D. one thousand eight hundred and fifty one between *John Charles Frémont* of the City of San Francisco and State of California, party of the first part, and *Joseph C. Palmer, Charles W. Cook, George W. Wright* and *Edward Jones* of the same place, parties of the second part, WITNESSETH that the said John Charles Frémont for and in consideration of the Sum of one dollar to him in hand paid by the said parties of the second part, at or before the ensealing and delivery hereof, the receipt whereof is hereby acknowledged, and for other good and valuable considerations not herein expressed, has granted, bargained, sold &

conveyed and does by these presents, grant, bargain, sell & convey to the said parties of the second part their heirs and assigns forever all his right, title, interest, estate, claim and demand both at law and in equity, and as well in possession as expectancy *of in and to the equal, undivided one half part of all that certain tract or parcel of land, situated in the County of Mariposa* and *State of California and known and described as follows*: viz Being all that tract or parcel of land in the San Joaquin Valley, called "las Mariposas" being ten leagues in extent and situated between the boundaries formed by the "Sierra Nevada" mountains, the "San Joaquin" river, the "Mercedes" river and the "Chauchiles river," which said tract of land was granted by General Micheltorena, Governor of California on the twenty ninth day of February AD 1844, to Ex Governor Juan B Alvarado and by said Juan B Alvarado sold & conveyed to said John Charles Frémont, the deed of conveyance being recorded in the Archives at Monterey, California, AD 1847.

To Have and To Hold, with all and singular the rights, privileges and hereditaments and appurtenances thereunto belonging or in any wise appertaining unto the said parties of the second part, their heirs and assigns forever, for their own use, benefit and behoof as fully as the same was held and possessed by the said John Charles Frémont.

In WITNESS whereof, I, the said John Charles Frémont have hereunto set my hand and affixed my seal, the day & year first above written at San Francisco, California.

JOHN CHARLES FRÉMONT. [*Seal*]

Signed, sealed & delivered in presence of us [the four members of Palmer, Cook & Company]

State of California
County of San Francisco

On this tenth day of September AD 1851. before me a Notary Public in and for said County, personally appeared John Charles Frémont, to me personally known to be the person described in and who executed the foregoing Instrument and acknowledged to me that he executed the same freely and voluntarily for the uses and purposes therein mentioned.

Witness my hand and official seal the day & year aforesaid.

[*Seal*]

HENRY H HAIGHT
Notary Public
San Francisco County, California

Filed Thursday October 13th. 1853 at 15 minutes of 5 o'clock PM
& recorded at request of Bradford Jones Esquire.

EDWARD C BELL RMC
By CHARLES GRAY, Dep RMC

Copy (Mariposa County Records, Book A of Deeds, pp. 323–25). By this instrument, Palmer, Cook & Company received a one-half interest in the Mariposa, although JCF still did not have a title from the U.S. government.

161. Frémont's Agreement with Edward F. Beale

[18 Sept. 1851]

I hereby acknowledge that I have received from the authorized agents of the U.S. Government in payment on a contract drafts payable to my order to the amount of $183,825; and that according to articles of agreement entered into by Lieut. E. F. Beale and myself he is entitled to 25 per cent. of the above amount after the reduction of the sum of $57,130, and a discount of 5 per cent. And I further hereby authorize James King of William & Co. at present holding said drafts to the amount of $153,575 to pay the above per centage, amounting to $29,376, to the order of said E. F. Beale; but in case interest should become due on the above drafts, by reason of protest or delay in payment, a proportionate amount of said interest shall be deducted from the sum to the said E. F. Beale.

Signed, JOHN C. FREMONT.

Printed in *Daily Alta California*, 2 Oct. 1855, in "Law Report," a column noticing activities in the Twelfth District Court, principally the case of Edward F. Beale v. Frémont. The plaintiff alleged that JCF had received payments of the drafts in the hands of James King of William & Co. about 1 Aug. 1854 and therefore by the terms of this agreement owed him $29,376 plus interest at the rate of 10 percent. The editor has been unable to locate additional information about the suit.

162. Frémont to Thomas Hart Benton

San Francisco, 1 Oct. 1851

[With this power of attorney, Frémont authorizes his father-in-law to bargain, sell, and convey or to lease all or a portion of the Mariposa grant, with the leases not to exceed seven years. He also permits him to modify or alter a number of drafts drawn in JCF's favor by George W. Barbour, Indian agent, upon the Secretary of Interior, Alexander H. H. Stuart. These amounted to $153,575 and had been placed by JCF in the hands of James King of William comformable to a contract that was also being sent to Benton. Frémont's signature was witnessed by Thos. Manson and P. W. Thompkins and notarized by John McCracken. The power of attorney was recorded in the Office of the Recorder of Deeds, District of Columbia, 22 Jan. 1852, and "Exd & Deld. to Lieut. Beale, 22 Jany. 1852." Copy, Office of the Recorder of Deeds, Washington, D.C.]

163. Frémont to David Hoffman

San Francisco, Oct. 1, 1851

My dear Sir:

You will think it strange that I have so frequently been forced to make my correspondence with you consist of a brief note. I will act differently by the next steamer. The object of this is simply to say to you that I received by last mail a copy of Mr. Flandin's note to you and to ask you to regard it merely as an unauthorized impertinence. He had no such power as it implied, & I have revoked the power which had been given to him for a special purpose. You will confer a favor on me by having the enclosed notice published in the Times. If Col. Benton could have been aware of the difficulties we have here between squatters & dishonest & thoughtless agents, he would have modified his opinion of my business capacities.

[*Two-thirds of a page has been blanked out.*][1]

The quartz work is acquiring a fixed, known value, & the quartz mining is taking the place of washing in the earth among common laborers. We therefore believe that next summer the estate would command a ready sale at much higher price than is now offered.

I will write you at some length by the next mail. In meantime remain yours truly,

JOHN C. FRÉMONT

[Enclosure]

[San Francisco, 1 Sept. 1851]

I, the undersigned John Charles Frémont, of the County of Mariposas, in the State of California, do hereby revoke and declare null and void all powers of attorney, general and special heretofore conferred by me, as well as any and all authority heretofore entrusted by me to any agencies, having reference especially to my estate of Mariposas, situate in the aforesaid county of Mariposas, State of California. And whereas certain of my former attornies or agents have undertaken to exercise undue and unwarranted authority in reference to the said estate of Mariposas, and whereas there is good reason to apprehend that unauthorized persons may illegally and fraudulently attempt to exercise rights and authority in over and upon the said estate of Mariposas—now therefore, I the aforesaid John Charles Frémont, do hereby distinctly advise and warn all persons whatsoever against entering into any contract of sale or lease, or engagement of any kind whatever in reference to the above estate of Mariposas, or any part thereof, saving and excepting with the Hon. Thomas H. Benton, of Missouri, and David Hoffman, Esquire, of the City of London, Engd. to whom I hereby renew and confirm the powers, heretofore entrusted, for making and executing leases upon the said estate of Mariposas, conformable to the written authority held by them, and whom I declare to be my sole and only attornies in and for that purpose; and I further declare that no other person has any right or authority to act in any way whatever in reference to the said estate of Mariposas, or for me in any other way whatever.

JOHN CHARLES FRÉMONT
San Francisco, Cala. Sepr. 1, 1851[2]

ALS and copy (NHi—David Hoffman Papers).
1. In a separate place in the Hoffman papers appears a copy of the material

266

that had been blanked out of the ALS letter. An endorsement reading "Letter 1 October Private part" makes the connection. The substance of the "Private part" also appears in the body of the letter as it was copied into Frémont v. Hoffman: Brief, Bill and Answer, p. 59. In the part which Hoffman deemed "private," JCF had written: "In regard to the sale of the Mariposa I have written to Col. Benton to ratify *provided* the purchasing party come fully up to their engagements within the time fixed. Otherwise and thereafter to entertain no proposals whatever from them. I am certainly disposed to rid myself of the trouble of managing the property and a *fixed income* would be better than waiting. But I regarded the purchase of Mr. Sargent as a mere speculation—on the other hand it is very probable that the title will be confirmed *this winter*." Hoffman added a note: "Benton had promised 2½ millions for all at least and 1½ for half. See what Flandin writes—1,000,000 not thought of for [all], but as to the ½."

2. The revocation of power of attorney was endorsed in Hoffman's hand: "Proposed advt. of Col. Frémont's. Recd. by me 19 Nov. 1851. By letter dated *1 October*." When the abbreviated version appeared in the London *Times*, 20 Nov. 1851, it was dated 1 Oct. 1851 and read: "Whereas there is a good reason to apprehend that unauthorized persons have illegally and fraudulently attempted to exercise rights and authority in, over, and upon my estates of Mariposa in California, I, the said John Charles Frémont, do hereby distinctly warn and advise all persons whomsoever against entering into any contract, in Europe, for sale, or lease, or engagement of any kind whatsoever in reference to my said estates in California, except with my only authorized representative in Europe, David Hoffman, Esq., of London."

164. Frémont to David Hoffman

SAN FRANCISCO, CALIFORNIA
October 8, 1851

MY DEAR SIR,

I have just completed executing a number of leases which cover a large extent of ground at the Mariposas. For this reason together with the difficulties always following the least uncertainty of title, I have decided to make no more leases, or in any way to take any farther action in regard to the Mariposas property, until after the judicial or legislative settlement of the question. I therefore write this note with the object of advising you of this determination, to the end that you may not take any farther action upon the subject in Europe. I send by this mail a notice[1] to the above effect to be published in the New York papers, and you will oblige me by causing the enclosed notice to be published in the Times newspaper. The course I have hitherto pursued has caused me a large unproductive outlay, and as I have great reason to believe that the question of title will be definitively settled in the course of the coming year, I have thought it most advisable to stop all my present business, in that connection, and so avoid all embarassment that might perhaps result to me from continuing to act in the present confused condition of this state.

I have to make you my thanks for the satisfactory and able manner in which you have acted for me, and will be happy to resume our business relations & again avail myself of your able services when I again resume operations. I have all reason to believe that they will then be resumed with force and great profit, as our quartz rock is now assuming a fixed, undoubted value. Mr. Moffat, who is of the government assaying & coining establishment in this city, has just assured me that he is now obtaining from his mine at the rate of one thousand ($1000) dollars *per diem*. His mining establishment is about 10 miles from the town of Mariposas, & has just now got fairly into operation. His operations will be the commencement of an era in mining here. Mr. Moffat informs me that he has expended about $70000, all of which is from stock taken here.[2]

I am about leaving today for the Mariposas and fearing I should be detained there too late for the mail of the 15th write this. Please send me a statement of my business with you, and be kind enough to inform Mr. Robert of my determination. I shall write to you regularly & frequently & trust to hear regularly from you, hoping notwithstanding the interruption of our business relations, to have with you a steady correspondence. Yours truly,

JOHN CHARLES FRÉMONT

David Hoffman, Esqre
London, England

ALS (NHi—David Hoffman Papers). Endorsed: "Received 18 Dec."

1. JCF's enclosure not found. See Doc. No. 182 for Hoffman's version of JCF's notice to end leasing. It was not published in the *Times* as JCF requested.

2. Formerly a New York assayer, John Little Moffat had spent some time as a mining man in the Georgia goldfields. In addition to his assay and gold brokerage business at Clay and DuPont streets in San Francisco, he was a partner and director of the Merced Mining Company, which had commenced operations in April on the "Great Johnson Vein" at Mount Ophir northwest of Mariposa (CRAMPTON, 189–91).

165. David Hoffman to Frémont

41 Conduit Street, Hanover Square, 24 Oct. 1851

[The Chagres Mail, with dates from California as late as 6 Sept., had arrived but Hoffman had not been favored with letters from JCF. He had thought his own communiqués of late July and early August so important that he had sent them in triplicate by various routes. He was grateful for Mrs. Frémont's letter (1 Aug. 1851) received through Charles F. Mayer.

Notes how he had "quietly" yet "continuously" availed himself of his position in society to disseminate "widely and significantly yet with dignity sound impressions of the honorable nature of your own private as well as public character, and the great & curious quality of your estates." It could all have been done "much more easily and much more readily" had he and Robert had the desired information from JCF.

He hopes that the advance party of the Mineurs Belges is in California and acceptable to JCF. He has no doubt found Vander-Maesen "anxiously bent" on extracting gold by dissolving the quartz. When Mons. Derriey[1] of Paris, the "gérant" in the Mineurs Belges, has "tidings" that his emissaries are satisfied with what they find, he will promptly send out heavy machinery and perhaps as many as 300 men.

Hoffman notes that a second operation from Belgium is intended, that "Le Nouveau Monde (French) is in high vigor and adding a double to their last named amount of Capital," and that the Nouveau Monde (English) is "ripe." He writes that he is enclosing a prospectus for the latter company and that their engineers, the Taylors,[2] are first-rate. "In this company is our friend Capt. W. K. Smith," who had been energetic in its promotion. The company and its operations would have been much more forward had JCF replied when their contract was transmitted.

Hoffman hopes that a desirable contract can be concluded with the Bonaparte family. One of the contractors in that private association would be Le Chevalier Cipriani,[3] Sardinia's consul general in California, who would introduce £12,000 into California operations.

The British Mutual is renovating its financial power "with much vigor"; Andrew Smith's company was remodeled "under first rate auspecies"; the Comte de la Garde's[4] second company is forming; Mayles' [Moyle's?] Cornish company is in progress; and five more contracts

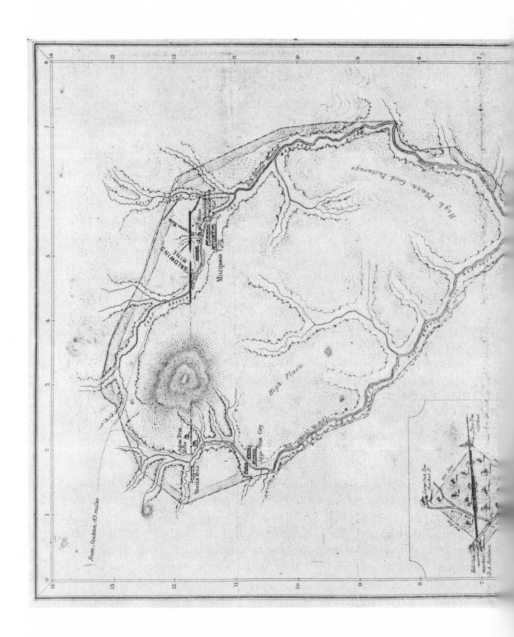

270

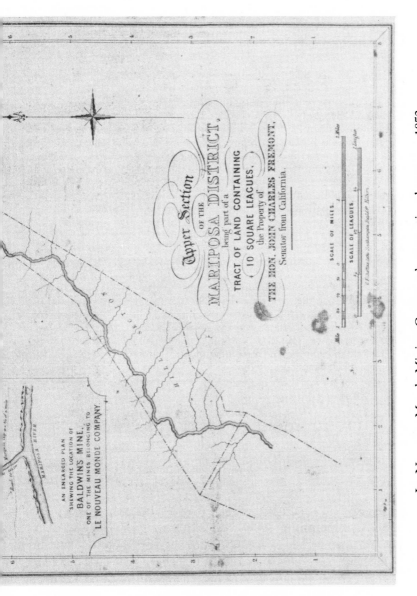

Le Nouveau Monde Mining Company's promotional map, ca. 1852.
The original size of the map was 8½" x 14⅛" and was printed
in London by C. F. Cheffins, Lithographers. Courtesy of
M. A. Goodspeed, Jr., Chevy Chase, Maryland.

are being sought. The Agua Fria, the Ave Maria, and the West Mariposa profess to fight under JCF's standard, but Hoffman is skeptical that the gentlemen in these companies would do much in California. The stock exchange was promptly to be their theater of action. As to the Sargent affair, he has no doubt that JCF would promptly annihilate it. Sender's copy.]

1. Charles Derriey had been collector of taxes for the town of Auxerre, France.

2. This is a reference to the prestigious firm of John Taylor and Sons, which had been established early in the nineteenth century and which was still in business in London in the mid-1950s. The senior Taylor had been born in Norwich in 1779 and had early gained a reputation for his successful management of Wheal Friendship Mine, Tavistock. The firm not only would inspect and report on mining property all over the world but would endeavor to promote companies and manage mines (see BURT for two of John Taylor's essays on "Cornish Mining" and "The Economy of Mining").

3. Leonetto Cypriani may never have obtained a lease from JCF, but he did acquire mining claims at various points near the Merced River, many of which had been discovered by Louis Victor Nivault (Mariposa County Records, Quartz Claims A, pp. 60–62).

4. Hoffman wrote about the interest of the "Comte de la Garde" in organizing companies for mining on the Mariposa, but JBF wrote about his friendly interest in her and her husband when they went to Paris in 1852 and how his influence put them on the "*liste intime*" so that they might receive invitations to the fêtes and balls connected with the government of Louis Napoleon. JBF's "grand seigneur" of Old France was Augustin Pelletier, Comte De Lagarde (b. 1780), who returned from exile after the restoration of the Bourbons and became a general, ambassador, and a member of the Chambre des Pairs (J. B. FRÉMONT [1], 253–315; LAROUSSE, 10:66).

166. Frémont to David Hoffman

SAN FRANCISCO, CALA., Oct. 29, 1851

MY DEAR SIR,

By the last mail I received yours of August 16th, which was therefore about two months on its way. Many things grow old, and many changes are operated here in the course of two months, and this makes efficient correspondence difficult. I notice that Gregory's Express lately carried bullion through to Liverpool in 37 days; and it may be well to use this means in any more important communications, where time enters into the question. Agreeably to my letter by last mail, I proceed to give you current intelligence, which will about amount to a reply to your last letter. [So far, no company from Europe has commenced operations on the Mariposas]. The Director of the Nouveau Monde Company arrived here [a few months since, but entirely without funds to commence even preliminary work at the mine, & without means to make that ordinary respectable appearance which I reasonably looked for in the agent of such a company. I had repeated interviews with the gentlemen and Mr. Cavallier, who is also an agent for the company, & who made a favorable impression here as a man of business.[1] The time accorded to the company for commencing operations had already expired when the director arrived, & I did not feel disposed to permit one of our best locations to be occupied by a company without means to open it, holding it only for purposes of speculation, and resulting in discredit to the mine. We have already seen the evils of this thing, & are wary of speculators, and fearful of being ourselves compromised. It was therefore, or if not therefore, at least as the proper course, agreed that Mr. Cavallier, about to return to France, should endeavor to procure such an employment of capital as should be a guarantee to me that the company intend to mine seriously, and that in the meantime no location should be made. With such as understanding] I have approved their lease, [extended the term within which they are to commence operations], and engaged to have a good location ready for them. Should the *Mineurs Belges* arrive in working condition, we will put them immediately on a good vein, [and the same in regard to the *Mineurs Français*]. But they must have money to open the mines properly & to put up good machinery. [I am not able to tell you how much money Stockton & Aspinwall expended at the vein where they failed. But these facts I do know, namely:] They[2] sunk a shaft perhaps 40 feet deep, & drove in two adits about the same distance, put up an engine of SEVEN horse power & a set of stamps & during the four consecutive months that the machine was kept running, the ore yielded them a little over forty-one (41) dollars the ton. It is a matter of notoriety at the Mariposas that the people employed on the vein did not know how to work it. [I learned a few days since that examinations had been made of the tailings from their mill, that is, of the ore which had passed through & the result was that about ten cents of gold was found to the ordinary miner's washing pan. These few details are sufficient to satisfy you that their work showed nothing for the value of the vein. Other companies now are at work on the same vein, & in a short time I will send you the result]. We are daily gaining confidence in the richness of the veins & in their performance. We have also discovered a beautiful method of obtaining the gold from the rock, and about the 1st of Jany. I will give you a statement of results. I have decidedly declined any sale of the Mariposas. To my next I must reserve what I shall further have to say; and in the mean time, remain with regard, truly yours,

J. C. Frémont

ALS NHi—(David Hoffman Papers). Endorsed: "Important." Penciled on the letter: "Rec'd Dec. '51 before letter of 8 Oct." Bracketed material was deleted from the letter as printed in HOFFMAN, 59.

1. Probably Edmund Cavallier, who was residing in San Francisco in 1854 (San Francisco *Daily Herald*, 2 April 1854). It is not clear from JCF's letter that Cavallier actually came to California with the Nouveau Monde Company.

2. In the printed version "One party" was substituted for "They."

167. Frémont and George W. Wright's Contract with Adam Johnston

[1 and 11 Nov. 1851]

We the undersigned hereby agree to sell to Adam Johnston, U.S. Indian Agent, Twelve hundred head of Beef Cattle now on the little Mariposa averaging five hundred pounds each, at the sum of Seventy-five Dollars per head to be delivered to the Indians of the valley of San Joaquin as per order from Adam Johnston Agent.

Also 1000 half sacks of Flour to be delivered on the Little Mariposa at the Rancho of Col. J. C. Fremont for the use of the Indians of the Valley of San Joaquin.

Nov. 1st 1851   (signed) G. W. WRIGHT for
John Charles Fremont

Received San Francisco Nov. 11. 1851 of Coln. John Charles Fremont Twelve hundred head of cattle and one thousand half sacks of Flour delivered on the little Mariposa river for the support of the Indians in the Valley of San Joaquin for which drafts have been drawn upon the Secretary of the Interior of the date of this receipt.[1]

(signed) ADAM JOHNSTON
U.S. Indian Agent
Valley of San Joaquin

Copy (M. A. Goodspeed, Jr., Collection). In the same collection is a private memorandum by George W. Wright indicating that the half-sacks of flour were sold at $30 each and that a total of $120,000 was received in drafts on the Secretary of the Interior. Wright maintained that Johnston understood that there were not sufficient cattle on the Mariposa to fulfill the terms of the contract immediately, but that supplies would be available eventually for daily or weekly deliveries.

Wright then arranged to purchase 2,634 head of cattle from Felix Argenti, who in turn claimed them from Mariano G. Vallejo in settlement of a debt. In April 1852 Alexander Godey drove the cattle from Vallejo's Sucol Ranch to the Mariposa. Still later Wright testified that at $16 per head he had paid Argenti twice the value of the cattle. The high price was given because Argenti had been willing to take the Johnston drafts, already protested, and had agreed not to look to JCF "in any event" for payment (Deposition of George W. Wright, 22 Jan. 1857, in Orestes P. Quintard v. Fremont, M. A. Goodspeed, Jr., Collection).

1. The Court of Claims ultimately decided that the federal government had a total financial responsiblity of $60,000 under this contract. Since there was "no clear and distinct evidence of delivery" of the flour, no claim for its provision was allowed, and since an inferior kind of cattle was delivered, the "beef claim" was reduced from $90,000 to $60,000 (Frémont, for the use of Jackson, v. The United States, 2 *Court of Claims Reports*, Dec. Term, 1866, pp. 461–81). Jackson and Munro held drafts for $20,000, but since the court had earlier decided that an action had to be in the name of the original party to the contract, so as to protect the equitable right of all the holders of the drafts, they probably had to give JCF a portion of their recovery of $13,333.33. Two years later the court declared Frémont theoretically entitled to recover $46,666 (two-thirds of $70,000 outstanding after the Jackson decision) upon the original contract and specifically $18,666, since $28,000 of the drafts were in his possession (although $14,000 had been lost by Wright). John Roach, as Baker's administrator, held $42,000, but the validity of his claim had yet to be established (John C. Frémont, in his own right, and for the use of Roach and another, executors of Baker, v. the United States, 4 *Court of Claims Reports*, Dec. Term, 1868, pp. 252–57).

168. Frémont to David Hoffman

SAN FRANCISCO, Nov. 4, 1851

MY DEAR SIR,

Accompanying this I send you the [San Francisco] Herald of Sunday. I am surprised that I do not oftener send the journals of the day here, as they almost always contain information of value relative to the gold mines. Did I tell you in my last anything of an improved method of extracting the gold which we have discovered on our place? As I do not remember having told you & cannot conveniently refer, I will run the risk of telling you the same thing twice. I should not say we have discovered, as it was discovered solely by a gentleman who is engaged in mining at the Mariposas—one of my lessees[1]—neither ought I to characterize it as an improved method, because in application and in principle both it is wholly new, and in practice proves admirably successful. As soon as I am at liberty to do so, I will describe it to you fully, and in the mean time you may judge of it by this statement, namely. His stamping mill is a small one, driven by an engine of seven horse power, and the powdered ore is, as usual, conducted from the mortars by water over what are called shaking tables, which of some 2 feet by 3, and of these there are three. By this discovery the ore which planed over a space of two inches square on one of these tables gave in 24 hours two ounces of amalgram, equal to about one third of an ounce of gold. This was an experiment on a small scale, but you can judge what it may be when applied in grand. Yours truly,

J. C. FREMONT

ALS (NHi—David Hoffman Papers).

1. In his 22 Dec. 1851 letter to Hoffman, JCF identifies the discoverer of the new process as Frederick Goodell.

169. David Hoffman to Frémont

41 Conduit Street, Hanover Square, 10 Nov. 1851

[Hoffman again laments that he is without advices from JCF. "Your last letter is one of the 11th May, and one from Mrs. Frémont of the 1st Aug."

JCF's economic interests were advancing even in the face of "the strange operations which are being worked in this Town under cover of your name and by means of some of your seven-year leases, now five, and forfeitable—possibly forfeited." They had been granted by JCF in "the faith" that the lessees would early operate with American capital and machinery. The Wright and Walbridge party was seeking to obtain capital with the Agua Fria, as was Sargent with his two leases now bearing the names of the West Mariposa and the Ave Maria. Sargent was also asserting that JCF's powers to Hoffman were revoked or superseded and that he and Col. Benton had arranged "a purchase of the half of your Estates, and in all probability the whole!!"

In spite of the disagreeable situation, Hoffman insists he is still operating "most importantly." "The Nouveau Monde on coming out today has passed immediately to a premium of £1.10 per share and will, we expect . . . rise much higher." In the company he had secured for JCF notes in the amount of £950 and £250 and 13,275 shares. Two thousand shares had also been obtained from Capt. Smith and Mr. Jackson for an extension of their seven-year leases to twenty-one. The London Mariposa Gold Mining Quartz Company had all its capital, and Lord Erskine's British Mutual, which had changed its name to the Quartz Rock Mining Company, had two-thirds of its capital. Draft.]

170. Frémont to the Philadelphia and California Mining Company

SAN FRANCISCO, Nov. 10th, 1851

GENTLEMEN:

The object of this note is to inform you, that I have become interested in the mining operations which you propose to carry on at Mariposa, and have consequently this day executed to you, a lease of mining land, of unusual extent and privileges.[1] In doing this I have acted principally on the representations of the Hon. Mr. Wright, who informs me that your Company, has at command large capital, which they design to employ in working the mines faithfully and giving them their full development for the benefit of all who may be concerned. Believing that mining operations so conducted would be eminently successful, and having at my command a large extent of mineral ground, I have associated myself with your enterprise, and have accordingly assigned to the Company, locations which, as you will see in the lease, are very large and which comprise the best situation and the most valuable veins at this time known to be on the place.

I am desirous to aid the operations of the Company by giving them all the advantages in my power, and to this end have granted them the right to occupy and work any more valuable vein which may hereafter be discovered, and will be glad, in other ways which may offer in the progress of the work, to contribute to their success,[2] and in the meantime, I am very respectfully, Your obedient servant,

JOHN CHARLES FRÉMONT

Messrs. Solomon Alter, John L. Newbold, and others
Philadelphia

Printed in Articles of Association of the Philadelphia and California Mining Company, pp. 15–16 (CHi). The brain-child of George W. Wright, the Philadelphia and California Mining Company had been in the process of organizing for more than a year. Along with Hiram Walbridge, Wright was one of the directors (and a few days later president) when the company made an agreement with Palmer, Cook & Company whereby the latter gave the Philadelphia company access to its 600-foot-square lease on the Mariposa River, which it had obtained from JCF and "upon which there is a large quartz vein of gold." In return the San Francisco banking firm received 11,000 of the 25,000 shares of stock valued at $20 a share (Articles of Agreement, 14 Feb. 1851, *ibid.*). The eastern company immediately sent H. S. Parke, a native of Philadelphia, to examine the veins on the Mariposa as well as most of the "theatres of active operations in California." Parke's official report extolled the possibilities of the New Britain and Heap veins upon which JCF had already granted leases to the company.

1. On 10 Nov. 1851 JCF, "for and in consideration of the sum of two hundred and fifty thousand dollars," specifically assigned two locations to the Philadelphia and California Mining Company. One was on the Heap and Sargent vein; the other one was on the New Britain (Philadelphia and California Mining Company Lease, 10 Nov. 1851, Mariposa County Records, Book D of Deeds, pp. 360–64). Fifty thousand dollars of the stipulated amount may have been in cash; the balance was certainly in shares, and the company soon reorganized in order to meet its agreements with JCF. In the new stock split and $2 million capitalization, JCF received 40,000 shares valued at $5 each. He and Senator William M. Gwin were added as directors of the company.

2. The company never really operated on the Mariposa. The steam engines and stamps it sent out in 1851 were thought to be too light and were "temporarily" stored at Stockton, but the Articles of Association, p. 20, assured the public that they had "a sufficient extent of valuable veins for the supply of a great many sub-companies."

171. David Hoffman to Frémont

LONDON, 20 Nov. 1851

[Acknowledges receipt of JCF's 1 Oct. letter—the first since 11 May—with his proposed advertisement, dated 1 Sept. "I now send you the advertisement inserted by me in 5 papers.[1] Under the excited state of this country it would not have been proper to insert *verbatim* the one prepared by you on the 1st Septr. for the *least idea* of your selling an acre in fee would go a large way to stop everything. . . . We are astonished that the *Nouveau Monde* contract, though sent to you 2 months ago, has not been ratified, and that it is said you refused them. . . . It was then thought very lightly of, but much higher now, since it has become united with a British Branch in London, to raise £200,000 after which I sent to you the new contract and Prospectus, embracing in all just 4200 feet by 600 feet—that is, 2400 feet lease by me and 1800 feet by my extension of the 7 year leases made to Capt. W. K. Smith and Baldwin, the three each of 600 feet."[2]

He relates that contracts are executed for JCF to receive about £14,800 in cash or about $74,000, a part of which Hoffman had received and the residue of which he hoped for in a few days. To this would be added £37,000 or about $185,000 which the lessees had deposited in the bank, with Hoffman's name as trustee, until sites were selected and the leases approved by JCF. Hoffman expected the total of £51,800 or $259,000 to be extended "to quite £80,000 or $400,000," and this for not more than 23,800 by 600 feet of land. In addition to cash, JCF would have 100,000 one-pound shares in the various companies.

Hoffman requests that JCF send him: "As neatly a prepared Power of Attorney as can be drawn [the original had a piece cut out], with the amplest powers"; specimens authenticated as to localities and depths; statements as to the location of his mines and especially those actually located, the known veins and their direction; all geological developments; and "as much of your replies to my previous questions as shall remain unanswered when you receive this letter."

He again expresses the hope that JCF will visit London and that Sargent will be driven off entirely. "I must add that I abhor the artful proceedings of General Wallbridge as to the Agua Fria, but I have observed profound silence as to him because really you never told me a syllable about him or the Agua Fria. He has done some good, and much mischief. He has yet but a 7 year lease, so far as I know, and I hope he will never get an extension to 21 years, except through your authorization to me. . . . They say P[almer], C[ook] & C[ompany] has sent an extension of the lease from you; but Col. W[albridge] expressly stated to me that no one had seen it, and yet when I applied to him to see it, he stated he had parted with it for a short time!!"

Hoffman notices that the advertisement in the New York *Herald* of

12 July 1851 had appeared again in both New York and London papers. Sender's copy.]

1. For Hoffman's advertisement, see Doc. No. 163, n. 2.
2. The new contract between Hoffman and Fabien Paganelli di Zicavo of Le Nouveau Monde Gold Mining Company was dated 8 Nov. 1851 and is in the M. A. Goodspeed, Jr., Collection. The prospectus was published in the London *Times*, 10 Nov. 1851.

172. David Hoffman to Frémont

LONDON, 25 Nov. 1851

MY DEAR SIR,

Your letter [of] 1 October sunk me to the earth! Surely Sir you have dealt harshly with yourself, cruelly with me, though I feel it to be quite impossible you intended it. You have taken the whole matter out of the hands of honesty, devotion, faith, to entrust it all to villainy. My only hope now is that your recent letter will show clearly that your eyes are opened and also that a paltry first payment will not be in time. I enclose copy of my last to Col. Benton and trust for all our sakes that rascality (under God) cannot be permitted to prevail. If all is made right by Co. B. and yourself your property is worth 10 times as much as Sargent promises. Why didn't my good counsels avail. Yours,

D.H.

Copy initialed (NHi—David Hoffman Papers). 1st endorsement: "Mariposa sold!!!" 2nd endorsement: "Probably not sent [I think now it did go] *Again*. It is quite impossible it could have been sent on the 25 Nov. if the 20 [?] Nov. letter went—also a mystery."

173. Francisca Villa de Dominguez to Frémont

[27 Nov. 1851]

Agreement made between D[on]a Francisca Villa de Dominguez of one part and Don Juan Carlos Fremont of the other part: Said

Senora has sold and by these presents does sell and make over in perpetual transfer to the said Senor Fremont and his heirs, for the sum of Two Thousand dollars to her paid and to her satisfaction, all the interest, right and ownership which she has in the tract of land called "Rancho de San Emidio," situated in the County of Santa Barbara and the same that was granted to the late Senor Don José Antonio Dominguez, the 14th day of July 1842, it being understood that the portion sold is the half of all the right and estates of said rancho, leaving the other half of the said rancho to the benefit of the sons and daughters of said Senora Da. Francisca Villa de Dominguez jointly with the half of the minerals which might hereafter be discovered.

We certify to this by our signatures and seals on this twenty-seventh day of November 1851, it being well understood, that if in the part purchased by the Señor Fremont there should turn out some mines, the said Da. Francisca and her heirs shall have the right to the half of them, and the Senior Fremont shall have the same right in the other part.

We certify to this by our signatures and seals date as above,

Assenting witnesses,   (Signed) FRANCISCA her mark VILLA DOMINGUEZ

Anast[asi]o Carrillo   (Signed) JOHN CHARLES FREMONT
Nicholas A. Den

State of California, County of Santa Barbara, this day twenty-seventh of November of the year 1851, appeared personally before me, Notary Public of said County, Da. Francisca Villa and Don John Charles Fremont, whom I certify and know to be the persons, who made and agreed to the foregoing instrument, and are described therein, and who declared to me to have made it fully and voluntarily for the purpose and uses therein mentioned there being as witnesses Don Anastasio Carrillo and Don Nicholas Den, I certify.

                                    (Signed) R. CARRILLO
Private Seal   Notary Public

I certify the foregoing to be a correct translation.

                                    (Signed) GEO. FISHER
                                              Sec.

Filed in Office February 10th 1853

                                    (Signed) GEO. FISHER, Sec.

Copy, translation (DNA-49, California Land Commission, vol. 19 [25], Record of Evidence, Case 556, pp. 39–40). The petition of the Dominguez heirs was rejected by the California Land Commission on 26 Dec. 1854, largely because the attorneys had mishandled the case and failed to submit the proper proofs (*ibid.*, no. 29 [vol. II], Decisions, p. 429). Rufus A. Lockwood petitioned for a second review and the title was confirmed on 19 June 1855 (*ibid.*, no. 17 [vol. XI], Evidence, pp. 667–68, 646–49, 667–68, 678–80, and no. 30 [vol. III], Decisions, pp. 73–74). The patent to this ranch of 17,709.79 acres was not given until 1866 (GATES [1]). By that time JCF's monetary difficulties had forced him to make a temporary consignment of his property to D. W. Perley, a San Francisco lawyer, but he succeeded in getting a reconveyance (Frémont to T. W. Park, 23 April 1860). He then deeded his undivided interest to Mark Brumagin to hold in trust for his niece, Frances Cornelia Frémont (called Nina), the wife of Henry M. Porter. The trust ended in 1867, and in 1869 she deeded all her rights to Edward F. Beale, who was building up his great empire known as Rancho El Tejon (Brumagin, Frémont, and Porter Indenture, 8 Jan. 1867, and Frances Cornelia Frémont Porter to Edward F. Beale, 18 Feb. 1869, Kern County Records, Bakersfield). Joseph C. Palmer and his wife, Martha, also had some rights in San Emigdio and made deeds to Robert Page and to Edward F. Beale in 1869 (unpublished paper on San Emigdio Rancho, compiled by Mrs. Douglas Allen, Bakersfield Public Library).

174. David Hoffman to Frémont

10 Conduit Street, LONDON, 9 Dec. 1851

[Expresses disappointment in not receiving the communiqué promised by JCF's letter of 1 Oct. "It is painful to me to have to write you that stagnation—at least suspension of the incomings for you has followed so immediately on the ripening of my long sown seed into a rich and golden harvest. . . . I was receiving (or about to receive) at the rate of 5000£ a day until Sargent published Col. Benton's letter and the Flandin contract. The shares and money must have exceeded £80,000 for remittance to you when the *stroke* came!" He expects an immediate reversal if JCF would confirm his powers fully, revoking all others, annul all of "Sargent's pretensions," and confirm all leases. "Confidence will return and your stock will go largely up. . . . All adhered to me personally, but Col. Benton has alarmed them greatly. My pen against him is, of course, restrained. It is now for *you alone* to save *your estate, your name*, and in some degree my *honour*. I wait your full reply." Sender's copy.]

175. Frémont to Benjamin D. Wilson

My dear Sir,

I have just received yours of the 23d. Novr., asking me information in regard to the contract. You will have already learned from Mr. [Henry] Mellus that in anticipation of difficulties I have paid in accepted checks on the House of Palmer, Cook & Co. (of this city) all of my liabilities in your neighborhood, except those of the purchase from [Antonio José] Côt. Among those paid in this will be included [William] Workman's. I find now that my anticipations were fully justified. The drafts given me in payment for cattle by the United States Commissioner, Col. G. W. Barbour have not been accepted by the government, but have been dishonored by the Secretary of the Interior on whom they were drawn & returned to me protested. For some of those which I had procured to be discounted here I am liable to action as the endorser. I shall now have to request Côt & Menendez also to receive accepted checks on Palmer, Cook & Co. for the amount which will be due them at the end of this month. This will give me time to perhaps meet their other payments as they become due. Palmer & Cook agree to make the advances in this way. This is the best arrangement I can make & under the circumstances I think it is a good one for those from whom we purchased, as there is no knowing how many sessions of Congress will lapse before the drafts are paid. Will you do me the favor to explain to Ro[w]land & Workman how things stand. The only inconvenience to them has been a little delay, which I hope they will overlook.

If there is any thing I can do for you here, let me know. The Land Commission has advertised to commence its sittings on the 31st of this month. One of the Commissioners, Mr. [Hiland] Hall, is sick with Panama fever, and his eldest son died of it at 12 last night. The Pacific came in last night, but I believe has not brought the other Commissioner, Harry J. Thornton![1] Yours truly,

John C. Frémont

B. D. Wilson, Esqre.
Los Angeles

ALS (CSmH).
1. In addition to Hall and Thornton, President Fillmore had appointed a

third Whig, James Wilson, to the Board of Land Commissioners. The commissioners were to consider claims in California and to determine whether they conformed to Mexican law. In 1853 President Pierce appointed an entirely new board.

176. Frémont to Charles F. Mayer

My DEAR SIR,

On my return to this City a few days since I had the pleasure to receive your note of October the 16th accompanying duplicates of letters from Messrs. Hoffman and Robert. A duplicate or perhaps the original of Mr. Hoffman's letters had already reached me some weeks since, and perhaps in my notes to him I may have acknowledged its receipt. Generally however, I have written briefly and always to some particular point.

Our friends are altogether wrong to infer that there is anything mysterious or unfair in the failure of their letters to meet me. In the first place there has been general complaint on the same subject, & in the second, I have been almost constantly in the remote interior, travelling from place to place, and much more rapidly than the mail, or the careless and chance means of transmitting by travellers. In this way, letters might (& have) have travelled after me for months and finally reached me when their contents were obsolete.

I will take care to exonerate you from any neglect of them, by informing them (or rather Mr. Hoffman) of your earnest representations to me on the score of my neglect. And now in regards that, "The replying to the many inquiries that were addressed to me by our friends on the subject of the Mariposas," I will simply say to you that I did not reply to those inquiries because of the absolute impossibility to do so.

All the knowledge in my power to give, was general and had been already given. As regards my title to the property, I believe it to be good, & fully believe that it will be recognized by the United States. More I could not say until the legal investigation had taken place. I had already described the place, its extent and character, its great fertility. I had mentioned its numerous gold veins and stated their character as far as partial analysis could give it (a means of information very uncertain) and I had informed them that gold was to be found nearly over all the land and up to the present I had occasionally informed them that whatever knowledge we had been able to obtain confirmed what we had previously reported. What more could be done? To obtain more required absolutely the very thing they were endeavouring to accomplish in England, namely such an employment of Capital as should open up these veins should [they] go down 2 and 3 and 500 feet into the earth, what the veins are, whether they get richer or poorer as we go down, whether they become larger or smaller—whether they become permanent and authorize employment of large capital, or whether they give out entirely. These are the only questions which they should require to be solved. I think that a few months will go some way to elucidate them. At present I can only say and shall say to Mr. Hoffman in my letter of today that we have upon the Mariposas a Gold vein apparently permanent (in the sense above mentioned) to which the history of gold mining the world over, as far as I am acquainted with it, affords no approximate parallel. I say a vein, we may have many such, we have *many* such, of the same superficial indications, but we cannot know them till we go down upon them. But of this one we know, and from it might reasonably argue that the others are so, and if I answered his question loosely, I should at once jump to the conclusion, and say that they are so. But in matters of business, where the information I give is expected to be a basis, I shall not state opinions as facts but wait until the facts develop themselves. In the meantime, ask them to remember that the thousand speculators who are holding California up to the view of the world write extravagantly, for or against, according to their local interests, and that California illustrated by the father of lies with a Cornucopia at his mouth would convey to them a good idea. I will shortly send a statement of the mine and in meantime remain Yours truly,

J. C. Frémont

Charles F. Mayer, Esq.
Baltimore, Md.

ALS (NHi—David Hoffman Papers). Mayer retained a copy and forwarded the original to Hoffman, who received it in Feb. 1852.

177. Teodoro Arellanes to Frémont

To the Colonel
Don Juan Fremont
San Francisco
Dear Sir:

I had the pleasure of receiving your kind letter of the 30th of last month and in reply, permit me to say that with respect to the delivery of the two hundred and fifty cattle my son Antonio Arellanes went to the Rancho de Guadalupe to meet Sr. Luna but since the said Sr. wanted to accept only selected [escogida] cattle my son was not in a position to deliver to him in this manner—because you will remember our agreement at the house of Don Nicolas Den[1]—that I promised you to deliver the two hundred and fifty cattle but it would be impossible for them to be selected first because I had no obligation and second that the weather did not permit setting up a rodeo—so you will see that I have tried in good faith to comply and only for this reason of wanting to receive selected cattle Sr. Luna did not take delivery—my son offered to deliver the cattle as they came in a small rodeo which could have been done—but Sr. Luna refused this saying that he would only accept selected cattle—which you must know was impossible, either according to our obligation or because of the weather which did not premit.

You must see that I have had enough expense in this affair—in getting a cavalcade and people etc. to fulfill my obligation to you—I am very sorry for you as well as for myself but what shall we do—it was not my obligation to deliver selected cattle—moreover the weather did not permit for the very bad state of the cavalcade and the cattle *Mariposa [pencilled in]*.

I hope that you will take into consideration these reasons which seem to me to be the true ones—and I shall always hold myself at your disposition. I sign myself as your attentive servant and friend, Q.S.M.B. [who kisses your hand].

Teodoro Arellanes

ALS in Spanish (M. A. Goodspeed, Jr., Collection). Translated by M. K. Swingle of the California Historical Society. Described by H. H. Bancroft as a "man of genial temper and gentlemanly manners, locally a kind of ranchero prince," Teodoro Arellanes was one of the owners of Rancho Guadalupe in the northwestern corner of Santa Barbara County (PIONEER REGISTER).

1. Nicholas Augustus Den (ca. 1812–62) was an Irish physician who in 1836 came to Santa Barbara, where he became a very wealthy land owner and stock raiser (PIONEER REGISTER).

178. Frémont to Abel Stearns

SAN FRANCISCO, Dec. 12, 1851

MY DEAR SIR,

I desire to sell my portion of the lots at the mission (San Francisco d'Asis). I think it better to sell now before any action of the commissioners, as there are parties here, Forbes & Co., I believe, who hold a title for the whole mission property.[1]

If you are desirous to sell, let me know in reply to this, and say what you would like to have done, or what you will probably ask for your property there. I remember that when you were last here you mentioned the subject to me, & were desirous to sell.

The drafts we had received from the Indian Commissioner, in payment for cattle, have been dishonored by the Department, & returned protested. There is no knowing when they will be paid, if ever; but fortunately for us I had made such arrangements that I shall not be much inconvenienced.

I shall be glad to hear from you at your earliest convenience. With regard, Yours,

JOHN C. FRÉMONT

Hon. Mr. Stearns
Los Angeles

ALS (CSmH—Stearns Collection). Endorsed: "Answered Eno. 13 de 1852."

1. In later years Mission San Francisco de Asís was more popularly known as "Mission Dolores." The orchard area, approximately seventy acres, had reputedly been given to José M. Andrade on 6 May 1846. Part of his claims was acquired by JCF and Stearns but, as JCF indicates here, there were other claimants to all or portions of the large and valuable mission property in San Francisco, including James R. Bolton, who with his partner William E. Barron was linked to Barron, Forbes, and Company of Tepic, Mexico (GATES [1], 28–30; Daily Alta California, 25 May 1850; House Report 243, 45th Cong., 2nd sess., Serial 1822).

Bolton had purchased the claim of the priest José Prudencio Santillan, who allegedly had received the entire mission, containing 29,717 acres, from Governor Pío Pico on 16 Feb. 1846 with the condition that he pay the debts of the mission. Bolton filed his petition for a patent with the California land commissioners and then sold the claim to JCF's business partner, George W. Wright, who in turn sold it to a group of investors in Philadelphia (Wright's deposition, 14 Nov. 1854, DNA-49, California Land Commission, Case No. 81, James R. Bolton v. United States, vol. V, Record of Evidence, 677–78). The investors organized a company known as the San Francisco Land Association, which worked to get a confirmation of the Santillan claim and the Noe Ranch claim. It was possible to own shares in either Santillan or Noe, or both, and Wright, Palmer, and JCF were among the many shareholders, with JCF's stock largely in Santillan.

The Land Commission confirmed the Santillan/Bolton claim in 1855 (U.S. Commission for ascertaining and settling private land claims in California, *Title papers, briefs of counsel, opinion of the board, and decree of confirmation in case no. 81, J. R. Bolton vs. the United States, for the lands of the ex-Mission of Dolores*, San Francisco, J. A. Lewis, 1855). The decision made squatters of the many people who were living on the mission lands and who thought they had good titles. They howled in protest. The U.S. Supreme Court reversed the decisions of the Land Commission and the District Court in 1859, holding that the grant lacked the proper documentation (64 *United States Reports*, 341–53). Ironically, a U.S. attorney used the Andrade grant against the Santillan, arguing that since the grant of the mission orchard lands was later by two months than the grant of all the mission lands, it raised the presumption that the earlier Santillan grant was invalid, or at least had become so by 6 May 1846. In resisting the Andrade claim a few years later, the United States introduced the Pueblo claim as a genuine grant, maintaining that an orchard would have been included in the four-league grant to the city (DWINELLE, 82).

The Philadelphia Land Association did not give up easily. It lobbied in Congress for a recognition of their investors' rights, and in 1876 the House Committee on Private Land Claims recommended (unsuccessfully) the enactment of legislation to allow the investors to try their claim again in the federal courts because of new evidence not previously available (House Report 344, 44th Cong., 1st sess., Serial 1709).

179. David Hoffman to Frémont

10 Conduit Street, Hanover Square, LONDON, 15 Dec. 1851.

[Introduces John Hamilton Clemment [Clement], superintendent of the Nouveau Monde Mining Company, who was going to the Mariposa with a staff of twenty-three, and requests that he be given the *very best possible selection that can be made.*" Clement had been previously employed by Taylor & Sons and had a practical knowledge of gold mining from twenty-five years' experience in Mexico. The organization of the Nouveau Monde in both France and England was "perfect" and the capital ample; more funds would be released after the company was in possession.

Robert was proceeding in a few days to see Benton, and Hoffman promises to send to JCF "by next steamer" a pamphlet "which will explain all" (Dec. 1851). Draft.]

180. David Hoffman to Frémont

16th December '51

My Dear Sir,

One day later than my letter of Introduction to Mr. Clemment [Clement], I have only to state that Mr. Sargent left here for New York to see Col. Benton. The *on dit* is that he carries with him only £10,000 or $50,000, but the next *on dit* an hour after is that it is only contracted to be sent to him in New York. If he had 20,000£ in cash, and security for all the rest, it would be madness to adopt him—New Contracts were offered me within the last three hours to the amount of £40,000 in addition to all the rest—but no one will do more than *deposit* your premiums, which will be at your call immediately after Col. Benton shall abandon his Enterprise—or *you* do the same effectually. I send the Globe paper,[1] which I pray you to read carefully. I am too much exhausted to write more. Yours faithfully,

DH

The mail has this moment arrived—not a line from you—the world here is *astounded*.

ALS (M. A. Goodspeed, Jr., Collection).
1. The *Globe*, 6 Dec. 1851, had contained an advertisement signed "Thomas Denny Sargent" in which Benton was represented as having written that Hoffman's leases since 7 July were not only "void but fraudulent."

181. Frémont to Pablo de la Guerra

San Francisco, Ca. Dec. 18, 1851

Dear Sir,

Accompanying this letter you will receive by Steamer Sea Bird the sum of two thousand dollars ($2000) which is the sum stipulated to be paid to the widow of [José Antonio] Dominguez for her interest in the rancho of San Emidio,[1] according to the deed executed before Sr. Carillo,[2] and which you kindly agreed to keep in your possession until I should be able to send the above sum of money. Accordingly, I will be greatly obliged to you if you will pay this sum to her, & send me the deed at some convenient opportunity.

It will reach me most safely & most directly by being sent for me to Messrs. Palmer, Cook & Co. of this city. With regard I am, Yours truly,

JOHN C. FRÉMONT

Hon. Dn. Pablo Noriega[3]
Santa Barbara

ALS (Old Mission, Santa Barbara Archive Library). Endorsed: "John C. Frémont to P. de la Guerra, Dec. 18, 1851."

1. By his 27 Nov. 1851 purchase of the interest of Francisca Villa de Dominguez, JCF acquired one-half interest (two leagues) in the ranch (Doc. No. 173).

2. Raimundo Carrillo, a notary public for Santa Barbara County.

3. The sons of José de la Guerra and Maria Antonia Carrillo, of whom Pablo was one, sometimes used their paternal grandmother's distinguished family name, Noriega (PIONEER REGISTER).

182. David Hoffman to Frémont

LONDON, 21 Dec. 1851

[Encloses the advertisement (printed below) he had prepared after the receipt of JCF's 8 Oct. letter, "which came to hand many days after" the 29 Oct. letter. "A Pamphlet [David Hoffman, *The Frémont Estate: An Address to the British Public, Respecting Col. Frémont's Leasing Powers to the Author, from June, 1850*] issued this day I have sent to Col. Benton and to Mr. Flandin and if you have not written to them, your estate is gone, or will be involved in great difficulties. . . ." JCF's "power to Colonel Benton" remains a mystery to Hoffman, who has carried out the contract of 12 Oct. with Prince Napoleon Bonaparte.[1] Refers to JCF's confirmation of the Agua Fria lease and notes: "If you had so instructed me it would have been done and my influence as your agent would have remained unimpaired." He intends drawing up a full statement for JCF. Draft.]

[*Hoffman's advertisement in the newspapers as printed in his pamphlet,*

The Frémont Estate, 60. *The advertisement did not appear in the London* Times.]

"NOTICE.—THE FRÉMONT PROPERTY.

"The Public are now finally informed, that all contracts for a lease, up to this 20th day of December, 1851, are valid, and are confirmed by Col. Frémont, by his letter received yesterday, by private hand, from San Francisco. No more contracts of lease will be executed by me after the *nineteenth* of December present—a determination I had previously come to. But my agency for further leasing is *only suspended* for a short time, as will appear by the following extract from his said letter; and all the existing *contracts* will be faithfully observed by me.

'I have to make you my thanks for the satisfactory and able manner in which you have acted for me, and will be happy to resume our business relations, and again avail myself of your able services, when I again resume my operations. I have all reason to believe that they will then be resumed with force and great profit, as our quartz rock is now assuming a fixed and undoubted value. I shall write to you regularly and frequently, and trust to hear regularly from you; hoping, notwithstanding the interruption of our business relations, to have your steady correspondence. Yours truly,

JOHN CHARLES FREMONT.

David Hoffman, Esq., London.'

"My leasing powers being now so happily suspended for a short time, the completion or carrying out of all the now existing contracts, or their speedy annulment, *ought* to follow. The course taken by Col. Fremont meets with my warmest approbation, especially as it has *no connection whatever* with the recent matter of Thomas Denny Sargent, as also appears by the letters of 1st October and 29th October; but arises solely out of Col. Fremont's present resolution, (having now retired from public life), to thoroughly develope his estate, and to possess me with the fullest acquaintance with his property, as preparatory to my renewal of my leasing powers. My agency for the execution of the now outstanding contracts remains as before; but for *no new* ones.

DAVID HOFFMAN."

1. Prince Napoleon was Joseph Charles Paul (1822–91), but known as Jérôme and also as Plon'-Plon': He was the son of the former king of Westphalia, Jérôme Bonaparte and his wife, Princess Catherine of Würtemberg. His older

brother, christened Jérôme, had died in 1847. His half-brother, Jérôme Napoleon, son of Elizabeth Patterson Bonaparte of Baltimore, was not involved in the companies that Hoffman hoped would be organized in France.

183. Frémont to David Hoffman

SAN FRANCISCO, CAL. Dec. 22. 1851

My dear Sir,

I have to acknowledge the receipt by the last mail of some packages of letters from yourself—a number were duplicates of letters already received & of old date. The accompanying letter which I send you is in way of part reply to points on which you make enquiries, & I presume, comprehends those points wh[ich] are of greatest interest to the British public. As regards my title to the Mariposas, the best answer I can make to you will be in communicating the action of the U.S. Commissioners upon it, which I think we shall have in 2 to 3 months. In the course of ten days the "*notice*" of the claim will be sent in to the Board, & I will perhaps find time to copy and send it to you. It will give you the history of the grant. In the mean time it will [be] sufficient to say to you that the grant was made by Micheltorena (who came here when Santa Anna was dictator) commanding general & governor of the Californias, & who by a special order of March 1842 (I think) was invested with the *supreme powers* of governnment. The grant was made *in consideration* of the public services of the grantee. These two points are, I suppose, sufficient to satisfy you. The following are answers to some other points proposed by you.

1. Heavy machinery can be taken to the mines as far as Stockton by water & thence by land.
2. *Any* weight whatever, at all likely to be required, can be taken to Stockton.
3. From Stockton the mode is by land carriage, & pieces of three tons may be carried to the mines of Mariposas.
4. I think that specimens would really be of no use to you, as they can be had of any conceivable witness, but then they do not indicate the character of the veins, which are not uniform.
5. No such minute survey has yet been made as to enable me to lay
6. down the veins on a map. The veins are numerous & the work
& just now would be very expensive. I shall wait until the title be

7. confirmed & I can get proper men to commence the work.

8. So soon as the title be confirmed we shall have complete protection against intruders.

9. I do not think there is water power capable of useful application, except in one or two localities on the place.

10. Coal has never been discovered on the place. I am told there is some on the opposite side (western) of the San Joaquin valley, near another property of mine, about 75 miles from Mariposas & 50 miles from the sea coast.[1] But this is not certain knowledge. I send you by Adams' Express a small specimen from a very large vein on that property. Will you please see what it contains & let me know at the earliest possible date. I shall take a receipt from Adams for the package & send it to you.

11. I cannot yet give you elevations.

12. These are the usual convenient facilities for transporting materials from the agricultural to the mining lands. Some agricultural land is dispersed throughout the mining land, but the main body of agricultural land is about 20 miles from the mining land. They in part run into each other.

13. There is no iron on the Mariposas property. There may be on the other above alluded to.

14. There are numerous machine shops, where machinery may be adjusted, at San Francisco.

15. are best answered by the accompanying letter.
&
16.

17. No machinery fit for use in this country can yet be transported across the Isthmus. By the Cape is the best way.

18. Agricultural lands range from four dollars to forty per acre—so far as my knowledge extends, for I have not made much enquiry. The price depends upon situation. Around this bay land is already high & next in value comes the land in the Sacramento and San Joaquin vallies.

19. I have several tracts in addition to the Mariposas & can therefore sell some land in fee. In small quantities I could not sell at less than ($4) four dollars per acre & in large at perhaps two dollars ($2). Valuable agricultural lands are not abundant, are generally in hands of individuals, & of course will rise in price, as the govt. will not have much to dispose of. By reference to your letter of August 11th. 1851, you will find the questions

which I have here replied to. I will keep the letter by me, & answer more strictly as I shall find myself able.

I have received a letter from the Nouveau Monde Company—Mr. Paganelli,[2] I believe, for I have it not by me. I reply by this mail. It is my intention to reserve a good location for that Company & the British Mutual, & for that purpose, among others, I shall go to the Mariposas in a few days. During a recent absence in the Southern part of the State, the Mineurs Belges arrived & went on to the Mariposas. I have sent on permission for them to occupy the houses on Stockton & Aspinwall's location, where they will be very comfortable during the winter. I shall propose to their director to examine the vein, which is a continuation of that on which the Mariposas Company is located, & of which you will remember Sir Henry Huntley speaks in his pamphlet. The yield at Stockton's mill, as I previously informed you, was forty-one (41$) dollars to the ton uniformly for a space of four consecutive months. From Mr. Goodell's[3] examination it appears that the mine was very unskillfully worked, & the gold not extracted from the ore, their process being very inefficient. I shall propose to the director of the Mineurs Belges to examine the ore carefully & thoroughly this winter, & if he likes that vein, I will give him the location. Pits & adits are already commenced where the work can be carried on under shelter & as the winter rains have now set in, it is the best thing he can do. It is storming heavily at this moment.

About the British Mutual? Can you tell me if it is finally registered? It was to have been done by the 10th July last. Have they deposited their funds in the manner, times, & amounts as stated in the contract? Frankly, I do not much like the permission you have given the Nouveau Monde to transfer without my consent. In granting leases, much is sometimes conceded to the character & position of the lessees.

I was gratified to know that Mr. Powles has been speaking to you in reference to a lease. He is the kind of man we want. A successful actual experience in a working company like that of St. John del Rey, is to me a great voucher for success here. Please show him Mr. Goodell's letter. He will understand it and know what calculations to base upon it.

Next year, I think we shall begin to know what our veins are & then I can give you more information. In the meantime you must be content with what you get from other sources. Mr. Goodell has great experience with machinery & is an enlightened practical miner. He thinks that we yet have no just conception of the great value and number of our veins. But we are daily making discoveries.

I believe that now I have brought up a little my correspondence with you, & now I can send from time to time such bits of information as present themselves. You have much to excuse in my infrequent letters, but I have been really borne down by business. Here, it is absolutely necessary to manage every thing myself, & I have been obliged to call in all my business & concentrate it in my own hands. I commence now to devote myself principally to my mining interests. Yours truly,

JOHN C. FRÉMONT

David Hoffman, Esqre.
London, Eng.

[*The next day JCF enclosed a clipping cut from the San Francisco Herald of 23 Dec. 1851, which read:*]

Rich Silver Mine—Messrs. Jacks & Woodruff have been receiving from some time past supplies of rich silver ore from a mine located in Southern California, about fifty miles from San Diego. This mine belongs to and is worked by a Spanish company, who keep their operations as secret as possible. They represent the vein as ten feet deep and fifteen varas wide, and capable of supplying an unlimited amount of ore. Messrs. J & W have smelted a quantity of the material, and it yields fifty per cent of pure silver. The ore itself is like galena, and contains a large proportion of lead. They have just received also a solid cubic block of auriferous quartz from Goodall & Co.'s mine, Mariposa county, weighing 125 pounds, and beautifully permeated and overlaid with gold. It is, for so large a piece of rock, one of the richest specimens yet found. It is worth from eight to ten dollars per pound.

The silver mine above mentioned is, we have reason to believe, on my property of San Emigio in the San Joaquin valley, & referred to in my letter of yesterday. The Mr. Goodall mentioned in the paragraph is Mr. Frederick Goodell, writer of the letter I send you, & the mine from [which] the block was taken is on my property & the same referred to in his letter to me. He is the inventor of the improvement for extracting gold which I mentioned to you in a previous letter. His statements may be relied on. He has put wages at a higher price than we are now paying, & put the yield of gold low. But his experience is the best & most reliable that I know of. He holds under a lease from me. Yours truly,

J. C. Frémont
Dec. 23

Hon. Mr. Hoffman
London

The above paragraph is cut from the *Herald* of today, F.

ALS (NHi—David Hoffman Papers). Addressed to Hoffman at 13 Half Moon Street, Piccadilly. Endorsed: "Recd. 14 Feb. '52."

1. A reference to his half-interest in Rancho San Emigdio (see Doc. No. 173).

2. Mons. Fabien Paganelli di Zicavo was gérant of the French branch of the Nouveau Monde.

3. Frederick Goodell not only had a mining claim in the Mariposa region by right of discovery, but also held leases directly from JCF and had subleased the mine and property of the Mariposa Mining Company. Within a few days of this letter to Hoffman, he would obtain from JCF a lease on a gold-bearing quartz vein below the works of Stockton & Aspinwall. See the Goodell claim and leases, dated 2 Aug., 16 Sept., 27 Oct., 29 Dec. 1851, and one cancellation, 19 Dec. 1852 (Mariposa County Records, Book 1, pp. 230, 275–80, 346–48, 471–72, and Book 2, pp. 19–22). With Ralph H. Lord he established a firm in San Francisco and in the spring of 1852 was in London trying to raise capital for the development of his interests on the Mariposa (Goodell to G. W. Wright, 30 April, 18 May, 1 June 1852, and to Joseph C. Palmer, 1 June 1852, M. A. Goodspeed, Jr., Collection).

184. Frémont to George W. Wright

San Francisco, Cal., Dec. 26, 1851

My dear Sir,

I was of course very much surprised on my arrival here to find you gone, & greatly regretted not to have seen you before you left. There were many points on which to agree, but we will do the best we can. All the requests contained in the letter you left for me shall be attended to. I have not yet been able to go to the Mariposas, but shall set out tomorrow afternoon. Another French Company, called "*The Belgian Miners*," have arrived there. They hold under lease from me, & their report to France will be of great importance. I will put them immediately on a good vein. During my absence in the South I obtained a good deal of information relative to mines. Ore from a very large vein was brought in, said to be silver ore, but the analyses made since it was brought here are very contradictory. I knew the locality & knew that it was covered by a private title. I therefore was able to buy half the interest in the whole place at a reasonable price & since my return here we have sold one fourth of the interest & the remainder *costs us nothing.*[1] By this mail I send a piece of the ore to England, & we shall know what it is. At all events we have gained a league and a half of good land, well watered, by the operation. We are engaged in other things, but they have not resulted. We have made a contract for removing the cattle during the winter from Vallejo's rancho to the Mariposas. How would good land sell per acre in the eastern market? I may have the control of a considerable quantity.

I trust, reasoning upon Col. Benton's letter of Novr. 9, to hear soon of the drafts being paid & I very much [hope] that you will be able to have my contracts with Wozencraft & Barbour confirmed by the Department. We all entertain hope that you will be able to get Beale the place of agent.[2] At all events we know that what can be done will be done. I write to Dr. Gwin by this mail, requesting his aid. It is reported here that Mr. [Hiland] Hall will not act as commissioner, & that consequently we shall have no commissioner for some months yet. But we trust that the President will send out others without delay. I mention this for your advisement. Wozencraft behaves badly. He has given to [Samuel J.] Hensley & others a contract for the supply of 1500 head of cattle.[3] He has himself gone below to Los Angeles, when Barbour ought to have gone, to make treaties with the Indians.[4] But I hope that your action will be such as to make his void. Yours truly,

J. C. Frémont

Hon. Mr. Wright
Washington.

ALS (CSmH).
1. He has sold one-half league, presumably for $2,000, of the two leagues he purchased from Francisca Villa de Dominguez on 27 Nov. 1851 (see Doc. No. 173).
2. Edward F. Beale was appointed Superintendent of Indian Affairs on 4 March 1852.
3. One who received a contract to supply 2,500 head of cattle at an average of 500 pounds each was Isaac Williams, owner of Rancho del Chino. According to "Orion" in the Los Angeles *Star*, 5 June 1852, he lost it because Wozencraft wanted $36,000 for his share of the profits rather than the $25,000 promised by

Williams. Three weeks later Wozencraft denied any truth in the story (see copies of letters from the Los Angeles *Star* in CSmH—George William and Helen Pruit Beattie Collection, B34 folder).

4. Barbour had planned to visit the tribes below Los Angeles when a threatened outbreak of Indians in the Tulare Valley forced him to go there. He subsequently went to San Francisco, where he learned that very little money had been appropriated for the Indian work in California. He asked for permission to go east and left his district in charge of Wozencraft. Trouble among the southern tribes prompted Wozencraft to go south in December with a military escort (ELLISON, 52, 54).

185. Frémont to William M. Gwin

SAN FRANCISCO, December 26th 1851

MY DEAR SIR,

The object of this note is to ask you to give me your aid in obtaining from the Department, a confirmation of the contracts made with the Indian Comms. & which I sent on by Lieut. Beale. You are aware of the circumstances of that transaction. I took up & carried through that contract at a time when no one else probably would have been found both willing & able to do so. Some consideration therefore ought reasonably to be shewn to us in any benefit that is hereafter to be derived.

Our friend Mr. Wright is thoroughly acquainted with this subject. He will be able to make you acquainted with particulars, if he has not already done so. Wozencraft has acted badly. He is now in the neighborhood of Los Angeles, treating with the Indians of Barbour's Dist. Before going down he gave to Hensley and others a contract for supplying 1500 head of cattle to the Indians in the San Joaquin. But this will be all set right if you have my contract confirmed. There should be but one agent for the management of these Indians. With proper subagents the work could then be carried on with more unity & more economically. Yours truly,

J. C. FRÉMONT

Hon. Mr. Gwinn
Washington City

LS (Lehigh University—Honeyman Collection).

186. Frémont to John McLoughlin

SAN FRANCISCO, CAL. Dec. 26th 1851

DEAR SIR,

I have to acknowledge the receipt of your letter of the 7th ult. which I read with satisfaction on account of the assurance it conveys to me of your continued good health. You refer to a statement made in Congress of an unfriendly disposition displayed by you to the immigrants arriving in Oregon from the Atlantic States,[1] and ask me to state what I saw of your conduct in 1843. I have not by me a copy of a report of that Journey made by me to Congress, but I am very sure that in it I made mention of your active and efficient kindness to the immigration of that year.[2] I was in the midst of that portion of the emigration which reached the lower Columbia in winter, many of them destitute or at least badly provided to meet the inclemency of winter. I had knowledge of several cases in which you aided the immigrants with stock and supplies without payment, together with valuable practical information to enable them to select their place of settlement. My general impression was that your disposition and acts were both unusually friendly to the immigrants, especially agreeable and useful to them at the close of their hard journey. I will make use of this occasion to repeat what I have always said publicly, and thank you for the kind and hospitable treatment I received from you in 1843. As we are now neighbors I am able to hope for an opportunity to reciprocate it but I can never hope to make it so agreeable, because I shall never find you in a situation to make hospitality so highly appreciated as yours was by me. With respect and regard I am Yours Truly,

JOHN C. FRÉMONT

Dr. John McLoughlin
Oregon City, Oregon

Copy (OrHi).
1. Oregon's first territorial delegate, Samuel R. Thurston (d. 9 April 1851), had charged that McLoughlin had tried to prevent the settlement of Oregon by Americans by emphasizing the hostility of the Indians, refusing aid to the travel-worn and destitute, and encouraging removals to California (see Thurston's speech, 26 Dec. 1850, *Congressional Globe*, 31st Cong., 2nd sess., Appendix, pp. 36–45). McLoughlin's biographers, HOLMAN, 246–52, and MONTGOMERY, 316–18, indicate the ulterior motives of Thurston and others in wishing to strip McLoughlin of his land claims.

2. See Vol. 2, pp. 566–67, for JCF's remarks on McLoughlin's kindness and hospitality to American immigrants.

187. John Duncan to Frémont

2, New Inn, Strand, London.
26th Dec. 1851.

To the Honourable John Charles Fremont,
San Francisco, California.
Sir,

In the absence of Mr. Thomas Denny Sargent, at New York, I take the liberty, as his solicitor, of addressing you, a liberty which I beg you to excuse: had he been in London he would himself have written to you, as following up his recent letter to you.

My letter is occasioned by the incessant attacks of your agent, Mr. Hoffman, made in print, upon Mr. Sargent and Colonel Benton; which attacks, while they every day tend to create a distaste in the public mind towards your mining property in California, do the grossest injustice to Mr. Sargent, who has from first to last conducted himself with the high bearing of a gentleman.

Should all Mr. Hoffman's long, confused, and jumbled letters, statements, advertisements, and pamphlets, be sent to you, as I presume they will, it will be difficult for you to find the actual facts. Assertions which are not facts, and scurrilous and unworthy language, such as I am sure must give you or any high minded man pain to read, you will find in abundance. I will, in very brief words, give you *actual facts*, which will serve to counteract prejudices which may be imbibed from Mr. Hoffman's communications to you—facts which you can probe to the bottom—facts which will show that towards you, the British public, Mr. Hoffman himself, and, indeed, everybody, Mr. Sargent has acted as a straightforward, honourable man of business.

Mr. Hoffman, being evidently of a slanderous disposition, and of uncontrollable pen and tongue, has attempted to injure me along with Mr. Sargent, because I have acted for the latter professionally. His slanders I disregard—I am amenable to public investigation and opinion: those who seek truth, and wish to find it, may examine all my transactions and operations from first to last, with Mr. Sargent; and I am satisfied that they can arrive at no other conclusion but that Mr. Hoffman is a reckless calumniator, and that the conduct of both Mr. Sargent and myself has been that of scrupulous integrity, and also of great forbearance towards Mr. Hoffman, except when his vile personal attacks provoked retaliation.

I proceed to the narrative of *actual facts*.

You will well remember, that on the 30th of April, 1850, you signed at Washington a lease of a gold mine to Mr. Sargent. He was to proceed to California to locate it. That lease did not contain any covenant for him to erect machinery by any fixed period, such as was introduced into the next lease you signed to him.

You will also well recollect, that on the 21st of May, 1850, you signed at Washington a lease to Mr. Sargent of *another mine*, which he was to proceed to California to locate.

On the 3rd of May, 1850, he parted with two-thirds of his interest in the first mentioned lease, to Messrs. Eldridge and Harpur [*sic*].

In the autumn of 1850 Mr. Sargent proceeded to California,[1] and located the first-mentioned lease, at a spot adjoining on the west to the mine of the Mariposa Company,—a mine called the Fremont Mine, intervening between the Mariposa Company's mine and Mr. Sargent's location. To this located mine Mr. Sargent at the time gave the name of the "Santa Maria." Its location, as you are aware, was on the banks of the Mariposa River.

At the same period, Mr. Sargent located the second mentioned lease on a gold quartz vein, situated on the bank of the Ave Maria River, and to this mine he gave the name of the "San Carlos."

The proper certificates of location were in each case signed by your then local agent at Mariposa, Mr. G. Heap.

Messrs. Sargent, Eldridge, and Harpur ordered and purchased, as you are probably aware, machinery to work the Santa Maria Mine; but experience (I believe your own) had with considerable loss discovered, that this machinery would be too light and useless.

Mr. Sargent then determined to come to England so soon as practicable, to endeavour to procure large capitals to work both these mines. He negotiated with Mr. Eldridge (Mr. Harpur being dead) to re-purchase the two-thirds interest in the Santa Maria Mine.

He arrived in London in the spring of 1851, and proceeded immediately to try to form a Company for working the San Carlos Mine, of which the whole, as a leasehold for seven years, was his own sole property; he did not then attempt anything with the Santa Maria Mine, as he did not possess the transfer of the two-thirds interest, held by Mr. Eldridge, and his title to it, in consequence, was not clear.

The friends to whom he applied for help, seeing the clause in the San Carlos lease, that the machinery ought to have been put up in one year, and that the lease was for seven years only, from May, 1850, applied to Mr. Hoffman to make the term twenty-one years, and to extend the period for putting up the machinery. Acting sensibly for your interests, that gentleman executed an instrument in due legal form, drawn up by himself, for both purposes. He received his fee for this, as described to me by Mr. Sargent, in the following manner: A person named Smith, who acted with Mr. Hoffman, in the matter, obtained from Mr. Sargent his acceptance at three months date for £225. The engagement made with Mr. Sargent was that the acceptance should not be used if Mr. Sargent should fail to form a Company to purchase the San Carlos lease, so extended to twenty-one years. Disregarding this engagement, and before the lease was sold to a Company, the acceptance was used; it was discounted; and the proceeds of discount were divided between Mr. Hoffman and Mr. Smith. The bill remaining in third hands—the discounters after it became due to prevent Mr. Sargent setting up to it the good defence he had as against Hoffman and Smith—he was vindictively arrested upon it and thus forced to settle it, in order to release himself from custody, at a time when his attendance on capitalists in London was hourly requisite.

Mr. Sargent and his friends, after obtaining this extension from Mr. Hoffman, continued their operations to form a Company and procure a capital. But at this period (say May and June, 1850 [1851]), even up to September, or rather October, the capitalists of England viewed with absolute indifference the project of working gold mines in California. He consequently made very little progress, although he formed good connections.

In June, Mr. Sargent went back to the United States, mainly to complete his arrangements with Mr. Eldridge as to obtaining an actual re-transfer of the two-thirds of the Santa Maria Mine. He met with Col. Benton and Mr. Flandin. They proposed to him to purchase the entire Mariposa estate from you. After negociations he agreed upon terms. *They were reduced to writing, and signed by Mr. Flandin and himself on 7th July, 1851, and attested to by Colonel Benton.* Not the least blame could attach to Mr. Sargent in this proceeding, as regards you: he simply agreed to buy what was offered to him on sale. Again, those acting for you, Col. Benton and Mr. Flandin, could not I presume be to blame, *because the contract of sale was made expressly conditional, that unless you should ratify it then it was to be null and void.*

Mr. Sargent, soon after signing this contract, returned to England, and Mr. Flandin and Col. Benton both thought fit to address letters to Mr. Hoffman, requesting him to stay all action on his part, as regards leases until you could be communicated with.

At these letters Mr. Hoffman took deep offense, and, in truth, the chance of sale of the estate seems to have driven him nearly mad with rage. What was Mr. Sargent's conduct on his arrival in England, and for months afterwards? To boast of having made the purchase, or assume any pretensions as owner in consequence?—Not in the least. Being conscious that there was in fact no sale at all, unless you confirmed it in due form,—he awaited your ratification. In the interval he received letters from Colonel Benton, which said that Mrs. Fremont approved of the sale; and also letters from Mr. Flandin, which copied a passage from one of your letters of the date of 1st September last, in these words:—

"It is rumoured in the papers, and not clearly intimated in a letter from Mr. Sargent, that you have sold the Mariposas: *if*, [*sic*] *so I entirely approve it.* I intend to send you a copy of the papers relating to the grant."

Such letters satisfied Mr. Sargent that the ratification would come; but still he remained wholly silent on the subject until the receipt of 10th November, from Col. Benton, hereafter mentioned.

I must now, in point of dates, go back in my narrative to explain Mr. Sargent's proceedings between August, when he arrived in England, and the end of November, when he received Col. Benton's said letter of the 10th of that month.

In the first place, he used his best endeavours to get the Company formed to work the San Carlos Mine. With that Company I personally had nothing to do. The parties who proposed to Mr. Sargent and to his agent in London, Mr. Green, to form the Company, did not succeed, and, therefore, he failed in this quarter to sell his San Carlos Lease.

Whilst these negociations were proceeding, (end of October) he was introduced to me by Mr. Green, for the purpose of my forming a Company for him and obtaining the capital to work the Santa Maria Mine,—the transfer of the two-thirds formerly vested in Mr. El-

303

dridge, having arrived in London, and being at Mr. Sargent's disposal on payment of about £600. I carefully examined all the documents, and found them correct. I saw that the lease was signed by yourself, and knew that it could be depended upon as the act of a gentleman of high honour and integrity. I accepted the business, and went immediately to work. As a practical man, knowing the English market for mining property, I advised, as a preliminary, to change the name of the mine from "Santa Maria," which I thought would be objectionable, to the "West Mariposa Mine." I was guided to the new name simply by the plain and straightforward fact that the Santa Maria Mine had its position to the *west* of, and closely adjacent to the Mariposa Mine (a known property), and upon the same gold quartz vein. I succeeded with my friends in less than three weeks in forming the Company, by the name of the "West Mariposa Gold Quartz Mining Company," and obtaining the capital. I delivered to the Company the original lease, signed by you, and verified to be your signature by the Hon. Abbott Lawrence, the American Ambassador. It was transferred by Mr. Sargent to the Company. The papers relating to the two-thirds were paid for and handed over to the Company, and the Title completed.

Mr. Sargent represented to the Directors of the Company the facts as to the sale of the Estate just as he knew them, not carrying them one whit farther than the documents in his hands established. He promised that should he, by your ratification of the sale, and by the completion of his part, become the purchaser, he would extend the term of the lease from seven to twenty-one years; and he further engaged, that if he did not become the purchaser, he would use his interest with you to extend the term of the lease, and to do every act in your power to give strength and ratification to it, and to co-operate with the Company in promoting its success. I am quite sure, that in these latter promises he only anticipated your own sentiments and feelings; and was protecting your interests, which could not be promoted by anything so much as by the outlay of the West Mariposa Capital upon a mine of which you were the Freeholder entitled to a sixth of the proceeds.

I have before stated, that this lease of the West Mariposa (Santa Maria) Mine did not contain any clause to put up machinery by a fixed period. No forfeiture of it, therefore, had taken place, or could take place; and Mr. Hoffman's aid, as your agent, to remove any forfeiture was consequently not wanted, and was not sought. In the face, also, of what had taken place on the 7th July, as to the sale of the Mariposa Estate to Mr. Sargent, and of the notices from Mr. Flandin and Col. Benton to Mr. Hoffman, it would not have been consistent of Mr. Sargent to apply to Mr. Hoffman for an extension to twenty-one years. He was not applied to. Now, I am sorry to say it of Mr. Hoffman, but his strange conduct drives me to the statement, that I sincerely believe that he was not applied to, and therefore did not get his fee,—and because his vanity was not flattered,—and, further, because he owed Mr. Sargent a grudge, as having dared, without his permission, to attempt to purchase your Mariposa Estate, he commenced a virulent and calumniating hostility towards the West Mariposa Company, which has unquestionably tended to its depression in the eyes of those, who are too careless, or who have not time, to enquire into actual truth, and who are carried away by bold assertions. In particular Mr. Hoffman has been ceaseless in intimating that the lease contains the same forfeiture clause as to putting up machinery in one year as other leases of yours do, *when such insinuations are positively false.* Have these attacks, founded in untruth and injustice, done you or your property any good? The contrary. Your bitterest enemy could not have devised any greater mischief to your real interests than your agent has practised by his impulsive love of rushing into print, and throwing about in all directions violent, coarse, and vulgar slanders.

Under his attacks the West Mariposa Company have remained calm. They know that they possess a valid lease for the remainder of the seven years. They have appointed Mr. Macdougall, of New York, a gentleman of character and experience in mining, to take possession of the Mine.[2] They are selecting a mining staff, and procuring machinery; and they intend to work the mine vigorously under his directions, for the benefit of the Shareholders as to five-sixths—and for your benefit as to one-sixth.

If the sale of your estate to Mr. Sargent should, from any circumstances, not be completed, they will be rejoiced to remain your lessees; and Mr. Macdougall will, in due time and form make the application to you to extend the term of the lease to twenty-one years, in like manner as you have done to the Agua Fria Company, which Company also, although of the highest standing, has not escaped from Mr. Hoffman's sarcasms and insinuations.

I will now briefly tell you the further facts relating to the San Carlos Mine. The Company I have referred to, seeking to purchase it, did not succeed in forming itself. The lease and papers were delivered back to Mr. Sargent, and handed to me. Mr. Hoffman had by this time so *spoiled the market for your leases*, that with the public I could do nothing. To that lease, as I have before explained, I possessed Mr. Hoffman's own ratification, and an absolute extension to twenty-one years; but still his publications and advertisements had been so prejudicial that I could not possibly form a new Company at that period.

A singular circumstance then occurred. The Directors of a Company called the "Ave Maria Company," which had obtained its capital from the public to work a gold mine on your estate, upon the Ave Maria River, applied to me, as Mr. Sargent's Solicitor, to purchase the lease of the San Carlos Mine. With the formation of that Company,—its basis—its prospectus—its operations—and its advertisements, neither Mr. Sargent nor myself ever had the least concern. Every director and officer of that Company can vouch for this fact. When applied to, *at the end of November*, to sell the San Carlos Mine, a representation was made to Mr. Sargent that he had already authorised the sale of it to the Company, and that because it was located on the banks of the Ave Maria River it had been called the Ave Maria Mine. Mr. Sargent denied, as was the fact, that he had ever authorized the sale of the lease. The original document, with Mr. Hoffman's deed extending it, was then in my hands; and he refused to treat with the Company upon any other footing than that they did now (end of November), knowing that he had the San Carlos Mine lease, apply to him to sell it to the Ave Maria Company, *as an application then for the first time made*. To this the Company assented; terms of sale were made, and the San Carlos lease was transferred to the Ave Maria Company. Their large paid up capital will be applied to work it. Their miners and machinery will start in a few days; and, therefore, your Lessee, Mr. Sargent, in his character as that Lessee, had done you every justice as his Landlord, *and will have brought upon two of your mines very large capitals*. He does not doubt for a moment but that you will duly appreciate his exertions—that you will rejoice at any success of his in the transactions of sale of these two leases—and that you will assist and co-operate with the agents and staff of both companies— the West Mariposa and the Ave Maria—and assent to every reasonable application their agents may make which will give energy to their operations and satisfaction to the Directors and Shareholders and the public in England who have depended on your high standing and honourable name.

I now arrive at the last few facts of this long narrative, the length of which you must excuse, and I know readily will; because your sense of justice will desire that Mr. Sargent should have the opportunity of clearing away the vile aspersions made upon his character.

Upon the 22nd of November there arrived from Col. Benton the letter of the 10th of November, of which a copy is enclosed. A few days afterwards another letter arrived from him, of which a copy is also enclosed.³ Neither of these letters did Mr. Sargent at the time print or publish. They were produced to the Directors of the West Mariposa Company, and to some persons sent by Mr. Hoffman's friends to inspect them. Can any possible blame attach to Mr. Sargent for receiving them—for believing them—for allowing them be read? Their authenticity was doubted. He placed them at once in the hands of two gentlemen of the highest character,—Sir Edward Belcher, a Captain in the Royal Navy,—and Mr. Ambrose Moore, a Director of one of the most opulent London Banks, to get them verified. They made enquiries in proper quarters, and when completed, they expressed their conviction that they were the genuine letters of Col. Benton, every word in his own hand-writing. Mr. Sargent then simply prepared himself to depart for New York, upon Col. Benton's invitation and, while thus occupied, Mr. Hoffman continued his public attacks, and fell foul of an East Mariposa Mine Company which had been formed without the least co-operation with Mr. Sargent in the first instance. Mr. Sargent did afterwards endeavour to assist that Company for your interests as well as his own, by promising a lease to it of mining ground on the Mariposa Estate; which lease, if confirmed by you, in case Mr. Sargent should see reason not to complete his purchase of the Freehold, would have carried the right to you to receive the royalties from the working of the East Mariposa Mine. Mr. Hoffman, looking to your interests, must have seen, that if he could help to collect another capital to work another mine upon your estate, viz.:—the East Mariposa Mine,—he should have assisted. But again, his head-strong vanity could brook nothing that did not come before the public under the sanction of his "Sole agency for Europe," and he has done his utmost to injure and destroy the East Mariposa Company.

That Company published a paragraph without consulting Mr.

Sargent, or asking his consent, to the effect that they had received a contract of lease from Mr. Sargent who "*had purchased*" the Mariposa Estate.

These were not his words—he never would have used such—Mr. Hoffman however instantly charged Mr. Sargent with the authorship, and made upon him a virulent personal attack in the "Globe Newspaper," and Mr. Sargent then, for the first time, published Colonel Benton's letter of the 10th of November, but confining that publication, by my advice, to the same daily paper, the "Globe," in which Mr. Hoffman's attack had appeared, and to two weekly newspapers, in which Mr. Sargent had also been personally attacked with much violence.

I here conclude the narrative. The result is that Mr. Sargent in a fair, honourable, and straightforward manner, has sold two of the leases held from you direct—the Santa Maria Lease, now West Mariposa, neither forfeited nor forfeitable—and the San Carlos Lease, now Ave Maria, extended, by Mr. Hoffman's own signature, to twenty-one years—and that large capitals will be sent from England to work them both; and, doubtless, they will be highly prosperous undertakings, and produce large royalties to you or to any purchaser from you, (be he Mr. Sargent himself or anybody else), should your gold quartz mines possess a richness equal to their reputation. Further, Mr. Sargent having signed a contract to buy your Estate, which he was invited by friends in your interest to do, has proceeded to New York, (upon Col. Benton's express invitation as holding your full power of attorney) to complete the purchase.

The result of the narrative, also, is to show, that Mr. Hoffman, although he had to thank the brilliant success of the West Mariposa Company, as the groundwork on which he was able to launch into new life the dead schemes of the Nouveau Monde and Golden Mountain Companies, has done his utmost to spoil the undertakings of the West Mariposa and Ave Maria Companies, and to drive them to return their capitals to the shareholders, instead of sending them to California to largely benefit your pocket.

I shall take the liberty of addressing you again, should I find it necessary, and I remain, with great respect, Sir, Your most obedient Servant,

JOHN DUNCAN

P.S.—1st. January, 1852. I have found myself compelled to print this letter, as the best answer to a long pamphlet issued by Mr. Hoffman. The public now have the actual facts.

Printed in DUNCAN, 4–12. John Duncan was a London solicitor and promoter of companies and would write *Practical Directions for Forming and Managing Joint-Stock Companies . . . under the Provisions of the "Joint Stock Companies Act, 1856,"* 2 pts. (London, 1856).

1. The *Daily Alta California*, 16 Aug. 1850, noted the arrival of Sargent, Eldridge, and Harper in the *Northerner* at San Francisco.

2. The West Mariposa Gold Quartz Mine Company's advertisement noted that John MacDougall's experience was in the mining operations of Cuba and Mexico (London *Times*, 11 Dec. 1851).

3. Not printed. In his two letters to Sargent, dated 10 and 12 Nov. from Washington, Benton wrote that he had received from JCF "his full, and regularly authenticated power of attorney, to ratify and carry into effect the conditional sale" of the Mariposa that had been made in July. He was going to St. Louis but would return in eight days after being telegraphed of Sargent's arrival in New York and readiness to complete the transaction (DUNCAN, 12–13).

188. Eulogio de Célis to Frémont

Sr. Don Juan Fremont   ANGELES December 31, 1851
DEAR SIR AND FRIEND:

Until the receipt of your letter I did not know the reason why the cattle of our agreement last July had not been moved, because my questions to Sr. Arellanes on the delivery had been answered saying that no one had presented himself to receive them and that the good weather had ended and afterwards there was no cavalcade to serve because of the bad weather. For my part I am very sorry that you were upset but the difficulties which you have suffered depend more on the season so badly chosen than on lack of compliance. You were present here at my agreement with Stearns on the delivery of the 1200 cattle which you know were to be delivered 20 days later than the notice; well, on receipt of the notice, he replied that he did not have a horse that would go 10 miles. And it is certain that the weather this year has been very bad. We had 12 days of continuous water. The fields next March will present a beautiful aspect.

The war, the uprisings and all that you have seen of the Indians, are some of the things that have always happened in this country. Hopefully, your trip to the Indian tribes will not be interrupted.

I believe that it is not necessary that I take steps in regard to Sr. Arellanes, convinced as I am that actually the failure to deliver the cattle was because he did not have the resources of men and horses, but loyally he will do soon, because I know that he hoped to make delivery in August. Thus I remain at your disposition, your affectionate servant QSMB [who kisses your hand],

Eulogio de Celis

ALS in Spanish (M. A. Goodspeed, Jr., Collection). Translated by M. K. Swingle of the California Historical Society.

Frémont in Europe

189. Frémont to David Hoffman—Letter 1

SAN FRANCISCO, Jany. 15th. 1852

MY DEAR SIR,

I have received your several letters of the 20th & 25th of November last and argue from them that it is absolutely necessary for me to go for a few days to London which I will accordingly do. I will endeavor to leave this on the 1st of February and connect at Chagres with the English steamer of the 28th. Will you do me the favor to address me a note at Southhampton, informing me which hotel I had best go to in London. I would not give you this trouble but that I shall have my family with me & might otherwise be inconvenienced. I think that my letters received by you after the 25th of November will satisfy you that you were somewhat hasty in the course you adopted. You will see that I have made every effort to stop the sale of the Mariposas—the only company arrived here recently is the Mineurs Belges. They arrived during my absence and went immediately to the Mariposas. I have not seen or heard from them, but tomorrow I send an agent there expressly to locate them.

The exaggerated statements in regard to yields of gold published in the London Times have furnished the foundation of an attack upon me in one of the newspapers, with the cooperation of a self styled geologist (there is no such office as *state geologist*).[1] The object of the attack was twofold—1st to discredit the title and thus give a chance for success in the London market to companies whose operations are on lands without the security of a title. 2dly to increase that chance by depreciating the Mariposas & exaggerating the value of other districts.

All this was produced by the success of your operations as described in the Times & copied in the Herald of this place. They will send copies of their articles to the London Mining Journal. I send you by various sources the only reply that I have thought proper to make.[2]

I will write to you again by the steamer of the 21st inst. & which will join the mail by which this letter goes. Yours truly,

JOHN CHARLES FRÉMONT

David Hoffman, Esqre.
London

ALS-JBF (NHi—David Hoffman Papers). Endorsed: "Recd, 1st March 1852."

1. JCF is referring to an editorial in the Stockton *Journal*, 14 Jan. 1852, which attacked his title and alluded to "grand company schemes" being organized in Europe for working the quartz mines of Las Mariposas. It especially mentioned the Nouveau Monde Mining Company and found it hard to believe that JCF had lent the influence of his name to such "a nefarious scheme." It cited John B. Trask, "state geologist," as the authority for the view that the value of the gold veins on JCF's claim was greatly exaggerated. The editor called for an explanation of the matter, alleging that "an outrageous fraud has been or is about to be perpetrated." See Stockton *Journal* material in *Daily Alta California*, 15 Jan. 1852.

2. JCF's reply was to collect testimonials of geologists and assayers as to the value of his property and to have them printed in the *Daily Alta California*, 16 Jan. 1852 (Doc. Nos. 192–94). He also brought suit for libel against Trask and the Stockton *Journal* (*Daily Alta California*, 9 Feb. 1852).

190. Frémont to David Hoffman—Letter 2

SAN FRANCISCO, Jany. 15th, 1852
9 o'clock P.M.

MY DEAR SIR,

I desire you to have published in the Times for which this letter will be your full authority, a notice "that all leases for land upon the Mariposas the holders of which have not complied with all their stipulations, particularly as regards time for putting up their machinery are hereby declared to be, and will be strictly held to be, forfeited." I have within the hour received your notice of the 11th [10th] November & send this in reply, having just mailed a letter which you will receive.

Sargent has no living lease from me. I have never renewed or extended any lease to him and no one else had the power to do so but yourself. He has applied to me, some time since for such extension, but I have not even answered his letter. He has no authority from me, no relation or connection with me, social, friendly, or legal, & I disown & repudiate everything coming from him purporting to come from me. So far from having any letters from Mrs. Frémont he is not even known to her by sight—his acquaintance with me amounting to a few business interviews in Washington in the spring of '50. Make any use of the above you please either in print or otherwise; the letters, *if written by Mrs. Frémont* must have been stolen ones addressed to her Father, otherwise they are forgeries.

Please inform Mr. Andrew Smith or other gentlemen who may reach this country during my absence with you that they will apply for information as to their locations to my solicitors Messrs. Jones Strode & Tompkins[1] or to the banking house of Palmer Cook & Co. Your transactions, as communicated to me up to the 20th of November, meet with my entire approval.

Bissell's company[2] which is referred to in the publication of today & which I send you commenced their operations in August last—the dividends of the other companies referred to are monthly dividends. I keep this open to enclose to you the slips from the printing office.

I will bring with me what evidence I judge necessary for the Mariposas title. The Commissioner's hold their first sitting on the 21st and the Mariposas title has been already laid before them. We shall now soon have the title so regulated & in such process of confirmation that we can go to work with increased strength & then agreeably to my former letters your operations can be resumed. Every day we are acquiring fixed knowledge & the publication of today which you can rely upon is in that respect very interesting.

A principal cause of failure in companies formed in the United States to operate in gold here, is in the agents they send. These immediately on arriving set themselves to work to make their own fortunes, using for that purpose the position in which they are placed by their company sending them. I do not charge this as universal, but as frequently the case within my knowledge. My object in saying it, is, that you may call to it, the attention of the companies formed for the Mariposas. It is of vital importance to their success that they should send only men of approved character who are directly interested in the success of their company. So far, I have seen nothing of, & heard nothing from the Belgian company, hearing accidentally that they had arrived at the Mariposas I sent to have comfortable houses put at their disposition for the winter & tomorrow send an agent to put them on their location.

The slips do not come from the press. I will endeavor to get them off by the express. Yours truly,

JOHN CHARLES FRÉMONT

David Hoffman Esqre.
London

ALS-JBF (NHi—David Hoffman Papers). Endorsed: "Recd. 1st March 1852."
1. A reference to the San Francisco legal firm of his brother-in-law, William Carey Jones.
2. "Bissell's company" is the Gold Hill Quartz Mining Company, which operated in Grass Valley in present-day Nevada County (see Doc. No. 192 and GUDDE [1], 134). G. W. P. Bissell was treasurer in Jan. 1852 when the company paid a dividend of 10 percent on its capital stock (unidentified newspaper clipping, Hoffman Papers). By the end of the year it had two mills, one having a steam engine of twenty-five horsepower, driving eighteen stampers, capable of crushing thirty tons per day, and the other sixty-five horsepower, driving ten stampers. The quartz was yielding from $45 to $50 per ton and the company was capitalized at $1 million (*Hunt's Merchants Magazine*, 27 [Dec. 1852], p. 753, citing San Francisco's *Placer Times and Transcript*).

191. Frémont to John L. Moffat

SAN FRANCISCO, January 1852

DEAR SIR:

A slanderous attack having been made upon my Mariposas property,[1] and through it upon me, directed, among other things, to discredit the value of the property as a gold-bearing tract, with the evident object of giving, by contrast, increased value to other portions of the mining districts, I have thought it advisable to apply to you, among other gentlemen, as eminently qualified, by your great experience, and connection with gold mining generally, and more particularly to California, for a written expression of your opinion in the case. The points on which I more particularly desire the expression of your knowledge are these:

1st. What is your opinion as to the general value and extent of the gold-bearing district of Agua Frio and Mariposas?

2d. Have you visited any particular localities there, and if so, what do you judge to be the quantity of gold contained in the average ton of vein?

3d. Were the mining operations at the Mariposas so conducted as to extract the greater portion of the gold from the rock?

4th. Have you at any time made a personal examination of the Mariposas mine, and if so, will you please state your opinion of its general character, and how much per ton you could obtain by proper working of the mine?

5th. Have any dividends been declared upon the capital stock, of any companies in California, and if so, what amount?

An early answer to these enquiries will greatly oblige. Yours,

J. C. Fremont

Printed in *Daily Alta California*, 16 Jan. 1852. Exact or similar letters were addressed by Frémont to Samuel Count Wäss and Frederick Goodell. For the replies, see Doc. Nos. 192–94.

1. This is a reference to the critical editorial in the Stockton *Journal*, 14 Jan. 1852, about which JCF had written to Hoffman (Doc. No. 189).

192. John L. Moffat to Frémont

San Francisco, January 15, 1852

Dear Sir:

I have the honor to acknowledge the receipt of your note growing out of the publication in a Stockton paper, of certain slanderous charges against you, in causing to be published in the English papers, greatly exaggerated statements of the richness of the veins on your claims in Mariposa County.

You ask my judgment on the general value and extent of the Agua Frio and Mariposa. I have twice visited the Mariposa vein, in March and July last. In both instances I judge from what I saw and what I learned, that it was producing then and have averaged for several months, forty dollars per ton, worked with close mortars and shaking tables. With better amalgamators, I am of opinion twice that amount could have been saved from the same ore.

I have not visited any other vein in that region than the Mariposa, with a view to form an opinion of its richness. It is a general characteristic of the veins in California that they improve as they go down, and such, so far as I could learn and observe, is the case with this one. It showed rich at the depth of forty-two feet, when I was there in July.

The mining operations at Mariposa, so far as the mechanism was concerned, were very good, but the plan then used can never be made, in my judgment, to save half the gold. The general character of the Mariposa rock is hard, and requires burning, after which it can be reduced with comparative ease.

Of the Agua Frio veins I cannot speak from my own knowledge, but to judge from what I was told, and from the great number that flocked there, I must conclude they are at least as rich as the Mariposa.

With regard to dividends on gold stock, the company of which Mr. [G. W. P.] Bissell is a director, at Grass Valley, the "Gold Mountain Mining Co." [the Gold Hill Quartz Mining Company] I believe is the name, have paid back the capital to those who advanced it, and divided ten per cent for the month of December. Three others I have heard of, but don't recollect the names, have divided one 10, one 11, and one 15 per cent [*per month*] on their capitals.[1] I have the honor to be very respectfully, Your friend,

JOHN L. MOFFAT

Printed in *Daily Alta California*, 16 Jan. 1852, and is a reply to JCF's letter of Jan. 1852 (Doc. No. 191).
1. See JCF to Hoffman, 17 Jan. 1852 (Doc. No. 195).

193. Frederick Goodell to Frémont

SAN FRANCISCO, Jan. 15, 1852

DEAR SIR:

In reply to your communication I can say that I have thoroughly tested the quartz vein known as the "Mariposa Vein" to the depth of forty-two feet, and found the quartz to increase in richness the deeper down I went. I have crushed the quartz to the extent of several hundred tons, and extracted the gold by the use of the shaking tables, which were on the place previous to my visiting Mariposa, and were very imperfect in their construction. I have also tested quartz from many veins upon your property, and the results varied from two cents to eight dollars and fifty cents from the pound of rock.

The vein known as the "Mariposa Vein," and upon which I have been operating, varies in thickness from three to twelve feet, and can supply one hundred tons of quartz per day for years to come, without a question of doubt. In my own opinion I do not think the vein can be exhausted in a century. The veins upon your property in the Mariposa and Agua Frio districts are numerous and rich in gold; and I am confident that large results can be realized by a judicious outlay of capital and the use of heavy and well constructed machinery. If unfavorable results have emanated in working on any vein in the districts I have named, it is to be attributed entirely to the light and imperfect machinery used, and the limited amount of capital expended without a knowledge of mining and machinery. In regard to the extent of the quartz veins upon your property, I feel perfectly safe in saying that they cannot be exhausted in this century. With reference to the letters recently published and signed by John B. Trask,[1] styling himself a geologist, I do not consider them worthy of notice. These letters, over the above named signature, make mention of the quartz veins, and the formation of the Mariposa and Agua Frio districts, and the statements therein made I know from personal explorations of that district to be entirely false and incorrect. I view the gentleman as one of the very many self styled geologists, who have, from interests best known to themselves, caused much injury to the mining interests of California.

As my time is very limited, I am compelled to be thus brief, intending at a future period to give you my views and experience more in detail. I am, sir, very respectfully, Your ob't. serv't.

FREDERICK GOODELL

Hon. John Charles Frémont, S. Francisco

P.S. In regard to your title to the Mariposa and Agua Frio districts, I had occasion to examine your title, in taking a lease from you, and found it satisfactory to me. In my mind there is not a question of doubt as to the validity of your title.

F.G.

Printed in *Daily Alta California*, 16 Jan. 1852.
1. Born in Roxbury, Mass., John B. Trask (1824–79) was a man of great erudition. He had been a member of the Mexican boundary survey and would

become the first state geologist of California as well as a founding member of its Academy of Sciences. In 1853 he published a map entitled *Topographical Map of the Mineral Districts of California*, which GUDDE [1], 424, terms a "landmark" in the cartography of the mining region. It and his *Map of the State of California*, also published in 1853, are reproduced in WHEAT [2].

194. S. Count Wäss to Frémont

[SAN FRANCISCO, 15 Jan. 1852]

MOST RESPECTED SIR:

Circumstances and misfortune having banished me from my beloved native country, the love of natural sciences, particularly those of Geology and Mineralogy, have induced me not only to visit California, but perhaps to find here a new and quiet home. In the first days of my arrival, I have been so happy as to enjoy your hospitality, on your property situated on the Mariposa Creek. Struck by the beauty and interestingness of the formation there, I was very soon decided to stay for a longer time in those quarters, which was greatly facilitated by your kind hospitality, and I have passed one whole year on the Mariposa Creek and its vicinity. In the first three or four weeks of my sojourn, I have paid particular attention especially to the auriferous formation, which is very interesting on your property. During this time I have examined more than thirty points of auriferous formations, having subjected the minerals to regular metallurgical operations and chemical assays, and I can not only ascertain, but chemically prove to you that with very few exceptions, almost all of them have showed traces of fine metal, and some of them gave the most satisfactory results which might be expected for the most advantageous and lucrative mining operations. Besides these points which I have examined, I have found a great many other points which I am sure would give, by a regular examination, the same results. But to prove the nature of the auriferous formations situated on your property, it is enough to give some account about the only two veins which have been opened and worked till this day, on your property, the so called Mariposa veins, where the works of the Mariposa Mining Company are established, and the Guadalupe vein, situated on the Agua Frio Creek. Having been employed by the Mariposa Mining Company to open the vein and point out the levels, I had the opportunity of examining that vein thoroughly, and I myself confess that I never saw a more perfect, more highly developed formation.

During my sojourn at Mariposa and the environs, I have made a great many excursions, partly to know the country, partly to acquire more knowledge of the metalliferous formations. I have visited Maxwell's Creek, the Merced, Bear Valley, Quartzville, and several other places, not only as visitor but employed by mining companies, to open their mines; but I feel happy to inform you, that neither of those places is superior to yours in regard to the richness of the metalliferous leads. I know very well the famous Adeline vein; it is nothing in comparison to that which was found on the top of the Mariposa vein in 1850, and in regard to locality, situation, water and abundance of fuel, the veins situated on your property are incomparably superior to any others I know.

Receive, Colonel, the regards and consideration of, Truly yours,

S. Count Wäss

San Francisco, Jan. 15, 1852.

Printed in *Daily Alta California*, 16 Jan. 1852. As noted earlier, Count Wäss had already extolled the splendid veins of the Mariposa property (Doc. No. 121, n. 4).

195. Frémont to David Hoffman

A duplicate of this goes on the 21st.
inst. San Francisco, Jany. 17, 1852

DAVID HOFFMAN, ESQRE.
MY DEAR SIR,

The words underlined "*one 10, one 11, and one 15 per cent*" should be followed by "per month," reading when corrected, "have divided, one ten, one eleven, & one fifteen per cent per month on their capitals."[1]

This correction is authorized by Mr. Moffat & will appear corrected as above in the weekly Alta California, which will leave this on the 21st by the Golden Gate, and will probably reach you as soon as this. Please publish the article in the Times and the Mining Journal. It is of importance that it should be immediately communicated to the editor of the Mining Journal as the slanderous article which called it forth has been sent to him. The Mr. Trask, alluded to in it is made to appear State Geologist, but there is no such office. He is simply a hireling, one of the many perambulating scourges in the country.

Mr. Goodell you already know from previous letters. Count Wass is the head of a firm of assayers & gold melters in this city. He came to Washington in 1850 with Gov. Ujházy (the Govt. of Komárom)[2] who applied to me for letters for him to this country. Enclosed is his advertisement in this City. Moffat is the head of the U.S. Assaying & Coining establishment here. Enclosed is his advertisement also.[3]

My agent left yesterday to look for the Mineurs Belges.

JOHN CHARLES FRÉMONT

ALS-JBF (NHi—David Hoffman Papers). Endorsed: "Recd. 1 March."
1. The correction is to the last informative sentence of Moffat's 15 Jan. letter to JCF (Doc. No. 192).
2. László Ujházy (1795–1870), a political exile like Wäss, helped found the city of New Buda, Iowa, before settling permanently near San Antonio, Tex. (GÁSPÁR).
3. Not found.

196. David Hoffman to Frémont

London, 23 Jan. 1852

[JCF's letters of 8 and 29 Oct. and 4 Nov. "were very acceptable to the friends of California and greatly the reverse to those few designing persons who hoped to find Thomas Denny Sargent the owner of your estate." Confidence was coming back and once even one of JCF's lessees expressed satisfaction with the selection of land, restrictions on the release of money would be removed and JCF would be able to draw for "defined" sums.

Since JCF's letter suspending his leasing powers, Hoffman had been "busily employed" in carrying into execution "those contracts previously made" by him. He had been to France to complete those there and to obtain the benefit of French law, which does not "charge stockholders *in solido*," as did British law. A French organization enabled him to obtain British capital, "mind," and machinery with comparative ease. He again promises a full statement on all the contracts—monies, stocks, and their value. This would have been done had it not been for the Paris visit and for the fifty to one hundred calls daily, "which rendered any continuous work even of a few hours absolutely impossible."

Mr. Andrew Smith would apprise him "of all things." An Amsterdam company was interested in a lease but, per JCF's "last instructions," had been rejected. "Many other contracts are applied for, and, of course, meet the same fate." Mr. Paul's[1] company was ready to go to the Mariposa as soon as Hoffman had more information about its status. Draft.]

1. In the summer of 1850 in London, a Mr. Paul had accompanied his showing of a painted panorama of JCF's route to Oregon and California with a lecture and sometimes with a printed pamphlet. He was often in communication with Hoffman, and he was probably the W. H. Paul whom Hoffman sent to meet the Frémonts on their arrival in Liverpool (Hoffman to Charles Mayer, 20 July 1850; telegram of W. H. Paul to Hoffman, 22 March 1852; Hoffman's 1852 itemization of payments to Paul, all in NHi—David Hoffman Papers).

197. Frémont to Joseph C. Palmer

SAN FRANCISCO, 26 Jan. 1852

[Frémont gives Palmer a power of attorney to receive all monies and merchandise; sell or exchange goods that may come into his possession; sell real estate; "receive, confirm, make, and execute any contracts, deeds, conveyances, or other instruments"; adjust all partnership accounts; compound for any debts; and prosecute for injuries, real and personal. He could do all with the same powers and to all intents and purposes with the same validity as if Frémont were personally present, and he could act through a substitute attorney. Frémont's signature was witnessed by Edward Bosqui, Palmer's clerk; notarized on 27 Jan. by E. H. Hodges; recorded 28 Jan. (Powers of Attorney, Liber 2, p. 132) at the request of Palmer by M. E. Flanagan, deputy recorder for San Francisco County. The original was temporarily filed again on 5 Jan. 1856 and recorded once more in the Recorder's Office, San Francisco County (Book C, pp. 394–95), by the request of R. A. Lockwood. ADS (CSf).]

198. Antonio María Pico to Frémont

[31 Jan. 1852]

Know all men by these presents, that I Antonio Maria Pico of the County of Santa Clara, State of California, have bargained and sold and do hereby bargain sell and convey to John Charles Fremont of the said State in consideration of the sum of five thousand dollars in hand paid all my right, title and interest in and to the Rancho or tract of land lying and being in the County of San Joaquin, in said State and on the river San Joaquin as the same was granted to me by Manuel Michael Torrena [Micheltorena] governor of California on the Twenty-eighth day of November one thousand eight hundred and forty three, with the description and boundaries set forth in said grant, to wit, "El Paraja conocido con el nombre del Pescadero por la parta di abajo colindante con el rancho de don Juan Maer con el don Jose Nouiga con Buenos Ayres al pass de Pescadero y el rio" containing eight Sitios de granada mayor more or less, my interest and share therein and which I now sell to said Fremont being one undivided half of said tract or Rancho; together with all the rights, privileges and interest therein, of what ever nature I may possess guaranteeing the said Fremont against any person claiming by under or through me, but not against any other person, to have and to hold the said demised premises, to the said Fremont his heirs and assigns forever IN TESTIMONY WHEREOF I have hereunto set my hand and seal this thirty first day of January one thousand eight hundred and fifty two.

Signed, Sealed and delivered in the presence of
ANTONIO M. PICO [<i>Seal</i>]

C. B. Shorce
State of California
County of San Francisco

On this 31st day of January A.D. 1852 before me a Notary Public duly qualified in and for said County personally appeared Antonio María Pico known to me to be the person described in [the record] and who executed the foregoing instrument who acknowledged to me that he executed the same freely and voluntarily, and for all the uses and purposes therein mentioned.

IN TESTIMONY WHEREOF I have hereunto set my hand and private seal (having as yet no Official Seal) on the day and year last above written.

[*Seal*]

JAMES VAN NESS

Not. Public

Recorded by request of Capt. Hold Sept. 21st 1853 at 11 o'clock A.M.

Copy (San Joaquin Deeds, vol. 4, p. 527, Court House, Stockton). The record is in typescript and is apparently a copy of an older document. Antonio María Pico had already sold half the property to Henry Naglee on 25 April 1849 (Papers relating to El Pescadero in CU-B—Halleck, Peachy, and Billings Correspondence, ca. 1852–67). A petition for a patent was filed in their names on 10 June 1852, but it was rejected by the California Land Commission. On appeal, it was confirmed by the District Court and also by the U.S. Supreme Court; the patent for the 35,546.39-acre rancho was issued in 1865 (DNA-49, California Private Land Claims, El Pescadero, Case 272).

Palmer, Cook & Company quickly came to have an interest in the rancho. An employee of the banking firm reported that the owners neglected it with the result that squatters pastured thousands of cattle upon the land and resisted their efforts to collect rents (BOSQUI, 82). JCF seems to have lost title temporarily, as he had in Rancho Emigdio, but succeeded in obtaining a reconveyance (Frémont to T. W. Park, 23 April 1862, CSf). In 1867 JBF, as "the owner in fee in her own right of an undivided one-fourth part" of the rancho, sold 6,672 acres for $11,000, payable in the stock of Wells Fargo's Express Company; in 1874, "in her own right and as Trustee for Francis Preston Frémont," she sold the remainder of her interest—one-sixteenth part containing 2,216 acres—for $8,400 in gold coin (JCF and JBF's agreement with Charles McLaughlin, 18 Nov. 1867; JBF's deed to H. W. Carpentier, 13 May 1874, San Joaquin Deeds, Court House, Stockton).

199. David Hoffman to Frémont

LONDON, 1 Feb. 1852

[Sends him the original engrossed contract for the Hoffman-Alverado Company and hopes very soon to send via New York every one of the engrossed contracts (perhaps eighteen or twenty) with a statement of all monies, premiums, shares, and royalties. The Quartz Rock Gold Mining Company of Mariposa (formerly British Mutual Gold Mining Company) was finally registered. The news that JCF had approved the Nouveau Monde Company would raise their stock at least ten shillings. Still hopes for specimens and frequent communiqués. Copy.]

200. Frémont to Benjamin D. Wilson

SAN FRANCISCO, February 1st. 1852

MY DEAR SIR,

I am sorry I can not send you down the amount of your bill, but will make arrangements to do so at an early day. I am about leaving the state for a few months—in the meantime Mr. Joseph C. Palmer, of Palmer Cook & Co. will act as my attorney in the same manner as if I were here. You will see the notice in the Alta California.

I write in haste on the eve of my departure[1] but hope to have the satisfaction to see you soon again. Yours very truly,

J. C. FRÉMONT

B. D. Wilson Esqre.
Los Angeles

ALS-JBF (CSmH).
1. JCF and his family sailed on the *S.S. Tennessee*, probably the day of the letter (San Francisco *Alta*, 1 Feb. 1852; San Diego *Herald*, 7 Feb. 1852).

201. David Hoffman to Frémont

LONDON, 8 Feb. 1852

[Writes that it is not within his physical ability to make JCF fully aware "of the condition of things" in London, but calls his attention to a number of points.

He has heard from private sources that the Sargent sale had been rejected by Benton (it had not been) and rejoiced for JCF's sake, since the purchasers would have involved him in ultimate difficulties. Hoffman could easily obtain $5 million for the Mariposa. He has endeav-

John Charles Frémont. From an oil painting
by William S. Jewett in 1852. Courtesy of the National
Portrait Gallery, Smithsonian Institution.

The town of Mariposa, sometime between 1850 and 1854.
Courtesy of the Henry E. Huntington Library.

ored to keep him informed of everything in London, but both he and the public have wondered at JCF's silence on some matters.

Hoffman encloses copies of Walbridge's advertisement in the *Times* (27 Jan. 1852) on the Agua Fria, which he labels "false in some respects" and intended for "stock jobbing purposes," and expresses his view that Walbridge's conduct was improper both to JCF and to himself. His own public letter to the members of the Stock Exchange (*Times*, 27 Jan. 1852) expressed doubts that JCF had given one-half of the Mariposa (he did not know about the 5 Sept. 1851 conveyance) to Palmer, Cook & Company for a share in the Agua Fria Mine, but did not impute any hostility to that firm or question JCF's right to enter into such an agreement. He wishes the extension of the Agua Fria leases had been done through his agency rather than by JCF directly, and he has no doubt that JCF would grant leases to the Ave Maria and the West Mariposa Gold Quartz Mine Company.

He encloses the 27 Jan. 1852 letter in which Walbridge had assured him that he had authority to terminate Hoffman's agency. He is pained that JCF has not had sufficient confidence in him to reveal his plans and policies, but he hopes he will let him know if he is discontented. In the meantime he will continue to sustain JCF's, his, and the contractees' interests. Two copies: a rough draft and a "fair copy made for Thomas H. Benton."]

202. Palmer, Cook & Company to Frémont

SAN FRANCISCO Feb 28. 1851 [1852]

DEAR COL.

The agent of the Agua Frio mine[1] has arrived, and leaves on Monday for the Country. The United States Surveyor General leaves same day to survey the ranch.[2] The Commissioners have settled one important point, the very one suggested by Lockwood,[3] that is, they sit as a tribunal executing a political trust, to decide titles as the Mexican Government would have decided them, and this obviates the difficulty apprehended from the decisions of the Supreme Court of the United States, that a judicial tribunal is not competent to execute a political trust—that settles the point. We received a letter from Wright by the last mail requesting us urge on you the importance of holding on, that he can raise all the money you may want to develop the resources of your ranch, that too before he knew of this important decision settling the whole matter of the claims—for you see at once it only requires a survey and the rest is a mere form—and the Commissioners will issue a patent of title at once. Very Respectfully Yours,

PALMER, COOK & CO

To Hon J. Charles Fremont
London

Copy (M. A. Goodspeed, Jr., Collection).

1. James Hepburn had left England on 17 Dec. 1851. He was the agent of the Agua Fria Mining Company, which had been promoted in London by Wright, Walbridge, Jackson, and Lakeman to carry on mining under the 17 Sept. 1850 lease obtained by Palmer, Cook & Company from JCF. The company was officially registered on 5 Oct. 1851, but in its amended return a week later the proposed capitalization of £200,000 was reduced to £100,000, with each share worth one pound and with one-third of the shares reserved for Palmer, Cook & Company, who were also to receive £6,000 in cash. "It was a grand affair," Walbridge wrote Wright, "and by far the greatest bargain that ever was made in this or any other country." The incorrigible Hoffman and the rumored sale of the Mariposa soon caused the company to move cautiously, to lock up one-half the promised shares to Palmer, Cook & Company, and to delay final arrangements until April 1852 (see Records of the Agua Fria Mining Company, Film Z-G-1, Reel 58, and Agua Fria Gold Mining Agreements, London, 16 and 17 April 1852, CU-B; Walbridge to Wright, London, 11 Feb. 1852, M. A. Goodspeed, Jr., Collection).

2. Surveyor General Samuel D. King appointed Allexey W. Von Schmidt to conduct the survey of Las Mariposas. It was completed in June 1852 (CRAMPTON, 206–7).

3. Jonathan A. Jessup, better known as Rufus A. Lockwood, was an eccentric legal genius who did win JCF's case with the California land commissioners. He then went off to Australia, but when the District Court overturned the decision of the land commissioners, Palmer persuaded him to return and add his name to the distinguished battery of legal counsel appealing the Mariposa case to the Supreme Court (BOOTH; Montgomery Blair to Minna, 22 April 1854, DLC—Montgomery Blair Papers). Ultimately the commissioners decided that it was unimportant whether their authority be termed "judicial" or "political." It came from Congress, the political power of government, but it was a power measured and limited by the act of 1851. The commissioners held that they were competent to pass on all classes of titles, complete or incomplete, and that in doing so they would take notice of the general history of Spain, Mexico, and California as well as all applicable laws, usages, customs, treaties, and even equity. The wisdom or policy of Mexican law was not the issue (Opinion of Hiland Hall, printed in John C. Frémont v. the United States, pp. 9–34, DNA-267).

203. Philip R. Fendall to Frémont

WASHINGTON, 28th Febr. 1852

DEAR SIR:

Edward Beale Esqr. informs me that he has received a letter from you from which it appears that you would have left California for London before you could have received Col. Benton's last letters to you concerning the sale of the Mariposas lands. Those letters stated, as I learnt from Col. Benton, the particulars and result of his negotiation with Mr. Thomas Denny Sargent on this subject. As I was professionally consulted by Col. Benton during that negotiation, Mr. Beale suggests that I should communicate to you the substance of the treaty, and I now accordingly do so.

On the 29th of January 1852 two agreements were executed, to which the parties were, yourself through your attorney, Col. Benton, and Mr. Sargent. One of them ratified the previous contract of sale of 7 July 1851 between Mr. Flandin as your attorney, and Mr. Sargent. The other recites that it had been so ratified; that the parties had mutually consented to dispense with the limit of four months stipulated in that contract as the term for carrying it into effect, and had agreed on a farther delay for that purpose, that you had by letter of attorney to Col. Benton given him full powers as to the sale and disposition of the Mariposas estate; that under his authority on the 29th day of January 1852 Col. Benton ratified that contract; and that the parties had agreed on certain modification of the terms of the contract.

The new agreement contained a mutual covenant for the performance of the conditions original and modified.

The modifications were as follows:

1st. Instead of the cash payment of 100,000 as originally stipulated, $25,000 to be paid in cash on the execution of the agreement; and 75,000 to be paid in London, on the delivery of the deed conveying all your title, and within eight days after Mr. Sargent or his agent in London should have been certified that possession of the premises had been delivered to his agent in California. If the $75,000 should not be paid as agreed on then the $25,000 paid by Mr. Sargent to be forever forfeited to you.

2nd. The sum of $30,000 the first annual payment to be paid in New York, in one payment, in twelve months from the date of the agreement.

3rd. The sum of $60,000 to be paid annually, from the date of the

331

payment of the 30,000, in quarter-yearly installments, in New York, until a perfect title to the lands should be made to Mr. Sargent, or until a final adjudication of your title should be made by the United States.

4th. The sum of 300,000 to be paid in New York on the delivery of a perfect title.

5th. Within one year after the delivery of a perfect title, such farther sum, with interest at the rate of six per cent as together with the previous payments shall amount to the purchase money of *one million dollars*, to be paid to you in New York.

6th. On the confirmation by the United States of your inchoate title, you are to make further reasonable conveyances for assuring Mr. Sargent's title.

On the same day, 29th January 1852, Mr. Sargent executed an agreement reserving to you the right within fifteen days after you should have received notice from his agent for receiving possession of the lands, to renounce and annul the whole contract; and providing in case of your disapproval for its utter nullity.

On the same day a deed was executed by you through your attorney Col. Benton, to Mr. Sargent, of your inchoate title to the Mariposas estate. The deed to be delivered on your confirmation of the sale and Mr. Sargent's payment of the $75,000 dollars.

On the same day a deed of mortgage was executed by Mr. Sargent on the Mariposas estate, to secure the payment of the $900,000 which would remain due after the payment of $25,000 down, and $75,000 on the delivery of the deed from you.

On the same day Mr. Sargent, in a letter to you renounces all claim to any account for moneys received by you from leases, rents, royalties, &c.

On the 31st January a covenant on your part for the release, within six months, of Mrs. Fremont's dower, was executed by Col. Benton.

Hoping that the advantages to you from the sale may be commensurate with the pains taken by Col. Benton to place the negotiation on proper grounds, and to bring it to a favorable result, I am, Dear Sir, Yours truly & respectfully,

P. R. Fendall

Col. Fremont
London

LS (CLU).

204. Frémont to Edward F. Beale

MY DEAR SIR:

I have learned that the opponents at Washington to your present appointment, strongly urge upon the President a charge that you were concerned in my contracts for the supply of cattle to the Indians in California. The object of the present note is to authorize and request you, in my name, to say upon all fitting occasions that those contracts were made by me, and in behalf of myself and Paul Leroy, Esq. a merchant of San Francisco;[1] that they were conducted in my name alone, as the sole responsible contracting party; that you were at the time these contracts were made in a different part of the country; that the first contracts were made, and arrangements for carrying them into execution completed, nearly a month before you were aware of anything in regard to them; that a large amount of capital and firm credit being necessary to carry through the business, and the credit of the Government Agents being very low in California, Mr. Leroy became alarmed and withdrew from the contract, I reimbursing the actual expenditures he had made. I then associated as partners, Major Savage and Capt. Vincenthaler, who also shortly afterwards retired from the contract, leaving me the sole risks and responsibilities of the transactions. Finally, that you are not, and never were a partner of mine in any transaction, or party to any contract in which I am or have been concerned. I trust that our known friendly relations will not prove an injury to you, and hope that I therefore, with safety to yourself, give to this charge in my name, the most peremptory denial, and to characterize it in the plainest terms, a falsehood, and to show this letter to the person you contradict, as the authority, holding me personally responsible.

Business of greater importance compels me to leave, on Wednesday, for England; but I will be back at an early day, and will give this subject my undivided attention. To carry out this contract I availed myself of an extensive credit among the old Californians; accomplished it at great risk of means and unusual long continued personal risk and expense. The profit to me will be large, but I ask it as my right from the honesty of the department. You are at liberty to make what use of this letter you please. Yours truly,

JOHN CHARLES FREMONT

Printed in Stockton *Journal*, 15 June 1852.
1. See Doc No. 133, n. 2. Paul Leroy not identified. The San Francisco city directories for 1851 and 1852 list "Theodore Leroy, merchant, 151 Montgomery St."

205. Frémont to Charles F. Mayer

IRVING HOUSE, March 10th. 1852

DEAR SIR,

I have barely a moment to acknowledge your letters, and say that I *do not confirm* the sale of the Mariposas. I will write from England. Yours truly,

(signed) JOHN C. FRÉMONT

Charles F. Mayer, Esq.
Baltimore

Copy (NHi—David Hoffman Papers).

206. David Hoffman to Frémont

23 March [1852]
10 Conduit Street, HANOVER SQUARE

MY DEAR SIR:

Welcome to Old England and sound sleep to Mrs. Frémont and yourself who I cannot think of disturbing in any way until tomorrow at 12 o'clock. In truth, my dear Sir, I am quite as much fatigued as your good self, having been in the City for three hours and received some monies on your a/c and finally closed two matters standing out since 12th November last. You have in London thousands of friends, and some *tens* (only) of cunning foxes. I pray you to be cautious. One Lakeman is worse infinitely than a distillation of Sargent—a mere *chevalier d'industrie*—a genteel vagabond very well looking and genteel enough, but artful as Satanas.

I shall do myself the great pleasure and honour of paying Mrs. Frémont my respects tomorrow at 12 o'clock if not too early for her. I have much to say to you of real interest. The calls on you will be very great. I hope we may have a couple of days to ourselves. Then all will be well and smooth as a summer's sea. Yours faithfully,

D. Hoffman

SC (NHi—David Hoffman Papers). Endorsed: "on arrival."

207. Frémont to David Hoffman

[Wednesday morning]
[24 March 1852]

My Dear Sir,

I have just received your note. I am unwell this morning and some engagements have crowded upon me which prevent my seeing you as early as twelve. If agreeable to you suppose we say three this afternoon. Yours truly,

J. C. Frémont
Wednesday mg.

Mr. Hoffman

ALS-JBF (NHi—David Hoffman Papers). Endorsed: "24 March 1852."

208. David Hoffman to Frémont

[24 March 1852]

Dear Sir:

I am extremely sorry to hear of your continued indisposition and especially that engagements should so early have pressed in upon you. I shall be with you at 3 o'clock—that hour, however, being the one selected by the Marchioness Wellesley to pay her respects to your Lady, but that can be deferred to another time. My natural desire was to see you before any business would press on you, as there are some funds in my hands I wished to place in yours at once. [*Hoffman indi-*

cates that the remaining portion of the original draft was cut from the letter sent to JCF:]< In very candour, my dear Sir, the presence in the same Hotel of Mr. Wright, the supposed representative of the Agua Fria, the alleged purchaser of ½ your estate for a bauble, and the presence of Mr. Heap, who the public regard as the representative of Sargent, clouds the matter with a mystery that surprises the public even on your very arrival in town—all that might have been easily avoided by one minutes conversation last night, which my earnest desire for your repose prevented and which Mr. Wright's action confirmed [?] >Yours faithfully,

D. HOFFMAN

Signed draft (NHi—David Hoffman Papers). Endorsed: "Altered."

209. David Hoffman to Frémont

24 March [1852]

DEAR SIR:

I called punctually at 3 o'clock; waited 25 minutes. Heard you were out during the morning, and had not received my last note.

I shall be happy to see you at No. 10 Conduit St—only a square from the Clarendon—at any hour you may name.

D. HOFFMAN

SC (NHi—David Hoffman Papers). Endorsed: "Mentioning call at 3 and waiting."

210. David Hoffman to Frémont

10 CONDUIT STREET
24 March '52
9 o'clock [Evening]

SIR:

I pass wholly by myself, but Mos. Derriey, a most respectable gentleman who has expended upon a small portion of your Estate a vast

336

sum now demands my deepest sympathies. I ask you to see him without fail privately—he may be relied upon fully. The universal public are astonished at this day's proceedings—all except the few talking creatures that would deceive angels of light. I cannot consent to be longer in an equivocal situation or the most innocent means of injuring so worthy a gentleman as Mos. D. There are also hundreds more who reposed on you alone, and who are resolved to see me fully sustained and themselves freed from solicitude. Mr. Heap regularly conveys all his news to those whom he serves—also Mr. Wright, with his Agua Fria, claims his portion and so does even Mr. Sargent. As for them all singly and collectively they cannot touch me, but must bring ruin on as splendid a prospect, industriously formed by me for you as ever dawned on the hopes of any man. Whether they are to be dashed to the winds by you or not rests now with yourself alone, and must be decided one way or the other without further delay.[1] Yours obediently,

D H

Initialed draft (NHi—David Hoffman Papers). Endorsed: "To introduce Mos. Derriey & sent by Post as Mos. D would not be seen."

1. On this evening Hoffman had a stormy interview with Wright, who implied that Hoffman had cast aspersions on the respectability of Palmer, Cook & Company and claimed that the Agua Fria was to have priority in the British market. In a subsequent meeting with Wright and during the half-hour interview that JCF ultimately granted him, Hoffman agreed not to continue his attacks but "to row in the same boat" as they desired. But when the press reported that one of JCF's first acts would be to attend a meeting of the Agua Fria Company, the old man had difficulty restraining his anger at this "unneutral act" (Hoffman to Wright, 25 and 27 March 1852, M. A. Goodspeed, Jr., Collection).

211. Frémont to David Hoffman

CLARENDON, March 25 [1852]

My DEAR SIR,

I have half an hour at my command this morning which I will devote to you, *en attendant* greater leisure, if you will do me the favor to call now. Yours truly,

JOHN C. FRÉMONT

David Hoffman, Esqre.

ALS (NHi—David Hoffman Papers). Endorsed: "25 March 1852."

212. David Hoffman to Frémont

[25 March 1852]

It is quite out of my power to be with you till one hour hence, viz before 1 o'clock. I regret that time presses with you so that you cannot accord to me more than half an hour on business that consumed more than two years of the most precious part of my life and with a devotion to you & your interests that knew no limits. I had hoped that you would call on me where are all my papers, instead of passing conversation for half an hour—after the whole public now know you rejected me all yesterday and saw certain persons during seven hours of the same day you appointed to see me.

My servant will take a verbal message from you whether you can see me at one o'clock. Yours faithfully,

D. HOFFMAN

SC (NHi—David Hoffman Papers). Endorsed.

213. Frémont to David Hoffman

Thursday afternoon [25 March 1852]

MY DEAR SIR,

In declining to see gentlemen on business matters just now, your note of this morning in regard to Mr. Dozziez [Derriey] (of the Mineur Belges) had escaped my mind. If you think that his interests require that he should see me, I will be at home after 9 this evening, or between 10 & 11 tomorrow morning as may be most agreeable to you. Yours truly,

J. C. FRÉMONT

D. Hoffman, Esqre.
Present

ALS (NHi—David Hoffman Papers). Endorsed: "25 March 1852."

214. David Hoffman to Frémont

[LONDON], 26 March 1852

[Finds that "it is deemed politic that the Ave Maria and the West Mariposa Companies should have leases, provided the stockholders call a meeting, remove all the present obnoxious Directors, constitute an approved new organization, and dedicate their funds to the purposes [?] paying the usual premium.

"If you agree to this, it can be done hereafter, but only after you have stated your intentions as to all other matters. This with your other arrangements will then produce entire harmony."[1] Signed copy. Endorsed: "About Ave Maria and West Mariposa, 27 [26] March 1852."]

1. This is a curious letter in view of the fact that JCF had abrogated Hoffman's leasing powers by his 8 Oct. 1851 letter.

215. David Hoffman to Frémont

CONDUIT STREET, [26 March 1852]

[Several gentleman-capitalists of high character and much influence wish personal interviews with JCF. They are disturbed that JCF had delayed receiving Hoffman. Signed copy. Endorsed: "27 [26] March."]

216. Frémont to David Hoffman

[27 March 1852]

MY DEAR SIR,

I will be happy to see the gentlemen named in your note of last night, but I think it will be expedient that you first give me a statement of the present condition of my affairs.

In my interview with these gentlemen, I ought to be thoroughly acquainted with their business relations to me. Please therefore to let me have such a statement as early as convenient, & I shall then be

prepared to see these gentlemen immediately. I have received, and replied to, a note on the subject of yours of this morning. Yours truly,

J. C. Frémont

David Hoffman Esqre.

ALS (NHi—David Hoffman Papers). Endorsed: "27 March 1852."

217. Frémont to David Hoffman

[Sunday, 28 March 1852]

My dear Sir,

I have appointed the Messrs. Lawford my solicitors.[1] Will it be convenient for you to meet me at their office, Drapers' Hall, at some time
between 12 and 1 tomorrow? Say 12½?

In the mean time I will Thank you to say to any gentlemen who
may apply to you on matters connected with the Mariposas estate that
these gentlemen are authorized to act for me and in my name, and
that whatever may be done by them will be sanctioned by me.

It will be well also to give them notice to place confidence in no
representations from any other quarter whatever. Yours truly,

J. C. Frémont
Sunday 28th March

David Hoffman, Esquire
10 Conduit St.

ALS (NHi—David Hoffman Papers).
1. E. J. H. and John Lawford not only handled JCF's legal problems with
Hoffman and Sargent but also defended the explorer in the action brought by
Anthony Gibbs and Sons in the Court of Exchequer. The U.S. government paid
the firm $2,150 for this latter service (Senate Ex. Doc. 109, 34th Cong., 1st sess.,
pp. 96–140, Serial 825).

218. David Hoffman to Frémont

London, [28 March 1852]

["I should have very good pleasure in meeting your solicitor Mr.
Lawford if I had the least previous intimation of the topics to be sub-

mitted to our joint consideration. There are (so far as I can imagine) only two—*viz*: the Sargent pretensions and the validity and faithfulness of my Agency." If the latter, he wants to know before giving a final reply about the meeting. Draft. Endorsed.]

219. Frémont to David Hoffman

CLARENDON HOTEL
[Sunday] Afternoon [28 March 1852]

MY DEAR SIR,

Your note is just received. I have put the whole Mariposas subject in Mr. Lawford's hands for the purpose of settling all the questions which have arisen or may arise in regard to it, and in order to know clearly what my liabilities are, and in order to know what are the advantages accruing or likely to accrue to me from any application of the property up to this time. I am indisposed to do this myself, having neither the time nor health necessary for it.

Many questions are daily arising out of your acts which comprise the greater part of what has been done upon the property in question, and you will oblige me if you will simply consider Mr. Lawford as being in my place, and meet me at his office prepared to give him the same facts and complete account of your agency that you were about to render to me.

If without further explanation you can give me your aid promptly and efficiently in the settlement of my affairs, you will confer a favor upon me, and for that purpose, I would be glad to know this evening if you can meet me at the time appointed at Mr. Lawford's tomorrow.

I desire to act with you now as always in a straightforward and cordial manner. Yours very truly,

J. C. FRÉMONT

David Hoffman, Esqr.
10 Conduit Street

LS (NHi—David Hoffman Papers).

220. David Hoffman to Frémont

[LONDON], 28 March 1852

[Will meet him at Mr. Lawford's office on Monday at 12:30. Copy.]

221. David Hoffman to Frémont

10 Conduit Street, HANOVER SQUARE, 29 March 1852

[He needs immediately the book statement sent to him on Saturday and hopes JCF will dispatch a messenger for it. He is preparing the résumé which he promised Mr. Lawford. Initialed draft.]

222. Frémont to David Hoffman

[ca. 29 March 1982]

MY DEAR SIR,

I hope you will not be inconvenienced by want of the book. I have place it [in] Mr. Lawford's hands to aid him in his study of the subject. I however herewith send the parchments. Yours very truly,

J. C. FRÉMONT

D. Hoffman Esqr.

ALS (NHi—David Hoffman Papers). Endorsed.

223. Frémont to David Hoffman

CLARENDON HOTEL
April 2d. 1852

MY DEAR SIR,

I acknowledge the receipt of your note of the 31st.[1] and will refer the points stated to Mr. Lawford. In regard to the leases I have informed gentlemen who have called upon me that they must wait until I am acquainted with what has been done before I can answer their questions.

Regretting that you health is not good I am Yours truly,

J. C. FRÉMONT

David Hoffman, Esqre.
Conduit St.

LS (NHi—David Hoffman Papers). Endorsed.
1. Not found.

224. David Hoffman to Frémont

[LONDON], 3 April 1852

[Sends two original letters, "one from Prince Jérôme Bonaparte to Mr. Robert in respect to the Company (en commandite) organized in France under the Presidency of the Prince, and with a Branch in London under the guidance of Geo. Thomas whom you have seen.[1] The other letter is from Mr. Hess (a confidential friend of the Prince) who replies to the Prince instead of Mr. Robert." The letters show that companies, shareholders, and even the general public sustain Hoffman. His exclusion from JCF's counsel has prevented the Mariposa owner from "rightly understanding" his moral, legal, and honorable position. JCF did great prejudice to himself by appointing a solicitor, and even the Sargent clique wonder at his course. Draft.]

1. Prince Jérôme Bonaparte's company and its London branch were not connected with Le Nouveau Monde Company, which listed Prince Louis Lucien Bonaparte as its president and which also had an English counterpart.

225. David Hoffman to Frémont

[LONDON], Sunday, 4 April 1852

[His first note of "today" did not reach JCF. A second note from the U.S. minister, Abbott Lawrence, has come. He will meet JCF at

Mr. Lawrence's at 9 o'clock. "His idea and mine was to go through the matter thoroughly for some consecutive days, but the rumour just reaches me that you intend going to Paris on Tuesday." Sender's copy.]

226. Frémont to David Hoffman

Clarendon Hotel
10½ Sunday Night [4 April 1852]

Dear Sir,

I have just received your two notes. I do not see what possible connection the Chancery Bill[1] can have with the interview you desire to have with me. I understood Mr. Lawford to say it was furnished at your request. In regard to the papers sent me by you on Saturday I understand these to be addressed to Mr. Lawford and not to me and I will accordingly transmit them to him. I do not feel that any preparation is necessary for an interview with me, neither have I any explanation to make. I will take occasion to repeat what I have already said, that I ask of you only such statement of the business you have done for me and such rendering of the account, you may have had with me as it is customary and proper that an agent should render to his principal. For this I do not understand that any explanations are necessary, beyond the statement itself, which is the clearest of all explanations. But, as your notes just received intimate a desire for an interview on business to extend through several days, I shall have to ask your leave to decline it, and to refer you again to Mr. Lawford. By adopting this course you will spare me a great deal of trouble and bring the affairs of your agency to a prompt settlement. I do not feel at liberty to use Mr. Lawrence's house as a place of business, nor do I wish to involve his name in any way with this business which has already been so much thrust upon the public notice. Yours truly,

John C. Frémont

David Hoffman Esqre.
10 Conduit Street

ALS (NHi—David Hoffman Papers). Endorsed: "Sunday Night 4 Apr. 1852. Wonder of wonders! Inconsistency of inconsistencies! Impudence of Impudences!!"

1. JCF had repudiated Benton's sale of the Mariposa to Sargent, and on 27 March Sargent filed a bill of complaint in the British Chancery. Hoffman had asked the Messrs. Lawford to see the bill.

227. David Hoffman to Frémont

10 Conduit Street, Hanover Square, 5 April 1852

[In responding to his employer's letter of 4 April, he notices that he might have information which would help JCF in his defense against Sargent's bill; that he has given an account of the various companies' monies and shares and that not until the 4 April letter did he know that an account of his agency's disbursements was desired; nor did he wish to substitute interviews for accounts. He is surprised that JCF is not sufficiently interested to take time to learn the details of his agency and reiterates his belief that they have a mutual duty to give a candid explanation to "the many and worthy individuals whose confidence in you through *myself*, has induced them to enlist their capital, character, credit and time in operations on the Mariposa Estate." He has no desire to make Mr. Lawrence's house a counting house, and if the Mariposa business had been thrust before the public, it was not his responsibility. He had not initiated controversial publications but had responded to antagonistic advertisements in order to protect JCF's interests and character as well as his own. He had published his pamphlet only after the journals refused to take his business advertisements, which would have refuted those of his opponents. Sender's copy.]

228. David Hoffman to Frémont

Private and also for Mrs. Frémont
10 Conduit Street, 8 April 1852

["I am still loyal to you, to your interests, and to the Companies legally formed by me under your powers to me. This will be the last effort made by me to save your property from serious injury, and your name in England from horrible abuse. You do not (because you will

345

not) understand the facts of your case, and the extreme peril of it (of your own creation, chiefly since your arrival). The present letter is private, but also will be submitted by me to your Solicitor according to your request. I make no difficulty on that matter. But if you refuse to read the present letter you thereby refuse to do *yourself* justice. It is for your sake alone that I ask you and *Mrs. Fremont* also to calmly read it, and you will then find that no truer friend ever existed than I shall prove myself to have been from May 1850 to the present hour.

"Your whole history (from the hour I met you several times at my brother's house in Baltimore with Mr. Nicollet and until your arrival) had inspired me with an extraordinary admiration of your character. I was much with Mr. N. during his illness in Baltimore and somewhat in Washington and greatly loved him. I came to this country only to stop here a short time and then to proceed to the Continent where I might economize until my little property should greatly rise in value. Your agency detained me here. I abandoned nearly every other enterprise and eventually every thing else, and with a zeal and devotedness that all admire and which you, and even your foes must admit or cannot deny, I battered down all prejudices against Calif. I encountered a mountain of doubt of yourself and property and, by my growing familiarity with Calif. '*Statistics*' I was enabled to gradually form a collection of *Statistics* from 1526 to 1852 in a very large folio volume, such an one as no where else exists and a more elaborate and truthful record than can any where be found. With this at my hand, I was enabled (though you gave me so little aid) to build up 21 Companies, more or less organized, dedicating only about 37,800 feet by 600 feet of your property which Companies in Premiums alone must have yielded you in cash before the present month of April at least £176,887 had not the Sargent matter and afterwards the Palmer, Cooke, & Co. matter (as brought out by the Agua Fria Advertisement) created the difficulties that compelled the Companies (and myself as a honourable man) to place the monies and shares in a Temporary Trusteeship and several Companies to rest upon their oars, all of which would have passed off had you met me on your arrival here in the way that everybody expected."

He proceeds to make a number of points:

1. JCF's course has alarmed the companies, and his selection of a solicitor, although an honorable one, has surprised the public.

2. The horrible things said about JCF privately in the City during

the last week would have been in the papers had it not been for Hoffman's vigilance.

3. Since his arrival in England, JCF had shown preference, much to the prejudice of his name and estate, for his previous enemies or their sympathizers, namely: Sargent, Duncan, Bates, [George K.] Huxley of the West Mariposa, the directors of the Ave Maria, Newton of the Agua Fria, Walker of the Carson Creek, Peabody ("friendly alone to the Agua Fria"), Lakeman, Green, Wright, Walbridge, [William] Hance of the Carson Creek, West Mariposa directors, [M. B.] Sampson of the *Times*, and Sir Roderick Murchison.

4. He had not taken the time to inform himself about the condition of his estate by reading Hoffman's letters.

5. He had not even read Hoffman's manuscript reply to the Duncan letter.

6. Hoffman had heard a report that JCF sympathized with Sargent and was sorry for the position in which Hoffman had placed himself.

7. Hoffman thinks higher of Wright than he does of Walbridge, but thinks Wright's coming out for the Agua Fria is indiscreet. Lakeman and Huxley may make money for themselves but would ultimately ruin JCF's legitimate and permanent interests.

8. Refers to Wright's speech at the meeting of the stockholders of the Agua Fria which had resulted in the continued depression of that company's stock and the appreciation of the shares of the other companies; "nothing now prevents their rising still more but your silence as to the three matters named by me in my letter of the 31st March" (not located).

9. Wright had showed him a very large map of the Mariposa region. He regretted that during the two years of his agency JCF had not been able to send him such a map. If it were correct, he would have been happy to possess it; if it were not, Wright ought not to exhibit it.

10. The public and press had expressed approval of his proceedings, but JCF seemed only to disapprove.

11. Sargent's bill in Chancery would not have been filed had JCF sustained Hoffman on his arrival.

12. Wright had discussed the Sargent case with him. "But Mr. Wright did not show me your written declamation of the Conditional Sale—nor did he allude to any written one on board ship, as stated in Sargent's Bill—but on the contrary he stated you had promptly re-

347

jected the sale at Chagres verbally and that Mr. Heap had advised you to make a written one which was done, he says, and also that Mr. Heap had offered to accompany you to England for the express purpose of sustaining by his evidence the written rejection at Chagres. This impressed me so highly as to the honorable course of Mr. Heap that I expressed to my friends a prompt desire to call on Mr. Heap and to express to him my gratification; and this would have been done had it not been for the idea subsequently imparted to me that my good feeling in this regard would not be reciprocated! . . . The Bill in Chancery states not only an actual authority to Flandin to make the Sale but also that he possesses your Title Deeds from Alverado &c. This is *new* to me!"

13. The *Mining Journal* had been too full to take the information from the California newspaper, which JCF had sent to Hoffman, but from the information he had prepared a long article which had appeared in the London *Sun* and the *Daily News*. His companies had united in publishing at their expense a separate edition of more than 5,000 copies.

14. The correspondence with Gen. Walbridge was a curious one, but he had kept it secret and was willing to bury all with reference to the Agua Fria, provided justice was done him by all.

15. He is preparing material for Lawford.

16. Hoffman was surprised at JCF's "small intimation" about Robert, who was then seriously ill, but hoped he would investigate and make amends if the rumor were untrue.

17. Has learned that JCF spent an evening with Sir Roderick Murchison. "I trust that Gentleman has by this time gotten over his absurdities as to Gold in California and in the Ural Mountains!" He had been the "Magnus Apollo" of opposition to the idea of quartz gold existing at all.

18. Hoffman is pained by JBF's unhappiness with him. Her alienation stemmed from the fact that he had published her 1 Aug. 1851 letter (Doc. No. 149) in his pamphlet and had defended JCF and his property at some expense to the reputation of her father.

19. He understands that JCF still wishes to sell his estate to someone else for about a million dollars instead of the larger sum he had mentioned to him. But that was his affair.

20. Fourteen months ago he had drawn a bill on JCF for £260 and was now surprised to learn that he knew nothing about it. As it was still outstanding, he would pay George Peabody immediately. He had

not received any compensation for either his disbursements or labors in JCF's behalf and yet was being treated as his debtor. Two copies, one of which appear in the Brief, Bill and Answer (in Chancery) of Frémont v. Hoffman.]

229. David Hoffman to Jessie B. Frémont

[LONDON], 8 April 1852, 9 o'clock

[He had waited last night some hours.[1] Was pained that she had not read his private letter of that day at the time of his call at the Clarendon Hotel. He is going to see Lawford. "I see clearly how all things can be set right, but surely not by still persisting in dealing with your best friend for two years as a *villain*!!" He was surprised not to find Wright, but his whereabouts were unknown. He would be happy to hear if JCF is released (i.e., from arrest) and, if not, where he might see him. Copy.]

1. Hoffman had waited for a message from JBF concerning her husband, who had been arrested on the evening of 7 April for the nonpayment of four drafts which he had drawn as governor of California upon the Secretary of State for supplies furnished to the battalion by one F. Hüttmann, but since sold to Anthony Gibbs and Sons of London. He spent the night in Sloman's Lock-up in Cursitor Street, Chancery Lane, while JBF sought bail. See Doc. No. 236 for Hoffman's version of the events of that evening.

230. Jessie B. Frémont to Hoffman

8th April/52
CLARENDON

Mr. Hoffman need not trouble himself to take the long drive into the City as Mr. Fremont has no longer any need of assistance. Mr. Wright went at once last night to Mr. Peabody, whom he found but after some delay. Mr. Fremont knew nothing of Mrs. Fremont's application to Mr. Hoffman [for bail money] and disapproves of it, knowing it was useless!

[*Unsigned*]

349

AL-JBF (NHi—David Hoffman Papers). Endorsed: "Mrs. Fremont's Finale!!" Also: "Quere by whom written? and *when* written, and where written." The date is not in the handwriting of either of the Frémonts and must have been added later, possibly by Hoffman.

231. Frémont's Public Notice on Leasing and Sale

[13 April 1852]

MARIPOSA ESTATE. I, the undersigned, John Charles Fremont, of San Francisco, in California, now residing in London, at the Clarendon Hotel, in Albemarle St., do hereby give notice to all whom it may concern that I am ready to carry into effect all such contracts or agreements for leases of parts of the Mariposas Estate, as are legally binding upon me, which have been duly made and entered into prior to the 20th of December, 1851, by Hon. David Hoffman, then acting as my attorney in London, under a power of attorney, bearing date May 1850, and which power was revoked in October 1851, and notice of such revocation was received by said David Hoffman on the 19th December following.

And I hereby invite all persons in possession of such contracts to transmit forthwith to my Solicitors, Messrs. E. J. H. and J. Lawford, of Draper's Hall, Throgmorton St., London, authentic copies of such contracts or agreements, and to apprise my said Solicitors when and where the originals can be inspected by them on my behalf.

And I further give notice that I repudiate and disclaim (as I always have repudiated and disclaimed) the sale alleged to have been made by Col. Benton to Thomas Denny Sargent, Esqr., on the 29th January 1852.

13 April 1852.   JOHN CHARLES FRÉMONT

Newspaper clipping (NHi—David Hoffman Papers). Probably from the London *Daily News*, 13 or 14 April 1852 (see Doc. No. 234). Also printed in *Weekly Alta California*, 26 June 1852.

232. Frémont to Thomas H. Benton

Clarendon House, LONDON, April 13 '52

. . . .

I have been arrested for $50,000 for California liabilities contracted during the war and which we brought before Congress in 1848. I spent one night in a "Sponging House," (ante room to the jail) being arrested at night, and was bailed out next day, by Mr. George Peabody, the eminent American merchant here. Offers of service from numerous friends, including Mr. Lawrence, the Barings, and others were promptly made. I have reason to believe that many others of these liabilities will be urged upon me. If I was [as] great a patriot as you, I would go to jail and stay there until Congress paid these demands, now over a million, but my patriotism has been oozing out for the last five years. As my detention here promises to be long, you will greatly contribute to our comfort by getting me appointed chargé to some neighboring power, to protect me from further arrests & help to pay expenses.[1]

. . . .

[JOHN C. FRÉMONT]

Excerpt from ALS of Thomas H. Benton to Daniel Webster, ca. 14 May 1852 (Microcopy No. M-872, Roll 6, Letters of Application and Recommendation during the Administration of James Polk, Zachary Taylor, and Millard Fillmore, 1845–53). Endorsed: "Received, May 15th '52."

1. In making the extract for Webster, Benton wrote that he was "confident that both the Secretary [of State] and the President will be glad to do anything for Mr. Frémont which circumstances and a sense of duty will permit."

233. Thomas Denny Sargent's Notice on the Sale of the Mariposa

[ca. 14 April 1852]

MARIPOSA ESTATE. I, the undersigned, Thomas Denny Sargent, of Washington, in the United States, now residing at the York Hotel,

London, do hereby give notice, that the sale of the Mariposas Estate of Honorable John Charles Fremont, of San Francisco, was duly and completely made to me on the 29th of January last, at Washington, by Colonel Thomas H. Benton, the father-in-law and legally constituted attorney for the express purpose of the said John Charles Fremont; and I have, in assertion of my rights as such purchaser, filed a bill in Chancery against the said John Charles Fremont; and I hereby give notice to all persons holding leases or contracts for leases from David Hoffman, Esqr., that the said Mariposas Estate being no longer vested in the said John Charles Fremont, but in me alone, any contracts or deeds signed by him in regard to such Hoffman leases or contracts will have no validity or effect unless recognized and confirmed by me.

THOMAS DENNY SARGENT

Printed in *Weekly Alta California*, 26 June 1852, which indicates that it came from the London *Daily News* of 15 April and was a reply to JCF's advertisement of 13 April 1852.

234. David Hoffman to Frémont

CONDUIT STREET, 14 April 1852

[Is leaving for Paris to visit his family. "Specimens *receipted* for by Col. Fremont as being sent by the Express" have not reached London. Four other specimens brought by Robert, and one sent later to Hoffman by JCF, are at his disposal. Hears that there is some advertisement by JCF in the *Daily News* (see Doc. No. 231). Copy.]

235. Frémont to Felix Argenti

LONDON April 21st. 1852

DEAR SIR,

I desire to say to you that I very much regret the delay you have experienced in obtaining payment at Washington for Col. Johnsons

Dfts. [Col. Adam Johnston's drafts.].[1] We have been using & shall continue to use urgent efforts to obtain from Congress an early appropriation, which the language of the authorities at Washington has fully justified us in expecting.

Should the payment however be delayed beyond the 30 of June I will endeavor from other sources to make provisions for the Dfts. you hold.[2] In the meantime I am with regard, Respectfully Yours,

(Signed)   J C FREMONT

Felix Argenti Esqr.
Morley Hotel [London]

Copy (CSmH). Enclosed in Argenti to John A. Rockwell, 4 April 1859. Argenti requested that Rockwell find the original letter and send it to him, since JCF was then contending—1859—that the banker had taken the drafts without recourse on him.

1. See Doc. No. 167 for the Frémont-Wright contract with Adam Johnston. Argenti claimed that $49,000 in drafts had been endorsed to him by JCF (House Report 127, 33rd Cong., 2nd sess., Serial 808). The 1857 deposition of George W. Wright in the Quintard case (M. A. Goodspeed, Jr., Collection) and the Frémont and Roach case imply $42,000 (4 *Court of Claims Reports*, Dec. Term, 1868, pp. 252–57).

2. JCF did not make provision for reimbursing Argenti, and the latter petitioned Congress for relief. The committee report was negative, alleging that Johnston had exceeded his authority and that there was no proof that the supplies provided earlier to the Indians by Commissioner Barbour were insufficient or that the beef had been used to feed the Indians. Argenti must look to either JCF or Johnston for redress of his grievance (House Report 127, 33rd Cong., 2nd sess., Serial 808).

Later Argenti began a suit in the 12th District Court of California (Argenti v. United States, CHi—Wright Papers), but it seems not to have reached final decision. However, it was sufficiently far along on 14 Jan. 1857 for JCF to write Montgomery Blair seeking to learn "what probably will be the decision" (DLC —F. P. Blair Family Papers). Somehow the drafts or a part of them passed into the hands of Orestes Quintard, who sought recovery from JCF in the New York Supreme Court (1857 deposition of George W. Wright in the Quintard case, M. A. Goodspeed, Jr., Collection). According to the testimony of JCF's attorney, Coles Morris, there was an out-of-court settlement. Quintard assigned the drafts to his own attorney, John Baker, and Baker agreed to release JCF from all personal liability on the payment of $10,000, which, according to Morris, JCF did pay. Baker unsuccessfully petitioned Congress on the drafts, and on his death his executors, of whom John Roach was one, and JCF brought an action to recover (see Frémont and Roach's case, 4 *Court of Claims Reports*, Dec. Term, 1868, pp. 252–57).

236. David Hoffman to Frémont

To the Honorable   29 April 1852
Col. J. C. FREMONT
DEAR SIR

I now feel it to be a duty I owe myself and even to you to state some matters, which, possibly are quite *unknown* to you, and which *may* be in some degree the cause of your total alienation from me since our meeting at your special request at Mr. Lawford's Office. What had however previously taken place was far from being satisfactory to me and my friends. But still I referred all to a hasty judgment on your part and also to the embarrassing circumstances in what you imagined yourself to be placed. I now allude chiefly to the circumstances attendant upon the provoking arrest—my belief now being that you are even to this hour wholly uninformed of what did occur on that painful night and the following morning, as respect myself, and you have been permitted to remain under the most mistaken impressions as to what was my deportment on that occasion, and therefore I proceed to state them and with no other view whatsoever then that you may possess the fullest means of forming a correct opinion before you *finally* act.

At about 9 o'clock of the night of your arrest, I was extremely unwell and had retired with a draft for my severe cold. My Servant entered my Chamber with the Message that Colonel and Mrs. Fremont desired to see me! My surprise was great and being really quite unwell, my reply was that I was too unwell and had retired for the night, but that I would pay my respects next morning. The servant returned with a new message that "*Mrs. Fremont must see me on very important business*," and a moment after, Mrs. Fremont and a strange Gentlemen were in my Parlour, where I had left my Secretary, Mr. Holmes (in all my confidence for two years). In a minute after, I entered from my Chamber, and at once saw that it was not Colonel Fremont but a strange Gentleman who then was engaged in something that seemed to me a slight altercation with my Secretary! I at once asked Mrs. Fremont and the strange Gentleman to be seated, but the latter still persisted in stating to Mr. Holmes that a private interview was required and both the Lady and Gentleman emphatically declined to be seated. My prompt words again were "pray be seated, the gentleman will at once retire," and he promptly did so. I then asked the Stranger twice, "Who have I the honour to see?" and no reply, but in a moment after, he gave me the name of "Mr. Heap." I again urged both to be seated—the Gentleman declined by action, and the Lady spoke emphatically. Mr. Heap never uttered a word after! The words that followed from Mrs. Fremont were, "Do you know me?" "I believe so Lady ——." "My husband is arrested." Mr. Hoffman reply, "I am grieved to hear it." Lady reading from the first lines of my private letter just received by her, "you *say* you are still *loyal* to Colonel Fremont." Mr. Hoffman, "I certainly am but have you read that letter?"[1] Lady, "oh no! its too long." Mr. Hoffman, "Do be seated." Lady, "No I want no *words*. I have no time for *that*. I want £4000 and must have it." Mr. Hoffman, "I certainly have no £4000 to give you. I have but £600 out of Bank, and that is a mere accident, being too unwell and too busy to deposit it." Lady, "Oh don't tell *me* that. I know all about it. I know you have the money *there*. I was told so. I must have it." Mr. Hoffman, "If you had read *that* letter you would have found your mistake. I have no money beyond the £600 out of Bank and none of it due to Colonel Fremont. The Company's money I cannot, and will not part with. Colonel Fremont is my *Debtor*—not my Creditor—I am really much pained at what you state." Lady, "Do you know *who* I am? Here is my name." (Taking up a pen and writing her name at full length). Mr. Hoffman, "I do not at all doubt it Madame, but I have no such a sum—nothing but the £600 not mine—nor his." Lady "Oh don't tell me so, I will have it. I know all about you. Well, will you then go his Bail?" Mr. Hoffman, "I will not I cannot, that will not be in my power." (Mr. Heap returns to the Carriage). Lady, "You are a great rascal—my father says so." Mr. Hoffman, "It is of no moment to me what he says. I know myself." The Lady remained a moment after descending a few steps to the first Landing and continuing her vituperation, "You talk too much and write too much. You cannot talk little." My reply I do not remember. Mrs. Fremont then joined Mr. Heap in the Carriage.

I instantly prepared to see the American Minister to devise some plan for Colonel Fremont's instant relief. I well knew that I *could* not be Bail and that moreover it required *two*, and that as a Foreigner I could not be one. I likewise knew that the Minister could not be one—certainly I should have thought of prompt means had the Lady been the least calm and not overwhelmed me with a shower of words against me that necessarily drove out all means of deliberation. But a few minutes after Mrs. Fremont's departure I called on Mr. Lawrence who had not yet returned from dinner at Lord Palmerston's. From there I proceeded to the Clarendon Hotel, hoping that Mrs. Fremont might be able by that time to inform me where Colonel Fremont was. At that Hotel, I wrote a respectful note to Mrs. Fremont asking for an interview. A Message came that she would see me. I necessarily felt greatly pained at her situation, and all the vituperation of the late Interview was wholly forgotten by me, and I entered her Parlour with an earnest wish to be of all the service in my power. I took my Seat by her, and was pleased to find her apparently calm. I stated that she had dealt with me severely, to which she replied, "My only regret is to have used such language to a Man of your age," or words to that effect. I then asked where Colonel Fremont could be found. The reply was, "I do not know." Mr. Hoffman, "Will you see Mr. Lawrence here?" Lady, "I left a Note for him and expect him soon." Mr. Hoffman, "I am just from his House but he is still out at dinner." Lady, "You did not, I hope, say any thing there." Mr. Hoffman, "Oh no, I asked for the Minister, and whether Mrs. Fremont had lately called, but I will now leave a note for Mr. Lawrence with you." Paper and Ink were then handed to me by Mrs. Fremont, and I wrote a kind note to Mr. Lawrence (and I left it open for him after reading it to her) which note, as also the one to her written in Mr. Wright's Room asking for the interview I trust you will read. Upon handing the note for Mr. Lawrence to Mrs. Fremont, she said, "You are the last person in the world that either Colonel Fremont or myself would have called on." Mr. Hoffman, "I am sorry *you* think so, I think I should have been the very first." Mr. Hoffman then rising, said, "As you do not know where Colonel Fremont can be found I do not see what I can now do further." The Lady also then rising said, "You seem to have a very impudent person with you," alluding to my Secretary. "Oh no, Madame, it was only that he was ungraciously pressured by Mr. Heap to leave the Room before I could give him a sign. I have so many strange visitors that I am obliged to have some rule. He is a very amiable and respectful Man, and retired as soon as requested by me." Mr. Hoffman then took his respectful leave and there the somewhat painful second interview ended. I then retired to my Lodgings, where I waited for some message from the Clarendon (should Mr. Lawrence be there as was confidently believed by Mrs. Fremont). But as 1 o'clock came, and no message I retired for the night and on the next morning early, by 9 o'clock, I addressed a kind note to Mrs. Fremont again tendering her my services and requesting to know whether she had learnt where Colonel Fremont could be found by me, which note you possibly may not have seen, and a copy is now sent.[2] A prompt reply (I think by 10½ o'clock) came to me, copy of which note I now also send to you. You will observe that this Note of reply to mine has no *date*, no signature, no place, and the handwriting is not known to me.[3] Whether it be your's or Mrs. Fremont's or Mr. Heap's, or Mr. Wright's, I cannot positively say. But of this I am quite sure, the note is most unjust to me, by whomsoever written, as my deportment upon the whole matter of your arrest was prompt—feeling—courteous—but *firm*; I well knew I *could not* be Bail; and I had done all in my power and all that justice and good breeding required at my hands. And again on the following day I think the 8th April, I addressed a volunteer letter to Mr. Lawford dictated in the kindest spirit respecting the probable cause of your unjust arrest expressing to that Gentleman (your now Representative) my indignation at that arrest, my desire to explain to Mr. Lawford my belief as to the source of that arrest and my reasons for believing it to be wholly a Government debt and not Your's and also what I thought ought to be *Your's* and his course in regard to the same, and also as to a Letter to be written at once to the United States to put a stop to such cruel arrests in future. Now Sir, if the four Letters I have named as being written by me on the occasion of your arrest *have* been seen by you, it is possible that you can justify the note seemingly addressed to me by Mrs. Fremont at the moment she supposed you were released? But if none of these have been seen by you, and if you are under the naked impression that I coldly and cruelly neglected to sympathise with Mrs. Fremont and yourself you are under a very great mistake indeed, and such an idea would be not only in total conflict with all I really did in the matter, but also with my whole character. I make these explanations only that the absolute truth may be known to you. All the rest is with yourself. Permit me in conclusion to make the following remarks and still in a spirit of kindness towards you but of resolution in repect to myself:

1. This is the first instance ever known to me where a Principal sees fit to voluntarily *stultify* himself, cast off all intercourse with his Agent, who alone knows all the facts, and all the Law of his Case, and place the whole in the hands of a total Stranger, himself overwhelmed with occupations, and where the Principal, the Agent, and the selected Solicitor are all placed in a false position, and all rendered alike—utterly useless, but where by *unity of action*, all would have been triumphant success.

2. Supposing, argumenti gratia [?] that I am a very great Rascal, still *that fact* was positively the very reason why both you and Mr. Lawford should have acted precisely the reverse of what has been done.

3. But Sir, you know and all know that my whole life is *sans reproche*. You cannot put your finger on a single transaction of that agency, nor of my life, that will not bear the closest scrutiny.

4. I sought not the Agency and had ten others which amounted to far more than your one: and yet I was obliged to abandon every thing for yours after I once became engaged in it. I had read your history, I remembered you as a young Man, I was charmed with Mr. Nicollet. I became enthusiastic in your Cause. And how have you treated me? Nay how have treated yourself? I confidently reply, in a way that must be your total ruin, if you do not with earnestness and great good sense, place all things as they were or should have been, at the moment of your arrival, and which would have been all right had you sailed for Southhampton instead of New York.

5. Is it possible Sir, that Mr. Lawford and yourself still commune with such persons as Mr. Lakeman and a dozen of the like. "Madness and confusion lie in *that* way." Regularity and Harmony is the way that has been pursued by me for two years. All of the Companies are composed of *business* Men, of means and of high character; but the *Ave Maria*, the *West Mariposa*, and the *Agua Fria* have done all kinds of strange things that *cannot* command public confidence. I well know that the Agua Fria were at £3.10.0 for £1 paid but what reduced them down to their present low condition since their [?] arrival? And what reduced all of the premiums to either *par* or to discount? Surely nothing else than your fatal selection of a Solicitor, thereby, casting off *first* all of my knowledge of the facts and the law of your case. *Second*, causing many persons to question, for the first time, your title, the *value* of your estate, your *consistency*, your *honour*, and even calling you the "Great Avaricious Repudiator!" Now Sir, who (but myself) manfully resisted all this even since your arrival, and amidst all the innuendos of yourself, your Solicitor, and your enemies. Who (but yourself) has nearly broken down and cast to the winds a great system built up by my influences and zeal, that would have poured into California more than 20,000,000 of dollars, and upon your estate a large portion of it? Can the *ruin* you have thus far caused be cured? I do not know.

6. The effect of all this strange condition of things since your arrival is to cause people to again suspect everything. Two years of labor

358

in removing all objections now put in jeopardy and all risked very unnecessarily provided your property is even approximating as valuable as stated.

In final conclusion, I have only further to state that my Communications to Mr. Lawford of this day bring the whole matter as clearly to his view as I possibly can, and to the full extent to which I mean to go in the matter with that gentleman.

The whole affair is susceptible of being brought within a very few words, and a very few and simple proceedings.

Where there is a "*good will*" there is always a "*good way*." I now think I have fully discharged my *duty to you*. The future must guide my steps under the Counsel of my friends, and also under my own sober deliberations. Yours,

D.H.

To Col. Fremont

SC (NHi—David Hoffman Papers). Endorsed: "Letter (after sending to Mr. L[awford] further accounts). *Important* to show the *unjust* feeling against Mr. Hoffman."
1. See Hoffman to JCF, 8 April 1852 (Doc. No. 228).
2. Doc. No. 229.
3. Doc. No. 230.

237. Frémont to Messrs. Howland & Aspinwall

Paris, April 30th. 1852

Messrs. Howland & Aspinwall
New York
Gentlemen:

Five days after sight of this my second of exchange (first of same tenor and date not paid) please pay to the order of Dr. H[arvey] Lindsley, of the City of Washington, D.C., the sum of one thousand dollars ($1000) and charge the same to the account of Your Obedt. Servt.

John Charles Frémont

ALS (PHi).

238. David Hoffman to Frémont

[LONDON], 4 May 1852

[Writes him about the article in the London *Times* of that morning wherein the California agent of the Nouveau Monde, John H. Clement, noticed that JCF's title and his ability to put parties in possession of mineral grants were so tenuous as to raise questions about the wisdom of the company establishing itself on his property. The implication was that the company would seek another field for its operations. Hoffman notes that JCF has the right to see the letter from Clement and all of the company's instructions to him. He must be first in protecting his interests; Hoffman could give him much information, but JCF has cast him off. Copy.]

239. Frémont to Joseph C. Palmer

LONDON
7 May 1852

DEAR SIR,

This letter will be handed to you by Mr. Franz Jacob Schmitz who goes to California on the part of the present holders of a Lease granted to Lord Erskine and others under the title of the British Mutual Gold Mining Company.[1] The object of this brief note is to ask you to give to Mr. Schmitz the advantage of your friendly aid and experience in getting his mining materials to the ground & to give him all possible aid in making the selection of his location at Mariposa. You will be careful to observe that possession be given him strictly in conformity to the Lease granted to the British Mutual & which you will find among the Mariposa papers left with you. If it be not already occupied please instruct Mr. Parkes[2] to put Mr. Schmitz in possession of the vein in rear of the point located by Wass, Molitor & Company and if that be taken up request Mr. Parks to give his aid in pointing out the best locations to ensure to this company a good position. The present is intended principally to remove any difficulties in Mr. Schmitz's way and to ensure him a friendly reception by the next Mail from London

or Paris. I will write you at length upon this subject with regard, I am
yours truly,

JOHN CHARLES FRÉMONT

Copy (NHi—David Hoffman Papers). Contained in the Frémont v. Hoff-
man, Brief, Bill, and Answer, p. 15.
    1. The company was now known as the Quartz Rock Mariposa Gold Mining
Company (see its papers on Film Z-6-1, Reel 58, CU-B).
    2. Formerly employed by the Philadelphia and California Mining Company,
Parke seemed now to be serving as JCF's agent on the Mariposa.

240. David Hoffman to Frémont

10 Conduit Street, HANOVER SQUARE, 13 July 1852

[Although the agency between them is now ended and Stephen
Lakeman is JCF's agent, still Hoffman feels he has a duty to state a
number of things.

1. He will soon file his answer to the bill of Chancery which JCF
filed against him on 12 June to obtain the agency contracts and papers. It has been delayed by his indisposition, the unprecedented heat,
and the recent death of his only brother (John Hoffman).

2. JCF has never asked for any *formal* account until he asked it
by his bill in Chancery, which he regards as a proceeding of great
incivility.

3. When JCF first spoke of having a solicitor, he put it upon the
grounds of his own lack of health and the need for objectivity, dis-
claiming hostility to Hoffman. "And upon those grounds you requested me, as a favor, to meet your solicitor, which I did."

4. He has served JCF conscientiously, laboriously, and with a regard for economy.

5. With his own money he has sustained the agency for two years.
Not a shilling has JCF paid.

6. All his contracts were legal, bona fide, and made long before
JCF's letter reached him on 20 Dec. JCF may break them all, but that
is his responsibility—moral as well as pecuniary. Some of the final
formalities were not drawn up until later, but the contracts are valid.

7. He claims to be his agent until at least 13 April 1852, when JCF

inserted his advertisement [Doc. No. 231], but even then his agency was not legally ended and he will claim essential disbursements to 15 July.

8. Lawford knows that the little informal account which Hoffman had rendered was not intended to bind either party. He had offered Lawford or his clerks the use of his office to make copies of all papers resulting from a two-year agency, but Lawford "was too much occupied, or too indolent" to accept, and imposed upon Hoffman "a physical and an intellectual impossibility." Hoffman then offered copies of the essential documents provided he was compensated for his disbursements and services, but replies were "equivalent to either *nothing* or to a *denial*, or to mere reference to you, whereas you had referred me to him."

9. He then offered to arbitrate his disbursement account and compensation, but did not receive replies. He offered to explain all things verbally but was refused. When he inquired if JCF might leave for California without paying him, Lawford again did not reply.

10. The solicitor had likewise refused Hoffman's request to peruse JCF's answer to Sargent's bill in Chancery.

11. Hoffman is mystified by JCF's lack of interest in information, his aloofness, and his treatment of him as though he were "dishonest, a fool and mere trickster!"

12. "It was cruelly false, in whoever asserted to you that I demanded £60,000 as a settlement." Furthermore, he has been straightforward and honest and has not speculated in the companies.

13. Robert's power of attorney has never been revoked, but he has made no contracts since 20 Dec. 1851 and he only demanded money for his disbursements from the time Hoffman ceased to pay him until the revocation of his power, along with his passage to Baltimore. JCF was legally bound to restore him to the United States, since he had sent him to London. Copy. Endorsed: "Sent to Paris through Mrs. H."]

241. David Hoffman to Frémont

10 Conduit Street, LONDON, 25 July 1852

[Lawford has not replied to his letter of 24 July or JCF to his of 13 July. News of the deaths of Henry Clay, a Baltimore friend, and his brother, have increased his gloom.

The disbursement account and all vouchers were ready and the account has been sent to Mr. Lawford. The answer to the bill in Chancery would be filed in a few days. Inquires if it is JCF's "fixed intention" to further waste him in mind and body. "Pay me reasonably my *Disbursement* and my *Compensation*. The papers are always yours upon those terms. I never demanded for a moment any specific sum. All was left to himself [Lawford], yourself, and to my Solicitor. Is that unfair?

"May you, Sir, never find persons disposed to torment you unnecessarily when you arrive at my age—now in my 67th year. And may you never find a *Stolid* Solicitor (with a hundred times more business on hand than he can comprehend) willing to add to your declining days a misery not at all your due." Copy. Addressed to JCF in Paris.]

242. Frémont to Messrs. Storer & Stephenson

Paris, July 26th 1852

Gentlemen,

I have this day been informed by Mr. Frederick Goodell, that he has received from you a letter in which it is stated that you have advanced to Major Genl. Wm. Gibbs McNeill,[1] the sum of five hundred pounds on my account. This information has caused me much surprise and the object of this note is to say to you (should the information I have received be correct) that this money has been obtained without my consent or authority. Genl. McNeill was authorized in writing, to demand and receive a certain specified sum of money, stipulated to have been paid to me under certain engagements, but neither he or any one else was authorized to borrow money of which I am not in need.

I write this for your guidance, as you will not look to me for repayment of any sums so advanced. Respectfully Your obedient servant,

John Charles Frémont

Messrs. Storer & Stephenson
No. 53 South Street, New York

ALS-JBF (NN—Miscellaneous Papers). Storer & Stephenson of New York were shipchandlers.
1. Formerly connected with the Corps of Topographical Engineers, McNeill's major generalship was due to a commission in the state militia of Rhode Island.

Since 1851 he had been in London promoting "great American mining projects," and seems to have had a stake in the Agua Fria. When a crisis occurred in that company's affairs at the end of May 1852, he went to Paris to seek JCF's return to London (CULLUM, 1:161–66; M. A. Goodspeed, Jr., Collection).

243. Frémont to William M. Gwin

PARIS, Avenue des Champs Elysees 61,
Dec. 20. 52

MY DEAR SIR,

I see by the papers your arrival at New York, & hasten to make you my earnest acknowledgements for your kindness & support in having obtained from Congress means to pay the War Drafts upon which I was sued in London. Your immediate departure for California prevented the prompt acknowledgement of the letter in which you informed me of the condition of things at the adjournment of Congress. I greatly hope that the present Congress will authorize the Secretary to make the payment, as otherwise the embarrassments which surround me will be greatly increased, & it would be very mortifying if Mr. George Peabody, who became my bail on the occasion, should be obliged to pay the drafts.

Will you do me the favor to forward the enclosed to Palmer, Cook & Co.? I write as strongly as possible to urge them to obtain the action of the Commission upon the Mariposas title, if it can possibly be had. My counsel promised me the ratification by several mails back, but we have been disappointed & have heard not a word by the last two mails. All our business here depends entirely on the ratification. Our success will be immense if we receive it, but if we do not, & soon, the result will be ruinous. There never has been so strong a feeling in favor of gold mining as at this time. All the companies are at high premiums, the Australian Agricultural Company (which the Mariposas might have rivalled) being at 180 pounds sterling premium per share. The Mariposa is kept back & daily weakened by the distrust in which the doubt of title & delay of the Commission to act has placed it. In the mean time Australia is rapidly becoming very popular, & absorbing capital immensely. If we do not soon get our title the Mariposa, so far as regards the quartz crushing on it & results, will be valueless.

This I should think as a State question, & apart from the friendly regard which I have had the pleasure to enjoy from you, would have interest for you. It is certain that the capital of several millions of pounds sterling which might have been employed at the Mariposas, will be so far as its results are concerned a clear loss to the state.

It has been proved upon the ground & in your own knowledge, that American capital never can work the ground, & the occasion to put English capital there is rapidly passing in the greater inducements held out in Australia where companies can obtain properties embracing several hundred thousand acres of land. Would you find the leisure to let me have a line in return & tell me what we may expect from the Land Commission & whether or not in the case of the Mariposas there is likely to be had an early decision. As you are aware probably, it has been argued & submitted & stands No. 1 on the Docket.

I trust that your visit to California was in all respects pleasant & satisfactory, and with our respectful regards & homage to Mrs. Gwin, I am very truly yours,

J. C. FRÉMONT

Hon. Wm. M. Gwin
U.S. Senate,
Washington City.

Pray put your reply under cover to John Lawford, Esqre., Drapers Hall, Throgmorton Street, London. He is my solicitor & through him letters reach me with least delay, ut supra.

ALS (CU-B).

244. David Hoffman to Frémont

45 Conduit Street, Hanover Square, 25 Jan. 1853

[Inquires if there is still not a means of ending honorably, justly, and advantageously the disagreeable misunderstanding that has arisen between them. JCF seemed to listen to mere rumors; Wright could never have been worthy of his confidence, and Lawford had, without knowledge, termed Hoffman's business "moonshine." He again refers to JCF's declaration that he had heard something derogatory of Robert's character and would like to know the accuracy of the report that he might govern his own conduct. The Nouveau Monde allege "that your course has *compelled* them to abandon the contracts, and to turn Squatters, appropriating the $200,000 raised upon your name, and through my toils and long continued influence here, and the exertions of Mr. Robert in Paris. They withheld all payments, all stock, but still they hold on to the contracts and *intimate* their intention to claim damages of you, instead of your demanding damages of them!" He would like to know "what is to be done with certain shares of the Nouveau Monde, the French side by agreement to be converted into English shares, and which were retained for you in security for the £12,000 debt due you by Capt. W. K. Smith, the French Company, and others, and which as I contend are yours, but which, the English branch claim as theirs!"

His present occupation is the publication of some volumes written by him in the United States (*Chronicles Selected from the Originals of Cartaphilus, the Wandering Jew*, 3 vols. [London: Thomas Bosworth, 1853]). When it was completed, he would establish himself in Paris.

His answer to the bill in Chancery has been filed nearly a month. Neither Mr. Marriott's[1] suggestion nor Mr. Lawford's threat of an attachment had hastened its filing. Draft.]

1. Hoffman sometimes writes "Marryat" in designating JCF's agent, who attempted on several occasions to settle the controversy over Hoffman's compensation. This would seem to be Frederick Marriott (1805–84), the founder of the present *Illustrated London News*, but who was in San Francisco in Jan. 1852 advertising himself as a "Loan, Stock and Money Agent" as well as a dealer in exchange on all nations (CROSS, 1:155–58, 296–98). In the "Resume of his Agency," Hoffman recounts how Marriott had sailed from San Francisco to New York with JCF (this would have been in Feb. 1852) and then had taken passage on the *Baltic* (a few days ahead of the Frémonts in the *Africa*) "to relieve the mind of Mr. Hoffman" on the Sargent contract.

Another British emigré to California in 1850, Frank S. Marryat, was also traveling home about this time, although he recollects not leaving California until March. He would call upon Hoffman in London and would leave an account of his experiences in the mines of Sonora and Tuttletown in *Mountains and Molehills; or, Recollections of a Burnt Journal* (London, 1855).

The identity of JCF's emissary is further confused by newspapers' listing of passengers. "F. Marriot" arrived in New York with the Frémonts; "F. Maryatt" sailed on the *Baltic* (New York *Herald*, 7 March 1852; New York *Daily Tribune*, 8 March 1852).

245. David Hoffman to Frémont

LONDON, 8 Feb. 1853

[Wrote on 25 Jan. and is yet without attention. Copy. Addressed to JCF in Paris.]

246. Frémont to David Hoffman

PARIS, Feb. 8th. 53

DAVID HOFFMAN, ESQRE.
SIR,

I have received your note of this morning, & in reply to your intimation that you remain without attention from me, I have to say first, that I must continue to treat with neglect any communications from you which speak abusively of gentlemen with whom I am connected; & secondly, that pending a legal controversy I judged a correspondence between us inexpedient, & not likely to produce any good result. But, whenever you really find it agreeable to your views to arrange the business between us, I see no difficulty in the way of a reasonable adjustment, without prejudice to the interests of either. It would simply be necessary to signify that you are disposed to undertake such a settlement in good faith, & to let alone the names & character of individuals, who are not parties to the questions at issue.

In such case we might proceed without recourse to the law. I remain, Sir, Your obedt. servt.

J. C. FRÉMONT

ALS (NHi—David Hoffman Papers). Endorsed: "*Impossible*, but in reply to mine of the 8th and received by me [the] 10th. But from the 25 Jan. to the 8 Feb. he was silent. If this was written on [the] Evening of the 8 Feb. Mr. Lawford was then there, and saw mine of the 25 Jan. and also Mr. Venness's respecting the L'Aígle d'or."

247. Frémont to David Hoffman

PARIS, Avenue des Champs Elyseés, 61; Feb 21. 53
DAVID HOFFMAN, ESQRE.
SIR,

In pursuance of our recent correspondence I have sent to Mr. Lawford some bases of an agreement upon which I think the question at issue may be satisfactorily settled.

I suppose that they will be immediately communicated to you. I am respectfully Your Obdt. Servt.

JOHN C. FRÉMONT

ALS (NHi—David Hoffman Papers).

248. David Hoffman to Frémont

Friday P.M., 25 Feb. 1853

[Refers to JCF's letter of 21 Feb. Neither he nor his solicitor has heard from Mr. Lawford about a settlement. Draft.]

249. David Hoffman to Frémont

45 Conduit Street, Hanover Square, 2 March 1853

[Has still not heard from Mr. Lawford about the bases of an arrangement (see JCF's letter of 21 Feb.). It would be beneficial to both of them to get rid of all solicitorships and the quibbling about trifles. On 1 Feb. Lawford had filed exceptions to Hoffman's answer, but he will delay his own answer to the exceptions in hopes that he and JCF can end their controversy. Draft.]

250. David Hoffman to Frémont

LONDON, Thursday, 9 March 1853

[Has not had a reply to his letter of 2 March, and Lawford has not communicated to him the proposed bases of an agreement as JCF had indicated he would do by his letter of 21 Feb. Lawford insists that an attachment will issue against his person on the next day for failure to answer the exceptions. He considers the case out of law and hopes the letter will reach JCF before Lakeman leaves Paris for London. Wishes to avoid the months of legal delay and expense which will surely occur if his answer is filed. Two copies, one dated 10 March, but the differences are minor.]

251. David Hoffman to Frémont

LONDON, Saturday, 26 March 1853

[Lakeman had called several times, but now he has not seen him for a number of days and wonders if JCF has changed his mind about a private settlement. Two weeks ago he had sent to his solicitors, Venning, Naylor, and Robins, the answer to the exceptions, but after the arrival of Lakeman "as your agent to settle," he had asked for its return and had been informed that the law proceeding against him had been suspended. Lakeman had indicated that one of the bases for settlement was that Hoffman continue his agency to those companies that he might be able to put into operation out of the twenty contracts he had made. Hoffman declined to do so on the score of health and family commitments. He has now been informed by his solicitors that Lawford requires that the answer be filed "this day" or he risks arrest. Hoffman desires to know if he is "in law, or in the process of some settlement?"

He notes that he has sent the Andrew Smith contract to Smith's son, who said he wanted to send it to JCF. Draft.]

252. Frémont to David Hoffman

61, Ave. des Champs Elysees, March 30. 53

SIR,

I have today returned to Paris after an absence of nearly a week & find here your letter of the 26th, postmarked 27th.

By a letter received this morning I learn that Mr. Lakeman was called by business to Liverpool on the 24th. & is likely to remain there for some days to come, being detained by indisposition.

Perhaps this absence may account for the delay which you inform me has occurred in approaching a settlement. Agreeably to your suggestion I gave Mr. Lakeman a written memorandum of the terms upon which the arrangement might be discussed. Of course, until your views should have been made known to me & it was ascertained that the settlement could not be made in a friendly manner, I would not be at liberty, nor would I desire, to change my mind, as you suggest I might have done.

Your intimation in regard to seeing me in Paris might become the most advisable course, but I should think that yourself & Mr. Lakeman might in a very brief period accomplish it. As Mr. Lakeman has undertaken the negociation it would perhaps not be proper to interfere with him until he expresses some doubt of his ability to accomplish it.

I will write by this mail to Mr. Lawford upon the subject of the suit, & hope that in the meantime no untoward circumstances may have occurred. I am respectfully Your Obedt. Servt.,

JOHN C. FRÉMONT

ALS (NHi—David Hoffman Papers). Addressed and postmarked.

253. David Hoffman to Frémont

LONDON, 31 March 1853

[Replies to JCF's letter of 30 March. Has received a letter from Lakeman and has advised him to remain at the Adelphi Hotel in Liverpool until he has recovered from his illness.[1] Signed copy.]

1. Lakeman was not able to effect a settlement between JCF and Hoffman. The documents do not clearly indicate the basis of negotiations, although Hoffman implied in his letter of 26 March 1853 that JCF wished him to resume his agency to those companies which he might be able to put into operation out of the twenty contracts he had made. He declined to do so on the grounds that his health and family commitments did not permit it. Since the negotiations continued for several additional weeks, there must have been other possibilities. No agreement, however, could be reached. Hoffman's attempt to communicate directly with JCF's solicitor was rebuffed, and his own counsel warned him that it was really in vain to attempt to travel out of the beaten track. The answer to the exceptions had still not been filed by 4 May, and for a time it seemed as though Hoffman might be arrested and sent to prison (Walter C. Venning to Hoffman, 16 April, 4 May 1853, and Hoffman to Venning, 5 May 1853). After other legal maneuvers the case was heard in the Vice-Chancellor's Court on 3 June, and Hoffman lost his attempt to withhold the documents until JCF compensated him for his services. Even the argument that the documents also pertained to the second agent, Robert, who was not a part of the defense, was insufficient to bar JCF's right to them (Venning, Naylor, and Robins to Hoffman, 24, 28 and 30 May 1853, Hoffman Papers; report of the decision in Frémont v. Hoffman, London *Times*, 6 June 1853).

JCF soon returned to the United States; Hoffman followed within a few months and died 11 Nov. 1854. Through the New York Supreme Court, his widow continued the legal struggle to obtain compensation for her husband's services, but was apparently unsuccessful (SPENCE).

254. Brantz Mayer to Frémont

BALTIMORE, 25 April 1853

MY DEAR COLONEL,

I have inexpressible pleasure in congratulating you on your success in confirming the Title to your California Lands.[1]

I suppose they will ultimately produce the full value of all your calculations as to their gold contents; though I doubt whether the quartz region will come properly into play until the loose gold shall have been thoroughly picked from the river bars and ravines.

I cannot say how much I have been pained at hearing of the estrangement between yourself and my old friend and professor Mr. David Hoffman.

I take the liberty to express myself thus, because my Brother and myself were the means of your first business union. Neither Mr. Charles Mayer nor myself is yet precisely aware *of the grounds* of your difference, but I am sure that it can only have occurred in consequence of misapprehension or irritation which may be obliterated.

For nearly twenty-four years my association with Mr. Hoffman was of the most intimate character. I know him to be exciteable, but with this exception I can safely and conscientiously say, that I am not aware of any fault that should create mortal enmity betwixt himself and others. In pecuniary affairs I know him to be the Soul of Honor; and from my correspondence with him about your affairs while you were in California, I am satisfied that no one ever had an agent who was impressed with a greater zeal for his principal's interest than you had in Mr. Hoffman. I think, if he is at fault, that it must be chargeable to an excess of his quality rather than to any thing else.

His letters inform me how much he was thwarted and mortified by Col. Benton's sale to Denny Sargent when you had expressly disavowed the authority in letters to him.

This placed him in a most awkward posture before the British public, and was well qualified to test his sensibilities.

I write this much, not only to say, "how are you" once more, but with the hope—the *hearty* hope—that I may be instrumental—in restoring the kindly relations of two gentlemen whom I esteem and honor so much. You will do me the justice to believe that I am not offering this hope as an intermeddler.

If Mrs. Fremont is still with you in Paris, pray be kind enough to bring me to her recollection and to offer her my respectful Compliments.

I am now occupied chiefly, as far as my eyes allow, in editing a leading paper in Baltimore. One of my last long articles is in furtherance of Col. Benton's Scheme of the Great Central Road to the Pacific, the published plan of which I suppose he has sent you.

When do you come home again? though after your toilsome life in the wilderness I dare say you have no objection to enjoying for a few years the mingled pleasures and science of Paris. I beg you to believe me very truly yr. friend,

Brantz Mayer

For the Honb. C. J.
Fremont, Paris

Copy (NHi—David Hoffman Papers).
1. The California Board of Land Commissioners had confirmed title on 27 Dec. 1852.

255. Frémont to Charles F. Smith

WASHINGTON CITY, D.C.
June 27, 1853

COL. C. F. SMITH, &c. &c. &c.
SIR,

Your note of the 21st was not received by me until this morning probably on account of my absence from the city to which I returned yesterday.

I had made some business engagements for tomorrow before receiving your note, but will ascertain then, the earliest time which will be convenient to the board and make an appointment accordingly.

I shall be happy to give any explanation or information in my power. Very respectfully,

J. C. FRÉMONT

ALS, RC (DNA-92, LR, 1852–54). Endorsed: "Rec. June 28/53. No answer." JCF would meet with the California Claims Board several times during the summer of 1853 and immediately on his return from the fifth expedition was asked to attend again to give information on "claims now held suspended" (Charles F. Smith to Frémont, Lbk, DNA-92, LS, 1852–55, Microfilm roll 9).

256. Certificates of John C. and Jessie B. Frémont Concerning Frémont's Absence from the Second Session of the 31st Congress

[7 July 1853 and 5 Jan. 1854]

I certify that after the close of the first Session of the 31st Congress I left Washington on my return to California—that a few days after leaving New York I was taken seriously ill & was confined to my stateroom during the whole voyage afterwards. That I was so ill on my arrival at San Francisco as to be unable to proceed to my proper residence at Mariposas, and remained accordingly confined in that city. And that I did not sufficiently recover my health in time to attend the second session of the 31st Congress. The reasons for my absence from my place were stated to the Senate by Col. Benton & will be found in the Journals of that body.

JOHN C. FRÉMONT
Washington City, July 7th. 1853.

I accompanied Col. Frémont to California in the fall of 1850— leaving New York on the Cherokee the 8th of October & arriving in San Francisco on the 21st of November. Col. Frémont was ill from neuralgic sciatica in the left leg & could not leave his room during the voyage. The sea air of San Francisco aggravated the disease and his physician, Dr. Bowie after attending him for six weeks in San Francisco, sent Mr. Frémont to San José for the benefit of its soft climate. Mr. Frémont was there all January & about the twelfth or fourteenth of February he went to the Mariposas. As the journey then had to be made on horseback, it required him to be sure of his strength before undertaking it, and previous to that time he could not bend his leg.

JESSIE BENTON FRÉMONT
Washington City Jany. 5th 1854.

AD (IU). JCF received a total compensation of $8,110.40 during his tenure as senator in the 31st Congress. He was paid as follows:

"Sept. 30, 1850	Mileage, 10,270 miles	$4,108.00
Sept. 30, 1850	Per diem, 230 days	1,840.00
Dec. 2, 1853	additional mileage, 3,686 miles, short charged	1,474.40
Feb. 11, 1854.	Per diem for detention by sickness on journey home, 86 days	688.00"

Senate Ex. Doc. 109, 34th Cong., 1st sess., p. 85, Serial 825.

257. Frémont to P. G. Washington

Monday July 11th 1853

DEAR SIR,

I have the pleasure to thank you for the gratification afforded me by your note of Saturday informing me that the Honble. Secy. of the Treasury has requested our Minister at London to pay the recent award of the English court against me.[1]

I will permit myself the pleasure to repeat my thanks in person, and in the meantime remain Yours very respectfully,

J. C. Frémont

Honble. P. G. Washington
Asst. Secty. of the Treasury

ALS-JBF (James S. Copley Collection, La Jolla, Calif.).

1. On 6 May 1853, in the Exchequer of the Pleas, Middlesex, William Gibbs, Henry Hucks Gibbs, John Hayne, and George Thomas Davy (referred to as the Messrs. Anthony Gibbs) had won a favorable verdict in their suit against JCF, which had led to his arrest shortly after his arrival in London. He was ordered to pay the amount of the four bills of exchange (£3,988 12s. 9d.) with interest at the rate of 6 percent, the rate given at Washington, D.C., and court costs. Since the jury had found that the rate of interest in California in the late 1840s had been 25 percent, the plaintiffs were later successful in having the full court order an increase in the interest rate to 25 percent for the period from 25 Oct. 1847 to 16 June 1853.

Fortunately for JCF, Senator Gwin and other friends had been at work, and under an act for his relief, approved 3 March 1853, Congress had authorized the Secretary of the Treasury to pay the drafts and costs of JCF's legal defense. To settle the judgment, the Secretary paid £9,933 7s. 9d. on 21 Sept. 1853 and ultimately $2,150.49 in defense fees. Many documents connected with the case and Messrs. E. J. H. and J. Lawford's itemization of attornies' fees may be found in Senate Ex. Doc. 109, 34th Cong., 1st sess., pp. 88–140, Serial 825.

During the preparation of his legal defense, JCF had considered returning to the United States for three months in an attempt to get all claims with respect to California settled by the American government, and his bail was willing that he do so. Ultimately, however, the defense and plaintiffs requested the Barons of the Exchequer to appoint special commissioners in San Francisco, Philadelphia, and Washington to take testimony about conditions in California in 1847 and the nature of JCF's authority. As one of its witnesses, the Philadelphia commission called James Buchanan, who had been Secretary of State during the Mexican War. Most of his testimony may be found in a little pamphlet entitled "Who Conquered California?" Ironically, it was issued in 1856 by the Young Men's Fremont and Dayton Central Union when JCF and Buchanan were vying for the presidency.

The Fifth and Final Expedition, 1853–54

258. Frémont Justifies His Forthcoming Expedition

[Fall 1853]

My own journeys through our interior mountains had already in 1847 satisfied me that a direct railroad route ought to be searched for along the parallel of 38°39'. Information acquired from all sources led me to believe that this range of country was certainly practicable, and that the most important points on either ocean might be connected, by a line which should be direct, and at the same time penetrate the mountains through a region admirably adapted for settlement and cultivation. With this view I had embraced in my original plan of explorations, (and so stated in one of my published journals,) an examination of the central section of the Rocky Mountains; comprehending the Three Parks, with the numerous valleys which enclose the head waters of the South Platte, the Arkansas, and the Del Norte on the one side, and the sources of the East Fork of the Great Colorado on the other.

Since 1847 my attention has been continuously occupied with this line, and with this section of the Rocky Mountains through which I have proposed that the great road should pass, entering the valley of the Colorado through the valley of the San Luis or Upper Del Norte. To this point my own examinations have been extended, with the satisfactory result of finding a way easy and good, through a broad and fertile country, allowing straight roads and choice of lines with continuous and expanded settlements. Such a line seems to comprehend all the advantages which ought to be combined in a trunk road to the Pacific. It is direct, central, and feasible of construction; it commands the most practicable pass, and best known route for a branch road into Oregon, and would be the means of forming a new and great state of this Union—the Switzerland of America.

With these views I attempted, but was prevented from exploring it in 1847. In 1848 I resumed the attempt in an expedition which was defeated in its complete result; but was successful so far as it went, and completely successful so far as it realized my own idea.

About this time finding myself owner of a property which promised to be of extraordinary value, I conceived the idea of wholly devoting it, as far as it would go, to the prosecution of the work; and on my return to Washington in 1850, I communicated it to Mr. Francis P. Blair and other friends, who highly approved of my plan, and through whom, without design on my part, it reached the public press.

In the fulfillment of this plan I visited England with the expectation of engaging foreign capital in the development of the property, so as to make it available to the enterprise. Protracted delays and difficulties growing out of the contest for my property with the government, blunted or paralyzed my efforts, and I had succeeded only to a limited extent, when information of the general movement at home in favor of the railroad reached me. I immediately arranged my affairs for an absence of six or eight months, provided the necessary instruments, and started for Washington. On my arrival I found the [U. States] exploring parties were fully organized, and the Government commands already disposed of. Finding myself prepared with time and instruments, and fairly engaged in the enterprise, which properly formed a continuation of my own plans, I have decided to carry it out by my private means. The property above referred to had diminished in value from the litigation of the United States; much of its absolute and immediately available wealth had been carried away, but it had become better defined, and I had recently received in England an offer of two millions [of dollars?] for half, dependent upon recognition of title. This realization of the property has been again subjected to indefinite delay by the recent appeal of the Government from their own tribunal, but I have decided to invest it, whenever it becomes available, in that part of the road which shall go through the state of California from San Francisco to its western frontier, at whatever point the road from the East should strike it.

Under this deprivation of resources, I can only go on with one branch of my intended enterprise, that of completing my examinations of the country between the Upper Del Norte and the valley of the San Joaquin. Upon this line I propose to make a double examination—going out before the snows fall, and returning in mid-winter. A winter exploration, in making me acquainted with the depth and prevalence of the snows, and the extent of their impediments to winter traveling, would enable me to judge practically of some points very material to the right decision of the question.

The field of operations reaches over an expanse of mountain wilderness extending the whole length of our domain from north to south. In view of the enduring and unchangeable character of the work, no line can be considered approximately determined until all possible information should have been obtained, so that the best route, under every aspect for the country, may be adopted. To meet the actions of the next Congress, will give ample employment to all the labor that can be brought to it, and my examinations therefore must necessarily contribute to the mass of materials for the solution of the question. Whatever may be the results at which I arrive, they shall be fairly communicated to the public, as an element in aid of their decisions.

Finally, and above every other consideration, I have a natural desire to do something in the finishing up of a great work in which I had been so long engaged. I do it with the object and the hope of adding to the favorable considerations which (I may be permitted to say) have recognized the disposition I had already shown to serve the country. A deference to this favorable opinion, which I should regret by any act to impair, makes the occasion for the present letter. I felt that some explanation was due to the public for taking part as a private individual in this public concern, and was unwilling to leave the motives of the present journey exposed to misconstructions. I judged therefore that a clear statement of them would not be considered improper or uncalled for.

Printed in the *American Journal of Science and Arts*, 2nd ser., 17 (May 1854): 447–49. Before the arrival of Almon W. Babbitt in Washington with news of JCF's travels as far as Parowan, Benton had sent the little article, which was an extract from a longer paper, to James D. Dana with the request that it be published. He also supplied the information that the more lengthy paper had been prepared by JCF before he set out on his fifth expedition, "but for particular reasons it was not printed at that time." It had been addressed to a gentleman, but Benton would not divulge the name (*ibid.*, and James D. Dana to Benton, 30 March 1854, PPAN).

259. Frémont to Theodore Bacon

WASHINGTON CITY, D.C.
August 6th. 1853

DEAR SIR,

Your note of the 19th inst. has been received—In reply I regret to say that the expedition which you desire to accompany will be carried out by such slight means as to render it impossible for me to comply with your desire which otherwise it would afford me pleasure to do. Respectfully yours,

J. C. FRÉMONT

Theodore Bacon Esqre.
New Haven, Conn.

ALS-JBF (James S. Copley Collection, La Jolla, Calif.). Endorsed: "Received August 20th." Born in 1834, Theodore Bacon was the son of Dr. Leonard Bacon, pastor for forty-one years of the First Church in New Haven and later a teacher in Yale's Divinity School. Young Bacon became an attorney in Rochester, N.Y. See his letters to Robert A. Brock (CSmH).

260. Frémont's Agreement with Delaware Hunters

WESTPORT, Mo., September 16, 1853

I have this day made an agreement through Jim Secondi[1] by which ten Delaware hunters, good men, are to accompany me on my journey to California and back to this country. The ten Delawares are to furnish their own animals, and are each to be paid $2 per day. They are to provide themselves with good animals, and if any of their animals should die upon the road I am to pay them for the loss.

They will of course be furnished by me with ammunition, and the saddles which are furnished are at my own cost.

JOHN C. FRÉMONT

Printed in "Message of the President of the U.S. communicating claims presented by and allowed to John C. Frémont," Senate Ex. Doc. 109, 34th Cong., 1st sess., pp. 37–38, Serial 825. JCF seems not to have met, at least in full, his obligations to the Indians. A Delaware delegation headed by James Secondi or Saghundai (George W. Manypenny writes "Sagondyne") pressed their claims upon the Indian Commissioner in 1854 and again in 1856 (*ibid.*). Allegedly they were still unpaid in 1886, and George Washington, one of the Delawares on the expedition, claimed that he had "a copy of a statement bearing the signatures of the ten Delawares, detailing the amount due each for the work and loss of animals" (Memorial of the Delaware Indians, Senate Doc. 16, 58th Cong., 1st sess., pp. 159–60, Serial 4563).

1. Secondi had been with JCF on the 1845–46 expedition but did not go on the Fifth. The names of the Delawares are given in Doc. No. 261, n. 2.

261. With Frémont: Solomon Nunes Carvalho's Account of the Fifth Expedition, 22 Aug.–25 Oct. 1853

CHAPTER I

On the 22d August, 1853, after a short interview[1] with Col. J. C. Fremont, I accepted his invitation to accompany him as artist of an Exploring Expedition across the Rocky Mountains. A half hour previously, if anybody had suggested to me, the probability of my undertaking an overland journey to California, even over the emigrant route, I should have replied there were no inducements sufficiently powerful to have tempted me. Yet, in this instance, I impulsively, without even a consultation with my family, passed my word to join an exploring party, under command of Col. Fremont, over a hitherto untrodden country, in an elevated region, with the full expectation of being exposed to all the inclemencies of an arctic winter. I know of no other man to whom I would have trusted my life, under similar circumstances.

Col. Fremont's former extraordinary explorations, his astronomical and geographical contributions to the useful sciences, and his successful pursuit of them under difficulties, had deeply interested me, and aided in forming for him, in my mind, the beau ideal of all that was chivalrous and noble.

His conquest of California, appointment as Governor by Commodore Stockton, the jealousy and persecution by General Kearney for not acknowledging him instead of Commodore Stockton as

Solomon Nunes Carvalho. Courtesy of
the Library of Congress.

commander-in-chief, his court-martial and subsequent finding of the court, are matters of American history, and they reflect no dishonor on the individual who was a distinguished example of the ingratitude of republics.

The recognition of his claims on the American public by the citizens of Charleston, S.C., who presented him with an elegant sword and golden scabbard, satisfied me that I had formed no incorrect estimate of his character, and made me feel an instinctive pride that I, too, drew my first breath on the same soil that gave birth to heroes and statesmen.

Entertaining these feelings, the dangers and perils of the journey, which Col. Fremont pointed out to me, were entirely obscured by the pleasure I anticipated in accompanying him, and adding my limited skill to facilitate him in the realization of one of the objects of the expedition—which was to obtain an exact description of the face of the country over which we were to travel.

The party consisted of twenty-two persons: among them were ten Delaware chiefs;[2] and two Mexicans.[3] The officers were: Mr. Egloffstien,[4] topographical engineer; Mr. Strobel, assistant;[5] Mr. Oliver Fuller, assistant engineer;[6] Mr. S. N. Carvalho, artist and daguerrotypist; Mr. W. H. Palmer, passenger.[7]

The expedition was fitted out, I think, at the individual expense of Col. Fremont.

Chapter II

The preparations for my journey occupied about ten days, during which time I purchased all the necessary materials for making a panorama of the country, by daguerreotype process, over which we had to pass.

To make daguerreotypes in the open air, in a temperature varying from freezing point to thirty degrees below zero, requires different manipulation from the processes by which pictures are made in a warm room. My professional friends were all of the opinion that the elements would be against my success. Buffing and coating plates, and mercurializing them, on the summit of the Rocky Mountains, standing at times up to one's middle in snow, with no covering above save the arched vault of heaven, seemed to our city friends one of the impossibilities—knowing as they did that iodine will not give out its fumes except at a temperature of 70° to 80° Fahrenheit. I shall not appear egotistical if I say that I encountered many difficulties, but I was well prepared to meet them by having previously acquired a scientific and practical knowledge of the chemicals I used, as well as of the theory of light: a firm determination to succeed also aided me in producing results which, to my knowledge, have never been accomplished under similar circumstances.

While suffering from frozen feet and hands, without food for twenty-four hours, travelling on foot over mountains of snow, I have stopped on the trail, made pictures of the country, re-packed my materials, and found myself frequently with my friend Egloffstien, who generally remained with me to make barometrical observations, and a muleteer, some five or six miles behind camp, which was only reached with great expense of bodily as well as mental suffering. The great secret, however, of my untiring perseverance and continued success, was that my honor was pledged to Col. Fremont to perform certain duties, and I would rather have died than not have redeemed it. I made pictures up to the very day Col. Fremont found it necessary to bury the whole baggage of the camp, including the daguerreotype apparatus. He has since told me that my success, under the frequent occurrence of what he considered almost insuperable difficulties, merited his unqualified approbation.

I left New York on the 5th September, 1853, having in charge the daguerreotype apparatus, painting materials, and half a dozen cases of Alden's preserved coffee, eggs, cocoa, cream, and milk, which he sent out for the purpose of testing their qualities.[8] There was in them sufficient nourishment to have sustained twenty men for a month. I purchased a ticket by the Illinois River to St. Louis, but the water was so low in the river that it was deemed advisable to cross over to Alton by stage, as I was afraid of being detained. The cases of instruments were very heavy, and the proprietor of the stage refused to take them; it being night, I remonstrated with him, telling him of the importance that they should arrive at St. Louis; he peremptorily refused to take them. I, of course, had to succumb, and remarked inadvertently how disappointed Col. Fremont would be in not receiving them. At the mention of Col. Fremont's name, he asked me if those cases were Fremont's? I told him, yes. He sang out for his boy to harness up an extra team of horses, and stow away the boxes. "I will put them through for Fremont, without a cent expense. I was with him on one of his expeditions, and a nobler specimen of mankind does not live about these parts." I was put through in good time, but he would not receive a cent for my passage, or freight of the boxes, which together would have amounted to eight dollars.

I arrived at St. Louis at twelve o'clock. Col. Fremont was at Col. Brant's house, where I immediately called. The Colonel was very glad to see me; he had telegraphed several times, and I had been anxiously expected. We left that same afternoon in the steamer F. X. Aubrey, for Kansas.[9] On board, I found Mr. Egloffstien, the topographical engineer, Mr. Oliver Fuller, and Mr. Bomar,[10] the photographist. Our journey was somewhat protracted by the shallowness of the water in the river, and we did not arrive at Kansas until the 14th.

CHAPTER III

When we landed, we met Mr. Palmer and several of the men who were to accompany the Expedition as muleteers, etc. The equipage of the camp that had been previously shipped from St. Louis, had arrived safely. As soon as our baggage was landed, it, together with the rest of the material, was transported by wagons to camp near Westport, a few miles in the interior.

Our tents were raised, and active preparation for our journey was immediately commenced. Several droves of mules came in next day from which Col. Fremont selected a few. Very near two prices were exacted by the owners; it being necessary that we should proceed without delay, we were obliged to submit to extortion.

Mr. Egloffstien, Mr. Bomar and myself, found comfortable quarters at a hotel where we put up, in order to be ready for the journey, our various apparatus.

Mr. Bomar, proposed to make photographs by the wax process, and several days were consumed in preparing the paper, etc. I was convinced that photographs could not be made by that process as quickly as the occasion required, and told Col. Fremont to have one made from the window of our room, to find out exactly the time. The preparation not being entirely completed, a picture could not be made that day; but on the next, when we were all in camp, Col. Fremont requested that daguerreotypes and photographs should be made. In half an hour from the time the word was given, my daguerreotype was made; but the photograph could not be seen until next day, as it had to remain in water all night, which was absolutely necessary to develop it. Query, where was water to be had on the mountains, with a temperature of 20° below zero? To be certain of a result, even if water would be procured, it was necessary by his process, to wait twelve hours, consequently, every time a picture was to be made, the camp must be delayed twelve hours. Col. Fremont finding that he could not see immediate impressions, concluded not to incur the trouble and expense of transporting the apparatus, left it at Westport, together with the photographer. The whole dependence was now on me. Col. Fremont told me if I had the slightest doubts of succeeding, it were better to say so now, and he would cancel the agreement on my part, and pay me for my time, etc.

On the night of the 20th, all hands slept in camp, a heavy rainstorm drenched us completely, giving to the party an introduction to a life on the prairies. The necessity of India-rubber blankets became evident, and I was dispatched to Westport to procure them. There were none to be had. I sent a man to Independence to purchase two dozen; he travelled thirty miles that night, and by ten next morning I had them in camp. They were the most useful articles we had with us; we placed the India-rubber side on the snow, our buffalo robes on the top of that for a bed, and covered with our blankets, with an India-rubber blanket over the whole—India-rubber side up, to turn the rain. We generally slept double, which added to our comfort, as we communicated warmth to each other, and had the advantage of two sets of coverings. During the whole journey, exposed to the most furious snow-storms, I never slept cold, although when I have been called for guard I often found some difficulty in rising from the weight of the snow resting on me.

The distribution of arms and ammunition to the men occupied a portion of the next day. Each person had a rifle and Colt's revolver. Some of the Delawares had horseman's pistols also.[11] The messenger Col. Fremont sent to the Delaware camp returned, with a number of braves, some of whom had accompanied Col. Fremont on a former expedition—he selected ten, among whom was a chief named Solomon, who had been with him before, and for whom Col. Fremont felt a great friendship. They were entertained with dinner, and after a smoke, each had a small quantity of the brandy we brought for medicinal purposes. They left us, to make preparations for the expedition, and to join us near the Kansas River, about one hundred miles westward.

A most amusing scene, although attended with some pain to the animals, was enacted today; it was the process of branding them with a distinctive mark. We had an iron made with the letter F, which we used to designate ours from those belonging to others.

A long rope with a noose and slip knot was fastened round the neck of the mule, the other round a tree; two men with another rope twisted it about its legs, when with a sudden jerk it was thrown to the ground; the red hot iron is now applied to the fleshy part of the hip— a terrible kicking and braying ensues, but it was always the sign that the work was done effectually.

In California, the most beautiful and valuable saddle horses are branded with a large unseemly mark on some prominent part of the body or neck, which would in this locality depreciate the value of the animals. I selected an Indian pony for myself; he was recommended as being a first rate buffalo horse; that is to say, he was trained to hunt buffaloes. This animal was given into my own charge, and I only then began to realize that I had entered into duties which I was un-qualified to perform. I had never saddled a horse myself. My seden-tary employment in a city, never having required me to do such offices; and now I was to become my own ostler, and ride him to water twice a day, besides running after him on the prairie for an hour sometimes before I could catch him. This onerous duty I finally performed as well as my companions. But, dear reader, follow me to a camp on the mountains of snow, where I exchanged my horse for a mule, at daylight, with the thermometer 20° below zero. Do you see, far away on the hill-side, an animal moving slowly? That is my mule; he is searching among the deep snows for a bite of blighted grass or the top of some wild bush to break his fast on. How will you get him? I will go for him; watch me while I tramp through the frozen snow. My mule sees me, and knowing that my errand is to prepare him for his day's journey, without first giving him provender to enable him to perform it, prefers to eat his scanty breakfast first, and moves leisurely along; his lariat, about thirty feet in length, trails along the ground. I have reached it, and at the moment I think I have him securely, he dashes away at a full gallop, pulling me after him through the snow; perfectly exhausted, I loose my hold; my hands lacerated and almost frozen. I lie breathless on the icy carpet. I am now a mile from camp, and out of sight of my companions. I renew my exertions, and gently approach him; this time he stands quiet, and I gather the rope in my hand, and pat him for a few minutes, and then mount him bare backed. The life and activity he possessed a few moments before, is entirely gone; he stands like a mule in the snow, determined not to budge a step. I coax, I kick him. I use the other end of the rope over his head; he dodges the blow; but his fore-feet are immovably planted in the snow, as if they grew there. I, worn out, and almost frozen, remain chewing the cud of bitter reflection, until one of my comrades comes to seek and assist me; he goes behind the mule and gives him a slight touch *à posteriori*; when, awakening from his trance, he starts at a hard trot into camp, quietly submits to be saddled, and looks as pleasantly at me as if he were inquiring how I liked the exercise of catching him. Similar scenes occurred daily; if it were not with myself it was with another. "Stubborn as a mule," is an o'er true adage, as I can fully testify.

A general examination of the equipage resulted in the knowledge that everything requisite for our journey, had been procured, and scales were in requisition to apportion the weight of luggage; 65 to 90 lb. for each mule. The personal luggage of the men was restricted to a certain number of pounds—and all useless apparel, books etc., etc., were packed up and sent back to town. We intended to pack on mules all the way, and it was necessary to take as little as possible of what we did not absolutely require.

A trial start was made, and the cavalcade started in excellent order and spirits, and we camped at the Methodist mission, about six miles from Westport.

CHAPTER IV

We remained at the Methodist Mission until the next day, when we proceeded to the Shawnee Mission,[12] a few miles further, and camped for the night. It was at this spot that Mr. Max Strobel made his appearance. He had been attached to Col. Stevens' expedition, but had left it on account of some misunderstanding with the officer in command. He requested Col. Fremont to allow him to accompany his expedition as a volunteer, and he would contribute his services as assistant topographer, &c. Col. Fremont hesitated, as his company was complete, but finally yielded to his continued entreaties. Col. Fremont who had been slightly indisposed during the day, finding himself worse, decided to return to Westport, requesting us to continue on our journey until we met the Delawares, and then to encamp and await his return. The Col. returned to Westport, accompanied by Mr. Strobel, for whom it was necessary to purchase an outfit.

24th.—We travelled during this day on the open prairie. The weather was hazy and considerable rain fell during the last twenty-four hours; we camped on the open plains for the first time. At dawn of day I was up; I found the weather perfectly clear; and in breathless expectation of seeing the sun rise, I saddled my pony, determined to ride away from the camp—made my way through the long grass, for a considerable distance, before I perceived any inclination on the part of the majestic king of day to awake from his royal couch. Gradually the eastern horizon assumed a warmer hue, while some floating clouds along its edge, developed their form against the luminous heavens. The dark grey morning tints were superseded by hues of the most brilliant and gorgeous colors, which almost as imperceptibly softened, as the glorious orb of day commenced his diurnal course, and illumined the vault above; a slight rustling of the long grass, caused by a deliciously pleasant zephyr, which made it move in gentle undulation, was all that disturbed the mysterious silence that prevailed. I alighted from my pony, and gave him the range of his lariat. I perceived, that he preferred a breakfast of fresh grass, to the contemplation of the sublime scene around me, to which he seemed totally indifferent.

My heart beat with fervent anxiety, and whilst I felt happy, and free from the usual care and trouble, I still could not master the nervous debility which seized me while surveying the grand and majestic works of nature. Was it fear? no; it was the conviction of my own insignificance, in the midst of the stupendous creation; the undulating grass seemed to carry my thoughts on its rolling surface, into an impenetrable future;—glorious in inconceivable beauty, extended over me, the ethereal tent of heaven, my eye losing its power of distant vision, seemed to reach down only to the verdant sea before me.

There was no one living being present with whom I could share my admiration. Still life, unceasing eternal life, was everywhere around me. I was far away from the comforts of my home, not even in sight of a wigwam of the aboriginal inhabitants of the forests.

A deep sigh of longing for the society of man wrestled itself from my breast. Shall I return, and not accomplish the object of my journey? No. I cannot; does not the grass, glittering in the morning dew in the unbroken rays of the sun, beckon me a pleasant welcome over its untrodden surface. I will onward, and trust to the Great Spirit, who lives in every tree and lonely flower, for my safe arrival at the dwelling of my fellowmen, far beyond the invisible mountains over which my path now lies.

27th.—To-day we met our Delawares, who were awaiting our arrival. A more noble set of Indians I never saw, the most of them six feet high, all mounted and armed *cap-a-pie*, under command of Captain Wolff, a "Big Indian," as he called himself. Most of them spoke English, and all understood it. "Washington," "Welluchas," "Solomon," "Moses," were the names of some of the principal chiefs. They became very much attached to Col. Fremont, and every one of them would have ventured his life for him.

Near the principal town of the Pottawatomies[13] we remained encamped until the end of September, awaiting Col. Fremont. Two or three stores with no assortment of goods, and about thirty shanties make up the town. I went to every house in the place for a breakfast, but could not get anything to eat except some Boston crackers, ten pounds of which (the whole supply in the town) I bought. My ride into the town was for the purpose of having strong boxes made to carry my daguerreotype apparatus. The baskets in which they had been packed being broken and unfit for use. There was not a carpenter, nor any tools to be had in town. There was a blacksmith's about ten miles from town, where it was likely I could procure them. It being absolutely necessary that I should have the boxes, I induced one of our Delawares to accompany me, carrying on our horses a sufficient quantity of dry goods box covers and sides to manufacture them. When we arrived at the blacksmith's house, the proprietor was absent. His wife, an amiable woman, prepared dinner for us, and gave us the run of the workshop, where I found a saw and hatchet; with these instruments I made the boxes myself, and by the time they were finished, the blacksmith returned. He refused to receive pay for my dinner, but charged for the nails, raw hide, etc., I covered the boxes with, and the use of his tools. The lady told me I was the first white man she had seen, except her husband, in three years. I gave some silver to the children, and mounting our horses, with a huge box before us on our saddles, we slowly retraced our way to camp, where we arrived at dark. Nobody in camp knew my errand to town, and I never shall forget the deep mortification and astonishment of our muleteers when they saw my boxes. All their bright hopes that the apparatus would have to be left, were suddenly dissipated. The expenses attendant on the manufacture of the boxes, and the material, were nearly five dollars, which I requested our quarter-master to pay, as Col. Fremont left him money for disbursement; he refused, at first, but was finally induced to do so under protest. I have every reason to believe that my baskets were purposely destroyed; and but for my watchful and unceasing care, they would have been rendered useless. The packing of the apparatus was attended with considerable trouble to the muleteers, and also to the officer whose duty it was to superintend the loading and unloading of the mules; and they all wanted to be rid of the labor. Hence the persecution to which I was subjected on this account. Complaints were continually being made to Col. Fremont, during the journey, that the weights of the boxes were not equalized. Twice I picked up on the road the tin case containing my buff, &c., which had slipped off the mules, from careless packing— done purposely; for if they had not been fortunately found by me, the rest of the apparatus would have been useless. On one occasion, the keg containing alcohol was missing; Col. Fremont sent back after it, and it was found half emptied on the road.

I am induced to make these remarks to show the perseverance and watchfulness I had to exercise to prevent the destruction of the apparatus by our own men.

CHAPTER V

After remaining at this camp two days, Mr. Strobel arrived with a letter from Col. Fremont to Mr. Palmer, stating that his increasing illness made it necessary that he should return to St. Louis for medical advice, and directed us to proceed as far as Smoky Hills, and encamp on the Saline fork of the Kansas River, where there were plenty of buffalo, and remain there until he joined us, which he hoped would be in a fortnight.[14]

The expedition, during encampment, was to be under the supervision of Mr. Palmer. Accordingly, we continued our journey, and crossed the Kansas River at its junction with the Republican, within half a mile from Fort Riley, thence to Solomon's Fork, in crossing which creek, some of the baggage of the camp became saturated with water.[15]

Immediately after crossing Solomon's Fork, we saw our first buffalo. As soon as he was discovered, our Delawares gave a whoop, and they all started, helter skelter, the officers and muleteers following leaving the baggage animals to take care of themselves. Our engineer, Mr. Egloffstien, after the first excitement had passed, suddenly drew rein—I did so likewise.

He remarked, "I have been at full speed for a mile, with both barometers slung across my back."

I never saw any one look so alarmed as he did. I had exchanged ponies, to give him an easy-going animal, so as not to shake the instruments, and now his rashness had probably injured them. He alighted and examined them; luckily, they were well packed with cotton, and they were not at all disarranged. Our buffalo was soon killed; and that night we made an encampment on a beautiful site near Salt Creek, and about four miles from the Kansas River, with buffalo steaks for supper.

[Extract from a Letter]

DEAR S——:[16]

We are now encamped, as it were, for a pleasure excursion, for all the day is employed in hunting, gunning, shooting at a mark with rifles, and preparing buffalo meat in all the modes in which it is said to be good.

I was much amused, the first day we encamped here, to see the Indians go into the woods on the creek, and bring out straight green sticks, the size of a small walking-cane, and proceed to divest them of their outer peeling—also pointing them at both ends.

I soon discovered their use; they cut the buffalo meat in strips about an inch thick, four wide, and twelve to fifteen long. The stick is then inserted in the meat, as boys do a kite stick; one end of the stick is then stuck in the ground, near the fire, and the process of roasting is complete—the natural juice of the meat is retained, in this manner, and I think it the most preferable way to cook game. The breast of a fat antelope prepared thus is a most fitting dish for a hungry man.

Several kinds of game were brought into camp this evening, buffalo, antelope, and deer, by the Indians, and our most successful gunner, Mr. Fuller, brought in two wild turkeys, three ducks, a rabbit, and a prairie hen, the result of his day's sport. Our cook for the nonce is making a splendid Olla Podrida. This is our first week in camp, and we are living sumptuously—coffee, tea, and sugar three or four times a day.

I have no control of the commissariat department, but I very much fear that we shall want some of the good things which are now being inconsiderately wasted. Our quarter-master is determined to enjoy himself—his motto is "dum vivimus vivamus."

While I am writing, I am smoking a pipe filled with "Kinni-kinick," the dried leaves of the red sumach; it is pleasant and not in-toxicating—a very good substitute for tobacco. The Delawares have been preparing some for their journey. They smoke it mixed with tobacco.

My quarter-box of Havanas are all gone, already; they were the only ones in camp, and every time I took out my pouch, I of course handed it round to my companions, which soon diminished my store. I close this letter by giving you a description of an Indian game, which our Delawares participated in last night.

A large fire of dried wood is brightly burning—around it sit, cross-legged, all our Delaware; behind them are the rest of us, standing looking on. I contributed the article (which was a large imitation seal ring, several of which I bought to exchange with the Indians for moc-casins) with which they amused themselves. One of them took the ring, and while the rest are chanting Highya, Highya, he makes sun-dry contortions of his limbs, and pretends to place it in the hands of the one next to him. This one goes through with the same antics, until all have had it or are supposed to have had it. The first one then guesses who has the ring; if successful, he wins the ring; if not, he contributes tobacco for a smoke; a pipe is filled, which is generally a tomahawk with a bowl at the butt-end; the handle is hollow, and communicates with the bowl, thus forming a weapon of war, as well as the calumet of peace; each one takes two or three puffs and then passes it around.

DEAR S——:

The duties of camp life are becoming more onerous as the weather gets colder. It is expected that each man in camp will bring in a cer-tain quantity of firewood! My turn came to day, and I am afraid I shall make a poor hand in using the axe; first I have not the physical strength, and secondly, I do not know how. I managed by hunting through the woods to find several decayed limbs, which I brought in on my shoulder. I made three trips, and I have at all events supplied the camp with kindling wood for the night.

I certainly, being a "Republican," do not expect to warm myself at the expense of another; therefore, arduous as it is, I must, to carry out the principle of equality, do as the rest do, although it is not a very congenial occupation.

* * * * * *

'Tis very strange how fallacious ideas of mankind obtain stronghold in the minds of those who should know better. The night previous to leaving home, I was asked how I could venture my life with such a man as Col. Fremont? "A mountaineer"—"an adventurer"—"a man of no education."

During my voyage up the Missouri, I had continual opportunities of conversing with Col. Fremont.

If you ever see Mr. —— and Mrs. ——, please say to them, that the character of Col. Fremont as a gentleman of "high literary attainments," "great mental capacity," and "solid scientific knowledge," is firmly established in my own mind.

These personal observations, added to the knowledge I gained of him from report, has brought me to the conclusion that he is not only a "man of education," but a "man of genius and a gentleman." One would suppose that the "conqueror of California," "the successful commander and governor," would have a little to say about himself—some deeds to vaunt of—some battle to describe. I found him reserved, almost to taciturnity, yet perfectly amiable withal. No one, to see him, would ever imagine that a man of great deeds was before him.

My estimation of character is seldom wrong. I may have been imprudent in undertaking this journey, which already "thunders in the index," and on which I shall have to encounter many personal difficulties; but, if I felt safe enough to impulsively decide to accompany him, without personally knowing him—how much safer do I now feel from the short time I have known him!

All the men in camp have the same opinion of him.

Yesterday, while discussing the merits of the most prominent men who were likely to be placed before the people for the "next President," I mentioned the name of "Col. Fremont." It was received with acclamation, and he is the first choice of every man in camp. So you see I am safe enough with the man—it is only the mountains which are the "stumbling blocks." Yet I have full faith that I shall return once more to you in safety.

*   *   *   *   *   *

Chapter VI

Kansas lies between the thirty-seventh and fortieth degrees of north latitude. The Indian Territory bounds it on the south, Utah and New Mexico on the west, Nebraska on the north, and Missouri on the east.

There are numberless streams of water in the Territory. The Arkansas which rises in the Rocky Mountains, runs nearly six hundred miles through it. Kansas River, which empties into the Missouri near Kansas City, has many forks of considerable size, viz., the Republican, Solomon Fork, Grand Saline Fork, Vermilion, Little Vermilion, Soldier Creek, Grasshopper Creek, Big Blue, Pawnee Fork, Walnut Creek, Wakarusa, and several others. The country is well watered, and on all the rivers grows timber of large size and in great variety. The river bottoms are very fertile, being covered with an alluvial black soil from twelve to twenty-four inches deep. These bottoms vary in width from four to seven miles.

Another bottom over which the waters must have once flowed, is elevated about sixteen feet from the river, and high up some sixty to seventy feet, lies the immense undulating prairie, teeming with buffalo, blacktail, deer, antelope, sage, and prairie chickens. Thousands of cayottes—a small wolf, make night hideous with their shrill discordant bark. The large white wolf is also found in great numbers on the rivers. We killed wild turkeys and ducks. The second bottoms are studded with groves of timber. The various kinds of oak, maple, elm, red-flowered maple, black walnut, locust, beech, box, elder, wild-cherry, and cotton-wood, attain a large size, and are to be found on the Kansas River and its many tributaries in quantities.

Grasses of a hundred different kinds, some of them rank and high, but the most of them possessing highly nutritive qualities, grow spontaneously on the prairies, and afford nourishment to immense quantities of game.

The water of the Kansas partakes in color of the character of the soil over which it passes. It is, I am inclined to believe, always turbid. I

397

found it quite unfit for daguerreotype purposes, and had to preserve many of my plates until we approached the crystal streams from the Rocky Mountains, to finish them. During our long camp on Salt Creek, our topographical engineer and myself explored the country for miles. Coal in abundance is to be obtained with but little exertion; in many instances it crops out on the surface of the ground. The general character of the formation of this country is the same as Missouri—a secondary limestone.

DEAR S——:

To-day we had a delightful jaunt through the woods which fringe the forests of Salt Creek. Cotton-wood, oak, elm, ash, hickory, grow luxuriously, some of them to an immense height. Our Delaware that accompanied Egloffstien and myself suddenly stopped, and pointed upward. There, at a height of over one hundred feet, suspended between two oaks, were grapevines loaded with rich luscious looking fruit.

How were we to obtain them? I could not climb so tall a tree. Mr. Egloffstien declined, and we both depended on our Delaware. He look very grave and said: "Suppose Delaware want grapes, he know how to get them."

By this time our desire increased to obtain the prize, which seemed to say, "Come and take me." I commenced climbing one tree, and my friend the other. When we had exerted ourselves, and had reached the first limb, on which we stopped to rest, we heard a grunt from our Delaware, and almost at the same moment, the whole vine came tumbling down on his head.

He purposely waited until we were in the trees, to see how "white men gathered grapes." He took hold of the grape vine, and with one tremendous pull, down it came; when we descended, he was quietly stowing away the choicest bunches in his hunting shirt. I never would have dreamed of destroying such a noble vine, to gratify my appetite.

The grapes were small, but sweet and well flavored. I ate a great many of them. I had been without fruit or vegetables for four weeks, and they were very grateful to me. I hope I shall not suffer for my imprudence. Good night.

BRANDY *VERSUS* POISON.

Previous to leaving New York, I had two tin flasks made, to contain about a quart each, which I intended to have filled with alcohol for daguerreotype purposes. At Westport, I purchased a quart of the best quality of old cognac, filled one of them for medicinal purposes, and carefully packed my flask in my daguerreotype boxes. One day during our camp at Salt Creek, one of our Indians being ill, I opened my flask and pouring out about an ounce, replaced it. I noticed, however, that a chemical action had taken place, turning the brandy exactly the color of ink. One of our mess saw me open my box and appropriate a portion of the contents of the bottle; I am not certain but that I tasted it myself.

The next day I had occasion to go to my box, when to my utter astonishment, my flask of brandy was gone. I immediately suspected the very person who afterwards proved to be the thief. Keeping my loss a secret, at dinner I carefully watched the countenances and actions of the whole party, and the effects of liquor were plainly visible on the person of this man.

"How excellent," said I, "would a bottle of old cognac be as a digester to our tough old buffalo bull.—Gentlemen, how would you like a drop?" "Bring it forward by all means, Carvalho. You have, I verily believe, Pandora's box; for you can produce everything and anything at a moment's notice, from a choice Havana to old brandy."

"With your leave, gentlemen, I will procure it. I have two flasks exactly alike; one contains poison, a mixture of alcohol, and some poisonous chemicals for making daguerreotypes; the other contains the best brandy to be had on the Kansas River."

I went to my box, and turning up my hands with an exclamation of surprise, announced to the mess that the "bottle containing the poison, and which I laid on the top of my box last night, is missing." Like Hamlet I looked into the face of the delinquent, and I never shall forget his expression when I remarked that "the liquid in the purloined flask was poison, and perfectly black, and although it would not kill immediately, an ounce will produce certain death in 48 hours."

"Gentlemen! I shall, in consequence, have to reserve the brandy to make another similar mixture, to substitute for alcohol; therefore I am sorry I cannot treat you as I intended."

Of course the innocent parties felt indignant that my flask had been stolen, and that one of their party was suspected.

The thief was discovered, although he nor any one else knew that I detected him. The next day I went to my box again, and in its proper place, I found my brandy flask about half full. Our friend had taken several strong pulls during the night and morning, and likely enough

399

he looked at the contents, and finding them black as ink, believed all about the poison, and fearing to die, replaced the flask, without detection. When I discovered it, I showed it around and also the color of the contents, and told them it was not poison but "good old brandy." I tasted a little, and divided it among the party.

The man that took it knew I suspected him, and his whole conduct to me during the journey, was influenced by that event, although I never taxed him with it.

Dear S——:

Yesterday being a fine, mild day, I thought I would examine my wardrobe, and have such articles as I had worn during the last three weeks washed. I collected three shirts, as many pairs of stockings, together with handkerchiefs, and drawers; I made up a dozen pieces; and I assure you, that how or by whom they were to be washed, never entered into my mind. I offered some compensation to one of our muleteers if he would wash them, but he was perfectly independent of the necessity of earning money in that way. I soon discovered, that I would have to become my own washerwoman; and obtaining some soap from the quarter master, I gathered up my duds, and made my way down the banks of the creek, to a convenient place, and there I entered upon my novitiate. I rubbed the skin off my hands during the operation, but after considerable application, I succeeded in cleansing them, and hung them out to dry. I doubled them up, and laid them carefully under my buffalo robe couch, last night; and this morning they are as smooth as if they had been "mangled." To-day I employed myself making a pair of buckskin mitts and moccasins, as I shall require them before many weeks; most of the Indians and muleteers are out, looking for a large black mule, the finest animal in the collection, which was missing last night.

Yesterday two beaver trappers came into the Delaware camp, and traded for sugar and coffee with the Delawares. I have my suspicions that our mule conveyed them away, as they are no longer on the creek where they set their traps yesterday.

I must leave off my journal, as it is my usual hour for rifle practice; I have become quite an expert; at one hundred paces, I have hit the "bull's eye" twice in five times, which is not bad shooting, considering I have had no practice since I was a member of a rifle volunteer company in Charleston, some twenty years ago.

Chapter VII

DELAWARE MEDICINE MAN

For several days, Capt. Wolff, the chief of our Delawares, had been ailing, this morning I noticed some unusual preparations in their camp, on inquiring I was told that, in the woods, Capt. Wolff, who was very sick, was undergoing the Indian ceremony of "incantation," by one of the tribe, who was "a great medicine man." The ceremony was conducted in secret, but I found out afterwards the place, and from the mode which was explained to me, I understood the rite perfectly. A small lodge, composed of the branches of trees, high enough for a man to sit upright in, was built; in this the patient was placed in a state of perfect nudity. "The Medicine Man," who is outside, takes a "pipe," filled with "kinnikinick and tobacco," and hands it in to the patient. While the Medicine Man recites the "all powerful words," the patient puffs away until the lodge is filled with smoke; when the poor devil is almost suffocated, and exhausted, he is taken out, wrapped in his blankets, and conveyed to his own lodge.

Feeling anxious about him, I went in to see him about an hour afterwards; I found him in a high state of febrile excitement, which had, no doubt, been increased by his extraordinary treatment; he complained of dreadful headache and pain in his back. He thought he was going to die. I told him if he would submit to my advice I thought I could cure him—he consented, and I administered ten grains of calomel, and four hours afterwards half oz. of Epsom salts. He is now considerably relieved; and I think by the morning he will be well. Indigestion was the cause of his suffering. I made him some of the arrowroot, which thanks to your usual foresight I found stowed away in my trunk. I shall reserve it for similar occasions.

Col. Fremont has not yet arrived.

Our quarter master has suddenly discovered that his commissariat is empty, and talks of sending to Fort Riley for fresh supplies to-morrow; if he does I will forward a package of letters to you, which please preserve from public eye.

Two Delawares and a muleteer are now preparing to go to "Fort Riley" for supplies. Capt. Wolff is better; by evening I hope he will be perfectly well. I think if I had not treated him he would have probably died. Another "incantation" would certainly have killed him. I shall continue to write to you. Most probably we shall be detained here a week longer; it is now the 20th October, and I am afraid Col. Fremont is seriously ill; you will, of course, have heard of his return, and I shall look forward to receive by him happy tidings from all those I love.

I have had occasion to observe that the immense clouds of smoke which filled the atmosphere continually during the time the prairies were on fire, were condensed during the cold of the night, sometimes forming rain, but always heavy dew, which I did not observe before the prairies were burning.

I think Prof. Epsy says that artificial rain can be produced by smoke from large fires, and from the observations I have made I coincide in that theory.

It is not unlikely that the Indians, who have from the earliest knowledge of the prairie country annually set the high rank grass on fire, did it to afford artificial moisture for the immense tracts of buffalo grass plains, on which subsist hundreds of thousands of buffalo, elk, and deer. No rain falls at certain seasons, and without dew the grass would be all burnt up by the scorching heat of the sun.

The Indians, I believe, practically put into operation the theory of Espy—knowing from experience that smoke is condensed into dew.

On the Kansas River the dew fell very heavily. I found it necessary while doing guard to cover myself with my India-rubber poncho, to prevent my clothes from becoming saturated with water.

*　*　*　*　*　*

Last night our camp was visited with a heavy storm of rain and sleet; it was bitter cold. It rained considerably yesterday, but the temperature was not lower than 65°. The wind increased during the night, and one sudden gust blew our cotton tent completely over, exposing us to the peltings of the merciless storm of sleet. Several of us essayed to raise the tent, but the ground had become saturated with moisture, and afforded no hold for our tent-pins, and we consequently lay down, wrapped ourselves in our India-rubber blankets, and bewailed our fate.

We presented an interesting picture when the daylight came. Many of our clothes, which were lying loosely in the tent, were blown some distance from camp, and we were all drenched to the skin. The weather cleared off at sunrise, and around a large camp-fire we dried our clothes and passed jokes on each other's distressing appearance. Winter seems to have suddenly set in; the thermometer indicated, at

402

sunrise, 34° ("*por peccados,*" as the Spaniards say.) Many of our animals pulled up their picket-pins, and sought shelter in the woods. My pony is missing, among others, and on *myself and no one else* devolves the delightful duty of finding him. I have put on, for the first time, my waterproof boots, as I have a wet road, and, probably, a long distance to walk, before I find my horse. He is safe enough on the creek; the Indians saw him while hunting up theirs.

CARVALHO, 17–49. In order to keep an approximate chronology of the documents, Carvalho's published account will be broken into several parts. Although copies of *Incidents of Travel and Adventure in the Far West; with Col. Fremont's Last Expedition . . .* were sold in 1856 in both New York and London, a volume with the date-line "1856" is extremely rare. One such copy may be found in the Everett D. Graff Collection in the Newberry Library, Chicago; Derby & Jackson of New York and Sampson Low, Son, & Co., 47 Ludgate Hill, London, are listed as English and American booksellers and publishers. The 1856 English release did not have an illustration; the American copies of the following year carried a frontispiece painted by Jacob A. Dallas and engraved by Nathaniel Orr, but neither of the very early editions contained the dedication to "Mrs. Jessie Benton Fremont" that appeared in all the subsequent printings. Many years later Solomon's son David indicated, probably erroneously, that the journal was originally printed by "George W. Childs, Public Ledger, Philadelphia, Pa., 1856," but Carvalho's nephew had written on 11 Sept. 1856 that the book was "in print by Derby & Jackson, Publishers, and will be out in about two or three weeks" (Carvalho file, Ben Roe Papers, Special Collections, University of Utah; Jacob S. Rittenband letter, printed in KORN, 37–38).

One can only speculate that had JCF not become involved in the presidential campaign of 1856, the book would never have been published—at least not in this country, since it might undercut JCF's own proposed book of travels which George W. Childs had contracted to bring out. Perhaps Jessie's influence with her husband or with Childs was responsible for the lifting of the probable ban on publication, and Carvalho's dedication to her is the expression of his gratitude.

A Spanish-Portuguese Sephardic Jew, Solomon Nunes Carvalho (1815–97) had been born in Charleston, S.C. When he met JCF, he has already won some favorable notoriety for his technique of protecting daguerreotypes from abrasion by the application of a thin coating of varnish or enamel that made it unnecessary to enclose them in cases and cover them with glass. For a biography of this artist and adventurer, see STURHAHN.

1. Presumably the interview with JCF had occurred in New York City, as Carvalho was then working at Jeremiah Gurney's studio at No. 349 Broadway.

2. The Delawares were contracted for at Westport (see Doc. No. 260). They actually joined the expedition one hundred miles farther west, near Uniontown, on 27 Sept. At one time or another, twelve were connected with the expedition, namely: Capt. Wolf, Wahalope, James Harrison, John Smith, Solomon Everett, Jacob Enis, Wahore, George Washington, Caperessis, Welluchas, John ? Moses, and John Johnny Cake. John Johnny Cake left the expedition on 30 Oct., as did a Wyandott boy named Amos. Solomon Everett had been on JCF's third expedition; Moses was probably the Moses who had served Gunnison for two weeks as a guide from Uniontown to Walnut Creek (PACIFIC RAILROAD REPORTS, 2:15 and p. 19). Three Wyandott Indians—Jos. Carter, Nick Carter, and Jno. Brown—

also served (roster compiled from CARVALHO and the unpublished diary of James F. Milligan, courtesy of David Miller).

3. The two Mexicans were Frank Dickson, the Americanized name for an employee from New Leon, Mexico, and Jose, who was picked up nearly naked in Mosca Pass (unpublished diary of James F. Milligan and CARVALHO). The Mormon George W. Bean remembered Jose as Vincente Chavez (BEAN, 93).

4. F. W. Egloffstein (ca. 1824–ca. 1898), a German baron, and a Mr. Zwanziger had been advertising themselves in St. Louis as "surveyors and topographical engineers" (*Daily Missouri Democrat*, 2 Sept. 1853). At Parowan Egloffstein withdrew from JCF's party and went to Salt Lake City, where he accepted the invitation of Lieut. E. G. Beckwith to act as topographer of his railroad survey in place of Richard Kern, who had been murdered by the Indians along with Capt. Gunnison. Later Egloffstein was with Joseph C. Ives in the survey of the Colorado River and during the Civil War became a colonel of the 103rd Regiment of New York Volunteers. For some of his illustrations, in addition to the one printed in this volume, see PACIFIC RAILROAD REPORTS, vol. 11; for additional biographical details, see TAFT [1], 262–64.

5. Max Strobel joined the expedition at the Shawnee Mission. He had just withdrawn from the northern railroad survey headed by Isaac I. Stevens, having been employed to aid the artist John M. Stanley (TAFT [1], 15). He later managed for nearly two years the mines and mills on JCF's Mariposa estate, and it was his map of the property that JCF took to England when he prepared to sell it to British investors. In May 1861 he was writing to Abel Stearns from Gold Hill, Nev., where he was working for the Crown Point Company. For Strobel and Stearns's interest in mines located in Soledad Canyon, near Los Angeles, see Strobel's correspondence (CSmH).

6. Greeley and M'Elrath's thirty-two-page *Life of Colonel Fremont* (1856) indicates that Oliver Fuller of St. Louis, "a tall, large and powerful looking man," had made a previous crossing to California, "principally on foot." As Carvalho will write later, his was the only death the expedition suffered.

7. The "passenger," William H. Palmer, was a brother of the banker Joseph C. Palmer, who became the administrator of his estate on his death in 1857 (Vital Records of Nantucket, Essex Institute, Salem, Mass.; Fitze Maurice to Mrs. E. Martin, 29 April 1882, CU-B—Jenkins Family Papers). In what seems to be a collusion suit, Joseph C. Palmer brought an action against JCF in the fall of 1854; because JCF had not sufficient moneys and chattels in the 12th Judicial District to satisfy the judgment, the sheriff seized Alcatraz Island, which JCF was claiming as his personal property since the United States had declined to recognize the purchase on its behalf (John C. Frémont by W. R. Gorman, sheriff, to William H. Palmer, 5 Feb. 1856, CU-B—Jenkins Family Papers; Vol. 2, pp. 317–18). At the public auction which followed, Edward Jones, another member of the banking firm, bought the property. JCF failed to redeem the premises within the allotted six months and, since Jones had assigned the certificate to William H. Palmer, the sheriff gave the formal deed to him.

Other members of the fifth expedition were James F. Milligan, who was noticed in the introduction, and JCF's mulatto servant and cook, Albert Lea, who was executed in 1861 for killing his wife (see JBF's article on him in *Alta California*, 27 Feb. 1861).

Some historians have accepted Jessie's statement that Alexander Godey was on the expedition, but he was not.

8. H. Schimper & Co. of San Francisco had Alden's products for sale in the spring of 1854 (San Francisco *Daily Herald*, 4 April 1854).

9. JCF had arrived in St. Louis on 2 Sept.; the party left on 8 Sept. (*Daily Missouri Democrat*, 3 and 9 Sept. 1853).

10. Bomar, a German, did not proceed with the expedition, as Carvalho will indicate shortly.

11. According to BIGELOW, 430, JCF also issued "sheath-knives."

12. The camps were first at the Shawnee Methodist Mission and then at the Baptist Mission (BARRY, 1180).

13. The camp was near Uniontown (BARRY, 1180).

14. On 27 Sept. JCF had boarded the *Clara* and returned to St. Louis (*Missouri Republican*, 28 Sept. 1853). BIGELOW, 431, dates Strobel's arrival at the Kansas camp as 1 Oct. After the expedition established camp in buffalo country, Palmer was to send Lea and the Indian Solomon back to Westport to meet JCF.

15. The expedition started for the Saline Fork on 6 Oct., taking a route up the south side of the Kansas and not the regularly traveled military road north of the river, which JCF would take when he rejoined his party.

16. Undoubtedly addressed to Sarah Solis, Carvalho's wife.

262. Excerpt from the Memoirs

[25–27 Oct. 1853]

Oct. 25. Went to Uniontown and nooned. This is a street of log-cabins. Nothing to be had here. Some corn for animals and a piece of cheese for ourselves. Lots of John Barleycorn which the men about were consuming. Uniontown is called a hundred miles from Kansas.

Oct. 26. High wind and select. Clouds scudding across the sky. About two o'clock we reached the pretty little Catholic Mission of Saint Mary's. The well-built, whitewashed houses, with the cross on the spire showing out above them was already a very grateful sight. On the broad bottoms immediately below are the fields and houses of the Pottawatamie Indians. Met with a hospitable reception from the head of the Mission. A clear sky promises a bright day for tomorrow. Learned here some of the plants which are medicinal among the Indians. Among them *Asarum Canadensis*—Jewel-weed—a narcotic; and *Oryngium Aquaticum*, a great remedy of the Pottawatamies for snake-bites.

Oct. 27. White frost covers the ground this morning. Sky clear and air still. With bowls of good coffee and excellent bread made a good breakfast. We already begin to appreciate food. Prepared our luggage, threw into the wagon the provisions obtained here, and at ten o'clock took leave of the hospitable priests and set out. I was never more impressed by the efficiency of well-directed and permanent missionary effort than here at this far-off mission settlement, where the progress and good order strike forcibly as they stand in great contrast with the neighboring white settlement.

MEMOIRS, 27–28. Immediately upon his return to St. Louis for medical assistance, JCF had telegraphed Jessie, who rushed to him. He also wrote to Benton, asking that he convey the following message: "Please request of Mr. Beale to put his best animals at my rancho, or at any other convenient place, where they may recruit, and exchange them for mine when I reach California. It is my intention to turn back immediately and make the return voyage with great rapidity. I had on my place, when I left California, upwards of twenty horses and mules. These animals, and the proposed exchange with Beale, would enable me to accomplish my purpose; but the animals ought to be all looked to and well cared for in the meanwhile." Benton wanted Beale to return overland with JCF, who ultimately chose a sea route.

By 15 Oct. JCF's health permitted him to leave St. Louis. Jessie accompanied him as far as Independence, which he left on 22 Oct. Lea and Solomon were waiting for him and Dr. Ebers at Westport. For details, see JBF to Elizabeth Blair Lee, Saint Louis, 14 Oct. 1853, NjP—Blair-Lee Papers; Benton to Beale, Washington, 3 Oct. 1853, printed in HEAP, 307–9; *Daily Missouri Democrat*, 19 Nov. 1853.

263. With Frémont: Solomon Nunes Carvalho's Account of the Fifth Expedition, 25 Oct.–26 Nov. 1853

CHAPTER VIII

MY FIRST BUFFALO HUNT.

At daylight, on the 25th October, the hunters were at breakfast. At our mess, feats of daring and gallant horsemanship were being related, while our roast was preparing. Weluchas, a most successful hunter, and as brave and daring an Indian as ever fashioned a moccasin or fired a rifle, approached me, remarking, "What for you no hunt buffalo—got buffalo pungo?" (horse). I had, while at breakfast, almost made up my mind to go—this, however, determined me. In quick time I had my horse saddled, and, fully equipped with rifle, navy revolver, and sheath knife, was all ready for a start. On this occasion our party consisted of eight Delawares and four white men, besides myself. I rode out of camp, side by side with Weluchas, who seemed gratified that I accompanied him. The buffaloes, from having been daily hunted for several weeks, had gone South about fifteen to twenty miles, and we had to ride that distance before we saw any game.

DISCOVERY OF A HERD.

After about three hours' gentle trotting, one of the party started a cayote, and we chased him until he disappeared in the brush. When we reached the brow of a hill, Weluchas ejaculated in deep, low tones, "Buffalo," "big herd"—"plenty cow." I turned my eyes, and, for the first time, beheld a large herd of buffaloes occupying an extensive valley, well wooded and watered, and luxuriant with the peculiar short curled grass, called "Buffalo grass" (*Lysteria Dyclotoides*), on which this animal principally feeds. I gazed with delight and astonishment at the novel sight which presented itself. There must have been at least 6,000 buffaloes, including cows and calves. It was a sight well worth travelling a thousand miles to see. Some were grazing, others playfully gambolling, while the largest number were quietly reclining or sleeping on their verdant carpet, little dreaming of the danger which surrounded them, or of the murderous visitors who were about to disturb their sweet repose.

THE FOE DISCOVERED BY THE SENTINEL—THE HERD IN MOTION.

Taking the word of command from Capt. Wolff, one of the finest proportioned men I ever beheld, we kept silent, to await the direction which the herd would take when they discovered us. An old bull was stationed several hundred yards in advance of the herd, as sentinel: they invariably follow him, as leader, even into danger. He soon espied us; and suddenly, as if by magic, the whole herd was in motion. We occupied such a position that they passed within rifle shot.

THE PURSUIT.

At a signal, the whole party, except myself, galloped after them. I was intensely absorbed by this mighty cavalcade passing with majestic stride, as it were, in review before me. My pony, anxious for the chase, fretted and champed at the bit. I singled out what I thought a fat cow (the bulls are tough and hard, and are only hunted by the Indians for their robes—their flesh never being eaten when cows can be obtained), and in a few seconds, I was riding at full speed. It requires a very fleet horse to overtake a buffalo cow. A bull does not run quite so

407

fast. After a chase of about two miles, I was near enough to take sight with my rifle, by stopping my pony. I fired and wounded him in the leg—reloaded, and started again at full speed, the buffalo running less swiftly. I fired again, but this time without effect. Not wishing him to get too far ahead of me, I took out my revolver, and got within pistol shot, when I discovered I had chased an old bull instead of a cow.

PERILOUS SITUATION

I fired my pistol four times at full speed, and was endeavoring to sight him again, when the bull suddenly turned upon me, within five yards of my horse. My well-trained pony instantly jumped aside. The bull, in turning, got his wounded leg in a painful position, and stopped, which gave me time and opportunity to save my life; for, with my total inexperience, I should not have been able to have mastered him. My horse jumped aside without any guiding from me, having been trained to this by the Indian from whom we purchased him. I reloaded my rifle, and took deliberate aim at a vital part. When dying, I approached the monster that had given me such a fright, when he turned his large black eyes mournfully upon me, as if upbraiding me with having wantonly and uselessly shot him down.

MODE OF ATTACK BY THE DELAWARES.

A Delaware Indian, in hunting buffaloes, when near enough to shoot, rests his rifle on his saddle, balances himself in his stirrup on one leg; the other is thrown over the rifle to steady it. He then leans on one side, until his eye is on a level with the object, takes a quick sight, and fires while riding at full speed, rarely missing his mark, and seldom chasing one animal further than a mile.

SOLITARY AND ALONE.

After recovering from my fright, and the intense excitement incidental to the chase, other sensations of a different character, although not less disagreeable, immediately filled my mind. I discovered that I was entirely alone, in an uninhabited, wild country, with not a human being in sight. I had chased my bull at least five miles. My companions had taken a different direction, nor was a single buffalo to be seen. My mind was fully alive to the perils of my situation. I had left my pocket compass in camp, and I did not know in what direction to look for it. I mounted my horse and walked to the top of a hill to see if I could find any traces of the party. I discovered looming in the distance, Smoky Hills some twenty miles off. My mind was in a slight degree relieved, although I was almost as ignorant of my geographical position as I was before. I did not despair, but unsaddling my horse, I gave him an hour's rest; the grass was fresh, and he appeared totally unconcerned at my situation.

PONY KILLED FOR MEAT.

Poor fellow! Little did I think that day, as he carried me, so full of life and high spirit, that in a few weeks he would be reduced to a mere skeleton, and that I should be obliged, in order to save my own life on the mountains of snow, to partake of his flesh. I shed tears when they shot him down, and I never think of his generous, willing qualities, but I lament the stern necessity that left his bones bleaching on the mountains.

IT'S AN ILL WIND THAT BLOWS NOBODY GOOD.

I re-saddled my pony, and turned his head in the direction of Smoky Hills, fervently hoping to fall in with some of our party; nor was I disappointed, for after riding about an hour, I discovered to the left of my course a horse without a rider. As I approached it, I recognized the animal, and in a little while I saw its owner, my friend Weluchas, walking slowly, with his eyes intently fixed on the ground. He told me he was looking for his tomahawk pipe, which he had dropped while hunting. I joyfully assisted him in finding it, after a persevering search of an hour. He had been at least an hour on the spot before I came up. To this lucky circumstance I attributed my arrival in camp that night, for when we resumed our journey, he took a course some six points variation from the one I was travelling. On our way we fell in with Capt. Wolff and another Delaware, who were busily engaged cutting up a fine fat cow. I was soon at work, but I gave up after an ineffectual attempt to cut the liver, which is very delicate eating, my knowledge of human anatomy not being of any service to me in dissecting buffaloes.

THE INCREDULITY OF THE INDIAN HUNTERS.

While journeying campwards I related to the party my adventure with the old bull. I, of course, finished it by stating I had slain him. Capt. Wolff looked at me with a most quizzical and incredulous smile, and emphatically remarked, in his broken English, "Carvalho no kill buffalo." I insisted that I had left him dead on the field. At this the whole party laughed at me. I felt annoyed, but soon found it was no use to contend with them. Weluchas, who was really my friend, and to whom I had rendered several services, such as bleeding him and curing him of fever, could not believe the statement I had made. Capt. Wolff, seeing me look offended, said, in these exact words:— "When Capt. Wolff kill buffalo, he cut out the tongue. Indian shoot buffalo, bring home tongue. Carvalho no bring buffalo tongue; he no kill buffalo." This was powerful argument, and the inference perfectly logical; and I soon changed the subject. Gentle reader, do you think I was equal to cutting out, by the roots, a tongue from the head of an old buffalo bull, after telling you that I did not succeed in getting out the liver of a young cow, after the animal was opened? Surely I was not; but even if I had been, the alarming situation I found myself in, at the time he fell, prevented me from attempting it, if I even had known it was the hunters' rule to do so.

RETURN TO CAMP.

My messmates, to whom I related my adventure, had not the slightest idea that I had lost my way in the chase. I came into camp with the rest of the party, that night, about seven o'clock, tired and hungry. After eating a hearty supper, I wrapped myself up in my blankets and was soon asleep, dreaming of the disputed honors I had gathered in my maiden hunt after a buffalo bull.

PRAIRIE ON FIRE.

Oct. 30.—During the day, the sun was completely obscured by low, dark clouds; a most disagreeable and suffocating smoke filled the atmosphere.

We were still encamped on the Saline fork of the Kansas River, impatiently awaiting the arrival of Col. Fremont, who had not yet returned from St. Louis.[1] His continued absence alarmed us for his safety, and the circumstance that the prairies were on fire for several days past, in the direction through which he had to pass to reach us, added to our anxiety.

Night came on, and dark clouds which overhung us like an immense pall, now assumed a horrible, lurid glare, all along the horizon. As far as the eye could reach a belt of fire was visible. We were on the prairie, between Kansas River on one side, Solomon's Fork on another, Salt Creek on the third, and a large belt of woods about four miles from camp on the fourth. We were thus completely hemmed in, and comparatively secure from danger.

Our animals had been grazing near this belt of woods, the day before, and when they were driven into camp at night, one of the mules was missing. At daylight a number of our Delawares, Mr. Egloffstien, our topographical engineer, and myself, sallied out in search of it.

After looking through the woods for an hour, we discovered our mule lying dead, with his lariat drawn close around his neck. It had become loose, and, trailing along the ground, got entangled with the branches of an old tree, where in his endeavors to extricate himself he was strangled.

We were attracted to the spot by the howling of wolves, and we found that he had been partially devoured by them. Our engineer, who wanted a wolfskin for a saddle-cloth, determined to remain to kill one of them.

I assisted him to ascend a high tree immediately over the body of the mule, untied the lariat, and attaching his rifle to one end of it, pulled it up to him.

The rest of the party returned to camp. About four o'clock in the afternoon, he being still out, I roasted some buffalo meat and went to seek him. I found him still on the tree, quietly awaiting an opportunity to kill his wolf.

A heroic example of perseverance on an eminence smiling at disappointment.

Mr. Egloffstien declined to come down; I told him of the dangers to which he was exposed, and entreated him to return to camp. Finding him determined to remain, I sent him up his supper, and returned to camp, expecting him to return at sundown.

About this time the prairie was on fire just beyond the belt of woods through which Col. Fremont had to pass.

Becoming alarmed for Mr. Egloffstien, several of us went to bring him in. We found him half-way to camp, dragging by the lariat the dead body of an immense wolf which he had shot. We assisted him on with his booty as well as we could.

My "guard" came on at two o'clock. I laid down to take a three hours' rest. When I went on "duty," the scene that presented itself was sublime. A breeze had sprung up, which dissipated the smoke to windward. The full moon was shining brightly, and the piles of clouds which surrounded her, presented magnificent studies of "light and shadow," which "Claude Lorraine" so loved to paint.[2]

411

The fire had reached the belt of woods, and seemingly had burnt over the tree our friend had been seated in all day.

The fire on the north side had burned up to the water's edge, and had there stopped.

The whole horizon now seemed bounded by fire.

Our Delawares by this time had picketed all the animals near the creek we were encamped on, and had safely carried the baggage of the camp down the banks near the water. When day dawned, the magnificent woods which had sheltered our animals, appeared a forest of black scathed trunks.

The fire gradually increased, yet we dared not change our ground; first, because we saw no point where there was not more danger, and, secondly, if we moved away, "Solomon," the Indian chief, who after conducting us to the camp ground we now occupied, had returned to guide Col. Fremont, would not know exactly where to find us again.

We thus continued gazing appalled at the devouring element which threatened to overwhelm us.

After breakfast, one of our Delawares gave a loud whoop, and pointing to the open space beyond, in the direction of Solomon's Fork, where to our great joy, we saw Col. Fremont on horseback, followed by "an immense man," on "an immense mule," (who afterwards proved to be our good and kind-hearted Doctor Ober;) Col. Fremont's "cook," and the Indian "Solomon," galloping through the blazing element in the direction of our camp.[3]

Instantly and impulsively, we all discharged our rifles in a volley.

Our tents were not struck, yet we wanted to make a signal for their guidance. We all reloaded, and when they were very near, we fired a salute.

Our men and Indians immediately surrounded Col. Fremont making kind inquiries after his health.

No father who had been absent from his children, could have been received with more enthusiasm and more real joy.

To reach us he had to travel over many miles of country which had been on fire. The Indian trail which led to our camp from "Solomon's Fork," had become obliterated, rendering it difficult and arduous to follow; but the keen sense of the Indian directed him under all difficulties directly to the spot where he had left us.

During the balance of the day, the camp was put in travelling order.

With the arrival of Col. Fremont, our commissariat had received considerable additions of provisions, more, in fact, than he had any good reason to suppose we had consumed during his absence.

The reverse was exactly the truth. The provisions intended for our journey had been lavishly expended, and surreptitiously purloined.

Twice it became necessary to send to Fort Riley to procure supplies.

The season had advanced, and it became imperatively necessary to continue onwards—we should have plenty of game until we got to Bent's Fort, where there always were kept large supplies of provisions, and where Col. Fremont intended to refit and replenish.

At midnight, the fire crossed the Kansas River. I was in a great state of excitement. I mounted my horse and rode out in the direction of the Kansas, to see if the fire had actually crossed; I suppose I must have advanced within half a mile, before I discovered that the prairie was on fire on this side of it. I turned round, and galloped as I thought, in the direction of camp, but I could not descry it. I continued onwards; but as there were woods all around Salt Creek, I had lost my landmarks, and was in a terrible quandary. I however reached Salt Creek, and with great difficulty returned to camp, after an absence of three hours.

At daylight, our animals were all packed, the camp raised, and all the men in their saddles. Our only escape was through the blazing grass; we dashed into it, Col. Fremont at the head, his officers following, while the rest of the party were driving up the baggage animals. The distance we rode through the fire, could not have been more than one hundred feet, the grass which quickly ignites, as quickly consumes, leaving only black ashes in the rear.

We passed through the fiery ordeal unscathed; made that day over fifteen miles, and camped for the night on the dry bed of a creek, beyond the reach of the devouring element.

CHAPTER IX

The cold was intense during our last encampment at Walnut Creek. About an hour after the midnight watch had been relieved, and while the last watch were warming their benumbed limbs before a large fire, one of the men on horse guard left his duty, and came into camp to warm himself—Col. Fremont, who was always on the "qui vive," suddenly appeared at the camp-fire. This was not unusual, that he should personally inspect the guard, but he took such times, when he was least expected—in order to see if the men did their duty properly.

The Colonel accosted the officer of the watch, and enquired if Mr. —— had been relieved? He replied that he had not, but gave as an excuse, the coldness of the weather. Col. Fremont lectured the officer, and had another man immediately sent out to take his place. He was highly displeased, and as a punishment, told Mr. —— that he expected he "would walk," during the next day's travel. I had been relieved a short time before, and I knew how cold I was, and that it was necessary to move about continually, to keep up the circulation of the blood; under the circumstances, I thought the punishment disproportionate to the offense.

I was a novice in camp life among Indians, and was not aware of the stern necessity required for a strict guardianship of the animals; but the sequel proved, that the "slight dereliction" from duty, as I thought it, involved the most serious consequences.

At day-light, when the animals were driven in to be loaded and packed for the day's journey, five of them were missing. The camp was, in consequence, delayed, while the animals were sought; half the day was lost in an ineffectual search. Our Delawares reported having discovered moccasin prints on the snow, and at once decided they were made by Cheyenne Indians, from their peculiar form.

The next day we followed a track made by "shod horses," which convinced us we were on the right scent. The Indians do not shoe their horses.

On the "divide," near the Arkansas River, we saw one of our mules grazing, but so worn out by the hard drive, that he was unable to continue, and the Indians left him on the prairie.

It took us several days to reach the village, which was situated on the part of the Arkansas River known as Big Timber[s], near Mr. Bent's house.

At this village we found the rest of the animals, and some of the thieves. On examining them, they confessed that they had watched our camp during the night, for an opportunity to run off our animals, but found them guarded, until one man left his watch, and went to warm himself at the camp fire, during which time they stole five of them, and if they had had an hour longer time, they would have stolen a great many more. They went so far as to point out the very man who went to the fire.

Mr. —— submitted to the walk with as good a grace as possible. We had a long journey that day, but he manfully accomplished it; and I heard him say, afterwards, that he richly deserved it.

Imagine twenty odd men, 600 miles from the frontiers, at the commencement of a severe winter, deprived of their animals, on an open prairie, surrounded by Camanches, Pawnees and other tribes of hostile Indians. I am fully convinced that but for the "watchfulness" of Col. Fremont, we should have been placed in this awkward predicament.

IMMENSE HERDS OF BUFFALO.

On the divide, between Walnut Creek and the Arkansas River, we travelled through immense herds of buffalo; at one time there could not have been fewer than two hundred thousand in sight.

All around us, as far as the eye could reach, the prairie was completely black with them; they at times impeded our progress. We stopped for more than an hour to allow a single herd to gallop, at full speed, across our path, while the whole party amused themselves with singling out particular ones, and killing them.

I essayed, at different times, to daguerreotype them while in motion, but was not successful, although I made several pictures of distant herds.

On this "divide" I saw numbers of prairie dogs, they ran to their holes on our approach; a small sized owl, most generally stood as sentinel near the hole. Our Delawares told me that the prairie dog, the owl, and the rattlesnake always congregate together—a strange trio.

The prairie after you pass Pawnee Fork, and also on the divide between Walnut Creek and the Arkansas River, is covered with a short grass, called buffalo grass.

Firewood or timber, only grows on the creek, and the artemisia entirely disappears.

We camped one night on the open prairie, without wood, near Pawnee Fork, a tributary of the Kansas. The thermometer was below freezing point, and there was no vestige of wood or timber to be seen.

I was busily engaged making my daguerreotype views of the country, over which I had to travel the next day. On looking through my camera I observed two of our men approaching over a slope, holding between them a blanket filled with something; curious to know what it was, I hailed them, and found they had been gathering "dried buffalo chips," to build a fire with. This material burns like peat, and makes a very hot fire, without much smoke, and keeps the heat a long

415

time; a peculiar smell exhales from it while burning, not at all unpleasant. But for this material, it would be impossible to travel over certain parts of this immense country. It served us very often, not only for cooking purposes but also to warm our half frozen limbs. I have seen chips of a large size—one I had the curiosity to measure, was two feet in diameter.

Our first camp on the Arkansas was visited by a number of Indian hunters, with the product of their skill, in the use of their bows and arrows, hanging across their horses. One of them borrowed my jack-knife, and cutting a piece of the raw antelope liver, deliberately ate it. I remember the peculiar feeling this exhibition excited in my bosom. I considered the Indian little better than a cannibal, and taking back my knife, turned from him in disgust.

I got bravely over it, however, in the course of my journey, as a perusal of these pages will show.

Chapter X

The Cheyenne village, on Big Timber[s], consists of about two hundred and fifty lodges, containing, probably, one thousand persons, including men, women and children.

I went into the village to take daguerreotype views of their lodges, and succeeded in obtaining likenesses of an Indian princess—a very aged woman, with a papoose, in a cradle or basket, and several of the chiefs. I had great difficulty in getting them to sit still, or even to submit to have themselves daguerreotyped. I made a picture, first, of their lodges, which I showed them. I then made one of the old woman and papoose. When they saw it, they thought I was a "supernatural being;" and, before I left camp, they were satisfied I was more than human.

The squaws are very fond of ornaments; their arms are encircled with bracelets made of thick brass wire—sometimes of silver beaten out as thin as pasteboard. The princess, or daughter of the Great Chief, was a beautiful Indian girl. She attired herself in her most costly robes, ornamented with elk teeth, beads, and colored porcupine quills—expressly to have her likeness taken. I made a beautiful picture of her.

The bracelets of the princess were of brass; silver ones are considered invaluable, and but few possess them.

416

Cheyenne Princess. From the "Prospectus" for Frémont's *Memoirs*.
Courtesy of the Henry E. Huntington Library.

After I had made the likeness of the princess, I made signs to her to let me have one of her brass bracelets. She very reluctantly gave me one. I wiped it very clean, and touched it with "quicksilver." It instantly became bright and glittering as polished silver. I then presented her with it. Her delight and astonishment knew no bounds. She slipped it over her arm, and danced about in ecstacy. As for me, she thought I was a great "Magician".

My extraordinary powers of converting "brass into silver" soon became known in the village, and in an hour's time I was surrounded with squaws entreating me to make *"presto, pass!"* with their "armlets and brass finger-rings."

Some offered me moccasins, other venison, as payment; but I had to refuse nearly all of them, as I had only a small quantity of quicksilver for my daguerreotype operations.

My "lucifer matches," also, excited their astonishment; they had never seen them before; and my fire water, "alcohol," which I used, also, to heat my mercury—capped the climax.

They wanted me to live with them, and I believe if I had remained, they would have worshipped me as possessing most extraordinary powers of necromancy.

I returned to camp with a series of pictures, and about a dozen pairs of moccasins, some elaborately worked with beads; all of which I stowed away in my boxes, and had the great gratification of supplying my companions with a pair, when they were most required, and when they least expected them.

The Pawnees and Cheyennes were at deadly war, at this time. During our visit to the Cheyenne camp, a number of warriors returned from a successful battle with the Pawnees, and brought in some twelve or fifteen scalps as trophies of their prowess. On the night of their arrival, they had a grand scalp-dance; all the men and most of the women were grotesquely attired in wolf, bear, and buffalo skins; some of them with the horns of the buffalo, and antlers of the deer, for head ornaments. Their faces were painted black and red; each of the chiefs, who had taken a scalp, held it aloft attached to a long pole. An immense fire was burning, around which they danced and walked in procession, while some of the women were beating drums, and making night hideous with their horrible howlings and discordant chantings. This was so novel and extraordinary a scene, that I rode into our camp, about three miles off, and induced Col. Fremont to accompany me to witness it. Mr. Egloffstien, succeeded in writing down the notes of their song; they have no idea of music; they all sing on the same key. I did not notice a single second or bass voice amongst them. We returned to camp about 12 o'clock, and left them all still participating in the celebration of their bloody victory. I accepted an invitation to dine with the chief; his lodge is larger, but in no other respects different from those of the others. We dined in it, on buffalo steaks and venison; a fire was burning in the centre; around the fire, were beds made of cedar branches, covered with buffalo robes, on which his two wives and three children slept. They use no furniture of any kind; there are hiding places under their beds, in which they place their extra moccasins and superfluous deer-skin shirts.

The women make the bows and arrows, and all their moccasins, dress and prepare their skins and buffalo robes, take down and put up their lodges when they move their villages, which is three or four times a year, and all the servile and hard work of the camp. The men hunt, fish, and go to war.

The Cheyennes possess a large number of fine horses, some of which they raise, while the most of them are stolen and taken as prizes in their forays with other tribes of Indians.

Chapter XI

Bent's House[4] is built of adobes, or unburnt brick, one story high, in form of a hollow square, with a courtyard in the centre. One side is appropriated as his sleeping apartments, the front as a store-house, while the others are occupied by the different persons in his employ. He has a large number of horses and mules.

Col. Fremont procured from him fresh animals for all the men, leaving behind us those which were thought unable to go through. At this time Mr. Bent had but a small quantity of sugar and coffee; he supplied us, however, with all he could spare, and a considerable quantity of dried buffalo meat, moccasins and overshoes for all the men; a large buffalo-skin lodge, capable of covering twenty-five men, and one small one for Col. Fremont; buffalo robes for each man besides stockings, gloves, tobacco, etc.

I breakfasted with Mr. Bent and Doctor Ober, on baked bread, made from maize ground, dried buffalo meat, venison steaks, and hot coffee; a treat that I had not enjoyed for a very long time.

Col. Fremont having entirely recovered his health, decided not to take the doctor over the mountains, but made arrangements with Mr. Bent to send him home by the first train of wagons; one of our white men, a Mr. Mulligan, of St. Louis, also remained, as an assistant to the doctor.[5] I had formed quite an attachment to Doctor Ober; he was a gentleman of extensive information, and his intellectual capacity was of the highest order. I have ridden by his side for many a mile, listening to his explanations of the sciences of geology and botany. When we passed a remarkable formation, he would stop and compare it with others of similar character in different parts of the world. I regretted very much the necessity there was for his remaining behind, but it was well for him that he did so; his age and make would have incapacitated him from enduring the privations and hardships which we had to encounter.

The weather continuing so cold I found it inconvenient to use my oil colors and brushes; accordingly I left my tin case with the doctor, who promised to take charge of them for me to the States.

When the weather is very clear, you can see the snowy peaks of the Rocky Mountains from Bent's house, which is seventy miles distant. Our friend the doctor wanted to obtain a nearer view of them, and proposed that I should accompany him. We started on a clear morning, for that purpose. I took my apparatus along; we rode thirty miles, but the weather becoming hazy, it entirely shut out our view of the mountains. We returned to camp late at night, after a tiresome day's ride.

The Arkansas River where we first struck it, which was at the crossing of the Santa Fé trail, is almost entirely bare of timber; the trunks of several giant cottonwood trees, which had probably been landmarks for early travellers to Mexico, still reared their enormous heads high into the Heavens, defying alike the storms of winter, and the axe and fire of the hungry pioneer, who in vain attempted to hew and burn them down. I measured one of them, its circumference was eighteen feet. We travelled up the river a great many miles, without seeing any timber at all, and relying for firewood on the drift logs, we found along the banks.

There are a great many islands in the Arkansas River, on which some few young cottonwoods are growing. We frequently encamped on these islands.

At "Big Timber," there is a considerable quantity of oak, and cottonwood of large growth. Game of all kinds abounds in it.

Bent's house is a trading post. Indians of the different tribes bring in their venison, buffalo meat, skins, and robes, which are exchanged for various descriptions of manufactured goods. Mr. Bent also receives the annual appropriation from Government, for the neighboring tribes of Indians which are distributed at this point. Bent's Fort, which is situated about thirty miles further up the Arkansas, was recently destroyed by the Indians,[6] and has not been rebuilt, from the scarcity of timber in its vicinity. All the material saved from the fort, was removed to Mr. Bent's house, on Big Timber. After a sojourn of a week, near Bent's trading house, the whole of which time was employed in refitting and preparing proper camp equipage for the journey over the mountains, we bade an affectionate adieu to our worthy doctor; and started in high spirits, the lofty summit of Pike's Peak in the distance glittering in the morning sun.

CARVALHO, 50–74.

1. A letter written by a member of the party, probably James F. Milligan, conveyed to St. Louisans the impatience of the camp "to get forward." The Indians were predicting a long and severe winter on the bases of the "fire light," as they called the aurora borealis, and the migration of the buffalo southward (*Daily Missouri Democrat*, 19 Nov. 1853).

2. This was Claude Gellée (1600–1682), but more often known as Claude Lorrain because of his birth at Champagne in Lorraine. Down to the middle of the nineteenth century he was regarded as the prince of landscape painters, partly because of his treatment of atmosphere and light (KITSON).

3. The four joined the main camp on 31 Oct., and the next day the expedition moved toward Bent's New Fort near the Big Timbers (*Daily Missouri Democrat*, 9 Dec. 1853). According to both JBF and Benton, JCF found his mules weak and some lame. The grass was gone and the camp had been too far from fort or trading post to procure corn. A. Ebers (not Ober) was the name of the homeopathic physician (MONTAGUE, 49). JBF indicates that he had experience at Gräfenberg, the water-cure place in Austria for "rheumatic generals and sciatic naval men," and that he recommended JCF go there, too. Ebers had also served in the Russian army in its war with the Turks in 1828 (JBF to Elizabeth Blair Lee, Saint Louis, 14 Oct. 1853, NjP—Blair-Lee Papers).

4. Bent's House or Bent's New Fort stood on the north bank of the Arkansas River, below the Big Timbers, and about thirty-eight miles downstream from the Old Fort, which William Bent had deliberately destroyed on 21 Aug. 1849. The new fort had just been completed when JCF's expedition arrived and probably furnished a better site for trade than the old location (LAVENDAR).

5. Milligan, and probably Ebers too, reached Westport on 23 April 1854 (BARRY, 1204).

6. The fort was destroyed not by the Indians but by Bent. See the account of its destruction in LAVENDAR.

264. Excerpts from Letters: Frémont to Jessie B. Frémont and Thomas H. Benton

"Big Timber," Upper Arkansas
November 26, 1853

In the early part of the month the weather was cold and bad, the thermometer usually at daybreak in the morning standing at 15° and 17° below the freezing point, but for the last ten days it is beautiful, yesterday and to-day quite warm at mid-day, and not a particle of snow to be seen; and this is at a time when our Surgeon Dr. Ebers, says that in Germany there is much snow. The expedition so far has been successful enough to gratify all our expectations, both in its general results and in its particular object. The coal formation reappears in this neighborhood, and I have come acquainted with a locality where the beds are said to be developed largely, and near the line of the road. The coal has been tried, and found to burn perfectly well. I have purchased sixteen fresh mules at this place, and laid in supplies for the winter struggle in the mountains, now appearing in view. I am determined to carry the enterprise through to the end, contending with the winter and every obstacle, prudently and cautiously, but never giving way. I have presents to conciliate the Indians, and our vigilance will prevent attacks. Our movement now will be a struggle with the winter. We have December and January, the mountains and the strength of the winter before us, and shall move slowly, but do good work. The astronomical, barometrical, and topographical work all go on well. After surmounting some difficulties with our *daguerre*, (which it required skill to do) it has been eminently successful, and we are producing a line of pictures of exquisite beauty which will admirably illustrate the country. We hope to get through in two months, and to make a complete winter exploration of the route.

Printed in *National Intelligencer*, 18 March 1854. The excerpts were made by Benton and embodied in his letter to the editor. He made a slightly different arrangement for James D. Dana, who published them in the *American Journal of Science and Arts*, 2nd ser., 17 (May 1854):449–50. In referring to the daguerreotypes, Benton or JCF wrote: "Every successive picture improves upon its predecessor, and those of yesterday were jewels. They were of the Cheyenne village here among the timber."

265. With Frémont: Solomon Nunes Carvalho's Account of the Fifth Expedition, 27 Nov. 1853–21 Feb. 1854

CHAPTER XII

We travelled up the Arkansas,[1] and passing the ruins, of Bent's Fort on the opposite side of the river, struck the mouth of the Huerfano; we followed that river to the Huerfano Valley—which is by far the most romantic and beautiful country I ever beheld. Nature seems to have, with a bountiful hand, lavished on this delightful valley all the ingredients necessary for the habitation of man; but in vain the eye seeks through the magnificent vales, over the sloping hills, and undulating plains, for a single vestige to prove that even the foot of an Indian has ever preceded us. Herds of antelope and deer roam undisturbed through the primeval forests, and sustain themselves on the various cereals which grow luxuriantly in the valley.

But where are the people?

Were there ever any inhabitants in this extraordinarily fertile country?

Will the progress of civilization ever extend so far in the interior?

At present, not even the smoke from an Indian wigwam taints the pure air which plays around, and imparts healthful vigor to my frame.

After crossing the Huerfano River, we saw the immense pile of granite rock, which rises perpendicularly to the height of four or five hundred feet, from a perfectly level valley. It appeared like a mammoth sugar loaf, (called the Huerfano Butte).* Col. Fremont expressed a desire to have several views of it from different distances.[2]

The main party proceeded on the journey, leaving under my charge the mules which carried our apparatus, and also the blankets and buffalo robes of the whole camp; it being necessary in equalizing the weight, to distribute the different boxes on three or four animals. Mr. Egloffstien, Mr. Fuller, and two Delawares, remained with me.

To make a daguerreotype view, generally occupied from one to two hours, the principal part of that time, however, was spent in packing,

---

*"The Orphan."

423

Entrance of Pass in Sierra Mojada or Wet Mountains. From the "Prospectus" for Frémont's *Memoirs*. Courtesy of the Henry E. Huntington Library.

and reloading the animals. When we came up to the Butte, Mr. Fuller made barometrical observations at its base, and also ascended to the top to make observations, in order to ascertain its exact height. The calculations have not yet been worked out.

If a railroad is ever built through this valley, I suggest that an equestrian statue of Col. J. C. Fremont, be placed on the summit of the Huerfano Butte; his right hand pointing to California, the land he conquered.

When we had completed our work, we found that we were four hours behind camp, equal to twelve miles. We followed the trail of our party, through the immense fields of artemisia, until night overtook us, travelling until we could no longer distinguish the trail.

Our arms were discharged as a signal to the camp; they answered it by firing off their rifles, but the wind being then high, we could not determine their exact distance or position. Then, taking counsel together, we determined to encamp for the night, on the side of a mountain covered with pines, near by.

We soon had a large fire burning, for the weather was intensely cold and disagreeable. Upon unloading our animals we found that we had with us all the baggage and buffalo robes of the camp, but nothing to eat or drink; the night was so dark that although not more than half a mile from a creek, we preferred to suffer from thirst rather than incur fresh danger which might lurk about it.

I had with me three tin boxes, containing preserved eggs and milk, but I preferred to go supperless to bed, rather than touch the small supply which I had, unknown to the rest, carefully hid away in my boxes, to be used on some more pressing occasion.

Our absence was most keenly felt by the camp, for they had to remain up, around their fires all night, not having any thing to sleep on.

We also watched all night, fearful that our animals should stray away, or that we should be attacked by Indians.

At day dawn we reloaded our animals, found our lost trail, and soon met some of our party whom Colonel Fremont had sent to look for us.

When we got to camp, they were all ready for a start, and waiting for us. A delicious breakfast of buffalo and venison had been prepared, and we discussed its merits with an appetite sharpened by a twenty-four hours fast.

Cochetopa Pass. From the "Prospectus" for Frémont's *Memoirs*.
Courtesy of the Henry E. Huntington Library.

At the very base of the Rocky Mountains, while we were approaching the Sand-hill Pass,[3] fresh bear track were discovered by our Delawares, who determined to follow in search of the animal. Diverging a little from our line among the trees on the side of the mountain, our bruin was first seen. "A bear hunt! a bear hunt!" was quickly re-echoed by the whole company. The baggage animals were left to themselves while Colonel Fremont and the whole party darted off at full speed to the chase.

Two of our Delawares who first spied him, were half a mile in advance, for they gave the reins to their animals the instant they saw the bear. His bearship seeing strangers approaching at full speed, and being unused to their ways, thought it most prudent to make himself scarce; he turned and slowly descended the hill in an opposite direction; our loud huzzas finally alarmed him and off he went in full tilt, the whole party surrounding him; the first shot from the Delaware brought him to his knees. Three shots killed him.

He was an enormous black bear, and very fat; I partook of but small quantities of it, it being too luscious and greasy for my palate. The meat was brought into camp and served several days for food for the whole party.

The next day I accompanied Col. Fremont into the Roubidoux Pass,[4] from the summit of which I had the first view into the San Louis [San Luis] Valley, the head waters of the "Rio Grande del Norte." On the opposite side forty miles across are the "San Juan Mountains," the scene of Col. Fremont's terrible disaster on a former expedition. He pointed out to me in the direction of the spot and with a voice tremulous with emotion, related some of the distressing incidents of that awful night. I made a daguerreotype of the pass with the San Louis Valley and mountains in the distance.

While exploring in the pass we accidentally came upon a Mexican, almost naked, who had deserted or been left behind by some hunters. Col. Fremont, whose great heart beats in sympathy for the suffering of his fellow men, made him follow to camp, and although he knew that this man would be an incubus upon the party from his inability to walk, allowed him to accompany the expedition, and supplied him with a part of his own wardrobe. The man subsequently proved perfectly worthless.[5]

On our way down from the pass, Col. Fremont took out his revolver, and at a distance of about twenty paces killed a small, white, delicately formed animal, very like an ermine. This was an excellent shot with a sightless pistol.

Chapter XIII

We entered the San Louis Valley through the Sand-hill Pass, and camped at the mouth. Travelling up the valley about twenty miles, we ascended one of the verdant and gentle slopes of the mountains, along which meandered a stream of living water, fringed on its banks with cottonwood and elms. We selected a camp-ground in an immense natural deer-park, and raised our tents under the shelter of wide-spreading cedars.[6]

Scarcely were we comfortably fixed, when a herd of black-tail deer came down the mountain to water within sight of our camp. Cautiously our Indian hunters sallied out, and ere many minutes, the sound of one, two, three—a dozen rifles were heard in quick succession. Every shot brought down a fine fat buck, and our supper that night, consisted of as fine roast venison as ever graced the table of an epicure.

Col. Fremont determined to remain here for several days in order to have a quantity of the meat cured for our use in the mountains. I exercised my skill in rifle shooting for the last time at this camp. Game of all kinds which had hitherto been plentiful, disappeared almost entirely after we left it.

We travelled up the San Louis Valley, crossing the Rio Grande del Norte [Saguache Creek], and entered the Sarawatch [Saguache] Valley through a perfectly level pass. Our journey continued along the valley until we came to the Cochotope,[7] where we camped.

That night it snowed on us for the first time. The snow obliterated the wagon tracks of Capt. Gunnison's expedition, but Col. Fremont's unerring judgment conducted us in the precise direction by a general ascent through trackless, though sparsely timbered forests, until we approached the summit, on which grew an immense number of trees, still in leaf, with only about four inches of snow on the ground.[8]

As we approached this dense forest, we soon perceived that the axe of the white man had forced a passage through for a wagon-road. Many of the larger trees on both sides of the track were deeply cut with a cross, as an emblem of civilization, which satisfied us that Capt. Gunnison and Lieut. Beale had penetrated through to the other side.[9] In this forest, we were surrounded by immense granite mountains, whose summits were covered probably with everlasting snow. The streams from them which had previously been running towards us, now took the opposite direction, supplying us with the gratifying proof that we had completed our travel to the summit, and were now descending the mountains towards the Pacific.[10] After issuing from these woods we camped on the edge of a rivulet.

At this camp Col. Fremont exhibited such unmistakable marks of consideration for me, that it induced my unwavering perseverance in the exercise of my professional duties subsequently, when any other man would have hesitated, and probably given up, and shrunk dismayed from the encounter.

Near by our camp, a rugged mountain, barren of trees, and thickly covered with snow, reared its lofty head high in the blue vault above us. The approach to it was inaccessible by even our surefooted mules. From its summit, the surrounding country could be seen for hundreds of miles. Col. Fremont regretted that such important views as might be made from that point, should be lost, and gave up the idea as impracticable from its dangerous character. I told him that if he would allow two men to assist me in carrying my apparatus up the mountain, I would attempt the ascent on foot, and make the pictures; he pointed out the difficulties, I insisted. He then told me if I was determined to go he would accompany me; this was an unusual thing for him and it proved to me, that he considered the ascent difficult and dangerous, and that his superior judgment might be required to pick the way, for a misstep would have precipitated us on to the rugged rocks at its base; and it also proved that he would not allow his men or officers to encounter perils or dangers in which he did not participate.

After three hours' hard toil we reached the summit and beheld a panorama of unspeakable sublimity spread out before us; continuous chains of mountains reared their snowy peaks far away in the distance, while the Grand [Gunnison] River plunging along in awful sublimity through its rocky bed, was seen for the first time. Above us the cerulean heaven, without a single cloud to mar its beauty, was sublime in its calmness.

Standing as it were in this vestibule of God's holy Temple, I forgot I was of this mundane sphere; the divine part of man elevated itself, undisturbed by the influences of the world. I looked from nature, up to nature's God, more chastened and purified than I ever felt before.

Plunged up to middle in snow, I made a panorama of the continu-

Black Canyon of the Gunnison River. By J. W. Stanley but based on a sketch made by F. W. Egloffstein during his 1853–54 expedition with Frémont. From *Reports of Explorations and Surveys . . . for a Railroad . . . to the Pacific Ocean*, vol. 2.

ous ranges of mountains around us. Col. Fremont made barometrical and thermometrical observations, and occupied a part of his time in geological examinations. We descended safely, and with a keen appetite, discussed the merits of our dried buffalo and deer meat.

CHAPTER XIV

Eating, sleeping, and travelling, continually in the open air, with the thermometer descending, as we gradually ascended the immense slopes of country between the frontiers of Missouri and the Rocky Mountains, until I have found myself in a temperature of 30° below zero, prepared my system for the intense cold, which we endured during our journey through that elevated country. Twice only did our party find it too cold to travel longer than half an hour, without stopping and making a large fire to keep ourselves from freezing. We were all mounted at the time, but we found it necessary to walk a greater part of the way, to keep up a circulation of the blood.

It is judiciously ordained by a kind Providence, that the cold as well as heat, gradually increases in intensity.

If the human body at a temperate heat, say 80° was suddenly exposed to a temperature of 30° below zero, in which we travelled without any extra clothing, no ill effect resulting, we should not have been able to exist for an hour.

Let us then humbly acknowledge that to the great Omnipotent, we owe our being and all the benefits we receive.

MY FIRST JOURNEY ON FOOT.

It was a very cold day in December; the snow covered the immense mountain, over which we had to travel, and right merrily we all followed each other's footsteps in the deep snow.

When we arrived at the foot of the rugged mountain, it was found necessary to dismount, and lead our animals along the intricate and tortuous path. As usual I was at the rear of the cavalcade; I threw the bridle over my pony's head, and followed slowly behind him. I plunged frequently up to my neck in chasms of snow. My efforts to extricate myself cost me some time, and when I regained my footing, I discovered my pony about fifty yards ahead, trying to regain the party. I redoubled my exertions to reach him—I halloed all to no purpose—I sank down exhausted on a rock, with the dreadful reality that I was alone, and on foot on the mountains of eternal snow, with a long day's journey before me.

Gathering fresh strength and courage from the serious position I found myself in, I scrambled up that mountain with a heart palpitating so loudly, that I could count its pulsations. In this manner, alternately resting, I reached the top. On looking on the other side, the only indication of the party, was their deep trail in the frozen snow.

I commenced descending, and at considerable distance below me, I fancied I saw a moving object under a tree; continuing in the track, slipping at times a distance of ten or fifteen feet, until some disguised rock brought me up, I reached the bottom, where I found my pony tied to a tree, immediately on the trail.

No shipwrecked mariner on beholding the approach of a friendly vessel to deliver him from certain death, ever felt greater joy than I did, when I realized that it was my horse which I saw.

This incident was most injurious to me, and I felt its effects for several days, both in body and mind. I mounted my pony, and arrived in camp at dark, some four or five hours after the rest of the party.

Captain Wolff saw my pony riderless, and suspecting that he had escaped from me, caught and tied him up in the place where he was sure to be found; thus repaying me a hundred fold for my medical advice and attendance on Salt Creek.

* * * * * *

HORSE STEAKS FRIED IN TALLOW CANDLES, AND BLANC MANGE FOR DESSERT.

At Bent's Fort, Col. Fremont had several pounds of candles made out of buffalo tallow; the want of convenient boxes to convey them, resulted in many of them being broken to pieces, so as to render them useless as candles. On the first of January, 1854, our men were regaled by unexpected, though not unwelcome luxuries.

I had reserved with religious care, two boxes containing one pound each, of Alden's preserved eggs and milk.—(The yolks of the eggs were beaten to a thick paste with a pound of loaf sugar, the milk was also prepared with powdered sugar, and hermetically sealed in tin cases).—These two tins I had stowed away in my boxes, being the remains of the six dozen which had been wantonly destroyed at our six weeks camp on Salt Creek.

Nobody knew I had them. A paper of arrow root, which my wife had placed in my trunk, for diet, in case I was sick, I had also reserved. These three comestibles, boiled in six gallons of water, made as fine a blanc mange as ever was *mangéd* on Mount Blanc. This "dessert" I prepared without the knowledge of Col. Fremont.

Our dinner, in honor of "New Year's Day," consisted, besides our usual "horse soup," of a delicious dish of horse steaks, fried in the remnants of our "tallow candles." But the satisfaction and astonishment of the whole party cannot be portrayed, when I introduced, as dessert, my incomparable blanc mange. "Six gallons of *bona fide*," nourishing food, sweetened and flavored! It is hardly necessary to say, that it disappeared in double quick time. The whole camp had a share of it; and we were all sorry that there was "no more left of the same sort."

*   *   *   *   *   *

Several days after we came down from the Cochotope Pass, it became necessary to ascend a very high and excessively steep mountain of snow. When we were half way up, one of the foremost baggage mules lost his balance, from his hind feet sinking deep in the snow. Down he tumbled, heels-over-head, carrying with him nearly the whole cavalcade, fifty odd in number, several hundred feet to the bottom.[11]

It was a serious, yet a most ludicrous spectacle, to witness fifty animals rolling headlong down a snow mountain, gaining fresh impetus as they descended, unable to stop themselves. The bales of buffalo robes, half buried in the snow, lodged against an old pine tree, the blankets scattered everywhere; my boxes of daguerreotype materials uninjured, although buried in the snow. Considerable time was occupied in searching after them.

I found myself standing up to my eyes in snow, high up the mountain, witnessing this curiously interesting, although disastrous accident; for, when we collected ourselves and animals together, we found that one mule and one horse were killed. This scene made a deep impression upon me. Night came upon us before we were ready to leave the spot. We camped on the same place of the night before.

A snow storm commenced raging, which detained us in this situation for another day; when, determined to cross the mountains, we all recommenced the ascent, and successfully arrived, though much exhausted, without further accident, at the top, and encamped on its summit in snow four feet deep.

That night the thermometer sank very low, and the men stood to their waists in snow, guarding the animals to prevent their running away in search of grass, or something to eat.

We descended the mountain the next day. Our tent poles, belonging to the large lodge, were broken by their contact with the trees in the winding path. The lodge, afterwards, became useless, and the men, myself among them, had to sleep out upon the open snow, with no covering but our blankets, etc.

Chapter XV

After descending a very steep mountain, on the snows of which we passed the coldest night I experienced during the journey, the thermometer, at daylight, being 30 degrees below zero, we camped on a creek fringed with willows and interspersed with cotton-wood. The country indicating that there might be game about, our Delawares sallied out in quest of some.

We at this time were on rations of meat-biscuit,* and had killed our first horse for food. Towards night, our hunters returned, and brought with them the choice parts of a fine fat, young horse that they had killed. He was one of three or four wild ones which they discovered grazing some four miles from camp.

Our men, in consequence, received a considerable addition to their stock of provisions, which, when cooked, proved much more palatable than our broken down horses.

The Delawares also discovered recent footprints of Utah Indians. This information caused Col. Fremont to double the guard and examine the arms of the whole party, who hitherto had been warned by him of the necessity there was for keeping them in perfect order.

Suddenly it occurred to me that my double-barrel gun might be out of order: I had used it as a *walking stick*, in descending the mountain that day; the snow was so deep that I was obliged to resort to that course to extricate myself from the drifts.

I quietly went to the place where I had laid it down, and attempted to fire it off; both caps exploded, but the gun did not go off, the barrels being filled with frozen snow. The quick ear of Col. Fremont heard the caps explode. He approached me very solemnly and gave me a lecture, setting forth the consequences which might have ensued

---

*A preparation made by saturating flour with the juices of boiled beef, and then baked into biscuit.

Utah Village, foothills of the west slope of the Rocky Mountains. From the "Prospectus" for Frémont's *Memoirs*. Courtesy of the Henry E. Huntington Library.

435

from a sudden attack of the Indians on our camp. "Under present circumstances, Mr. Carvalho," said he, "I should have to fight for you." His rebuke was merited, and had its effect throughout the camp, for all the men were most particular afterwards in keeping their arms in perfect order.

We travelled that day nearly twenty miles, and encamped outside of a Utah Indian village, containing a large number of lodges and probably several hundred persons.[12]

The men were mostly armed with rifles, powderhorns, and also with their Indian implements of warfare. On our mules was packed the balance of our "fat horse" of the night before.

These Indians received us very kindly, and during the evening we exposed our wares, viz.: blankets, knives, red cloth, vermilion, etc., etc., which we brought along to conciliate the Indians, and also to trade with them for horses and venison.

We made several purchases, and traded for several small lots of fat venison.

About nine o'clock, after placing double guard around our animals and while we were regaling on fat deer meat in Col. Fremont's lodge, we heard loud noises approaching the camp; voices of women were heard in bitter bewailment. I thought it was a religious ceremony of Indian burial, or something of the kind. Col. Fremont requested me to see from what it proceeded. I found the whole Indian camp in procession assembled around our lodge. The warriors were all armed, headed by a half-breed, who had been some time in Mexico, and had acquired a smattering of the Spanish language; this man acted as interpreter. Understanding the Spanish language, I gleaned from him that the horse our Delawares had killed the evening before, some twenty miles away, belonged to one of the squaws then present, who valued it very highly, and demanded payment.

On informing Col. Fremont, who denied himself to the Indians, he remarked that "we had no right to kill their horse without remunerating them for it." The man in charge of the baggage was deputed to give them what was a fair compensation for it.

The Indians having seen our assortment, wanted a part of everything we had, including a keg of gunpowder.

To this demand Col. Fremont gave an absolute refusal, and at the same time emphatically expressed his desire that the men should not sell, barter, or give away a single grain of gunpowder, on pain of his severest displeasure.

436

The Indians then threatened to attack us. Col. Fremont defied them. After considerable parleying, we succeeded in pacifying them.

As it was the intention of Col. Fremont to leave camp at an early hour, I unpacked my daguerreotype apparatus, at daylight, and made several views.

While engaged in this way, one of the Utah Indians brought into camp a beautiful three-year-old colt, and offered to trade him with me; he was a model pony—dark bay color, in splendid order, sound in wind and limb, and full of life and fire. My poor buffalo Pungo had, three days before, been shot down for food, and in consequence I was literally on foot, although I was using one of the baggage animals for the time.

With permission of Col. Fremont I traded for him; I gave him in exchange one pair of blankets, an old dress coat, a spoiled daguerreotype plate, a knife, half an ounce of vermilion and an old exhausted pony, which we would have been obliged to leave behind; previous to the trade, I had never mounted him, but I saw the Indian ride him, and his movements were easy and graceful. The Indian saddled him for me, as I was otherwise engaged and did not notice him during the operation. By this time the rest of the party were all mounted, and I never jumped on him until the last moment; he winced a little under the bit, the first one he ever had in his mouth, but cantered off at a round pace, I would not at that moment have taken $500 for him. I considered myself safely mounted for the rest of the journey.

After we had proceeded about two miles, my pony prancing and caracoling to the admiration of the whole party, I discovered that I had left my Colt's navy revolver in camp. I told Col. Fremont of my carelessness, and he smilingly sent one of the men back with me to look for it. I must confess I had not the slightest hopes of finding it, nor had he.

At the time we started, there must have been two hundred Utah men, women, and children at our camp, and if one of them had picked it up, it was most unlikely I should ever receive it again. They had shown some hostility, and although I was not afraid to go back, I thought some danger attended it—Frank Dixon accompanied me.

My pony finding his head turned homeward, commenced champing at his bit, and working his head and body endeavoring to get away. I prided myself on being a good horseman, but this fellow was too much for me.

He got the bit between his teeth and off he started at a killing pace for camp. In less than five minutes I found myself in a wild sage bush on the road; the saddle had slipped round his body, which was as smooth as a cylinder, while I, losing my balance, slipped off.

My pony was quietly grazing in the Indian camp, when I, riding double with Frank, arrived there. The most important thing, was my pistol; I proceeded immediately to the spot, and, hidden in the long grass, where I laid it down, I found it.

With the assistance of the Utahs, my pony was captured, and doubling the saddle-blanket, I attempted to draw the girth tightly—he resisted, and gave considerable trouble; but I was finally mounted, and away we cantered after our party, which we overtook after a couple of hours' ride.

This animal continued to trouble me every morning afterwards. On one occasion, I was saddling him, to perform which operation, I had to tie him to a tree, if one was at hand; at the time I now describe, he was tied to a tree, and in vain I endeavored to place the saddle on him, finally, he reared, and planted both feet on my breast, and I barely escaped with my life, yet my pride never suffered me to complain about it. Sometimes one of my comrades would assist me, but on this occasion, Col. Fremont saw my predicament; in a few minutes, his servant, "Lee," came to me, and said, "he was more accustomed to break horses than I was," and offered to exchange with me, until mine was more manageable.

This man rode a cream colored pacer, which Col. Fremont wanted to take through to California, if possible, as a riding horse for his daughter. I need not say how gladly I accepted this offer. I rode out of camp that morning much lighter in spirits, although suffering somewhat from the bruises I received. The horse I exchanged for, was a pacer, he had no other gait; and unaccustomed to it, I did not notice, until one of the Delawares pointed out to me, that there was any defect in him.

Captain Wolff was riding by my side during the day, and expressed in his Indian manner, how surprised he was that I had exchanged my fresh pony for a lame pacer, "one day more, that horse no travel, Carvalho go foot again!"

His prognostications proved, alas, too true, for on the second day, he was so lame that I could not ride him, and I remained on foot, while my beautiful pony was gallantly bearing the cook.

The horse, he said, was not lame when he gave him to me, and I could not prove that he was, so I was constrained to submit, but

I never saw this man galloping past me, while I was on foot, that I did not regret I was not brought up as an "ostler and professional horsebreaker."

Chapter XVI

When we left the Utah village, we travelled a long day's journey, and camped on the Grand River, thirty miles from the last camp; my pony behaved admirably well on the road, and I would not have parted with him on any account.

While at supper, the guard on the look-out gave the alarm that mounted Indians were approaching, the word was given to arm and prepare to receive them.

About fifty or sixty mounted Utah Indians, all armed with rifles, and bows and arrows, displaying their powder horns and cartouch boxes most conspicuously, their horses full of mettle, and gaily caparisoned, came galloping and tearing into camp.

They had also come to be compensated for the horse we had paid for the night before; they insisted that the horse did not belong to the woman, but to one of the men then present, and threatened, if we did not pay them a great deal of red cloth, blankets, vermilion, knives, and gunpowder, they would fall upon us and massacre the whole party.

On these occasions, Col. Fremont never showed himself, which caused the Indians to have considerable more respect for the "Great Captain," as they usually called him; nor did he ever communicate directly with them, which gave him time to deliberate, and lent a mysterious importance to his messages. Very much alarmed, I entered Col. Fremont's lodge, and told him their errand and their threats. He at once expressed his determination not to submit to such imposition, and at the same time, laughed at their threats; I could not comprehend his calmness. I deemed our position most alarming, surrounded as we were by armed savages, and I evidently betrayed my alarm in my countenance. Col. Fremont without apparently noticing my nervous state, remarked that he knew the Indian character perfectly, and he did not hesitate to state, that there was not sufficient powder to load a single rifle in the possession of the whole tribe of Utahs. "If," continued he, "they had any ammunition, they would have surrounded and massacred us, and stolen what they now demand, and are parleying for."

439

I at once saw that it was a most sensible deduction, and gathered fresh courage. The general aspect of the enemy was at once changed, and I listened to his directions with a different frame of mind than when I first entered.

He tore a leaf from his journal, and handing it to me, said: here take this, and place it against a tree, and at a distance near enough to hit it every time, discharge your Colt's Navy six shooters, fire at intervals of from ten to fifteen seconds—and call the attention of the Indians to the fact, that it is not necessary for white men to load their arms.

I did so; after the first shot, they pointed to their own rifles, as much as to say they could do the same, (if they had happened to have the powder), I, without lowering my arm, fired a second shot, this startled them.

I discharged it a third time—their curiosity and amazement were increased: the fourth time, I placed the pistol in the hands of the chief and told him to discharge it, which he did, hitting the paper and making another impression of the bullet.

The fifth and sixth times two other Indians discharged it, and the whole six barrels being now fired it was time to replace it in my belt.

I had another one already loaded, which I dexterously substituted, and scared them into an acknowledgment that they were all at our mercy, and we could kill them as fast as we liked, if we were so disposed.

After this exhibition, they forgot their first demand, and proposed to exchange some of their horses for blankets, etc.

We effected a trade for three or four apparently sound, strong animals; "Moses," one of the Delaware chiefs, also traded for one, but in a few days they all proved lame and utterly useless as roadsters, and we had to kill them for food.

The Indians with the consent of Col. Fremont, remained in camp all night; they had ridden thirty miles that day, and were tired. On this occasion, eleven men, fully armed, were on guard at one time.

The Indians who no doubt waited in camp to run our horses off during the night, were much disappointed in not having an opportunity. They quietly departed the next morning, while our whole camp listened to the energetic exclamation of Col. Fremont, that the "price of safety is eternal vigilance."

The crossing of the Grand River, the eastern fork of the Colorado,[13] was attended with much difficulty and more danger. The weather was excessively cold, the ice on the margin of either side of the river was over eighteen inches thick; the force of the stream always kept the passage in the centre open; the distance between the ice, was at our crossing, about two hundred yards. I suppose the current in the river to run at the rate of six miles an hour. The animals could scarcely keep their footing on the ice, although the men had been engaged for half an hour in strewing it with sand. The river was about six feet deep, making it necessary to swim our animals across; the greatest difficulty was in persuading them to make the abrupt leap from the ice to the roaring gulph, and there was much danger from drowning in attempting to get on the sharp ice on the other side, the water being beyond the depth of the animals, nothing but their heads were above water, consequently the greater portion of their riders' bodies were also immersed in the freezing current.

To arrive at a given point, affording the most facilities for getting upon the ice, it was necessary to swim your horse in a different direction to allow for the powerful current. I think I must have been in the water, at least a quarter of an hour. The awful plunge from the ice into the water, I never shall have the ambition to try again; the weight of my body on the horse, naturally made him go under head and all; I held on fast as a cabin boy to a main-stay in a gale of wind. If I had lost my balance it is most probable I should have been drowned. I was nearly drowned as it was, and my clothes froze stiff upon me when I came out of it. Some of the Delawares crossed first and built a large fire on the other side, at which we all dried our clothes standing in them.

It is most singular, that with all the exposure that I was subjected to on this journey, I never took the slightest cold, either in my head or on my chest; I do not recollect ever sneezing. While at home, I ever was most susceptible to cold.

The whole party crossed without any accident; Col. Fremont was the first of our party to leap his horse into the angry flood, inspiring his men, by his fearless example to follow.

"Julius Cæsar crossed the Rubicon with an immense army; streams of blood followed in his path through the countries he subdued, to his arrival at the Eternal City, where he was declared dictator and consul."

On a former expedition, Col. Fremont crossed the Grand River with a handful of men; but no desolation followed in his path. With the flag of his country in one hand and the genius of Liberty resting on his brow, he penetrated through an enemy's country, converting all

441

hearts as he journeyed, conquering a country of greater extent than Cæsar's whole empire, until he arrived at San Francisco, where he became military commandant and governor in chief of California, by the simple will of the people. Fremont's name and deeds, will become as imperishable as Cæsar's.

At last we are drawn to the necessity of killing our brave horses for food. The sacrifice of my own pony that had carried me so bravely in my first buffalo hunt, was made; he had been running loose for a week unable to bear even a bundle of blankets. It was a solemn event with me, and rendered more so by the impressive scene which followed.

Col. Fremont came out to us, and after referring to the dreadful necessities to which we were reduced, said "a detachment of men whom he had sent for succor on a former expedition, had been guilty of eating one of their own number." He expressed his abhorrence of the act, and proposed that we should not under any circumstances whatever, kill our companions to prey upon them. "If we are to die, let us die together like men." He then threatened to shoot the first man that made or hinted at such a proposition.

It was a solemn and impressive sight to see a body of white men, Indians, and Mexicans, on a snowy mountain, at night, some with bare head and clasped hands entering into this solemn compact. I never until that moment realized the awful situation in which I, one of the actors in this scene, was placed.

I remembered the words of the sacred Psalmist, (Psalm cviii. 4–7) and felt perfectly assured of my final deliverance.—"They *wandered* in the *wilderness* in a solitary way: They found no city to dwell in.

"*Hungry* and *thirsty* their souls fainted within them. Then they cried unto the Lord in their trouble, and he *delivered them* out of their distresses.

"And he led them forth by the *right way* that they might go to a *city of habitation*.

"Oh, that *men* would *praise the Lord* for his goodness, and for his wonderful works to the children of men."

It was a clear, cold night, on the Eagle Tail River, after a long fast, and a dreary walk, our men had returned supperless to sleep on their snowy bed, and with no prospect of anything to eat in the morning, to refresh them for another day's tramp. It was a standing rule in camp that a rifle discharged between the set of watch at night until daylight, was a signal that Indians were approaching, and this rule had been strictly observed, as a safeguard to the party. I have seen our camp on

Salt Creek surrounded with wolves—they even came within its precincts and stole our buffalo meat, but our Delawares would never allow an arm to be discharged. On this occasion, Mr. Fuller was on guard, and it was a few days before he gave out. We had been twenty-four hours without a meal, and as may be supposed, he was as hungry as the rest of us; while patrolling up and down the river on the banks of which we were encamped, his keen eye discovered a beaver swimming across the stream; he watched it with rifle to his shoulder, and as it landed, he fired and killed it.[14]

The sudden discharge of a rifle during a still night, under overhanging mountains, and in the valley of the river where we expected to find Indians, made a tremendous explosion. The sound reverberated along the rocks, and was re-echoed by the valley. Instantly the whole camp was on duty. Col. Fremont who had been making astronomical observations, had but a few moments previously retired to rest. He rushed out of his lodge, completely armed, the party assembled around it and all were filled with the utmost anxiety and alarm. We did not know the number or character of the enemy, but we were all prepared to do battle to the death. In a few moments, one of the Delawares approached camp dragging after him an immense beaver, which he said Mr. Fuller had killed for breakfast. The sight of something to eat, instead of something to fight, created quite a revolution of feeling; and taking into consideration the extremity, which caused Mr. Fuller to break through the rule, Col. Fremont passed it off quietly enough. Poor Fuller did not realize the excited condition of the camp, until he was relieved from duty. Our beaver was dressed for breakfast, when Fuller told Col. Fremont that he was so anxious and delighted at seeing the beaver, that he entirely forgot the rule of the camp.

Chapter XVII

The divide between Grand River and the Green River,[15] (the eastern and western forks of the Colorado) is barren and sterile to a degree. At the season that we crossed, there was no water between the two rivers, a distance of about forty miles. Capt. Gunnison's wagon trail was still plainly visible at the crossing of a gully, now however without water.

That party must have had great difficulty in transporting their wagons across it. From its appearance, a tremendous body of water must have forced a passage through the gully, at that time. Dwarf artemisia grows sparsely on this sandstone formation.

At the roots of the artemisia still remained small quantities of dry powdered snow. To allay my thirst, I have put my head under the bush, and lapped the snow with my tongue. The descent into the valley of the Green River was over most dangerous projections of different strata of rock, thrown into its present state by some convulsion of nature.

When we arrived at the [Green] river, we saw on the high sand bluffs, on the opposite side, several Indians, whose numbers soon increased. As our party was much exhausted for want of wholesome food, we were buoyed up with hopes that we could obtain supplies from them.

We crossed the river,[16] and were conducted by the Indians to a fertile spot on the western bank of it, where their village was. We found that they lived on nothing else but grass-seed, which they collected in the fall. Their women parch it, and grind it between stones. In this manner it is very palatable, and tastes very much like roasted peanuts.

This, their only article of food, was very scarce, and we could procure only a small supply. I parted with everything out of my daguerreotype boxes that I did not require, and several articles of necessary clothing, for about a quart of it. It is very nourishing, and very easy of digestion. The quantity I had, lasted me for three days. I made a hearty meal of it the night we camped among them.

To the sustaining properties of this cereal, I firmly believe, I owe the strength which enabled me to undergo the physical exertion that was required to reach the settlements.

Each man procured a more or less quantity.

Col. Fremont purchased a lame horse, in very good condition, which was slaughtered at this camp; and an incident occurred which proved to me the real character of one of my companions.

At the killing of this horse, nearly all the men were present. They had not tasted food for nearly two days, and were, consequently, ravenous, and thought of nothing else but satisfying the cravings of hunger. As soon as the horse was slaughtered, without exception, every one cut off a piece, and roasted it at the different camp fires. This was contrary to camp discipline; and, a complaint was made to Col. Fremont, by one of the Delawares, of what was going on, Mr. —— was among the first to cut off pieces from the meat, and he devoured larger quantities than the rest of us. When Col. Fremont was ap-

444

proaching, he took his pencil and paper out of his pocket, and seating himself by the fire, appeared to be deeply absorbed in his occupation. The rest of us remained where we were, partaking of the roast. Col. Fremont lectured us all for not waiting until supper, to eat our respective shares, and pointed this "gentleman" out as an exception, and as one who exercised "great self-denial." At the same moment, he had a piece of meat, *covered up in the cinders, at his feet*!

This "gentleman," instead of avowing his complicity, encouraged the mistake of Col. Fremont, by his continued silence. If he ever reads this journal, he will recognize himself, and, probably, not thank me for withholding his "name" from the public.

One of the most tiresome and unpleasant of duties devolves on those of the party who are at the end of the cavalcade. This duty is, driving up the animals which, either from exhaustion or other causes, linger on the road. Stopping on the trail to make daguerreotypes, generally placed me in the rear; and I have often overtaken the muleteers with a dozen lazy or tired animals, using, in vain, all their endeavors to make them go ahead. As a rule, I always assisted them, sometimes on foot, and in the earlier part of the journey on horseback. When a mule takes a stand, and determines not to budge a step, it requires a man with an extraordinary stock of patience to wait upon his muleship's leisure.

The idea frequently suggested itself, that I should change my professional card-plate, and add instead, *my name with "M.D."* attached, as significant of my new office.

DINNER ON PORCUPINE.

A large porcupine was killed and brought into camp to-day by our Delawares, who placed it on a large fire burning off its quills, leaving a thick hard skin, very like that of a hog. The meat was white, but very fat, it looked very much like pork. My stomach revolted at it, and I sat hungry around our mess, looking at my comrades enjoying it. The animal weighed about thirty pounds.

RELIEVE THE GUARD.

I was awakened one night by a rude push from the officer of the guard, who was a huge "Delaware." "Carvalho, go watch horse." "Twelve o'clock." I put my head out of my buffalo robe, and received a pile of fresh snow upon me. I had laid myself down on a snowbank, before a scanty fire of artemisia. I had my clothes on, and wrapped in my buffalo robe, I had sought a few hours sleep until my turn to guard arrived.

I came into camp exhausted, from a ten mile travel on foot, over an irregular and broken road. I had stopped to make daguerreotypes; in consequence, I was detained, and did not get to camp until near eight o'clock.

With some difficulty I threw off the heavy snow which enveloped me, and soon discovered that a northeast snow storm was furiously raging. The fire was extinguished, and six inches of snow now lay on the ashes. I took hold of my gun from under my buffalo robe, and asked the Delaware, "where the animals were."

He pointed in the direction, and replied,—"horses on the mountain, one mile away." I looked out, but could not see ten feet ahead. I thought of the remark my good old mother made on a less inclement night, when I was a boy, and wanted to go to play. "I would not allow a cat to go out in such weather, much less my son."

Dear soul! how her heart would have ached for me, if she had known a hundredth part of my sufferings.

I followed in the direction given me, and succeeded in finding the animals. I relieved my companion, and walking in snow up to my waist, around the animals for two hours, formed my sole occupation.

There was no grass. The horses and mules were hungry, and whenever they could steal a chance, they would wander out of the corral, and give us trouble to hunt them back; on this night they were very restless, and gave the guard continual exercise, which was also necessary to keep the life within them; it was comparatively easy to walk around in the track; but when one went astray, every step you took, plunged you two feet deep in the snow, making it a most tiresome and arduous task. The two hours seemed at least six, before I was relieved, when groping my way down the mountain side, I followed the trail to camp; by this time the last guard had made a fresh fire of artemisia, which consumes quickly, and burns brightly while consuming. I laid on a fresh pile, and by its light I saw the living graves of my companions; there they lay, with snow underneath them for a bed, and the "cold mantle of death," as it were, above them for a coverlid.

Cold, tired and hungry, I rested myself before the fire, and warmed my frozen limbs.

Some little distance from the fire, now covered with snow, lay the frozen meat of the horse we had killed the night before; all in the

446

camp were fast wrapped in sleep. I was the only one awake. Taking out my jackknife, I approached the pile of meat intended for the men's breakfast, and cutting about a half pound of the liver from it, I returned to the fire, and without waiting to cook it, I consumed it raw—the finer feelings of my nature were superseded by the grosser animal propensities, induced most probably from the character of the food we had been living upon for the last forty days.

I filled my pipe, and sat wrapped in my robe, enjoying the warmth of my fire, determined to remain by it until my tobacco was consumed.

The wind, which had been blowing from the N.E., now chopped round to the N.W., dissipating the snowclouds. The glorious queen of night shone forth in resplendent brilliancy. With the change of wind came an increase of cold—the thermometer, at daylight that morning indicated 20° below zero. One of my feet which was much blistered became numbed, and gave me intense pain. I took off my moccasin, and rubbing my foot in the snow to create circulation, I partially relieved it.

Finding it more comfortable, lying down, I crept under the snowy robe, and made the comparison of the warm rooms, feather beds, and silken canopies of the St. Nicholas wedding-chamber, with our snow-wreathed pillows, airy rooms, and the starry canopy of heaven.

CHAPTER XVIII

CARELESS PACKING OF THE MULES.

From careless packing of the mules, many of our party were often detained on the road. A bale of blankets or buffalo robes, would be displaced while descending some steep mountain; the mule, finding himself free from his load, would dart off in an opposite direction at full speed; a chase ensued, sometimes for over an hour before he could be captured, repacked, and again placed on the trail.

After performing a most arduous and difficult day's journey of fifteen miles, over continuous ranges of snowy ridges, we discovered that the mule on which was packed the bales of red cloth and blankets, intended for trading with the Indians, was missing. The muleteers did not remember to have seen him during the day. The animal was well trained, and was considered as one of the most willing and docile mules in the lot. Two men were sent back to look for him; it was easy to see if he had left the track, for the snow was unbroken except on the trail make by our own party.

447

The men not returning in good time, we became alarmed; they, however, made their appearance late in the night, with our lost mule; he was found standing, exactly in the same place where he was packed, behind a tree.

When the animals were driven out of camp, he was partly out of sight, escaped the vigilance of the men, and remained stationary, until our men found him in the evening; a lapse of at least twelve hours.

This incident is related to show the value of Mexican mules as faithful beasts of burthen, on which a great deal of dependence can always be placed. I consider them much preferable for travelling over the plains and mountains; they possess greater powers of endurance under privations. A mule will thrive on provender, that would starve a horse. If a mule gives out from exhaustion; with a day's rest, and a good meal, he will start on his journey, and appear as fresh as he ever was; but if a horse once stops and gives up, it is over with him, he is never fit for travel again. I suppose the noble and willing spirit of the horse, incites him to work until he is incapable of further exertion.

COL. FREMONT'S HORSE.

Col. Fremont started from Westport with a splendid dark bay horse; he was the pride of the party; he was always at the head of the cavalcade, and would sometimes look around, as it were disdainfully on his more humble companions. He felt his breeding, and I have no doubt, knew that he was carrying a gallant officer on his back. The Indians on the plains would have stolen him, and the Indians of the mountains would have given half-a-dozen mustangs for him. Mr. Palmer's horse gave out, and, was consequently on foot. We had at this time, the Doctor's mule, which we called "the Doctor," after he left us at Bent's Fort—running loose, as a spare animal, to carry the scientific apparatus. Col. Fremont the next day, rode the Doctor, and mounted Mr. W. H. Palmer on his own horse, which he continued to ride for ten days, until he was so exhausted for want of food, that he stopped on the road, and could not be brought into camp. Mr. Palmer came into camp on foot, and told Col. Fremont that his horse was left about five miles on the road, that it was impossible to bring him in.

I shortly afterwards heard Col. Fremont give orders to the Delaware camp, to send out a couple of men to find the horse and shoot it through the head. He had too much affection for the noble animal, to allow him to become a living sacrifice to the voracious wolves. The finer feelings of his heart seemed to govern all his actions, as well towards man as beast.

When it became necessary to slaughter our animals for food, I refrained from eating it in the vain hope of killing game, until exhausted nature demanded recuperation. I then partook of the strange and forbidden food with much hesitation, and only in small quantities. The taste of young fat horse is sweet and nutty, and could scarcely be distinguished from young beef, while that of the animal after it is almost starved to death, is without any flavor; you know you are eating flesh, but it contains no juices—it serves to sustain life, it contains but little nutritive matter, and one grows poor and emaciated, while living on it alone. Mule meat can hardly be distinguished from horse meat, I never could tell the difference. During one of the intervals when we were, from our own imprudence, entirely without food, a Delaware killed a cayotte [coyote], brought it into camp, and divided it equally between our messes—my share remained untouched. I had fasted 24 hours, and preferred to remain as many hours longer rather than partake of it. The habits of the horse and mule are clean; their food consists of grass and grain; but I was satisfied that my body could receive no benefit from eating the flesh of an animal that lived on carrion. Those who did partake of it were all taken with cramps and vomiting.

An old raven that had been hovering around us for several days, "to gather the crumbs from the rich man's table," paid at last the penalty of his temerity by receiving a rifle ball through his head. One of the men picked the feathers from its fleshless body and threw the carcass on the ground before us. It lay there undevoured when we left camp. I have no doubt it subsequently gave employment to a brother raven.

A RAIN STORM.

At the close of a long day's journey we descended into a fertile, although unknown, narrow valley, covered with dense forests of trees; a clear stream of water glided over its rocky bed, in the centre, and immense high sandstone mountains enclosed us; we chose a camp near the entrance of the valley, having deviated from our course, which was over the table land 500 feet above us, to obtain wood and water.

It is not at all improbable that our party were the first white men that ever penetrated into it—it was in reality a primeval forest. Our

449

feet sank deep into the bed of dead leaves, huge trunks of trees in all stages of decay lay strewed around us, while trees of many kinds, were waving aloft their majestic limbs covered with spring foliage, shading our pathway. On the margin of the river grass of good quality grew in abundance, which afforded a delightful meal for our wearied animals. Although there was no snow visible around us, still the weather was cold and raw, the heavens were filled with floating clouds which seemed to increase as the night advanced. Large camp fires were soon burning, and another of our faithful horses was shot for food.

Selecting as I thought a comfortable place for my sleeping apartment, I made up my bed, placing as usual my India-rubber blanket on the decayed leaves. After supper I laid myself down to rest my exhausted body.

I had been on foot all day, travelling over a rugged country of volcanic formation, with an apology for moccasins on my lacerated and painful feet. I slept soundly until twelve o'clock, when I felt the cold water insinuating itself between my clothes and body. I uncovered my head, over which I had my robe and blankets, to find it raining fast and steadily. In an hour, I found myself laying in water nearly a foot deep. I could not escape from my present situation. Wrapping my India-rubber closely around me, I remained perfectly passive, submitting to the violence of the heaviest and most drenching rain-storm I experienced on the whole journey.

Darkness reigned supreme. Our camp-fires were extinguished, and but for the occasional ejaculations of our men, only the furious raging of the tempest, and the roar of the streams that came bounding in torrents from the table land above, could be heard. My blankets and robe became saturated with water, while my clothes were wet to the skin.

I had ample time to reflect on my position; but while I experienced much personal inconvenience from the storm, the parched earth, over which we had travelled miles without a drop of water, received fresh sustenance from the refreshing shower. The dry and withered grass on our forward path, would be replaced by young tender shoots for our animals to sustain themselves. It is a happy thing for us that futurity is impenetrable, else my fond and fragile friends at home would endure more anguish than they do now, in the ignorance of the situation their husband and son is placed in.

Morning at last dawned, and with it appeared the sun, dissipating the clouds. Our camp equipage was all soaked. The daguerreotype apparatus was unhurt; my careful precaution always securing it against snow or rain. My polishing buffs I used the next day, when we ascended the mountain; I found them perfectly dry, and worked successfully with them. We remained late in camp the next morning to dry our blankets, etc. This was the first and only real storm of rain, we encountered in a six months' journey.

CHAPTER XIX

Mr. Egloffstien, Mr. Fuller, and myself were generally at the end of the train, our scientific duties requiring us to stop frequently on the road. Mr. Fuller had been on foot several days before any of the rest of the party, his horse having been the first to give out. On this occasion, we started out of camp together. We were all suffering from the privations we had endured, and, of the three, I was considered the worst off. One of my feet became sore, from walking on the flinty mountains with thin moccasins, and I was very lame in consequence. Mr. Fuller's feet were nearly wholly exposed. The last pair of moccasins I had, I gave him a week before; now his toes were out, and he walked with great difficulty over the snow. He never complained when we started in the morning, and I was surprised when he told me he had "given out."

"Nonsense, man," I said; "let us rest awhile, and we will gather fresh strength." We did so, and at every ten steps he had to stop, until he told us that he could go no further.

Mr. Fuller was the strongest and largest man in camp when we left Westport, and appeared much better able to bear the hardships of the journey than any man in it. I was the weakest, and thought ten days before that I would have given out, yet I live to write this history of his sufferings and death, and to pay this tribute to his memory.

The main body of the camp had preceded us, and they were at least four miles a-head. Both Mr. Egloffstien and myself offered our personal assistance; Mr. Fuller leaned upon us, but could not drag one foot after the other—his legs suddenly becoming paralyzed. When we realized his condition, we determined to remain with him; to this he decidedly objected—"Go on to camp," said he, "and if possible, send me assistance. You can do me no good by remaining, for if you do not reach camp before night, we shall all freeze to death."

He luckily had strapped to his back his blue blankets, which we carefully wrapped around him. In vain we hunted for an old bush or

451

something with which to make a fire—nothing but one vast wilderness of snow was visible. Bidding him an affectionate farewell, and promising to return, we told him not to move off the trail, and to keep awake if possible.

Limping forward, Egloffstien and myself resumed our travel; the sun had passed the meridian, and dark clouds overhung us. The night advanced apace, and with it an increase of cold. We stopped often on the road, and with difficulty ascended a high hill, over which the trail led; from its summit I hoped to see our camp-fires; my vision was strained to the utmost, but no friendly smoke greeted my longing eyes. The trail lost itself in the dim distance, and a long and weary travel was before us. Nothing daunted, and inspired by the hope of being able to render succor to our friend, we descended the mountain and followed the trail.

It now commenced to snow. We travelled in this manner ten long hours, until we came upon the camp.

Mr. Egloffstien and self both informed Col. Fremont of the circumstance, and we were told that it was impossible to send for Mr. Fuller.

Overcome with sorrow and disappointment, I fell weeping to the ground. In my zeal and anxiety to give assistance to my friend, I never for a moment thought in what manner it was to be rendered. I had forgotten that our few remaining animals were absolutely necessary to carry the baggage and scientific apparatus of the expedition, and that, with a furiously-driving snow-storm, it was almost folly to attempt to find the trail.

While we were speaking at our scanty fire of the unfortunate fate of our comrade, Col. Fremont came out of his lodge, and gave orders that the two best animals in camp should be prepared, together with some cooked horse-meat. He sent them with Frank Dixon, a Mexican, back on the trail, to find Mr. Fuller. We supposed him to have been at least five miles from camp.

There was not a dry eye in camp that whole night. We sat up anxiously awaiting the appearance of Mr. Fuller. Col. Fremont frequently inquired of the guard if Mr. Fuller had come in?

Day dawned, and cold and cheerless was the prospect. There being no signs of our friend, Col. Fremont remarked that it was just what he expected.

Col. Fremont had allowed his humanity to overcome his better judgment.

452

At daylight, Col. Fremont sent out three Delawares to find the missing men; about ten o'clock one of them returned with Frank Dixon, and the mules; Frank had lost the trail, he became bewildered in the storm, and sank down in the snow, holding on to the mules. He was badly frozen, and became weaker every day until he got to the settlements. Towards night, the two Delawares supporting Mr. Fuller, were seen approaching; he was found by the Delawares awake, but almost senseless from cold and starvation; he was hailed with joy by our whole camp. Col. Fremont as well as the rest of us, rendered him all the assistance in our power; I poured out the last drop of my alcohol, which I mixed with a little water, and administered it to him. His feet were frozen black to his ankles, if he had lived to reach the settlements, it is probable he would have had to suffer amputation of both feet.

Situated as we were, in the midst of mountains of snow, enervated by starvation and disease, without animals to carry us, and a long uncertain distance to travel over an unexplored country; could any blame be attached to a commander of an expedition, if he were to refuse to send back for a disabled man? I say, no, none whatever. Twenty-seven of our animals had been killed for food, and the rest were much reduced, and without provender of any kind in view. If this event had occurred six days later, there would have been no animal strong enough to carry Mr. Fuller into camp.

But suppose he had been disabled while in camp, and unable to proceed, could blame attach to his comrades if he were deserted, and left to die alone? This frightful situation was nearly realized on several occasions. I again answer, no, not any—the safety of the whole party demanded their immediate extrication from the dangers which surrounded them; every hour, every minute, in these mountains of snow, but increased their perils; on foot, with almost inaccessible rugged mountains of snow to overcome, with no prospects of food except what our remaining animals might afford—to stop, or remain an indefinite time with a disabled comrade, was certain death to the whole party, without benefiting him; his companions being so weak, that they could not carry him along. I made up my mind on one occasion, not to leave camp, my exhausted condition reminded me of the great difficulty and bodily pain which I endured, to reach camp the night before. I was fully prepared to remain by myself, and await my fate. I probably should have done so, but for the fond links which bound me to life, exercising a magic influence which inspired me with fresh courage, and determination. If such had been the case, might not my friends, in the excess of their grief have exclaimed, "Alas! for my poor son, who was left by his companions to perish in the mountains of snow." It would have been difficult to have persuaded my old parents, of the utter impossibility of preventing it. They would have attached cruelty and neglect, to the whole party, and laid their son's death at the door of their leader.

How is it in war, when the superior force of the enemy demands an immediate retreat by the opposing army, without permitting time to carry the wounded off the field? How is it with a man who falls overboard during a storm, when imminent peril to the vessel and crew would follow an attempt to rescue him? The life of one must be sacrificed for the safety of the whole.

Chapter XX

After we crossed the Green River,[17] the whole party were on foot. The continued absence of nutritious food made us weaker every day. One of my feet was badly frozen, and I walked with much pain and great difficulty; on this occasion my lameness increased to such a degree, that I was the last man on the trail, and my energy and firmness almost deserted me. Alone, disabled, with no possibility of assistance from mortal man, I felt that my last hour had come; I was at the top of a mountain of snow, with not a tree to be seen for miles. Night approached, and I looked in vain in the direction our party had proceeded, for smoke or some indication that our camp was near. Naught but a desert waste of eternal snow met my anxious gaze—faint and almost exhausted, I sat down on the snowbank, my feet resting in the footsteps of those who had gone before me. I removed from my pocket the miniatures of my wife and children, to take a last look at them. Their dear smiling faces awakened fresh energy, I had still something to live for, my death would bring heavy sorrow and grief to those who looked to me alone for support; I determined to try and get to camp, I dared not rest my fatigued body, for to rest was to sleep, and sleep was that eternal repose which wakes only in another world. Offering up a silent prayer, I prepared to proceed. I examined my guns and pistols, so as to be prepared if attacked by wolves or Indians, and resumed my lonely and desolate journey. As the night came on, the cold increased; and a fearful snow storm blew directly in my face, almost blinding me. Bracing myself as firmly as I could against the blast, I followed the deep trail in the snow, and came into camp about ten o'clock at night. It requires a personal experience to appreciate the intense mental suffering which I endured that night; it is deeply engraven with bitter anguish on my heart, and not even time can obliterate it.

Col. Fremont was at the camp fire awaiting my arrival. He said he knew I was badly off, but felt certain I would come in, although he did not expect me for an hour.

My haggard appearance sufficiently indicated what I suffered. As I stood by the fire warming my frozen limbs, Col. Fremont put out his hand and touched my breast, giving me a slight push; I immediately threw back my foot to keep myself from falling. Col. Fremont laughed at me and remarked that I had not "half given out," any man who could act as I did on the occasion, was good for many more miles of travel. He went into his tent, and after my supper of horse soup, he sent for me, and then told me why he played this little joke on me; it was to prevent my telling my sufferings to the men; he saw I had a great deal to say, and that no good would result from my communicating it. He reviewed our situation, and the enervated condition of the men, our future prospects of getting into settlements, and the necessity there was for mutual encouragement, instead of vain regrets, and despondency; the difficulties were to be met, and it depended on ourselves, whether we should return to our families, or perish on the mountains; he bade me good night, telling me that in the morning he would endeavor to make some arrangements to mount the men.

The next day, he called the men together and told them he had determined to "cache" all the superfluous baggage of the camp, and mount the men on the baggage animals, as a last resource. Nothing was to be retained but the actual clothing necessary to protect us from the inclemency of the weather.

A place was prepared in the snow, our large buffalo lodge laid out, and all the pack saddles, bales of cloth and blankets, the travelling bags, and extra clothes of the men, my daguerreotype boxes, containing besides, several valuable scientific instruments, and everything that could possibly be spared, together with the surplus gunpowder and lead, were placed in it, and carefully covered up with snow, and then quantities of brush to protect it from Indians. I previously took out six sperm candles from my boxes, and gave them to Lee, the

Colonel's servant, in charge; they were subsequently found most useful. A main station was made at this place, so as to be able to find it if occasion demanded that we should send for them.[18]

The men now were all mounted; a large mule was allotted to me, and we again started, rejoicing in having animals to carry us. After this, every horse or mule that gave out, placed a man on foot without the possibility of procuring others, and it was necessary in consequence of the absence of grass, to allow the mules to travel as light as possible; we therefore relieved them frequently by walking as much as we were able.

BEAVER DAMS ON THE SEVEIR RIVER.

When we got to the crossing of the Seveir [Sevier] River,[19] I was almost certain I was within the precincts of civilization. I saw numberless large trees cut down near the roots, appearing to have been hewn with an axe; some of them laid directly across the river; in one place there were three trees lying parallel with each other, evidently intended, I supposed, as a bridge across it; at this spot, the stream was not more than thirty feet wide; no other indication of civilization being around us, I supposed we occupied an old camping ground of Indians. I was doomed to disappointment again; the beavers had constructed the dams, and cut down the trees, and not until I had closely inspected the work, could I believe that they were not the work of men.[20]

MANNER OF DIVIDING THE HORSE MEAT.

When an animal gave out, he was shot down by the Indians, who immediately cut his throat, and saved the blood in our camp kettle. (The blood I never partook of.) The animal was divided into twenty-two parts as follows:—Two for Col. Fremont and Lee, his cook; ten for the Delaware camp, and ten for ours. Col. Fremont hitherto had messed with his officers; at this time he requested that we should excuse him, as it gave him pain, and called to mind the horrible scenes which had been enacted during his last expedition—he could not see his officers obliged to partake of such disgusting food.

The rule adopted was, that one animal should serve for six meals for the whole party.

If one gave out in the meantime, of course it was an exception, but otherwise on no consideration was an animal to be slaughtered, for every one that was killed placed one man on foot, and limited our chance of escape from our present situation.

If the men chose to eat up their six meals in one day, they would have to go without until the time arrived for killing another.

It frequently happened that the white camp was without food from twenty-four to thirty-six hours, while Col. Fremont and the Delawares always had a meal.

The latter religiously abstained from encroaching on the portion allotted for another meal while many men of our camp, I may say all of them, not content with their daily portion, would, to satisfy the cravings of hunger, surreptitiously purloin from the pile of meat at different times, sundry pieces thus depriving themselves of each other's allowances.

The entrails of the horses were well shaken (for we had no water to wash them in) and boiled with snow, producing a highly flavored soup, peculiar to itself, and readily distinguished from the various preparations of the celebrated "Ude" of gastronomic memory. The hide was roasted so as to burn the hair and make it crisp, the hoofs and shins were disposed of by regular rotation.

Our work was never done. When we got to camp all the men off duty, were dispatched to gather firewood to burn during the night. One might be seen with a decayed trunk on his shoulder, while a half dozen others were using their combined efforts to bring into camp some dried tree.

Col. Fremont at times joined the men in this duty—when it was peculiarly difficult in procuring the necessary material to prevent us from freezing while we were in camp.

One night we camped without wood, the country around was a waste of snow; we laid down in our blankets, and slept contentedly till morning, and re-commenced our journey without any breakfast.

I have been awakened to go on "guard" in the morning watch, when, looking around me, my companions appeared like so many graves, covered with from eight to ten inches of snow.

Some of our animals would eat the snow, others would not. To keep them alive we had to melt snow in camp kettles and give it them to drink, which process was attended with much fatigue and trouble.

We lived on horse meat fifty days. The passions of the men were so disturbed by their privations, that they were not satisfied with the cook's division of the hide; but one man turned his back, while another asked him who was to have this piece, and that, and so on, until all was divided, and the same process was gone through with in the sharing of the delectable horse soup.

Chapter XXI

Four days before we entered the Little Salt Lake Valley [Parowan Valley], we were surrounded by very deep snows; but as it was necessary to proceed, the whole party started, to penetrate through what appeared to be a pass, on the Warsatch Mountains. The opening to this depression was favorable, and we continued our journey, until the mountains seemed to close around us, the snow in the cañon got deeper, and further progress on our present course was impossible.

It was during this night, while encamped in this desolate spot, that Col. Fremont called a council of Capt. Wolff and Solomon of the Delawares—they had been sent by Col. Fremont to survey the cañon, and surrounding mountains, to see if a passage could be forced. On their return, this council was held; Capt. Wolff reported it impossible to proceed, as the animals sank over their heads in snow, and he could see no passage out. The mountains which intercepted our path, were covered with snow four feet deep. The ascent bore an angle of forty-five degrees, and was at least one thousand feet from base to summit. Over this, Captain Wolff said it was also impossible to go. "That is not the point," replied Col. Fremont, "we must cross, the question is, which is most practicable—and how we can do it."

I was acting as assistant astronomer at this time. After the council, Col. Fremont told me there would be an occultation that night, and he wanted me to assist in making observations. I selected a level spot on the snow, and prepared the artificial horizon. The thermometer indicated a very great degree of cold; and standing almost up to our middle in snow, Col. Fremont remained for hours making observations, first with one star, then with another, until the occultation took place. Our lantern was illuminated with a piece of sperm candle, which I saved from my pandora box, before we buried it; of my six sperm candles this was the last one. I take some praise to myself for providing some articles which were found most necessary. These candles, for instance, I produced when they were most required, and Col. Fremont little thought where they were procured.[21]

The next morning, Col. Fremont told me that Parowan, a small settlement of Mormons, forty rods square, in the Little Salt Lake Val-

458

ley, was distant so many miles in a certain direction, immediately over this great mountain of snow; that in three days he hoped to be in the settlement, and that he intended to go over the mountain, at all hazards.

We commenced the ascent of this tremendous mountain, covered as it were, with an icy pall of death, Col. Fremont leading and breaking a path; the ascent was so steep and difficult, that it was impossible to keep on our animals; consequently, we had to lead them, and travel on foot—each man placed his foot in the tracks of the one that preceded him; the snow was up the bellies of the animals. In this manner, alternately toiling and resting, we reached the summit, over which our Delawares, who were accustomed to mountain travel, would not of themselves have ventured. When I surveyed the distance, I saw nothing but continued ranges of mountains of everlasting snow, and for the first time, my heart failed me—not that I had lost confidence in our noble leader, but that I felt myself physically unable to overcome the difficulties which appeared before me, and Capt. Wolff himself told me, that he did not think we could force a passage. We none of us had shoes, boots it was impossible to wear. Some of the men had raw hide strapped around their feet, while others were half covered with worn out stockings and moccasins; Col. Fremont's moccasins were worn out, and he was no better off than any of us.

After we were all rested, Col. Fremont took out his pocket compass, and pointing with his hand in a certain direction, commenced the descent. I could see no mode of extrication, but silently followed the party, winding round the base of one hill, over the side of another, through defiles, and, to all appearance, impassable cañons, until the mountains, which were perfectly bare of vegetation, gradually became interspersed with trees. Every half hour, a new snow scape presented itself, and as we overcame each separate mountain, the trees increased in number.[22]

By noon, we were in a defile of the mountains, through which was a dry bed of a creek.[23] We followed its winding course, and camped at about two o'clock in a valley, with plenty of grass. Deer tracks were visible over the snow, which gave fresh life to the men. The Delawares sallied out to find some. Col. Fremont promised them, as an incentive to renewed exertions, that he would present the successful hunter, who brought in a deer, a superior rifle.

They were out several hours, and Weluchas was seen approaching, with a fine buck across his saddle.

He received his reward, and we again participated in a dish of wholesome food.

We had now triumphantly overcome the immense mountain, which I do not believe human foot, whether civilized or Indian, had ever before attempted, from its inaccessibility; and on the very day and hour previously indicated by Col. Fremont, he conducted us to the small settlement of Parowan, in Little Salt Valley, which could not be distinguished two miles off, thus proving himself a most correct astronomer and geometrician.

Here was no chance work—no guessing—for a deviation of one mile, either way, from the true course, would have plunged the whole party into certain destruction. An island at sea may be seen for forty miles; a navigator makes his calculations, and sails in the direction of the land, which oftentimes extends many miles; when he sees the land, he directs his course to that portion of it where he is bound; he may have been fifty miles out of his way, but the well-known land being visible from a great distance, he changes his course until he arrives safely in port.

Not so with a winter travel over trackless mountains of eternal snow, across a continent of such immense limits, suffering the privations of cold and hunger, and enervated by disease.

It seems as if Col. Fremont has been endowed with supernatural powers of vision, and that he penetrated with his keen and powerful eye through the limits of space, and saw the goal to which all his powers had been concentrated to reach. It was a feat of scientific correctness, probably without comparison in the records of the past. His firmness of purpose, determination of character, and confidence in his own powers, exercised under such extraordinary circumstances, alone enabled him, successfully, to combat the combination of untoward and unforeseen difficulties which surrounded him, and momentarily threatened the annihilation of his whole party.

It is worthy of remark, and goes to show the difference between a person "to the manor born," and one who has "acquired it by purchase." That in all the varied scenes of vicissitude, of suffering and excitement, from various causes, during a voyage when the natural character of a man is sure to be developed, Col. Fremont never forgot he was a gentleman; not an oath, no boisterous ebullitions of temper, when, heaven knows, he had enough to excite it, from the continued blunders of the men. Calmly and collectedly, he gave his orders, and they were invariably fulfilled to the utmost of the men's abilities. To the minds of some men, excited by starvation and cold, the request of an officer is often misconstrued into a command, and resistance follows as a natural consequence; but in no instance was a slight request of his received with anything but the promptest obedience. He never wished his officers or men to undertake duties which he did not readily share. When we were reduced to rations of dried horse meat, and he took his scanty meal by himself, he was, I am sure, actuated by the desire to allow his companions free speech, during meal time; any animadversion on the abject manner in which we were constrained to live would, no doubt, have vibrated on his sensitive feelings, and to prevent the occurrence of such a thing, he, as it were, banished himself to the loneliness of his own lodge.

Col. Fremont's lodge, at meal time, when we had good, wholesome buffalo and deer meat presented quite a picturesque appearance. A fire was always burning in the centre; around it cedar bushes were strewn on which buffalo robes were placed. Sitting around, all of us on our hams, cross-legged, with our tin plates and cups at each side of us, we awaited patiently the entrance of our several courses; first came the camp kettle, with buffalo soup, thickened with meat-biscuit, our respective tin plates were filled and replenished as often as required. Then came the roast or fry, and sometimes both; the roast was served on sticks, one end of which was stuck in the ground, from it we each in rotation cut off a piece. Then the fried venison. In those days we lived well, and I always looked forward to this social gathering, as the happiest and most intellectually spent hour during the day. Col. Fremont would often entertain us with his adventures on different expeditions; and we each tried to make ourselves agreeable.

Although on the mountains, and away from civilization, Col. Fremont's lodge was sacred from all and every thing that was immodest, light or trivial; each and all of us entertained the highest regard for him. The greatest etiquette and deference were always paid to him, although he never ostensibly required it. Yet his reserved and unexceptionable deportment, demanded from us the same respect with which we were always treated, and which we ever took pleasure in reciprocating.

MR. FULLER'S DEATH.

The death of Mr. Fuller filled our camp with deep gloom; almost at the very hour he passed away, succor was at hand. Our party was met by some Utah Indians, under the chieftainship of Ammon, a brother of the celebrated Wakara, (anglicized Walker) who conducted us into the camp on Red Creek Cañon.[24] At this spot our camp was informed by Mr. Egloffstien, that our companion in joy and in sorrow, was left to sleep his last sleep on the snows. The announcement took some of us by surprise, although I was prepared for his death at any moment. I assisted him on his mule that morning, and roasted the prickles from some cactus leaves, which we dug from the snow, for his breakfast; he told me that he was sure he would not survive, and did not want to leave camp.

A journey like the one we had passed through, was calculated to expose the thorough character of individuals; if there were any imperfections, they were sure to be developed. My friend, Oliver Fuller, passed through the trials of that ordeal victoriously. No vice or evil propensity made any part of his character. His disposition was mild and amiable, and generous to a fault. Slow to take offense, yet firm and courageous as a lion; he bore his trials without a murmur, and performed his duties as assistant astronomer and engineer to the hour he was stricken down. After he was unable to walk, he received the assistance of every man in camp.

His companions who were suffering dreadfully, though not to such an imminent degree, voluntarily deprived themselves of a portion of their small rations of horse meat to increase his meal, as he seemed to require more sustenance than the rest of us. His death was deeply regretted.

Not having any instruments by which a grave could be dug in the frozen ground, Col. Fremont awaited his arrival at Parowan, from which place he sent out several men to perform the last sad duties to our lamented friend.[25]

I was riding side by side with Egloffstien after Mr. Fuller's death, sad and dejected. Turning my eyes on the waste of snow before me, I remarked to my companion that I thought we had struck a travelled road. He shook his head despondingly, replying "that the marks I observed, were the trails from Col. Fremont's lodge poles." Feeling satisfied that I saw certain indications, I stopped my mule, and with very great difficulty alighted, and thrust my hand into the snow, when to my great delight I distinctly felt the ruts caused by wagon wheels. I was then perfectly satisifed that we were "saved!" The great revulsion of feeling from intense despair to a reasonable hope, is impossible to be described; from that moment, however, my strength perceptibly left me, and I felt myself gradually breaking up. The nearer I approached the settlement, the less energy I had at my command; and I felt so totally incapable of continuing, that I told Col. Fremont, half an hour before we reached Parowan, that he would have to leave me there; when I was actually in the town, and surrounded with white men, women and children, paroxysms of tears followed each other, and I fell down on the snow perfectly overcome.[26]

I was conducted by a Mr. [William] Heap to his dwelling, where I was treated hospitably.[27] I was mistaken for an Indian by the people of Parowan. My hair was long, and had not known a comb for a month, my face was unwashed, and grounded in with the collected dirt of a similar period. Emaciated to a degree, my eyes sunken, and clothes all torn into tatters from hunting our animals through the brush. My hands were in a dreadful state; my fingers were frost-bitten, and split at every joint; and suffering at the same time from diarrhœa, and symptoms of scurvy, which broke out on me at Salt Lake City afterwards. I was in a situation truly to be pitied, and I do not wonder that the sympathies of the Mormons were excited in our favor, for my personal appearance being but a reflection of the whole party, we were indeed legitimate subjects for the exercise of the finer feelings of nature. When I entered Mr. Heap's house I saw three beautiful children. I covered my eyes and wept for joy to think I might yet be restored to embrace my own.

During the day I submitted to the operation of having my face and hands washed, and my hair cut and combed. Our combs might have been lost, and this would account for the condition of our hair, but how about the dirty faces? Alas, we had no water, nothing but frozen snow; and although we laved our faces with it, we had no towels to wipe with, and the dirt dried in.

Mr. Heap was the first Mormon I ever spoke to, and although I had heard and read of them, I never contemplated realizing the fact that I would have occasion to be indebted to Mormons for much kindness and attention, and be thrown entirely among them for months.

It was hinted to me that Mr. Heap had two wives; I saw two matrons in his house, both performing to interesting infants the duties of maternity; but I could hardly realize the fact that two wives could be reconciled to live together in one house. I asked Mr. Heap if both these ladies were his wives, he told me they were. On conversing with them subsequently, I discovered that they were sisters, and that there originally were three sets of children; one mother was deceased, and she was also a sister. Mr. Heap had married three sisters, and there were living children from them all. I thought of that command in the bible—"Thou shalt not take a wife's sister, to vex her." But it was no business of mine to discuss theology or morality with them—they thought it right.

These two females performed all the duties which devolve on a country home. One of them milked the cow, churned the butter, and baked the bread; while the other cared for the children, attended to the making, washing, and ironing of the clothes. Mr. Heap was an Englishman, and his wives were also natives of London. Mr. Heap was a shoemaker by trade, and a preacher by divine inspiration. Mammon was the god he worshipped, for he gave away nothing without an equivalent—not even a piece of old cloth to line a pair of moccasins with. His wives differed from him in this respect, daily they furnished "Shirt-cup," the "Utah," with everything edible, for numbers of miserable Indians who surrounded their door. The eldest in particular, was a kind-hearted woman; they all, however, showed me as much attention as they could afford, for one dollar and fifty cents a day, which amount Col. Fremont paid for my board while with them, a period of fourteen days.

Chapter XXII

I remained from the 8th to the 21st February at Parowan. I was very ill during the whole time; I was so much enervated by diarrhœa, that my physician advised me not to accompany the expedition; the exertion of riding on horseback would have completely prostrated me, my digestive organs were so much weakened, and impaired, by the irregular living on horse meat, without salt or vegetables, that I was fearful that I should never recover. Col. Fremont was very anxious for me to continue, but yielded to the necessity of my remaining; he supplied me with means to reach home, and on the same day he bade me farewell, to continue his journey over the Sierra Nevada, I left for great Salt Lake City, in a wagon belonging to one of a large company of Mormons, who were on their way to "Conference." I was so weak, that I had to be lifted in and out like a child. To the kind attentions of Mr. Henry Lunt, President of Cedar City, Coal Creek, and his lady, I was indebted for some necessaries, viz.—sugar, tea and coffee, which it was impossible to purchase; they also offered me the use of their wagon, which was better adapted to an invalid, than the one I occupied. Mr. Egloffstien also accompanied me; his physical condition being similar to my own, he could not continue with Col. Fremont; he successfully managed, notwithstanding his illness, to make topographical notes all the way to Great Salt Lake City, a distance of three hundred miles, which we accomplished in ten days, passing through all the different Mormon settlements on the road, particulars of which I shall give in my journal, from Salt Lake City. We arrived at Great Salt Lake City on the night of the 1st of March 1854, and took lodgings at Blair's hotel; in the morning I learned that Lieut. Beckwith and Captain Morris, with the remnant of Captain Gunnison's expedition, were hybernating in the city. I called on Lieut. Beckwith, who invited me and my friend to mess at their table, at E. T. Benson's, one of the Mormon apostles, which I gladly accepted, and that night I found myself once more associating with intelligent gentlemen. The arrival of my friend, Egloffstien, proved very timely; the massacre of the lamented Captain Gunnison and his officers, deprived Lieut. Beckwith of the services of their topographical engineer, to which situation Mr. Egloffstien was immediately appointed, and Lieut. Beckwith generously invited me to accompany the expedition, free of any expense, which I respectfully declined, as I intended to reach California by the Southern route, over the trail of Colonel Fremont, in 1843. To the kindness of Lieut. Beckwith I was also indebted for a supply of painting materials, which I could not have procured elsewhere, and by the use of which, I was enabled to successfully prosecute my profession, during my residence in that city.

Messrs. Kincaid and Livingston,[28] cashed Col. Fremont's bills on California, without any discount, and contributed many luxuries which were not on sale, and I feel deeply grateful to them for their disinterested friendship. After I was comfortably settled, I called on Governor [Brigham] Young, and was received by him with marked attention. He tendered me the use of all his philosophical instruments and access to a large and valuable library.

CARVALHO, 75–141.

1. After Ebers and Milligan withdrew, the latter wrote: "the expedition now consists of 21 mens [*sic*] and 54 shod animals" (unpublished diary, 25 Nov.).

2. The expedition had moved up the Arkansas River to the mouth of the Huerfano and followed it into the mountains. JCF wrote that they entered the mountains on 3 Dec. (Doc. No. 267).

3. In the 1850s JCF's "Sandhill Pass" was better known as Williams Pass, after "Old Bill," the guide of his fourth expedition. Today it is called Medano Pass. The expedition had worked its way over the Wet Mountain Range and

would descend through the forbidding peaks of the Sangre de Cristo Range to the San Luis Valley by way of this pass.

4. Ten miles below Medano Pass is Mosca Pass, or, in the nomenclature of the nineteenth century, Robidoux Pass.

5. The addition of the Mexican, whom Carvalho later refers to as Jose (see also Doc. No. 261, n. 3), makes twenty-two, which is in agreement with Carvalho's count on p. 385. He is described as "worthless" because he was a party to the theft of the equipment which the expedition cached prior to the arrival at Parowan (CARVALHO, 195–96).

6. The camp was in junipers—not cedars—near present Crestone, Colo. The "stream of living water" is the Crestone drainage, which is actually composed of several streams, some of which quickly disappear into the sand. Since they all head on the mountain and are so close together, Carvalho might have viewed them as one stream (Patricia Joy Richmond to Mary Lee Spence, 17 Jan. 1983).

7. In the Utah language Cochetopa signifies "Buffalo Gate"; the Mexicans have the same name for it, "El Puerto de los Cibolos" (HEAP, 137). This Continental Divide pass has an altitude of 10,160 feet. The men reached it on 14 Dec. (Doc. No. 267).

8. Beale had used North Cochetopa Pass during June 1853; however, he, and later Gunnison, both entered the San Luis Valley via Sangre de Cristo Pass (present La Veta Pass), which is south of both Medano and Mosca passes.

9. DELLENBAUGH, 437, thinks the crosses were the work of Mexicans, who, like the buffalo and the Indians, had used the pass for many years.

10. The party went down Cochetopa Creek to Tomichi Creek, thence to the present-day Gunnison River (Carvalho's Grand River) where Gunnison, Colo., now stands.

11. The accident occurred as the party was attempting to avoid the deep chasm of the Gunnison River, by swinging south to traverse at higher elevations the canyons and mesas which characterize the topography of the area adjacent to it.

12. The *Memoirs* map indicates that JCF's route around the impenetrable canyon of the Gunnison River was to the south, via the watersheds of Cimarron and Cedar creeks, almost anticipating the future route taken by U.S. Highway 50. He probably came upon the Indian village in the Uncompahgre Valley.

13. Since 1921 JCF's "Grand River, the eastern fork of the Colorado," has been called the Colorado. Following the Uncompahgre, the party again reached the Gunnison and followed it down to the Colorado River, which the men crossed with extreme difficulty as Carvalho indicates here. They were now in the vicinity of Grand Junction.

14. Carvalho recalls the time and place of the beaver-shooting incident incorrectly. Most likely it occurred during the last week of January when the expedition found itself in desperate condition, approaching the eastern face of the Wasatch Mountains.

15. The men had made their way through Grand Valley for about a hundred miles. They now leave the watershed of the Colorado River and climb the sterile plateau separating it from Green River.

16. Diverging from Gunnison's trail on the divide between the Colorado and Green rivers, JCF traveled southwest, following the course of a dry stream to the Green, where a crossing was made opposite the mouth of the San Rafael River— approximately twenty miles south of the present town of Green River, Utah.

17. The *Memoirs* map indicates that from the Green River the expedition as-

cended the valley of the San Rafael River in a northwesterly direction until some unidentifiable point was reached just beyond the 39th parallel. Apparently JCF then realized that continued travel on the present course would take the expedition beyond the purview of his envisioned central railroad route. Consequently, he turned his party to the southwest and searched the base of the San Rafael Reef for an opening that would permit passage to the Wasatch Mountains along the 38th parallel.

18. Internal evidence suggests that the cache was made in Grass Valley.

19. The *Memoirs* map indicates that JCF turned west from his line of march along the front of the San Rafael Reef at or about latitude 38° 30′ and ascended to Thousand Lake Mountain via a route that approximates the northern boundary of Wayne County, Utah. The party subsequently descended to Rabbit Valley and made a long camp before crossing the upper headwaters of Fremont River to gain the divide of the Great Basin and enter Grass Valley. Proceeding south on a course parallel to Otter Creek, the expedition crossed the East Fork of the Sevier River to enter Circle Valley where they encamped near the confluence of the two Seviers.

20. At this point JCF's route intersected that of Parley P. Pratt's southern exploring expedition, which in 1849 had traveled by wagon through Sevier Valley to Parowan Valley over much the same route that JCF would take. In fact, Fremont Pass, to be noted later, was originally named Brown's Pass by Pratt's party, for the Mormon captain, John Brown, who discovered it on 16 Dec. 1849 (BROWN, 108–9).

21. From their desolate camp at the mouth of Choke Cherry Creek in Circleville Canyon, JCF and Carvalho conducted their last astronomic observation.

22. The party had crossed Dog Valley to arrive at Fremont Pass, the dividing ridge separating the watershed of the Sevier Ridge from that of Little Salt Lake.

23. Descending from the pass via Fremont Wash, the expedition went into camp early in the afternoon, selecting a site in the broadening canyon where it first breaks through the Hurricane Cliffs.

24. It was on Red Creek that the Mormons had established the little settlement of Paragonah in the fall of 1852, but they were forced temporarily to abandon it the next year because of Indian hostility. The settlers moved to Parowan, some four or five miles southeast.

Wahkara was known to JCF—the two had exchanged blankets at Pinto Creek in 1844. The day after his meeting with JCF, Ammon and his braves encountered Almon W. Babbitt and his party, who were traveling from Salt Lake City to Washington, D.C., via Los Angeles and San Francisco, and told of the hungry party of Americans. When Babbitt arrived in Parowan that night, 8 Feb., he learned that JCF had gotten in but was too "worn down" to talk that evening. Early the next morning they met, as JCF's letter to Benton (Doc. No. 267) indicates.

25. In his account as published in BIGELOW, 441, Carvalho implies he was a member of the burial detail. So also were Simeon F. Howd and a Mr. David of Parowan. Fuller was buried about one and one-half miles from Muley Point, which virtually divides Fremont Wash from Parowan Valley (FISH, 46).

26. Various dates have been given for the arrival, but the letters of JCF and Almon W. Babbitt state clearly that it was 8 Feb. 1854. Founded in 1851, Parowan was intended to be the agricultural base for the various coal and iron works being established in the area. It had all the appearance of a fort, with walls twelve feet high and five feet thick at the base, a watch tower, and inner and outer gates (DRIGGS). The man on the lookout had reported the entrance of a

body of men into the north end of the valley when JCF was yet twenty miles distant from the settlement (Letter of Elder J. C. L. Smith in *Desert News*, 16 March 1854).

27. JCF's hosts were the Stake president, John Calvin Lazelle Smith, and his family.

28. More frequently written "Livingston and Kinkead," this firm of merchants and traders especially catered to overland emigrants. Their supply trains came to Utah from Iowa. For an indication of JCF's financial arrangements, see Doc. No. 266, n. 1.

266. Frémont to Thomas H. Benton— Letter 1

PARAWAN, IRON CO., UTAH TERR., Feb. 9, '54

MY DEAR SIR:

You will have the pleasure personally to hear from our friend Mr. Babbitt, who does me the kindness to take charge of my letters, good accounts of my health and present condition, and of the time when I shall probably see you. I am particularly fortunate in having met him here, as I shall owe to his kindness and valuable assistance the means of continuing my journey, without such extraordinary delay as would have rendered it comparatively useless, or the alternative of continuing it on foot.[1] Let me suggest to you (what you would doubtless do without any suggestion) the great importance of a full conversation with Mr. Babbitt, in regard to the recent railroad movements here, and the winter which has just passed.

Commending him to your kindest consideration, I am sincerely &c.

JOHN C. FREMONT

Hon. Mr. Benton, Washington City

Printed in San Francisco *Daily Herald*, 15 March 1854. The letter was submitted to the journal by Almon W. Babbitt, who had met JCF in Parowan and who was carrying dispatches to Washington for Brigham Young's government in Utah. Compare it with the lengthier version published by Benton in the *National Intelligencer*, 12 April 1854 (Doc. No. 267).

Babbitt had been a member of the Illinois state legislature, a Mormon trustee in Nauvoo, and a publisher of the *Western Bugle* in Council Bluffs before coming to Utah, where he had been very active in the government. After he returned from this particular Washington mission, he acted as defense counsel for the six Indians who were indicted for the murder of Gunnison and his men. Babbitt, in turn, was murdered by Cheyennes near New Fort Kearny in 1856 and was buried on the plains he may have crossed as many as twenty times (RIDD).

1. Babbitt's letter in the San Francisco *Daily Herald*, 15 March 1854, details the "valuable assistance": "The Colonel was out of ready money, but had evidence that he could draw on Palmer, Cook & Co., and other responsible banking houses in this city, for any amount. This would not buy horses and mules at that place [Parowan], it being only a small settlement, having no storekeeper or other business man there. I knowing the reputation of the banking houses in this city, and at the same time being well acquainted with the Bishop of the Mormon Church at that place, made the arrangement that he could furnish the horses and mules to Col. Fremont for the journey, and pay it out of tithing money in hand, and take a draft on Palmer, Cook & Co. for the whole amount in favor of Gov. Young."

On his return to Washington, JCF called on the Utah territorial delegate, John Bernheisel, and thanked him for the kindness he had received from the Mormon people (Bernheisel to Brigham Young, 14 June 1854, Bernheisel Papers, Archives, Historical Department of the Church of Jesus Christ of Latter-Day Saints, Salt Lake City).

267. Frémont to Thomas H. Benton— Letter 2

PARAWAN, IRON COUNTY*
UTAH TERRITORY, Feb. 9, 1854

DEAR SIR:

I have had the good fortune to meet here our friend Mr. Babbitt, the Secretary of the Territory, who is on his way to Washington, in charge of the mail and other very interesting despatches, the importance of which is urging him forward with extreme rapidity. He passes directly on this morning, and I have barely a few moments to give you intelligence of our safe arrival and of our general good health and reasonable success in the object of our expedition.

This winter has happened to be one of extreme and unusual cold. Here, the citizens inform me, it has been altogether the severest since the settlement of this valley. Consequently, so far as the snows are concerned, the main condition of our exploration has been fulfilled. We

---

*Valley of the Parawan, about 60 miles east of the meadows of Santa Clara, between 37 and 38 degrees of north latitude, and between 113 and 114 degrees of west longitude; elevation above the sea about 5,000 feet.

entered the mountain regions of the Huerfano River on the 3rd of December, and issued from it here on the 7th of this month arriving here yesterday afternoon. We went through the Cochatope Pass on the 14th December, with four inches—not feet, take notice, but inches—of snow on the level, among the pines and in the shade on the summit of the Pass.

This decides what you consider the great question, and fulfills the leading condition of my explorations; and therefore I go no further into details in this letter.

I congratulate you on this verification of your judgment, and the good prospect it holds out of final success in carrying the road by this central line. Nature has been bountiful to this region, in accumulating here, within a few miles of where I am writing vast deposits of iron, and coal, and timber, all of the most excellent quality; and a great and powerful interior State will spring up immediately in the steps of the Congressional action which should decide to carry the road through this region. In making my expedition to this point I save nearly a parallel of latitude, shortening the usual distance from Green River to this point by over a hundred miles. In crossing to the Sierra Nevada I shall go directly by an unexplored route, aiming to strike directly the Tejon Passes at the head of the San Joaquin valley, through which in 1850 [1851] I drove from two to three thousand head of cattle that I delivered to the Indian Commissioners. I shall make what speed I possibly can, going light, and abandoning the more elaborate survey of my previous line, to gain speed.

Until within about a hundred miles of this place we had daguerreotyped the country over which we passed, but were forced to abandon all our heavy baggage to save the men, and I shall not stop to send back for it. The Delawares all came in sound, but the whites of my party were all exhausted and broken up, and more or less frost-bitten. I lost one, Mr. Fuller, of St. Louis, Missouri, who died on entering this valley. He died like a man, on horseback, in his saddle, and will be buried like a soldier on the spot where he fell.

I hope soon to see you in Washington. Mr. Babbitt expects to see you before the end of March. Among other documents which he carries with him are the maps and report of Captain Gunnison's party. Sincerely and affectionately,

JOHN C. FREMONT

Col. Benton, Washington

P.S.—This is the Little Salt Lake settlement, and was commenced three years since. Population now four hundred, and one death by sickness since the settlement was made. We have been most hospitably received. Mr. Babbitt has been particularly kind, and has rendered me very valuable assistance.

Printed in *National Intelligencer*, 12 April 1854, the day after Babbitt arrived in Washington. Actually the letter is embodied within a letter from Benton to the editor of the journal. Also printed in BIGELOW, 443–44. Benton had probably extracted—and perhaps elaborated on—information from private letters. Compare with Doc. No. 266.

268. Frémont to Abel Stearns

SAN FRANCISCO, Apr. 20, 1854

DEAR SIR:

In a recent conversation with your agent here, Mr. Scott,[1] I learned that the Andrade grant is now before the Board and will probably be disposed of in the course of a month or two.[2] Should it be confirmed, I think that it would be expedient to assume some control over the property, and to this end I am desirous to have my now undivided portion separated and set off. In the course of conversation with Mr. Scott I referred to this subject and was informed by him that he had no power to act in the case. I have therefore thought it advisable to write immediately to yourself and request that you will instruct your agent to take the necessary steps for making the division. I would be glad to hear from you in reply as soon as may suit your convenience, and in the meantime am, with regard, respectfully yours,

JOHN C. FRÉMONT

Hon. Abel Stearns
Los Angeles

ALS (CSmH—Stearns Collection). Endorsed: "Answered 10 May."
1. A native New Yorker, Jonathan R. Scott had practiced law in Missouri before coming to Los Angeles, where he became associated with Lewis Granger and Benjamin Hayes. A man of great physical strength and stature, he had the reputation of being a tornado in court (ROBINSON, 31, 43).
2. For information on the Andrade grant, see JCF to Stearns, 12 Dec. 1851 (Doc. No. 177).

269. Frémont's Railroad Exploration

[21 April 1854]

During the last thirty-five years Colonel Benton has toiled inde-
fatigably for the interests of the West. The opening of a wagon road
from Independence to Santa Fe, long treated with ridicule by Honorable Senators, was for many years his favorite project. Since his success in the attainment of that, the Pacific Railroad, by a central route,
has become his favorite scheme, and he has succeeded in bringing,
directly and indirectly, a vast amount of valuable information on the
topography and resources of the interior of the country before the
public. Much of this information has been obtained by the dauntless
energy of his son-in-law, Col. Fremont, who arrived but a few days
since from his adventurous trip across the continent in mid-winter.
The purpose of undertaking the journey at such a time was to ascertain what amount of snow lay on the proposed route in the depth of
winter, and to demonstrate completely that the road could be traversed at all seasons of the year.

On the 15th of October Col. Fremont left St. Louis and on the 1st
of November started from the frontier with his party of eight Americans, and ten Delaware Indians; all of them experienced moun-
taineers, and men who placed great confidence in Col. Fremont, as he
in them.

The route up the Kansas and across to the Arkansas was made
over a beautiful country. On the 30th November the party arrived at
Bent's Fort, where they saw the last white man until they arrived at
the Mormon settlements. From the Fort they travelled up the Arkansas and the Huerfano. The country here is hilly, very well watered,
covered with grass and well timbered with pine. The soil is of a sandy
cast, and in the valleys is very rich. On the 5th the party entered the
mountains, crossed the divide between the Huerfano and the head
waters of the Rio Grande at the Sand Hill Pass (sometimes called
Williams Pass), and passing over to the Cochetope Pass, crossed to the
waters of the Pacific. The Cochetope Pass, in the main range of the
Rocky Mountains, was crossed on the 14th December, and had then
but four inches of snow.

After crossing the summit, the party struck down one of the tributaries of the Grand [Colorado] River to that stream, which they fol-

lowed down to near the Spanish trail, and then went off due west to the Mormon settlement of Parowan, where they arrived on the 8th of February. The country from the backbone to Grand River is covered with excellent pine timber, and a great deal of the soil is of an excellent quality. Indeed, the whole country east of Grand River to the western line of Missouri, a distance of 800 miles, is so suitable for tillage and grazing that the farms can touch each other for the whole distance. From Grand River to Parowan, about 150 miles, is a country without timber, and with a poor soil, but otherwise favorable for the construction of a road.

Just before getting into Parowan, one of the party, a Mr. O. Fuller, of St. Louis, died. He was a brave and energetic man, but the cold, exertion, and hard fare were too much for him, and he died in his saddle. From the time the party entered the mountains until they reached Parowan, they encountered a good deal of difficulty. It was midwinter; the grass was in many places bad; the animals required a great deal of attention and game was wild and scarce. Col. Fremont was determined to pursue his course, and to make all the explorations which the strength of himself and party would permit. The party arrived at the Mormon settlement travel worn and much reduced in flesh. They remained there twelve days, which sufficed to place them in excellent condition.

On the 21st of February, Col. Fremont left the hospitable people of Parowan to cross the Sierra Nevada.[1] His course was a little south of west. The country was hilly, and in many places mountainous.[2] About 100 miles from Parowan the party crossed the river [rim] of the Great Basin, and reached the watershed of the Rio Virgin, which empties into the Colorado. Thence the distance to Owen's Range [Inyo-White Mountains], which was struck on latitude 37, was about 200 miles over the same kind of country.[3] Indeed, Col. Fremont did not know at what precise point he left the Great Basin. Here and there were fertile valleys, but the greater portion of the soil is of a sterile character. The mountains are composed of short irregular ranges, generally running north and south, covering nearly the whole country, and are well timbered with pine. Col. Fremont reached Owen's Mountain on the 21st of March. It was covered with snow, and presented no pass, and the party turned to the north [south] following the foot of the mountain about 60 miles to the end of the range.[4] Here they saw the first human beings since leaving Parowan.[5] These were the Horse-thief Indians, living just at the southern point of the range. They had large bands of California horses, and appearances indicated that they were constantly receiving additions to their herds from California. The whites attacked a party of them, and took 30 horses.[6] One of the party was wounded by an arrow, but not seriously.

About the 1st inst. they crossed the Sierra Nevada near latitude 36.[7] The pass was very favorable, and the slopes were so gradual, and the country so favorable for a road, that Col. Fremont says that he could have started in a buggy from the spot where he camped the day before crossing, fifteen miles beyond the summit, and have travelled driven to a point 35 miles on this side of the divide without injury to a horse. Indeed, many of the party would not believe that they had reached the summit.[8] This pass, which is at the head of a creek entering Kern River from the East, was previously unknown, so far as we know.[9]

Col. Fremont arrived in this city on the 16th, well and so hearty that he is actually some 14 pounds heavier than ever before. The principal result of his trip has been to establish the practicability of the route at all seasons. The Mormons say that the last winter has been unusually severe, and the church officers at Parowan, offered to give Col. Fremont a certificate to that effect. The greater portion of the route from Bent's Fort to Parowan had been surveyed by Capt. Gunnison, and reported to be not only practicable but favorable. This portion of the central route, is undoubtedly better than the corresponding portion in the same longitude of any other route. It is more direct, through a more fertile country, well provided with water and timber, favorable topographically, and will command the trade and the support of the Mormons at Salt Lake.

The route pursued by Col. Fremont from Parowan to the Sierra Nevada not having been direct, would not be suitable for the road. The road might go from Parowan direct to the Sierra Nevada, in latitude 36, or perhaps might follow the Spanish trail—now the road from Salt Lake to San Bernardino—down to the 36th parallel, and thence west to the pass.

Col. Fremont has not had time to arrange his papers, and most of his calculations are still to be made, and we expect that when a detailed narrative of his journey shall be published, it will create a strong impression on the public mind in favor of the central route. The season did not permit of extensive zoological, botanical or geological researches, yet a considerable portion of the journey having been made over country never before examined by civilized man, the report will no doubt add much to the present stock of knowledge about the country near the southern rim of the Great Basin.

Excerpt from the account of the expedition as printed in *Daily Alta California*, 21 April 1854. JCF had arrived in San Francisco five days before, and this is the first known report of the entire expedition. The only other known report is the account—equally sketchy—which he gave to the editor of the *National Intelligencer* approximately two months later (Doc. No. 274).

1. Through the good offices of Babbitt, Mormon bishop Tarlton Lewis assumed the responsibility of procuring the necessary horses and mules for the expedition, while Jesse N. Smith, district attorney and county clerk, gathered the required rations and camp equipment. When all was ready, the exploring party, now reduced in size by at least four persons, was guided as far as present-day Enterprise by the bishop's son, Samuel, a veteran of the Mormon Battalion, and his unidentified friend. Later John Steel, the mayor and recorder, lamented that JCF, who had determined the latitude of Parowan as being N 37° 50' 41", took away the survey maps of Iron County which had been lent to him and which were valued at $20.

2. Although JCF's course between Parowan and the Sierra Nevada is not indicated on the *Memoirs* map with the desired completeness, nevertheless a reconstruction of the expedition's route can be made by carefully observing the intricate cartographic details which lay astride his trail. Plainly, this corridor-like pattern is the result of first-hand experience.

The southwest direction carried the men past Cedar City, the site of the fledgling Mormon ironworks. They entered the Antelope Range via Leach Canyon, thus anticipating, in part, the future route of Utah Highway 56. After traversing the range, the party descended Meadow Valley Creek to the floor of the Escalante Desert. It was here that JCF's trail converged with that made in 1849 by the wagons of those ill-fated gold seekers, who had deflected from the Old Spanish Trail and the guidance of Jefferson Hunt, in an attempt to reach California in twenty days. Continuing west in the wagon tracks of the Death Valley parties, the expedition traveled up Shoal Creek to its source, which is almost on the present-day boundary dividing Utah and Nevada. In this instance, it coincides with the rim of the Great Basin. Between the Escalante Desert and the Sierra Nevada, JCF's trail and the tracks of the Forty-niner wagons would alternately run together and cross many times before California was reached (courtesy of Todd Berens).

3. Approximately eighty miles beyond Parowan, the expedition crossed the rim of the Great basin and descended into Clover Valley via Clover Creek, a minor affluent of the Virgin River. Following the course of that stream for nearly ten miles, the party turned northwest to enter the watershed of Meadow Valley Wash, crossing its main stream at mile one hundred. Continuing in the same direction, JCF left the watershed of the Virgin River for the last time and re-entered the Great Basin, opting to cross the divide in the Highland Mountains at Stampede Gap (elevation 7,315 feet) rather than at the nearer and lower Bennett Pass. Descending from the higher elevation in a more westerly direction, the exploring party crossed Dry Lake Valley to enter the watershed of the White River, a disrupted sluggish stream. During the Pluvial period it had

475

flowed to the Colorado River via the Virgin, but since that time had been reduced to a trickle of its former glory.

Following the White River northward to the 38th parallel, JCF struck westward and crossed Timber Pass at the northern end of the Seaman Range. Entering Coal Valley, he swung to the southwest, crossed the Golden Gate Range to
Garden Valley, and went across Sand Spring Valley via the gap at the north end
of the Worthington Mountains.

Turning west after clearing the southernmost projections of the Quinn Canyon and Reveille ranges, the expedition crossed the Kawich Mountains via Cedar
Pass and descended to the floor of Cactus Flat. They made their way through the
low gap in the Cactus Range and arrived at the head of Stonewall Flat, a forty-
mile-long trough-like basin containing numerous playa lakes. It terminates
abruptly at its western end (in latitude 37° 30′) in the Palmetto and Magruder
mountains. Most likely, it was in this basin that JCF's trail and the wagon tracks
of the Death Valley parties crossed for the last time. JCF's expedition would go
west over the Palmetto Mountains via Lida Pass; the luckless emigrants had
turned south and into Death Valley.

Descending from Lida Pass via Palmetto Wash, JCF crossed Fish Lake Valley
and began his ascent of the White Mountains, the last barrier remaining between him and Owens Valley. Perhaps using the same route as the future California State Highway 168, the expedition entered Deep Springs Valley by a narrow canyon, and crossed the divide at or near Westgard Pass (elevation 7,276
feet) to arrive on the floor of Owens Valley in latitude 37°. This put him near the
present-day city of Big Pine, Calif. (courtesy of Todd Berens).

4. Proceeding southward down Owens Valley on the same route used by the
Kern-Walker-Talbot party during the winter of 1845 (Vol. 2, Doc. No. 5), JCF
made an attempt to cross the Sierra Nevada at some point opposite the source of
Kings River—most likely Kearsarge Pass (elevation 11,823 feet). Finding the
pass blocked by deep snow, he abandoned his plan for a 37th parallel crossing,
and turned south again fully expecting to find lower passes leading into the San
Joaquin Valley along a more advantageous, albeit indirect, route. Subsequently,
after a journey of some sixty miles, the expedition found itself opposite the
southern terminus of the Sierra Nevada—Owens Peak (compare with Doc.
No. 274).

5. After leaving Parowan, they met one or two bands of Diggers (Interview
with the Delawares, *Daily Missouri Democrat*, 7 June 1854).

6. The Delawares did not mention the skirmish with the Indians or the taking of horses, and it is doubtful that it occurred. They reported that when they
went into California they were all on foot, having but one mule left (*ibid.*).

7. The *Memoirs* map indicates that the expedition bypassed Freeman Canyon
(California State Highway 178), the natural entrance to Walker Pass, and instead
entered the watershed of the Kern River via Hum pa ya mup Pass, or Bird
Spring Pass, ten miles to the south. JCF's oversight in missing his objective is
understandable when considered in the light of the topographical nature of the
region. When reviewed from the floor of the Indian Wells Valley, Walker Pass is
hidden from observation by the foothills of the Kiavah Mountains, whereas Bird
Spring Pass is silhouetted against the horizon, giving the appearance of a natural
corridor leading out of the valley (courtesy of Todd Berens).

8. JCF's alleged description of the crossing of Bird Spring Pass may sound
exaggerated and overly optimistic. When compared with some of his previous
experiences in surmounting the Sierra Nevada, his "find" was decidedly a cause

for boasting. He might be judged negligent, however, in remaining silent regarding the nature of Kern River Canyon and the Greenhorn Mountains beyond the pass, for they later proved to be an even greater barrier to the construction of a railroad.

9. Apparently neither JCF nor the editor of the *Daily Alta California* knew of the survey work conducted by Lieut. Robert S. Williamson of the Corps of Topographical Engineers in the southern Sierra passes during Aug. 1853. Traveling with Williamson's Pacific Railroad survey party that summer were Alexander Godey and Charles Preuss, members of JCF's earlier expeditions. They identified for Williamson the passes used by JCF's exploring parties in 1844 and 1845.

270. Committee of the Pioneer Society of California to Frémont

[San Francisco, 29 April 1854]

Dear Sir:

The Pioneer Society, being desirous of testifying their high regard and esteem for you as one of the first pioneers who opened the road to this flourishing State, beg leave to offer you a dinner,[1] to be given at such time as may suit your convenience. Hoping that this may receive your favorable consideration, we are, very respectfully, Your obedient servants,

J. R. Snyder
D. S. Turner
Wm. Van Voorhies
J. C. Low

G. F. Lemon
Selim Franklin
S. Brannan

Committee of Invitation

San Francisco, April 29, 1854.

Printed in *Daily Alta California*, 1 May 1854. The Society of California Pioneers had been organized in Aug. 1850. Men residing in California prior to 1 Jan. 1849 and their male descendants were entitled to the first class of membership (soulé, 283).

1. When Montgomery Blair heard of the society's resolution to offer the dinner, he wrote to his wife that JCF was again becoming popular and that "people have begun to think with renewed admiration of his service to the country & his heroic character" (25 April 1854, DLC—Montgomery Blair Papers).

271. Frémont to the Pioneer Society of California

San Francisco, April 30, 1854

Gentlemen:

I have this moment received your invitation on behalf of the Pioneer Society to dine with them at such time as will suit my convenience. I find difficulty in expressing my gratification at this mark of kindness towards me. It is delightful termination of a long and difficult journey to be thus welcomed by old friends, who having themselves encountered them, know the difficulties and hardships incident to the undertaking. A feast with *them* would, under the circumstances of the occasion, be peculiarly gratifying to me; but I must content myself for the present with the satisfaction of receiving, in your invitation, renewed proof of their favorable considerations of my public efforts to explore the country, and make known a region which has so suddenly and unexpectedly assumed a controlling influence in the affairs of men. This cherished object of my labors for so many years takes me to the East by the steamer of tomorrow, in order that I may, at the earliest moment, lay before the public the results of my recent successful efforts to complete my previous surveys, and I regret, therefore, that it is out of my power to accept your generous hospitality.[1] I am gentlemen, truly yours,

J. C. Fremont

Messrs. Snyder, Lemon, Turner, Franklin, Voorhies, Brannan and Lowe, Committee.

Printed in *Daily Alta California*, 1 May 1854.
1. After JCF's return to California on 19 Sept. 1854, the society, over the signatures of Thomas O. Larkin, Jacob R. Snyder, Philip A. Roach, O. P. Sutton, and William Van Voorhies, again tendered him a public dinner, which JCF again declined (see letters dated 9 and 21 Oct. in *Weekly Alta California*, 28 Oct. 1854).

272. Frémont to George Engelmann

STEAMER CORTES, at sea, May 7th. 1854

MY DEAR SIR,

This will be handed to you by my friend & assistant, Mr. Max F. Strobel, who in seeing our Delaware Indians safely on their way home will go as far as your city.[1] I know that you will be glad to hear of our welfare & the general good success of our journey, and have therefore taken the liberty of giving Mr. Strobel a letter of introduction to your friendly regard. I had the satisfaction to receive at San Francisco your note, containing some supplementary Barometrical data & will perhaps have occasion to reply more particularly, so soon as I can refer to it at Washington. Will you have leisure to look over & determine our Geological fragments? Collection I cannot call them. Snow, fatigue & anxiety did not leave room but for the most scanty gleaning. Still, as the country we passed over has so much occupied your attention, & its geological connection are so familiar to you you will be able to establish something of interest from what we have done. So soon as I arrive in Washington I will arrange the specimens & forward them to you with such notes as I may be able to add in explanation. Yours very truly,

J. C. FRÉMONT

ALS (MoSB). Addressed to "Dr. G. Engelman, St. Louis, Mri. Favor of Mr. Strobel." Endorsed: "Rec. June 6th. Ans. June 12th and June 24."

1. Strobel and seven Delawares arrived at St. Louis on 5 June. An eighth Indian, John Smith, had died aboard the steamboat coming up from New Orleans and was buried at B. F. Allain's plantation, Diamond Point, in Arkansas (*Missouri Republican*, 6 June 1854). Several called at the offices of the *Daily Missouri Democrat* and since one or two of them could speak English very fluently, the editor received a graphic description of the route (which he did not record) and many amusing details of camp life. "They speak," he wrote, "with gusto of their feasts upon mule meat, and seem even to relish their weary wandering along the base of the Sierra Nevada before they found a pass" (*Daily Missouri Democrat*, 7 June 1854). No mention was made of the other two Delawares who supposedly accompanied the expedition.

273. Abel Stearns to Frémont

ANGELES May 10th. 1854

HON JOHN C. FREMONT
DEAR SIR:

Yours of date April 20th is at hand, and owing to having been absent did not answer it per last Steamer.

In regard to the land at the Misn. Dolores [San Francisco de Asis], our agreement will be complyed with as soon as confirmed and a division made. Your testimony with regard to boundaries of the land, and occupation by Leidesdorff and afterwards by yourself, on my account, will be important in the case. If you cannot declare with regard to the occupation by Leidesdorff, you can with regard to the boundary at least the starting points.

For which purpose I desire that you will see Mr. Scott, my agent, and confer with him with regard to the testimony you may be able to give. Mr. W[illiam] Buckler I understand has arrived at S. Francisco from Canton,[1] his testimony might be of service in the case—you can place all confidence in Mr. Scott with regards what testimony will be necessary to obtain a confirmation by the Board. I cannot leave here at present but intend soon to be in San Francisco, where I hope to see you. Very Respectfully Yours,

ABEL STEARNS

ALS, SC (CSmH).
1. According to an 1856 article on the Mariposa, probably written by George W. Wright, Canton was in the Guadalupe Valley (New York *Herald*, 27 Feb. 1856). GUDE [1] does not list Canton as a gold camp but, according to Bertha Schroeder, a long-time resident of Mariposa, there were several hundred Chinese in the Guadalupe Valley in 1856.

274. Frémont to the Editors of the *National Intelligencer*

[WASHINGTON, 13 June 1854]

GENTLEMEN:

While the proceedings in Congress are occupying public attention, more particularly with the subject of a Pacific Railway, I desire to offer to your paper, for publication, some general results of a recent winter expedition across the Rocky Mountains, confining myself to mere results, in anticipation of a fuller report, with maps and illustrations, which will necessarily require some months to prepare.

The country examined was for about three-fourths of the distance—from the Missouri frontier, at the mouth of the Kansas river, to the valley of Parawan, at the foot of the Wahsatch Mountains, within the rim of the Great Basin, at its southeastern bend—along and between the 38th and 39th parallels of latitude; and the whole line divides itself naturally into three sections, which may be conveniently followed in description.

The *first* or eastern section consists of the great prairie slope, spreading from the base of the *Sierra Blanca* [1] to the Missouri frontier, about 700 miles; the *second* or middle section, comprehends the various Rocky Mountain ranges and interlying valleys, between the termination of the Great Plains at the foot of the *Sierra Blanca*, and the Great Basin of the Parawan Valley and Wahsatch Mountains, where the first Mormon settlement is found, about 450 miles; the *third* or western section comprehends the mountainous plateau lying between the Wahsatch Mountains and the *Sierra Nevada*, a distance of about 400 miles.

The country examined was upon a very direct line, the travelled route being about 1,550 miles over an air-line distance of about 1,300 miles.

The First Section.—Four separate expeditions across this section, made before the present one, and which carried me over various lines at different seasons of the year, enable me to speak of it with the confidence of intimate knowledge. It is a plain of easy inclination, sweeping directly up to the foot of the mountains which dominate it as highlands do the ocean. Its character is open prairie, over which summer travelling is made in every direction.

For a railway or a winter-travelling road, the route would be, in consideration of wood, coal, building-stone, water, and fertile land, about two hundred miles up the immediate valley of Kansas (which might be made one rich continuous cornfield), and afterwards along the immediate valley of the Upper Arkansas, of which about two hundred miles, as you approach the mountains, is continuously well adapted to settlements as well as to roads. Numerous well watered and fertile valleys—broad and level—open up among the mountains, which present themselves in detached blocks—outliers—gradually closing in around the heads of the streams, but leaving open approaches to the central ridges. The whole of the inter-mountain region is abundant in grasses, wood, coal, and fertile soil. The *Pueblos* above Bent's Fort, prove it to be well adapted to the grains and vegetables common to the latitude, including Indian corn, which ripens well, and to the support of healthy stock, which increase well and take care of themselves summer and winter.

The climate is mild and the winters short, the autumn usually having its full length of bright open weather, without snow, which in winter falls rarely and passes off quickly. In this belt of country lying along the mountains, the snow falls more early and much more thinly than in the open plains to the eastward; the storms congregate about the high mountains and leave the valleys free. In the beginning of December we found yet no snow on the *Huerfano* River, and were informed by an old resident,[2] then engaged in establishing a farm at the mouth of this stream, that snow seldom or never falls there, and that cattle were left in the range all the winter through.

This character of country continued to the foot of the dividing crest, and to this point our journey resulted in showing a very easy grade for a road, over a country unobstructed either by snow or other impediments, and having all the elements necessary to the prosperity of an agricultural population, in fertility of soil, abundance of food for stock, wood and coal for fuel, and timber for necessary constructions.

Our examinations around the southern headwaters of the Arkansas, have made us acquainted with many passes, grouped together in a small space of country, conducting by short and practicable valleys from the waters of the Arkansas just described, to the valleys of the *Del Norte* and East Colorado. The *Sierra Blanca*, through which these passes lie, is high and rugged, presenting a very broken appearance, but rises abruptly from the open country on either side, narrowed at the points through which the passes are cut, leaving them only six or eight miles in length from valley to valley, and entirely unobstructed by outlying ranges or broken country. To the best of these passes the ascent is along the open valley of watercourses, uniform and very gradual in ascent. Standing immediately at the mouth of the *Sand Hill Pass*[3]—one of the most practicable in the *Sierra Blanca*, and above those usually travelled—at one of the remotest headsprings of the *Huerfano* River, the eye of the traveller follows down without obstructions or abrupt descent along the gradual slope of the valley to the great plains which reach the Missouri. The straight river and the open valley form, with the plains beyond, one great slope, without a hill to break the line of sight or obstruct the course of the road. On either side of this line hills slope easily to the river, with lines of timber and yellow autumnal grass, and the water, which flows smoothly between, is not interrupted by a fall in its course to the ocean. The surrounding country is wooded with pines and covered with luxuriant grasses, up to the very crags of the central summits. On the 8th of December we found this whole country free from snow and Daguerre views taken at this time show the grass entirely uncovered in the passes.

Along all this line the elevation was carefully determined by frequent barometrical observations, and its character exhibited by a series of daguerreotype views, comprehending the face of the country almost continuously, or at least sufficiently so, to give a thoroughly correct impression of the whole.

Two tunnel-like passes pierce the mountains here, almost in juxtaposition, connecting the plain country on either side by short passages five to eight miles long. The mountains which they perforate constitute the only obstruction, and are the only break in the plane or valley line of road from the frontier of Missouri to the summit hills of the Rocky Mountains, a distance of about 850 miles, or more than half way to the San Joaquin valley. Entering one of these passes from the eastern plain, a distance of about one mile upon a wagon road, already travelled by wagons, commands an open view of the broad valley of *San Luis* and the great range of *San Juan* beyond on its western side. I here connected the line of the present expedition with one explored in 1848–'49 from the mouth of the Kansas to this point, and the results of both will be embodied in a full report.

At this place the line entered the middle section, and continued its western course over an open valley country, admirably adapted for settlement, across the *San Luis* valley, and up the flat bottom lands of the Sah-watch[4] to the heights of the central ridge of the Rocky Mountains. Across those wooded heights—wooded and grass-covered up to and over their rounded summits—to the Coocha-to-pe pass, the line followed an open easy wagon-way, such as is usual to a rolling country. On the high summit lands were forests of coniferous trees, and the snow in the pass was four inches deep. This was on the 14th of December. A day earlier our horses' feet would not have touched snow in the crossing. Up to this point we had enjoyed clear and dry pleasant weather. Our journey had been all along on dry ground; and travelling slowly along waiting for the winter, there had been abundant leisure for becoming acquainted with the country. The open character of the country, joined to good information, indicated the existence of other passes about the head of the Sah-watch. This it was desirable to verify, and especially to examine a neighboring and lower pass connecting more directly with the Arkansas valley, known as the Poow-che [Poon-che].[5]

But the winter had now set in over all the mountain regions, and the country was so constantly enveloped and hidden in clouds which rested upon it, and the air so darkened by falling snow, that exploring became difficult and dangerous, precisely where we felt most interested in making a thorough examination. We were moving in fogs and clouds, through a region wholly unknown to us, and without guides, and were therefore obliged to content ourselves with the examination of a single line, and the ascertainment of the winter condition of the country over which it passed; which was in fact the main object of our expedition.

Our progress in this mountainous region was necessarily slow, and during ten days which it occupied us to pass through about one hundred miles of the mountainous country bordering the eastern side of the Upper Colorado valley, the greatest depth of snow was, among the pines and aspens, on the ridges about two and a half feet, and in the valleys about six inches. The atmosphere is too cold and dry for much snow, and the valleys, protected by the mountains, are comparatively free from it, and warm. We here found villages of Utah Indians in their wintering ground, in little valleys along the foot of the highest mountains and bordering the more open country of the Colorado valley. Snow was here (December 25) only a few inches deep—the grass generally appearing above it, and there being none under trees and on southern hillsides.

The horses of the *Utahs* were living on the range, and notwithstanding that they were used in hunting, were in excellent condition. One which we had occasion to kill for food had on it about two inches of fat, being in as good order as any buffalo we had killed in November on the eastern plains. Over this valley country—about 150 miles across—the Indians informed us that snow falls only a few inches in depth, such as we saw it at the time.

The immediate valley of the Upper Colorado for about 100 miles in breadth, and from the 7th to the 22d of January, was entirely bare of snow, and the weather resembled that of autumn in this country.

The line here entered the body of mountains known as the *Wah-satch* and *An-ter-ria* [6] ranges, which are practicable at several places in this part of their course; but the falling snow and destitute condition of my party again interfered to impede examinations. They lie between the Colorado valley and the Great Basin, and at their western base are established the Mormon settlements of Parawan and Cedar City. They are what are called fertile mountains, abundant in water, wood, and grass, and fertile valleys, offering inducements to settlement and facilities for making a road. These mountains are a great store-house of materials—timber, iron, coal—which would be of indispensable use in the construction and maintenance of the road, and are solid foundations to build up the future prosperity of the rapidly-increasing Utah State.

Salt is abundant on the eastern border mountains, as the *Sierra del Sal*, being named from it. In the ranges lying behind the Mormon settlements, among the mountains through which the line passes, are accumulated a great wealth of iron and coal, and extensive forests of heavy timber. These forests are the largest I am acquainted with in the Rocky Mountains, being in some places twenty miles in depth of continuous forest; the general growth lofty and large, frequently over three feet in diameter, and sometimes reaching five feet, the red spruce and yellow pine predominating. At the actual southern extremity of the Mormon settlements, consisting of the two enclosed towns of Parawan and Cedar City, near to which our line passed, a coal mine has been opened for about eighty yards, and iron works already established. Iron here occurs in extraordinary masses, and some parts accumulated into mountains, which come out in crests of solid iron thirty feet thick and a hundred yards long.

In passing through this bed of mountains about fourteen days had been occupied, from January 24th to February 7th, the deepest snow we here encountered being about up to the saddle-skirts, or four feet; this occurring only in occasional drifts in the passes on northern exposures, and in the small mountain flats hemmed in by woods and hills. In the valley it was sometimes a few inches deep, and as often none at all. On our arrival at the Mormon settlements, February 8th, we found it a few inches deep, and were there informed that the winter had been unusually long-continued and severe, the thermometer having been as low as 17° below zero, and more snow having fallen than in all the previous winters together since the establishment of this colony.

At this season their farmers had usually been occupied with their ploughs, preparing the land for grain.

At this point the line of exploration entered the *third* or western section, comprehending the mountainous *plateau* between the Wahsatch Mountains and the Sierra Nevada of California. Two routes here suggested themselves to me for examination, one directly across the *plateau*, between the 37th and 38th parallels; the other keeping to the south of the mountains and following for about 200 miles down a valley of the *Rio Virgen*—Virgin river—thence direct to the Tejon Pass, at the head of the San Joaquin valley. This route down the Virgin River had been examined the year before with a view to settlement this summer by a Mormon exploring party under the command of Major Steele[7] of Parawan, who (and others of the party) informed me that they found fertile valleys inhabited by Indians who cultivated corn and melons, and the rich ground in many places matted over with grape vines. The Tejon Passes are two, one of them (from the abundance of vines at its lower end) called *Caxon de las Uvas*.[8] They were of long use, and were examined by me and their practicability ascertained in my expedition of 1848–'49, and in 1851 I again passed through them both, bringing three thousand head of cattle through one of them.

Knowing the practicability of these passes, and confiding in the report of Major Steele as to the intermediate country, I determined to take the other (between the 37th and 38th parallels), it recommending itself to me as being more direct towards San Francisco, and preferable on that account for a road, if suitable ground could be found; and also as being unknown. The Mormons informed me, that various attempts had been made to explore it, and all failed for want of water. Although biased in favor of the Virgin river route, I determined to examine this one in the interest of geography, and accordingly set out for this purpose from the settlement about the 20th of February, travelling directly westward from Cedar City (eighteen miles west of Parawan).[9] We found the country a high table land, bristling with mountains, often in short isolated blocks, and sometimes accumulated into considerable ranges, with numerous open and low passes.

We were thus always in a valley and always surrounded by mountains more or less closely, which apparently altered in shape and position as we advanced. The valleys are dry and naked, without water or wood; but the mountains are generally covered with grass and well wooded with pines; springs are very rare, and occasional small streams are at remote distances. Not a human being was encountered between the Santa Clara road, near the Mormon Settlements and the *Sierra Nevada*, over a distance of more than 300 miles. The solitary character of this uninhabited region, the naked valleys without watercourses, among mountains with fertile soil and grass and woods abundant, give it the appearance of an unfinished country.

Commencing on the 38th, we struck the Sierra Nevada on or about the 37th parallel about the 15th March.[10]

On our route across we had for the great part of the time pleasant and rather warm weather; the valley grounds and low ridges uncovered, but snow over the upper parts of the higher mountains. Between the 20th of February and 17th of March we had several snowstorms, sometimes accompanied with hail and heavy thunder; but the snow remained on the valley ground only a few hours after the storm was over. It forms not the least impediment at any time of the winter. I was prepared to find the Sierra here broad, rugged, and blocked up with snow, and was not disappointed in my expectation. The first range we attempted to cross carried us to an elevation of 8,000 or 9,000 feet and into impassable snows, which was further increased on the 16th by a considerable fall.

There was no object in forcing a passage, and I accordingly turned at once some sixty or eighty miles to the southward, making a wide sweep to strike the *Point of the California mountain* where the Sierra Nevada suddenly breaks off and declines into a lower country. Information obtained years before from the Indians led me to believe, that the low mountains were broken into many passes, and at all events I had the certainty of an easy passage through either of Walker's passes.

When the Point was reached I found the Indian information fully verified; the mountain suddenly terminated and broke down into lower grounds barely above the level of the country, and making numerous openings into the valley of the San Joaquin. I entered into the first which offered (taking no time to search, as we were entirely out of provisions and living upon horses), which led us by an open and almost level hollow thirteen miles long to an upland not steep enough to be called a hill, over into the valley of a small affluent to Kern River; the hollow and the valley making together a way where a wagon would not find any obstruction for forty miles.

The country around the passes in which the Sierra Nevada here terminates, declines considerably below its more northern elevations. There was no snow to be seen at all on its eastern face, and none in the pass; but we were in the midst of opening spring, flowers blooming in fields on both sides of the Sierra.

Between the point of the mountains and the head of the valley at the Tejon the passes generally are free from snow throughout the year, and the descent from them to the ocean is distributed over a long slope of more than 200 miles. The low dry country and the long slope, in contradistinction to the high country and short sudden descent and heavy snows of the passes behind the bay of San Francisco, are among the considerations which suggest themselves in favor of the route by the head of the San Joaquin.

The above results embody general impressions made upon my mind during this journey. It is clearly established, that the winter condition of the country constitutes no impediment, and from what has been said, the entire practicability of the line will be as clearly inferred. A fuller account hereafter will comprehend detailed descriptions of the country, with their absolute and relative elevations, and show the ground upon which the conclusions were based. They are contributed at this time as an element to aid the public in forming an opinion on the subject of the projected railway, and in gratification of my great desire to do something for its advancement. It seems a treason against mankind and the spirit of progress which marks the ages, to refuse to put this one completing link to our national prosperity and the civilization of the world. Europe still lies between Asia and America: build this railroad and things will have revolved about: America will lie between Asia and Europe—the golden vein which runs through the history of the world will follow the iron track to San Francisco, and the Asiatic trade will finally fall into its last and permanent road, when the new [ancient] and the modern Chryse throw open their gates to the thoroughfare of the world.

I am, gentlemen, with much regard, respectfully yours,

J. C. FRÉMONT

Washington, June 13.

Printed in *National Intelligencer*, 14 June 1854, and in many other journals throughout the country, including the *Missouri Daily Democrat*, 19 June 1854, and *Daily Alta California*, 20 Nov. 1854. Both chambers of the 33rd Congress ordered the letter to be printed. See Senate Misc. Doc. 67, 1st sess., Serial 705, and House Misc. Doc. 8, 2nd sess., Serial 807. Except for punctuation, the changes that had been made in the congressional printing are indicated by brackets. JCF's letter of 14 June 1854 is remarkably similar to his 1 April 1850 letter to the railroad convention in Philadelphia (Doc. No. 54).

1. "Sierra Blanca" is JCF's term for the Sangre de Cristo Range in particular, and to the ranges and peaks comprising the southern Rocky Mountains in general. The name does not appear on any of JCF's maps.

2. The old resident was either R. L. Wootton or Charles Autobees (LECOMPTE, 35:59).

3. Presently known as Medano Pass.

4. Saguache.

5. Poncha Pass, with an elevation of 9,010 feet, is at the northern end of the Sangre de Cristo Mountains.

6. The name "An-ter-ria" is one of the geographical misnomers of JCF's third expedition, and refers to a river which he had not personally observed but which he set down on his "Map of Oregon and Upper California" on the strength of information supplied to him by mountain men and/or Indians while traversing the Wasatch Mountains on his eastward journey in 1844. His map incorrectly indicates that the Green River is joined by an affluent called "Anteree R." in latitude 38° 30′. The error in both name and latitude is apparent when compared with modern topographical maps. JCF's "Anteree R." is actually the San Rafael River, and the correct latitude is 30° 45′. Consequently, when the fifth expedition crossed the Green at the mouth of the San Rafael River in Dec. 1853, the misnomer An-ter-ria was applied to the watershed of the San Rafael, inadvertently identifying the great anticlinal uplift behind it as the An-ter-ria Range rather than the San Rafael Swell. Evidently the error was detected following the publication of the surveys of the Gunnison party, for the name does not appear on the *Memoirs* map.

As to the origin of the name itself, An-ter-ria could very well be a corruption of Antero (or vice versa), the name of a mid-nineteenth-century Yampa Ute who was chief of the tribe of Indians which occupied the region that included the San Rafael Swell.

7. Maj. John Steele.

8. In recent times the canyon has become known as the Grapevine, and is the route of Interstate 5. Its summit is now called Tejon Pass but was formerly known as Fort Tejon Pass, after the military post established in the canyon by Edward F. Beale during 1853. The original Tejon Pass was located approximately fifteen miles to the northeast (GUDDE [2], 333, and ABELOE, 123–24).

9. JCF and his party set out from Parowan on 21 Feb. Cedar City was southwest of Parowan.

10. Having arrived at the eastern base of the Sierra Nevada near present-day Big Pine, Calif., JCF sought a passage that would carry him over the mountains on a route contiguous with the 37th parallel. However, he was thwarted by deep snow in his attempt to breach the mountain barrier at this point in the range. Therefore, he reluctantly turned southward to enter the San Joaquin Valley through a lower pass just beyond his "Point of the California mountain"— present-day Owens Peak (elevation 8,400 feet), which he reached a week later (Doc. No. 269).

275. Charles F. Smith to Frémont

Office of the Board &c.
WASHINGTON, D.C.
June 21, 1853 [1854]

SIR:

There are many claims before this Board[1] for examination which require such explanation or approval as can only be obtained from you, & which is necessary for their being favorably acted upon by the Board.

Will you then at your earliest leisure attend before the Board for the above purpose, say at 12 o'clock tomorrow. If you cannot come tomorrow will you please let the Board know by mail, when you can make it convenient to appear.

By direction of the Board:

C. F. SMITH
Col. U.S. Army
Presdt. of the Bd.

Lbk (DNA-92, LS, 1852–55). In the left-hand margin: "Enclosed to Hon. T. H. Benton same date."

1. The Army Appropriation Act, approved 31 Aug. 1852, authorized and empowered the Secretary of War to appoint three competent and disinterested officers of the army to examine and report to Congress upon all remaining unpaid claims resulting from JCF's operations in California in 1845. Secretary of War C. M. Conrad named Brevet Col. Charles F. Smith, Lieut. Col. Charles Thomas, and Maj. Richard B. Lee to undertake the task. Details about individual claims and their disposition may be found in RG 92, California Claims Board, 1847–55, Microfilm rolls 6, 7, 8, and 9. A printed summary may be found in "Message of the President of the U.S. communicating, in compliance with a resolution of the Senate of the 11 Aug. 1856, copies of claims presented by and allowed to John C. Fremont," Senate Ex. Doc. 109, 34th Cong., 1st sess., pp. 54–81, Serial 825.

Three hundred sixty-three claims were filed with the board, amounting in the aggregate to $989,185.29. Of this amount $149,236 were recommended for payment, $9,129.40 recommended for allowance, $157,317.65 disallowed, $307,927.36 did not require action by the board, $147,800 were withdrawn, and $28,570.37 were registered. Congress then appropriated money to pay the claims accepted by the board. On 3 April 1855 the Secretary of War abolished the board and assigned its unfinished business to Col. Thomas.

276. Frémont to Abel Stearns

WASHINGTON CITY,
July 2d. 1854.

DEAR SIR

Yours of the 10th May I received here by the last mail. I stayed in San Francisco but a few days. I saw Mr. Scott once but was so unfavorably impressed by him that I made no attempt to see him again. He called upon me on the subject at Palmers.

From what I learned the case will not come up before I reach San Francisco again, but in case of accident I mentioned the subject to my friend Judge [Montgomery] Blair and told him where the evidence necessary to the claim could be had. The claim of evidence is complete both as regards the boundaries of the land and the occupation of Leidesdorff & myself and the expensive improvements in fencing and defending the land. The starting point can be perfectly well established and to these points there is much better evidence than Mr. Buckler's though his may serve.

I am quite sorry that Mr. Scott did not show me some letters from you, in order that I might have known what degree of confidence to place in him. I was in a great hurry when he called upon me & one does not like to talk important business with men upon their mere assertion that they are agents.

I shall soon have the satisfaction to see you and would return immediately to California but am just now occupied in endeavoring to obtain from Congress payment for a claim of more than two hundred thousand dollars.

As Congress adjourns of the 4th of August this must be decided during the present month and I will then immediately leave for San Francisco. Your very truly,

J. C. FRÉMONT

LS (CSmH). Endorsed.

277. Frémont to William H. Emory

SIR:

In a letter published in the Washington *Union* on the 8th inst., over your signature, I observe the following language:

"Ever since my campaign with General Kearney in 1846, *in which a member of Mr. Benton's family was dismissed from the army,*" &c.

As this statement does me manifest injustice, and conveys a false impression to the public, I have to invite your attention to it, and ask a public correction through the same medium. Your obedient servant,

J. C. FREMONT

To Major Wm. H. Emory, Topographical Corps.

Printed in New York *Times*, 14 July 1854. In the "correction" Emory published some of the court-martial proceedings against JCF, including his 19 Feb. 1848 letter of resignation from the army. With tongue in cheek, Emory then wrote: "It will be seen by these documents that my statement is substantially correct; but I have no objection to make the statement more full since he has called my attention to it and to say that, for acts committed in the campaign of 1846, he was subsequently tried at Washington and by sentence of a general Court-Martial—approved by the President—was dismissed from the service of the United States; but that the sentence was remitted, and that he was ordered to join his regiment in Mexico, but tendered his resignation, which was accepted, and his connection with the army was terminated."

The hostility between Emory, on the one hand, and Frémont and Benton on the other, was unrelenting; in fact, Emory's 8 July 1854 letter had been an answer to Benton's verbal attack upon him.

278. Frémont to Reverdy Johnson

WASHINGTON, August 9th. 1854

MY DEAR SIR,

A mistake prevented me from getting yours of yesterday until this morning. The contract with Johnson [Adam Johnston] was made on the eve of my departure for England in '51—and the drafts left by me with the house of Palmer Cook & Co. for the purpose of collection in the event that the government ratified the contract. They were endorsed by me for this purpose and it was clearly understood that they were never to be used for any purpose. I have never received one dollar on account of them. To pay them is impossible. There are no funds any where to meet them & whatever is to be done in the case must be the subject of an arrangement with Palmer Cook & Co. I will make this a special business when I arrive in San Francisco, for which place I hope to be able to set out on the 5th of next month.

I will thank you to keep me advised of any thing in reference to them which it may be important for me to know and in the meantime am very truly yours,

J. C. FRÉMONT

Hon. Reverdy Johnson
Baltimore

ALS-JBF (James S. Copley Collection, La Jolla, Calif.).

279. Frémont to Brantz Mayer

WASHINGTON, August 17th. 1854

DEAR SIR,

Your note finds me on the eve of departure for California and I think I can most satisfactorily oblige you by looking at the condition of things in San Francisco & giving you immediately my opinion. Things there change so fast that what was good three months ago may not be good now. Yours truly,

J. C. FRÉMONT

Brantz Mayer, Esqre.
Baltimore

ALS-JBF (Haverford College).

280. Frémont to George Engelmann

NEW YORK, August 20th. 1854

MY DEAR SIR,

I have to thank you for your two letters together with the pamphlet containing meteorological observations.

Since my return I have been devoted to such severe business that all more agreeable intercourse was laid aside in the expectation of an interval of leisure which I find I am not to have.

I start suddenly for California tomorrow leaving many things unfinished. I write more especially to say to you that I have asked Mr. Coles Morris, of No. 39 William Street, this city, to pay to you for Mr. Eggloffstien one hundred dollars which is the amount remaining due him. As you said in yours we are both disappointed. He has many good qualities but is not a good topographer for such service as we are engaged in.

I was obliged to engage Strobel to fill his place for which I have given him about seven hundred dollars including his work here.

As the expedition was made with private means, they do not permit me to be liberal beyond what is fairly and reasonably due to all who have taken part in it.

Until my return I have postponed all barometrical and other calculations and will write to you on my return home. Yours truly,

J. C. FRÉMONT

ALS-JBF (MoSB). Endorsed: "Recd. Sept 4. Ans. to Mr. Morris Sept. 5th."

281. Frémont to Abel Stearns

SAN FRANCISCO Octr. 3. 1854

DEAR SIR,

I received in Washington your letter in reply to mine of April last from this place.[1] I regret not to have been here at the time of your visit to this place, the more especially as, I suppose, you are not likely to repeat it immediately.

In regard to the Mission property I would be glad if some arrangement could be made by which it might be rendered available—that is to say, my portion of it, as I am not disposed to keep it, but would prefer to sell & I think the present as good a time for this purpose as any other. I think that the division might be made & the portion set off definitely with advantage to the interest of both parties.[2]

I should be glad to hear from you soon in answer & meanwhile remain Yours truly,

JOHN C. FRÉMONT

Hon Abel Stearns,
Los Angeles

ALS (CSmH).
1. See JCF to Stearns, 20 April 1854 (Doc. No. 268). For information relating to the subject of their correspondence—property connected with the Mission San Francisco de Asís—see Doc. No. 178.
2. The Andrade claim was eventually rejected by the California Land Commission and the District Court, but before that JCF had conveyed away his interest (GATES [1], 29).

282. *Geographical Memoir upon Upper California, in Illustration of His Map of Oregon and California*

Editorial note: In the spirit of 1850, Professor James Rhoads noticed in *Sartain's Union Magazine of Literature* that, after the mission of Christ, the three greatest events in the world had been connected with the rise and progress of the United States: "Columbus marked a pathway to a new-found world; Washington guided and sustained the patriots who consecrated that world to the advancement of human rights and human welfare; and Fremont lifted the veil which, since time first began, had hidden from view the real El Dorado." The California that Frémont so simply, precisely, and eloquently describes in this memoir is an "El Dorado," with a mild and salubrious climate, capable of sustaining a considerable population in agriculture, timbering, and maritime activity.

Like the map it was designed to illustrate, the *Memoir* is not confined to an examination of the California west of the Sierra, but also depicts the terrain, rivers, and climate of the opposite side—Frémont's Great Basin. Scant are its comments on Oregon, although the latter country as far north as the 49th parallel was well represented on the map, largely through the surveys of Charles Wilkes. While Frémont and Charles Preuss acknowledge their indebtedness on the face of the map "to other authorities," they do not mention by name

Wilkes or William H. Emory, whose map of his march to the Pacific with Stephen Watts Kearny had helped in delineating the topography of the Southwest. Frémont was not on friendly terms with either officer.

The 1848 map of Oregon and California was published as Map 5 in the Map Portfolio volume, which accompanied Vol. 1 of the *Expeditions*. Being a primary record of exploration, it was used in combination with Table III of the appendix to this *Memoir* to trace the third expedition's route west and its movements after reaching California. The commentary may be found in Vol. 2, especially in the editorial notes to Doc. Nos. 3, 5, and 22, and is not repeated here.

Donald Jackson indicated in the Map Portfolio how Preuss was able to mark the first gold strikes on the map, probably while it was in the hands of the lithographer and several months after Frémont had submitted the *Memoir* to the Senate. Consequently, other than quicksilver, the *Memoir* does not mention the mineral wealth of California. Frémont does notice the arrival of the Mormons in the Valley of the Great Salt Lake, and Preuss shows their settlements along the eastern shore of the lake and locates "Mormon Fort" near the north end of Utah Lake. Actually the "fort" would not be constructed until 1849.

On 5 June 1848 the Senate ordered printed 20,000 copies of both the map and the *Memoir* and ten days later requested an additional hundred of each for the Topographical Bureau. In January 1849 the House ordered 20,000 copies of the *Memoir* (without the appendix) and 10,000 copies of the map. Later in the year William McCarty of Philadelphia brought out a commercial edition, without the map but enlarged with extracts from numerous other travelers. Many a Fortyniner was able to purchase it for twenty-five cents.

In the 1880s the Frémonts would dust off the 1848 Senate document, reprinted here, and incorporate large portions of it into the *Memoirs* of the explorer's life.

GEOGRAPHICAL MEMOIR

On the second day of February, in the year 1847, during my absence on my third expedition of topographical survey, in the western part of this continent, a resolve was passed by the Senate directing the construction of two maps—one of the central section of the Rocky

Mountains, and the other of Oregon and Upper California—from the materials collected by me in the two previous expeditions, and with the additions which the then existing expedition might furnish; and Mr. Charles Preuss, my assistant in the first and second expeditions, was employed to commence the work.

On my return to the United States, in the month of September last, I found Mr. Preuss closely engaged upon the work on which the Senate had employed him; and, from that time to the present, I have myself given all the time that could be spared from other engagements to supply the additions which the last expedition has enabled me to make. Conceiving that the map of Oregon and California was of the most immediate and pressing importance, I first directed my attention to its preparation, in order to bring it into a condition as soon as possible to be laid down before the Senate; which is now done.

In laying this map of Oregon and Upper California before the Senate, I deem it proper to show the extent and general character of the work, and how far it may be depended on as correct, as being founded on my own or other surveys, and how far it is conjectural, and only presented as the best that is known.

In extent, it embraces the whole western side of this continent between the eastern base of the Rocky mountains and the Pacific ocean, and between the straits of [Juan de] Fuca and the Gulf of California, taking for its outline, on the north, the boundary line with Great Britain, and on the south, including the bay of San Diego, the head of the gulf of California, the rivers Colorado and Gila, and all the country through which the line of the late treaty with Mexico would run, from *El Paso del Norte* [El Paso, Tex.] to the sea. To complete the view in that quarter, the valley of the Rio del Norte [Rio Grande] is added, from the head of the river to El Paso del Norte, thereby including New Mexico. The map has been constructed expressly to exhibit the two countries of Oregon and the Alta California together. It is believed to be the most correct that has appeared of either of them; and it is certainly the only one that shows the structure and configuration of the interior of Upper California.

The part of the map which exhibits Oregon is chiefly copied from the works of others, but not entirely, my own explorations in that territory having extended to nearly two thousand miles. The part which exhibits California, and especially the Great Basin, the Sierra Nevada, the beautiful valley of Sacramento and San Joaquin, is chiefly from my own surveys of personal view, and in such cases is given as correct.

497

Where my own observations did not extend, the best authorities have been followed.

The profile view in the margin, on the north side of the map, exhibits the elevations of the country from the *South Pass* in the Rocky mountains to the bay of San Francisco, passing the Utah and the Great Salt lake, following the river Humboldt through the northern side of the Great Basin, crossing the Sierra Nevada into the valley of the Sacramento, where the emigrant road now crosses that sierra forty miles north of Nueva Helvetia. This line shows the present travelling route to California. The profile on the south side of the map exhibits the elevations of the country on a different line—the line of exploration in the last expedition—from the head of the Arkansas by the Utah and Salt lake, and through the interior of the Great Basin, crossing the Sierra Nevada into the Sacramento valley at the head of the *Rio de los Americanos*. These profile views are given merely for their *outlines*, to show the structure of the country between the Rocky mountains and the sea, and the rise and fall occasioned by mountains and valleys. Full and descriptive profile views on a large scale are wanted, marking the geological structure of the country, and exhibiting at their proper altitudes the different products of the vegetable kingdom. Some material is already collected for such a purpose, extending on different lines from the Mississippi to the Pacific, but not sufficient to complete the work.

The Arabic figures on different parts of the map indicate the elevation of places above the level of the sea; a knowledge of which is essential to a just conception of the climate and agricultural capacities of a country.

The longitudes established on the line of exploration of the last expedition are based on a series of astronomical observations, resting on four main positions, determined by lunar culminations. The first of these main positions is at the mouth of the *Fontaine qui Bouit* river [Fountain Creek], on the Upper Arkansas; the second is on the eastern shore of the Great Salt lake, and two in the valley of the Sacramento, at the western base of the Sierra Nevada. This line of astronomical observations, thus carried across the continent, reaches the Pacific ocean on the northern shore of the bay of Monterey.

In my published map, of the year 1845, the line of the western coast was laid down according to Vancouver. When the newly established positions were placed on the map now laid before the Senate, it was found that they carried the line of the coast about fourteen miles west, and the valleys of the Sacramento and San Joaquin about twenty miles east; making an increase of more than thirty miles in the breadth of the country below the Sierra Nevada. Upon examination, it was found that these positions agreed, nearly, with the observations of Captain Beechey, at Monterey. The corrections required by the new positions were then accordingly made; the basin of the Sacramento and San Joaquin valleys was removed to the eastward, and the line of the coast projected farther west, conformably to my observations, retaining the configuration given to it by the surveys of Vancouver.

The error, in the position of the San Joaquin, Sacramento, and Wahlahmath [Willamette] valleys still exists upon the most authentic maps extant; and it appears that, upon the charts in general use, a greatly erroneous position is still given to the coast.

By the return of the United States sloop-of-war Portsmouth, Commander [John B.] Montgomery, from the Pacific ocean, it is learned that two British ships of war are now engaged in making a new survey of the gulf and coast of California. It is also known that an American whale ship was recently lost on the coast of California in consequence of the errors in the charts now in general use, locating the coast and islands, from Monterey south, too far east.*

The astronomical observations made by me across the continent, in this my third expedition, were calculated by Professor [Joseph S.] Hubbard, of the national observatory, (Washington city,) during the present winter; and a note from him on the subject of these observations is added as an appendix to this memoir. My attention having been recently called to this subject, (the true position of the coast of California,) I find it worthy of remark that the position given to this coast on the charts of the old Spanish navigators agrees nearly with that which would be assigned to it by the observations of the most eminent naval surveyors of the present day. The position adopted for Monterey and the adjacent coast, on the map now laid before the Sen-

---

*Naval—The United States sloop-of-war Portsmouth, Commander John B. Montgomery, arrived at Boston on Friday, from the Pacific ocean, last from Valparaiso, February 23. Commander Montgomery states that the British frigate "Herald," and the brig "Pandora," are engaged in making a new survey of the gulf and coast of California.

The whale ship "Hope," of Providence, was recently lost on the coast, in consequence of an error in the charts now in general use, which locate the coast and islands from Monterey to Cape St. Lucas from fifteen to forty miles too far to the eastward.—*National Intelligencer.*

ate, agrees nearly with that in which it had been placed by the observations of *Malaspina*,* in 1791.

In constructing this map it became necessary to adopt the coast line of the Pacific, as found in maps in general use, to give it completeness. It was no part of my design to make a chart of the coast. Finding an error when I came to lay down the Bay of Monterey, I altered my map to suit it. I knew nothing then of any errors in the coast. It is satisfactory now to find that my astronomical observations correspond with those previously made by Beechey and Belcher, and very gratifying to be able to add some testimonial to the correctness of those made by Malaspina long before either of them. Vancouver removed the coast line as fixed by Malaspina, and the subsequent observations carry it back.

In laying this map before the Senate, and in anticipation of the full work which my explorations (with some further examinations) may enable me to draw up hereafter, I deem it a proper accompaniment to the map to present some brief notices of CALIFORNIA, with a view to show the character of the country, and its capability or otherwise to sustain a considerable population. In doing this, no general remarks applicable to the whole of California can be used. The diversity in different parts is too great to admit of generalization in the description. Separate views of different parts must be taken; and in this brief sketch, the design is to limit the view to the two great divisions of the country which lie on the opposite sides of the SIERRA NEVADA, and to the character of that mountain itself, so prominent in the structure of the country, and exercising so great an influence over the climate, soil, and productions of its two divisions.

SIERRA NEVADA

This Sierra is part of the great mountain range, which, under different names and with different elevations, but with much uniformity

---

*Of this skillful, intrepid, and unfortunate navigator, Humboldt (Essay on New Spain) says: "The peculiar merit of his expedition consists not only in the number of astronomical observations, but principally in the judicious method which was employed to arrive at certain results. The longitude and latitude of four points on the coast (Cape San Lucas, Monterey, Nootka, and Fort Mulgrave) were fixed in an absolute manner."

of direction and general proximity to the coast, extends from the peninsula of California to Russian America, and without a gap in the distance through which the water of the Rocky mountains could reach the Pacific ocean, except at the two places where the Columbia and Frazer's river respectively find their passage. This great range is remarkable for its length, its proximity and parallelism to the sea coast, its great elevation, often more lofty than the Rocky mountains, and its many grand volcanic peaks, reaching high into the region of perpetual snow. Rising singly, like pyramids, from heavily timbered plateaus, to the height of fourteen and seventeen thousand feet above the sea, these snowy peaks constitute the characterizing feature of the range, and distinguish it from the Rocky mountains and all others on our part of the continent.

That part of this range which traverses the ALTA CALIFORNIA is called the *Sierra Nevada*, (Snowy mountains)—a name in itself implying a great elevation, as it is only applied, in Spanish geography, to the mountains whose summits penetrate the region of perpetual snow. It is a grand feature of California, and a dominating one, and must be well understood before the structure of the country and the character of its different divisions can be comprehended. It divides California into two parts, and exercises a decided influence on the climate, soil, and productions of each. Stretching along the coast, and at the general distance of 150 miles from it, this great mountain wall receives the warm winds, charged with vapor, which sweep across the Pacific ocean, precipitates their accumulated moisture in fertilizing rains and snows upon its western flank, and leaves cold and dry winds to pass on to the east. Hence the characteristic differences of the two regions—mildness, fertility, and a superb vegetable kingdom on one side, comparative barrenness and cold on the other.

The two sides of the Sierra exhibit two different climates. The state of vegetation, in connexion with some thermometrical observations made during the recent exploring expedition to Calfornia, will establish and illustrate this difference. In the beginning of December, 1845, we crossed this Sierra, at latitude 39° 17' 12", at the present usual emigrant pass [Donner Pass], at the head of the Salmon Trout [Truckee] river 40 miles north of New Helvetia, and made observations at each base, and in the same latitude, to determine the respective temperatures; the two bases being, respectively, the *western* about 500, and the *eastern* about 4,000 feet above the level of the sea; and the Pass, 7,200 feet. The mean results of the observations were, on the *eastern* side, at sunrise, 9°; at noon, 44°; at sunset, 30°; the state of vegetation and the appearance of the country being at the same time (second week of December) that of confirmed winter; the rivers frozen over, snow on the ridges, annual plants dead, grass dry, and deciduous trees stripped of their foliage. At the *western* base, the mean temperature during a corresponding week was, at sunrise 29°, and at sunset 52°; the state of the atmosphere and of vegetation that of advancing spring; grass fresh and green, four to eight inches high, vernal plants in bloom, the air soft, and all the streams free from ice. Thus December, on one side of the mountain, was winter; on the other it was spring.

THE GREAT BASIN

East of the Sierra Nevada, and between it and the Rocky mountains, is that anomalous feature in our continent, the GREAT BASIN, the existence of which was advanced as a theory after the second expedition, and is now established as a geographical fact. It is a singular feature: a basin of some five hundred miles diameter every way, between four and five thousand feet above the level of the sea, shut in all around by mountains, with its own system of lakes and rivers, and having no connexion whatever with the sea. Partly arid and sparsely inhabited, the general character of the GREAT BASIN is that of desert, but with great exceptions, there being many parts of it very fit for the residence of a civilized people; and of these parts, the Mormons have lately established themselves in one of the largest and best. Mountain is the predominating structure of the interior of the Basin, with plains between—the mountains wooded and watered, the plains arid and sterile. The interior mountains conform to the law which governs the course of the Rocky mountains and of the Sierra Nevada, ranging nearly north and south, and present a very uniform character of abruptness, rising suddenly from a narrow base of ten to twenty miles, and attaining an elevation of two to five thousand feet above the level of the country. They are grassy and wooded, showing snow on their summit peaks during the greater part of the year, and affording small streams of water from five to fifty feet wide, which lose themselves, some in lakes, some in the dry plains, and some in the belt of alluvial soil at the base; for these mountains have very uniformly this belt of alluvion, the wash and abrasion of their sides, rich in excellent grass, fertile, and light and loose enough to absorb small streams. Between these mountains are the arid plains which receive and deserve the name of desert. Such is the general structure of the interior of the Great Basin, more Asiatic than American in its character, and much resembling the elevated region between the Caspian sea and northern Persia. The rim of this Basin is massive ranges of mountains, of which the Sierra Nevada on the west, and the Wah-satch and Timpanogos chains on the east, are the most conspicuous.[1] On the north, it is separated from the waters of the Columbia by a branch of the Rocky mountains, and from the gulf of California, on the south, by a bed of mountainous ranges, of which the existence has been only recently determined. Snow abounds on them all; on some, in their loftier parts, the whole year, with wood and grass; with copious streams of water, sometimes amounting to considerable rivers, flowing inwards, and forming lakes or sinking in the sands. Belts or benches of good alluvion are usually found at their base.

Lakes in the Great Basin.—The Great Salt lake and the Utah lake are in this Basin, towards its eastern rim, and constitute its most interesting feature—one, a saturated solution of common salt—the other, fresh—the Utah about one hundred feet above the level of the Salt lake, which is itself four thousand two hundred above the level of the sea, and connected by a strait, or river, thirty-five miles long.

These lakes drain an area of ten or twelve thousand square miles, and have, on the east, along the base of the mountain, the usual bench of alluvion, which extends to a distance of three hundred miles, with wood and water, and abundant grass. The Mormons have established themselves on the strait between these two lakes, and will find sufficient arable land for a large settlement—important from its position as intermediate between the Mississippi valley and the Pacific ocean, and on the line of communication to California and Oregon.

The Utah is about thirty-five miles long, and is remarkable for the numerous and bold streams which it receives, coming down from the mountains on the southeast, all fresh water, although a large formation of rock salt, imbedded in red clay, is found within the area on the southeast, which it drains. The lake and its affluents afford large trout and other fish in great numbers, which constitute the food of the Utah Indians during the fishing season. The Great Salt lake has a very irregular outline, greatly extended at time of melting snows. It is about seventy miles in length; both lakes ranging nearly north and south, in conformity to the range of the mountains, and is remarkable for its predominance of salt. The whole lake waters seem thoroughly saturated with it, and every evaporation of the water leaves salt behind. The rocky shores of the islands are whitened by the spray, which leaves salt on everything it touches, and a covering like ice forms over the water, which the waves throw among the rocks. The shores of the lake in the dry season, when the waters recede, and especially on the south side, are whitened with encrustations of fine white salt; the shallow arms of the lake, at the same time, under a slight covering of briny water, present beds of salt for miles, resembling softened ice, into which the horses' feet sink to the fetlock. Plants and bushes, blown by the wind upon these fields, are entirely encrusted with crystallized salt, more than an inch in thickness. Upon this lake of salt the fresh water received, though great in quantity, has no perceptible effect. No fish, or animal life of any kind, is found in it; the *larvae* on the shore being found to belong to winged insects. A geological examination of the bed and shores of this lake is of the highest interest.

Five gallons of water taken from this lake in the month of September, and roughly evaporated over a fire, gave fourteen pints of salt, a part of which being subjected to analysis, gave the following proportions:

Chloride of sodium (common salt)	97.80 parts
Chloride of calcium	0.61 "
Chloride of magnesium	0.24 "
Sulphate of soda	0.23 "
Sulphate of lime	1.12 "
	100.00

Southward from the Utah is another lake of which little more is now known than when Humboldt published his general map of Mexico. It is the reservoir of a handsome river, about two hundred miles long, rising in the Wahsatch mountains, and discharging a considerable volume of water. The river and lake were called by the Spaniards, *Severo*, corrupted by the hunters into *Sevier*. On the map, they are called *Nicollet*, in honor of *J. N. Nicollet*, whose premature death interrupted the publication of the learned work on the physical geography of the basin of the Upper Mississippi, which five years of labor in the field had prepared him to give.[2]

On the western side of the basin, and immediately within the first range of the Sierra Nevada, is the Pyramid lake, receiving the water of Salmon Trout river. It is thirty-five miles long, between four and five thousand feet above the sea, surrounded by mountains, is remarkably deep and clear, and abounds with uncommonly large salmon trout. Southward, along the base of the Sierra Nevada, is a range of considerable lakes, formed by many large streams from the Sierra. Lake Walker, the largest among these, affords great numbers of trout, similar to those of the Pyramid lake, and is a place of resort for Indians in the fishing season.

There are probably other collections of water not yet known. The number of small lakes is very great, many of them more or less salty, and all, like the rivers which feed them, changing their appearance and extent under the influence of the season, rising with the melting of the snows, sinking in the dry weather, and distinctly presenting their high and low water mark. These generally afford some fertile and well-watered land, capable of settlement.

Rivers of the Great Basin.—The most considerable river in the interior of the Great Basin is the one called on the map Humboldt river, as the mountains at its head are called Humboldt river mountains— so called as a small mark of respect of the "*Nestor of scientific travellers*," who has done so much to illustrate North American geography, without leaving his name upon any one of its remarkable features. It is a river long known to hunters and sometimes sketched on maps under the name of Mary's, or Ogden's, but now for the first time laid down with any precision. It is a very peculiar stream, and has many characteristics of an Asiatic river—the Jordan, for example, though twice as long—rising in mountains and losing itself in a lake of its own, after a long and solitary course. It rises in two streams in mountains west of the Great Salt lake, which unite, after some fifty miles and bears westwardly along the northern side of the basin towards the Great Sierra Nevada, which it is destined never to reach, much less to pass. The mountains in which it rises are round and handsome in their outline, capped with snow the greater part of the year, well clothed with grass and wood, and abundant in water. The stream is a narrow line, without affluents, losing by absorption and evaporation as it goes, and terminating in a marshy lake, with low shores, fringed with bulrushes, and whitened with saline encrustations. It has a moderate current, is from two to six feet deep in the dry season, and probably not fordable anywhere below the junction of the forks during the time of melting snows, when both lake and river are considerably enlarged. The country through which it passes (except its immediate valley) is a dry sandy plain, without grass, wood, or arable soil; from about 4,700 feet (at the forks) to 4,200 feet (at the lake) above the level of the sea, winding among broken ranges of mountains, and varying from a few miles to twenty in breadth. Its own immediate valley is a rich alluvion, beautifully covered with blue grass, herd grass, clover, and other nutritious grasses; and its course is marked through the plain by a line of willow and cotton wood trees, serving for fuel. The Indians in the fall set fire to the grass and destroy all trees except in low grounds near the water.

This river possesses qualities which, in the progress of events, may give it both value and fame. It lies on the line of travel to California and Oregon, and is the best route now known through the Great Basin, and the one travelled by emigrants. Its direction, nearly east and west, is the right course for that travel. It furnishes a level unobstructed way for nearly three hundred miles, and a continuous supply of the indispensable articles of water, wood, and grass. Its head is towards the Great Salt lake, and consequently towards the Mormon settlement, which must become a point in the line of emigration to California and the lower Columbia. Its termination is within fifty miles of the base of the Sierra Nevada and opposite the Salmon Trout river pass—a pass only seven thousand two hundred feet above the level of the sea, and less than half that above the level of the Basin, and leading into the valley of the Sacramento, some forty miles north of Nueva Helvetia. These properties give to this river a prospective value in future communications with the Pacific ocean, and the profile view on the north of the map shows the elevations of the present travelling route, of which it is a part, from the South pass, in the Rocky mountains, to the bay of San Francisco.

The other principal rivers of the Great Basin are found on its circumference, collecting their waters from the Snowy mountains which surround it, and are, 1. BEAR RIVER, on the east, rising in the massive range of the Timpanogos mountains and falling into the Great Salt lake, after a doubling course through a fertile and picturesque valley, two hundred miles long. 2. The UTAH RIVER and TIMPANAOZU or TIMPANOGOS [Provo River], discharging themselves into the Utah lake on the east, after gathering their copious streams in the adjoining parts of the *Wah-satch* and Timpanogos mountains. 3. NICOLLET [Sevier] River, rising south in the long range of the *Wah-satch* mountains, and falling into a lake of its own name, after making an arable and grassy valley, two hundred miles in length, through mountainous country. 4. SALMON TROUT [Truckee] river, on the west, running down the Sierra Nevada and falling into Pyramid lake, after a course of about one hundred miles. From its source, about one-third of its valley is through a pine timbered country, and for the remainder of the way through very rocky, naked ridges. It is remarkable for the abundance and excellence of its salmon trout, and presents some ground for cultivation. 5. CARSON and WALKER rivers, both handsome clear water streams, nearly one hundred miles long, coming like the preceding, down the eastern flank of the Sierra Nevada and forming lakes of their own name at its base. They contain salmon trout and other fish, and form some large bottoms of good land. 6. OWENS RIVER, issuing from the Sierra Nevada on the south, is a large bold stream about one hundred and twenty miles long, gathering its waters in the Sierra Nevada, flowing to the southward, and forming a lake about fifteen miles long at the base of the mountains. At a medium stage it is generally four to five feet deep, in places fifteen; wooded with willow and cotton wood, and makes continuous bottoms of fertile land, at intervals rendered marshy by springs and small affluents from the mountain. The water of the lake in which it terminates has an unpleasant smell and bad taste, but around its shores are found small streams of pure water with good grass. On the map this has been called OWENS river.

Besides these principal rivers issuing from the mountains on the circumference of the Great Basin, there are many others, all around, all obeying the general law of losing themselves in sands, or lakes, or belts of alluvion, and almost all of them an index to some arable land, with grass and wood.

Interior of the Great Basin.—This interior of the Great Basin, so far as explored, is found to be a succession of sharp mountain ranges and naked plains, such as have been described. These ranges are isolated, presenting summit lines broken into many peaks, of which the highest are between ten and eleven thousand feet above the sea. They are thinly wooded with some varieties of pine, (*pinus monophyllus* characteristic,) cedar, aspen, and a few other trees; and afford an excellent quality of bunch grass, equal to any found in the Rocky mountains.

Black tailed deer and mountain sheep are frequent in these mountains; which, in consideration of their grass, water and wood, and the alluvion at their base, may be called fertile, in the radical sense of the word, as signifying a capacity to produce, or bear, and in contradistinction to sterility. In this sense these interior mountains may be called fertile. Sterility, on the contrary, is the absolute characteristic of the valleys between the mountains—no wood, no water, no grass; the gloomy artemisia the prevailing shrub—no animals, except the hares, which shelter in these shrubs, and fleet and timid antelope, always on the watch for danger, and finding no place too dry and barren which gives it a wide horizon for its view and a clear field for its flight. No birds are seen in the plains, and few on the mountains. But few Indians are found, and those in the lowest state of human existence; living not even in communities, but in the elementary state of families, and sometimes a single individual to himself—except about the lakes stocked with fish, which become the property and resort of a small tribe. The abundance and excellence of the fish, in most of these lakes, is a characteristic; and the fishing season is to the Indians the happy season of the year.

Climate of the Great Basin.—The climate of the Great Basin does not present the rigorous winter due to its elevation and mountainous structure. Observations made during the last expedition, show that around the southern shores of the Salt Lake, latitude 40° 30', to 41°, for two weeks of the month of October, 1845, from the 13th to the 27th, the mean temperature was 40° at sunrise, 70° at noon, and 54° at sunset; ranging at sunrise, from 28° to 57°; at noon, from 62° to 76°; at four in the afternoon, from 58° to 69°; and at sunset, from 47° to 57°.

Until the middle of the month the weather remained fair and very pleasant. On the 15th, it began to rain in occasional showers, which whitened with snow the tops of the mountains on the southeast side of the lake valley. Flowers were in bloom during all the month. About the 18th, on one of the large islands in the south of the lake, *helianthus* [sunflower], several species of *aster, erodium cicutarium* [filagree], and several other plants, were in fresh and full bloom; the grass of the second growth was coming up finely, and vegetation, generally, betokened the lengthened summer of the climate.

The 16th, 17th, and 18th, stormy with rain; heavy at night; peaks of the Bear river range and tops of the mountains covered with snow. On the 18th, cleared with weather like that of late spring, and continued mild and clear until the end of the month, when the fine weather was again interrupted by a day or two of rain. No snow within 2,000 feet above the level of the valley.

Across the interior, between latitudes 41° and 38°, during the month of November (5th to 25th) the mean temperature was 29° at sunrise, and 40° at sunset; ranging at noon (by detached observations) between 41° and 60°. There was a snow storm between the 4th and 7th, the snow falling principally at night, and sun occasionally breaking out in the day. The lower hills and valleys were covered a few inches deep with snow, which the sun carried off in a few hours after the storm was over.

The weather then continued uninterruptedly open until the close of the year, without rain or snow, and during the remainder of November, generally clear and beautiful; nights and mornings calm, a light breeze during the day, and strong winds of very rare occurrence. Snow remained only on the peaks of the mountains.

On the western side of the basin, along the base of the *Sierra Nevada*, during two weeks, from the 25th *November* to the 11th *December*, the mean temperature at sunrise was 11°, and at sunset 34°; ranging at sunrise from zero to 21°, and at sunset from 23° to 44°. For ten consecutive days of the same period, the mean temperature at noon was 45°, ranging from 33° to 56°.

The weather remained open, usually very clear, and the rivers were frozen.

The winter of '43–'44, within the basin, was remarkable for the same open, pleasant weather, rarely interrupted by rain or snow. In fact, there is nothing in the climate of this great interior region, elevated as it is, and surrounded and traversed by snowy mountains, to prevent civilized man from making it his home, and finding in its arable parts the means of a comfortable subsistence; and this the Mormons will probably soon prove in the parts about the Great Salt lake. The progress of their settlement is already great. On the first of April of the present year, they had 3,000 acres in wheat, seven saw and grist mills, seven hundred houses in a fortified enclosure of sixty acres, stock, and other accompaniments of a flourishing settlement.

Such is the Great Basin, heretofore characterized as a desert, and in some respects meriting that appellation; but already demanding the qualification of great exceptions, and deserving the full examination of a thorough exploration.

MARITIME REGION WEST OF THE
SIERRA NEVADA

West of the SIERRA NEVADA, and between that mountain and the
sea, is the second grand division of California, and the only part to
which the name applies in the current language of the country. It is
the occupied and inhabited part, and so different in character—so
divided by the mountain wall of the Sierra from the Great Basin
above—as to constitute a region to itself, with a structure and configuration—a soil, climate, and productions—of its own; and as northern Persia may be referred to as some type of the former, so may Italy
be referred to as some point of comparison for the latter. North and
south, this region embraces about ten degrees of latitude—from 32°,
where it touches the peninsula of California, to 42°, where it bounds
on Oregon. East and west, from the Sierra Nevada to the sea; it will
average, in the middle parts, 150 miles; in the northern parts 200—
giving an area of above one hundred thousand square miles. Looking
westward from the summit of the Sierra, the main feature presented
is the long, low, broad valley of the Joaquin and Sacramento rivers—
the two valleys forming one—five hundred miles long and fifty
broad, lying along the base of the Sierra, and bounded to the west by
the low coast range of mountains, which separates it from the sea.
Long dark lines of timber indicate the streams, and bright spots mark
the intervening plains. Lateral ranges, parallel to the Sierra Nevada
and the coast, make the structure of the country and break it into a
surface of valleys and mountains—the valleys a few hundred, and the
mountains two to four thousand feet above the sea. These form
greater masses, and become more elevated in the north, where some
peaks, as the Shastl [Shasta], enter the regions of perpetual snow.
Stretched along the mild coast of the Pacific, with a general elevation
in its plains and valleys of only a few hundred feet above the level of
the sea—and backed by the long and lofty wall of the Sierra—mildness and geniality may be assumed as the characteristic of its climate.
The inhabitant of corresponding latitudes on the Atlantic side of this
continent can with difficulty conceive of the soft air and southern productions under the same latitudes in the maritime region of Upper
California. The singular beauty and purity of the sky in the south of
this region is characterized by Humboldt as a rare phenomenon, and
all travellers realize the truth of his description.

The present condition of the country affords but slight data for forming correct opinions of the agricultural capacity and fertility of the soil. Vancouver found, at the mission of San Buenaventura, in 1792, latitude 34° 16′, apples, pears, plums, figs, oranges, grapes, peaches, and pomegranates growing together with the plantain, banana, cocoa nut, sugar cane, and indigo, all yielding fruit in abundance and of excellent quality. Humboldt mentions the olive oil of California as equal to that of Andalusia, and the wine like that of the Canary islands. At present, but little remains of the high and various cultivation which had been attained at the missions. Under the mild and paternal administration of the "*Fathers*," the docile character of the Indians was made available for labor, and thousands were employed in the fields, the orchards, and the vineyards. At present, but little of this former cultivation is seen. The fertile valleys are overgrown with wild mustard; vineyards and olive orchards, decayed and neglected, are among the remaining vestiges; only in some places do we see the evidences of what the country is capable. At San Buenaventura we found the olive trees, in January, bending under the weight of neglected fruit; and the mission of San Luis Obispo (latitude 35°) is still distinguished for the excellence of its olives, considered finer and larger than those of the Mediterranean.

The productions of the south differ from those of the north and of the middle. Grapes, olives, Indian corn, have been its staples, with many assimilated fruits and grains. Tobacco has been recently introduced; and the uniform summer heat which follows the wet season, and is uninterrupted by rain, would make the southern country well adapted to cotton. Wheat is the first product of the north, where it always constituted the principal cultivation of the missions. This promises to be the grain growing region of California. The moisture of the coast seems particularly suited to the potato and to the vegetables common to the United States, which grow to an extraordinary size.

Perhaps few parts of the world can produce in such perfection so great a variety of fruits and grains as the large and various region enclosing the bay of San Francisco and drained by its waters. A view of the map will show that region and its great extent, comprehending the entire valleys of the Sacramento and San Joaquin, and the whole western slope of the Sierra Nevada. General phrases fail to give precise ideas, and I have recourse to the notes in my journal to show its climate and productions by the test of the thermometer and the state of the vegetable kingdom.

VALLEYS OF THE SACRAMENTO
AND SAN JOAQUIN

These valleys are one, discriminated only by the names of the rivers which traverse it. It is a single valley—a single geographical formation—near 500 miles long, lying at the western base of the Sierra Nevada, and between it and the coast range of mountains, and stretching across the head of the bay of San Francisco, with which a *delta* of twenty-five miles connects it. The two rivers, San Joaquin and Sacramento, rise at opposite ends of this long valley, receive numerous streams, many of them bold rivers, from the Sierra Nevada, become themselves navigable rivers, flow toward each other, meet half way, and enter the bay of San Francisco together, in the region of tide water, making a continuous water line from one end to the other.

The valley of the San Joaquin is about 300 miles long and 60 broad, between the slopes of the coast mountain and the Sierra Nevada, with a general elevation of only a few hundred feet above the level of the sea. It presents a variety of soil, from dry and unproductive to well watered and luxuriantly fertile. The eastern (which is the fertile) side of the valley is intersected with numerous streams, forming large and very beautiful bottoms of fertile land, wooded principally with white oaks (*quercus longiglanda*, Torr. and Frem.) in open groves of handsome trees, often five or six feet in diameter, and sixty to eighty feet high. Only the larger streams, which are fifty to one hundred and fifty yards wide, and drain the upper parts of the mountains, pass entirely across the valley, forming the *Tulárè* lakes and the San Joaquin river, which, in the rainy season, make a continuous stream from the head of the valley to the bay. The *foot hills* of the Sierra Nevada, which limit the valley, make a woodland country, diversified with undulating grounds and pretty valleys, and watered with numerous small streams, which reach only a few miles beyond the hills, the springs which supply them not being copious enough to carry them across the plains. These afford many advantageous spots for farms, making sometimes large bottoms of rich moist land. The rolling surface of the hills presents sunny exposure, sheltered from the winds, and having a highly favorable climate and suitable soil, are considered to be well adapted to the cultivation of the grape and will probably become the principal vine growing region of California. The uplands bordering the valleys of the large streams are usually wooded with evergreen oaks, and the intervening plains are timbered with groves or belts of evergreen and white oaks among prairie and open land. The surface of the valley consists of level plains along the Tulárè lakes and San Joaquin river, changing into undulating and rolling ground nearer the foot hills of the mountains.

A condensed notice from observations, made during several journeys through the valley, will serve to give some definite ideas of its climate and character.

We left the upper settlements of New Helvetia on the 14th December, and, passing through the groves of oak which border the Rio de los Americanos, directed our course in a southeasterly direction across a plain toward the Rio de los Cos-um-nes, a handsome, well wooded stream, about thirty yards wide. The Cos-um-ne Indians, who give name to this river, have been driven away from it within a few years, and dispersed among other tribes; and several farms, of some leagues in extent, have already been established on the lower part of the stream. We encamped at one of these, about eight miles above the junction of the Cos-um-ne river with the Mo-kel-um-ne, which a few miles below enters a deep slough in the tide water of the San Joaquin *delta*.

At this place the temperature at sunset was 55°, and at sunrise 27°.

Our road on the 15th was over the plain between the Cos-um-ne[s] and Mo-kel-um-ne rivers, inclining toward the mountains. We crossed several wooded sloughs, with ponds of deep water, which, nearer the foot hills, are running streams, with large bottoms of fertile land; the greater part of our way being through open woods of evergreen and other oaks. The rainy season, which commonly begins with November, had not yet commenced, and the Mo-kel-um-ne river was at the low stage usual to the dry season, and easily forded. This stream is about sixty yards wide, and the immediate valley some thirty or forty feet below the upland plain. It has broad alluvial bottoms of very fertile soil—sometimes five hundred yards wide, bounded by a low upland, wooded with evergreen oaks. The weather in the evening was calm, the sky mottled with clouds, and the temperature at sunset 52°.

Leaving the Mo-kel-um-ne, (December 16,) we travelled about twenty miles through open woods of white oak, crossing in the way several stream beds—among them the Calaveras creek. These have abundant water with good land above; and the Calaveras makes some remarkably handsome bottoms. Issuing from the woods, we rode about sixteen miles over an open prairie, partly covered with bunch grass, the timber reappearing on the rolling hills of the river Stanislaus in the usual belt of evergreen oaks. The river valley was about forty feet below the upland, and the stream seventy yards broad, making the usual fertile bottoms, which here were covered with green grass among large oaks. We encamped in one of these bottoms in a grove of the large white oaks previously mentioned, as *quercus longiglanda* (*Torr. and Frem.*) This oak is a new species, belonging to the division of white oaks, distinguished by the length of its acorn, which is commonly an inch and a half, and sometimes two inches. This long acorn characterizes the tree, which has accordingly been specified by Dr. Torrey as *quercus longiglanda*—(long acorn oak.*) The tree attains frequently a diameter of six feet, and a height of eighty feet, with a wide spreading head. The many varieties of deciduous and evergreen oaks, which predominate throughout the valleys and lower hills of the mountains, afford large quantities of acorns, which constitute the principal food of the Indians of that region. Their great abundance, in the midst of fine pasture lands, must make them an important element in the agricultural economy of the country.

The day had been very warm, and at sunset the temperature was 55°, and the weather clear and calm.

At sunrise next morning, the thermometer was at 22°, with a light wind from the Sierra N. 75° E., and a clear pure sky, in which the blue line of the mountain showed distinctly. The way, for about three miles, was through open woods of evergreen and other oaks, with some shrubbery intermingled. Among this was a *lupinus* of extraordinary size, not yet in bloom. Emerging from the woods, we travelled in a southeasterly direction, over a prairie of rolling land, the ground becoming somewhat more broken as we approached the To-wal-um-ne [Tuolumne] river, one of the finest tributaries of the San Joaquin. The hills were generally covered with a species of geranium, (*erodium cicutarium*,) a valuable plant for stock, considered very nutritious. With this was frequently interspersed good and green bunch grass, and a plant commonly called *bur clover*. This plant, which in some places is very abundant, bears a spirally twisted pod, filled with seeds, which remains on the ground during the dry season, well preserved, and affords good food for cattle until the spring rains bring out new grass. We started a band of wild horses on approaching the river, and

---

*The names of plants mentioned in this memoir rest on the authority of Dr. Torrey, by whom the specimens have been examined.

the Indians ran off from a village on the bank—the men lurking around to observe us. About their huts were the usual acorn cribs, containing each some twenty or thirty bushels. We found here excellent grass, and broad bottoms of alluvial land, open-wooded, with large white oaks of the new species. The thermometer, at sunset, was at 54°.5, with a calm, clear atmosphere. Multitudes of geese and other wild fowl made the night noisy.

In the morning, the sky was clear, with an air from S. 55 E., and a hoar frost covering the ground like a light fall of snow. At sunrise, the thermometer was at 24°.5. Our course now inclined more towards the foot of the mountain, and led over a broken country. In about 17 miles we reached the river Aux-um-ne [Merced], another large affluent to the San Joaquin, and continued about six miles up the stream, intending to reach, gradually the heart of the mountains at the head of the *Lake Fork* [Kings River] of the Tulárè.

We encamped on the southern side of the river, where broken hills made a steep bluff, with a narrow bottom. On the northern side was a low, undulating wood and prairie land, over which a band of about three hundred elk was slowly coming to water where we halted, feeding as they approached.

December 19th. The weather continued clear and pleasant. We continued our journey in a southeasterly direction, over a broken and hilly country, without timber, and showing only scattered clumps of trees, from which we occasionally started deer. In a few hours' ride we reached a beautiful country of undulating upland, openly timbered with oaks, principally evergreen, and watered with small streams.[3] We came here among some villages of Indians, of the horse-thief tribes, who received us in an unfriendly manner; and, after a busy night among them, we retreated the next morning to a more open country of the lower hills. Our party was then a small one of 16 men, encumbered with cattle, which we were driving to the relief of the main body of the expedition, which had been sent southward from Walker's lake, in the basin, along the eastern base of the Sierra Nevada, and to which a valley in the mountains, on the Tulárè Lake Fork, had been appointed as a place of meeting.

In the evening, we encamped at an elevation of 1,000 feet above the sea, latitude 37° 07' 47", still among the hills, on a spring hollow, leading to the Upper Joaquin river. The day had been mild, with a faint sun and cloudy weather; and, at sunset, there were some light clouds in the sky, with a northeasterly wind, and a sunset temperature of 45°; probably rendered lower than usual by the air from the mountains, as the foot-hills have generally a warmer temperature than the open valley. Elk were numerous during the day, making, on one occasion, a broken band, several miles in length.

On the 21st, the thermometer at sunrise was 32.6; the sky slightly clouded, and, in the course of the morning, the clouds gathered heavy in the southwest. Our route lay in a southeasterly direction, toward the Upper Joaquin, crossing, among rolling hills, a large stream and several sandy beds of affluents to the main river. On the trees along these streams, as well as on the hills, I noticed mosses. About 2, in the afternoon, we reached the Upper San Joaquin. The stream was here about 70 yards wide, and much too deep to be forded. A little way below, we succeeded in crossing, at a rapid made by a bed of rock, below which, for several miles, the river appeared deep and not fordable. We followed down the stream for six or eight miles, and encamped on its banks, on the verge of the valley plain. At evening, rain began to fall, and, with this, the spring properly commenced. There had been a little rain in November, but not sufficient to revive vegetation.

December 22.—The temperature at sunrise was 39°. There had been heavy rain during the night, with high winds, and this morning, there was a thick fog, which began to go off at 8 o'clock, when the sun broke through. We crossed an open plain, still in a southeasterly direction, reaching, in about twenty miles, the *Tulares Lake* river. This is one of the largest and handsomest streams in the valley, being about 100 yards broad, and having, perhaps, a larger body of fertile land than any other. The broad alluvial bottoms are well wooded with several species of oaks. This is the principal affluent to the Tulàrè lake, (the bullrush lake,) a strip of water, about 70 miles long, surrounded by lowlands, rankly overgrown with bullrushes, and receiving all the rivers in the southern end of the valley. In times of high water, the lake discharges into the Joaquin, making a continuous water line through the whole extent of the valley.

We ascended this river to its sources in the Sierra Nevada, about 50 miles from the edge of the valley, which we reached again on the 7th of *January*, in the neighborhood of the Tulàrè lake. We found the temperature much the same as in December. Fogs, which rose from the lake in the morning, were dense, cold, and penetrating, but, after a few hours, gave place to a fine day. The face of the country had been much improved by the rains which had fallen while we remained in the mountains. Several humble plants, among them the golden flowered violet (*viola crysantha*) and *erodium cicutarium*, the first valley flowers of the spring, which courted a sunny exposure and warm sandy soil, were already in bloom on the southwestern hill slopes. In the foot hills of the mountains the bloom of the flowers was earlier. We travelled among multitudinous herds of elk, antelope, and wild horses. Several of the latter, which we killed for food, were found to be very fat. By the middle of *January*, when we had reached the lower San Joaquin, the new green grass covered the ground among the open timber on the rich river bottoms, and the spring vegetation had taken a vigorous start.

The mean temperature in the Joaquin valley, during the journey, from the middle of December to the middle of January, was at sunrise 29° and at sunset 52°, with generally a faint breeze from the snowy mountains in the morning, and calm weather at the evening. This was a lower temperature than we had found in the oak region of the mountains bordering the valley, between 1,000 and 5,000 feet above the level of the sea, where, throughout California, I have remarked the spring to be more forward than in the open valleys below.

During a journey through the valley, between the head of the Tulárè lakes and the mouth of the San Joaquin, from the 19th January to the 12th February, the mean temperature was 38° at sunrise, and 53° at sunset, with frequent rains. At the end of January, the river bottoms, in many places, were thickly covered with luxuriant grass, more than half a foot high. The California poppy, (*Eschscholtzia Californica*,) the characteristic plant of the California spring; *memophila insignis*, one of the earliest flowers, growing in beautiful fields of a delicate blue, and *erodium cicutarium*, were beginning to show a scattered bloom. Wild horses were fat, and a grisly bear, killed on the 2d February, had four inches thickness of fat on his back and belly, and was estimated to weigh a thousand pounds. Salmon was first obtained on the 4th February in the To-wal-um-né river, which, according to the Indians, is the most southerly stream in the valley in which this fish is found. By the middle of March, the whole valley of the San Joaquin was in the full glory of spring; the evergreen oaks were in flower, *geranium cicutarium* was generally in bloom, occupying the place of the grass, and making on all the uplands a close *sward*. The higher prairies between the rivers presented unbroken fields of yellow and orange colored flowers, varieties of *Layia* and *Eschscholtzia Californica*, and large bouquets of the blue flowering *nemophila* nearer the streams. These made the prevailing bloom, and the sunny hill slopes

517

to the river bottoms showed a varied growth of luxuriant flowers. The white oaks were not yet in bloom.

Observations made in the valley, from the bend of the Joaquin to the Cós-um-nè[s] river, give, for the mean temperature, from the 10th to the 22d March, 38° at sunrise, and 56° at sunset, the dew point being 35°.7, at sunrise, and 47°.6 at sunset, and the quantity of moisture contained in a cubic foot of air being 2.712 grains, and 4.072 grains, respectively.

A sudden change in the temperature was remarked in passing from the *To-wal-um-ne* to the *Stanislaus* river, there being no change in the weather, and the wind continuing from the northwest, to which we were more directly exposed on reaching the Stanislaus river, where we opened on the bay. In travelling down to the Stanislaus the mean temperature for five days (from the 11th to the 16th) was 40°.3 at sunrise, 73° at 4 p.m., and 63° at sunset; and detached observations gave 66° at 9, a.m., 77° at noon, and 87° at 2, p.m.

The dew point was 38°.0, 55°.5, 54°.3 at sunrise, at 4 in the afternoon, and at sunset; and the moisture contained in a cubic foot of air 2.878 grains, 5.209 grains, and 4.927 grains, respectively.

North of the Stanislaus for five days (from 16th to the 21st) the mean was 36°.6 at sunrise, 57° at 4, p.m., and 49° at sunset. The dew point was 34°.9 at sunrise, 37°.1 at 4, p.m., and 40°.9 at sunset, and the quantity of moisture in a cubic foot of air 2.671 grains, 2.983 grains, and 3.216 grains at the corresponding times. At sunrise on the 16th, on the To-wal-um-ne, the thermometer was at 43°, and at sunrise of the next morning, on the Stanislaus, at 35°.

The temperature was lowest on the night of the 17th. At sunrise of the morning following the thermometer was at 27°, and it was remarked that the frost affected several varieties of plants. On the 20th and 21st there were some showers of rain, the first since the end of February. These were preceded by southwesterly winds.

During December and the first part of January, which was still at the season of low waters, we were easily able to ford all the Joaquin tributaries. These begin to rise with the rains, and are kept up by the melting snows in the summer. At the end of January, the Joaquin required boating throughout the valley, and the tributaries were forded with difficulty.

In the latter part of March, of a dry season, (1844,) we were obliged to boat the Stanislaus, To-wal-um-ne, and Aux-um-ne, and the San Joaquin was no where fordable below the bend where it is joined by the slough of the Tulárè lake. On the 13th of March, 1846, we were obliged to boat the San Joaquin, the river being no where fordable below the junction of the slough, and the Indians guided us to some difficult fords of the large tributaries, where we succeeded to cross with damage to our equipage. In July of the same year, we boated the San Joaquin below the Aux-um-ne, it being no where fordable below the bend.

In June, 1847, the Joaquin was no where fordable, being several hundred yards broad as high up as the Aux-um-ne river, even with its banks, and scattered in sloughs over all its lower bottoms. All the large tributaries, the Aux-um-ne, To-wal-um-ne, Stanislaus, and Mo-kel-um-ne, required to be boated, and were pouring down a deep volume of water from the mountains, one to two hundred yards wide. The high waters came from the melting snows, which, during the past winter, had accumulated to a great depth in the mountains, and, at the end of June, lay in the approaches to the Bear river pass, on a breadth of ten or fifteen miles, and this below the level of 7,200 feet. In rainy seasons, when the rains begin with November, and the snows lie on the mountains till July, this river is navigable for 8 months of the year—the length of time depending on the season.

The Cos-um-ne was the last tributary of the San Joaquin, and the last river of its valley coming down from the Sierra Nevada. The *Rio de los Americanos* was the first tributary of the valley of the Sacramento, also coming down, like all the respectable tributaries of both rivers from the snowy summit and rainy sides of the great Sierra. The two valleys are *one*, only discriminated in description or reference by the name of the river which traverses the respective halves, as seen in the map. We entered the part of the valley which takes the name of its river, *Sacramento*, on the 21st day of March, going north, and continued our observations on that valley.

We remained several days on the Rio de los Americanos, to recruit our animals on the abundant range between the Sacramento and the hills. During this time the thermometer was at 35° at sunrise, 54° at 9 o'clock in the morning, 63° at noon, 63° at 2 in the afternoon, 61° at 4, and 53° at sunset; the dew point at corresponding times being 34°.0, 49°.9, 46°.6, 49°.4, 51°.6, 43°.7; and the quantity of moisture in a cubic foot of air being 2.519 grs., 4.235 grs., 3.808 grs., 4.161 grs., 4.484 grs., 3.469 grs.

We left the Rio de los Americanos on the 24th, ten miles above the mouth, travelling a little east of north, in the direction of the Bear river settlements, at the foot of the Emigrant Pass. The road led among oak timber, over ground slightly undulating, covered with grass intermingled with flowers. The thermometer at 4 was 76°, and at sunset 60°; the weather clear.

At sunrise of the 25th, the temperature was 36°, with an easterly wind and clear sky. In about thirty miles travel to the north, we reached the rancho of Mr. [Sebastian] Keyser, on Bear river; an affluent to *Feather* river, the largest tributary of the Sacramento. The route lay over an undulating country—more so as our course brought us nearer the mountains—wooded with oaks and shrubbery in blossom, with small prairies intervening. Many plants were in flower, and among them the California poppy, unusually magnificent. It is the characteristic bloom of *California* at this season, and the Bear river bottoms, near the hills, were covered with it. We crossed several small streams, and found the ground miry from the recent rains. The temperature at 4 in the afternoon was 70°, and at sunset 58°, with an easterly wind, and the night bright and clear.

The morning of the 25th was clear, and warmer than usual; the wind southeasterly, and the temperature 40°. We travelled across the valley plain, and in about 16 miles reached Feather river at 26 miles from its junction with the Sacramento, near the mouth of the *Yuva* [Yuba], so called from a village of Indians who live on it. The river has high banks—20 or 30 feet—and was here 150 yards wide, a deep, navigable stream. The Indians aided us across the river with canoes and small rafts. Extending along the bank in front of the village, was a range of wicker cribs, about twelve feet high, partly filled with what is there the Indians' staff of life—acorns. A collection of huts, shaped like bee hives, with naked Indians sunning themselves on the tops, and these acorn cribs, are the prominent objects of an Indian village.

There is a fine farm, or *rancho*, on the Yuva, stocked with about 3,000 head of cattle, and cultivated principally in wheat, with some other grains and vegetables, which are carried, by means of the river, to a market in San Francisco. Mr. [Theodor] Cordua, a native of Germany, who is proprietor of the place, informed me that his average harvest of wheat was about twenty-five bushels to the acre, which he supposed would be about the product of the wheat lands in the Sacramento valley. The labor on this and other farms in the valley is performed by Indians.

The temperature here was 74°. at 2 in the afternoon, 71°. at 4, and 69°. at sunset, with a northeasterly wind and clear sky.

At sunrise of the 27th the temperature was 42°., clear, with a north-easterly wind. We travelled northwardly, up the right bank of the river, which was wooded with large white and evergreen oaks, interspersed with thickets of shrubbery in full bloom. We made a pleasant journey of twenty-seven miles, and encamped at the bend of the river, where it turns from the course across the valley to run southerly to its junction with the Sacramento. The thermometer at sunset was at 67°, sky partially clouded, with southerly wind.

The thermometer at sunrise on the 28th was at 46°.5., with a northeasterly wind. The road was over an open plain, with a few small sloughs or creeks that do not reach the river. After travelling about fifteen miles we encamped on *Butte* creek, a beautiful stream of clear water about fifty yards wide, with a bold current running all the year. It has large fertile bottoms, wooded with open groves, and having a luxuriant growth of pea vine among the grass. The oaks here were getting into general bloom. Fine ranchos have been selected on both sides [of] the stream, and stocked with cattle, some of which were now very fat. A rancho [Esquón] here is owned by [Samuel] Neal, who formerly belonged to my exploring party. There is a *rancheria* (Indian village) near by and some of the Indians gladly ran races for the head and offals of a fat cow which had been presented to us. They were *entirely* naked. The thermometer at 2 in the afternoon was at 70°, two hours later at 74°, and 65° at sunset; the wind east, and sky clear only in the west.

The temperature at sunrise the next day was 50°, with cumuli in the south and west; which left a clear sky at 9, with a northwest wind, and temperature of 64°. We travelled 20 miles, and encamped on Pine creek, another fine stream, with bottoms of fertile land, wooded with groves of large and handsome oaks, some attaining to six feet in diameter, and forty to seventy feet in height. At 4 in the afternoon the thermometer showed 74° and 64° at sunset; and the sky clear, except in the horizon.

March 30.—The sun rose in masses of clouds over the eastern mountains. A pleasant morning, with a sunrise temperature of 46°.5, and some *mosquitoes*—never seen, as is said, in the coast country; but at seasons of high water abundant and venomous in the bottoms of the Joaquin and Sacramento. On the tributaries nearer the mountain but few are seen, and those go with the sun. Continuing up the valley, we crossed in a short distance a large wooded creek having now about thirty-five feet breadth of water. Our road was over an upland prairie of the Sacramento, having a yellowish, gravelly soil, generally two or three miles from the river, and twelve or fifteen from the foot of the eastern mountains. On the west it was 25 or 30 miles to the foot of the mountains, which here made a bed of high and broken ranges. In the afternoon, about half a mile above its mouth, we encamped on Deer creek, another of these beautiful tributaries to the Sacramento. It has the usual broad and fertile bottom lands common to these streams, wooded with groves of oak and a large sycamore, (*platanus occidentalis*,)[4] distinguished by bearing its balls in strings of three to five, and peculiar to California. Mr. [Peter] Lassen, a native of Germany,[5] has established a rancho here, which he has stocked, and is gradually bringing into cultivation. Wheat, as generally throughout the north country, gives large returns; cotton, planted in the way of experiment, was not injured by frost, and succeeded well; and he has lately planted a vineyard, for which the Sacramento valley is considered to be singularly well adapted. The seasons are not yet sufficiently understood, and too little has been done in agriculture, to afford certain knowledge of the capacities of the country. This farm is in the 40th degree of latitude; our position on the river being in 30°. 57′.00″., and longitude 121°.56′.44″. west from Greenwich, and elevation above the sea 560 feet. About three miles above the mouth of this stream are the first rapids—the present head of navigation—in the Sacramento river, which, from the rapids to its mouth in the bay, is more than 200 miles long, and increasing in breadth from 150 yards to 600 yards in the lower part of its course.

During six days that we remained here, from the 30th March to 5th April, the mean temperature was 40° at sunrise, 52°.5 at 9 in the morning, 57°.2 at noon, 59°.4 at 2 in the afternoon, 58°.8 at 4, and 52° at sunset; at the corresponding times the dew point was at 37°.0, 41°.0, 38°.1, 39°.6, 44°.9, 40°.5; and the moisture in a cubic foot of air 2.838 grs., 3.179 grs., 2.935 grs., 3.034 grs., 3.766 grs., 3.150 grs., respectively. Much cloudy weather and some showers of rain, during this interval, considerably reduced the temperature, which rose with fine weather on the 5th. Salmon was now abundant in the Sacramento. Those which we obtained were generally between three and four feet in length, and appeared to be of two distinct kinds. It is said that as many as four different kinds ascend the river at different periods. The great abundance in which this fish is found gives it an important place among the resources of the country. The salmon crowd in immense numbers up the Umpqua, Tlamath [Klamath], and Trinity rivers, and into every little river and creek on the coast north of the Bay [of] San Francisco, ascending the river Tlamath to the lake near its source, which is upwards of 4,000 feet above the sea, and distant from it only about 200 miles.

In the evening of the 5th we resumed our journey northward, and encamped on a little creek, near the Sacramento, where an emigrant from "the States" was establishing himself, and had already built a house. It is a handsome place, wooded with groves of oak, and along the creek are sycamore, ash, cotton wood, and willow. The day was fine, with a northwest wind.

The temperature at sunrise the next day, (April 6th,) was 42°, with a northeasterly wind. We continued up the Sacramento, which we crossed in canoes at a farm on the right bank of the river. The Sacramento was here about 140 yards wide, and with the actual stage of water, which I was informed continued several months, navigable for a steamboat. We encamped a few miles above, on a creek wooded principally with large oaks. Grass was good and abundant, with wild oats and pea vine in the bottoms. The day was fine, with a cool north-westerly breeze, which had in it the air of the high mountains. The wild oats here were not yet headed.

The snowy *Peak of Shastl* bore directly north, showing out high above the other mountains. Temperature at sunset 57°, with a west wind and sky partly clouded.

April 7.—The temperature at sunrise was 37°, with a moist air; and a faintly clouded sky indicated that the wind was southerly along the coast. We travelled toward the Shastl peak, the mountain ranges, on both sides of the valleys, being high and rugged, and snow-covered. Some remarkable peaks in the Sierra, to the eastward are called *the Sisters*, and, nearly opposite, the Coast Range shows a prominent peak, which we have called Mount Linn.[6]

Leaving the Sacramento, at a stream called *Red Bank creek*, and continuing to the head of one of its forks, we entered on a high and somewhat broken upland, timbered with at least four varieties of oaks, with *mansanita (arbutus Menziesii)* [*Arctostaphylos* sp.] and other shrubbery interspersed. A remarkable species of pine, having leaves in threes, (sometimes six to nine inches long,) with bluish foliage, and a spreading, oak-shaped top, was scattered through the timber. I have remarked that this tree grows lower down the mountains than the other pines, being found familiarly associated with the oaks, the first met after leaving the open valleys, and seeming to like a warm climate. Flowers were as usual abundant. The splendid California poppy characterized all the route along the valley. A species of clover was in bloom, and the berries of the *mansanita* were beginning to redden on some trees, while on others they were still in bloom. We encamped at an elevation of about 1,000 feet above the sea, on a large stream called Cottonwood creek, wooded on the bottoms with oaks, and with cottonwoods along the bed, which is sandy and gravelly. The water was at this time about twenty yards wide, but is frequently fifty. The face of the country traversed during the day was gravelly, and the bottoms of the creek where we encamped have a sandy soil.

There are six or seven *rancherias* of Indians on the Sacramento river between the farm where we had crossed the Sacramento and the mouth of this creek, and many others in the mountains about the heads of these streams.

The next morning was cloudy, threatening rain, but the sky grew brighter as the sun rose, and a southerly wind changed to northwest, which brought, as it never fails to bring, clear weather.

We continued 16 miles up the valley, and encamped on the Sacramento river. In the afternoon (April 8) the weather again grew thick, and in the evening rain began to fall in the valley and snow on the mountains. We were now near the head of the lower valley, and the face of the country and the weather began sensibly to show the influence of the rugged mountains which surround and terminate it.

The valley of the Sacramento is divided into upper and lower—the lower two hundred miles long, the upper about one hundred; and the latter not merely entitled to the distinction of upper, as being higher up on the river, but also as having a superior elevation of some thousands of feet above it. The division is strongly and geographically marked. The Shastl peak stands at the head of the lower valley, in the forks of the river, rising from a base of about 1,000 feet, out of a forest of heavy timber. It ascends like an immense column upwards of 14,000 feet, (nearly the height of Mont Blanc,)[7] the summit glistening with snow, and visible, from favorable points of view, at a distance of 140 miles down the valley. The river here, in descending from the upper valley, plunges down through a *cañon*, falling 2,000 feet in twenty miles. This upper valley is 100 miles long, heavily timbered, the climate and productions modified by its altitude, its more northern position, and the proximity and elevation of the neighboring mountains covered with snow. It contains valleys of arable land, and is deemed capable of settlement. Added to the lower valley, it makes the whole valley of the Sacramento 300 miles long.

April 9.—At 10 o'clock the rain which commenced the previous evening had ceased, and the clouds clearing away, we boated the river, and continued our journey eastward toward the foot of the Sierra. The Sacramento bottoms here are broad and prettily wooded, with soil of a sandy character. Our way led through very handsome, open woods, principally of oaks, mingled with a considerable quantity of the oak-shaped pine. Interspersed among these were bouquets or thickets of *mansanita*, and an abundant white-flowering shrub, now entirely covered with small blossoms. The head of the valley here (lower valley) is watered by many small streams, having fertile bottom lands, with a good range of grass and acorns. In about six miles we crossed a creek 20 or 25 feet wide, and several miles farther descended into the broad bottom of a swift stream about 20 yards wide, called Cow creek, so named as being the range of a small band of cattle, which ran off here from a party on their way to Oregon. They are entirely wild, and are hunted like other game. A large band of antelope was seen in the timber, and five or six deer came darting through the woods. An antelope and several deer were killed. There appear to be two species of these deer—both of the kind generally called black-tailed; one, a larger species frequenting the prairies and lower grounds; the other, much smaller, and found in the mountains only. The mountains in the northeast were black with clouds when we reached the creek, and very soon a fierce hail storm burst down on us, scattering our animals and covering the ground an inch in depth with hailstones about the size of wild cherries. The face of the country appeared as whitened by a fall of snow, and the weather became unpleasantly cold. The evening closed in with rain, and thunder rolling around the hills. Our elevation here was between 1,000 and 1,100 feet. At sunrise the next morning the thermometer was at 33°. The surrounding mountains showed a continuous line of snow, and the high peaks looked wintry. Turning to the southward, we retraced our steps down the valley, and reached Mr. Lassen's, on Deer river, on the evening of the 11th. The Sacramento bottoms between Antelope and Deer river were covered with oats, which had attained their full height, growing as in sown fields. The country here exhibited the maturity of spring. The California poppy was every where forming seed pods, and many plants were in flower and seed together. Some varieties of clover were just beginning to bloom. By the middle of the month the seed vessels of the California poppy, which, from its characteristic abundance, is a prominent feature in the vegetation, had attained their full size; but the seeds of this and many other plants, although fully formed, were still green colored, and not entirely ripe. At this time I obtained from the San Joaquin valley seeds of the poppy, and other plants, black and fully ripe, while they still remained green in this part of Sacramento—the effect of a warmer climate in the valley of the San Joaquin. The mean temperature for 14 days, from the 10th to the 24th of April, was 43° at sunrise, 58° at 9 in the morning, 64° at noon, 66° at 2 in the afternoon, 69° at 4, and 58° at sunset (latitude 40°.) The thermometer ranged at sunrise from 38° to 51°, at 4 (which is the hottest of those hours of the day when the temperature was noted) from 53° to 88°, and at sunset from 49° to 65°. The dew point was 40°.3 at sunrise, 47°.3 at 9 in the morning, 46°.1 at noon, 49°.2 at 2 in the afternoon, 40.°2 at 4, and 46.°6 at sunset; and the quantity of moisture in a cubic foot of air at corresponding times was 3. grs. 104, 3. grs. 882, 3. grs. 807, 4. grs. 213, 4. grs. 217, 3. grs. 884, respectively. The winds fluctuated between northwest and southeast, the temperature depending more upon the state of the sky than the direction of winds—a clouded sky always lowering the thermometer fifteen or twenty degrees in a short time. For the greater number of the days above given the sky was covered and the atmosphere frequently thick, with rain at intervals from the 19th to the 23rd.

On the 25th May we returned to this place (Lassen's) from an excursion to the Upper Sacramento. The plants we had left in bloom were now generally in seed; and many, including the characteristic plants, perfectly ripe. The mean temperature of a few days ending May was 54°.7 at sunrise, 70°.6 at noon, and 67°.3 at sunset. Travelling south into the more open and wider part of the valley, where the bordering mountains are lower and showed less snow, the temperature increased rapidly. At the *Buttes*—an isolated mountain ridge about six miles long and about 2,690 feet above the sea—the mornings were pleasantly cool for a few hours, but before ten the heat of the sun became very great, though usually tempered by a refreshing breeze. The heat was usually greatest about four in the afternoon. The mean temperature from May 27th to June 6th was 64° at sunrise, 79° at nine in the morning, 86° at noon, 90° at two in the afternoon, 91° at four, and 80° at sunset, ranging from 53° to 79° at sunrise—from 85° to 98° at four in the afternoon—and from 73° to 89° at sunset. The place of observation was at the eastern base of the *Buttes*, about 800 feet above the sea, latitude 39° 12', and one of the warmest situations in the Sacramento valley. At corresponding times the dew point was at 56°.5, 62°.4, 66°.5, 68°.2, 66°.6, 66°.9, and the quantity of moisture in a cubic foot of air 5. grs. 253, 6. grs. 318, 7. grs. 191, 7. grs. 495, 7. grs. 164, and 7. grs. 269, respectively. We felt the heat here more sensibly than at any other place where our journeying brought us in California. The hunters always left the camp before daylight, and were in by nine o'clock, after which the sun grew hot. Game was very fat and abundant; upwards of eighty deer, elk, and bear were killed in one morning. The range consisted of excellent grasses, wild oats in fields, red and other varieties of cover, some of which were now in mature seed and others beginning to flower. Oats were now drying in level places where exposed to the full influence of the sun, remaining green in moister places and on the hill slopes.

The mean temperature at the open valley between the Buttes and the American fork from the 8th to the 21st June, was 57° at sunrise, 74° at nine in the morning, 85° at noon, 87° at two in the afternoon, 88° at four, and 77° at sunset; ranging at sunrise from 51° to 61°; at 4 from 81° to 97°, and at sunset from 71° to 85°. The dew point at corresponding times was 52°.8, 58°.8, 62°.1, 66°.8, 62°.5, 60°.7 and the quantity of moisture in a cubic feet of air being 4.685 gr., 5.700 grs., 6.320 grs., 7.217 grs., 6.377 grs., 5.973 grs., respectively.

Western slope of the Sierra Nevada.—The western flank of this Sierra belongs to the maritime region of California and is capable of adding greatly to its value. It is a long, wide slope, timbered and grassy, with intervals of arable land, copiously watered with numerous and bold streams, and without the cold which its name and altitude might imply. In length it is the whole extent of the long valley at its base, five hundred miles. In breadth, it is from forty to seventy miles from the summit of the mountain to the termination of the foot hills in the edge of the valleys below, and almost the whole of it available for some useful purpose—timber, pasturage, some arable land, mills, quarries—and so situated as to be convenient for use, the wide slope of the mountain being of easy and practicable descent. Timber holds the first place in the advantages of this slope, the whole being heavily wooded, first with oaks, which predominate to about half the elevation of the mountain, and then with pines, cypress, and cedars, the pines predominating; and hence, called the pine region, as that below is called the oak region, though mixed with other trees. The highest summits of the Sierra are naked, massive granite rock, covered with snow, in sheltered places, all the year round. The oaks are several varieties of white and black oak, and evergreens, some of them resembling live oak. Of the white oak there are some new species attaining a handsome elevation, upon a stem six feet in diameter. Acorns of uncommon size, and not bad taste, used regularly for food by the Indians, abound on these trees, and will be of great value for stock. The cypress, pine, and cedar are between 100 and 250 feet high, and five to twelve feet in diameter, with clean solid stems. Grass abounds on almost all parts of the slope; except toward the highest summits, and is fresh and green all the year round, being neither killed by cold in the winter, nor dried by want of rain in the summer. The foot hills of the slope are sufficiently fertile and gentle to admit of good settlements; while valleys, coves, beaches, and meadows of arable land are found throughout. Many of the numerous streams, some of them amounting to considerable rivers, which flow down the mountain side, make handsome, fertile valleys. All these streams furnish good water power. The climate in the lower part of the slope is that of constant spring, while above, the cold is not in proportion to the elevation. Such is the general view of the western slope of the great Sierra; but deeming that all general views should rest upon positive data, I add some notes taken from actual observations made in different ascents and descents in the winter and spring of 1845–'46, and in different degrees of latitude from 35° to 41°.

December 4, 1845—Descent from the pass, at the head of Salmon Trout river, latitude 39° 17', elevation 7,200 feet. At 3 in the afternoon the temperature at 46°, at sunset 34°, at sunrise next morning 22°, the sky perfectly clear; no snow in the pass, but much on the mountain tops. Here the present emigrant road now crosses. A fork of bear river (a considerable stream tributary to Feather river, which falls into the Sacramento) leads from the pass, and the road follows it; but finding this a rugged way, we turned to the south, and encamped in a mountain meadow of good green grass. A yellow moss very abundant on the north sides of the pines.

December 6.—The route over good travelling ground, through open pine forest on a broad, leading ridge, affording an excellent road. A species of cedar (*Thuya gigantea*) occurred, often of extraordinary height and size. *Pinus lambertiani* was one of the most frequent trees, distinguished among cone-bearing tribes by the length of its cones, sometimes sixteen or eighteen inches long. The Indians eat the inner part of the burr, and large heaps of them were seen where they had been collected. Leaving the higher ridges, and gaining the smoother spurs, and descending about 4,000 feet, the face of the country changed rapidly. The country became low, rolling, and pretty; the pines began to disappear, and varieties of oak, and principally an evergreen resembling oak, became the predominating forest growth. These oaks bear great quantities of large acorns, the principal food of all the wild Indians. At a village of a few huts which we came upon there was a large supply of these acorns—eight or ten cribs of wicker work, containing about twenty bushels each. The best acorns are obtained from a large tree belonging to the division of white oaks, which is very abundant, and generally forms the groves on the bottom lands of the streams—standing apart, with a clean undergrowth of grass, giving them the appearance of cultivated parks. It is a noble forest tree, already mentioned as a new species, sixty to eighty feet high, with a tufted summit of spreading branches, and frequently attains a diameter of six feet. The largest we measured reached eleven feet. The evergreen oaks generally have a low growth with long branches and spreading tops. Some of them are suitable for ship timber, and have already been used for that purpose.

At our evening encampment of the 8th, which was at an elevation of five hundred feet above the sea, latitude 38° 53', and distant from the seacoast about one hundred miles, the temperature at sunset was 48°, the sky clear and calm, weather delightful, and the vegetation that of early spring. We were still upon the foothills of the mountains, where the soil is sheltered by woods, and where rain falls much more frequently than in the open Sacramento valley, near the edge of which we then were. I have been in copious, continuous rains of eighteen or twenty hours' duration in the oak region of the mountain, when not a drop fell in the valley below. Innumerable small streams have their rise and course through these foot hills, which never reach the river of the valley, but are absorbed in its light soil. The large streams coming from the upper parts of the mountain make valleys of their own, of fertile soil, covered with luxuriant grass and interspersed with groves. This is the general character of the foot hills throughout the entire length of the Sacramento and San Joaquin valleys—a broad belt of country, and probably destined to become a vine growing, as well as a grain and pastoral country.

December 9.—Entered the valley of the Sacramento. Fresh, green grass for eight or ten miles into the valley, cattle feeding upon it, or lying under the shade of trees—the shade being pleasant to our own feelings. Further in, towards the middle of the valley, where the spring rains had not yet commenced, the country looked parched and dry, the grass eaten down by the cattle, which were quite fat and fine beef.

Ascent, December and January, 1845–46, latitude 37°. Entering the mountain by the *Rio Reyes* [Kings River], of Tulárè lake, (December 24), we found its general character very similar to what it was in the northern part, (latitude 39°,) the timber perhaps less heavy and more open, and the mountain generally more rough, extremely rocky in the upper parts, but wooded up the granite ridges which compose its rocky eminences. At the elevation of 3,500 feet the ridges were covered with oaks and pines intermixed, and the bottom lands with oaks, cottonwood, and sycamores. Small varieties of evergreen oaks reached the observed height of 9,480 feet, at which elevation *pinus lambertiani,* and other varieties of pine, fir, and cypress, were large and lofty trees. During the latter part of December and first days of January the average temperature of the oak region, going to about 5,000 feet above the sea, was, at sunrise, 34°.6, and at sunset 50°.5. In the piney region, between this height and 1,100 feet, the average at sunrise was 28°.7, and at sunset, 30°.4. The lowest observed temperature was at sunset of January 1, when the sky had entirely cleared after a severe snow storm. The thermometer then stood at 8°.5, the elevation above the sea being 9,400 feet. Descending to the oak region, spring weather, rain and sunshine, prevailed. At an elevation of 4,500 feet the temperature, at the night encampment of the 3d day of January, was 38° at sunset, and the same at sunrise, the grass green, and growing freshly under the oaks. The snow line was then at about 6,000 feet above the level of the sea. Rain had begun to fall in the valley of the San Joaquin in this latitude (37°) on the 20th of December, and snow at the same time upon the summit of the mountain. The mean temperature of the mountain during this ascent and descent (December 24 to January 8) was 31°.6 at sunrise, 40°.4 at sunset.

Descent by Mr. Kern's party, latitude 35°.30′, December and January. Mr. Kern, with a detached party, had crossed the Sierra about one hundred miles further south, nearly opposite the head of the Tulárè lakes, and remained encamped in a valley or cove, near the summit of the Sierra, at the head of Kern's river, from December 27th to January 17th; the cove well wooded with evergreen oaks, some varieties of pine, firs and cedars, maintaining the usual majestic growth, which characterizes the cone-bearing trees of the Sierra. Until the 12th of January the weather almost that of summer, when the rains commenced, which was almost three weeks later than in latitude 37°. The 17th there was a fall of snow, washed off in the cove by a rain in the afternoon, the high ridges remaining covered a foot deep. The mean temperature in the cove from December 27th to January 17th was at sunrise 26°, at noon 60°, at sunset 52°. After that, snow and rain, alternated with sunshine, snow remaining on the ridges, and winter set in fairly on all the upper half of the mountain.

Ascent about latitude 41°, (April and May,) April 26, 1846—head of the lower Sacramento valley. Left the river Sacramento, going up one of the many pretty little streams that flow into the river around the head of the lower valley. On either side low, steep ridges were covered along their summits with pine, and oaks occupied the somewhat broad bottoms of the creek. Snowy peaks made the horizon on the right, and the temperature at noon was 71°, but the day was still and hot. The small streams are numerous here and have much bottom land; grass and acorns abundant, and both of excellent quality. Encamped in the evening in latitude 40° 38′ 58″, elevation above the sea 1,080 feet, temperature at sunset 56°, weather pleasant. Grisly bears numerous, four being killed by the hunters after we had encamped.

April 27.—Found a good way along a flat ridge, a pretty, open mountain stream on the right, the country beginning to assume a mountainous character, wooded with mingled oak and long leaved pine, and having a surface of scattered rocks, with grass and flowers. At noon, crossing a high ridge, the thermometer showed 61°. At night, at an elevation of 2,460 feet, we encamped on a creek that went roaring into the valley; temperature at sunset 52°.

28th, continued up the stream on which we had encamped, the country rising rapidly, clothed with heavy timber. On crossing one of the high ridges, snow and *pinus lambertiani* appeared together. An hour before noon reached the pass in the main ridge, in an open pine forest, elevation 4,600 feet, thermometer at 50°, latitude near 41°. Snow in patches, and deciduous oaks mixed with the pines.

Returning upon a different line, towards the lower valley of the Sacramento, near its head, we found in the descent a truly magnificent forest. It was composed mainly of a cypress and a lofty white cedar (*Thuya gigantea*) 120 to 140 feet high, common in the mountains of California. All were massive trees; but the *cypress* was distinguished by its uniformly great bulk. None were seen so large as are to

531

be found in the coast mountains near Santa Cruz, but there was a greater number of large trees—seven feet being a common diameter—carrying the bulk eighty or a hundred feet without a limb. At an elevation of four thousand six hundred feet the temperature at sunset was 48°, and at sunrise 37°. Oaks already appeared among the pines, but did not yet show a leaf. In the meadow marshes of the forest grass was green, but not yet abundant, and the deer were poor. Descending the flanks of the mountain, which fell gradually towards the plain, the way was through the same deep forest. At the elevation of about 3,000 feet the timber had become more open, the hills rolling, and many streams made pretty bottoms of rich grass; the black oaks in full and beautiful leaf were thickly studded among the open pines, which had become much smaller and fewer in variety, and when we halted near midday, at an elevation of 2,200 feet, we were in one of the most pleasant days of late spring; cool and sunny, with a pleasant breeze, amidst a profusion of various flowers; many trees in dark summer foliage, and some still in bloom. Among these the white spikes of the horse-chesnut, common through the oak region, were conspicuous. We had again reached summer weather, and the temperature at noon was 70°.

In the afternoon we descended to the open valley of the Sacramento, 1,000 feet lower, where the thermometer was 68° at sunset, and 54° at sunrise. This was the best timbered region that I had seen, and the more valuable from its position near the head of the lower valley of the Sacramento, and accessible from its waters.

Bay of San Francisco and dependent country.—The bay of San Francisco has been celebrated, from the time of its first discovery, as one of the finest in the world, and is justly entitled to that character even under the seaman's view of a mere harbor. But when all the accessory advantages which belong to it—fertile and picturesque dependent country; mildness and salubrity of climate; connexion with the great interior valley of the Sacramento and San Joaquin; its vast resources for ship timber, grain and cattle—when these advantages are take. into the account, with its geographical position on the line of communication with Asia, it rises into an importance far above that of a mere harbor, and deserves a particular notice in any account of maritime California. Its latitudinal position is that of Lisbon; its climate is that of southern Italy; settlements upon it for more than half a century attest its healthiness; bold shores and mountains give it grandeur; the extent and fertility of its dependent country give it great resources for agriculture, commerce, and population.

The bay of San Francisco is separated from the sea by low mountain ranges. Looking from the peaks of the Sierra Nevada, the coast mountains present an apparently continuous line, with only a single gap, resembling a mountain pass. This is the entrance to the great bay, and is the only water communication from the coast to the interior country. Approaching from the sea, the coast presents a bold outline. On the south, the bordering mountains come down in a narrow ridge of broken hills, terminating in a precipitous point, against which the sea breaks heavily. On the northern side, the mountain presents a bold promontory, rising in a few miles to a height of two or three thousand feet. Between these points is the strait—about one mile broad, in the narrowest part, and five miles long from the sea to the bay. Passing through this gate,* the bay opens to the right and left, extending in each direction about 35 miles, having a total length of more than 70, and a coast of about 275 miles. It is divided, by straits and projecting points, into three separate bays, of which the northern two are called San Pablo and Suisoon [Suisun] bays. Within, the view presented is of a mountainous country, the bay resembling an interior lake of deep water, lying between parallel ranges of mountains. Islands, which have the bold character of the shores—some mere masses of rock, and others grass covered, rising to the height of three and eight hundred feet—break its surface, and add to its picturesque appearance. Directly fronting the entrance, mountains a few miles from the shore rise about 2,000 feet above the water, crowned by a forest of the lofty *cypress*, which is visible from the sea, and makes a conspicuous landmark for vessels entering the bay. Behind, the rugged peak of *Mount Diavolo* [Diablo], nearly 4,000 feet high, (3,770), overlooks the surrounding country of the bay and San Joaquin. The immediate shore of the bay derives, from its proximate and opposite relation to the sea,

---

*Called *Chrysopylae* (Golden gate) on the map, on the same principle that the harbor of *Byzantium* (Constantinople afterwards) was called *Chrysoceras* (golden horn). The form of the harbor, and its advantages for commerce (and that before it became an entrepot of eastern commerce), suggested the name to the Greek founders of Byzantium. The form of the entrance into the bay of San Francisco, and its advantages for commerce (Asiatic inclusive), suggest the name which is given to this entrance.

the name of *contra costa* (counter-coast, or opposite coast). It presents a varied character of rugged and broken hills, rolling and undulating land, and rich alluvial shores backed by fertile and wooded ranges, suitable for towns, villages, and farms, with which it is beginning to be dotted. A low alluvial bottom land, several miles in breadth, with occasional open woods of oak, borders the foot of the mountains around the southern arm of the bay, terminating on a breadth of twenty miles in the fertile valley of St. Joseph, a narrow plain of rich soil, lying between ranges from two to three thousand feet high. The valley is openly wooded with groves of oak, free from underbrush, and after the spring rains covered with grass. Taken in connexion with the valley of San Juan, with which it forms a continuous plain, it is fifty-five miles long and one to twenty broad, opening into smaller valleys among the hills. At the head of the bay it is twenty miles broad, and about the same at the southern end, where the soil is beautifully fertile, covered in summer with four or five varieties of wild clover several feet high. In many places it is overgrown with wild mustard, growing ten or twelve feet high, in almost impenetrable fields, through which roads are made like lanes. On both sides the mountains are fertile, wooded, or covered with grasses and scattered trees. On the west it is protected from the chilling influence of the north-west winds by the *cuesta de los gatos*, (wild-cat ridge), which separates it from the coast. This is a grassy and timbered mountain, watered with small streams, and wooded on both sides with many varieties of trees and shrubbery, the heavier forests of pine and cypress occupying the western slope. Timber and shingles are now obtained from this mountain; and one of the recently discovered quicksilver mines is on the eastern side of the mountain, near the Pueblo of San Jose. This range terminates on the south in the *Anno* [Año] *Nuevo* point of Monterey bay, and on the north declines into a ridge of broken hills about five miles wide, between the bay and the sea, and having the town of San Francisco on the bay shore, near its northern extremity.

Sheltered from the cold winds and fogs of the sea, and having a soil of remarkable fertility, the valley of St. Joseph (San José) is capable of producing in great perfection many fruits and grains which do not thrive on the coast in its immediate vicinity. Without taking into consideration the extraordinary yields which have sometimes occurred, the fair average product of wheat is estimated at fifty fold, or fifty for one sown. The mission establishments of *Sana* [Santa] *Clara* and *San*

José, in the north end of the valley, were formerly, in the prosperous days of the missions, distinguished for the superiority of their wheat crops.

The slope of alluvial land continues entirely around the eastern shore of the bay, intersected by small streams, and offering some points which good landing and deep water, with advantageous positions between the sea and interior country, indicate for future settlement.

The strait of Carquines [*Carquinez*], about one mile wide and eight or ten fathoms deep, connects the San Pablo and Suisoon bays. Around these bays smaller valleys open into the bordering country, and some of the streams have a short launch navigation, which serves to convey produce to the bay. Missions and large farms were established at the head of navigation on these streams, which are favorable sites for towns or villages. The country around the Suisoon bay presents smooth low ridges and rounded hills, clothed with wild oats, and more or less openly wooded on their summits. Approaching its northern shores from *Sonoma* it assumes, though in a state of nature, a cultivated and beautiful appearance. Wild oats cover it in continuous fields, and herds of cattle and bands of horses are scattered over low hills and partly isolated ridges, where blue mists and openings among the abruptly terminating hills indicate the neighborhood of the bay.

The *Suisoon* is connected with an expansion of the river formed by the junction of the Sacramento and San Joaquin, which enter the Francisco bay in the same latitude, nearly, as the mouth of the Tagus at Lisbon. A delta of twenty-five miles in length, divided into islands by deep channels, connects the bay with the valley of the San Joaquin and Sacramento, into the mouths of which the tide flows, and which enter the bay together as one river.

Such is the bay, and the proximate country and shores of the bay of San Francisco. It is not a mere indentation of the coast, but a little sea to itself, connected with the ocean by a defensible gate, opening out between seventy and eighty miles to the right and left, upon a breadth of ten to fifteen, deep enough for the largest ships, with bold shores suitable for towns and settlements, and fertile adjacent country for cultivation. The head of the bay is about forty miles from the sea, and there commences its connexion with the noble valleys of the San Joaquin and Sacramento.

Coast country north of the bay of San Francisco.—Between the Sacramento valley and the coast, north of the bay of San Francisco, the

535

country is broken into mountain ridges and rolling hills, with many very fertile valleys, made by lakes and small streams. In the interior it is wooded, generally with oak, and immediately along the coast presents open prairie lands, among heavily timbered forests, having a greater variety of trees, and occasionally a larger growth than the timbered region of the Sierra Nevada. In some parts it is entirely covered, in areas of many miles, with a close growth of wild oats, to the exclusion of almost every other plant. In the latter part of June and beginning of July, we found here a climate sensibly different from that of the Sacramento valley, a few miles east, being much cooler and moister. In clear weather, the mornings were like those of the Rocky mountains in August, pleasant and cool, following cold clear nights. In that part lying nearer the coast, we found the mornings sometimes cold, accompanied with chilling winds; and fogs frequently came rolling up over the ridges from the sea. These sometimes rose at evening, and continued until noon of the next day. They are not dry, but wet mists, leaving the face of the country covered as by a drizzling rain. This sometimes causes rust in wheat grown within its influence, but vegetables flourish and attain extraordinary size.

I learned from Captain [Stephen] Smith, a resident at *Bodega*, that the winter months make a delightful season—rainy days (generally of warm showers) alternating with mild and calm, pleasant weather, and pure bright skies—much preferable to the summer, when the fogs and strong northwest winds, which prevail during the greater part of the year, make the morning part of the day disagreeably cold.

Owing probably to the fogs, spring is earlier along the coast than in the interior, where, during the interval between the rains, the ground becomes very dry. Flowers bloom in December, and by the beginning of February grass acquires a strong and luxuriant growth, and fruit trees (peach, pear, apple, &c.) are covered with blossoms. In situations immediately open to the sea the fruit ripens late, generally at the end of August, being retarded by the chilling influence of the northwest winds: a short distance inland, where intervening ridges obstruct these winds and shelter the face of the country, there is a different climate and a remarkable difference in the time of ripening fruits; the heat of the sun has full influence on the soil, and vegetation goes rapidly to perfection.

The country in July began to present the dry appearance common to all California as the summer advances, except along the northern coast within the influence of the fogs, or where the land is sheltered by forests, and in the moist vallies of streams and coves of the hills. In some of these was an uncommonly luxuriant growth of oats, still partially green, while elsewhere they were dried up; the face of the country presenting generally a mellow and ripened appearance, and the small streams beginning to lose their volume, and draw up into the hills.

This northern part of the coast country is heavily timbered, more so as it goes north to the Oregon boundary (42°,) with many bold streams falling directly into the sea.

The country between the bays of San Francisco and Monterey.—In the latter part of *January*, 1846, a few shrubs and flowers were already in bloom on the sandy shore of Monterey bay (lat. 36° 40'). Among these were the California poppy, and *nemophilia insignis*.

On the 5th February I found many shrubs and plants in bloom, in the coast mountains bordering St. Joseph's valley, between Monterey and the bay of San Francisco; and vegetation appeared much more green and spring-like, and further advanced, than in the plains. About the middle of February I noticed the *geranium* in flower in the valley; and from that time vegetation began generally to bloom. Cattle were obtained in February, from ranchos among the neighboring hills, extremely fat, selected from the herds in the range.

During the months of January and February rainy days alternated with longer intervals of fair and pleasant weather, which is the character of the rainy season in California. The mean temperature in the valley of St. Joseph—open to the bay of San Francisco—from the 13th to the 22d of February, was 50° at sunrise, and 61° at sunset. The oaks in this valley, especially along the foot of the hills, are partly covered with long hanging moss—an indication of much humidity in the climate.

We remained several days, in the latter part of February, in the upper portion of the coast mountain between St. Joseph and Santa Cruz. The place of our encampment was 2,000 feet above the sea, and was covered with a luxuriant growth of grass, a foot high in many places. At sunrise the temperature was 40°; at noon 60°; at 4 in the afternoon 65°; and 63° at sunset; with very pleasant weather. The mountains were wooded with many varieties of trees, and in some parts with heavy forests. These forests are characterized by a cypress (*taxodium*) of extraordinary dimensions, already mentioned among the trees of the Sierra Nevada, which is distinguished among the forest trees of America by its superior size and height. Among many which we

537

measured in this part of the mountain, nine and ten feet diameter was frequent—eleven sometimes; but going beyond eleven only in a single tree, which reached fourteen feet in diameter. Above two hundred feet was a frequent height. In this locality the bark was very deeply furrowed, and unusually thick, being fully sixteen inches in some of the trees. The tree was now in bloom, flowering near the summit, and the flowers consequently difficult to procure. This is the staple timber tree of the country, being cut into both boards and shingles, and is the principal timber sawed at the mills. It is soft, and easily worked, wearing away too quickly to be used for floors. It seems to have all the durability which anciently gave the cypress so much celebrity. Posts which have been exposed to the weather for three quarters of a century (since the foundation of the missions) show no marks of decay in the wood, and are now converted into beams and posts for private buildings. In California this tree is called the *palo colorado*. It is the king of trees.

Among the oaks is a handsome lofty evergreen species, specifically different from those of the lower grounds, and in its general appearance much resembling hickory. The bark is smooth, of a white color, and the wood hard and close grained. It seems to prefer the north hill sides, where some were nearly four feet in diameter and a hundred feet high.

Another remarkable tree of these woods is called in the language of the country *madrono*.[8] It is a beautiful evergreen, with large, thick, and glossy digitate leaves, the trunk and branches reddish colored, and having a smooth and singularly naked appearance, as if the bark had been stripped off. In its green state the wood is brittle, very heavy, hard, and close grained; it is said to assume a red color when dry, sometimes variegated, and susceptible of a high polish. This tree was found by us only in the mountains. Some measured nearly four feet in diameter, and were about sixty feet high.

A few scattered flowers were now showing throughout the forests, and on the open ridges shrubs were flowering; but the bloom was not yet general.

On the 25th February, we descended to the coast near the northwestern point of Monterey bay, losing our fine weather, which in the evening changed into a cold southeasterly storm, continuing with heavy and constant rains for several days.

During this time the mean temperature was 53° at sunrise, 56°.5 at 9h., a.m., 57°.5 at noon, 54°.5 at 2h. in the afternoon, 53°.4 at 4, and

52°.7 at sunset. On the 28th, a thick fog was over the bay and on the mountains at sunrise, and the thermometer was at 38°—15° below the ordinary temperature—rising at 9 o'clock to 59°. These fogs prevail along the coast during a great part of the summer and autumn, but do not cross the ridges into the interior. This locality is celebrated for the excellence and great size of its vegetables, (especially the Irish potato and onions), with which, for this reason, it has for many years supplied the shipping which visits Monterey. A forest of *palo colorado* at the foot of the mountains in this vicinity, is noted for the great size and height of the trees. I measured one which was 275 feet in height and fifteen feet in diameter, three feet above the base. Though this was distinguished by the greatest girth, other surrounding trees were but little inferior in size and still taller. Their colossal height and massive bulk give an air of grandeur to the forest.

These trees grow tallest in the bottom lands, and prefer moist soils and north hill sides. In situations where they are protected from the prevailing northwest winds, they shoot up to a great height; but wherever their heads are exposed, these winds appear to chill them and stop their growth. They then assume a spreading shape, with larger branches, and an apparently broken summit.

The rain storm closed with February, and the weather becoming fine, on the 1st of March we resumed our progress along the coast. Over the face of the country between Santa Cruz and Monterey, and around the plains of St. John, the grass, which had been eaten down by the large herds of cattle, was now every where springing up; flowers began to show their bloom, and in the valleys of the mountains bordering the Salinas plains, (a plain of some fifty miles in length, made by the Salinas river,) wild oats were three feet high, and well headed, by the 6th of March.

During three days that we remained on one of these mountains, at an elevation of 2,200 feet above the sea, and in sight of Monterey, the mean temperature was 44° at sunrise, 55° at 9 in the morning, 60° at noon, 62° at 2 in the afternoon, 57° at 4, and 53° at sunset. At the same hours, the dew point was at 42°.0, 48°.1, 52°.8, 54°.9, 52°.9, 51°.6, and the quantity of moisture in a cubic foot of air, 3.283 grs., 3.982 grs., 4.726 grs., 4.972 grs., 4.682 grs. and 4.558 grs., respectively. The weather remained bright and pleasant; fogs sometimes covering the mountains at sunrise, but going off in a few hours. These are open mountains, untimbered; but fertile in oats and other grasses, affording fine range for cattle. Oaks and pines are scattered thinly over their

539

upper parts, and in the higher and more exposed situations the ever-green oaks show the course and influence of the northwest winds, stunted and blighted by their chillness, bent to the ground by their force, and growing in that form.

Descending into the valley of the San Joaquin, (March 11th,) we found almost a summer temperature, and the country clothed in the floral beauty of advanced spring.

Southern country and rainy season, (*latitudes 32°—35°*.)—South of *Point Concepcion* the climate and general appearance of the country exhibit a marked change. The coast from that cape trends almost di-rectly east, the face of the country has a more southern exposure, and is sheltered by ranges of low mountains from the violence and chilling effect of the northwest winds; hence the climate is still more mild and genial, fostering a richer variety of productions, differing in kind from those of the northern coast.

The face of the country along the coast is generally naked, the lower hills and plains devoid of trees, during the summer heats parched and bare, and water sparsely distributed. The higher ridges and the coun-try in their immediate vicinity are always more or less, and sometimes prettily, wooded. These usually afford water and good green grass throughout the year. When the plains have become dry, parched and bare of grass, the cattle go up into these ridges, where, with cooler weather and shade, they find water and good pasture. In the dryest part of the year we found sheep and cattle fat, and saw flowers bloom-ing in all the months of the year. Along the foot of the main ridges the soil is rich and comparatively moist, wooded, with grass and water abundant; and many localities would afford beautiful and productive farms. The ranges of the *Sierra Nevada* (here approaching its termina-tion) still remain high—some peaks always retaining snow—and af-ford copious streams, which run all the year. Many of these streams are absorbed in the light soil of the larger plains before they reach the sea. Properly directed, the water of these rivers is sufficient to spread cultivation over the plains. Throughout the country every farm or *rancho* has its own springs or running stream sufficient for the sup-port of stock, which hitherto has made the chief object of industry in California.

The soil is generally good, of a sandy or light character, easily culti-vated, and in many places of extraordinary fertility. Cultivation has always been by irrigation, and the soil, seems to require only water to produce vigorously. Among the arid brush-covered hills south of San

540

Diego we found little vallies converted by a single spring into crowded gardens, where pears, peaches, quinces, pomegranates, grapes, olives, and other fruits grew luxuriantly together, the little stream acting upon them like a principle of life. The southern frontier of this portion of California seems eminently adapted to the cultivation of the vine and the olive. A single vine has been known to yield a barrel of wine; and the olive trees are burdened with the weight of fruit.

During the month of *August* the days are bright and hot, the sky pure and entirely cloudless, and the nights cool and beautifully serene. In this month fruits generally ripen—melons, pears, peaches, prickly fig, (*cactus tuña,*) & c.,—and large bunches of ripe grapes are scattered numerously through the vineyards, but do not reach maturity until the following month. After the vintage, grapes are hung up in the house and so kept for use throughout the winter.

The mornings in September are cool and generally delightful—we sometimes found them almost cold enough to freeze—the midday hours bright and hot, but a breeze usually made the shade pleasant; the evenings calm, and nights cool and clear when unobscured by fogs. We reached the southern country at the end of July; and the first clouds we saw appeared on the 6th *September* at sunset, gradually spreading over the sky, and the morning was cloudy, but clear again before noon. Lightning at this time was visible in the direction of Sonora, where the rainy season had already commenced, and the cloudy weather was perhaps indicative of its approach here. On some nights the dews were remarked to be heavy; and as we were journeying along the coast between San Diego and Santa Barbara, fogs occasionally obscured the sunset over the ocean, and rose next morning with the sun. On the wooded plain, at the foot of the San Gabriel mountain, in the neighborhood of Santa Barbara, and frequently along the way, the trees were found to be partly covered with moss.

Country between the Santa Barbara mountain and Monterey, (lat. 34° 30' to 36° 30'.)—About the middle of *September* we encamped near the summit of the *Cuesta de Santa Ines* [Ynez], (Santa Barbara mountain,) on a little creek with cold water, good fresh grass, and much timber; and thenceforward north along the mountain behind the *Santa Ines* mission, the country assumed a better appearance, generally well wooded and tolerably well covered with grass of good quality—very different from the dry, naked and parched appearance of the country below Santa Barbara. The neighboring mountain exhibited large timber, redwood or pine, probably the latter. Water was frequent in small running streams. Crossing the fertile plain of *San Luis Obispo*, (lat. 35°,) a sheltered valley noted for the superiority of its olives, we entered the *Santa Lucia* range, which lies between the coast and the *Salinas*, or *Buenaventura* river[9] (of the bay of Monterey.) We found this a beautiful mountain, covered thickly with wild oats, prettily wooded, and having on the side we ascended (which is the water shed) in every little hollow a running stream of cool water, which the weather made delightful. The days were hot, at evening cool, and the morning weather clear and exhilarating. Descending into the valley, we found it open and handsome, making a pleasing country, well wooded, and everywhere covered with grass of a good quality. The coast range is wooded on both sides and to the summit with varieties of oaks and pines. The upper part of the Salinas valley, where we are now travelling, would afford excellent stock farms, and is particularly well suited to sheep. The country never becomes miry in the rainy season, and none are lost by cold in the mild winter.

The good range, grass and acorns, made game abundant, and deer and grisly bear were numerous. Twelve of the latter were killed by the party in one thicket.

Lower down, in the neighborhood of San Miguel, the country changed its appearance, losing its timbered and grassy character, and showing much sand. The past year had been one of unusual drought, and the river had almost entirely disappeared, leaving a bare sandy bed with a few pools of water. About fifteen miles below San Miguel it enters a gorge of the hills, making broad thickly wooded bottoms, and affording good range and abundance of water, the bed being sheltered by the thick timber. The lower hills and spurs from the ranges, bordering the river, are very dry and bare, affording little or no grass. Approaching the mission of Soledad the river valley widens, making fertile bottoms and plains of arable land, some fifteen to twenty miles broad, extending to Monterey bay, and bordered by ranges of mountain from two to three thousand feet high. These ranges have the character of fertile mountains, their hills being covered with grass and scattered trees, and their vallies producing fields of wild oats, and wooded with oak groves. Being unsheltered by woods, water is not abundant in the dry season, but at the end of September we found springs among the hills, and water remained in the creek beds.

On the evening of the 25th September, *cumuli* made their appearance in the sky, and the next morning was cloudy with a warm southerly wind and a few drops of rain—the first of the rainy season. The weather then continued uninterruptedly dry through all October—fair and bright during the first part, but cloudy during the latter half. At the end of the month the rainy season sat in fully, consisting generally of rain squalls with bright weather intervening, and occasional southeasterly storms continuing several days. The previous seasons had been very short and light for several years, and the country had suffered from the consequent drought. The present season commenced early, and was very favorable. Much rain fell in the low country, and snow accumulated to a great depth in the high mountains. The first rains changed the face of the country. Grass immediately began to shoot up rapidly, and by the end of the first week of *November* the dead hue of the hills around Monterey had already given place to green.

A brief sketch of the weather during a journey in this year from the mission of *San Juan Bauptista* [Bautista] (latitude 37°) to *los Angeles* will exhibit the ordinary character of the season.

In the valley of San Juan, during the latter half of *November*, there was no rain; the weather, generally, pleasant and bright, with occasional clouds. The night clear and cool, occasionally cold; the mornings clear and sharp, with hoar frost sometimes covering the ground. The days were warm and pleasant, and the evenings mild and calm. On some mornings a thick fog settled down immediately after sunrise, but in a few hours cleared off into a pleasant day.

The falling weather recommenced on the 30th, with a stormy day of spring; blue sky in spots, rapidly succeeded by masses of dark clouds and pouring rain, which fell heavily during [the] greater part of the night.

The morning of the 1st *December* was partially clear, but rain recommenced in a few hours, with sky entirely clouded. The weather brightened at noon, and from a high point of the hills bordering the St. Juan river valley, up which we were travelling, snow was visible on summits of the dividing range between the San Joaquin valley and the coast. It rained heavily and incessantly during the night, and continued all the next day. In the night the sky cleared off bright with a north wind, but clouded up at morning, with rain and a broken sky. There were showers of rain during the day, with intervals of bright and hot sun; and the sky at sunset was without a cloud.

During the day and night of the 4th, there were occasional showers. The sky was tolerably clear on the morning of the 5th, with a prospect of fair weather. The tents were frozen, and snow appeared on the near ridges. We were then in a small interior valley of the mountains, bordering the *Salinas* river, and about 1,000 feet above the sea.

December the 6th was a beautiful day, followed by a cold frosty night.

The next day we descended to the valley of the *Salinas* river, the weather continuing clear and pleasant during the day. Snow appeared on the mountains on both sides of the valley, and a cloud from some of them gave a slight shower during the night. Several successive days were clear, with hot sun; the nights cold, starry, and frosty. The new grass on the hills was coming out vigorously. The morning of the 10th was keen and clear, with scattered clouds, and a southerly wind, which brought up showers of rain at night, followed by fog in the morning.

On the 12th, at the mission of *Santa Margarita*, in the head of the Salinas valley, rain began in the afternoon, with a cold wind, and soon increased to a southeasterly storm, with heavy rain during all the night. The 13th was cloudy, with occasional showers. During the night the weather became very bad, and by morning had increased to a violent and cold southeasterly rain storm. In the afternoon the storm subsided, and was followed by several days of variable weather.

By the 19th, the country where we were travelling between *San Luis Obispo* and the *Cuesta of Santa Ines*, showed a handsome covering of grass, which required two weeks more to become excellent: There were several days of warm weather, with occasional showers and hot sun, and cattle began to seek the shade.

The 23d was a day of hard rain, followed by fine weather on the 24th, and a cold southeasterly rain storm on the 25th.

During the remainder of the year, the weather continued fair and cool.

No rain fell during the first half of *January*, which we passed between Santa Barbara and Los Angeles: the days were bright and very pleasant, with warm sun; and the nights, generally, cold. In the neglected orchards of the San Buenaventura and Fernando missions, the olive trees remained loaded with the abundant fruit, which continued in perfectly good condition.

About the 14th day, a day of rain succeeded by an interval of fine weather, again interrupted by a rainy, disagreeable southeaster on the 23d. During the remainder of the month the days were bright and pleasant—almost of summer—sun and clouds varying; the nights clear, but sometimes a little cold; and much snow showing on the mountain overlooking the plains of San Gabriel.

In the first part of *February*, at *Los Angeles*, there were some foggy and misty mornings, with showers of rain at intervals of a week. The weather then remained for several weeks uninterruptedly and beautifully serene, the sky remarkably pure, the air soft and grateful, and it was difficult to imagine any climate more delightful. In the meantime the processes of vegetation went on with singular rapidity, and, by the end of the month, the face of the country was beautiful with the great abundance of pasture, covered with a luxuriant growth of *geranium*, (*erodium cicutarium*,) so esteemed as food for cattle and horses, and all grazing animals. The orange trees were crowded with flowers and fruit in various sizes, and along the foot of the mountain, bordering the San Gabriel plain, fields of orange colored flowers were visible at the distance of fifteen miles from Los Angeles.

In the midst of the bright weather there was occasionally a cold night. In the morning of March 9 new snow appeared on the San Gabriel mountain, and there was frost in the plain below; but these occasionally cold nights seemed to have no influence on vegetation.

On the 23d and 27th of March there were some continued and heavy showers of rain, about the last of the season in the southern country. In the latter part of April fogs began to be very frequent, rising at midnight and continuing until 9 or 10 of the following morning. About the beginning of May the mornings were regularly foggy until near noon; the remainder of the day sunny, frequently accompanied with high wind.

The climate of maritime California is greatly modified by the structure of the country, and under this aspect may be considered in three divisions—the *southern*, below Point Concepcion and the Santa Barbara mountain, about latitude 35°; the *northern*, from Cape Mendocino, latitude 41°, to the Oregon boundary; and the *middle*, including the bay and basin of San Francisco and the coast between Point Concepcion and Cape Mendocino. Of these three divisions the rainy season is longest and heaviest in the north and lightest in the south. Vegetation is governed accordingly—coming with the rains—decaying where they fail. Summer and winter, in our sense of the terms, are not applicable to this part of the country. It is not heat and cold, but wet and dry, which mark the seasons; and the winter months, instead of killing vegetation, revive it. The dry season makes a period of consecutive drought, the only winter in the vegetation of this country, which can hardly be said at any time to cease. In forests, where the soil is sheltered; in low lands of streams and hilly country, where the ground remains moist, grass continues constantly green and flowers bloom in all the months of the year. In the southern half of the country the long summer drought has rendered irrigation necessary, and the experience of the missions, in their prosperous day, has shown that, in Calfornia, as elsewhere, the dryest plains are made productive, and the heaviest crops produced by that mode of cultivation. With irrigation a succession of crops may be produced throughout the year. Salubrity and a regulated mildness characterize the climate; there being no prevailing diseases, and the extremes of heat during the summer being checked by sea breezes during the day, and by light airs from the Sierra Nevada during the night. The nights are generally cool and refreshing, as is the shade during the hottest day.

California, below the Sierra Nevada, is about the extent of Italy, geographically considered in all the extent of Italy from the Alps to the termination of the peninsula. It is of the same length, about the same breadth, consequently the same area, (about one hundred thousand square miles,) and presents much similarity of climate and productions. Like Italy, it lies north and south, and presents some differences of climate and productions, the effect of difference of latitude, proximity of high mountains, and configuration of the coast. Like Italy, it is a country of mountains and vallies: different from it in its internal structure, it is formed for *unity*; its large rivers being concentric, and its large vallies appurtenant to the great central bay of San Francisco, within the area of whose waters the dominating power must be found.

Geographically, the position of this California is one of the best in the world; lying on the coast of the Pacific, fronting Asia, on the line of an American road to Asia, and possessed of advantages to give full effect to its grand geographical position.

———

The map of Oregon and California, presented with this memoir, is only a past performance of the Senate's order of February 2, 1847. That order contemplated a topographical and descriptive map, for which there is some material on hand, but not enough to complete the work on the plan required, or in a way to do justice to the subject. As now laid before the Senate, it may be assumed to be the best that has yet appeared, but is still imperfect and incomplete. With the knowledge already acquired in the expeditions which I have conducted, and which enable me to know what parts of the country most require examination, one year more of labor in the field would furnish me additional materials sufficient to complete a map of these countries, with topographical and descriptive maps of their most valuable parts, and a general map of the whole from the Mississippi river to the Pacific ocean. Having been many years engaged in this geographical labor, and having made so much progress in it, I should be much gratified with an opportunity to complete it in the public employ; and I respectfully submit the subject to the consideration of your honorable body.

This geographical memoir, as stated in the beginning, is only a preliminary sketch in anticipation of a fuller publication, which the observations of the last expedition would justify, but not sufficient to give the full view of Oregon and California which the increasing importance of those countries demands. The publication of the results of this expedition, with or without further additions from another exploration, is respectfully submitted to your consideration. The results of the previous two expeditions were published by order of the Senate, and disposed of according to its pleasure. No copy-right was taken; and whatever information the journals of the two expeditions contained, passed at once into general circulation. I would prefer a similar publication of the results of the last expedition; but being no longer in the public service, an arrangement for the preparation and the superintendence of the publication would be necessary.

All which is respectfully submitted:

J. Charles Frémont

Washington, *June*, 1848.

1. Today the mountains east of Great Salt Lake are known simply as the Wasatch, with Mount Timpanogos (11,705 feet) being the highest peak.

2. JCF's attempt to rename Sevier River and Lake failed.

3. The streams together make the Mariposa River (excerpt from the *Memoirs*, printed in Vol. 2, p. 34).

4. *Platanus racemosa*.

5. Lassen was a Dane.

6. Not the present Mount Linn in Tehama County, but another high peak to the west.

7. Mount Shasta towers 14,162 feet above sea level in northern California; at 14,781 feet, Mont Blanc in France is the highest mountain in the Alps.

8. Madroña or *Arbutus menziesii*.

9. San Buenaventura was the Wilkes party's name for the Salinas (GUDDE [2], 41).

APPENDIX.

I. Note from Professor Hubbard, (of the National Observatory, Washington city,) describing the instruments used by J. C. Frémont in making the astronomical observations in his third or last expedition, and the methods followed by Professor Hubbard in reducing them.

II. A table of astronomical observations made by J. C. Frémont at the four principal stations determined in this third expedition, namely: 1. The mouth of Fontaine Qui Bouit, on the upper Arkansas. 2. Southeastern shore of the Great Salt lake. 3. Lassen's farm, Deer creek, in the valley of the Sacramento. 4. The Three Buttes, valley of the Sacramento.

III. A table of latitudes and longitudes, deduced from the foregoing astronomical observations, calculated by Professor Hubbard.

IV. Meteorological observations made in the Great Basin from December 16, 1843, to February 22, 1844.

V. Meteorological observations made in the Sacramento and San Joaquin valleys from March 9 to April 11, 1844.

I.

Note from Professor Hubbard.

The instruments employed in the determination of astronomical positions were—
A portable transit instrument, by Young, of Philadelphia.
A sextant, by Troughton.
A sextant, by Gambey.
Two pocket chronometers, (Nos. 438 and 443,) by Appleton.

The transit instrument was made by Mr. William J. Young, of Philadelphia. The length of the telescope was 26 inches, the diameter of the object glass $2\frac{1}{2}$ inches, and the axis 16 inches between the shoulders. A circle was attached to the instrument, having a diameter of 11 inches, graduated to read to 10 seconds, and furnished with 3 verniers. The stand was of iron, and 4 feet in height.

Of the sextants, the one by Gambey, a new instrument, was most frequently used. The other, by Troughton, is the same that was carried in the previous exploration, and was now only used in observing at night, its divided arc being more readily illuminated than that of the other. The index errors of both were carefully and often determined, in order that any possible change of adjustment might be readily detected.

The sextant observations consist of single altitudes of a star or the sun for time, and of Polaris or a star in the south, for latitude. They have been reduced in the usual manner, the formulæ being too well known to need quoting. All the latitudes, and the several links of the chain of longitudes connecting the primary stations, depend upon the data thus furnished. In deducing the differences of longitude, in order to obviate, so far as possible, all error arising from eccentricity of the sextant or any like cause, comparison has been made, when practicable, with observations in the same quarter of the heavens.

The rates of the chronometers depend entirely upon sextant observations. The comparison of these rates, determined at different times and under different circumstances of climate and usage, has shown that but one of the chronometers (No. 438) was entitled to confidence. All differences of longitude from the principal stations have therefore been determined by this one, and the results thus obtained are, as will hereafter be seen, highly satisfactory. The following are the observed rates, deduced, with but a single exception, from altitudes of the sun; the sign + indicates a gaining rate :

549

Locality.	Dates of observation.	Rate of 443.	Rate of 438.
		s.	s.
Bent's fort......	1845, Aug. 3 to Aug. 15	+ 2.020	+ 3.386
Camp at Salt lake	" Oct. 14 to Oct. 20	+ 0.883	3.317
Laguna farm.....	1846, Feb. 11 to Feb. 19	— 1.754	2.146
	" Mar. 30 to April 14	....	2.193
	" April 14 to May 22	....	+ 2.980

The whole route has been divided into three distinct lines. The first, commencing at Bent's fort, extends to the camp of January 4, 1846. The chronometers were then for a time subjected to a rapid travel over a rough road, and their rates were thereby changed. The second line commences with the Laguna farm, between which

and the camp of January 4 no observations were made, and extends to the camp of March 30—April 14, where the chronometers stopped, and another change of rate took place. The last line extends from this camp to that of June 7, after which date no more longitudes were determined.

By combining the above rates for the same line, giving to each a weight equivalent to the number of days elapsed between the observations on which it depends, we get the following:

Rates of chronometer No. 438.

s.

August 21, 1845 to January 4, 1846........... .... + 3.363
February 18, 1846, to March 30, 1846......... + 2.175
April 14, 1846, to June 7, 1846............ .... + 2.980

The transit instrument has given, by moon culminations, the longitudes of four camps with an accuracy much more than sufficient for ordinary geographical purposes. These camps being connected, as we have already seen, by chronometric differences, an excellent check of the whole work is thus afforded. When we remember that an error of one second of time in the observed transit of the moon induces an average error in the resulting longitude of the place of nearly seven minutes of arc, the agreement of these independent determinations, thus referred to the same point, is unexpectedly great. The following is the method by which the transit observations have been reduced:

An estimated longitude for each of the camps in question, gave the means of computing with sufficient accuracy the "the tabular mean time of transit" of the stars observed; their places in the heavens being taken from the catalogue of the British Association. The "observed mean time of transit" was next to be obtained. Where the passage of the star over all the wires had been observed, the mean, reduced to the middle wire, gave at once the time sought. For the purpose of correcting imperfect transits, a determination of the equatoreal intervals of the transit wires was necessary. These wires were originally seven in number; their intervals are given below (I.) They were broken out after the 21st of October, 1845, and were replaced by a set of five (II,) which in their turn were broken, and the last set (III) inserted. Of these last, the second wire was broken before the commencement of observations, and the reduction of the mean to the middle wire, of course includes the correction for the deficiency. The following, then, are the adopted intervals of the several wires and the mean of the whole from the middle wire:

No.	Dates.	A.	B.	C.	Mean.	E.	F.	G.
	1845.	s.	s.	s.	s.	s.	s.	s.
I.	Aug. 12 to Oct. 21	+55.49	+36.78	+18.52	+00.69	—18.12	—34.63	—53.18
	1846.							
II.	April 14 to April 23	....	36.59	17.99	00.00	18.14	36.45	
III.	June 4 to June 6....	+54.96	....	+18.84	—05.17	—17.41	—35.19	—51.95

From this table, the corrections to the mean of wires for imperfect transits have been deduced by dividing the sum of the intervals for the wires observed by the product of the number of wires into the cosine of the star's declination. In the single case of an imperfect transit of the moon, allowance has been made for the moon's motion during the interval of time indicated by the correction.

In deducing the instrumental and chronometer errors by comparison of the observed and computed times of transit, the formula of M. Hansen has been employed.

Denoting by L the latitude of the place.

D the declination of the star.

Z the zenith distance of the star.

i the correction of instrument for error of level.

n the correction of instrument for deviation at the pole.

c the correction of instrument for error of collimation.

Then the reduction of the observed transit to the meridian has the form

$$i \sec L - n \sin Z \sec L \sec D + c \sec D.$$

The value of one division of the level tube accompanying the instrument was unknown; and the instrument itself being in California, this value could not be determined; but, knowing from the observing-books that the axis was always kept as nearly horizontal as possible, we may neglect the constant term i sec L, or rather may include it in the chronometer correction, and this without affecting the observed right ascensions.

Denote also by A the computed mean time of star's transit.

T the observed mean time of star's transit.

$\triangle$T the correction of the chronometer.

Then every observation will give an equation of the following form:

$$O=T+\triangle T-A-\sin Z \sec L \sec D\ n+\sec D\ c.$$

Or for brevity:

$$O=T+\triangle T-A-a\ n+b\ c.$$

putting a and b for the co-efficients of n and c. By help of this formula, approximate values were obtained for n and c from two or more observations. These were generally taken on different days, and the equations furnished by them were only limited by the condition that the value of c should remain constant for these days, allowance being afterwards made for the error of this assumption. The values of n and c thus obtained, were substituted in the equation furnished by each observation. The mean of the chronometer corrections thus determined, being compared with the individual results, a new set of equations of condition was arranged, of the following form:

$$O=d\triangle T-a.\ dn+b.\ dc.$$

where $d\triangle T$ is the residual quantity obtained by the above comparison. The solution of these differential equations by the method of least squares, gave the corrections of n and c, which, applied to the assumed, gave the most probable values. The assumed and adopted n and c are given below. The application of these final values to the original equations gave now the most probable chronometer correction, and this, applied to the corrected transit of the moon's limb, gave the mean time of transit, and finally the right ascension.

Table of assumed and adopted values of n and c.

Date.	Assumed.		Adopted.	
	n.	c.	n.	.c.
	s.	s.	s.	s.
1845, August 21, 22.........	+ 3.702	—3.237	+ 3.702	—3.237
October 20...........	+ 1.633	—3.237	+ 1.343	—3.062
1846, April 14..............	+ 1.02	+0.183	+ 1.648	+0.890
16............	+52.07	+0.183	+52.265	—0.084
June 4................	} + 0.574	—0.145	{ + 0.574	—0.145
5..............			{ + 0.689	—0.183

The following longitudes were assumed as the basis of the comparison of the observed with the tabulated moon culminations:

		h.	m.	s.
I.	1845, August 22	6	58	30
II.	1845, October 20..............	7	29	31
III.	1846, April 14................	8	08	20
IV.	1846, June 4.................	8	01	52

4

By help of these, the moon's $\mathcal{R}$ and hourly motion at transit were computed from the moon-culminating list of the Nautical Almanac, using fourth differences. A comparison of the computed $\mathcal{R}$ with that observed, gave the numerator—the hourly motion being the denominator—of the fraction expressing the correction of the assumed longitudes. Those corrections, and the resulting longitudes, are as follows:

	m.	s.	h.	m.	s.
I.	+0	15.52	6	58	45.52
II.	−1	15.65	7	28	15.35
III.	−0	37.54	8	07	42.46
IV.	+4	36.70	8	06	28.70

Camps I and II, as well as III and IV, being connected by chronometric differences, it becomes important to test the results above given by a comparison of the two differences. We have then

	m.	s.	m.	s.
By lunars..........................	29	29.83	1	13.76
By chro...........................	29	33.83	1	10.67
L—C		−4.00		+3.09

The chronometric difference is adopted as the most exact—apportioning the errors of the other among the longitudes by lunars, remembering that camp II is determined by a single culmination, while at each of the others two were observed, we should now have, were the lunar tables correct, the best system of longitudes. Mr. S. C. Walker states that a correction of the present residual errors of the lunar tables, would increase all the longitudes depending upon moon culminations by about six seconds of time. Adding, therefore, six seconds to the above corrected longitudes, we get finally, as the basis of the whole work, the following adopted longitudes.

	h.	m.	s.	°	′	″
I. Mouth of the Fontaine-qui-bouit, August 22, 1844	6	58	50.72=104	42	41	
II. Camp at Salt Lake, October 14, 20....................	7	28	24.55=112	06	08	
III. Lassen's farm, Deer creek, April 14, 1846	8	07	46.92=121	56	44	
IV. Buttes Sacramento valley, June 4, 1846	8	06	36.24=121	39	01	

Upon these and the sextant observations, is based the accompanying table of latitudes and longitudes.

J. S. HUBBARD

OBSERVATIONS

WITH

THE TRANSIT INSTRUMENT

Date. 1845.	Reference No.	Object.	Declination	TRANSITS OBSERVED.						
				I.	II.	III.	IV.	V.	VI.	VII.

CAMP AT THE MOUTH OF

Date. 1845.	Reference No.	Object.	Declination	I.	II.	III.	IV.	V.	VI.	VII.
			° ′	s.	s.	s.	s.	s.	s.	s.
Aug. 21	1	η Piscium.......	+ 14 33	24.5	04.0	22.4	42.5	00.5	18.0	36.5
	2	Moon's II L...	+ 13 51	59.4	18.5	38.4	58.0	16.4	35.0	54.4
	3	θ¹ Arietis........	+ 19 11	54.4	14.5	33.4	52.5	12.0	30.4	50.0
Aug. 22	4	α Aquilæ	+ 8 28	48.0	06.4	25.0	44.4	02.0	19.0	37.0
	5	β Ceti..........	− 18 50	3 0	52.0	11.0	31.0	50.0	08.0	28.0
	6	Polaris........	+ 88 29	53.5	38.5	12.0	57.4	11.5	45.5	17.0
	7	i Draconis, S. P.	+114 31	36.0	51.5	05.5	22.0	....	....	....
	8	θ¹ Arietis........	+ 19 11	00.0	19.4	39.0	59.0	17.4	35.0	55.0
	9	ψ Arietis........	+ 17 01	46.0	06.0	25.0	45.0	03.5	20.5	40.0
	10	Moon's II L...	+ 15 30	47.0	07.4	26.5	46.5	05.5	23.4	43.4

CAMP ON THE

Date. 1845.	Reference No.	Object.	Declination	I.	II.	III.	IV.	V.	VI.	VII.
Oct. 20	11	Polaris.......	+ 88 29	....	....	....	....	27.0	00.2	46.8
	12	β Ursæ Min. S.P.	+105 13	14.8	04.0	51.2	49.0	32.5	30.5	21.0
	13	γ¹ Eridani........	− 13 57	27.3	46.5	06.0	24.0	43.5	01.0	19.0
	14	β Orionis	− 8 23	33.5	53.5	12.0	29.2	49.0	05.2	23.2
	15	α Leporis.......	− 17 56	16.0	35.0	54.7	13.0	33.2	50.8	09.7
	16	χ¹ Orionis........	+ 20 14	34.3	54.3	13.5	33.5	53.5	09.8	30.2
	17	χ⁴ Orionis .....≻..	+ 20 08	03.8	23.0	42.5	02.5	22.5	39.5	59.0
	18	Moon's II L...	+ 19 41	45.5	05.8	26.0	45.5	05.4	22.5	43.0
	19	ζ Geminorum ...	+ 20 47	05.0	24.0	44.0	03.4	23.0	40.0	00.0

LASSEN'S FARM, DEER CREEK,

Date. 1845.	Reference No.	Object.	Declination	I.	II.	III.	IV.	V.	VI.	VII.
April 14	20	α Virginis.......	− 10 20	....	57.2	16.0	34.3	53.0	11.2	....
	21	β¹ Scorpii........	− 19 21	....	54.6	14.3	33.2	52.5	11.0	....
	22	Moon's II L...	− 19 05	....	11.0	31.5	51.3	10.5	31.0	....
	23	35 Draconis......	+ 76 59	....	15.0	39.2	56.5	....	....	....
	24	μ¹ Sagittarii......	− 21 05	....	36.5	56.5	15.5	35.2	54.5	....
April 16	25	ρ Cassiopeæ, S.P.	+123 22	....	....	08.5	40.0	14.5	48.2	....
	26	β Cassiopeæ, S.P.	+121 42	....	09.5	34.0	59.3	25.2	51.0	....
	27	β Corvi	− 22 33	....	35.0	55.0	14.5	33.0	54.0	....
	28	α Cassiopeæ, S.P.	+124 19	....	40.2	07.5	35.4	04.0	32.0	....
	29	Polaris, S. P.	+ 91 30	....	30.0	33.0	02.0	45.2	04.0	....
	30	58 Ophiuchi	− 21 36	....	38.0	58.2	18.0	37.0	56.3	....
	31	μ¹ Sagittarii.....	− 21 05	....	53.5	13.5	33.2	52.5	11.7	....
	32	Moon's II L...	− 18 29	....	17.5	37.6	58.0	17.2	37.0	....

ment, determining the four principal positions mentioned in his me-
fessor Hubbard.

Mean of obs'd. wires.	REDUCTIONS TO		Observed transit.	Computed transit.	Chronometer fast.	Reference No.
	Mid. wire.	Meridian.				

THE FONTAINE-QUI-BOUIT.

H. M. S.	M. S.	M. S.	H. M. S.	H. M. S.	H. M. S.	
15 44 41.20	+ 0 00.72	— 0 05.29	15 44 36.63	15 20 57.04	0 23 39.59	1
16 21 57.16	0 00.72	0 05.29	16 21 52.59	....	....	2
16 30 52.47	+ 0 00.73	— 0 05.09	16 30 48.11	16 07 08.36	0 23 39.75	3
10 01 43.11	+ 0 00.71	— 0 05.64	10 01 38.18	9 37 58.02	0 23 40.16	4
14 53 30.29	0 00.73	— 0 07.61	14 53 23.41	14 29 45.08	0 23 38.33	5
15 21 25.06	+ 0 26.32	+ 0 14.54	15 22 05.92	14 58 25.22	0 23 40.70	6
16 05 28.75	— 1 06.78	— 0 03.23	16 04 18.74	15 40 34.95	0 23 43.79	7†
16 26 57.83	+ 0 00.73	0 05.06	16 26 53.50	16 03 12.48	0 23 41.02	8
16 39 43.71	0 00.73	0 05.18	16 39 39.26	16 15 58.46	0 23 40.80	9
17 10 45.67	+ 0 00.73	— 0 05.25	17 10 41.15	....	....	10

SALT LAKE.

12 25 24.67	—22 22.51	— 1 13.08	12 01 49.08	11 06 38.20	0 55 10.88	11†
13 47 46.14	— 0 02.64	+ 0 06.63	13 47 50.13	12 52 34.16	0 55 15.97	12†
14 47 23.90	+ 0 00.72	— 0 03.82	14 47 20.80	13 52 08.92	0 55 11.88	13
16 03 29.37	0 00.70	0 03.63	16 03 26.39	15 08 13.81	0 55 12.58	14
16 22 13.20	0 00.73	0 03.95	16 22 09.98	15 26 58.70	0 55 11.28	15
16 41 32.73	0 00.74	0 03.39	16 41 30.08	15 46 14.99	0 55 15.09	16
16 51 01.83	0 00.74	0 03.39	16 50 59.18	15 55 44.04	0 55 15.14	17
17 30 44.81	0 00.74	0 03.39	17 30 42.16	....	....	18
17 51 02.77	+ 0 00.74	— 0 03.38	17 51 00.13	16 55 45.67	0 55 14.46	19

SACRAMENTO VALLEY.

15 51 34.34	....	— 0 00.76	15 51 33.58	11 44 45.72	4 06 47.86	20
18 30 33.12	....	0 01.02	18 30 32.10	14 23 43.80	4 06 48.30	21
19 14 51.06	....	— 0 01.02	19 14 50.04	....	....	22
20 23 36.90	+ 1 20.78	+ 0 09.70	20 30 07.38	16 23 19.30	4 06 48.08	23
20 38 15.64	....	— 0 01.06	20 38 14.58	16 31 26.13	4 06 48.45	24
14 15 57.80	— 0 16.56	— 2 03.19	14 13 38.05	10 06 43.24	4 06 54.81	25
14 29 59.80	....	2 08.41	14 27 51.39	10 20 58.16	4 06 53.23	26
14 54 14.30	....	1 05.42	14 53 08.88	10 46 15.59	4 06 53.29	27
15 00 35.82	....	2 00.06	14 53 35.76	10 51 41.74	4 06 54.02	28
16 03 58.84	....	33 48.98	15 30 09.86	11 23 18.86	4 06 51.00	29†
20 01 17.50	....	1 04.38	20 00 13.12	15 53 17.58	4 06 55.54	30
20 31 32.88	....	1 03.85	20 30 29.03	16 23 34.37	4 06 54 66	31
21 09 57.46	....	— 1 03.00	21 08 54.46	....	....	32

Date. 1845.	Reference No.	Object.	Declination	TRANSITS OBSERVED.						
				I.	II.	III.	IV.	V.	VI.	VII.

THREE BUTTES, SA

			° ′	s.	s.	s.	s.	s.	s.	s.
June 4	33	γ Virginis........	− 0 36	....	....	54.7	13.0	30.2	48.7	05.0
	34	Moon's I L....	− 8 24	10.0	....	48.2	07.0	25.2	43.8	01.2
	35	Polaris, S. P...	+ 91 31	25.2	....	....	....	....	13.5	23.0
	36	a Virginis.......	− 10 22	23.0	....	01.7	19.0	37.7	55.7	12.7
	37	φ Centauri......	− 41 21	55.0	. ..	42.0	06.5	30.5	54.8	17.0
	38	θ Centauri......	− 35 37	40.7	....	25.2	47.7	09.7	31.6	52.3
	39	ι Lupi.....,.,..	− 45 21	24.7	....	15.6	41.8	07.7	33.0	56.5
	40	5 Ursæ Minoris .	+ 76 23	....	....	36.0	54.2	11 0	26.5	38.2
	41	δ Ursæ Minoris .	+ 74 47	....	....	58.0	10.0	16 8	23.7	29.0
June 5	42*	θ Virginis	− 4 43	....	....	....	....	40.2	....	16.0
	43	Polaris, S. P ..	+ 91 31	51.0	54.5	....	50.0	....	....	34.2
	44	a Virginis.......	− 10 22	32.2	50.0	07.3	24.3	42.7	....	20.2
	45	ω Cassiopeæ,S.P	+112 45	34.5	52.0	04.2	....	....	....	....
	46	ε Cassiopeæ,S.P.	+117 06	....	55.3	16.5	40.2	57.5	....	38.2
	47	φ Centauri......	− 41 21	02.2	25.0	48.5	10.0	36.2	....	....
	48	Moon I L.....	− 12 11	20.5	39.2	57.5	15.0	35.2	....	13.0
	49	θ Centauri.....	− 35 37	48.5	09.0	31.2	52.0	15.2	....	00.2
	50	χ Virginis.......	− 9 33	00.2	17.5	35.5	52.5	12.0	....	49.2
	51	λ Virginis.......	− 12 39	05.5	22.5	40.0	57.2	17.2	....	54.5
	52	5 Ursæ Minoris..	+ 76 23	16.5	28.8	45.2	58.2	19.0	....	51.6
	53	a² Libræ	− 15 24	34.5	52.3	10.2	26.6	48.2	....	25.2
	54	β Ursæ Minoris..	+ 74 47	....	....	....	10.2	25.6	....	43.0

* Instrument reversed between observations 41 and 42.

557

Mean of obs'd. wires.	REDUCTIONS TO		Observed transit.	Computed transit.	Chronometer fast.	Reference No.
	Mid. wire.	Meridian.				

CRAMENTO VALLEY.

H. M. s.	M. s.	M. s.	H. M. s.	H. M. s.	H. M. s.	
11 49 30.32	− 0 17.14	− 0 00.62	11 49 12.56	7 41 07.60	4 03 04.96	33
12 16 17.57	− 0 05.30	0 00.72	12 16 06.55	....	....	34
12 12 40.57	+ 6 46.18	0 16.69	12 19 10.06	8 11 05.46	4 08 04.60	35
12 32 24.97	− 0 05.26	0 00.72	12 32 18.99	8 24 14.59	4 08 04.40	36
13 04 14.30	0 05.90	0 01.17	13 04 07.23	8 56 01.28	4 08 05.95	37†
13 12 54.53	0 06.36	0 01.05	13 12 47.12	9 04 41.92	4 08 05.20	38
13 24 49.88	0 07.35	− 0 01.21	13 24 41.32	9 16 36.71	4 08 04.61	39
13 44 09.19	1 12.84	+ 0 01.28	13 42 57.63	9 34 52.72	4 08 04.91	40
14 07 15.50	− 0 05.32	+ 0 01.09	14 07 11.27	9 58 07.06	4 08 04.21	41
12 13 58.10	− 0 37.03	− 0 00.43	12 13 20.64	8 05 14.71	4 08 05.93	42
12 20 47.42	− 5 04.71	0 33.56	12 15 09.15	8 07 10.32	4 07 58.83	43†
12 23 19.45	+ 0 05.26	0 00.50	12 28 24.21	8 20 18.69	4 08 05.52	44
12 43 50.23	− 1 30.14	0 02.67	12 42 17.42	8 34 11.41	4 08 06.01	45
12 54 29.54	+ 0 09.31	0 02.31	12 54 36.54	8 46 30.48	4 08 06.06	46
12 59 48.38	0 22.83	0 00.93	13 00 10.28	8 52 05.37	4 08 04.91	47
13 04 10.07	0 05.40	0 00.53	13 04 14.94	....	....	48
13 08 46.02	0 06.36	0 00.83	13 08 51.55	9 00 46.01	4 08 05.54	49
13 15 47.82	0 05.24	0 00.51	13 15 52.55	9 07 47.30	4 08 05.25	50
13 21 52.82	0 05.30	− 0 00.53	13 21 57.59	9 13 52.18	4 08 05.41	51
13 38 36 55	0 21.97	+ 0 03.06	13 39 01.58	9 30 56.77	4 08 04.81	52
13 53 22.83	+ 0 05.36	− 0 00.56	13 53 27.63	9 45 22.11	4 08 05.52	53
14 03 46.27	− 1 33.75	+ 0 02.67	14 02 15.19	9 51 11.13	4 08 04.06	54†

† Omitted in taking the mean.

III.—A table of latitudes and longitudes deduced from the foregoing astronomical observations, calculated by Professor Hubbard.

Date.	Latitude. (° ′ ″)	Longitude. (° ′ ″)	Locality.
1845.			
Aug. 16	38 02 22	103 33 20	Bent's Fort.
22	38 15 18	104 42 41	Mouth of the Fontaine-qui-bouit.
26	38 25 44	105 22 17	Arkansas river, at mouth of the great *cañon*, left bank.
28	38 43 17	105 39 50	Sheep river—Utah pass.
29	38 50 35	105 49 56	Head water of a tributary to the Arkansas river, (heading in the ridge between Platte and Arkansas waters.)
30	38 49 43	106 17 56	Piney fork of the Arkansas, three miles above its mouth.
Sept. 1	39 05 12	106 30 03	On the lake fork of the Arkansas, on the western shore of the upper lake, near the inlet.
2	39 20 38	106 27 45	Heal waters of the main branch of the ARKANSAS river.
4	39 33 48	106 32 03	On Piney river—an affluent of Grand river of the Colorado of the gulf of California.
5	39 39 12	106 44 21	Williams's fishery—Piney river.
8	39 46 24	107 08 55	Grand river of the gulf of California.
12	29 56 54	107 44 57	White river, (affluent of Green river of the Colorado,) at "*flat prairie.*"
13	39 57 36	107 47 26	Forks of White river.
17	39 55 57	108 45 08	Guthrie's creek, (of White river.)
21	40 03 55	109 05 28	"War Eagle camp," White river.
25	40 04 00	109 53 43	GREEN RIVER of the Colorado, left bank, one and a half mile above the mouth of White river.
27	40 11 40	110 16 35	Lake fork, (of the Uintah,) two miles above its mouth.
29	40 19 38	110 52 05	Duchénes fork, (of the Uintah.)
Oct. 1	40 27 42	111 10 49	Morin's fork.
2	40 32 05	111 21 31	On a branch of the *Timpana-ozu* or Timpanogos river, (of the Utah lake.)
4	40 28 04	111 39 44	Timpanogos river.
6	40 13 12	111 54 55	Timpanagos river.
10	40 09 53	111 47 51	Pimquan creek, shore of the Utah lake.
12	40 33 27	112 02 32	Outlet of Utah lake, at mouth of Hughes's creek.
14	40 45 53	112 06 08	Station creek, southeastern shore of the Great Salt lake.
18	40 58 48	.. .. ..	Summit of peak of Antelope island, in the southern part of Great Salt lake.
21	40 42 19	.. .. ..	Spring point, (extremity of a promontory at south end of Salt lake, opposite Antelope island.)
23	40 39 15	112 51 11	Spring in valley, opening on southern shore of the Great Salt lake.
25	40 38 17	113 05 09	Valley, near southwestern shore of Salt lake.
30	41 00 28	114 11 09	Pilotpeak creek.
Nov. 1	40 43 49	114 26 22	Spring at head of ravine.
3	40 42 13	114 55 45	Whitton's spring.

Date	Lat.	Long.	Locality
8	40 17 16	115 46 00	Crane's branch (of the south fork of Humboldt river.)
9	39 53 26	115 54 11	Head of south fork of Humboldt river.
11	39 47 01	116 33 39	Connor's spring.
14	39 11 57	117 14 12	Basil's creek.
16	38 49 21	117 16 52	Boiling springs.
17	38 33 17	117 24 29	Moore's creek.
21	38 23 11	118 24 51	Secondi's spring—Sheep mountain.
24	38 35 11	118 32 19	Eastern shore of lake Walker.
26	38 56 36	118 52 54	Walker river, three miles above its mouth in lake Walker.
Dec. 1		119 05 23	Walker river, at its most northern bend.
2	39 33 48	119 30 24	Salmon Trout river, above the lower canon.
3	39 30 51	119 51 52	Salmon Trout river.
4	39 22 09	120 02 50	Salmon Trout river, at the forks.
6	39 17 12	120 15 20	Pass in the Sierra Nevada, at head of Salmon Trout river.
7	39 11 06	120 44 24	On affluent to north fork of the Rio de los Americanos.
8	39 04 11	121 07 48	On Martin's fork (of Sacramento valley)
12	38 53 05	121 08 49	On Hamilton's creek, (Sacramento valley.)
18	38 34 18	121 19 26	Rio de los Americanos, (opposite Grimes's house.)
20	37 29 56	120 14 11	Aux-um-ne river, (of the San Joaquin.)
1846. Jan. 4	37 07 47	119 23 32	On an affluent to the upper San Joaquin.
	36 53 56	119 02 21	On the Tularé lake fork, (Rio Reyes,) one mile below the junction of Taplin and Stepp's forks.
Feb. 18	37 13 32	121 39 08	The Laguna, in the valley of San Jose, (of Francisco bay.)
22	37 09 57	121 54 55	Road from San Jose to Santa Cruz, on the Cuesta de los Gatos.
23	37 08 45	121 52 40	Road from San Jose to Santa Cruz, near summit of the Cuesta de los Gatos.
Mar. 1	36 58 43	121 48 51	Uva Maron creek, (Bernardo Castro's,) bay of Monterey.
2	36 54 41	121 34 00	On the Pajaro river, (of the bay of Monterey,) one-fourth of a mile below Anser's house.
4	36 46 07	121 30 43	Gomez run, at edge of Salinas plain.
14	37 25 53	120 35 55	Towalumne river.
22	38 34 18	121 19 26	Rio de los Americanos, opposite Grimes's house.
26	39 07 45	121 30 21	Feather river, mouth of Yuva river.
27	39 27 17	121 32 35	Bend of Feather river.
28	39 39 05	121 27 55	Butte creek, (Neal's rancho.)
29	39 52 58	121 52 58	Pine creek.
April 14	39 57 04	121 56 44	Deer river, (opposite Lassen's house,) half a mile above its mouth in the Sacramento.
25	40 23 58	122 03 27	Mouth of Nozah river, (of the Sacramento.)
26	40 38 58	121 57 24	Brant's creek.
27	40 50 33	121 47 18	Campbell's creek.
29	40 58 43	121 07 59	Upper Sacramento, above Fall river.
30	41 17 17	121 01 23	Upper Sacramento river, at upper end of Round valley.
May 1	41 48 49	121 15 24	Eastern shore of lake Rhett.

III.—TABLE OF LATITUDES AND LONGITUDES—Continued.

Date.	Latitude.	Longitude.	Locality.
	° ′ ″	° ′ ″	
1846.			
May 4	42 10 52	121 28 53	McCrady river.
6	42 17 56	121 52 45	Denny's branch (of Tlamath lake.)
7	42 33 13	121 58 51	Ambuscade creek, (of Tlamath lake.)
11	42 36 35	121 58 45	Corral creek, (of Tlamath lake.)
12	42 41 30	121 52 08	Torrey river, (of Tlamath lake.)
14	42 21 23	121 41 23	We-to-wah creek, (southeastern end of Tlamath lake.)
19	40 53 19	121 05 57	Russell's branch.
20	40 39 52	121 19 05	Poinsett river, (of the upper Sacramento.)
21	40 31 54	121 36 16	Myers's branch, (Sierra Nevada.)
27	39 39 05	121 40 43	Butte creek.
31	39 12 03	121 38 04	"*Buttes of the Sacramento,*" (on a small run at southeastern base.)
June 7	39 14 41	121 33 36	"*Buttes of the Sacramento,*" (on a small run or spring at northeastern base.)

IV.—*Meteorological observations, made in the Great Basin, from December 17, 1843, to February 21, 1844.*

Date.	Time.	Ther.	Locality.	Remarks.
1843.		°	° ′ ″	
Dec. 17	Sunset	52.0	Lat. 42 57 22—on Summer lake	
18	Sunrise	34.0	....do	
18	Sunset	48.0	Lat. 42 42 37	
19	Sunrise	29.0	....do	
19	Sunset	46.0	....Fitzpatrick river	
20	Sunrise	36.0	....do	
20	Sunset	39.0	....Lake Abert	
21	Sunrise	33.0	....do	
21	Sunset	43.0	....do	Fresh wind from SE. all day.
22	Daylight	39.0	....do	Wind south; overcast.
23	Daylight	38.0	....open, sandy plain	Rain during the night.
23	Sunset	39.0	....on side of a ridge	Cloudy; a little rain.
24	Daylight	31.0	....do	
24	Sunset	37.0	Lat. 42 23 25—Christmas lake	Fair day; light breeze from south.
25	Daylight	32.0	....do	
25	Sunset	33.0	....ponds south of Christmas lake	Wind south; fair.
26	Daylight	22.0	....do	Clouds rising around the horizon.
26	Sunset	30.0	Lat. 42 00 09—Boundary creek	Cloudy; light SE. wind.
27	Daylight	20.0	....do	Clear; wind SE.
27	Sunset	23.0	....open, sage covered plain	Calm; sun faint.
28	Daylight	18.0	....do	Calm; reddish clouds over sky.
28	Sunset	34.0	....hill side	Gentle southeast breeze—threatening snows.
29	Daylight	33.0	....do	Light snow falling.
29	Sunset	19.0	Lat. 41 27 50—aspen grove, on small stream among mountains	Thick snow greater part of day; evening and night clear; wind WSW.
30	Daylight	14.0	....do	
30	Sunset	19.0	....in cañon of same stream	Fair; wind S. 80° W.
31	Daylight	17.0	....do	Fair.
31	Sunset	27.0	Lat. 41 19 55—on small stream, in open barren valley	
1844.				
Jan. 1	Daylight	24.0	....do	Fair; moderate SW. wind.
1	Sunset	28.0	....same stream	Fair; light clouds in the east.

IV.—METEOROLOGICAL OBSERVATIONS—Continued.

Date.	Time.	Ther.	Locality.	Remarks.
1844. Jan. 2	Daylight	26.0	...same stream	Thick snow falling.
3	Daylight	20.0	...barren valley	Thick dense mist.
3	Sunset	23.0	Lat. 40 48 15—on hill torrent; no water	Still misty—stars visible.
4	7h. a. m.	20.0	...do...at point of ridge, Mud lake	Very dense fog.
4	Sunset	24.0	...at point of ridge, Mud lake	Dense mist all day.
5	6h. 30m., a. m.	12.0	...do......do	Very dense fog.
5	Sunset	22.0	...do......do	Wind NE.; dense mist.
6	Sunrise	8.0	Lat. 40 39 46—boiling spings	Mist breaking away; clear, bright sunshine.
6	Sunset	21.0	...do	Clear; nearly calm.
7	7h. a. m.	6.0	...do	Slight mist.
7	Noon	31.0	...do	Clear.
7	Evening	24.0	...do	Clear sunset.
8	8h. a. m.	20.0	...do	Fresh breeze NE.; bright clouds in the west.
8	Noon	35.0	...do	Clear; wind from SW. Temperature of the largest spring, at its edge, 206°.
8	Evening	30.0	...do	
9	7h. 30m. a. m.	23.0	...on small creek; Cottonwood camp	A little snow falling.
9	Sunset	33.0	...do	Clear.
10	7h. a. m.	22.0	...east foot of mountain, on west side of the Pyramid lake	
10	Sunset	29.0	...do	Overcast.
11	Sunrise	15.0	...do	Day fair; bright sun.
11	Sunset	20.0	northerneast'n shore Pyramid lake	Threatening bad weather; snow storm during greater part of the forenoon.
12	Sunrise	33.0	...do	Wind SW.; partially overcast; snow falling heavily again at evening.
12	Sunset	28.0	...eastern shore of Pyramid lake	Overcast; wind S. 20° E.
13	Sunrise	29.0	...do	Snow falling thick; wind variable.
13	Sunset	31.0	...southeastern shore Pyramid lake	Nearly clear; wind N. 10° W.
14	Sunrise	26.0	...do	Wind N. 10° W.; elevation 4,500 feet.
14	Sunset	28.0	...near south end of Pyramid lake	Clear—partially.
15	Sunrise	31.0	...do	
15	Sunset	34.0	Lat. 39 51 13—outlet of Salmon-trout river, of Pyramid lake	Clear and calm.

563

Day	Time	Temp.	Location	Remarks
16	Sunrise	34.0	....do......	Clear; mild and pleasant.
16	Sunset	35.0	Salmon-trout river	Fair; light wind N. 50° W. all day.
17	Sunrise	17.0	...do...	Fair.
17	Sunset	42.0	Carson river	Calm; sun bright.
18	Sunrise	28.0	...do...	Reddish clouds in east.
18	3h., p. m.	49.5	Lat. 39 24 16	Wind S. 20° W.
18	Sunset	39.0	Carson river	Smoky.
19	Sunrise	37.0	...do...	Snow falling from daybreak until 11h. a. m.
19	Sunset	35.0	Lat. 39 19 21	Partly clear.
20	Sunrise	14.0	...do...	Fair.
20	1h. p. m.	41.0	...do...	Wind west; fair.
20	Sunset	32.0	...do...	Overcast; wind SW.
21	Sunrise	30.0	...do...	Snow falling fast; wind SW.; snow ceased at 10h, a. m.; sun shone out.
21	Sunset	29.0	Lat. 39 01 53—Walker river, north fork; open prairie bottom	Calm; clear sky.
22	Sunrise	30.0	...do......	Wind S. 25° W.; clouds in horizon; light snow falling from 9h. a. m. to 1h. p. m.
22	4h. p. m.	37.0	Lat. 38 49 54—Walker river, north fork, at mouth of cañon	Sky clear; high SW. wind.
22	Sunset	36.0	...do...	do.
23	Sunrise	40.0	...do...	Moderate west wind; dark clouds in north.
23	Sunset	42.0	Lat. 38 36 19—Walker river, south fork	Calm; sky nearly clear.
24	Sunrise	45.0	...do...	Fair and pleasant.
24	Sunset	36.0	Lat. 38 24 28—on a stream, among high mountains	
25	Sunrise	2.0	...do......	Sky clear; sun bright.
26	Sunrise	2.0	Lat. 38 18 01—south fork Walker river; valley in the mountains	Day fair; nearly fair.
26	11h. a. m.	30.0	...do...	Perfectly clear; calm, river frozen over; snow a foot deep on the ice; elevation 6,310 feet.
26	Sunset	47.0	...do...	Calm.
27	Sunrise	12.0	...do...	Fair and pleasant.
27	Sunset	33.0	branch of same river; higher up in the mountains	Bright, pure sky.
28	Sunrise	27.0	...do...	Sky unclouded all the day.
28	Sunset	40.0	open ridge of upper mountains; north fork of Walker river	Clear.
29	Sunrise	34.0	...do...	Clear; sun bright; moderate SE. wind.
30	Sunrise	31.0	Walker river, north fork	Reddish clouds in horizon to E. and N.; wind SE.
30	Sunset	39.0	...do...	Calm and cloudy.

Clouds breaking away.

IV.—METEOROLOGICAL OBSERVATIONS—Continued.

Date.	Time.	Ther.	Locality.	Remarks.
1844.		°	° ′ ″	
31	Sunrise	25.0	........Walker river, north fork......	Cumuli in SE. and N.; snowing during greater part of the day.
Feb. 1	Sunrise	27.0	Lat. 38 37 18—Carson river............	Overcast; snow falling.
1	Noon	40.0	...................do..............	Snowing all day.
1	Sunset	24.0	...................do..............	Clear and frosty.
2	Sunrise	24.0	...................do..............	
2	Sunset	35.0	........branch of Carson river; summit parts of mountains.......	Calm; clear; bright sunshine; elevation 6,760 feet.
3	Sunrise	14.0	.......do.........do.......	Nearly clear; calm.
3	3h. 45m. p. m.	28.0	.......branch of Carson river.......	Nearly calm.
3	Sunset	26.0	...................do..............	Overcast.
4	Sunrise	20.0	...................do..............	Light white clouds in the east.
4	Sunset	40.0	Lat. 38 42 26—upper part of Sierra Nevada, branch of Carson river.	Elevation 7,400 feet.
4	9h. p. m.	12.0	...................do..............	Strong SW. wind.
5	Sunrise	10.0	...................do..............	
5	Noon	48.0	...................do..............	Clear; moderate SW. wind.
5	Sunset	24.0	...................do..............	
6	Sunrise	16.0	...................do..............	Sky unclouded; light breeze SW.
6	Noon	37.0	...................do..............	Sky unclouded; calm.
6	Sunset	26.0	...................do..............	
7	Sunrise	9.5	...................do..............	Clear.
7	Sunset	28.0	.......same stream; higher up.......	Sky perfectly clear the whole day; light variable winds.
8	Sunrise	0.0	...................do..............	Sun shining full on the valley; cloudless; calm. When the rays of the sun fell on the high peaks, the thermometer was at 2°.5.
8	3h. 40m. p. m.	38.0	.......near the central ridge.......	Light easterly breeze; nearly clear; elevation 7,920 feet.
8	Sunset	36.0	...................do..............	Wind east; white clouds rising in horizon.
9	Sunrise	29.0	...................do..............	Strong SW. wind; light scud driving rapidly.
9	Noon	44.0	...................do..............	Moderate WSW. wind; nearly clear; a few wind clouds in the west.
9	Sunset	24.0	...................do..............	Wind variable; nearly clear; a few wind clouds in the west.
10	Sunrise	35.0	...................do..............	Nearly calm; cloudy in SW.
10	Noon	42.0	Lat. 38 41 57—immediately at foot of central ridge	Wind SE.; white clouds in W.; elevation 8,050 feet.
10	Sunset	37.0	...................do..............	Moderate SE. wind; sky partially overcast.

11	Sunrise	......do......	33.0	Entirely overcast; wind shifting.
11	Noon	......do......	35.0	Clouds breaking away; violent gusts of wind from W.
11	Sunset	......do......	33.5	Clearing off; moderate wind N. 80° W.
12	Sunrise	......do......	32.5	Calm; sky nearly clear.
12	Sunset	......do......	35.0	Sky clear; gentle west breeze.
13	Sunrise	......do......	33.0	Calm; cumuli in east; sun faint.
13	Sunset	......do......	35.0	Overcast; calm.
14	Sunrise	......do......	21.0	Sky clear; moderate westerly wind.
14	Sunset	......do......	22.5	Calm; sky nearly clear.
15	Sunrise	......do......	31.0	Calm; clouds in SW.; sun faint.
15	Noon	......do......	41.0	Calm; watery clouds moving from SW. to NE.
15	Sunset	......do......	31.5	Calm; sky nearly clear.
16	Sunrise	......do......	30.0	Wind SW.; rain clouds in E.
16	Sunset	......do......	33.0	Clear; moderate S. wind.
17	Sunrise	......do......	23.0	Entirely clear; calm.
17	Sunset	......do......	32.0	do. do.
18	Sunrise	......do......	22.5	Sky very clear; nearly calm.
18	Sunset	......do......	31.0	Calm; rain clouds in W.
19	Sunrise	......do......	23.0	Cloudless sky; calm.
19	Sunset	......do......	32.0	Cloudless sky; gentle breeze S. 60° E.
20	Sunrise	Lat. 38 44 00—summit of Sierra Nevada, at head of the *Rio de los Americanos*..	22.0	Clear; calm; elevation 9,338 feet.
20	Sunset	......do......	37.0	Sky clear; fresh wind S. 70° W.
21	Sunrise	......do......	32.0	Moderate west wind; scattered watery clouds.

V.—*Meteorological observations made in the Sacramento and San Joaquin valleys, from March 9 to April 12, 1844, (a dry season.)*

Date.	Time.	Thermometer.	Locality.	Remarks.
1844. Mar. 9	Sunset	62.0	Lat. 38 34 42—New Helvetia, (Sacramento valley)	Light grayish clouds in south; moderate SE. wind.
10	Sunrise	34.0	do.	Light grayish clouds; sky clear; calm.
10	Sunset	63.0	do.	Sky cloudy; wind SW.
11	Sunrise	45.0	do.	Sky partially overcast; slight rain falling.
11	Sunset	56.0	do.	Sky clear; no air stirring.
12	Sunrise	31.0	do.	Sky unclouded; calm.
12	Sunset	63.0	do.	Clear sky; fresh SW. wind.
13	Sunrise	35.0	do.	No clouds; calm.
13	Noon	75.0	do.	Strong westerly breeze.
13	Sunset	68.0	do.	Light watery clouds in horizon; wind from NW.
14	Sunrise	45.0	do.	Moderate wind, N. 10° W.; unclouded.
14	Sunset	76.0	do.	Clear; perfectly calm.
15	Sunrise	44.0	do.	Calm and cloudless.
15	Sunset	74.0	do.	Reddish clouds around setting sun.
16	Sunrise	40.0	do.	No wind; sky clear.
16	Noon	84.0	do.	No air stirring; sky clear.
16	Sunset	58.0	do.	Sky clear; calm.
17	Sunrise	46.0	do.	Slight haze in north; calm.
17	Sunset	63.0	do.	Clear; calm.
18	Sunrise	38.0	do.	do.
18	Sunset	64.0	do.	Sky unclouded; no wind.
19	Sunrise	41.0	do.	Few scattering clouds in west.
19	Sunset	68.0	do.	Calm; unclouded.
20	Sunrise	40.0	do.	Slight breeze N. 10° E.; white clouds in east.
20	Noon	81.0	do.	Clear sky; no wind.
20	Sunset	70.0	do.	Sky cloudy; calm.
21	Sunrise	41.0	do.	Dark clouds in east; wind N. 70° W.
21	Sunset	64.0	do.	Scattered wind clouds; wind west.
22	Sunrise	36.0	do.	

Date	Time	Temp.	Locality	Remarks
22	Sunset	64.0	......do......	Very cloudy; wind S. 10° E.
23	Sunrise	44.0	......do......	Sky nearly clear; moderate SW. wind
23	Sunset	63.0	......do......	Reddish clouds in west; wind SW.
24	Sunrise	42.0	......do......	Sky clear; calm.
24	Sunset	54.0	Cos-um-ne river, (San Joaquin valley)	Clear; wind S. 80° W.
25	Sunrise	45.0	Cos-um-ne river.	Cloudy in east; sun faint; calm.
25	Sunset	63.0	Lat. 38 08 23–Mo-kel-um-ne river.	Cloudy in horizon; gentle westerly breeze.
26	Sunrise	36.0	Lat. 38 02 48–Arroyo de los Calaveras.	Sun faint; partially overcast.
26	Sunset	58.0	......do......	Calm; nearly clear.
27	Sunrise	45.0	Stanislaus river.	Sky overcast; no wind.
27	Sunset	60.0	......do......	Very cloudy; appearance of rain; high west wind.
28	Sunrise	44.0	......do......	Calm; clear.
29	Sunrise	36.0	......do......	A few dark clouds in east; calm.
29	Sunset	60.0	......do......	Cloudy; sun faint.
30	Sunrise	53.0	......do......	Overcast; slight rain falling.
30	Noon	55.0	......do......	Incessant rain; moderate wind S. 15° W.
30	Sunset	56.0	......do......	Sky clouded; wind SW.
31	Sunrise	54.0	......do......	Heavy rain; wind S. 80° W.
31	Noon	62.0	Lat. 37 15 43......do......	Rain.
31	Sunset	58.0	......do......	Clearing off; wind SW.
April 1	Sunrise	52.0	To-wal-um-ne river	Sky nearly clear; calm.
1	Sunset	60.0	......do......	Dark clouds coming up in west; calm.
2	Sunrise	48.0	......do......	Cloudy; light easterly wind.
2	Noon	62.0	......do......	Rain from SW.; overcast.
2	Sunset	54.0	......do......	Fresh wind S. 15° E.; clearing off.
3	Sunrise	43.0	Aux-um-ne river......do......	Sky nearly clear; wind E.
3	Sunset	56.0	......do......	A few clouds in SE.; strong breeze N. 60° W.
4	Sunrise	41.0	Lat. 37 08....San Joaquin river	Slight rain falling; wind S. 60° W.
4	Sunset	60.0	..do....	Raining; wind from SW.
5	Sunrise	37.0	Lat. 36 49...do...	Sky clear; calm.
5	Sunset	68.0	......do......	do.
6	Sunrise	35.0	......do......	Sky cloudless; no wind.
6	Noon	90.0	......do......	Sky nearly clear; light SE. breeze.
6	Sunset	72.0	......do......	Wind S. 40° E.; cloudy in NE.
7	Sunrise	49.0	near Lake Fork, (Rio Reyes).	Overclouded; raining.
8	Sunset	35.0	Lat. 36 24 50–Lake Fork, (Rio Reyes).	Sky nearly clear; wind N. 60° W.
8	Sunrise	52.0	...do...do...	Heavy clouds in west; moderate wind S. 80° W.
9	Sunrise	38.0	......do......	Sky clear and calm.
9	Sunset	52.0	Lat. 36 08 38–Small stream; affluent to Tulare lake	Dark cumuli in west; light breeze N. 55° W.

V.—METEOROLOGICAL OBSERVATIONS—Continued.

Date.	Time.	Thermom- eter.	Locality.	Remarks.
1844. Ap'l 10	Sunrise	36.0	....	Perfectly clear; no air.
10	Sunset	56.0	Lat. 35 49 10–Small stream; affluent to the Tulare lake................	
11	Sunrise	37.0	..do....do...........do.....	Nearly clear; calm.
11	Sunset	57.0	............a large stream; affluent to Tulare lake..............	Sky overcast; calm.
12	Sunrise	32.0	..............do........do.......	Cloudy in horizon; high wind N. 45° W. Smoky; sun faint; calm.
12	Sunset	62.0	...........a large stream; affluent to smaller Tulare lake........	Dense smoke; sun obscured.

POSTSCRIPT.

Mineral salt.—The mineral or rock salt, of which a specimen is placed in the Congress Library, was found in the place marked by Baron Humboldt in his map of New Spain, (northern half,) as derived from the journal of the missionary *Father Escalante*, who attempted, towards the close of the last century, to penetrate the unknown country from Santa Fé, of New Mexico, to Monterey, of the Pacific ocean. The adventurous missionary does not seem to have got farther, and that was a great deal at that time, than the south end of the Utah lake, called Lake Timpanogos—a term signifying Rock river. Southeast of that lake is the chain of the Wah-satch mountains, constituting in that place the rim of the Great Basin. In this mountain, at the place where Humboldt has written "*Montagnes de Sel Gemme*," (Rock Salt mountain,) this mineral is found. Its locality, the head waters of a small creek, tributary to the Utah lake, on its southeast, in thick strata of red clay.

The crystallized salt, formed from the spray of the lake on whatever it touches—plants, shrubs, &c.—and of which a specimen is also in the Congress Library, was taken from the southeastern shore of the Great Salt lake. That specimen shows a formation of more than an inch thick of pure crystallized salt on the stem of a small twig, less than the size of a common goose quill.

570

283. *Plantae Frémontianae*; Descriptions of Some New Plants Collected by Col. J. C. Frémont in California. By John Torrey, F.L.S.

Editorial note: With ten plates of drawings prepared by Isaac Sprague, Torrey's twenty-page botanical memoir had been accepted for publication by the Smithsonian Institution in September 1850 while Frémont was in Washington serving the new state of California as senator. It was not printed, however, until April 1853, shortly before the explorer returned from Europe to make his last expedition; it forms a part of vol. VI of the *Smithsonian Contributions to Knowledge*.

Frémont's preserved dried plant collection, the basis of this memoir, was small compared with "the take" of many contemporary naturalists. In introducing the description of the plants, Torrey notes specifically the several mishaps which befell the plants gathered on the first two expeditions. During the course of the third expedition the botanist twice received specimens from Frémont. The first batch came overland from Bent's Fort, the second by sea in the *Erie* from California in 1847. Within the latter group, Torrey wrote a fellow scientist, "there must be a thousand species of plants," as well as "several cases of pine cones, fruit, &c." Later the botanist of the California State Geological Survey, William Henry Brewer, estimated that "about six hundred" numbered specimens came from the third expedition, but Joseph Ewan, who has written the notes to this memoir and provided a list of species for incorporation into the index, thinks this figure is too large.

Some of the specimens were puzzles for years. Frémont reported *Carpenteria* from the "headwaters of the San Joaquin," a plant not rediscovered until thirty years later at Grapevine Spring in Fresno County. The paradoxical snow plant (*Sarcodes sanguinea*) was evidently first made known to botanists from his collection and probably was taken in Yuba County, although Frémont apparently lost the record of where he had found it.

Frémont promised Torrey more plants from the collection he would make on his fourth expedition. None survived the San Juan experience; the second half of the journey yielded specimens but disaster struck again, this time through Creutzfeldt. "I had collected many fine plants along the Gila and in Sonora," Frémont wrote Torrey, "but the man to whom I entrusted their collection although professing to be a botanist, permitted them to get wet repeatedly and many are ruined & the rest he did not even label."

Torrey lauds the explorer's important services to science, although obviously he was disappointed in the collection and in the refusal of the U.S. government to fund further Frémont's explorations and a general account of the botany of California. As for Frémont, he assured the scientist in the fall of 1850 that as soon as he returned to California, he would direct a person in his employ "to collect the Spring plants of our neighborhood." Torrey seems never to have received such specimens, and after 1850 correspondence between the botanist and the explorer appears virtually to have ceased.

DESCRIPTIONS

OF

SOME NEW PLANTS

COLLECTED BY

COLONEL J. C. FRÉMONT, IN CALIFORNIA.*

The important services rendered to science by that distinguished traveller, Colonel Frémont, are known to all who have read the reports of his hazardous journeys. He has not only made valuable additions to the geographical knowledge of our remote possessions, but has greatly increased our acquaintance with the geology and natural history of the regions which he explored. His First Expedition was made in the year 1842, and terminated at the Rocky Mountains. He examined the celebrated South Pass, and ascended the highest mountain of the Wind River Chain, now called Frémont's Peak. The party moved so rapidly (travelling from the frontier of Missouri to the Mountains and returning in the short space of four months) that much time could not be given to botany. Nevertheless a collection of 350 species of plants was made, of which I gave an account in a Botanical Appen-

---

*An Abstract of this memoir was read before the American Association for the Advancement of Science, at its meeting held in New Haven, 1850, and published in the volume of its Proceedings.

dix to his first Report. The Second Expedition of Colonel Frémont, that of 1843 and 1844, embraced not only much of the ground which he had previously explored, but extensive regions of Oregon and California. In this journey, he made large collections in places never before visited by a botanist; but, unfortunately, a great portion of them was lost. In the gorges of the Sierra Nevada, a mule loaded with some bales of botanical specimens gathered in a thousand miles of travel, fell from a precipice into a deep chasm, from whence they could not be recovered. A large part of the remaining collection was destroyed, on the return of the Expedition, by the great flood of the Kansas river. Some of the new and more interesting plants that were rescued from destruction, were published in the Botanical Appendix to Colonel Frémont's Report of his Second Expedition.

Very large collections were also made in his Third Exposition in 1845 and the two following years; but again, notwithstanding every precaution, some valuable packages were destroyed by the numerous and unavoidable mishaps of such a hazardous journey. Very few of the new genera and species that were saved have as yet been published, excepting several of the Compositae, by Dr. Gray, in order that the priority of their discovery might be secured for Colonel Frémont. There was still another journey to California made by that zealous traveller; the disastrous one commenced late in the year 1848. Even in this he gleaned a few plants, which, with all his other botanical collections, he kindly placed at my disposal. I had hoped that arrangements would have been made by the Government for the publication of a general account of the Botany of California; but as there is no immediate prospect of such a work being undertaken, I have prepared this memoir on some of the more interesting new genera discovered by Colonel Frémont. The drawings of the accompanying plates were made by Mr. Isaac Sprague, of Cambridge, Massachusetts, who ranks among the most eminent botanical draughtsmen of our day.[1]

SPRAGUEA. Nov. Gen.

Calyx disepalus, persistens.; sepalis suborbiculatis, basi cordatis, emarginatis, membranaceis, patentibus. Corollae petala 4, aestivatio imbricata, libera, duobus exterioribus sepalis alternantibus, interioribus sepalis oppositis. Stamina 3, petalis opposita. Ovarium uniloculare. Ovula 8–10, basilaria. Stylus filiformis, apice trifidus; lobis intus

573

stigmatosis. Capsula membranacea, compressa, unilocularis, bivalvis. Semina 2–5, lenticulari-compressa, nigra, nitida, estrophiolata.— Herba Californica, perennis, glabra; caulibus 1–5, scapiformibus, e caudice brevi ortis, remote squamosis; floribus confertis scorpioideo-spicatis; spicis pluribus, aphyllis, umbellatis, terminalibus.

Spraguea Umbellata. Tab. I.

Hab.—Forks of the Nozah river, in the foot-hills of the Sierra Nevada of Northern California. In flower and fruit, May 22. Other specimens, not ticketed, were in the collection, perhaps obtained on the same ground a little earlier in the season.

The root of this remarkable plant is short and tapering, soon dividing into a tuft of thick fleshy fibres. The caudex is short and thick, throwing up from its summit from one to five or six simple scape-like branches, which are from three inches to a span high, and somewhat diverging. All the proper leaves are situated at the crown of the caudex, forming a dense rosulate cluster. They are from an inch to nearly two inches in length, of a fleshy consistence, obovate-spatulate, with a long tapering base, obtuse, and perfectly entire. The scapes are furnished with several lanceolate distant scales, which are scarious on the margin. Spikes six to twelve in a terminal spreading umbel, at first conspicuously scorpioid, and gradually unfolding from the base upwards. The peduncles are about half an inch long, and the ovate bracts at their base form an involucrum. Flowers closely imbricated, on short pedicels. The calyx consists of two persistent hyaline sepals, which are right and left of the axis; they are nearly orbicular, emarginate, undulate on the margin, obscurely veined, and of a pale rose-color, except the broad green midrib. Petals four, obovate, rose-color, much shorter than the calyx, two of them nearly opposite the sepals, the others alternate with them, gelatinous-colliquescent after flowering, as in many other Portulacaceae, and in a withered state, remaining attached to the summit of the young fruit like an indusium. The stamens are constantly but three, and are inserted opposite three of the petals; the fourth (belonging to a lateral petal) wanting: filaments longer than the petals: anthers ovate, fixed by the middle, two-celled, opening longitudinally. The ovary is globose-ovoid, much compressed, one-celled, and contains from eight to ten ovules, on conspicuous stalks, which arise from a basilar placenta. Style slender, as long as the stamens, undivided; the stigma minute and three-lobed. Capsule membranaceous, much compressed, two-valved; the valves parallel with the persistent sepals. Seeds lenticular, black and shining, with a crustaceous testa. Embryo hippocrepiform, embracing mealy albumen.

This remarkable plant undoubtedly belongs to the family of the Portulacaceae; and, judging from the description, it seems to be a near ally of the Chilian genus Monocosmia of Fenzl. In the latter, however, there is but a single stamen; the ovules are only from two to four in number; the style is very short as well as two-cleft, and the habit is different.

I have dedicated this genus to Mr. Isaac Sprague, of Cambridge, Massachusetts, so well known as a botanical draughtsman, and especially for the admirable illustrations of the Genera of the Plants of the United States, by himself and Dr. Gray.

FRÉMONTIA. Nov. Gen.

Calyx basi tribracteatus, patenti-campanulatus, quinque-partitus, subpetaloideus basi foveolatus aestivatione quincuncialis. Corolla nulla. Stamina quinque: filamenta vix ad medium monadelpha: antherae oblongo-lineares, biloculares, subanfractuosae, extrorsae; loculis longitudinaliter dehiscentibus. Ovarium quadriquinque-loculare: ovula in loculis plurima, biseriatim inserta, horizontalia, anatropa: stylus filiformis, subincurvus: stigma indivisum, acutiusculum. Capsula* ovata, turgida, plerumque quinquelocularis, loculicide dehiscens, pilis rigidis stellatis dense vestita; loculis polyspermis. "Semina ovata, glabra."— Frutex Californicus, stellato-pubescens; foliis alternis cordatis, lobatis; stipulis nullis vel caducis; pedunculis oppositifoliis unifloris; floribus amplis flavis.

---

*Just as this memoir was sent to press I received from the Rev. Mr. A. Fitch a collection of plants which he obtained while acting as a missionary in California. In his extensive travels through that country he availed himself of favorable opportunities of collecting botanical specimens, which from time to time he placed at my disposal. In the last parcel, which he brought home himself, I was greatly pleased to find the Frémontia. I am now able to describe the fruit of this rare plant, but unfortunately the only capsule that was received had shed its seeds, the characters of which I have given from the verbal description of Mr. Fitch.

HAB.—Sources of the Sacramento, in the northern part of the Sierra Nevada of California. Also hill-sides, Mariposa county, especially near the gold works of the Merced Company; flowering in May.— Rev. Mr. A. Fitch.

A beautiful shrub, usually from three to four feet high, but occasionally reaching a height of ten feet, and having very much the appearance of an ordinary fig-tree. The bark is of a brownish gray color; the wood is hard, and apparently of slow growth. Most of the leaves and flowers are produced at the extremity of very short lateral branches or spurs. The former are petiolate, roundish in outline, from three fourths of an inch to an inch, or sometimes even three inches, in diameter,* three to seven-lobed; the lobes entire, or crenate-toothed, of a thick (and when old of a somewhat coriaceous) texture, green and sparsely stellate-pubescent on the upper surface, ferruginous-tomentose underneath; the petioles from four to six lines long. In the specimens from Mariposa county, the leaves of the young shoots are less deeply and more numerously lobed. The peduncles are about as long as the petioles, stout, straight or somewhat recurved. Immediately under each flower, and closely applied to the calyx, are three small lanceolate bracts. The calyx is sulphur-yellow widely campanulate, about an inch and a quarter in diameter, deeply five-parted; the segments roundish-obovate, and usually with a short abrupt point, or sometimes mucronate. Externally the calyx is sparsely stellate-pubescent, and on the inside at the base it is densely villous. The stamens are equal, shorter than the calyx, and opposite to its segments: the filaments are glabrous, the upper half filiform, spreading and distinct; the lower part united into a tube which embraces the ovary and nearly conceals it: the anthers are about three lines long, extrorse, adnate, tortuous, and incurved at each end. In the bud they are four-celled, but only two-celled in the expanded flower; the cells are distinct and open longitudinally their whole length. Under the microscope the pollen appears triangular-globose and reticulated. The ovary is ovoid, and densely clothed with short conical hairs or processes. It is usually five-celled;[†] each cell containing eight or ten horizontal anatropous

---

*The plate of Fremontia was engraved and printed before the specimens with larger leaves were obtained.

†Only four cells are represented in the plate, and no more were found in the flowers first examined.

ovules: the style is about one third longer than the stamens, and gradually tapers towards the summit, where it terminates in a minute undivided stigma. The capsule is about as large as that of Hibiscus Syriacus, and is closely covered with short stiff reddish stellate hairs; a portion of the calyx remaining at its base. At maturity it splits loculicidally nearly to the base into five valves. Only two or three seeds ripen in each cell; and these are smooth, resembling those of the Ochra.

This genus is a near ally of the celebrated Cheirostemon of Humboldt, the Hand-tree of Mexico. The latter differs, however, in the form and texture of the calyx, the lobes of which are deciduous; in the much longer stamineal column and secund mucronate free portion of the filaments; in the straight parallel anther-cells, and in some other characters of less importance.

The genus Cheirostemon has long been regarded as an anomalous member of the order Bombaceae, which by many botanists is reduced to a tribe of Sterculiaceae. It differs, as does also Frémontia, from the rest of the tribe in the apetalous flowers, imbricated calyx, and definite stamens; characters which, in this family, are of sufficient value to constitute a distinct division, which may be called FRÉMONTIEAE. The genus Ochroma of Swartz, another anomalous Bombacea, has some resemblance to Cheirostemon, as Kunth noticed many years ago, especially in its five-lobed stamineal crown and in the subimbricated calyx; but in most other respects it resembles its congeners.

Those Bombaceae which have the stamineal tube five-cleft at the summit, with each segment bearing two anthers, may be regarded as composed of ten stamens, the filaments of which are monadelphous below and pentadelphous above; the upper portions of the filaments being united in pairs, with (usually) one-celled anthers. This view may be taken of Fremontia as well as of Cheirostemon.

In my memoir on Batis, published in the present volume, I have given the reason for relinquishing the former genus Frémontia, and my intention of bestowing the name on a new plant from California, first detected by the distinguished traveller himself, whose valuable services to North America Botany it is thus intended to commemorate.[2]

LIBOCEDRUS. Endl.[3]

LIBOCEDRUS Endl. Synops. Conif. p. 42; Gen. Pl. Suppl. IV. pars 2, No. 1794. THUYAE species auct.

L. ramulis compressis subancipitis; foliis late ovatis breviter acuminatis apice serrulatis longe decurrentibus, lateralibus carinatis, facialibus planis; strobilis ovato-oblongis erectis; squamis infra apicem spina tuberculiformi recurva auctis, superioribus multo majoribus; seminibus bialatis, ala altera maxima.

HAB.—Upper waters of the Sacramento, particularly from lat. 38° 40′ to about 41° N. lat., where it was also found (without fruit) by the botanists of the United States Exploring Expedition, and by Dr. G. W. Hulse.

A noble tree, sometimes attaining a height of 120 or even 140 feet; and a trunk of seven feet in diameter is not uncommon. It rises from 80 to 100 feet without a limb. The leaves are four-ranked, as usual in this genus, very small, and closely imbricated; their bases prolonged downward and contracted, with strongly-marked longitudinal lines where the two exterior overlap the two interior ones. In the younger branchlets, the decurrent bases are from two to three times longer than their diameter, and in the older ones, about four times longer. None of the leaves are acerose. The two interior of each joint are marked on the face with a slight depression, beneath which there is often a small obscure gland, although none appears externally. The staminiferous aments terminate the branchlets. They are ovoid-oblong, and from two to three lines in length. The stamens are from twelve to fourteen, four-ranked; the connective produced into a suborbicular excentrically peltate scale, and bearing on its under surface about four oblong anther-cells, which open longitudinally. The seminiferous aments are nearly an inch in length, ovate-oblong, and consist of four scales, of which the two exterior are very short, the two interior rounded externally, with the flattened septum-like axis prolonged between them, and equalling them in length; all the scales mucronate with a short recurved point below the tip. Beneath each interior scale are two seeds. These are furnished with two very unequal wings.

This tree much resembles Callitris quadrivalvis in its foliage. It has probably been confounded by some botanists with Thuya gigantea of Nuttall, from which, however, it can be distinguished by the foliage alone; the long decurrent bases of the leaves being characteristic of the Libocedrus. Endlicher has described three other species of this genus, all of which are natives of South America and New Zealand. Our L.

decurrens is most nearly related to L. Chilensis *Endl.* (Thuya Chilensis *Hook. Lond. Jour. Bot.* 2, p. 199. t. 4).

COLEOGYNE. Nov. Gen.

Calyx basi bibracteolatus, coriaceus, petaloideus, quadrisepalus; sepalis basi connatis persistentibus. Corolla nulla. Stamina numerosa; filamentis ima basi disci tubaeformi inserta. Ovarium uniovulatum, uniloculare, tuba disci inclusum: ovulum hemitropum: stylus lateralis, filiformis, intus longitudinaliter stigmatosus. Fructus . . . —Frutex Californicus, ramosissimus, rigidus; ramulis saepe subspinescentibus; foliis parvulis, oblongis, crassis, oppositis, confertis, brevissime petiolatis; lamina decidua, stipulis cum petiolo minutissimo persistentibus; floribus solitariis, terminalibus, basi bracteis trifidis suffulti.

Coleogyne Ramosissima. Tab. IV.

Hab. Sources of the Mohave and Virgin Rivers, tributaries of the Colorado of the West, in the mountains of Southern California. Flowering in April and May.

A shrub with the aspect of Krameria, five to six feet high, and clothed with a grayish bark; the branches spreading, short, crowded, and mostly opposite. Leaves crowded toward the summit of short, spur-like branches, which often become spiny, appearing fasciculate, but truly opposite. They are oblong, on very short pedicles, from five to eight lines long, rather obtuse, tapering at the base, very thick and coriaceous, marked with five longitudinal ribs on the upper surface, but flattish underneath, clothed with appressed hairs, which are fixed by the middle. The stipules are minute and scale-like, partly adherent to the short and persistent petiole, from which the lamina of the leaf falls away, their minute points giving to the spurs a squarrose appearance. The flowers are about half an inch in diameter, terminal, solitary, on short stalks, and are subtended by two (or sometimes four) trifid bracts which resemble the ordinary leaves, except that the points of the stipules are more strongly produced, and the articulated lamina is much smaller. The persistent sepals are ovate or obovate, coriaceous, somewhat united at the base, obtuse or mucronate at the summit, spreading, one or more of them rarely furnished with a single lateral tooth. Externally they are hairy like the leaves, but glabrous and yellowish on the inner surface; the two outer are flat, the two inner ob-volute or half equitant. There are from thirty to forty stamens, which are about as long as the calyx: the filaments slender, distinct, except at the base, where they are confluent with a singular sheath which encloses the pistil: anthers oblong-cordate, introrse, two-celled, opening longitudinally. Pollen very minute, obtusely triangular. The sheath arises from the base of the calyx, and is about the length of the stamens. It gradually tapers from below upwards, and is somewhat five-toothed at the summit. The pistil is solitary and simple; the ovary sessile and oblong: style lateral, arising from a little below the middle of the ovary, tortuous, exserted, very villous, the upper third compressed, somewhat recurved, and stigmatose on one side. Ovule single in all the specimens examined, hemitropous on a very short funiculus, which is inserted opposite the origin of the style. Ripe fruit unknown: probably an achenium. In a partially mature state the seed appeared to be destitute of albumen, and the broad flat cotyledons could be distinctly seen. The radicle is erect.

It is difficult to refer this puzzling genus with certainty to any natural order hitherto indicated. Its nearest affinities are doubtless with Rosaceae, and with the suborder Chrysobalaneae; from which it differs in its opposite leaves, persistent stipules, lateral stigma, and solitary ovules, as well as in habit. One undoubted genus of this suborder, and three anomalous genera referred here by most botanists, are apetalous. In several others, the filaments are united at the base; in two or three there are lateral or interior sterile filaments; and in Trilepisium there is a tube between stamens and pistils, as well as a solitary ovule. The sheath or tube may be regarded as belonging to the androecium either by the deduplication of the interior stamens, or as consisting of the monadelphous filaments of an abortive inner series of stamens.

Coleogyne also resembles some of the proper Rosaceae with solitary carpels; especially those of the Tribe Dryadeae, *Torr. & Gr.* In its elongated lateral stigma, it is like Purshia. To Cliffortia, it is allied in its foliage and stipules, as well as in other respects. Finally, we are inclined to place this new genus in Rosaceae, between Chrysobalaneae and Dryadeae; although it is more nearly related to the former than to the latter. The opposite leaves, which are so closely approximated that I was not aware of their true arrangement until the engraving of the plant was finished, are not found in any other Rosaceae, so far as I know.

EMPLECTOCLADUS, Nov. Gen.

Calyx obconico-campanulatus; tubo ad faucem nudo haud contracto; limbo aequaliter quinquepartito, persistente. Petala 5, erecto-patentia. Stamina 10–13, biserialia. Pistilla 1–2 (plerumque solitaria) unilocularia: ovula 2, collateralia, pendula. Stylus brevissimus, crassus, subobliquus: stigma capitatum. Fructus . . . —Frutex Californicus, ramosissimus; ramis rigidis, patentibus, subspinescentibus; foliis minutis, spathulatis, e gemmis subglobosis quasi fasciculatis; stipulis minutis deciduis; floribus subsolitariis, sessilibus, terminalibus, parvulis.

EMPLECTOCLADUS FASCICULATUS. TAB. V.

HAB.—Sierra Nevada of California; probably in the southern part of the range.

A shrub, with numerous widely spreading branches, which have a knobbed appearance from the short rounded buds or spurs; the bark smooth and of an olive color. The leaves are crowded on the spurs, three to four lines long, cuneate-spatulate, obtuse, sessile, of a thick and somewhat coriaceous texture, flat, marked with a single nerve underneath, sparsely hirsute with mostly deciduous hairs, and furnished with minute scarious stipules. The flowers are mostly solitary, surrounded by the closely set leaves, and are scarcely more than a fourth of an inch in diameter. Externally the calyx is glabrous, but woolly inside; the teeth short and obtuse. The petals are apparently white, ovate-oblong, obtuse, about one line and a half long, and are destitute of a claw. There are usually about eleven stamens, the slender filaments of which are inserted in two rows near the summit of the calyx-tube, the superior or exterior ones being about as long as the petals: anthers subglobose-didymous, introrse; the cells distinct, opening longitudinally. Pollen obtusely triangular (as is also the case in Adenostoma and many other Rosaceae). Pistils usually solitary, but sometimes in pairs, seated at the bottom of the calyx, and free from it. The ovary is ovoid, abruptly contracted above into a very short and somewhat oblique style, which is terminated by a depressed-capitate stigma. There are two ovules, which are anatropous, and suspended from the summit of the cell opposite the style. Nothing is yet known of the ripe fruit.

The only specimens of this plant brought by Colonel Frémont had

581

unfortunately lost their labels, so that we have no certain information as to its precise station, and of the size which it attains. Neither, for want of the fruit, can we determine its nearest affinities. It is probable, however, that the genus belongs to the Tribe Dryadeae. In many respects it resembles Adenostoma of that tribe, but it differs in the even calyx without glands* in the throat; in being almost destitute of a style, as well as in the mode of inflorescence, the form of the ovary, &c. There may also be considerable difference in the fruit, as the appearance of the ovary seems to indicate. The generic name is derived from Ἔμπλεκτος, *entangled*, and κλάδος, *a branch*.

CHAMAEBATIA, Benth. Plant. Hartw. p. 308.[†]

Calycis tubus turbinato-campanulatus; limbus persistens, laciniis 5 aestivatione valvatis. Petala 5. Stamina numerosa, pluriseriata, ad faucem calycis inserta. Ovarium in fundo calycis unicum, erectum, liberum: stylus ex apice ovarii erectus, latere interiore fere ad medium fissus et stigmatifer. Ovula 2, erecta, anatropa. Achenium siccum, calyce subinclusum. Semen unicum erectum.—Frutex Californicus, ramosissimus; foliis tripinnatisectis, segmentis ultimis confertis numerosissimis; stipulis lineari-lanceolatis; floribus cymosis albis.

CHAMAEBATIA FOLIOLOSA, Benth. l. c. TAB. VI.

HAB.—Higher parts of the Sierra Nevada, as well as on the sides of the foothills; in great abundance: Colonel Frémont. Mountains of the Sacramento: Mr. Hartweg and Mr. Shelton.

A shrub, growing from two to three feet high, of agreeable bal-

---

*The so-called glands in the throat of Adenostoma are only lobes of the free margin of the disk.

†The plant on which this genus was founded was first discovered by Colonel Frémont, in his second expedition, while traversing the Sierra Nevada and other parts of California, early in the year 1844, as well as in his third expedition. His specimens were too imperfect for description. It was afterwards found in good condition, but without mature fruit, by the well known and zealous botanical collector, Mr. Hartweg. Mr. Bentham kindly offered me the privilege of describing this fine new genus, but I thought the right fairly belonged to him, as he first determined its character and affinities. I have but little to add to the accurate description which he has given of it in his Plantae Hartwegianae.

samic odor,[4] with very smooth bark, and numerous upright branches; the young twigs clothed with a glandularly pubescent epidermis, which easily separates. The leaves are broadly ovate in outline, about two inches long, tripinnately dissected; the ultimate segments oval and obtuse, scarcely half a line long, hispidulous-pubescent, each tipped with a minute gland. Stipules minute, adnate to the petiole. The cymes are four–five-flowered, and terminate the young shoots: each pedicel is subtended by a foliaceous bract, which is toothed or pinnatifid. The flowers are about three fourths of an inch in diameter. Externally the calyx is glandularly pubescent, and the inside of the tube is densely woolly. The petals are white, obovate, emarginate, with a very short claw. There are fifty or more stamens, the filaments of which are inserted in several series in the throat of the calyx. The pollen is obtusely triangular. The ovary is ovoid; one-celled, with two collateral and erect ovules, which arise from the base of the cell: style as long as the stamens, nearly straight, and with a longitudinal stigmatose fissure or groove on the inside (as in Cercocarpus). Achenium oblong, compressed, almost wholly enclosed in the persistent and membranaceous calyx, apiculate with the base of the style. The seed is erect, with amygdaloid cotyledons, and a short inferior radicle.

The foliage of this plant is so different from that of most other Rosaceae, that it was at first sight taken for a Mimosa or Acacia. It clearly belongs to the subtribe Cercocarpeae, *Torr. & Gr.*,[*] although it differs in its valvate calyx. The aestivation of Cercocarpus is difficult to determine, as the calyx is open in the very young flower-bud, and the teeth are very short; it seems, however, to be imbricated. The characters of the subtribe Eudryadeae must be altered, for the calyx in Cowania (described by Don, Endlicher, and Zuccarini as valvate) is certainly imbricate in all the species. Dr. Englemann noticed this character in his genus Greggia[†] (which is Cowania plicata, *Don*, and C. purpurea, *Zucc.*)[‡] There will be nothing therefore to distinguish the subtribes, as they now stand, but the number of ovaries in the

---

*Flora of North America, 1. p. 426.

†Bot. Append. to Wislizenus's Tour in Northern Mexico, p. 114.

‡A remarkable new species of Cowania, with entire linear leaves (C. ericaefolia, *Torr.*), has very recently been found on the Rio Grande, by Dr. Parry of the Mexican Boundary Commission. It will be described in the appendix to the second part of Dr. Gray's Plantae Wrightianae, now in press, and soon to be published.

flower, which being a character of no great importance, they may be united; and then Cowania will stand next to Purshia, to which it is very nearly allied in habit.

CARPENTERIA, Nov. Gen.

Calycis tubo late hemisphaerico, basi ovarii adnato; limbo 5–6–(rarius 7–) partito, laciniis valvatis persistentibus. Petala 5–6, orbiculari-obovata, aestivatione convoluta. Stamina numerosa: filamenta filiformia. Styli in unicum coadunati, brevi: stigmata 5–7, lineari-oblonga, distincta. Capsula (nisi basi) libera, 5–7, locularis, loculicide dehiscens: placentae subglobosae, intra loculos projectae, polyspermae. Semina divergentia, oblonga; testa utrinque laxa, reticulata, ad hilum crenata.—Frutex Californicus; foliis oppositis integerrimis; floribus magnis, albis, in cymis racemosis simplicibus terminalibus dispositis.

Carpenteria Californica. Tab. VII.

Hab.—Sierra Nevada of California, probably on the head waters of the San Joachin.

A shrub, with upright dichotomous branches, and a loose grayish bark, which is disposed to separate in plates. Leaves from two to three inches long, elliptical-oblong, gradually tapering at the base into a petiole, the margins (when dry) narrowly revolute, glabrous above, densely and minutely tomentose underneath, and with scattered appressed hairs. These hairs are muricate-scabrous, as in Philadelphus, Decumaria, Deutzia, and Jamesia. Stipules wanting. The cyme is on a long straight peduncle, and is from five to seven-flowered. The pedicels are from an inch and a half to two inches and a half in length. They are furnished at the base with oblong foliaceous bracts, which resemble the leaves, but are smaller; and about half an inch below the flower, there is a pair of subulate bracteoles. The (fructiferous) calyx is very obtuse and almost truncate at the base, tomentose externally, with the segments ovate, acute, entire, and spreading. The petals are white, about three fourths of an inch long, nearly orbicular, and alternate with the segments of the calyx. There are fifty or more stamens, which are inserted with the petals at the base of the free portion of the calyx: the filaments are slender, shorter than the petals, glabrous, and furnished with subglobose, two-celled, didymous anthers, which open longitudinally. The pollen is subglobose and simple. The ovary was destroyed by insects in the withered flowers that were found with the specimens. The styles are combined, and the oblong stigmas are free. Capsule broadly ovoid-conical, crowned with the united styles; the thin exocarp finally separating from the coriaceous endocarp, and persistent at the base, so as to resemble accessory valves. The endocarp opens longitudinally on the back. The placentae are large, subglobose from a narrow base, projecting into the cavity of the cells, and covered with very numerous seeds, which radiate in all directions. The seeds are oblong, anatropous; the reticulated testa a little produced at each end, but not enough to form a wing, crenate at the hilar extremity. Nucleus oblong, nearly as long as the seed. The embryo is in the axis of fleshy albumen, which it nearly equals in length; with ovate plano-convex cotyledons, and a cylindrical thick radicle.

The only specimens of this plant brought home by Colonel Frémont, were in fruit; but I found attached to them a few withered and imperfect flowers. These materials, however, were sufficient to show the essential characters of nearly all the organs. The genus is very near Philadelphus: which differs, however, in the usually tetramerous flowers, in the calyx adhering to the greater part of the ovary and fruit, in the form of the placentae, and in the seeds being strongly imbricated and pendulous, as well as fimbriate at the hilum. In very old fruit of Philadelphus, especially after it has been exposed to the action of frost, the exocarp separates as in this genus, but not in such regular valves. The same character exists also in Decumaria.

This genus is named in memory of my excellent departed friend, the late Professor Carpenter of Louisiana, who for many years laboriously and successfully investigated the Botany of his native State, but who was suddenly arrested in his career, while preparing an account of his researches.[5]

HYMENOCLEA, Torr. & Gray.

Hymenoclea, Torr. & Gray, in Emory. Rep. p. 143 (sine char.); Gray, Pl. Fendl. p. 79.

Capitula monoica, homogama, glomerato-spicata. Mas. Involucrum Franseriae, 5–6—lobum, 15–20—florum. Receptaculum parvum, paleis scariosis unguiculatis obovato-dilatatis vel spathulatis onustum. Corolla cyathiformis, quinquedentata. Antherae conniventes, vix connatae, appendicula deltoidea inflexa superatae. Stylus apice radiato-pencillatus. Fem. Involucrum fructiferum obovoideum seu fusiformi-clavatum, coriaceum, clausum, uniloculare, apice in rostrum tubiforme superne scariosum pervium desinens, extus squamis 9–12 magnis scariosis persistentibus, aut spiraliter imbricatis, aut univerticillatis, insigniter alatum.—Frutices Neo-Mexicani, Texani, et Californici, in aridis salinis vigentes, ramosissimi, glabrati, foliosi; foliis alternis filiformibus, inferioribus pinnato-triquinquepartitis, summis integerrimis; capitulis axillaribus et terminalibus.—Gray, Pl. Fendl. l. c.

Hymenoclea Salsola, Torr. & Gray, l. c. Tab. VIII.

H. involucro fructifero strobiliformi squamas a basi ad apicem spiraliter dispositas suborbiculares undique gerente.

Hab.—Sandy saline uplands, near the Mohave River, Southern California; flowering in August.

This singular plant, looking, when in fruit, so much like one of the Chenopodiaceae, is a stout shrub, attaining the height of about two feet, with numerous branches which are invested with a loose and pale bark. The leaves are mostly entire, from one to inches long, and scarcely a line wide, semiterete (when dry), paler, and somewhat hoary underneath. Only the lower ones are from three to five parted. In the axils of the leaves, along the upper branches are clustered the sessile little heads of flowers. The staminate heads are hemispherical, and consist of a somewhat hairy involucre of five obtuse, undulate or crenate lobes, enclosing from fifteen to twenty minute flowers, which contain not even the rudiment of an ovary. The corolla is glabrous and five-lobed. The chaff, which is nearly as long as the corolla, is obovate or oblong, with a long and narrow claw. Although destitute of an ovary, the flower contains a slender filiform style, which at length projects through the included tube of anthers, and is furnished with a capitate pencillate stigma. The fructiferous involucre is the most conspicuous part of the plant. It is about one third of an inch in diameter, of an obovoid form, and is surrounded, in a spiral manner, with usually ten broad spreading winglike scales of a silvery color. The scales are thickened and indurated at the base. The achenium is of a dark purple color, and is completely enclosed in the coriaceous body of the involucre. It is tipped with the long and persistent style, which is much exserted through the tubular rostrum.

The only specimens of this plant which I have ever seen, were collected by Colonel Frémont, in the place above mentioned. Afterwards another species of the same genus was discovered by Major Emory on the Gila River, and is briefly noticed in the Botanical Appendix to his Report, under the name of H. monogyra, *Torr. & Gray.* The same plant has since been found in California by Colonel Frémont; at Ojito, in New Mexico, by the late Dr. Gregg; and in Texas by Mr. Charles Wright. It is described by Dr. Gray, in his Plantae Fendlerianae, p. 79. In my specimens of *H. monogyra* from the Gila, the scales in several of the fructiferous involucra are broad, and not contracted at the base. The sterile heads are rather smaller than in *H. Salsola*, and the chaff is spatulate.

This genus is very nearly allied to Franseria, but differs in the remarkable winglike scales of the fructiferous involucre, as well as in habit. Perhaps the following interesting plant, found by Colonel Frémont on his return from California in 1849, may unite Franseria and Hymenoclea.

Franseria.

FRANSERIA DELTOIDEA (sp. nov.): caule erecto suffruticoso glabriusculo; foliis deltoideis indivisis eroso-denticulatis subtus dealbatis; involucris foemineis subglobosis bilocellatis bifloris; squamis lanceolatis breviter spinescentibus, margine submembranaceis, exterioribus latioribus.

HAB.—On the Gila River, Southern California [present Arizona]: collected by Colonel Frémont, in returning [to California] from his fourth journey. Found also by Dr. C. C. Parry, on the same river.

Stem apparently suffrutescent, with slender angular branches, which are clothed with a deciduous pubescence. The leaves are deltoid, or deltoid-ovate, scarcely an inch long, obtuse or subcordate at the base, irregularly erose-toothed, tomentose on both sides, almost white underneath, except the reticulated veins. The heads are not larger than a small pea, and are disposed in racemose spikes, which are about two inches long. The sterile ones are pedicellate, with the involucre pubescent, 5–6-toothed, and about fifteen-flowered. Corolla of the sterile flowers tubular-infundibuliform and glabrous; the bracteole or chaff at its base broadly ligulate. The fertile involucre is sessile; the base surrounded with imbricated broadly ovate membranaceous mucronate bracts, which are crenulate on the margin; scales numerous, membranaceous on the margin, terminating in a sharp stout scabrous spine, which is often a little curved or uncinate at the tip. Styles filiform and obtuse.

A remarkable species, partaking of the character both of Hymenoclea and Franseria. There is a transition from the broad and somewhat membranaceous bracts at the base of the fertile head, to the lower scales of the involucre, and from these, with a broad base and spiny top, to the narrow prickles that occur in many species of Franseria.

A genuine and apparently new species of the latter genus occurs among the plants collected in California by Colonel Frémont. It belongs to the section Centrolaena of De Candolle, and may be thus characterized.

FRANSERIA ALBICAULIS: frutescens, incano-pubescens; foliis bipinnatifidis, laciniis oblongis vel lineari-oblongis obtusis integris vel pauci-dentatis; capitulis dense spicato-racemosis; involucro masculo 8-dentato, fructifero biloculari aculeis lanceolato-subulatis rigidis incurvis armato.

HAB.—Southern California [Arizona], probably on the Gila: Colonel Frémont. It was also found, without flower or fruit, by Major Emory, on the sandhills of the Gila; and is the plant referred to in my botanical appendix to his Report, as an apparently new species of Ambrosia.

A shrub with numerous branches, which are clothed with a short whitish pubescence. The leaves are about an inch long, grayish pubescent on both sides, and pinnately or bipinnately divided; the narrow ultimate segments being from one to three inches in length. The heads are about the size of a small pea, and are disposed in close leafless spiked racemes. Some of the racemes are wholly staminate; others have fertile heads intermixed. Sterile heads on short pedicels, with the involucre obtusely 7–8-toothed. The chaff is filiform and bearded. Corolla five-toothed. The fructiferous involucres are globuse, and thickly covered with rather rigid, compressed, curved prickles, which are slightly roughened, and about as long as the semidiameter of the involucre.

This species is near F. dumosa *Gray*, described in my Botanical Appendix to Frémont's Second Report; but it differs in the more divided leaves, and in the rigid, nearly glabrous, curved, and larger scales of the involucre.

AMPHIPAPPUS, Torr. & Gray.

Capitulum plerumque sexflorum, heterogamum; nempe flore radii unico ligulato, femineo, fertili, et floribus disci quinque, tubulosis, hermaphroditis, sed sterilibus. Involucrum obovoideum, squamis septem ad novem, subaequalibus, concavis, subcarinatis, appresso-imbricatis. Receptaculum angustum, subalveolatum. Ligula brevis, obovata, discum vix superans: corolla disci e tubo gracili infundibuli-formis, limbo profunde quinquefido. Styli rami breves Linosyridis; appendiculo ovato-deltoideo superati. Achenium radii oblongum, compressum, villosum, pappo uniseriali paleaceo (e squamellis pluribus setaceis varie modo concretis) achenio dimidio breviore superatum. Achenia disci infertilia, turbinata, pappo piloso uniseriali elongato in-structa; setis rigidulis, tortuosis, denticulatis, valde inaequalibus, inter-dum subramosis.—Frutex Californicus, ramosissimus; foliis alternis, brevibus, obovato-spathulatis, integerrimis, subsessilibus; capitulis dense corymbosis; floribus aureis.*

AMPHIPAPPUS FRÉMONTII, *Torr. & Gray, l. c.* Tab. IX.

Hab.—Interior of California, in the mountains between 35° and 36° of North latitude; particularly on the Mohave River and other tributaries of the Colorado: flowering in April.

A smoothish shrub, growing about a foot and a half high, with numerous slender, whitish, corymbose branches. The leaves are from half an inch to three fourths of an inch long, nearly glabrous, of a rather thick texture, mucronate at the tip, and tapering at the base into a short petiole. The flowers are yellow, in numerous heads, which are three or four lines long, in clusters of from three to five each, and disposed in somewhat naked corymbs. The involucres are nearly glabrous; and the oblong obtuse scales are of a pale straw color. There is but a solitary ray-flower, the ligule of which is obovate, entire, and about one third as long as the involucre. Its achenium is villous, and crowned with a paleaceous pappus of five or six scales, which are deeply cut into several unequal subulate segments, or rather consist of bristles variously united. The disk flowers are usually five in number, infundibuliform, with a slender tube, 5-cleft; the segments revolute. Stamens at length exserted; the anthers furnished with a subulate ap-

---

*Amphipappus, Torr. & Gray, in Bost. Journ. Nat. Hist. 5. p. 4.

pendage at the tip. The achenia of the disk are apparently always infertile, though containing a large and well formed ovule. They are crowned with a setose pappus which is nearly as long as the corolla. Its bristles are usually very tortuous, and sometimes forked or rather united in pairs, at the base.

This rare Composita belongs to the subtribe Asterineae of the tribe Astereae, and to the division Chrysocomeae. It resembles in many respects Solidago, particularly the sections Euthamia and Chrysoma of that genus, from which it differs in the involucre and in the dimorphous pappus. In its involucre and general habit it more nearly resembles Guttierrezia, and might be referred to that genus were it not for the truly pilose or setose pappus of the disk-flowers.

SARCODES, Nov. Gen.

Calyx quinquesepalus, marcescens; sepalis concavis, basi vix gibbosis. Corolla campanulata, persistens, quinquelobata; lobis ovatis, erectis. Stamina 10, hypogyna: filamenta subulato-filiformia: antherae oblongae, biloculares, didymae, fere ad basim introrsum affixae; loculis sacculaeformibus, apice oblique truncatis, foramine amplo hiantibus. Ovarium hemisphaericum, quinquelobatum, quinqueloculare; loculis multiovulatis. Ovula horizontalia, anatropa. Stylus elongato-columnaris: stigma capitatum, subquinquelobum. Discus nullus. Capsula depresso-globosa, subquinqueloba, quinquelocularis. Semina numerosissima, ovata, aptera; testa reticulata. Embryo in basi albuminis, minutissimus, indivisus.—Herba Californica, carnosa, rubra; caule simplici, squamis carnosis vestito, in spicam conferte bracteatam desinens; floribus pedicellatis.

Sarcodes Sanguinea, Tab. X.

Hab.—Valley of the Sacramento; the precise locality not recorded, but probably on the Yuba River.

A very interesting plant, belonging to the small group of Monotropeae. It is of a fleshy texture and blood-red color. The stems are apparently clustered, and spring from a thick coralloid root. They are from six to ten inches high, perfectly simple, and clothed with long erect scales, which are broader below, and gradually become narrower above, where they pass into bracts. The lowest scales are broadly ovate and clasping, very thick, and of a firmer texture than the others: upper ones an inch or two inches long, and two or three lines wide, rather obtuse, ciliate on the margin. The flowers are numerous (from 30 to 50), about as large as in *Hypopithys lanuginosa*, and occupy the upper half of the stem, each subtended and partly concealed by a long bract. All of them are decandrous. Peduncles of the lower flowers are nearly an inch long; of the upper flowers much shorter. The calyx is composed of five appressed, oblong, obtuse, glandularly pubescent sepals, which are imbricated in aestivation. The corolla is about one third larger than the calyx, monopetalous, obtusely five-lobed, without gibbosities at the base, and glabrous. The stamens are hardly more than half the length of the corolla, and arise from its base: the glabrous filaments are somewhat flattened. The anthers are attached to the filament by the back towards the base. They are about two lines long, and consist of two oblong, tubular, saccate cells, which in the bud are erect,* and almost or quite divided into two loculi. Each cell is obliquely truncated at the apex, where it opens by a large hole. The pollen is simple, very minute, and somewhat hemispherical. The ovary is distinctly five-lobed, and with as many cells, into which protrude the large placentae, covered with innumerable oblong anatropous ovules. The style is erect, stout, above the length of the filaments, and terminates in a capitate, slightly five-lobed stigma. The capsule is similar in form to the ovary, only larger. It is of a chartaceous texture, and apparently opens by chinks at the margin of the valves, which do not separate from the axis. Seeds covering the large two-lobed placentae, ovoid, obtuse at the base; the reticulated testa covering closely the nucleus, except at the apex, where it is produced into a short, conical, oblique appendage. The embryo is exceedingly minute, obovoid, undivided, and situated near the base of fleshy and oily albumen, with the radicle pointing to the hilum.

This genus is intermediate between Hypopithys and Schweinitzia. Like the former, it has a long style; but it differs from it in the gamopetalous corolla, the two-celled biporose anthers, close testa, &c.

---

*The anthers of Schweinitzia, while in flower-bud, are singularly turned to one side at a right angle, so that one cell stands directly over the other. Even in the expanded flower, they do not become perfectly erect. My friend, Dr. Gray, in his admirable description of this genus (*Chloris Bor.-Amer.* p. 17), gives me credit for adopting, in my Flora of the Northern and Middle States, published in 1824, the true view of the position of the anthers of Pyrola. It was in the Flora of New York (1843) that I corrected the error: in the former work the prevailing view was given.

Schweinitzia, which has a similar corolla, differs in its short thick style, and in the form as well as the insertion of the anthers.

There can be no doubt respecting the position of the embryo in this genus and in Pterospora. After much patient dissection, I have obtained it repeatedly in both genera. The ripe seeds of Monotropa and Hypopithys I have not examined, but they have anatropous ovules, and therefore the radicle must be next the hilum. Lindley and De Candolle, however, state that the embryo is situated at the *apex* of the albumen; but this I am convinced is a mistake. As, therefore, all the genera of this group but one have two-celled anthers, there would seem to be nothing to distinguish Monotropeae from Pyroleae, except the parasitic habit, the want of verdure, and the erect position of the anthers in the flower bud. There is, however, a leafless species of Pyrola which serves as a connecting link between them; and I have already alluded to the half turning of the anthers in the unexpanded flowers of Schweinitzia. In comparing these groups, there is still another character which, I believe, has been hitherto overlooked. Some years ago,* I remarked that the pollen in all the Ericaceae that I had examined was compound, consisting of three or four united spherules, as in Epacridaceae. At that time, I had only looked at the pollen of the Ericeae proper, and the Vaccineae. Afterwards, I found that, in Monotropeae, the pollen is simple; while, in Pyroleae, it is compound, consisting usually of three united grains; but these are not so easily observed as in the suborders just noticed.

The genus Galax, which was first referred to Ericaceae by Michaux,[†] and afterwards to a separate tribe of Pyrolaceae by De Candolle, ought, perhaps, to be the type of an order, or at least of a suborder. It is remarkable for its monadelphous stamens and truly one-celled anthers. From genuine Pyroleae it differs besides in its simple pollen, wingless seeds, and cylindrical, axile, divided embryo. According to Sir. J. E. Smith,[‡] it was referred by Mr. Dryander to Saxifragaceae; and the late Prof. D. Don placed it in his heterogeneous order Galacineae, which was characterized so as to include Francoa.

Endlicher enumerates among Pyroleae the little known genus Shortia,[§] although Dr. Gray gives no opinion of its affinities, merely

---

*Flora of the State of New York, i. p. 229.
† Michx. Fl. Bor.-Am. ii. p. 48.
‡ Grammar of Botany, p. 164.
§ Gray in Sill. Amer. Jour. 42, p. 48.

observing, that it has the habit of Pyrola and the foliage of Galax. It seems to be more nearly related to the latter than to the former. Until, however, the flowers of this plant (of which only a single specimen, in fruit, is extant) are obtained, it will be impossible to determine its place in the system with certainty.

Of the five genera and seven species that constitute the suborder Monotropeae, so far as at present known, four of the genera and five of the species are peculiar to North America.

Several of the species have a very wide range, both in latitude and longitude. Monotropa uniflora* occurs from Canada to Florida, and from the Atlantic to the Pacific coasts. On the western side of the continent it seems to be confined to Oregon. Hypopithys lanuginosa is spread almost as widely. H. multiflora, if it be really indigenous to North America, has not been found within the limits of the United States. The rare Schweinitzia is a somewhat southern genus, never having been observed in a higher latitude than Baltimore; while Pterospora is exclusively northern, the State of New York being its limit to the south, although it has been found as far west as the Cascade Mountains of Oregon. Sarcodes is wholly a Californian genus.

1. Isaac Sprague (1811–95) of Hingham, Mass., who had been apprenticed to a carriage painter, accompanied Audubon on his Missouri River expedition of 1843 as artist "especially to draw plants and views for backgrounds." Later Asa Gray published 186 plates by Sprague in his *Genera florae Americae boreali-orientalis illustrata* (1848–49). Some drawings were prepared by Sprague for an unfinished *Trees of North America* during this Frémont period. His drawings illustrated *First Lessons in Botany* (1857), which shows both Gray's and Sprague's names on the title page.

2. Torrey commemorated Frémont in 1843 but the eponym he gave, *Fremontia vermicularis*, is a synonym of *Sarcobatus vermiculatus* (Hook.) Torr. Therefore, though Torrey in 1853 hoped to rescue his intention, the International Rules of Botanical Nomenclature forbad the reuse of the name *Fremontia* as Torrey proposed. Noting the duplicate name, F. V. Coville renamed the shrub in the *Report of the Death Valley Expedition* (1893), which Torrey had described in 1853 as *Fremontia*, to be *Fremontodendron*. The small-leaved form of the polymorphic species *Fremontodendron californicum* drawn by Sprague is the historic type specimen preserved in the Torrey Herbarium, now at the New York Botanical Garden.

3. Incense cedar, called *Libocedrus* in Vol. 1, p. 633, is separated from the southern hemisphere conifer by latest studies as *Calocedrus decurrens*.

4. The "agreeable balsamic odor" enticed woodsmen to gather the foliage for

---

Monotropa Morisoniana is certainly nothing but *M. uniflora*, in which the flower is always erect after fertilization.

bedding, but to their dismay the twigs soon lost their springiness and "mountain misery" was their verdict.

5. William Marbury Carpenter (1811–48), who knew Audubon as a boy in West Feliciana Parish of Louisiana and Edgar Allan Poe at West Point, accompanied Lyell on field excursions during his visit to Louisiana in 1846. In 1838 he wrote to Benjamin Silliman from Jackson College, La., regarding the fossilization of cedar, hickory, poplar, etc. in the vicinity of Port Hudson.

EXPLANATIONS OF THE PLATES.

Plate I. SPRAGUEA UMBELLATA

Fig. 1. Plan of the flower.
2. A flower, magnified.
3. One of the sepals, magnified.
4. A petal, more magnified.
5. A stamen, seen in front, magnified.
6. The pistil, showing a longitudinal section of the ovary, more magnified.
7. A ripe dehiscent capsule, with the persistent sepals, equally magnified.
8. A seed, highly magnified.
9. Longitudinal section of the same.

Plate II. FRÉMONTIA CALIFORNICA

Fig. 1. Plan of the flower. The ovary should have been represented as 5-celled.
2. The androecium, magnified.
3. An anther, with the free portion of its filament magnified; front view.
4. The same; side view.
5. Transverse section of an anther, showing the two loculi of each cell.
6. Pistil, considerably magnified.
7. Longitudinal section of a flower, only part of the calyx remaining, equally magnified.
8. An ovule, more highly magnified.
9. One of the stellate hairs, highly magnified.

Plate III. LIBOCEDRUS DECURRENS

Fig. 1. A branch bearing male aments, of the natural size.
2. Portion of the same, magnified.

3. A branch bearing mature fertile aments, of the natural size.
4. An anther, seen from the inside, magnified.
5. The same seen from the outside.
6. A mature cone, of the natural size.
7. A seed, slightly magnified.
8. Vertical section of the same, more magnified.
9. The embryo separated, and still more magnified.

Plate IV. COLEOGYNE RAMOSISSIMA

Fig. 1. Plan of the flower.
2. A flower-bud, magnified.
3. A bract, equally magnified.
4. An expanded flower, moderately magnified.
5. A stamen, front view, more magnified.
6. The same, seen from behind.
7. A flower laid open longitudinally, magnified.
8. The pistil, equally magnified.
9. A leaf, magnified.
10. One of the centrally fixed hairs.

Plate V. EMPLECTOCLADUS FASCICULATUS

Fig. 1. A flower, on its short branch or spur, magnified.
2. The same laid open, and more magnified.
3. A petal, magnified.
4. A stamen, back view, equally magnified.
5. Front view of the same.
6. A grain of pollen, highly magnified.
7. Pistil, moderately magnified.
8. Longitudinal section of the same.
9. An ovule, more magnified.

Plate VI. CHAMAEBATIA FOLIOLOSA

Fig. 1. A flower, magnified.
2. The same laid open longitudinally, more magnified.
3. A stamen, front view, more magnified.
4. The same, back view.
5. The fruit enclosed in the calyx, magnified.

6. Longitudinal section of the same, somewhat more magnified.

Plate VII. CARPENTERIA CALIFORNICA. Tab. VII

Fig. 1. A petal of the natural size.
2. Front view of a stamen.
3. Back view of the same.
4. A capsule, with the persistent calyx, showing the manner in which the exocarp separates: slightly magnified.
5. Longitudinal section of a capsule, exposing one of the placenta, more magnified.
6. Transverse section of the same. The notches in the margin indicate the lines of dehiscence of the exocarp.
7. A separate cell, or carpel, after the removal of the exocarp.
8. A seed, highly magnified.
9. Longitudinal section of the same, equally magnified.
10. Embryo, still more highly magnified.

Plate VIII. HYMENOCLEA SALSOLA

Fig. 1. A staminate head, moderately magnified.
2. The involucre of the same, with a single staminate flower, and the chaff at its base.
3. A staminate flower laid open.
4. One of the stamens, considerably magnified.
5. Style and stigma of the sterile flower.
6. Fructiferous involucre, magnified four or five times.
7. The same, cut open longitudinally, showing the enclosed achenium and the seed.
8. Transverse section of the fructiferous involucre.
9. An achenium, with its persistent styles.
10. The embryo.

Plate IX. AMPHIPAPPUS FRÉMONTII

Fig. 1. A head of flowers, magnified.
2. The ray-flower, more magnified.
3. Pappus of the same, laid open, highly magnified.
4. A disk-flower, moderately magnified.

5. Pappus of the same, highly magnified.

6. Branches of the style, showing the stigmatic lines.

Plate X. SARCODES SANGUINEA

Fig. 1. Plan of the flower.

2. A flower, moderately magnified.

3. Front view of a stamen.

4. The same, seen from the inside; the anther cut transversely to exhibit its two cells: both more magnified than fig. 1.

5. Vertical section of a magnified flower, showing all the organs in their relative situations.

6. The pistil, with one of the stamens, magnified.

7. Transverse section of the ovary.

8. An ovule, highly magnified.

9. A ripe seed, more magnified.

10. Vertical section of the same.

11. The embryo detached, very highly magnified.

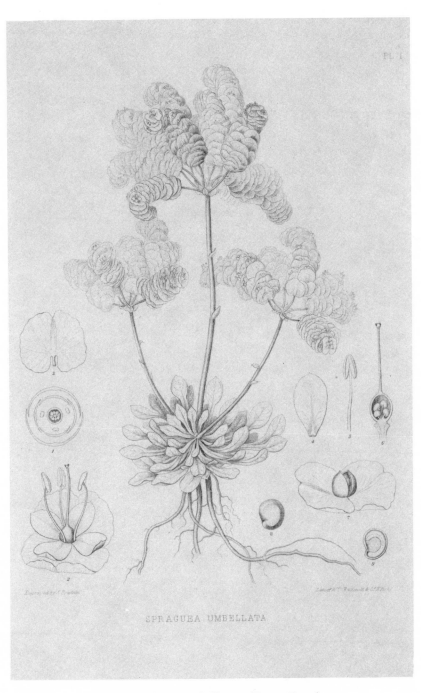

SPRAGUEA UMBELLATA

Calyptridium umbellatum (Pussy Paws)

599

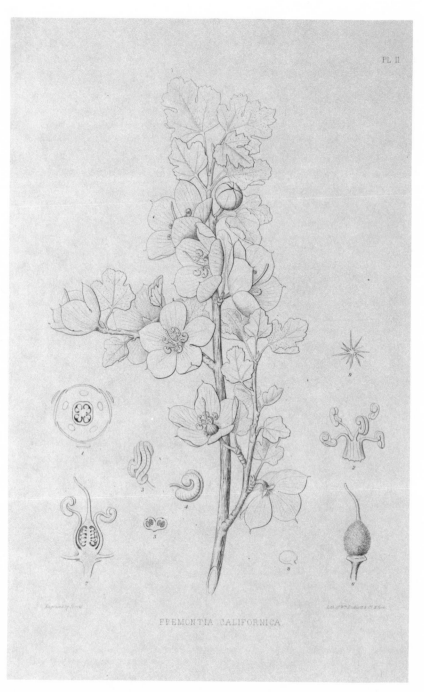

FREMONTIA CALIFORNICA.

Fremontodendron californicum

Pl. III

LIBOCEDRUS DECURRENS.

Calocedrus decurrens (Incense Cedar)

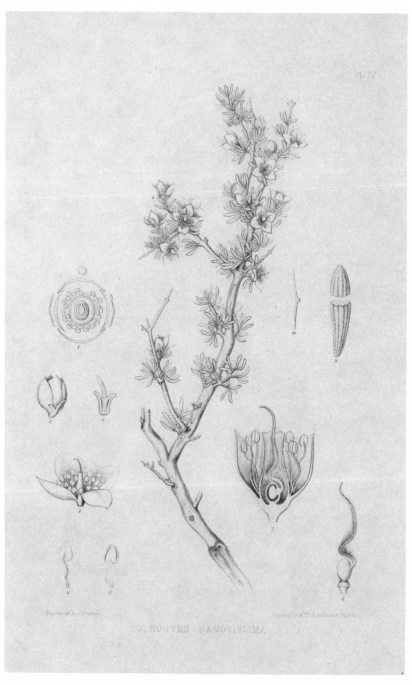

Coleogyne ramosissima (Blackbush)

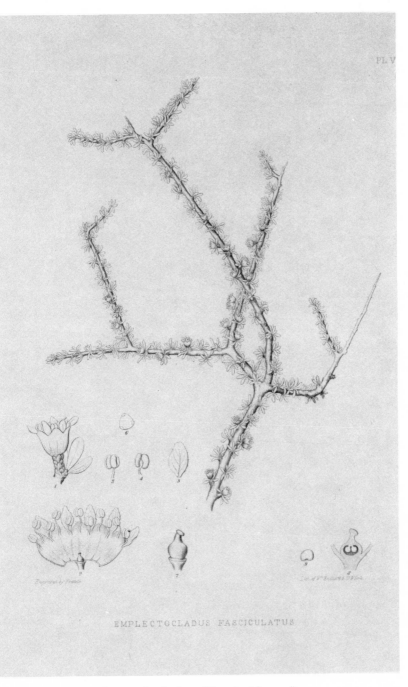

EMPLECTOCLADUS FASCICULATUS

Prunus fasciculata (Desert Almond)

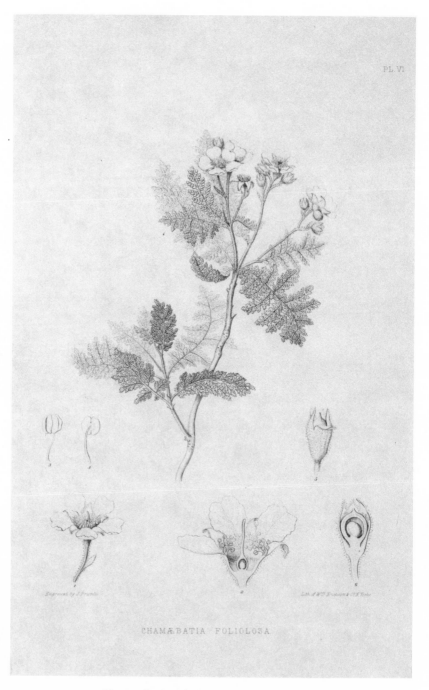

CHAMÆBATIA FOLIOLOSA

Chamaebatia foliolosa (Mountain Misery)

604

CARPENTERIA CALIFORNICA.

Carpenteria californica

605

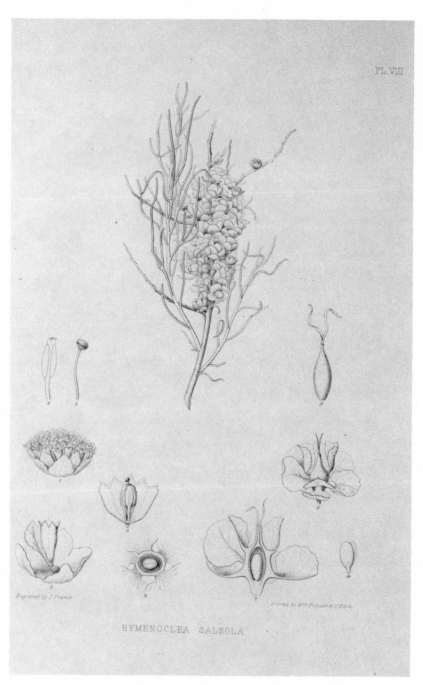

HYMENOCLEA SALSOLA

Hymenoclea salsola (Burrobrush)

606

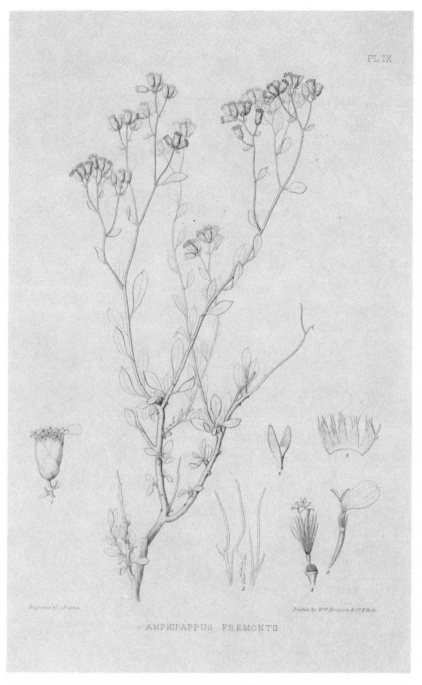

AMPHIPAPPUS FREMONTII

Amphipappus fremontii (Chaff-bush)

607

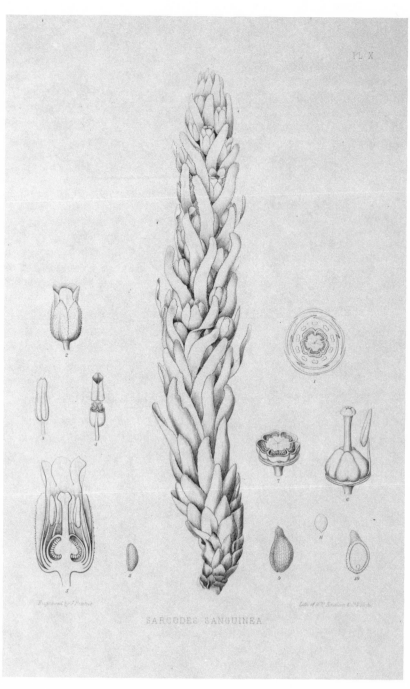

Sarcodes sanguinea (Snow Plant)

608

APPENDIX
FRÉMONT'S EARLY MINING LEASES AND
HOFFMAN'S COMPANIES AND/OR CONTRACTS

Early Mining Leases on the Mariposa
Granted by John C. Frémont

Lessee	Date and Evidence
Baldwin, Daniel A.	30 May 1850 (prospectus of the Nouveau Monde Company)
Beale, Edward F.	1850 or 1851 (Doc. No. 135, JCF to Hoffman, 1 May 1851)
Clark, John C., and George W. Guthrie	1850 (mentioned in their replacement lease of 5 Sept. 1851, Mariposa County Records, Book 1, pp. 267–71)
Goodell, Frederick	Two leases: 27 Oct. 1851 and 29 Dec. 1851 (Mariposa County Records, Book 1, pp. 471–72, and Book 2, pp. 19–22)
Lacharme, Louis	ca. 1 May 1850 (reference in Doc. Nos. 135 and 138)
Palmer, Cook & Company (Mariposa Vein)	Early 1850 (Doc. No. 121, JCF to Mayer, 29 Nov. 1850; Doc. No. 135, JCF to Hoffman, 1 May 1851).
Palmer, Cook & Company (Agua Fria Vein)	17 Sept. 1850 (Doc. No. 110)
Philadelphia and California Mining Company	10 Nov. 1851 (Doc. No. 170)
Sargent, Thomas Denny	Two leases: 30 April 1850 (Doc. No. 67) and 21 May 1850 (DUNCAN)

Smith, William King	Probably two leases, 3 July 1850 (Memorandum of Agreement between David Hoffman and Nouveau Monde Gold Mining Company [M. A. Goodspeed, Jr., Collection] and scattered references in Hoffman Papers)
Stockton & Aspinwall	Before June 1850 (Doc. No. 90, JCF to Baldwin, 22 June 1850; Doc. No. 100, JCF to Hoffman, 25 July 1850)
Werth, John J.	Before June 1850 (Doc. No. 90, JCF to Baldwin, 22 June 1850)

Contracts and/or Companies which David Hoffman claimed to have negotiated for operations on the Mariposa

1. Alta California
2. Alverado Company
3. Borradail contract
4. Count de la Garde contract
5. East Mariposa Company (after the Sargent-Duncan clique was ousted)
6. Golden Mountain
7. Gough contract
8. Great Montezuma
9. Henry Wise contract
10. Hoffman-Alverado Company
11. Le Nouveau Monde
12. Martelli contract
13. Les Mineurs Belges (British)
14. Les Mineurs Belges (French)
15. Prince Jérôme Napoleon's contract
16. Quartz Rock Mariposa Gold Mining Company
17. Turin contract
18. Valentine contract
19. Warner & Flight contract
20. Wellesley & Stafford protocols
21. Wilmar & Barillon protocol

Of the above, three companies actually sent out men and equipment to the Mariposa: Le Nouveau Monde, the Quartz Rock Mariposa Gold Mining Company, and Les Mineurs Belges. Lessee and engineer of the Golden Mountain, Andrew Smith, also went to California.

BIBLIOGRAPHY

ABELOE   Hoover, Mildred B., and Hero E. and Ethel Grace Rensch. *Historic Spots in California*. Rev. by William N. Abeloe. 3rd ed. Stanford, Calif., 1966.

ARMSTRONG   Armstrong, Leroy, and J. O. Denny. *Financial California: An Historical Review of the Beginnings and Progress of Banking in the State*. San Francisco, 1916.

ARRINGTON   Arrington, Joseph E. "Skirving's Moving Panorama: Colonel Frémont's Western Expeditions Pictorialized," *Oregon Historical Society Quarterly*, 65 (June 1964):133–72.

BARNES   Barnes, Will C. *Arizona Place Names*. Rev. and enlarged by Byrd H. Granger. Tucson, Ariz., 1960.

BARRY   Barry, Louise. *The Beginning of the West: Annals of the Kansas Gateway to the American West, 1540–1854*. Topeka, Kans., 1972.

BARTLETT   Bartlett, Ruhl Jacob. *John C. Frémont and the Republican Party*. Columbus, Ohio, 1930. No. 13 in Ohio State University Studies, Contributions in History and Political Science.

BEAN   Horne, Flora D. Bean, comp. *Autobiography of George Washington Bean, a Utah Pioneer of 1847 and His Family Records*. Salt Lake City, Utah, 1945.

BEATTIE   Beattie, George William, and Helen Pruitt Beattie. *Heritage of the Valley: San Bernardino's First Century*. Pasadena, Calif., 1939.

BIEBER   Bieber, Ralph, ed. *Exploring Southwestern Trails, 1846–1854*. Glendale, Calif., 1938.

BIGELOW   Bigelow, John. *Memoir of the Life and Public Services of John Charles Fremont. . . .* New York, 1856.

BIOG. DIR. CONG.   *Biographical Directory of the American Congress*. Washington, D.C., 1961.

BOOTH   Booth, Newton. "Rufus A. Lockwood," *Overland Monthly*, 4 (May 1870):393–404.

BOSQUI   Bosqui, Edward. *Memoirs*. Oakland, Calif., 1952.

BRANDON   Brandon, William E. *The Men and the Mountain: Frémont's Fourth Expedition*. New York, 1955.

BRECKENRIDGE [1]   Breckenridge, Thomas E. Reminiscences. Ms and typescript. Western Historical Manuscripts Collection, University of Missouri.

BRECKENRIDGE [2] ————. "The Story of a Famous Expedition," *Cosmopolitan*, 21 (Aug. 1896):400–408.

BROWN Brown, John. *Autobiography of Pioneer John Brown, 1820–1896*. Ed. by John Z. Brown. Privately printed, Salt Lake City, 1941.

BUNNELL Bunnell, L. H. *Discovery of the Yosemite, and the Indian War of 1851, Which Led to That Event*. Chicago, 1880.

BURT Burt, Roger, ed. *Cornish Mining: Essays on the Organisation of Cornish Mines and the Cornish Mining Economy*. Newton Abbot, Devon, England, 1969.

CARVALHO Carvalho, S. N. *Incidents of Travel and Adventure in the Far West; with Col. Fremont's Last Expedition across the Rocky Mountains: Including Three Months' Residence in Utah, and a Perilous Trip across the Great American Desert, to the Pacific*. New York, 1857.

CHAMBERS Chambers, William N. *Old Bullion Benton, Senator from the New West: Thomas Hart Benton, 1782–1858*. Boston, 1956.

COLTON Colton, Walter. *Three Years in California*. New York, 1850.

CRAMPTON Crampton, Charles Gregory. "The Opening of the Mariposa Mining Region, 1849–1859, with Particular Reference to the Mexican Land Grant of John Charles Frémont." Ph.D. dissertation, University of California, Berkeley, 1941.

CROSS Cross, Ira B. *Financing an Empire: History of Banking in California*. 2 vols. Chicago, 1927.

CULLUM Cullum, George W. *Biographical Register of the Officers and Graduates of the U.S. Military Academy . . . 1802 to 1890*. 3rd ed. 3 vols. Boston, 1891. Supplementary vols. under various editors to 1950.

DAKIN Dakin, Susanna Bryant. *A Scotch Paisano: Hugo Reid's Life in California, 1832–1852*. Berkeley, Calif., 1939.

DAB *Dictionary of American Biography*. 20 vols. and 5 supplements. New York, 1928–55.

DELLENBAUGH Dellenbaugh, Frederick S. *Fremont and '49*. New York, 1914.

DRIGGS Driggs, Nevada W. "When Captain Fremont Slept in Grandma McGregor's Bed," *Utah Historical Quarterly*, 41 (Spring 1973): 178–81.

DUNCAN Duncan, John. *Fremont Gold Mines and Property, California. An Answer to the Pamphlet of Mr. David Hoffman by John Duncan, Solicitor to Thomas Denny Sargent, Esq*. London, 1852.

DWINELLE Dwinelle, John W. *The Colonial History of the City of San Francisco*. 3rd ed. San Francisco, 1866.

ECCLESTON   Crampton, C. Gregory, ed. *The Mariposa Indian War, 1850–1851, Diaries of Robert Eccleston: The California Gold Rush, Yosemite, and the High Sierra*. Salt Lake City, Utah, 1957.

ELLISON   Ellison, Joseph. "Indian Policy in California, 1846–1860," *Mississippi Valley Historical Review*, 9 (June 1922):37–67.

FAVOUR   Favour, Alpheus. *Old Bill Williams, Mountain Man*. Chapel Hill, N.C., 1936.

FISH   Krenkel, John H., ed. *The Life and Times of Joseph Fish, Mormon Pioneer*. Danville, Ill., 1970.

J. B. FRÉMONT [1]   Frémont, Jessie Benton. *Mother Lode Narratives*. Ed. and annotated by Shirley Sargent. Ashland, Ore., 1970.

J. B. FRÉMONT [2]   ———. *Souvenirs of My Time*. Boston, 1887.

J. B. FRÉMONT [3]   ———. "A Year of American Travel," *Harper's New Monthly Magazine*, 55 (Nov. 1877):905–16; 56 (Dec. 1877):84–96.

FRÉMONT   Frémont, John Charles. *Geographical Memoir upon Upper California, in Illustration of His Map of Oregon and California*. Senate Misc. Doc. 148, 30th Cong., 1st sess. Washington, D.C., 1848, Serial 511.

GÁSPÁR   Gáspár, Stephen. "Four Nineteenth-Century Hungarian Travelers in America." Ph.D. dissertation, University of Southern California, 1967.

GATES [1]   Gates, Paul W. "The Frémont-Jones Scramble for California Land Claims," *Southern California Quarterly*, 56 (Spring 1974):13–44.

GATES [2]   ———. "The Land Business of Thomas O. Larkin," *California Historical Quarterly*, 54 (Winter 1975):323–44.

GAY   Gay, Theressa. *James W. Marshall, the Discoverer of California Gold: A Biography*. Georgetown, Calif., 1967.

GOETZMANN   Goetzmann, William H. *Army Exploration in the American West, 1803–1863*. New Haven, Conn., 1959.

GONZALES   Gonzales, John Edmond. "The Public Career of Henry Stuart Foote (1804–1880)." Ph.D. dissertation, University of North Carolina at Chapel Hill, 1958.

GRIVAS   Grivas, Theodore. *Military Governments in California, 1846–1850*. Glendale, Calif., 1963.

GUDDE [1]   Gudde, Erwin G. *California Gold Camps: A Geographical and Historical Dictionary of Camps, Towns, and Localities Where Gold Was Found and Mined; Wayside Stations and Trading Centers*. Ed. by Elisabeth K. Gudde. Berkeley, Calif., 1975.

GUDDE [2]   ———. *California Place Names: The Origin and Etymology of Current Geographical Names*. 3rd ed. Berkeley, Calif., 1969.

GUINN   Guinn, James M. *Historical and Biographical Record of Los Angeles*. Chicago, 1901.

HAFEN & HAFEN   Hafen, LeRoy R., and Ann W. Hafen, eds. *Frémont's Fourth Expedition: A Documentary Account of the Disaster of 1848–49*. Glendale, Calif., 1960.

HALL   Hall, Frederic. *History of San José and Surroundings with Biographical Sketches*. San Francisco, 1871.

HART'S ANNUAL ARMY LIST   *Hart's Annual Army List*. 76 vols. London, 1840–1915.

HEAP   Heap, Gwinn Harris. *Central Route to the Pacific*. . . . With related material on railroad explorations and Indian affairs by Edward F. Beale, Thomas H. Benon, Kit Carson, and Col. E. A. Hitchcock, and other documents, 1853–54. Ed. by LeRoy R. Hafen. Vol. 7 of *The Far West and the Rockies Historical Series, 1820–1875*. Glendale, Calif., 1957.

HEFFERNAN   Heffernan, William Joseph. *Edward M. Kern: The Travels of an Artist-Explorer*. Bakersfield, Calif., 1953.

HEITMAN   Heitman, Francis B. *Historical Register and Dictionary of the United States Army*. 2 vols. Washington, D.C., 1903. Reprinted, Urbana, Ill., 1965.

HINE [1]   Hine, Robert V. *Bartlett's West: Drawing the Mexican Boundary*. New Haven, Conn., 1968.

HINE [2]   ————. *Edward Kern and American Expansion*. New Haven, Conn., 1962.

HOFFMAN   Hoffman, David. *The Fremont Estate: An Address to the British Public, Respecting Col. Fremont's Leasing Powers to the Author, From June, 1850*. London, 1851.

HOLMAN   Holman, Frederick Van Voorhies. *Dr. John McLoughlin, the Father of Oregon*. Cleveland, Ohio, 1907.

HULBERT   Hulbert, Dorothy P., ed. "The Trip to California; An Explanatory Notice of the Panorama, Presented for the First Time to the Public, at the Theatre des Variétes (Paris) August 8, 1850," *Frontier and Midland*, 14 (1934):160–61, 168–69.

HUNTLY   Huntly, Henry V. "Report of Sir Henry Vere Huntly Dated November 24, 1850, to the Directors of the Anglo-California Gold Mining and Dredging Company," *California Historical Society Quarterly*, 12 (March 1933):73–76.

K. M. JOHNSON   Johnson, Kenneth M. *The New Almaden Quicksilver Mine with an Account of the Land Claims Involving the Mine and Its Role in California History*. Georgetown, Calif., 1963.

JOHNSON & DAVIS   Johnson, William E., and Edwin Adams Davis. "Micajah McGehee's Account of Frémont's Disastrous Fourth Exploring Expedition, 1848–1849," *Journal of Mississippi History*, 14 (April 1952):91–118.

KITSON   Kitson, Michael. "Claude Lorrain," in *Encyclopedia of World Art*. 15 vols. New York, 1959–67. 9:340–44.

KORN   Korn, Bertram Wallace, ed. *Incidents of Travel and Adventure in the Far West by Solomon Nunes Carvalho*. A centenary ed. Philadelphia, 1954.

LARKIN   Hammond, George P., ed. *The Larkin Papers: Personal, Business, and Official Correspondence of Thomas Oliver Larkin, Merchant and United States Consul in California*. 10 vols. Berkeley, Calif., 1951–64.

LAROUSSE   Larousse, Pierre. *Grand dictionnaire universel de XIX siècle*. . . . 17 vols. Paris, [1865–90?].

LAVENDAR   Lavendar, David. *Bent's Fort*. New York, 1954.

LECOMPTE   Lecompte, Janet. "Charles Autobees," *Colorado Magazine*, 35 (1958):139–53, 219–25, 303–8; 36 (1959):58–66, 202–13.

LIFE   *Life of Colonel Frémont*. Greeley & M'Elrath, 1856.

MC GEHEE [1]   McGehee, Micajah. Ms journal [to Pima villages]. Undated. 1 vol. 218 pp. DLC.

MC GEHEE [2]   ———. Typescript diary of Micajah McGehee [to California], 1848–49. Undated. 172 pp. LU.

MC KELVEY   McKelvey, Susan D. *Botanical Exploration of the Trans-Mississippi West, 1790–1850*. Jamaica Plain, Mass., 1955.

MALONEY   Maloney, Alice Bay. "A Botanist on the Road to Yerba Buena," *California Historical Society Quarterly*, 24 (Dec. 1954):321–25.

MARTIN   Martin, Thomas S. *With Frémont to California and the Southwest, 1845–1849*. Ed. with an intro. and notes by Ferol Egan. Ashland, Ore., 1975.

MEMOIRS   Frémont, John Charles. *Memoirs of My Life . . . Including in the Narrative Five Journeys of Western Exploration during the Years 1842, 1843–4, 1845–8, 1853–4. Together with a Sketch of the Life of Senator Benton in Connection with Western Expansion by Jessie Benton Frémont*. Only vol. 1 published. Chicago, 1887.

MITCHELL   Mitchell, Annie Rosaline. *Jim Savage and the Tulareño Indians*. Los Angeles, 1957.

MONTAGUE   Montague, William L. *The Saint Louis Business Directory for 1853–54*. St. Louis, Mo., 1853.

MONTGOMERY   Montgomery, R. G. *The White-headed Eagle, John McLoughlin, Builder of an Empire*. New York, 1934.

NEVILL   Nevill, Ralph. *London Clubs: Their History and Treasures*. New York, 19—?.

NEVINS   Nevins, Allan. *Frémont: Pathmarker of the West*. New York, 1955.

NEVINS & MORGAN   Nevins, Allan, and Dale L. Morgan, eds. *Geographical Memoir upon Upper California in Illustration of His Map of Oregon and California by John Charles Frémont*. With a reproduction of the map. San Francisco, 1964.

NIEMEIER   Niemeier, Jean G. *The Panama Story*. Portland, Ore., 1968.

PACIFIC RAILROAD REPORTS   *Pacific Railroad Reports*. 13 vols. Washington, D.C., 1855–60.

PARKER   Parker, Franklin. "George Peabody, Founder of Modern Philanthropy." 3 vols., facsimile. Ed.D. dissertation, George Peabody College for Teachers, 1956.

PARKHILL   Parkhill, Forbes. *The Blazed Trail of Antoine Leroux*. Los Angeles, 1965.

PHILLIPS   Phillips, Catherine Coffin. *Jessie Benton Frémont: A Woman Who Made History*. San Francisco, 1935.

PIONEER REGISTER   Bancroft, Hubert Howe. *Register of Pioneer Inhabitants of California, 1542–1848*. Reprinted from vols. 2–5 of *History of California*, published in 1885 and 1886. Los Angeles, 1964.

PREUSS   Preuss, Charles. *Exploring with Frémont*. Trans. and ed. by Erwin G. and Elisabeth K. Gudde. Norman, Okla., 1958.

RATHER   Rather, Lois. *Jessie Benton Frémont at Black Point*. Oakland, Calif., 1974.

RICHMOND   Richmond, Patricia Joy. "Trail to Disaster: The Route of John C. Frémont's Fourth Expedition from Big Timbers into the San Juan Mountains of Southern Colorado." Unpublished paper. Crestone, Colo.

RIDD   Ridd, Jay Donald. "Almon Whiting Babbitt, Mormon Emissary." M.A. thesis, University of Utah, 1953.

ROBBINS   Robbins, Christine Chapman. "John Torrey (1796–1873): His Life and Times," *Bulletin of the Torrey Botanical Club*, 95 (Nov.–Dec. 1968):519–645.

ROBINSON   Robinson, William W. *Lawyers of Los Angeles: A History of the Los Angeles Bar Association and of the Bar of Los Angeles County*. Los Angeles, 1959.

ROYCE   Royce, Sarah. *A Frontier Lady: Recollections of the Gold Rush and Early California*. Ed. by Ralph Henry Gabriel. Lincoln, Nebr., 1977. Reprint of 1932 ed. published by Yale University Press.

SCHARF   Scharf, J. Thomas. *The Chronicles of Baltimore: Being a Complete History of "Baltimore Town" and Baltimore City from the Earliest Period to the Present Time*. Baltimore, Md., 1874.

SIMMS   Simms, William Gilmore. *Letters*. Collected and ed. by Mary C. Simms Oliphant *et al*. 5 vols. Columbia, S.C., 1952–56.

SMITH   Smith, Elbert B. *Francis Preston Blair*. New York, 1980.

SOULÉ   Soulé, Frank, John H. Gihon, and James Nisbet. *The Annals of San Francisco*. . . . New York, 1854.

SPENCE   Spence, Mary Lee. "David Hoffman: Frémont's Mariposa Agent in London," *Southern California Quarterly*, 60 (Winter 1978):379–403.

STANTON   Stanton, William. *The Great United States Exploring Expedition of 1838–1842*. Berkeley, Calif., 1975.

STEEL   Steel, Edward M. *T. Butler King of Georgia*. Athens, Ga., [1964].

STEPHENS   Stephens, Frank. *A History of the University of Missouri*. Columbia, Mo., 1962.

STURHAHN   Sturhahn, Joan. *Carvalho: Portrait of a Forgotten American*. New York, 1976.

SUNDER   Sunder, John E. "British Army Officers on the Santa Fe Trail," *Bulletin of the Missouri Historical Society*, 23 (Jan. 1967):147–57.

TAFT   Taft, Robert. *Artists and Illustrators of the Old West, 1850–1900*. New York, 1953.

TAYLOR   Taylor, Bayard. *Eldorado*. 2 vols. New York, 1850. Facsimile, Palo Alto, Calif., 1968.

TORREY   Torrey, John. *Plantae Frémontianae; Or, Description of Plants Collected by Col. J. C. Fremont in California*. Smithsonian Contributions to Knowledge. Washington, D.C., 1853.

TWITCHELL   Twitchell, R. E. *The Leading Facts of New Mexican History*. 2 vols. Cedar Rapids, Iowa, 1912.

UPHAM   Upham, Charles Wentworth. *Life, Explorations and Public Services of John Charles Fremont*. Boston, 1856.

VILES   Viles, Jonas. *The University of Missouri: A Centennial History*. Columbia, Mo., 1939.

VOELKER   Voelker, Frederic. "William Sherley (Old Bill) Williams," in *The Mountain Men and the Fur Trade of the Far West*, ed. by LeRoy R. Hafen. 10 vols. Glendale, Calif., 1965–72. 8:365–94.

WEBB   Bieber, Ralph P., ed. *Adventures in the Santa Fe Trade 1844–1847 by James Josiah Webb*. Glendale, Calif., 1931.

WHEAT [1]   Wheat, Carl I. *Mapping the Transmississippi West, 1540–1861*. 5 vols. San Francisco, 1957–63.

WHEAT [2]   ———. *The Maps of the California Gold Region, 1848–1851: A Biblio-Cartography of an Important Decade*. San Francisco, 1942.

WHEELER   Wheeler, Alfred. *Land Titles in San Francisco and the Laws Affecting the Same with a Synopsis of All Grants and Sales of Land within the City*. San Francisco, 1852.

WHO WAS WHO   *Who Was Who, 1897–1916*. London, 1920.

WICKMAN   Wickman, John E. "Political Aspects of Charles Wilkes's Work and Testimony, 1842–1849." Ph.D. dissertation, University of Indiana, 1964.

WOODHAM-SMITH   Woodham-Smith, Cecil. *The Reason Why*. Reprinted, New York, 1960.

YOUNG   Young, Stark. "Cousin Micajah," *Saturday Evening Post*, 207 (13 April 1935):18–19, 37–40.

Index

The following abbreviations are used: JCF for John Charles Frémont; JBF for Jessie Benton Frémont. The Appendix is not indexed.

Arkansas River (*continued*)
420; headwaters of, described by
JCF, 481–82
Armstrong, C.: surveyor of the town
of Mariposa, 159n
Arnold and Dent: chronometer of, 23
Artificial rain: Espy theory of, 402
Asarum canadense L., 405
Aubry, François X.: identified, 89;
ride of, 93; mentioned, 80
Autobees, Charles, 489
Auxumne River. *See* Merced River
Ave Maria Mine, xlviii, 272, 301–8
passim
Ave Maria Mining Company, 306,
308, 339, 358

Babbitt, Almon W.: arrives in Washington, lvii, 381n; identified,
468n–469n; meets JCF at Parowan, 467n, 468, 469; good offices
of, 475
Bacon, Theodore: letter from JCF,
382
Bacon, William: and 1848 expedition,
52, 55n, 82; arrives at Little Colorado River settlement, 84
Bailey, Jacob W., 36n
Baldwin, Daniel A.: letter from JCF,
168–69; mining lease of, 168–69,
279
Baldwin's Mine, 169n
Baltimore *Sun*: letter from JCF,
200–205
Barbour, George W.: Indian commissioner, xl, xli; letter from JCF,
237–38; letters to JCF, 238–39,
241, 242; beef contracts and Indian
treaties, 238n, 241, 262, 263; and
Indian troubles, 298n
Bates, Joshua, li
Beadle, Benjamin: and 1848 expedition, 52, 55n, 83; death noted, 84,
97

Beale, Edward F.: and report of California gold, xxv, 85; arrives in
California, xxxiii; and JCF's Indian
beef contracts, xl, xlii; regard for
Benton, xliii; superintendent of Indian affairs, xliii; explores central
railroad route, lii, liii; misses JCF
in San Francisco, lxiii; rents JCF's
house on Black Point, lxxiii; and
Gila journey, 142, 143n; letters
from JCF, 142, 333; JCF's mining
lease to, 231, 235; files suit against
JCF, 265n; uses North Cochetopa
Pass, 466n; establishes fort at Fort
Tejon Pass, 489n; mentioned, 81,
406n, 428
Beale, Mary Edwards: marriage of,
116n; eye ailment of, 194; daughter
of, 143n
Beall, Benjamin L.: furnishes supplies
to JCF, 51, 92, 97
Bear Flag Revolt, lxxv
Bear River, Calif., 520
Bear River, Utah, 506
Bear Valley, Mariposa, Calif., lxviii
Beaver: as food, 443
Beckwith, Edward G., 404, 465
Beechey, Frederick W.: and survey of
California coast, 17–32 passim,
499, 500
Beef contracts: proposals of JCF,
236–39; receipts of JCF, 260–62;
payments to JCF, by drafts, 262n;
Beale's interest in, 264; Wright's
contract for JCF, 274; legal cases
connected with, 275n; drafts re-
jected, 283; JCF seeks aid for, 297,
298; JCF's partners in, 333; legal
cases connected with, 353n
Belcher, Edward: and survey of Cali-
fornia coast, 17–32 passim, 500
Belt, George, lviii
Benino Creek, 98n
Bennett Pass, 475n

Franseria deltoidea (Bur sage): description of, 587–88

Franseria dumosa: description of, 588

Freeman, J. S., xxviii

Freeman Canyon, 476n

Frémont, Ann: death of, liii

Frémont, Benton, xxiii, 48, 49n

Frémont, Frances Cornelia (Nina), liii, 282n

Frémont, Frank Preston, lviii

Frémont, Jessie B.: blames Williams for 1848 disaster, xxv; accompanies JCF to frontier, xxiii–xxiv, 406n; describes Isthmus crossing, xxxiiin; arrives in California, xxxiii, 111n; is presented to Queen Victoria, li; describes Black Point, lxxiii; letters to Torrey, 15, 74–75; asks about plants, 74–75; letters from JCF, 75–86, 422; on isolation of Mariposa, 229n–230n; letter to Mayer, 251–54; and Hoffman, 348; letter to Hoffman, 349; and JCF's arrest, 354–57; on JCF's absence from Senate, 374; Carvalho dedicates book to, 403

Frémont, John C.: and California claims, xx, 6–14, 49, 373; controversy with Wilkes, xx, 5, 16–34, 37–40, 41; wishes to continue explorations, xxi, 546–47; urges replacement of Larkin, xxi; attempts to purchase Rancho del Chino, xxxii; meets JBF in San Francisco, xxxiii, 111n; is anxious to become governor of California, xxxiii; appointed Mexican Boundary Commissioner, xxxiv, 112; sawmill business of, xxxiv; at Happy Valley, xxxiv; elected U.S. Senator, xxxv; donates books, xxxv; has "Chagres fever," xxxvi, 129, 137; supports mint for San Francisco, xxxvi, 137, 150–51; defends California against Clay, xxxvi, 139–40; draws short Senate term, xxxvi, 195; re his surveys and railroad route, xxxvi, 113, 122, 129–36, 474, 480–88; and mining legislation, xxxvii, 214–18, 225; and California land titles, xxxvii, 219–20, 225–27; seeks reelection to Senate, xxxviii, 212; establishes *Argus,* xxxviii; his Senate reelection blocked, xxxviii; offers to buy Los Alamitos, xl, 229; obtains loan, xl; is arrested in London, li, 349, 351; in Paris, li, 359; sues Hoffman, lii, 361; borrows from Lakeman, liii; settles with Corcoran & Riggs, lxx; land claims and property of, lxxi–lxxiii, 187, 190n, 280–82, 287, 324–25, 471; legacy of, lxxiii–lxxvii; and plants, 3, 571, 572–73; cancels sale of Mariposa, 1, 334; arrives in England, 1, 334; ignores Hoffman, 1, 335–45 passim; and Agua Fria Mine and lease, 1, 195–98; requests credit for third expedition property, 40–41; promises to botanize Mount Shasta region, 48; borrows from Aubry, 93; is a democrat, 121; traces history of Mariposa purchase, 123–24; re cattle contract with Célis, 125–26; and controversies with Foote, 142–43, 200–205; and biographies of himself, 143, 152–53; empowers Robert and Hoffman to raise European capital, 156–58; medals awarded to, 160–61, 170, 205–7; re quicksilver mines, 161–62; recommends Beale, 162–63, 297; and Indian agencies, 166–68; may abandon English enterprise, 171–72; and Washington Monument, 178; leaves for California, 207; neuralgia of, 211, 373–74; re-

Halleck, Henry W., xxxvi

Halsey, Absalam A., 240

Hammond, Marcus C. M.: and sketch of JCF, 153n

Harazthy, Agoston: and opposition to state government, 150

Hardscrabble: 1848 expedition at, 50, 76

Hardscrabble Creek, 52n

Harper, Alexander H.: sublessee of Sargent, xlviii, 301

Harrison, James, 403n

Hays, John C., lxii

Heap, Gwinn H.: re JCF's 1848–49 route, xxx; agent of Sargent, 1; encounters JCF at Isthmus, 1; with Beale, liii; JCF's agent for Las Mariposas, 144, 155; in London, 336, 337, 355

Heap, William, 463–64

Heap Vein, 144n

Helianthus, 508

Henry, Joseph, 48, 49

Hensley, Samuel J.: and JCF-Célis contract, 7–8, 126; and beef contract, 297

Hepburn, James: and Agua Fria, xlvii, 330n

Herald, 5

Heydenfeldt, Solomon, xxxviii

Highland Mountains, 475n

Higley, Horace, lxii

Hitchcock, Charles M., 199

Hitchcock, Horace P.: letter from JCF, 190–91

Hoe & Company: JCF requests mill stones of, 85

Hoes, Cantine, 164

Hoffman, David: becomes JCF's London agent, xlv–xlvi, 155n, 156–58; on Sargent, xlvii, 146–50, 255, 256, 259, 260; and reaction to sale of Mariposa, xlix; refuses to relin-

quish papers to JCF, lii, 361–62; death of, lii; and Nicollet and Mayers, 158n; and attitude toward JCF, 189n–190n; and royalty scale, 194; laments lack of information from JCF, 199, 242; JCF's confidence in, 231; on Wright and Walbridge, 233, 234, 245, 255, 279; anxiety over manipulations in London, 244–51, 255; changes JCF's public notice, 265–67; his optimism about companies, 269; JCF ignores, 335, 338, 339, 347; writings of, 366; thinks JCF's suit unjust, 362–63; pleads for private settlement, 365–66, 368–69; loses case, 371n

—letters: from miscellaneous, 349; from JCF, 158–59, 180–82, 186–89, 208–9, 220–21, 230, 230–32, 234–36, 265–66, 267–68, 272–74, 275–76, 292–96, 313–14, 314–16, 321–22, 335, 337, 338, 339–40, 341, 342–43, 344, 367, 368, 370

—letters: to miscellaneous, 349; to JCF, 164, 174, 192–94, 198, 199, 222, 223–24, 227–28, 233, 234, 240, 242, 244–50, 254, 256–57, 259–60, 269–71, 276–77, 278–80, 282, 288–89, 290–91, 322–23, 325–26, 326–29, 334–35, 335–36, 336–37, 338, 339, 340–41, 342, 343, 343–44, 345, 345–49, 352, 354–58, 360, 361–62, 362–63, 365–66, 367, 368, 369

Hoffman, Mary (Mrs. David): and suit against JCF, lii, liin

Hoffman, Ogden: and Las Mariposas decision, xli, lxii

Hoffman–Alverado Company, 325

Hope, 5

Howard, Volney E., lxi

Howd, Simeon F., 467n

Lester, C. Edwards: letters from JCF, 143, 152, 153; sketch of JCF, 173

Lewis, Rodman Price, 198

Lewis, Samuel, 475n

Lewis, Tarlton, 475n

Libocedrus decurrens. See Calocedrus decurrens

Lida Pass, 476n

Lindsley, Dr. Harvey, 359

Linnard Thomas Beasley, 46

Little Colorado River settlements, 79, 81, 87n, 88n

Livingston and Kinkead, 465, 468n

Lockwood, Rufus A.: and JCF's land cases, lx, 282n, 329; identified, 330

Longe (mountaineer), 55n, 56n

Lorrain, Claude. *See* Gellée, Claude

Los Alamitos (rancho of Stearns), 229

Loughborough, John: and map, 136n

Lugo, Antonio Maria, xxxiin

Lunt, Henry, 464

McAllister, Hall, lxii

McCorkle, Joseph W.: letter from JCF, 225–27; identified, 227n

McDougall, James A.: supports payment to JCF, xlin

McDougall, John: and West Mariposa Gold Mining Company, 305

McDowell, James: withdraws from 1848 expedition, 58n

McGehee, Charles G., xxvii

McGehee, Edward (father of Micajah), 159, 160n

McGehee, Edward (brother of Micajah), 56n

McGehee, James Stewart, xxvii

McGehee, Micajah: member of 1848 expedition, xxii, 52; value of his diary, xxvi–xxviii; and JCF's attempted purchase of ranch, xxxii; identified, 56n; with Kern party, 83; on suggested cannibalism, 89n; at Las Mariposas, 159

McKee, Ellen L., xxvii

McLaughlin, Ann L., xxvii

McLoughlin, John: letter from JCF, 299

McNabb, Theodore: and cattle drovers, xlii; member of 1848 expedition, 55n; goes with JCF for relief, 78, 81

McNeill, William G., 363

Madroña. *See Arbutus menziesii*

Malaspina, Alessandro: and California coastal survey, 32, 34, 500; Humboldt on, 500n

Manuel (Indian boy): and 1848 expedition, 52, 56n; JCF reports death of, 82; saved, 84

Manzanita. See Arctostaphylos sp.

Marcy, William L.: letter to JCF, 6; letters from JCF, 6–14, 199

Mariposa Battalion, xliii, 221n

Mariposa Mine, 196, 210n

Mariposa Mining Company, 222, 223n, 231; founders of, xlviin

Marriott, F., 366

Marshall, John: and petition of, 140, 141n

Martha, xxiii

Martin, Thomas S.: and 1848 expedition, xxviii, 52, 55n; goes with Vinsonhaler, 82, 83; arrives at Little Colorado River settlement, 84

Mason, Richard B., xxxvi, 117n; and JCF's California liabilities, 6–13 passim

Maxwell, Lucien B.: in Taos, 51, 80

Mayer, Brantz: and friendship with Hoffman, xlv, 158n; letter to JCF, 371–72; letter from JCF, 493

Mayer, Charles F.: solicitor to JCF, xlv, 158; and strictures on JCF, 207n; letters from JCF, 159, 160, 171–72, 207, 210–11, 284–85, 344; letter from JBF, 251–54

Mayhew & Company: JCF requests

Nisqually (in Puget Sound): observations at, 22, 32

N. menziesii, 517, 537

Noel, Gerard J., 66

Noe Ranch, lxxii

North Cochetopa Pass, xxix, lvi, 428, 433, 466n, 472, 483. *See also* Cochetopa Pass

Nouveau Monde Mining Company: and Merced Mining Company, lxix; delays in forming, 224; Hoffman's terms with, 228; plans to send machinery, 234; arrives without operating funds, 273; may locate off Las Mariposas, 360; mentioned, li, 169n, 260, 269, 277, 279, 294

Oaks, 513–42 passim. Interior live oak: *see Quercus wislinzeni;* JCF's long acorn: *see Q. lobata;* California black: *see Quercus kelloggii.*

Ober, Dr. *See* Ebers, A.

Ocampo, Francisco: furnishes cattle to JCF, xl

Oregon, xxxv, 136n

Orr, Nathaniel, 403

Oryngium aquaticum. See Eryngium aquaticum

Oso House, Mariposa County, Calif., lxiii

Otter Creek, 467n

Owens, Richard: in Taos, 51, 80; plans to go to Missouri, 89n

Owens Lake, lxxvii

Owens Peak, 473, 476n, 498n

Owens Range. *See* Inyo-White Mountains

Owens River, lxxvii, 507

Owens Valley, 476n

Pacific Railroad: favored by Benton, liii, lviii, 113, 472; JCF favors central route, xxxvi, 122, 129–36, 380, 474, 480–88

Packard, Albert, 118, 119n

Palmer, Joseph G.: and Mariposa Mining Company, xlviin; and anxiety about JCF, lvii; and San Francisco Land Association, lxxii; owns home on Point San Jose, lxxiii; identified, 259n; letter from JCF, 360; sues JCF, 404n

Palmer, William H.: and fifth expedition, liv, 385, 387, 488; identified, 404n

Palmer, Cook & Company: bankers to JCF, xxv, xl; involved in Indian drafts, xl, xliii, 283, 492–93; and Las Mariposas interests, xlv, lxiii, lxx; promote Agua Fria Mine, xlviii; cede Las Mariposas interests to JCF, lxiii; and Agua Fria lease, 195–98; enter Mariposa as squatters, 210; and Mariposa Mining Company, 231; letter to JCF, 329–30

Palmetto Mountains, 476n

Palo colorado (redwood). *See Sequoia sempervirens*

Panama, 111, 116

Pandora, 5

Parke, H. S., 278n

Parowan, Utah, 458, 460, 485; JCF arrives at, lvii, 463; JCF determines latitude of, 475n

Parrott, John C.: receives mortgage on Mariposa, 255

Parry, Charles C., 583n, 587

Pass of the Rio del Norte (Williams Pass), xxix

Patterson, Robert M.: re assay office in San Francisco, 136–37, 150–51, 172, 174, 177; letters to JCF, 136, 137–38, 149, 150–51, 172, 174–77; letters from JCF, 137, 145, 151,

177–78, 186; and assay of JCF's California gold, 149, 184, 186
Paul, W. H., 323
Peabody, George: bail for JCF, li, 349, 364
Peacock, 4n
Peel, Edmund, 66
Perlot, Jean-Nicolas, 166n
Perry, Edward, 53n
Perry's Creek, 98n
Philadelphia, 212n
Philadelphia and California Mining Company: letter and lease from JCF, 277–78
Pico, Andrés: and cattle, 125–26
Pico, Antonio María, lxxii; letter to JCF, 324–25
Pico, Pío, lxxii
Pico-Gulnack *diseño,* lix
Pierce, Franklin, lxiii
Pines, 541, 542. Sugar: *see Pinus lambertiana*
Pine Tree Mine, lxix
Pinto Creek, 467n
Pinus lambertiana (Sugar pine), 528, 530, 531
Pinus monophyllus. See P. monophylla
Plantae Frémontianae, 571–608
Platanus occidentalis. See Platanus racemosa
Platanus racemosa, 522, 547
Plume, John V., 117
P. monophylla, 507
Point Concepción, 540, 545
Pool Table Mountain, xxix
Poonche (Poncha) Pass, 484, 489n
Poppies, California (*Eschscholtzia californica*), 517, 520, 524, 525, 526, 537
Portsmouth, 18, 19
Powers, Cyrus: letter from JCF, 165
Powles, Mr. (President, San Juan del Rey Mining Company), 193, 244, 294

Pratt, George C., 127
Pratt, Parley P., 467n
Preuss, Charles: at San Jose, xxiv; work on 1848 map, 5, 495–97; member of 1848 expedition, 52, 55n, 73; goes with JCF for relief, 78, 81; comments on cannibalism, 87n; mentioned, lix, lxxiv, 477n
Price, Rodman M., 205n
Proue, Raphael: member of 1848 expedition, 52, 55n; death of, 78, 81, 97
Provo River, 506
Prunus fasciculata (Desert Almond): description of, 581–82
Pseudotsuga menziesii, 16
Pueblo (El Pueblo de San Carlos), Colo., 52n
Pyramid Lake, 505

Q. longiglanda. See Q. lobata
Q. lobata (Valley Oak), 4, 512, 514
Quartz Rock Mariposa Gold Mining Company, li, 223, 224, 233n, 277, 294, 360; Hoffman's terms with, 228
Queen Victoria, li
Quercus kelloggii, 528, 532
Quercus wislinzènii, 513, 514
Quicksilver mines: Guadalupe, New Almaden, San Juan Bautista, 161–62

Rabbit Valley, 467n
Rancho del Chino, xxxii
Ransom, Leander, lxii
Reading, Pierson B., lxxv; letter from JCF, 164
Red Bank Creek, 523
Reid, Hugo, 123, 127n
Remington, Frederick, xxviii
Rhett, Robert Barnwell, 43
Rhoads, James: re JCF's work, 495

Rich, William, xxxii n, xxxiii n
Richardson, H. S., 227 n
Richmond, Patricia J.: re JCF's 1847–48 route, xxix, 87 n
Riley, Bennet, 116, 117 n, 124
Rincones Creek, xxx, 53 n, 98 n
Rio Grande, xxix, xxx, xxxi, 50, 76–80 passim, 87 n, 95, 131–35 passim, 379, 472, 482
Rio Hondo, 79
Roach, Philip A., 478 n
Robert, Richard: works in Europe for JCF, xlv–xlvi, 154–58, 180–81; dedication to JCF, 250; letters from JCF, 154–55, 183–85; letters to JCF, 243, 254, 257–58; mentioned, 362, 366
Robidoux Pass. *See* Mosca Pass
Robinson, Charles, 227 n
Rohrer, Henry: member of 1848 expedition, 52, 55 n, 82, 83; death of, 83, 84, 97
Rowland, John, xxxiii; and cattle contracts, xl
Royce, Sarah: travels by JCF's journals, lxxv
Russell, William H., 10, 13
Ruxton, George, xxviii

Sacramento River: Wilkes's error in position of, 19, 22, 26, 28, 29, 37, 38; description of, 512, 519–27 passim
Sacramento Valley: and San Joaquin Valley, 512; description of, 519–27 passim, 529–31, 536
Saguache Creek, lvi, 86 n, 428
Saint Mary's Catholic Mission: described by JCF, 405
St. Vrain, Ceran, 80, 86 n, 89 n
Salinas River, Ariz. *See* Salt River
Salinas River, Calif., 539, 542, 544, 547 n

Salmon Trout River. *See* Truckee River
Salt River, Ariz., xxviii
San Buenaventura Mission, 544
San Carlos Mine. *See* Ave Maria Mine
San Carlos River. *See* San Francisco River
Sand Hill Pass. *See* Medano Pass
San Diego, lxxvii; soil, climate, and fruit of, 540–41
Sand Spring Valley, 476 n
San Emigdio (San Emidio) Ranch, lxxii; JCF purchases half of, 280–82, 289–90
San Francisco Bay, 32; description of, 532–35; coast north of, 535–37; area between Monterey and, 537–40
San Francisco, Calif.: town lots of JCF in, lxxi
San Francisco Land Association: Wright, Palmer, and JCF's interest in, lxxii; and Santillan and Noe claims, 288 n
San Francisco River (in Ariz.), xxxi
San Fernando Mission, 544
San Gabriel: plains of, 545
Sangre de Cristo Pass. *See* La Veta Pass
Sangre de Cristo Range, xxix, lvi, 53 n, 98 n, 489 n
San Joaquin River, 512–19 passim, 521
San Joaquin Valley, 476 n, 543; and Sacramento Valley, 512; description of, 512–19 passim
San Jose, 537; description of town and valley, 534–35
San Juan Bautista Mission, 543
San Juan del Rey Mining Company: and Morro Velho Mine, 183 n
San Juan Mountains, 50, 427, 483